D1795833

An Academic Green Paper on European Contract Law

Private Law in European Context Series

VOLUME 2

Series Editors
Martijn Hesselink
Ugo Mattei
Horatia Muir Watt

For the

Society of European Contract Law (SECOLA)

Massimo Bianca   Hugh Collins   Stefan Grundmann (President)
Ewoud Hondius   Sophie Stijns

Contract law is probably the most dynamic area of European Private Law and also the fundamental private law discipline in all national legal systems. SECOLA was founded to assist the study of European contract law and to enhance its quality. SECOLA organises an open, truly international and interdisciplinary discussion platform. The focus of the Society is upon newly enacted European Community legal measures, on core concepts in the field of European contract law, and on proposals for further legislation. The Society organises one or two international conferences each year, arranges for the publication of scholarly discussions in the field including books to be published in this series, and assists with other network activities. In addition, Secola is building up an information platform, systematically structured and containing all relevant European legal measures in full text in all official languages of the Community, together with their transposition into national laws and with reference to the pertinent scholarly literature (see www.secola.org).

This volume was realised jointly with the Leuven Centre for a Common Law of Europe of the Katholieke Universiteit Leuven (www.commonlawofeurope.be), which has the very similar aim of fostering the understanding of comparative law and research into the general principles common to the laws of the Member States of the European Union. Research and understanding in this field are prerequisites for the successful harmonisation and potential unification of private law in Europe.

A list of previous titles in the series may be found at the end of this volume.

An Academic Green Paper on European Contract Law

Edited by

Stefan Grundmann and Jules Stuyck

KLUWER LAW INTERNATIONAL
THE HAGUE / LONDON / NEW YORK

Published by Kluwer Law International
P.O. Box 85889, 2508 CN The Hague, The Netherlands
sales@kli.wkap.nl
http://www.kluwerlaw.com

Sold and distributed in North, Central and South America by
Kluwer Law International
101 Philip Drive, Norwell, MA 02061, USA
kluwerlaw@wkap.com

In all other countries, sold and distributed by
Kluwer Law International
Distribution Centre, P.O. Box 322, 3300 AH Dordrecht, The Netherlands

Library of Congress Cataloging-in-Publication Data

An academic greenpaper to European contract law / edited by Stefan Grundmann and Jules Stuyck.
        p. cm. – (Private law in European context series; v. 2)
    Includes bibliographical references and index.
    ISBN 9041118535 (hb: alk. paper)
        1. Contracts–European Union countries–Codification. I. Grundmann, Stefan, 1958-
    II. Stuyck, Julien. III. Series.

                                                                    2002030040

Printed on acid-free paper

ISBN: 90-411-1853-5

Printed and bound in Great Britain by MPG Books Limited, Bodmin, Cornwall.

Preface

Contract law is the core area of private law, all lawyers are trained in it and with party autonomy it is the purest expression of the market economy approach aimed at private party initiative. The Communication from the EC Commission on European Contract Law of July 2001 puts the question of a European Contract Law Code on the political agenda. Now all three legislative bodies in Europe take such a Code into consideration. The Commission sees several options, two of which are legislative options and would bring a new initiative: improving existing EC legislation and/or introducing a European Code. This second option has two alternatives: a European Code substituting national contract laws (Exclusive European Code) or one, which supplements them (Optional European Code).

This is where the Communication ends – and work begins. Bringing structure into a developing area is the most natural field of expertise of academia. The full potential of all three options has to be discussed in principle and also in some detail. There is more than enough space for improvement of existing European Law. Above all the discussion on the different design models still has to start. Important questions are *i.a.* how much flexibility and how much lee-way to party autonomy and private initiative will be given in future European contract law. What is on the agenda now is the constitution of contract making in Europe, a comprehensive European System of Contract Laws – a high quality contract law and the framework for it. This and the discussion of the options mentioned are the real tasks for a genuinely European and open discussion – and the content of this book in which all options are discussed in detail.

This is not only the first detailed discussion of all options and a first mapping of these options. The discussion is also highly representative of European academia in general. The conference in Leuven on which this book is based was organised by the Society of European Contract Law (SECOLA) representing about 300 members, mostly from academia, in collaboration with the Centre for a Common Law of Europe of the Katholieke Universiteit Leuven. The conference had a truly European representation, with more than 100 professors from all Member States and more than 200 participants. We also noted the presence and the intervention of all those who initiated the very drafting of proposals for a European Code so far – namely Lando, v. Bar and Gandolfi – and many of the outstanding members of the different groups such as Basedow, Beale, Bianca, Drobnig, Wilhelmsson and others and at the same time the presence of all those who, so far, most prominently took the one possible alternative view and insisted on the potential of decentralised rule-making, coming from legal and economic theory, namely van den Bergh, de Geest, Kerber, Kirchner and many (more pragmatic) English and Scandinavian scholars. The attendees and speakers included the initiators of the idea of making a European Code optional only and thus maintaining more space for experimentation, innovation and individual solutions, which would be better adapted to heterogeneous needs. The conference saw the first systematic and comprehensive discussion of this core issue of European private law development by all protagonists, in a fairly interdisciplinary way with input from economic and sociological theory, and by such a large public with academics, practising lawyers and specialists in legislation. The conference was probably the first event in academia focusing on the European Contract Law Code development bringing together all sides, all important countries and all relevant disciplines and their protagonists: a true market place of ideas. The genuinely academic discussion can best be put under the heading of 'An Academic Green Paper on European Contract Law'. We now present it to a large public.

We owe our thanks to the two institutions named and to those responsible for the organisation. We would like to name in particular among our assistants and secretaries: Christian Runkel, Annette St. Quintin and Majo Werrebrouck.

Above all, we would like to thank Evelyne Terryn and Tom Van Dyck. They deserve a very special mention for their intensive editing work. The book would not have this form without them.

We wish to mark how grateful we are to all persons named. The two editors feel that this book could be the start of an ongoing undertaking and found it a highly rewarding joint experience.

Erlangen and Leuven, Summer 2002

Survey of Contents

Detailed Table of Contents

Abbreviations

AcP	Archiv für die civilistische Praxis
AG	Aktiengesellschaft
All E.R.	All England Law Reports
Am. J. Comp. L.	American Journal of Comparative Law
British J. Law and Society	British Journal of Law and Society
Building L. R.	Building Law Reports
Cambridge L. J.	Cambridge Law Journal
CJEL	Columbia Journal of European Law
CMLR	Common Market Law Reports
CMLRev	Common Market Law Review
Columbia J. of Transnat'l Law	Columbia Journal of Transnational Law
Colum. L. Rev.	Columbia Law Review
Cornell Int'l Law J.	Cornell International Law Journal
CR	Computer und Recht
ECR	European Court Reports
ELJ	European Law Journal
ELR	European Law Review
ERPL	European Review of Private Law
European J. of Law and Economics	European Journal of Law and Economics
EuZW	Europäische Zeitschrift für Wirtschaftsrecht
EWS	Europäisches Wirtschafts- und Steuerrecht
Fordham Int'l Law J.	Fordham International Law Journal
GRUR Int.	Gewerblicher Rechtsschutz und Urheberrecht Internationaler Teil
Harv. L. Rev.	Harvard Law Review
Hastings Int'l & Comp. L. Rev.	Hastings International and Comparative Law Review
Hastings Law J.	Hastings Law Journal
ICLQ	International and Comparative Law Quarterly
Int'l Rev. L. & Econ.	International Review of Law and Economics
IPRax	Praxis des Internationalen Privat- und Verfahrensrechts

ABBREVIATIONS

J. Consumer Pol'y	Journal of Consumer Policy
J. of Common Market Studies	Journal of Common Market Studies
J. of Int. Economic Law	Journal of International Econonic Law
J. of Public Economics	Journal of Public Economics
J T DrEur	Journal des tribunaux. Droit Européen
JZ	Juristenzeitung
Maastricht J. of Eur. and Comp. L.	Maastricht Journal of European and Comparative Law
MLR	Modern Law Review
NJW	Neue Juristische Wochenschrift
RabelsZ	Rabels Zeitschrift für ausländisches und internationales Privatrecht
REDC	Revue européenne de droit de la consommation
RIDC	Rivista Internazionale di Diritto Comune
RIW	Recht der Internationalen Wirtschaft
RTD Civ.	Revue trimestrielle de droit civil
TPR	Tijdschrift voor Privaatrecht
Tulane Law Rev.	Tulane Law Review
Turku Law J.	Turku Law Journal
VuR	Verbraucher und Recht
W. L. R.	Weekly Law Reports
WPNR	Weekblad voor Privaatrecht, Notariaat en Registratie
Yale L. J.	Yale Law Journal
ZEuP	Zeitschrift für Europäisches Privatrecht
ZfRV	Zeitschrift für Rechtsvergleichung
ZIP	Zeitschrift für Wirtschaftsrecht

Part I
The Green Paper Process and the Need for Academic Input

1. An Academic Green Paper on European Contract Law – Scope, Common Ground and Debated Issues

Stefan Grundmann and Jules Stuyck

I. THE BACKGROUND

1. Communication from the Commission and Resolution by the Parliament on European Contract Law

a) European Contract Law now on the Political Agenda

The Communication from the European Commission on European Contract Law of July 2001[1] puts the question of a European Contract Law Code on the political agenda. Now all three branches of the Community legislature, including the Commission, which has the right of initiative in traditional Community legislation (Articles 94, 250(1), 251(2) EC), have taken the drafting and adoption of such a Code into consideration. The European Parliament had already initiated the process in 1989.[2] The Council urged the Commission to propose measures and alternatives in this respect at its Tampere meeting in 1999.[3] With its Communication of July 2001, the Commission accepted this invitation.

---

[1] Communication from the Commission to the Council and the European Parliament on European Contract Law, COM(2001) 398 final, EC OJ 2001 C 255/1. The four Directorates General concerned with contract law (Health and Consumer Protection; Internal Market; Justice and Internal Affairs; Enterprise) and the Legal Service were involved in the formulation process.

[2] Resolution of the European Parliament of 26 May 1989 on the approximation of private laws of the Member States, OJ 1989, C 158/400; Resolution of the European Parliament of 6 May 1994 on the approximation of private laws of the Member States, OJ 1994, C 205/518.

[3] European Council of Tampere 1999, SI(1999)800, point 39. In earlier days the the presidency of the Netherlands had taken up the initiative of the European Parliament. See A. Hartkamp, M. Hesselink, E. Hondius, C. Joustra and C. du Perron (eds.), *Towards a European Civil Code* (2nd edn, Nijmegen, The Hague *et al.*, Ars Aequi Libri and Kluwer, 1998, 1st edn 1994); see, for instance, E. Jayme, 'Ein Europäisches Zivilgesetzbuch – die Initiative der Niederlande', *Praxis des Internationalen Privat- und Verfahrensrechts (IPRax)* (1997), 375.

S. Grundmann and J. Stuyck (eds.), An Academic Green Paper on European Contract Law, 3–35
© 2002 *Kluwer Law International. Printed in Great Britain.*

and in which cases uniformity. Consequently, these issues form the core of the discussion in this book. The advantages and disadvantages of both Options IVa and IVb are discussed in Parts III and IV below. A map of core potential designs is given in Part IV, section A.

c) The Resolution of the European Parliament

As early as November 2001, the European Parliament reacted to the Communication from the Commission of July 2001.[10] The Parliament seems to favour strong optional elements[11] – very much like the large majority in academia in Leuven. The Parliament also set a very tight schedule for making progress and considered strong and ongoing consultation of academia to be paramount.[12]

2. The Meeting of European Academia in Leuven

a) Large Representation in Leuven

So far, and to the knowledge of the editors of this book, the Communication and Resolution have been discussed at conferences in Trier, Oxford and Leuven.[13] The conference in Leuven can certainly be seen as very representative of European academia. Although most participants were lawyers – the most important group of academics involved in contract law matters – distinguished economists, and last but not least, scholars specialising in law and economics, also participated in the discussions.

The papers presented at the conference thus constitute an Academic Green Paper on European Contract Law, existing and to come. The conference in Leuven can be seen as such, first, because representation was truly European, with more than 100 professors from all Member States and more than 200 participants. Second, the conference benefited from the presence of the very initiators of the drafting of proposals for a European Restatement or Code: namely Professors Lando, von Bar and Gandolfi,[14] and many of the members

---

[10]   Resolution of the European Parliament on the Approximation of Civil and Commercial Laws of the Member States, COM (2001) 398 – C5-0471/2001 – 2001/2187 (COS).

[11]   *Ibid.*, point 11.

[12]   *Ibid.*, point 14 and 16; see in more detail on the whole process D. Staudenmayer, *infra* Ch. 2.

[13]   The first conference organised and edited by R. Schulze, the second by S. Grundmann and J. Stuyck, this volume and www.secola.org.

[14]   This is, first: O. Lando and H. Beale (eds.), *Principles of European Contract Law, Parts I and II* (The Hague etc., Kluwer, 2000) (1st part pub. 1996); on this recently Hesselink and de Vries (eds.), *Principles of European Contract Law* (The Hague etc., Kluwer, 2001); R. Zimmermann, Die 'Principles of European Contract Law', Teile I und II, *Zeitschrift für Europäisches Privatrecht (ZEuP)* (2000), 391. This is, second: G. Gandolfi (ed.), *Code européen des contrats – avantprojet* (Milan, Giuffré, 2001) (with short commentaries, for instance, by H. Sonnenberger and F. Sturm, 'Der Entwurf eines Europäischen Vertragsgesetzbuchs

of diverse groups that are intensively involved with the debate, such as Professors Basedow, Beale, Bianca, Drobnig, Wilhelmsson and others. Only very few were unable to attend. The three initiators – and all the other scholars named – explained their views in different sections of the conference and also took the floor very actively in other sections. Third, the conference was very representative because of the presence of a large number of those from legal and economic theory who insist on the potential of decentralised rule-making, like Professors Van den Bergh, de Geest, Kerber, or Kirchner[15] and many (more pragmatic) English and Scandinavian scholars. Fourth, because Professor Kirchner who (to our knowledge) was the first to propose the idea of an optional European Code explained his views.[16] Finally, the conference has gained from the fact that, content-wise, the core camps in European contract law were also well represented, including those more inspired by consumer protection needs[17] or those more inclined towards a business law explanation of contract law,[18] those

---

der Akademie Europäischer Privatrechts wissenschaftler – ein Meilenstein', *Recht der Internationalen Wirtschaft (RIW)* (2001), 409 and 'Der Entwurf eines Europäischen Vertragsgesetzbuchs', *Juristenzeitung (JZ)* (2001), 1097). This is, third: Ch. v. Bar, 'The Study Group on a European Civil Code', *Festschrift for Henrich* (2000), 1; also Unidroit, *Principles of International Commercial Contracts* (Rome, Unidroit, 1994) (with literature www.unidroit.org.).

[15] See, for Instance, R. van den Bergh, 'Economic criteria for applying the subsidiarity principle in the European Community – the case of competition policy', (1996) 16 *International Review of Law and Economics*, 363; *id.*, 'The subsidiarity principle and the EC Competition Rules – the costs and benefits of decentralisation', in: D. Schmidtchen and R. Cooter (eds.), *Constitutional Law and Economics of the European Union* (Cheltenham, Elgar, 1998), 149; G. de Geest, *infra*, Ch. 23, with further references; W. Kerber, 'Rechtseinheitlichkeit und Rechtsvielfalt aus ökonomischer Sicht', in: S. Grundmann (ed.), *Systembildung und Systemlücken in Kerngebieten des Europäischen Privatrechts – Gesellschaftsrecht, Arbeitsrecht, Schuldvertragsrecht* (Tübingen, Mohr, 2000), 67; *id.*, 'Interjurisdictional competition within the European Union', 23 *Fordham International Law Journal* S217 (2000); V. Vanberg and W. Kerber, 5 *Constitutional Political Economy* 193 (1994); Ch. Kirchner, 'Ein Regelungsrahmen für Rechtseinheitlichkeit und Rechtsvielfalt in der Gemeinschaft', in: Grundmann *Systembildung und Systemlücken* above, xx. Clearly in this sense also H. Beale, H. Collins, see papers below, or H. Collins, 'European Private Law and the Cultural Identity of States', (1995) *ERPL* 353.

[16] Ch. Kirchner, 'Europäisches Vertragsrecht', in: L. Weyers (ed.), *Europäisches Vertragsrecht* (Baden-Baden, Nomos, 1997), 103; and in a monograph a habilitation thesis directed by him: A. Schwartze, *Europäische Sachmängelgewährleistung beim Warenkauf – optionale Rechtsangleichung auf der Grundlage eines funktionalen Rechtsvergleichs* (Tübingen, Mohr, 2000).

[17] G. Howells and T. Wilhelmsson, *EC Consumer Law* (Aldershot, Ashgate, 1997); N. Reich, *Europäisches Verbraucherrecht – eine problemorientierte Einführung in das europäische Wirtschaftsrecht* (3rd edn, Baden-Baden, Nomos, 1996).

[18] R. van den Bergh, *infra*, Ch. 17, with further references; S. Grundmann, *Europäisches Schuldvertragsrecht* (Berlin/New York, de Gruyter, 1999); Kirchner 'Europäisches

adopting a comparative law approach,[19] those more focusing on the European *lex lata* of contract law,[20] and at the same time those with an interest in economic or sociological theory.

The conference was organised by the Society of European Contract Law (SECOLA), representing more than 200 scholars from all over Europe[21] and its board members, Professors Grundmann, Bianca, Collins and Stijns, jointly with the Centre for a Common Law of Europe at the Catholic University of Leuven, namely Professors Stuyck and van Gerven, both also (founding) members of SECOLA. About 1,000 invitations were sent out – to persons and to most (in many Member States to all) law faculties.

b) Importance of National Private Law Circles Not Present in Leuven?

One important proviso must be made, however. The attendees as well as the speakers who were present in Leuven represent the academic circles with a strong interest in the Europeanisation of private law. These circles, however, encompass probably not more than 10–20 per cent of private law scholars in the Member States. The view stated here is therefore a view which represents a certain kind of expertise in Europeanisation of private law; and it also seems to be the view in legal scholarship which is most in favour of Europeanisation.

Verbraucherrecht', no. 16 above; also J. Drexl, *Die wirtschaftliche Selbstbestimmung des Verbrauchers – eine Studie zum Privat- und Wirtschaftsrecht unter Berücksichtigung gemein-schaftsrechtlicher Bezüge* (Tübingen, Mohr, 1998).

[19] J. Basedow, 'Codification of Private Law in the European Union: the making of a Hybrid', (2000) *ERPL* 35; Ch. v. Bar, his *Gemeineuropäisches Deliktsrecht* 2 vols. (Munich, Beck, 1996/1999); M. Bussani and U. Mattei (eds.), *Making European Law – Essays on the Common Core Project* (Trento, Univ. Trento, 2000) – for the Trento initiative on the common core of private law in the Member States, see for instance R. Zimmermann and S. Whittaker (eds.), *Good Faith in Contract Law – the Common Core of European Private Law* (Cambridge, Cambridge University Press, 2000) (see www.jus.initn.it/dsg/common-core/home.html); Hartkamp *et al.*, *Towards a European Civil Code*, no. 3 above; Lando and Beale (eds.), *Principles of European Contract Law*, n. 14 above; W. van Gerven, with his series of comparative case law textbooks, see W. van Gerven, J. Lever and P. Larouche, *Cases, Materials and Texts on National, Supranational and International Tort Law* (2nd edn, Oxford etc., Hart, 2000); H. Beale, A. Hartkamp, H. Kötz and D. Tallon, *Cases, Materials and Texts on National, Supranational and International Contract Law* (Oxford etc., Hart, 2002); E. Schrage and J. Beatson, *Cases, Materials and Texts on National, Supranational and International Unjust Enrichment Law* (Oxford etc., Hart, 2002).

[20] Reich *Europäisches Verbraucherrecht*, n. 17 above; Drexl *Die wirtschaftliche Selbstbestimmung*, n. 18 above; Grundmann *Europäisches Schuldvertragsrecht*, n. 18 above; Howells and Wilhelmsson *EC Consumer Law*, n. 17 above; Schwartze *Europäische Sachmängelgewährleistung beim Warenkauf*, n. 16 above.

[21] See for membership and support by the major academic institutions in European Contract Law, www.secola.org.

Therefore, the reservations which have been made against more intensive unification or in favour of maintaining elements of flexibility and diversity by a large majority even in this forum in Leuven have to be taken very seriously. It is not impossible that the majority view in legal academia in general could go in a direction opposite or less favourable to any more harmonisation or unification. Indeed, among many scholars, the *acquis communautaire* has the image of being fragmentary and unsystematic[22] and at the same time tending towards over-regulation (this latter criticism is less widespread and is disputed).[23]

Ideas or proposals shared by a large majority on the conference in Leuven should not be questioned only because there might be important opposition in purely national law-oriented circles as long as this opposition does not express itself. After all, these are ideas or proposals which found large acceptance in those circles which really studied the questions, i.e. among experts.

---

[22] See, for instance, G. Broggini, 'Conflitto di leggi, armonizzazione e unificazione nel diritto europeo delle obbligazioni e delle imprese', *Festschrift for Heini* (1995), 73, 85 ('disordinato'); H. Heiss, 'Europäisches Vertragsrecht in statu nascendi?', *Zeitschrift für Rechtsvergleichung (ZfRV)* 36 (1995) 54, 55 *et seq.*; J. Taupitz, 'Privatrechtsvereinheitlichung durch die EG – Sachrechts- oder Kollisionsrechtsvereinheitlichung?', *Juristenzeitung (JZ)* 1993, 533, 535; B. Tilleman and B. Du Laing, Ch. 6 below in this volume; and (not only referring to Community law): N. Irti, *L'età della decodificazione* (3rd edn, Milan, Giuffré, 1989); elements of system are shown in: Grundmann (ed.), *Systembildung und Systemlücken*, n. 15 above, and Grundmann *Europäisches Schuldvertragsrecht*, n. 18 above; *id.*, (2001) *ERPL* 505, 517–521 (EC Contract Law mainly concentrated in and mostly also exhausting one branch of contract law which is regulation – as opposed to facilitative law); H. Hirte, *Wege zu eine europäischen Zivilrecht* (Stuttgart etc., Boorberg, 1996), 22–26; N. Reich, *Privatrecht und Verbraucherschutz in der Europäischen Union* (Bonn, Zentrum für Europäisches Wirtschaftsrecht 45, 1995), 30 *et seq.*; and now, on a broad dogmatic basis, habilitation thesis by K. Riesenhuber, *Systemdenken im Europäischen Vertragsrecht* (forthcoming).

[23] See, for instance, M. Martinek, 'Unsystematische Überregulierung und kontraintentionale Effekte im Europäischen Verbraucherschutzrecht oder: Weniger wäre mehr', in: S. Grundmann (n. 15) 511, passim (for huge parts of consumer contract law); H.-D. Assmann, 'Die Regelung der Primärmärkte für Kapitalanlagen mittels Publizität im Recht der Europäischen Gemeinschaft', *Aktiengesellschaft (AG)* 1993, 549, 560; *id.*, 'Die rechtliche Ordnung des europäischen Kapitalmarkts – Defizite des EG-Konzepts einer Kapitalmarktintegration durch Rechtsvereinheitlichung "von oben"', *ORDO* 1993, 87, 103 (for capital market law); opposite, for instance, for the Directive 1999/44/EC of the European Parliament and of the Council of 25 May 1999 on certain aspects of the sale of consumer goods and associated guarantees, OJ EC 1999 L 171/12: H. Beale and G. Howells, 'EC harmonisation of consumer sales law – a missed opportunity?', (1997) 12 *Journal of Contract Law* 21.

II. COMMON GROUND – AN INCREASED CHALLENGE AND AN INCREASED ROLE FOR ACADEMIA

1. High Quality, Not Integration, is the Main Concern

There was unanimity – as far as participants who took the floor on this question – that the ultimate scope of a process of Europeanisation of contract law (and of other private law) must be a high quality contract law.[24] In this, decreased transaction costs (such as in the case of cross-border transactions) is only one parameter. What is the use of European contract law if it does not properly serve the needs of the parties, but merely creates a 'European'-wide possibility to enter into (bad) agreements? Transaction costs are one parameter; high quality contract law is a much more important one.

This is noteworthy in several respects. First, the approach taken by the Communication from the Commission is still one where obstacles to integration are the prime concern.[25] The Resolution of the Parliament seems to be less exclusively concentrated on this aspect, but again does not seem to question the assumption of the proposal that more unification increases quality. Such an assumption, however, has been questioned by comparative law scholars over twenty years[26] and it contradicts economic theory in the area.[27]

High quality should be the prime concern. It can certainly not – at least not without a thorough discussion – be equated with 'more unification'.

A quality-oriented approach, it should be conceded, is not a traditional one in private international law either, at least on the Continent.[28] Private international law scholars on the Continent always proposed to take private international law decisions irrespective of the quality of substantive law. Conversely, in

---

[24] See in particular, and very decidedly, authors who took quite different views in the core question how far unification should go, namely: Ch. v. Bar, H. Collins, S. Grundmann and W. Kerber, O. Lando, J. Stuyck, W. van Gerven and Th. Wilhelmsson, and A. Schwartze, all in this volume.

[25] COM(2001) 398 final, 10–14. It is obvious that the questions are aimed at fulfilling the prerequisites of Art. 95 EC.

[26] Pathbreaking: P. Behrens, 'Voraussetzungen und Grenzen der Rechtsfortbildung durch Rechtsvereinheitlichung', *RabelsZ* 50 (1986) 19; H. Kötz, 'Rechtsvereinheitlichung – Nutzen, Kosten, Methoden, Ziele', *RabelsZ* 50 (1986) 1; today, for instance, in: Lord R. Goff, 'Coming together – the Future', B. Markesinis (ed.), *The Coming together of the Common Law and the Civil Law – The Clifford Chance Millennium Lectures* (Oxford, Hart, 2001), 239, 241 et passim.

[27] See G. de Geest, Ch. 23 in this volume; S. Grundmann and W. Kerber, Ch. 20 in this volume; R. van den Bergh, Ch. 17 in this volume (all with ample further references).

[28] See, most prominently, G. Kegel, 'The crisis of private international law', *Recueil des Cours* 1964-II, 95; still today G. Kegel and K. Schurig, *Internationales Privatrecht* (8th edn, Munich, Beck, 2000/01), 114–130; also Vrellis, 'La justice "materielle" dans une codification du droit international privé', *Festschrift for Droz* (1996), 541.

9

the process of Europeanisation of private law, the quality of substantive law is the ultimate scope and concern. The question how high quality can be achieved is, however, debated. And if high quality is the main concern – and academics seem to be virtually unanimous in thinking that it should be – this debate is a core issue and one which should be taken very seriously (see below, sections 2 and 4).

2. The Role of Academia so far (Option II) and in the Future

a) Comparative Law Database in Contract Law already fairly broad

There was unanimity in Leuven that the comparative law database in European contract law is already fairly broad, a fact which was also considered in the Communication.[29] There are the restatements,[30] which may be expected to be refined in the next few years.[31] Furthermore, there is at least one textbook, and one case law textbook following.[32] In addition, there is a host of books on Europeanisation of private law and contract law which have been published in recent years.[33] All this activity takes place mainly in the area of facilitative law, not of regulation.

In contrast, existing EC law on contracts touches more upon areas of mandatory regulation rather than traditional facilitative (core) contract law. More particularly, it concerns rules protecting consumers or it attempts to assure a general smooth-functioning, by and large undistorted competition.[34] These are

---

[29]   See COM(2001) 398 final, 5–7 (paras. 1–9).

[30]   See Lando and Beale (eds.), *Principles of European Contract Law*, n. 14 above; Unidroit *Principles of International Commercial Contracts*, n. 14 above.

[31]   See v. Bar 'The Study Group on a European Civil Code', n. 14 above.

[32]   H. Kötz and A. Flessner, *Europäisches Vertragsrecht* (Tübingen, Mohr, 1st part 1996) (transl. T. Weir, 1997); and see the series of books on comparative case law refered to in n. 19 above.

[33]   For instance, partly also more about the *lex lata* (regulation) in European Contract Law, M. Franzen, *Privatrechtsangleichung durch die Europäische Union* (Berlin/New York, de Gruyter, 1999); M. van Hoecke and F. Ost (eds.), *The Harmonisation of European Private Law* (Oxford etc., Hart, 2000); S. Leible, *Wege zu einem Europäischen Privatrecht – Anwendungsprobleme und Entwicklungsperspektiven des Gemeinschaftsprivatrechts* (forthcoming); F. Osman (ed.), *Vers un code européen de la consommation – Codification, unification et harmonisation du droit des Etats-membres de l'Union Européenne* (Brussels, Bruylant, 1998); O. Remien, *Zwingendes Privatrecht und die Grundfreiheiten des EG-Vertrags* (not yet published); J. Smits, *The Making of European Private Law – Towards a Ius Commune as a Mixed Legal System* (Schoten, Intersentia, 2001).

[34]   For these two areas as the core areas of EC Contract Law so far, see S. Grundmann, (2001) *ERPL* 505, 515 *et seq.* and 518–521; *id.*, 'Europäisches Handelsrecht – vom Handelsrecht des laissez faire im Kodex des 19. Jahrhunderts zum Handelsrecht der sozialen Verantwortung', *Zeitschrift für das gesamte Handelsrecht (ZHR)* 163 (1999) 635, 650–652 and 665–676; see also W. van Gerven, *infra* Ch. 26.

areas of the law where traditionally comparative law is less developed. But even in these areas of the law, there is not only a very substantial *acquis communautaire*, but also two commentaries already covering the whole area.[35] And again, a host of books have been published in recent years, including one systemising the whole area.[36]

Therefore, it seems that the material substance needed for further drafting already in part exists both in the area of facilitative law and mandatory regulation (with the view to enhance the protection of consumers or guarantee undistorted competition). To a large extent, this is due to scholars and groups of scholars; in the area of facilitative law, they did the compilation, in the area of regulation, they helped in the preparation and systemised the body of law. This makes it difficult to imagine that a more systematic rule-making in European contract law would not be accompanied by, monitored very intensively or even effectively done by academia.

This observation does not, however, render obsolete the apparent need for putting European contract law more on the agenda of private law scholarly discussion in the Member States. The competing drafts would need consideration and discussion. It is to be noted that there was consensus amongst the participants in Leuven that the following question requires further consideration in particular and very much does so now: should there be one European Code only or should there be a European System of Contracts Laws? Furthermore, what was also considered to need particular attention is the additional question how such a European system should look like in detail, with its substantive rules and its specific drafting.[37] Needless to say, the outcome of the Leuven conference will require an ongoing process and dedicated follow up.

b) European Legal Education still to be Strengthened

One of the main concerns of many participants was that legal education is still very national. In most Member States European substantive law and comparative law is not very important in the broader context of the curriculum; at times it is even marginal. Giving European substantive and comparative law a more important role in legal education therefore seemed a *conditio sine qua non* for

---

[35] Grundmann *Europäisches Schuldvertragsrecht*, n. 18 above; C. Quigley, *EC Contract Law* (London etc., Kluwer, 1997); see also M. Wolf (ed.), 'Sekundärrecht A. Verbraucher- und Datenschutzrecht', in: Vol. 3 of E. Grabitz and M. Hilf (eds.), *Das Recht der Europäischen Union* (looseleaf, commentary, Munich, Beck, 1/2001).

[36] Riesenhuber *Systemdenken im Europäischen Vertragsrecht*, n. 22 above. Among the other books see those cited in nn. 7 and 33 above and – a classic already – Howells and Wilhelmsson *EC Consumer Law*, n. 17 above and Reich *Europäisches Verbraucherrecht*, n. 17 above.

[37] See Grundmann, Kerber and de Geest, *infra* Chs. 20 and 23 in particular.

achieving a comprehensive body of European contract law in the next decade and for establishing some kind of assurance that this body of law would be properly applied by the many lawyers who would be practising in the area. Professor van Gerven even proposed the setting up of a Curriculum Committee at the European level.

One could, for instance, take the Maastricht comparative and European law teaching experience, the key of which is that a Maastricht diploma is recognised for the Dutch legal profession. This should be introduced for several schools in the Member States, giving a truly European education the chance to compete with traditional education, i.e. giving European legal education the chance to enter the market of the legal profession. The curriculum could even be quite different from the Maastricht approach, possibly more interdisciplinary or more business law-oriented (where economies of scale and thus internationalisation are particularly important). Again, the materials available in that context are already more wide-ranging than ten years ago, and this trend will probably continue in the next few years.

c) Active Role of Academia in European Legislation

The strong involvement of academia in the different areas of Europeanisation of contract law seems to speak very intensively for a lead role also in the process of establishing a European Contract Law Code (if possible within a European System of Contract Laws). Professor Tilleman's view that academia did not have experience in the drafting of laws found no response, not even among practising lawyers. The general view was rather that, indeed, academia may lack ultimate democratic legitimacy,[38] but not expertise. Denying the latter seems to ignore the most important recent examples – not to say important historic codifications. Probably the two most important (quasi-) complete reforms of the law of contracts in the last decade – in The Netherlands and now also in Germany – were possible only because of committees which were heavily influenced, if not dominated, by academia.[39] One should even change perspective more fundamentally and not primarily calculate and compare the weight of different parts of the

---

[38] See, in particular, van Gerven and Mattei, *infra* Chs. 26 and 15.

[39] For Germany: Art. 1 des Gesetzes zur Modernisierung des Schuldrechts vom 26.11.2001, *BGBL. (German O.J.)* 2001 I, p. 3138 and (Prof.) U. Huber, in: Bundesminister der Justiz (ed.), *Gutachten und Vorschläge zur Überarbeitung des Schuldrechts* (Cologne, Bundesanzeiger, 1981), Vol. 1, 647 (basic system of the law on breach of contract) and 911 (Sales Law); Bundesminister der Justiz (ed.), *Abschlußbericht der Kommission zur Überarbeitung des Schuldrechts* (Cologne, Bundesanzeiger, 1992) (6 of the 16 members were from academia, many others partly involved were, too); and also the revision of the governmental proposal (see *Bundestags-Drucksache* 14/7052; 'Gesetzesentwurf der Bundesregierung: Entwurf eines Gesetzes zur Modernisierung des Schuldrechts vom 11.5.2001', *Bundesrats-Drucksache* 338/01) was done by two professorial commissions.

legal community. The exclusive alternative academia or practitioners (including ministerial staff) does not seem fruitful. As to system building, academia typically has more know-how; as to political choices, the ministries have to take responsibilities; as to problems in practice, input is equally important. What should be deduced from these younger important law reforms is combining the systematic as well as the interdisciplinary, fundamental and comparative law approach, which is so typical for legal scholarship with a pragmatic input (based on sound empirical investigation) coming from practice and from legislative bodies. It remains to be seen whether European academia is capable of accepting views from practice and whether European policy-makers are capable of allowing academia and its kind of systematic expertise to play a lead role in the process. The capacity and maturity of both sides to enter into a real debate will eventually decide the quality of future European Contract Law.

3. Flanking Measures

European legal education, restatements based on comparative law research, a genuinely European discussion of existing European contract law and the compilation of comparative law textbooks (including comparative case law books) are all useful and already existing flanking measures for the development of European contract law. They are flanking measures for the application of current European contract law which notably consists of harmonisation. In a Community where, for the time being, harmonisation is the only tool available to achieve a certain degree of European contract law, an evolution which is already paramount. It is to be expected, however, that the importance of harmonisation measures will increase considerably under a European Civil or Contract Law Code or a European System of Contract (or Civil) Laws. Such Code or System would be unthinkable in, say, ten years from now, without an intensive strengthening of these flanking measures in academia today.

Among many potential flanking measures, one was proposed with particular fervour – and the proposal was accepted by all attendees commenting on it. This proposal is based on the somewhat paradoxical observation that on the one hand Justices at the European Court of Justice often were, and probably still are, specialists in mainly constitutional law and public law, while on the other hand European substantive law is composed mainly of rules of private law, including business law. This paradoxical observation may lead us to propose the setting-up of a private and business law Chamber at the European Court of Justice or the Court of First Instance, consisting of private and business law-trained (and oriented) justices.[40] Reference to the US Supreme Court or the House of Lords is not itself an argument that would militate against the setting-up of such a Chamber (at least not currently), since private and business

---

[40]   See van Gerven, *infra* Ch. 26.

law-trained justices are almost in the majority there today. Indeed, having a high private and business law representation in the European Court of Justice – even better, a separate private and business law chamber – seems to be (another) *conditio sine qua non* for the introduction of a (System of) European Contract Law(s) and even for a high standard in the application of the existing *acquis communautaire*.

4. A Common European Tool – Common Ground and Debate

Whereas there seems to exist almost a consensus as to the three points discussed so far (quality orientation; much higher engagement of academia and European legal education; and a private and business law chamber at the European Court of Justice) during the Leuven conference we have been able to notice the existence of both common ground (which will be discussed in a) and b) below) and debate (which will be discussed in c) and d) below) regarding the questions relating to a common European tool in the area of contract law.

a) A Common European Tool Now

There can be no doubt (and it was not questioned) that it is still desirable to improve the *acquis communautaire*. The various possibilities for achieving this are discussed in Part II of this book. The question remains, however, if such improvement should involve the realisation of a European System of Contract Laws or the drafting of a European Contract Law Code.

It was not really questioned either whether the *acquis communautaire* should be introduced into any common European tool to come. Only Professor Van den Bergh cautiously considered cutting back on it very substantially, whereas Professors Grundmann and Kerber argued that most of the acquis consists solely of information rules and that therefore centralised rule-making does not much hinder experimentation, innovation and adaptability to heterogeneous preferences.[41]

Perhaps the most astonishing finding of the Leuven conference was that there was such a large majority for – and in the end not even express opposition to – the idea of having a common European tool of contract law.[42] The condition was, however, that this tool be optional in the sense that contractual parties – and not Member States – have as a matter of principle the option between different sets of rules (both at the Community and at the national level). With

---

[41] R. van den Bergh, *infra* Ch. 17; Grundmann and Kerber, *infra* Ch. 20; also Grundmann, Kerber and Weatherill (eds.), *Party Autonomy*, n. 7 above.

[42] Apart from all speakers in Part IV (and those who advocate in principle a European Code replacing national contract laws), see explicitly R. van den Bergh, J. Drexl and N. Reich, *infra* Chs. 17, 7 and 19 respectively.

few exceptions (most decidedly Van den Bergh), the participants seemed to accept that the choice could be restricted in those areas which at present fall under the scope of the *acquis communautaire* of contract law regulation.

The quasi-unanimity for such *optional* standard of unification, as a common denominator, effectively embodies the concerns which proponents of diversity have expressed (most impressively Beale and Van den Bergh). The constitutional implications are also less acute in this case.[43] Even under Aricle 95 EC, one could well argue that cross-border transactions seem to be favoured by the new instrument whenever the parties concerned themselves choose it as being the better solution for their needs (such party choice being inherent in an optional European Code solution). In this constellation, it is also particularly easy to put forward the two arguments which found virtually unanimous acceptance in favour of a European tool: First, such European tool should have the potential of reducing transaction costs (i.e. through economies of scale in a larger market with a uniform body of law). It can be noted in this context that the potential of the European tool may be particularly self-explanatory, as its benefits are demonstrated each time the cost bearers themselves (i.e. the parties) have opted in. Second, the European tool may also have the potential to increase contract law quality. Harmonisation and elaboration of a uniform tool would thus become a source of law reform;[44] again this will become still more evident, if, indeed, the European Code will actually be chosen by the parties concerned.

b) Concerns of Legitimacy and Practicability – Favouring a Restricted Scope Now

A first batch of important concerns was those of legitimacy and legal basis, and more specifically involved concerns about using Article 95 EC as a legal basis and outvoting Member States and potentially also Parliaments.[45] In addition, the position seemed virtually unanimous that a European Code has to be voted (also) by the European Parliament.[46] The concerns formulated by Professor van

---

[43] On the implications of the *Tobacco Advertising Judgment* of the ECJ (case C-376/98, *Germany v. Parliament and Council*, [2000] ECR I- 8419) for the (limited) powers conferred on the Community legislature to harmonise national laws, see different contributions to this book, in particular J. Basedow and W. Van Gerven; see also S. Weatherill, 'The European Commission's Green Paper on European Contract Law: Context, Content and Constitutionality', *Journal of Consumer Policy*, 24 (2001) 339–399.

[44] See very decidedly in this sense, Ch. v. Bar, *infra* Ch. 9; W. van Gerven, *infra* Ch. 26 (no traditional Civil Code in Europe being drafted by a democratically legitimised legislator and under market economy conditions); see also S. Grundmann, in: M. Bianca and S. Grundmann (eds.), *EU Sales Directive – Commentary* (Schoten/Oxford, Intersentia/Hart, 2002), *Introduction* para. 19 *et seq.* (for the EU Sales Directive).

[45] See W. van Gerven, in this volume, Ch. 26; for questions of competence also, J. Basedow and B. Tilleman / B. Du Laing, in this volume, Chs. 10 and 6 respectively.

[46] See also Resolution (n. 10 above), point 21.

Gerven, that it would contradict comity if four or five Member States were outvoted in a question so fundamental for their legal system,[47] were taken very seriously and found large acceptance amongst the speakers. Professor Lando replied for the proponents of a Code which would substitute national laws. He proposed to proceed as with the Euro – in two different speeds, leaving out those Member States, which would not be willing to adopt the European Code.[48] This means that a Convention would be preferred, and that a European Code substituting various national laws would potentially have a restricted scope of territorial application. It should be noted, however, that this concern may not exist if only an optional European Code were to be drafted.[49]

A second concern was that of practicability intertwined, however, with a more fundamental opposition to a far-reaching unification. Even among the scholars who propose a European Code which would substitute national laws in the long run, many propose that in a first stage such European Code should be either optional or restricted (for instance, restricted to cross-border cases only).[50] Some passages in the Resolution seem to indicate that this is also the opinion of the European Parliament.[51]

There is, however, also an alternative set of arguments, which has been expressed by a large audience perhaps for the first time in Leuven. This argument proceeds as follows. A European System of Contract Laws with a strong optional character should be introduced now, but will subsequently serve as a durable framework designed to keep flexibility, innovation and experimentation alive in the long run and to serve heterogeneous preferences more adequately than a European world with one regulation only.[52] Both sets of arguments, although quite different in

---

[47]   See W. van Gerven, *infra* Ch. 26. Basing the European Code on Arts. 95 and 251, 205 EC would mean that Great Britain, Ireland, Denmark, Sweden and Finland – all states more inclined to diversity and against European codification – could be outvoted.

[48]   In this sense also, U. Drobnig, *infra* Ch. 21.

[49]   See also from the competence side: U. Drobnig, *infra* Ch. 21 (for a Code covering only cross-border cases).

[50]   See J. Basedow, M. Bianca, M. Bussani and U. Drobnig, *infra* Chs. 10, 8, 11 and 21; also U. Mattei, *infra* Ch. 15 (full Code and full application right now, but only minimal European Code). The view that an optional Code could be a solution of transition is often expressed; see, for instance, H. Schulte-Nölke, 'Ein Vertragsgesetzbuch für Europa?' *Juristenzeitung (JZ)* 2001, 917, 920; A. Staudinger, 'Die Mitteilung der Kommission zum Europäischen Vertragsrecht', *Verbraucher und Recht (VuR)* 2001, 353, 358 *et seq.*; explicitly opposite: S. Grundmann / W. Kerber and J. Smits, *infra* Chs. 20 and 24 respectively.

[51]   Resolution (n. 10 above) point 11.

[52]   See more in detail, *infra*, Part IV and in particular S. Grundmann / W. Kerber, G. de Geest and Ch. Kirchner, *infra* Chs. 20, 23 and 25 (heterogeneous preferences). On experimentation also H. Beale and G. Howells, *infra* Chs. 4 and 5 respectively; Th. Wilhelmsson, 'Private Law in the EU – Harmonised or Fragmented Europeanisation', (2002) *ERPL* 77.

approach, seem to favour the elaboration of a European System of Contract Laws with a strong optional character, which would first need to be tested.

c) A European Code Only v. A European System of Contract Laws Including a European Code

The central discussion during the conference was focused on the choice between two options: a European Code only, or a European System of Contract Laws including a European Code (Options IVa and IVb: see Parts III and IV below). The advantages of centralised rule-making[53] that were often mentioned throughout the conference involved, first, those accepted in legal and economic literature, namely: a common set of rules can help to reduce (transaction) costs in cross-border cases (i.e. economies of scale in the gathering of information about the law). The second and third advantages that were identified are less well-known to current economic theory. The second advantage is considered to be the fact that a European Code would potentially result in 'better' and more modern law.[54] Perhaps the most striking examples were even given by opponents of a solution with one European Code only: none of the traditional national Codes was democratically legitimised (except for the new Dutch Code, and now also the revision of the German Code); and the traditional Codes did not come into existence in a modern market economy with its problems (including market deficiencies) and regulatory approach.[55]

A third advantage is considered to be the symbolic value of a European Code for the development of the Union. Especially during the oral discussions this perceived advantage was not only frequently put forward, but often also questioned. Moreover, the view that opposition to a solution with a European Code was necessarily retrograde, was firmly contested. Furthermore, one codification may be perceived as a prototypical idea for national states (such as the national states of the nineteenth century), while the refined interplay of laws and competences in a system of checks and balances may be perceived as a more flexible, modern and appropriate solution for big conglomerates. Therefore, it might well be that a system combining unity and pluralism in the central part of private law is a much more impressive symbol for Europe.[56]

The opponents of a solution with one European Code only and the proponents of an optional European Code design, i.e. a European System of Contract

---

[53]   The arguments in favour of and against centralised and decentralised rule-making are systemised in the two contributions of R. van den Bergh and S. Grundmann and W. Kerber, *infra* Chs. 17 and 20 respectively.

[54]   See references in n. 44 above.

[55]   See for these two points: W. van Gerven, *infra* Ch. 26; S. Grundmann and W. Kerber, *infra* Ch. 20.

[56]   See, in particular, Th. Wilhelmsson, *infra* Ch. 22.

17

Laws,[57] could point to a virtually unanimous economic literature which has made it very plausible that there also exist strong advantages in decentralised rule-making (and which has quite impressive empirical evidence for this).[58] The advantages relating to decentralised rule-making are basically those of parallel experimentation leading to various tests of varied knowledge and thus a reduction of knowledge problems in a complex world (competition as a discovery procedure). Other related advantages of decentralised rule-making are considered to be the existence of increased innovation in a dynamic world due to more experimentation and better capacity to serve heterogeneous preferences which are normal in a pluralistic world.

One of the most significant findings of the conference was not so much that there are arguments for centralised rule-making and arguments for decentralised rule-making, but rather that many scholars accept and agree that the prime challenge is to have them combined. At least two of the advantages named for centralised rule-making also seem to be consistent with a European System of Contract Laws including a European Code, because such system could also serve as a symbol of unity (and at the same time of a pluralistic Europe) and because the argument of law reform could appear even more convincing if parties who have the freedom to opt in and out, at the end of the day decide to choose the European Code. As to the third advantage of centralised rule-making that we identified above (standardisation and economies of scale) Professors Grundmann and Kerber argued that a two-level system would not necessarily increase complexity, so that the advantages of uniformity and standardisation would not be lost.[59] This set of arguments – combined with the idea that a European System of Contract Laws with an optional European Code is at least more practicable in the near future – are a very strong case for designing a European System of Contract Laws with an optional European Code now. At the end of the Leuven conference, there seemed to remain on the panel and in the audience no more than about five strong proponents of a solution with a European Code only.

d) Debate over Design Questions

Debated far less were design questions about the content of a European Code – whether such Code would be drafted within or outside a European System of

---

[57] See below chapters 17–19 and 20–26 respectively.

[58] Like stock prices in company law, see R. Romano, 'Law as a product – some pieces of the incorporation puzzle', (1985) 1 *Journal of Law, Economics, and Organization* 225, 242–265; id., *The Genius of American Corporate Law* (Washington, D.C., AEI Press, 1993), esp. 20 (survey), 60–75; and Kostel, 'A public choice perspective on the debate over Federal v. State corporate law', (1993) 79 *Virginia Law Review* 2129, esp. 2140–2154.

[59] See in detail: S. Grundmann and W. Kerber, *infra* Ch. 20.

Contract Laws. The issues which were nonetheless debated included, first, whether there should be a split between consumer law and general private law (or commercial law)[60] (to this question was added subsequently the question whether the Community should have a Consumer Contracts Code).[61] Second, the issue was raised whether a European Code needs a general part.[62] Third, and finally, the issue was raised whether the European Code should contain a comprehensive set of general rules[63] or rather focus on detailed rules.[64]

---

[60] In favour of such a split, for instance, G. Howells and J. Smits, *infra* Chs. 5 and 24; against it, referring to the fact that no modern national Code upholds such a split and that the fundamental explanation of consumer measures speaks for a general private law integration: S. Grundmann, 'Consumer Law, Commercial Law, Private Law – how can the Sales Directive and the Sales Convention be so similar?', (presentation SECOLA Conference in Rome, www.secola.org = (German version) *Archiv für civilistische Praxis (AcP)* 202 (2002) 40; E. Hondius, 'Consumer Law and Private Law – the case for integration', in: W. Heusel (ed.), *Neues Europäisches Vertragsrecht und Verbraucherschutz – Regelungskonzepte der Europäischen Union und ihre Auswirkungen auf die nationalen Zivilrechtsordnungen (New European Contract Law and Consumer Protection – the concepts involved in Community regulations and their consequences for domestic civil law) – (Le nouveau droit des contrats et la protection des consommateurs – concepts de la réglementation communautaire et leurs con-séquences pour le droit civil national* (Cologne, Bundesanzeiger, 1999), 19; B Tilleman / B. Du Laing and W. van Gerven, *infra* Chs. 6 and 26 respectively; also A. Schwartz, 'Legal implications of imperfect information in consumer markets', (1995) 151 *JITE* 31, esp. 35–46.

[61] As a number of directives already existing are focused on consumer contracts, this step seems to impose itself. In this sense, for instance, G. Howells, *infra* Ch. 5. On the other hand, for the last consumer contracts measure, the EU Sales Directive (see n. 23), the European legislator stressed that it is meant as a first step to general European private law, see COM(95) 520 final, 6; concurring, E. Hondius, *Consumer Guarantees – Towards a European Sale of Goods Act* (Rome, Unidroit 18, 1996), 20 *et seq.*; and also Grundmann (n. 44 above), *Introduction* para. 24 *et seq.*

[62] This has also to do with the question whether a European Code should cover contracts only, all obligations or even all patrimonial law. The German Civil Code, with its high degree of abstraction, has two or even three general parts for the typical contract which imposes duties on both parties, as it treats obligations generally. This is the general part, the general part on obligations and within this part the general rules on all obligations (as opposed to those flowing from contracts with duties for both sides). This made it less obvious, for instance, where to fit in rules on formation of contracts in the Schuldrechtsmodernisierungsgesetz of 2001 (see reference in n. 39 above).

[63] Thus, for instance, O. Lando, *infra* Ch. 14, stressing the potential of innovation inherent in such a design.

[64] Thus, for instance, G. Howells, J. Smits and Th. Wilhelmsson, *infra* Ch. 5, 24 and 22 respectively, and even more so G. de Geest, *infra* Ch. 23. Replacing directives by regulations (for instance W. van Gerven, *infra* Ch. 26) is another topic. Directives can be very detailed, regulations can be minimal. They are different only in the question whether transposition is needed for the European standard. On this topic as well, G. Howells and B. Tilleman / B. Du Laing, *infra* Chs. 5 and 6.

Although these questions – just like the debate on the scope of a European Code (contracts, obligations, all patrimonial law, etc.) – were not at the heart of the discussions in Leuven, they seem to merit a further detailed consideration.

III. ENHANCING CONTRACT LAW HARMONISATION (OPTION III)

Contract law harmonisation is the only option which is actually already in place. It focuses on mandatory law reducing the freedom of contract rather than on facilitative law. These rules of mandatory law are mainly concerned with the protection of consumers in situations of asymmetric information and undistorted competition in markets.[65]

The existence of harmonised contract law creates the opportunity for an evaluation of the harmonisation exercise. Since contract law harmonisation does not cover facilitative law, which is traditionally the much larger body of contract law, the harmonisation exercise would amount to a mere reduction of some remaining major obstacles to the functioning of the Internal Market, but would leave the broad area of facilitative contract law unaltered. The goal of introducing a comprehensive contract law at the Community level would thus not be achieved.

1. The Need for More Thorough Empirical Research (Schwartze)

The editors of this book strongly feel the need of more thorough empirical research in relation to the different sets of assumptions underlying the views that were adopted at the Leuven conference. For instance, empirical research should be conducted as to the significance and impact of the transaction costs incurred by diverging national contract laws, and as to which extent such transaction costs would be reduced by the adoption of a single European Code. This was also the basic idea behind the contribution by Professor Schwartze (Chapter 3). The advantages of a future European Code are so difficult to measure that, in order to be able to conduct such empirical research, one should start with existing law, and then apply fundamental principles of statistical empirical research to the very case of contract law in the internal market. The central theme is that the existence of more cross-border transactions in certain fields (see *supra* n. 7) denotes the existence of more cross-border contracts in these fields. On the other hand, an increased number of cross-border contracts of a certain type may well be the result of enhanced legal security for the type of contracts concerned. The paper isolates three conditions which have to be fulfilled cumulatively in order to measure in the best possible way the impact which harmonisation, and as a consequence higher legal security, may have had on the number of cross-border contracts. The paper proposes, first, a set of rules

---

[65]   See references in n. 34 above.

which is in existence long enough that results before and after harmonisation can be compared. Second, it proposes a particular field in which the effect of harmonisation can be fairly well isolated from other parameters of influence: possible strong factors in this respect are that preferences differ from country to country, that costs of transportation may have changed, and that other transactions influencing the transaction that is being scrutinised became easier (for instance methods of payment may have become easier). Moreover, Schwartze excludes as insignificant those contracts which are mostly national, above all labour contracts. He sees the conditions named (harmonisation with a certain history, possibility of isolating the influence of harmonisation from that of other factors, and the cross-border character) best fulfilled in the area of consumer credits, life insurance and investment services.[66] On this basis, a broad empirical investigation should be carried out.

2. Some Particular Ways of Enhancing Contract Law Harmonisation

a) Finding the Remaining Traps First (Beale)

The first plea for continuing contract law harmonisation (Chapter 4) is based on the assumption that there is still some potential for reducing hidden impediments for cross-border trade. Professor Beale argues that most of traditional heavy (i.e. internationally) mandatory national law is today subject to harmonisation and thus taken care of.[67] On the other hand, he is not convinced that there is a considerable adverse impact of diverging facilitative laws[68] – the burden of proof being on those who advocate change. More specifically, Beale does not want to sacrifice the charm and the advantages of diversity, and above all the potential of experimentation, without clear evidence of the advantages of uniform

---

[66]   See Council Directive 87/102/EEC of 22.12.1986 for the approximation of the laws, regulations and administrative provisions of the Member States concerning consumer credit, OJ EC 1987 L 42/48; amended in OJ EC 1990 L 61/14 and 1998 L 101/17; Council Directive 93/22/EEC of 10 May 1993 on investment services in the securities field, EC OJ 1993 L 141/27; amended in EC OJ 1995 L 168/7. As for life insurance, the relevant rules were introduced in the second and third generation of directives. See references (also for literature) in Grundmann *Europäisches Schuldvertragsrecht*, n. 18 above 4.30–1/2/3 and 4.31–1/2/3 'Fundstellenverzeichnisse'; Quigley *EC Contract Law*, n. 35 above 310–321. See also the references for the block exemption for the insurance business which also concerns standard term insurance contracts.

[67]   Thus, H. Beale seems to suggest that more stringent national rules should no longer hinder cross-border trade. See for this question the references in S. Grundmann and W. Kerber, *infra* Ch. 20; and the explanations of J. Drexl, *infra* Ch. 7 going again in the more integrative direction.

[68]   In this sense, for instance, also W. van Gerven and Th. Wilhelmsson, *infra* Chs. 26 and 22 respectively.

law for these types of rules. According to Beale, quite a few points seem to indicate that the advantages related to a uniform law approach are not significant. Consumers do not plan so much according to the law anyway; if a European Code contained in central parts principles (general clauses) such as the ones proposed by Lando and Beale, there would still be diversity in their application. What the paper is concerned with are the 'traps' still existing – such as the one that there is strict liability in one Member State (host country) and no insurance coverage for these cases in another Member State (home country) because the regime there is not one of strict liability. This is a classical problem of *dépeçage* in private international law.[69] According to Beale, the *acquis communautaire* could still be considerably improved by systematically uncovering these traps. In this Beale sees the real importance of works like those of the Study Group on a European Civil Code.

b) European Consumer Law – the Minimal and Maximal Harmonisation Debate and Pro Independent Consumer Law Competence (Howells)

Professor Howells (Chapter 5) contends that most initiatives taken in the area of European contract law served a sensible goal (i.e. consumer protection) but were unsatisfactory because of compromises being introduced. Indeed, according to Howells, most measures are diluted by lobbyism after a rather promising proposal by the Commission.[70] This speaks against conceiving harmonisation of consumer contract law as a maximum standard disallowing more intensive protection in national law. There is even a risk of *de facto* maximum standards under a minimum harmonisation approach, as shown in the area of misleading advertising. Howells isolates two important reasons for the rather low consumer protection standard at the Community level: first, the existence of the concept of subsidiarity (Art. 5 EC) and (even more so) second, the main rule of competence that is contained in Article 95 EC. Article 95 EC can only be used if the Community measure at stake furthers integration. However, consumer protection is at best an additional objective of equal importance, but it is certainly not the primary objective of a measure taken on the basis of Article 95 EC.[71] In order

---

[69] See Ekelmans, 'Le dépeçage du contrat dans la Convention de Rome du 19 juin 1980 sur la loi applicable aux obligations contractuelles', *Festschrift for Vander Elst* (1986) 243; G. Kegel and K. Schurig *Internationales Privatrecht*, n. 28 above 123–125; Reese, 'Dépeçage – a common phenomenon in choice of law', (1973) 73 *Colum. L. Rev.* 58.

[70] See H. Beale and G. Howells, 'EC harmonisation of consumer sales law – a missed opportunity?', (1997) 12 *Journal of Contract Law* 21.

[71] In case of furthering the so-called active consumer, going out to buy abroad, both objectives may, however, coincide. See, in particular for the EU Sales Directive criticised by Beale and Howells (n. 70 above): E. Deards, 'The proposed Guarantees Directive – is it fit for the Purpose?', (1998) 21 *J. Consumer Pol'y* 99, 114; Grundmann (n. 44 above), *Introduction* para. 17.

to increase the consumer protection quality of legal measures in the Community, Howells proposes to make the scope of consumer protection an independent source of Community competence and make the rules more precise and detailed. In view of the free trade inspiration of the Treaty, Howells sees legal measures for the protection of consumers as a priority in the harmonisation process.

c) Increasing Consistency in Existing Harmonisation (Tilleman/Du Laing)

The contribution by Professors Tilleman and Du Laing (Chapter 6) is characterised by a concern about the inconsistencies in existing European contract law and, conversely, the possibilities of enhancing the existing legislation. According to the authors, those concerns should be taken care of first before engaging in an all-embracing piece of legislation at the European level. Tilleman and Du Laing mention in particular the inconsistency within concepts of European contract law itself (such as the concept of consumers or professionals or the rescission rights which are defined not once and for all but anew in each directive), the separation of consumer law from the rest of private law through the adoption of directives limited to consumer contracts, and the fact that European contract law itself sometimes maintains two different regimes (as for product liability), or leads to a dual transposition in some Member States (the authors refer in this context to the EU Sales Directive). The authors furthermore point to the divergence which subsists even in harmonised areas. Finally, Tilleman and Du Laing extensively discuss the relevant questions of competence.

3. Additional Measures Needed for Really Levelling the Playing Field (Drexl)

Professor Drexl (Chapter 7) starts with a description of the distinctive features of the minimum harmonisation approach under the White Paper of 1985 which envisaged on the one hand only approximation of national laws, harmonisation of core questions and only at a minimum level, while on the other hand, mutual recognition of national laws for the remaining issues. Drexl's paper, however, goes beyond the harmonisation approach as set out by the White Paper. More specifically, he distinguishes different sets of mandatory rules and default rules. For consumer contracts, he finds that most of the rules are mandatory, especially under Article 5 of the Rome Convention on the law applicable to contractual obligations,[72] which also renders them mandatory in cross-border cases. With regard to consumer contract rules, Drexl furthermore refers to the possibility that national law can be (and often is) more stringent, i.e. protects consumers more intensively. If Article 5 of the aforementioned Rome Convention applies (i.e. if the host country rule applies, which is also typically the consumer's home country law) minimum harmonisation would not lead to a level playing field for

---

[72]   See consolidated version EC OJ 1998 C 27/34.

suppliers. In other words, suppliers in their relation with EU consumers may still have to comply with potentially fifteen different regimes. Therefore, Drexl questions the legal competence of the Community for such design of harmonisation. He therefore proposes to draft mandatory consumer protection rules not only as minimal standards, but at the same time as maximum standards. This would also cancel out a potential hypertrophy of protection (which would be costly and take away freedom of choice).[73] In this context, Drexl favours standards which are designed for private law as a whole, not only for consumer contracts. At most, these rules would have the peculiarity of being mandatory in the consumer field. Alternatively, during the discussions at the conference, he considered the possibility of no longer applying Article 5 of the Rome Convention, at least in the areas where there is already harmonisation and thus apply, in those fields, the principle of mutual recognition.[74] As to default rules, Drexl favours a European Code which would be optional, based on Article 308 EC and which would only apply to cross-border cases. Such a Code could lower transaction costs without penetrating into the realm of national law competence.[75]

IV. A EUROPEAN CODE REPLACING NATIONAL LAWS (OPTION IVa)

1. Progressive Codification (Bianca)

Professor Bianca (Chapter 8) argues that the EU needs a unique Civil Code in order to establish equality and to remove obstacles to free movement of goods and services, but he concedes that this can only be achieved progressively. According to this author, the adoption of the Directive on consumer sales and guarantees can be seen as a preparatory step, paving the way to the adoption of a fully fledged European regulation on the contract of sale.

2. In Favour of a European Contract Law or a Civil Code Replacing National Laws

a) Gradually Proceeding Towards a Comprehensive European Code (v. Bar)

Professor von Bar (Chapter 9) has strongly defended the idea of a European Civil Code. The role of academia in the preparation of such European Civil

---

[73] Pathbreaking, J. Drexl *Die wirtschaftliche Selbstbestimmung des Verbrauchers*, n. 18 above.

[74] For this view, see references, *infra*, 295, 316 n. 48. This view has basically also been taken by S. Grundmann / W. Kerber and by Ch. Kirchner, *infra* Chs. 20 and 25. For the consequences of such an approach see more in detail, *infra*, 295, 315–318. For an analysis of the problem see J. Stuyck, 'Patterns of Justice in the European Constitutional Charter – Minimum Harmonisation in the Field of Consumer Law', *Festschrift for Reich* (1997), 279, esp. 285 *et seq.*

[75] For this solution see also, *infra*, 295, 311 *et seq.* (S. Grundmann and W. Kerber) and Ch. 21 (U. Drobnig).

Code is essential. Von Bar believes that the Communication has created a momentum for scholars to carefully draft a restatement, or rather a 'statement' depicting at least the major parts of patrimonial law, including not only consumer protection law, but also the law of obligations in general, as well as essential parts of property law. According to this influential author, a legally binding text will be necessary, but the approximation of the laws will probably have to be achieved at a differentiated speed according to the cost–benefit analysis which each jurisdiction will have to make for itself.

Von Bar defends the gradual programme presented by the Commission on European Contract Law and the Study Group on a European Civil Code, which seems to have convinced the European Parliament. Phase one would be characterised by (i) the drafting of commented and annotated 'principles', (ii) the promotion of the study of these 'principles' at the universities, (iii) the acknowledgement by the European institutions that Community legislation affecting private law would use a terminology consistent with the 'principles' and (iv) the reference to the 'principles' in tenders with private law subjects. Phase one should be closed with a careful evaluation of the results achieved. An intermediate scenario which could be contemplated is that of allowing parties to voluntarily give effect to the 'principles' as the law governing their relationships, whether cross-border or not.

b) Solid Comparative Law Basis Existing Only for a Contract Law Code (Basedow)

Professor Basedow (Chapter 10) remarks that scholarly work has not been directed to the drafting of a European Civil Code, which would include matters such as family law, succession, or even labour and company law. A realistic approach would focus instead on the law of contracts, including securities in movables and could be extended, at a later stage, to other obligations.

Basedow does not agree with the view that Article 95 EC is not a sufficient legal basis for comprehensive Community legislation in the field of contract law.[76] In his view, legislation that helps to overcome psychological barriers can be justified as measures necessary for the establishment of the internal market. Even in a narrow interpretation of Article 95 EC, the Community would be empowered and obliged to continue its harmonisation programme with regard to these areas and issues of contract law which are the subject of different mandatory regulations at the national level. At the Leuven conference, Basedow gave the example of insurance contract law. The Commission abandoned its original idea to harmonise this area. As a consequence, insurance companies are at present unable to offer coverage in all Member States on the basis of the same policy, as far as small risks are concerned. The contract is governed by

---

[76] See his article in *CML Rev*, 1996, 1069 *et seq.*

the law of the policyholder and that law differs tremendously from Member State to Member State. In his contribution Basedow also illustrates his point with the law of contracts for the carriage of goods, sureties in goods and factoring, unfair contract terms and direct marketing to consumers.

It can be pointed out finally that Basedow argues in favour of a European Act on general contract law, not only to complete the Internal Market, but also for educational reasons (the present legal education, based on national law, tends to promote an attitude amongst lawyers which is hostile to Community law) and for cultural reasons (what we need is a 'common grammar'). In this context, reference can be made to our earlier comments on the subject of legal education and the symbolic value and psychological effects of a European Code (see for instance II.2.b and II.4.c)

c) The Policies and Interests Behind a Potential Codification Process (Bussani; Hesselink)

Bussani (chapter 11) begins with a description of the status quo. He finds fragmentation, partly between legal measures (directives), partly between types of contracts (consumer contracts, pure business contracts).

After considering the question whether a potential Code has an impact far abroad as well, i.e. does not play a geopolitical role and stressing strong ties with neighbouring areas, Bussani discusses his core theme, the rationale for a European Code. Partly he questions it, stressing the losses in freedom of experimentation and innovation brought about by such a Code. Partly, however, he also sees advantages. Based on an analysis of historical precedent, Bussani could imagine that a European Code, which would certainly be a systematic one, could make scholars regain importance and prestige in the legal community because these are items in which their expertise traditionally lies.

Hesselink (chapter 12) similarly asks the question who wins from a European Code and does so, as he states, 'with (moderate) left-wing ideological sympathies'. The core argument Hesselink makes is that each way of drafting furthers certain interests and similarly does the very drafting of such a Code. Hesselink is in principle in favour of a European Code, a European ideal and dimension, but clearly advocates as much freedom for plurality as possible – as Europe in his eyes is pluralistic, if anything. He would not advocate a European Code which did not have a thorough welfarist content. He is therefore in favour of uniformity mainly with respect to mandatory law, and for several sets of rules for general contract law. What Hesselink perhaps does not really make explicit is that this is very much already the status one would have if the *acquis communautaire* was supplemented by an optional Code.

d) Models For a European Code Presented (Gandolfi, Lando)

Professor Gandolfi (Chapter 13) starts with a description: in his eyes, harmonisation was good as a first step, but this has its limits. He makes reference to the distinction between mere harmonisation of 'objectives' ('*Ziele*', the term used in the German version of Art. 249(3) EC) and harmonisation of 'results', which goes further but still is harmonisation only. Fragmentation is one problem for Gandolfi, as well as consumer orientation.

Gandolfi would see progressive codification in a sense as natural if this means that not all can be achieved at once and, still more important, that it can always be changed again. He is, however, clearly opposed to the idea of a mere restatement, even though comparative law seems to be of some use for his proposal of a European Code.

This Code should not be optional, because the law is already not optional, but mainly because of the negative experience with such a Code, namely The Hague Uniform Sales Law of 1964 which English could have chosen but never did. And this Code should not be restricted to cross-border cases because otherwise two regimes – difficult to handle – would be installed.

For the proposed Code, Gandolfi thinks that a model is necessary. The Italian Code has been chosen (mediating between France and Germany) and the Civil Code MacGregor. The ease of application (enhancing the functioning of the internal market) and the suppression of negative external effects are seen as main advantages. Gandolfi opts for a detailed Code, indeed he sees this as the main condition for the advantages named.

Lando (Chapter 14) shares some of the foundations on which Gandolfi's proposal is based: that non-uniform law acts as a non-tariff trade barrier and that harmonisation is too fragmentary in order to convince. Lando then describes similarities which make a European Code feasible: judges behave the same way, the roots are Roman all over Europe, the socio-economic circumstances are very similar. Lando admits that opposition is a strong impediment for such a Code, but thinks that it has to be overcome.

The rest of the paper is dedicated to the question how to proceed. The opinion about the flanking measures referred to above, Lando explicitly states, is shared by virtually all authors. This, however, is not sufficient in Lando's eyes; this does not yet create simple rules. A good European Code is possible although directives may not be well drafted. Lando cites as an example the Vienna Convention on International Sales. He then describes the two parts of the Principles of European Contract Law, part I (1995) dedicated to performance, part II (1999) to formation and content. They could serve as a model for a European Code. The main aim is simplicity. If the cross-border trade increased more significantly within the Community than world-wide then, Lando holds, the CISG should have a companion in the Community *a maiore*.

e) A Hard, Often Mandatory, but Slim Code Now (Mattei)

Professor Mattei (Chapter 15) criticises 'softness' and advocates the immediate start of a political process leading to codification of European private law. The 'postmodernist' paradigm shift in codification proposals (from traditional codes to 'model codes', 'restatements' and the like) is illustrative of the change in relationship between the law and the market: the market governs the law rather than the other way round. In this context private law default rules are favoured, as proxies of what parties would have agreed upon. Mattei wonders whether this is not 'yet another strategy to justify and grant legitimisation to rapacious and self-serving corporate behaviour'.

In the European context (where the judiciary does not play the same role as in the US), emphasis on softness in the making of private law is likely to mean lawlessness and a free battleground for exploitative business interests, Mattei claims.

On the issue of what a European Code – a hard Code, according to this author – should contain, Mattei suggests that it should be minimal, containing only those fundamental principles that can readily be used by courts to force market actors to internalise social costs. The minimal hard civil code should by no means be limited to the law of contracts. From the perspective of social and economic sciences, contracts, torts, property, restitutions and corporations are all part of the fundamental rules of the game.

f) A Framework Code Only – Besides National Laws (Schwintowski)

According to Professor Schwintowski (Chapter 16) Europe is on its way to a European Civil Code. It is based on the logic of harmonisation of civil law. After the Euro, the Code could become a second building block on the way to a better embodiment of the European idea. The Code, because of its unifying effect, has become particularly desirable and urgent in view of the expansion of Europe towards the east. According to this author, the Code should be a supplement to, not a substitute for, national codes; it should be limited to essential matters (i.e. essential aspects of contract law), be clear, simple and comprehensible. It should furthermore reflect those rules which, today, are generally accepted throughout the European Union and supplement these with a small number of other indispensable rules, in particular information and transparency requirements. The details should be filled out by the respective national law.

3. Against a European Code Replacing National Laws

a) Virtually All Economic Arguments Contradicting such a Code (Van den Bergh)

As the title of his presentation clearly indicates ('Forced Harmonisation of Contract Law in Europe – Not to be Continued') Professor Van den Bergh (Chapter 17) is very critical about the ongoing process of harmonisation in the Community, including of course the adoption of a European contract law Code.

According to this author, the argument that harmonisation of laws increases legal certainty and facilitates cross-border trade should not be accepted too readily. On the one hand, the relevant benefits (reduced transaction costs) have not yet been quantified. On the other hand, the costs of harmonisation (including the administrative costs of legal changes and the disadvantages flowing from reduced diversity) are neglected. The advantages of competition between legal rules should not be underestimated.

From an economic perspective there is no strong case in favour of harmonisation of contract law. Rules of European law could strengthen competition between legal rules (and the resulting benefits) by providing non-binding rules as an additional choice. In the area of facilitative law the competition will be won by the least costly rules, while spontaneous harmonisation may also occur in areas of interventionist law if preferences are homogeneous with respect to a minimum level of legal protection. Van den Bergh exemplifies this point by referring to the evolution in the law of contract remedies. In Anglo-American law the principal remedy for breach of contract is the award of damages, whilst in civil law countries it is specific performance. However, much in line of what law and economics scholars have argued (namely that a contract would require performance in all circumstances, except those in which non-performance would result in greater joint wealth), the legal systems have converged in that they accept exceptions to the basic rule.

The European legislature should also review and improve the existing legislation to prevent welfare losses. This review must also include the possibility of 'repatriating' competences to the Member States if the latter have a competitive advantage over the EC in enacting efficient rules of contract law (the principle of subsidiarity).

b) Transaction Costs and Subsidiarity in European Contract Law (Collins)

Professor Collins (Chapter 18) argues that the Communication on Contract Law eschews many of the most important questions. Considerations of competitiveness could and should broaden the discussion.

The key issue, according to Collins, is whether rules at the EC level can reduce transaction costs in commercial transactions. The answer is positive, on condition that there is a compulsory uniform law. In addition, the real benefits would only emerge if these rules become reasonably certain or predictable. Collins' view is that this goal can probably only be achieved by tackling regulation on a case-by-case basis, dealing with one transaction at a time.

Finally, good commercial laws are not only uniform, but they must also meet the other kinds of standards by which we judge commercial law, such as clarity, predictability, and fairness. The unification of EC contract law also offers the opportunity of improvement, an opportunity Collins hopes will not be lost.

29

V. AN OPTIONAL EUROPEAN CODE SUPPLEMENTING, NOT SUBSTITUTING NATIONAL LAWS (OPTION IVB)

Part IV of this book is concerned with the optional European Code – within a European System of Contract Laws. The idea of an optional European Code is not fresh, the well-known debate on the *Societas Europaea*, which continued for over more than two decades, was finally resolved in October 2001.[77] Indeed, for a company lawyer it would seem strange to argue that complexity is in itself a sufficient reason to restrict the choice that parties have between different legal forms of companies. Moreover, as in so many other fields, it may well be that new combinations of known elements have the ability to generate additional gains (and progress). Drafters of a European Code should perhaps not be too afraid of the competition by national contract laws and face the challenge with more confidence: provided that it is well-drafted, it may be expected that because of advantages in the economies of scale, such optional European Code will anyway impose itself in the large majority of cases.[78]

1. A Map of Potential Designs and Basic Elements of Evaluation (Grundmann/Kerber)

Professors Grundmann and Kerber (Chapter 20) set up a map of the potential design alternatives. They include the scenario of a European Code supplementing national laws on the one hand, and different possible scenarios of an optional European Code on the other. In their set-up, the authors attempt to combine to the best extent possible the legal and the economic perspective. More particularly, the authors put forward a basic idea that it would be beneficial to combine the advantages of centralised rule-making (which is universally accepted in legal and economic literature) with the advantages of decentralised rule-making (which is equally universally accepted at least in economic literature). To a large extent it would be possible to have both the economies of scale which a uniform law can further and the openness to innovation, experimentation and heterogenous preferences which a multitude of laws can better serve. The latter design could be more complex than that of a European Code substituting the respective national laws but would potentially better serve the aim, which the authors identify as the prime aim, i.e. a high quality of (European) contract law (and thus not only for the sake of facilitating cross-border commerce). The basic design dimensions of the authors' map are twofold (see also the graph on p. 313):

---

[77] Council Regulation (EC) No. 2157/2001 of the Council of 8 October 2001 on the Statute for a European Company (SE), EC OJ 2001 L 291/1; Council Directive 2001/86/EC of 8 October 2001 supplementing the Statute for a European Company with regard to the involvement employees, EC OJ 2001 L 294/22.

[78] See Ch. Kirchner, *infra* Ch. 25.

first, who chooses the applicable law; should it be (1) the European Union (EU law only), (2) the Member States, (3) the European Union (for a minimum or maximum) and the Member States (for the rest), or (4) the contract parties, potentially also again only for the rest? Second, which rules are at stake; should it be (1) mandatory substantive rules, (2) mandatory information rules, or (3) default rules – all three having particular characteristics which speak in favour of different options?

The authors then run through all twelve of these design situations (4×3), each time describing the precise situation, giving the main practical examples (and also some of the potential future examples) and finally also some elements of evaluation. In summary, the authors favour in principle a set of uniform information rules at the EC level, to which are added very few mandatory substantive rules at the EC level. The rest of the mandatory substantive rules should nonetheless remain at the national level (giving parties some choice as to the latter). For the default rules, the authors favour in principle full sets of rules (EC and national, no split competences), while contract parties should be entitled to choose a particular set.

2. Some Particular Design Proposals

a) Cross-Border Only (Drobnig)

Professor Drobnig (Chapter 21) proposes for the time being a European Code for cross-border situations only, drawing on the experience of the UN Sales Convention. His argument advocates that traditional private international law in the European Union – though to a certain extent unified in the Rome Convention on the law applicable to contracts[79] – does not help parties to avoid particular information costs: for instance, one party or even both parties will be required to gather information about the foreign law governing the contract in question, which may be different in each new cross-border case. Drobnig notices, however, that this would change should one European Code be applicable to cross-border cases.[80]

He furthermore argues that there would not be problems of competence either for such a European Code. It could even serve as an alternative in purely domestic situations, i.e. where parties would opt in. However, Drobnig does not favour the application of the European Code to contracts falling under Articles 5 and 6 of the Rome Convention (consumer contracts and labour contracts). Otherwise, these provisions would be undermined. This, however, takes out quite an important range of contracts. The author therefore points out in quite a detailed manner the importance of the law of collateral, which is ancillary to

---

[79] See reference in n. 72 above.

[80] U. Drobnig, *infra* Ch. 21. In this sense also, for instance, H. Beale, *infra* Ch. 4.

contract law. In this context, diversity is still a major impediment to cross-border contracts, because collateral can collapse once the goods cross borders.

b) Restatement Only (Wilhelmsson)

Professor Wilhelmsson (Chapter 22) starts out with a critique of a potential European Code which would replace national laws.[81] According to Wilhelmsson, it would have mainly three disadvantages. First, it would be too static, because even national codes (the adoption of which generally does not require qualified majority) are not changed as often as smaller pieces of law. Second, it would be too abstract and not speak the language of the persons concerned which is particularly problematic in a bigger European Union, where understanding is a problem anyway. Third, it would probably be heavily influenced by classical liberal values of laissez faire, while it would risk to less reflect the principles underlying the contemporary welfare state.

Wilhelmsson therefore proposes a restatement, which could be chosen as well as a set of legal rules, but which in addition should serve as a vehicle of standardisation (a system of drawers) capable of facilitating discussion and circulation of differing legal ideas. The restatement should be rather detailed but also be apt to change quickly – perhaps its 'validity' should even be restricted in time. It could be recognised by a political body, for instance the Community legislator, and this could potentially even happen to two or three restatements (not too many in order not to endanger the function as a vehicle of communication). The restatement should be accompanied by solid legal acts of harmonisation at all instances where obstacles are actually created by diversity and harmonisation is therefore necessary for integration.

c) A Detailed European Code with a System of Options and a Multi-Layered Contract Law for Europe (De Geest and Smits)

Professor De Geest (Chapter 23) starts from a similar basic assumption as Grundmann and Kerber and also Kirchner. His design is aimed at combining the advantages of centralised rule-making (i.e. mainly standardisation) and those of decentralised rule-making (i.e. mainly experimentation, innovation and the serving of heterogeneous preferences). One major concern is that of transparency in a two-level system. De Geest proposes to draft an extremely detailed European Contract Law Code which would run parallel to national laws. According to this author, all rules – including judge-made rules – should be integrated into this Code. He does not distinguish between different kinds of rules (for instance, mandatory substantive rules, mandatory information rules and default rules). In

---

[81] See more in detail T. Wilhelmsson, (2002) *ERPL* 77.

his system, each rule in the Code should, besides the actual substantive significance of it, have a second-level indication. This indication is about who may opt out of this particular rule: the Member States, the judges, the parties etc. Thus he aspires not only to achieve ultimate transparency, but also to have the cost advantages of uniform law and in addition to maintain flexibility and experimentation.

On the other hand, Professor Smits' paper (Chapter 24) is concerned with the questions of how detailed rules should be and who should have rights to opt in or opt out. As to the first question,[82] Smits believes that a European Code on the basis of general principles of contract law would have adverse effects. Smits is not really sympathetic with national codes based on generalisation and general principles, but he is nonetheless convinced that, because of the underlying common tradition, national legal communities can handle such codes successfully. This is different in the Community – generalisation which has its problems anyway cannot be handled at the EC level because an underlying common tradition is lacking. Among the many diverging tendencies which Smits has come across in existing European contract law he cites the fragmentation due to punctual directives, the split between consumer law and other private (mainly commercial) law, multiculturalism and the multitude of rule-makers.

As to the second question, Smits is in favour of an optional European Code and more specifically one open to party choice. Only such optional Code could cope with the natural diversity. Smits predicts that, because legal security is lacking, parties would rarely choose a European Code containing mainly principles. And if Member States chose to opt in such Code the problem identified in the context of the first question (i.e. the risk that the Code cannot be handled properly) might become omnipresent. With regard to the choice between a detailed European Code which parties can opt for or which Member States can opt for, Smits prefers the first solution because border lines would still subsist if the Member States had the option.

3. An Optional European Code and the Problem of Knowing about the Best Design (Kirchner)

Professor Kirchner, one of the early proponents of an optional European Code[83] is in his paper (Chapter 25) not so much concerned with a particular kind of design of an optional European Code. Kirchner rather focuses on the argument that it is difficult for parties to detect which law is best fit and that this choice should therefore not be left to parties, but made and preempted by the (European)

---

[82] More in detail J. Smits, 'The future of European Contract Law: on diversity and the temptation of elegance', in: *Towards a European Ius Commune in Legal Education and Research* (Maastricht, forthcoming); comment S. Grundmann.
[83] Ch. Kirchner (n. 16).

legislator. The argument goes further that parties, and in particular consumers, cannot decide rationally in view of their wealth maximisation on an informed basis. Upon his careful analysis of this argument, Kirchner first points out that, by only harmonising, not enough unity can be achieved to reap the benefits of standardisation. Therefore, the author concludes that a real European Act seems necessary. However, in order to keep the system flexible, there should always be the possibility of opting out. Enterprises would then develop their offers on the basis of the European Code including typically only some core clauses which deviate from it and for which different prices are set. Kirchner's idea about the core problem of informed party choice is strikingly simple: in the beginning, there may not be enough knowledge about the quality of the different sets of laws, but there will probably be enough risk takers. These will get to know the quality. After a certain while, this – secondary – knowledge will enter in the market – like the one about an evaluation of firms on stock exchanges has entered in the market, although certainly not all investors can process the information which allows an appropriate evaluation of the different firms. On the basis of this secondary information, generated by the initial risk takers, the best set of rules has advantages over the others. The European set of rules, however, shall have the additional advantage in that it advances the economies of scale and thus should be chosen typically unless one national set is far superior in content.

4. A Curriculum of How to Proceed (van Gerven)

Professor van Gerven (Chapter 26) does not discuss directly the question of whether a European Code should substitute or supplement the respective national laws. He does not propose a particular design of it either. He rather sets up a curriculum of how to proceed – and this within a whole broad framework of measures. Ultimately, he is concerned with three issues. First, the legitimacy of the Code, which mainly involves democratic legitimacy; second, a broad involvement of all parties concerned; and third, enough time for the fulfillment of all the necessary framework conditions in order to avoid creating disruptive effects.

In six chapters he proposes to start codification where there is already harmonisation (i.e. the basic decisions, which are already taken at the EC level) and to strive there now for uniformity (i.e. the replacement of directives by regulations); to very carefully assess democratic legitimacy and not to exploit shaky rules on EC competence (i.e. tying in the European and various national Parliaments as much as possible and use a convention, not a directive or regulation, as a legislative tool); to listen to all parties concerned and to have all professions taking part in the legislative process, which shall involve many steps; to start important implementing flanking measures now, mainly in comparative law teaching and education of the professions; and never to haste the process and bundle all the efforts in a European Law and a European Curriculum Commission.[84]

In the line of van Gerven's ideas, mainly because of concerns about legitimacy and about the level of involvement of all parties concerned, it might seem appropriate to give the ultimate decision on the adoption of a European Code to the parties themselves. Van Gerven leaves unanswered the question whether, indeed, the European Code should be optional or whether it should replace national laws. Conversely, he points to drafting of the Dutch civil code, which was based on broad discussion and clear democratic will of improving the law, which took over 40 years of drafting. Striving for quality and investing time shall be again the core issues for an appropriate drafting process. Professor van Gerven at the end of the day admonishes each reader by referring to the succinct but sage expression: *Festina lente.*

---

[84]   In this sense first W. Snijders, 'The organisation of the drafting of a European Civil Code', (1997) *ERPL* 483 who had such an important say in the (last stages of) drafting of the Dutch Civil Code.

2. The Commission Communication on European Contract Law and its Follow-Up

*Dr. Dirk Staudenmayer**

On 11 July 2001 the Commission adopted its Communication on European Contract Law,[1] which has received much attention in academic discussion.[2] In the following, the main contents of the Commission Communication will first be summarised. In addition, the political and institutional context will be described, which is important for the understanding of the Communication and the future prospects. Finally, I will try to demonstrate how – according to the Council report[3] and the European Parliament (EP) resolution[4] concerning the Communication – these future prospects could develop.

I. THE COMMISSION COMMUNICATION ON EUROPEAN CONTRACT LAW

1. Scope of the Communication

First of all, it should be emphasised that the Communication essentially deals with contract law. Therefore the Communication explicitly mentions contracts of sale and service contracts (including service contracts in the area of financial

---

* Principal Administrator, Directorate-General Health and Consumer Protection for the European Commission. The author chaired the Commission inter-services working group which prepared the Communication. However, this article expresses exclusively his personal opinion and does not, in any way, bind the European Commission.

[1] COM(2001) 398 final of 11.7.2001, OJ C 255, 13.9.2001.

[2] Cf. Schulte-Nölke, 'Ein Vertragsgesetzbuch für Europa?', *JZ* 2001, 917 *et seq.*, Leible, 'Die Mitteilung der Kommission zum Europäischen Vertragsrecht-Startschuss für ein Europäisches Vertragsgesetzbuch', *EWS* 2001, 471 *et seq.*, Staudinger, 'Die Mitteilung der Kommission zum Europäischen Vertragsrecht, *Verbraucher und Recht* 2001, 353 *et seq.*, Von Bar, *Zeitschrift für Europäisches Privatrecht* (2001), 799 *et seq.*, Grundmann, 'Harmonisierung, Europäischer Kodex, Europäisches System der Vertragsrechte', *NJW* (2002), 393; *id.*, 'Internationales Privatrecht als Verfassungsordnung', *RIW* (2002), 329; Weatherill, The European Commission's Green Paper on European Contract Law, (2001) 24 *J. Consumer Pol'y*, 339.

[3] Council Report on the need to approximate Member States' legislation in civil matters, 13017/01 – JUSTCIV 129.

[4] European Parliament resolution on the approximation of the civil and commercial law of the Member States, 15. 11. 2001, A 5 –0384/2001.

S. Grundmann and J. Stuyck (eds.), An Academic Green Paper on European Contract Law, 37–55
© 2002 *Kluwer Law International. Printed in Great Britain.*

services). However, general rules on the conclusion, validity and interpretation of contracts as well as performance, non-performance and remedies are also covered by the Communication because they provide the essential background for the more specific rules on particular contracts.

The scope of the Communication was criticised in the EP resolution[5] and has been criticised in academic comments.[6] Surprisingly, these criticisms do not focus on company law or labour law where there is undoubtedly a certain relevant Community *acquis*. It is more the absence of coverage of areas like tort law or property law which is criticised. The reason given for this criticism is basically that these areas have a close link with contract law and the development of a European contract law could not be realised without a coherent overall concept which includes from the beginning the underlying principles of these other areas of law.[7]

While such reasoning is not unjustified, one should not overlook that the Communication to some extent goes beyond the area of pure contract law. It also mentions rules on security interests in movable goods and the law of unjust enrichment because of the economic linkage of those rules with contracts and the exchange of goods and services. Tort law is considered only in so far as it is already part of the *acquis*, which means, essentially, product liability. In this context, it is interesting to note that according to a very recent ECJ case, remedies for damages can be inferred directly from Article 81 of the Treaty.[8]

The reason for this exercise of restraint is that the Communication is intended to focus on the areas that are most relevant for cross-border transactions. This restriction is also caused by the currently available legal bases in the Treaty for a potential Community initiative. It is true that the Communication does not include a discussion of a legal base – we will come back to this point later.[9] In order to ensure the existence of a legal base, one would have to take as a working hypothesis the most ambitious option of the Communication, Option IV. On the basis of this option, if the Communication's scope were too large, then it would probably not be covered by the existing legal bases.

Finally, the Communication strongly emphasises the principles of subsidiarity and proportionality.[10] Taking into account this emphasis, it would be difficult to justify such an extension of its scope.

It is for this reason that the Communication explicitly states that it does not deal with areas such as family law. It is all the more surprising that the Council,

---

[5] See n. 4, point 9.
[6] See von Bar (n. 2, 800, 801); Staudinger (n. 2, 355).
[7] See von Bar (n. 2, 801).
[8] ECJ, 20.9.2001, C-453/99 *Courage and Crehan*, [2001] ECR I-6297.
[9] See III.4.
[10] See n. 1, points 42–44.

as the body representative of the Member States, puts emphasis on family law in its report to the European Council of Laeken.[11]

2. The Need for a Community Initiative in the Area of Contract Law

In the Communication the Commission asks for comments from the Community institutions and all stakeholders on two broad questions. The first question is whether there is any need for an EC initiative in the area of contract law.

a) 'Critical Mass' of Piecemeal Legislation

A discussion of the necessity of an EC initiative should start with a simple statement of fact. During the last 20 years the harmonisation of contract law by means of EC directives has progressed considerably. This is particularly true in the area of consumer contract law. The objectives and the central rules of the numerous Directives on contract law are described in the second annex to the Communication. Annex III tries to put the contents of these harmonisation measures into a certain systematic structure.[12] Looking at the existing 'acquis communautaire', however, it is obvious that the EC legislator has followed a 'piecemeal' approach, whereby the rules on certain types of contracts or on certain forms of marketing have been harmonised; but EC action has not gone beyond this sometimes rather narrow scope. Even within harmonised areas only certain aspects, sometimes explicitly,[13] have been harmonised.

The idea has already been suggested that the relevant harmonising measures have reached a 'critical mass'.[14] The most recent examples are the Directives on

---

[11] Points 3, 4 and 14–20 and a part of the conclusions of the Council report deal with family law.

[12] This is emphasised by Schulte-Nölke (n. 2, 918).

[13] Cf. for example Article 1(2) und (3) of Directive 94/47/EC of the European Parliament and of the Council of 26 October 1994 on the protection of purchasers in respect of certain aspects of contracts relating to the purchase of rights to use immovable properties on a timeshare basis (EC OJ L 280, 83).

[14] Staudenmayer, 'EG – Richtlinie 1999/44/EG zur Vereinheitlichung des Kaufgewährleistungsrechts', in: Grundmann, Medicus and Rolland (eds.), Europäisches Kaufgewährleistungsrecht (2000), 28; Staudenmayer, 'Perspektiven des europäischen Vertragsrechts', in: Schulze and Schulte-Nölke (eds.), Die Schuldrechtsreform vor dem Hintergrund des Gemeinschaftsrechts (1st edn, 2001), 419. See also Staudinger (n. 2, 353) and Däubler-Gmelin, 'Die Entscheidung für die sogenannte Große Lösung bei der Schuldrechtsreform', NJW (2001), 2283.

the sale of consumer goods and associated guarantees,[15] on late payments[16] and on electronic commerce.[17] This 'critical mass' should lead the European legislator to fundamental reflection on the future of European contract law. This assessment has also been shared by the EP Legal Affairs Committee, which has adopted it in the explanatory statement of its report to the plenary.[18] The Communication adopted by the Commission is the first important step in such reflection.

The need for such reflection leads to the main question, underlying the whole first part of the Communication: should the European legislator continue with the existing 'piecemeal' approach or – despite, or perhaps because of this approach – do problems exist which necessitate a new approach in European contract law?

b) Internal Market Problems

The Communication mentions the proper functioning of the internal market as the first area where problems could exist. The diversity of national contract laws may have resulted in obstacles to the smooth functioning of the internal market. The Commission asks the addressees of the Communication, in particular industry, retail associations, legal practitioners and consumers' associations, to report any problems in as much detail as possible. It also mentions examples of potential problems that could lead to obstacles to the proper functioning of the internal market. This paper will deal with only one example in specific detail: the information costs for economic operators willing to conclude cross-border transactions.

It is true that in the case of big companies and important transactions basically all the central legal questions are addressed in very detailed written contracts. However, this does not apply to the mass of cross-border contracts, where in most cases the application of only one national law is foreseen. In either case it is necessary to be informed about the foreign law. In the latter case, the necessity

---

[15] Directive 1999/44/EC of the European Parliament and of the Council of 25 May 1999 on certain aspects of the sale of consumer goods and associated guarantees, EC OJ L 171/12). See Staudenmayer, 'The Directive on the Sale of Consumer Goods and Associated Guarantees – A Milestone in European Consumer and Private Law' (2000) *ERPL*, 547.

[16] Directive 2000/35/EC of the European Parliament and of the Council of 29 June 2000 on combating late payments in commercial transactions, EC OJ L 200/35. See Schulte-Braucks, 'Zahlungsversug in der Europäischen Union', *NJW* (2001), 103 and Schmidt-Kessel, 'Die Zahlungsversugrichtlinie und ihre Umsetsung', *NJW* (2001), 97.

[17] Directive 2000/31/EC of the European Parliament and of the Council of 8 June 2000 on certain legal aspects of information society services, in particular e-commerce, in the Internal Market, EC OJ L 171/1.

[18] Cf. Explanatory statement of working document of 6.11.2001 of the Legal affairs and Internal Market Committee, PE 294.922.

of being informed as to the contents of the chosen foreign law is especially significant for the party whose law has not been chosen as the applicable law. This party is in all likelihood the economically weaker party. But even in the first case, in the event of litigation it will often be necessary to go back to the applicable law, which will need to provide answers to difficult questions and to deal with points that were simply not foreseen at the time of conclusion of the contract.

In addition to imposing information costs, this situation can reduce legal certainty. Unless the enterprise consults lawyers with training and experience in the foreign law concerned, it can never be sure that the legal advice it has received on foreign law is completely accurate, covers all necessary aspects and suggests what is economically the most favourable solution. For consumers and small and medium-sized enterprises, such problems can even create a threshold effectively preventing the conclusion of cross-border transactions. This is particularly relevant for consumers, because their national law in most cases is not the law applicable to the contract. This may be because the law of the trader is chosen as the applicable law under standard terms, or because under Article 4 of the Rome Convention the applicable law is to be the law of the other contracting party. Article 5 of the Rome Convention does not help the consumer in a significant way because it does not apply in the case of an active consumer who wants to take advantage of the Internal Market through his own initiative. For small and medium-sized enterprises and – even more obviously – for consumers, it will be disproportionate, in the light of the economic value of the transaction, to pay for proper legal advice before the conclusion of the contract. There can be also distortions of competition, which have been described elsewhere.[19]

c) *Uniform Application of Community Law*

The second kind of problems that might lead to a new approach, and in relation to which the Commission is seeking reactions from the addressees of the Communication, are problems concerning the uniform application of Community law. The Communication mentions two levels on which problems could exist: within EC law itself and in the relationship between EC law and national law.

a) Within EC law itself, possible problems could relate to the consistency of one legislative instrument with another. This could be for several reasons. First, commercial developments in some areas of the economy have led to the creation of new types of contracts and to new situations which did not exist at the time

---

[19] Basedow, 'A Common Contract Law for the Common Market' (1996) 33 *CMLRev* 1174 *et seq.*

when the relevant legislative instruments were adopted by the EC. Another reason is the nature of EC law as negotiated law.[20] The legislative procedures in the Council and the EP may lead to political compromises within one institution or between the two institutions, which are necessary for the adoption of the instrument concerned, but do not sufficiently safeguard the overall consistency of EC law.[21] It is true that compromises between different political interests are also concluded within national legislatures, but within the EC there is an additional layer of compromises, namely between different national legal orders. Finally, another reason for a possible lack of consistency could be changing political priorities, for example, changes over the longer term in the degree of attention paid to certain aspects of the Internal Market or of consumer protection.[22]

This can be illustrated with one concrete example, which is also mentioned in the Communication. The Doorstep Selling Directive, the Timeshare Directive and the Distance Selling Directive state different time periods for the right of withdrawal which they give to the consumer. This varies from seven days in the Doorstep Selling Directive[23] and seven working days in the Distance Selling Directive,[24] to ten days in the Timeshare Directive.[25] At the time of adoption, the parallel application of, for instance, the doorstep selling and timeshare directives was not considered to be a problem. Under Article 3(2)(a) of the Doorstep Selling Directive, that directive does not apply to contracts for the construction, sale and rental of immovable property or contracts concerning other rights relating to immovable property. The Timeshare Directive only applies to immovable goods. However, commercial practice has developed and numerous timeshare contracts now include service elements.

Such a contract was the subject matter of the decision of the ECJ in the *Travel Vac* case.[26] In that case the timeshare contract contained not only timeshare rights, but also several service elements. These included the maintenance of the

---

[20] See Timmermans, 'How can one improve the quality of Community legislation?' (1997) 34 *CMLRev* 1232.

[21] See Eckert, 'Europäisierung des Privatrechts – Die Bedeutung der Richtlinien der Europäischen Union für die Schaffung einer einheitlichen Rechtsordnung', in: Festschrift Söllner, *Europas universale rechtsordnungspoitische Aufgabe im Recht des dritten Jahrtausends* (2000), 243, 250.

[22] See Rittner, 'Ein Jahrhundert BGB-Deutsche Rechtseinheit und Europäisches Privatrecht', *JZ* (1995), 851; Schulze, Das Gemeinschaftsprivatrecht und die Europäische Integration, *Deutsche Richter Zeitung* (1997), 373.

[23] Art. 5(1) of Council Directive 85/577/EEC of 20 December 1985 to protect the consumer in respect of contracts negotiated away from business premises (EC OJ L 372, 31).

[24] Art. 6(1) of Directive 97/7/EC of the European Parliament and of the Council of 20 May 1997 on the protection of consumers in respect of distance contracts (EC OJ L 144, 19).

[25] Art. 5(1) first indent (see n. 9).

[26] ECJ, 22.4.1999, C-423/97, ECR I–2195.

building, the management of the timeshare, access to common parts of the timeshare complex and membership of a club allowing the consumer to exchange his timeshare rights in accordance with the club rules. As it now happens quite often, the economic value of the service elements was higher than the value of the timeshare rights. This commercial development occurred after the adoption of the Timeshare Directive.

The ECJ stated that as a matter of principle it was possible to apply both the Doorstep Selling Directive and the Timeshare Directive, or, more precisely, their national implementing laws, simultaneously to the same contract. According to the ECJ's reasoning, neither of the Directives explicitly excludes the application of the other. More importantly, it would be contradictory to the consumer protection objective of the directives to exclude the protection of, for instance, the Doorstep Selling Directive, simply because the contract in question was a timeshare contract. The ECJ decided that the timeshare contract, because of its overwhelming service elements, would not fall outside the scope of the Doorstep Selling Directive.

If the national legislator, in its implementing law, has not gone beyond the different deadlines of the directives (which is possible given the traditional minimum harmonisation clause in consumer protection directives) and unified the deadlines, the question would be which of the different deadlines applies. In the *Travel Vac* case this question was not relevant, as the Member State in question was in breach of the Treaty and had not yet implemented the Timeshare Directive. More generally, however, the problem is real.

b) Concerning problems arising in the relationship between EC law and national law, the Communication mentions the use of abstract terms. In national law, abstract terms are often complemented by a whole set of provisions of national law with definitions and detailed rules which elaborate more specifically on the meaning of the abstract term in question. Such a 'legislative background' does not exist in EC law. Abstract terms are not only used with different meanings in different directives, but there is no general, horizontal act giving a generally applicable definition and specific provisions for more detailed questions.[27]

A concrete example for this is the term of damage contained in a number of directives. For example, in Article 5(2) the Package Travel Directive[28] creates a liability on the organiser/retailer for damages. A preliminary ruling has been made by the ECJ on the interpretation of the provision on damages in the

---

[27] See Remien, 'Ansätse für ein Europäisches Vertragsrecht', *Zeitschrift für Vergleichende Rechtswissenschaft* 1988, 87, 116; Müller-Graff, 'Europäisches Gemeinschaftsrecht und Privatrecht', *NJW* (1993), 22.

[28] Council Directive 90/314/EEC of 13 June 1990 on package travel, package holidays and package tours (EC OJ L 158).

Directive.[29] The preliminary ruling had to deal with the question of whether the Member States, in implementing of Article 5(2), have to provide for compensation for 'moral damage' (e.g. unrecoverable holiday time spent in hospital). Most Member States, in implementing the directive, applied their general rules on contract law. In some systems there is compensation for 'moral damage', in others not.

This example demonstrates two potential problems. The first is the non-uniform application of a provision of a directive in practice. It is perfectly possible that two consumers having bought the same travel package from the same tour operator suffer the same damage because of the same event. However, the legal results could be different, because different national laws are applicable; for example, under Article 5 of the Rome Convention one consumer may receive compensation while the other may not. One could say that this different result is a consequence of the nature of a directive, which gives Member States leeway in adopting implementing measures. However, this does not change the fact that a difference in result is hardly satisfying.

The second problem concerns the consequences of the interpretation by the ECJ of such a provision, which uses abstract terms. On the one hand, the ECJ could interpret a directive within the context of the whole of EC law, that is, taking into account that the same term has been used in other directives and its meaning in those directives. There are indeed a number of directives which use the term 'damage' in the context of a remedy, or even define that term. For instance, Article 17(2) of the Commercial Agents Directive[30] and Article 9 of the Product Liability Directive.[31] The first provision does not contain a definition, but at least gives some examples of what damages could be covered. The latter provision even contains a definition of damage. However, the definition applies only for the purposes of that Directive and leaves the question of the 'moral damage' to the Member States.[31a]

On the other hand, the ECJ may – and has indeed done so – interpret the abstract term in question in the light of the terms of the relevant directive only. This could lead to the result that the same abstract term, such as, for example, 'damage', which has only one meaning in national law, could be given differing interpretations in EC law, depending on the directive in question. This result would then be transferred to the national legal systems of the Member States

---

[29]   ECJ, 12.3.2002, C-168/00 *Simone Leitner/TUI Deutschland GmbH & Co KG*, not yet published in the ECR.

[30]   Council Directive 86/653/EEC of 18 December 1986 on the coordination of the laws of the Member States relating to self-employed commercial agents (EC OJ L 382, 17).

[31]   Council Directive 85/374/EEC of 25 July 1985 on the approximation of the laws, regulations and administrative provisions of the Member States concerning liability for defective products (EC OJ L 210, 29).

[31a] The conclusions of the Advocate General, points 34, 35.

via the obligation to interpret national law in conformity with the relevant directive. As a consequence, there would be varying interpretations of the same abstract term, both in EC law and in national law. This would not be a satisfying result.

3. Options

Where problems do exist in the areas mentioned above, the Communication suggests four options for discussion, emphasising that these are not exhaustive and could, furthermore, be combined.

a) Leaving the solution to the market

The first option basically consists in leaving the solution to the market.[32] Industry and retail associations could, for example (obviously within the limits set by competition law) advise and support enterprises wishing to conclude cross-border transactions. The assistance offered by such associations could range from general information to specific advice. The Commission could, to a certain extent and within certain limits, promote such activities; however, this option does not foresee legislative intervention.

b) 'Restatement' option

The second option could be called the 'Restatement' option. Similar (but not identical, because of different circumstances) to the 'Restatements' drawn up by the American Law Institute,[33] this solution could consist in the creation of common principles of European contract law in problematic areas. The Commission could promote such activities. These common principles could be useful for contracting parties in drafting their contracts[34] and for judges and arbitrators in deciding cases where different national laws are involved. Last but not least, they could also be a guideline for national legislators taking national legislative initiatives in these areas. However, the common denominator of these different purposes is that the common principles would be not mandatory, but rather purely optional guidelines.

c) 'Review' option

The third option could be called the 'review' option. The existing *acquis* would be reviewed in order to eliminate possible inconsistencies, fill possible gaps,

---

[32] See the sceptical statements of Staudinger (n. 2, 355); Leible (n. 2, 475).

[33] See Staudinger (n. 2, 354).

[34] However, as Staudinger (n. 2, 355) points out, they would need to be integrated into the contract and could not – according to Article 3 of the Rome Convention – just be chosen as applicable law.

adapt existing measures to commercial developments and in general improve the existing *'acquis communautaire'*.[35] However, it would not go beyond the areas regulated by existing EC law.

d) New EC instrument

Finally, the fourth option would be the adoption by the EC of a new legislative instrument.[36] Within the fourth option a number of variants exist which could result from the combination of three basic criteria.

The first criterion is the nature of the legal measure. It could be a directly applicable regulation,[37] a directive which leaves Member States some freedom in relation to the implementing measures they adopt, or a non-binding recommendation.[38]

The second criterion is the scope of applicability of the new instrument. Should the new instrument be chosen by the parties by way of a choice of law clause in their contract, or should it be applicable by default? In the first case, the contracting parties would not apply the national law determined by the normal rules of private international law as the law applicable to the contract, but would choose – for example, as in the case of the European Company statute – European contract law, because it fitted their purpose better.[39] In the latter case, one could imagine that contracting parties, as for instance within the framework of the UN Convention on the International Sale of Goods, might waive the application of European contract law in favour of the application of national law because they consider national law to be more appropriate.

The last criterion has to reply to the question, whether national law should be replaced as in traditional harmonisation, or if it should co-exist parallel to European contract law. Finally, there must be clarification as to the extent to which European contract law should contain mandatory provisions, for example in the area of consumer law.

A new instrument resulting from the choice of the fourth option would combine these criteria. One could, for example, imagine that an automatically applicable regulation would provide a safety net of fallback provisions. A few of these provisions could be mandatory, for example if they concerned consumer protection. However, in respect of the majority of the provisions, it would be important to maintain the principle of contractual freedom, which provides parties with the possibility, in drawing up their contract, of selecting any solutions

---

[35] See Staudinger (n. 2, 356); Leible (n. 2, 474).

[36] See Schulte-Nölke (n. 2, 917).

[37] See Basedow, 'Codification of Private Law in the European Union: the making of a Hybrid' (2001), *ERPL* 47.

[38] See Staudinger (n. 2, 358).

[39] See Basedow, (2001) *ERPL* 44.

to specific problems which they consider appropriate. Furthermore, in such a scenario the parties could opt out of the regulation and provide for the application of the national law of a particular state instead of the law provided for by the regulation.

The Communication does not contain any consideration of the legal basis for an instrument adopted within the context of the fourth option.[40] This is so for various reasons. First, it is in line with the open-ended and consultative character of the Communication. It must first be clarified whether and, if so, where problems exist. In addition, the other options do not raise questions in relation to the legal basis for any Community action. The first two options do not require a legislative initiative and the third option would necessarily have Article 95 of the Treaty as the legal base as all the existing Directives are based on this provision. It would give the false impression that the Commission had already decided which option would be preferable.

The second reason is the present state of integration. It is obvious that the Treaty as presently worded provides three possible legal bases, each with different conditions: Articles 65, 95 and 308. Of these, Article 95 would seem to be the most appropriate.[41] However, a discussion of these articles as a possible legal basis for the fourth option would be premature. The fourth option would necessarily have to be a long-term project. However, given that the next intergovernmental conference has already been scheduled for 2004, the development of the possible legal bases is still open.

In the case that the Community would really consider a legislative initiative on the basis of Article 95, the consultation launched by the Commission Communication concerning eventual problems gains even more significance. This results from the recent *Tobacco Judgment* of the ECJ.[42] The ECJ stated that, in the case of an EC directive issued on the basis of Article 95 of the Treaty, the divergence of national laws would not in itself create a sufficient need for internal market harmonisation. There must be actual or at least probable obstacles to the functioning of the internal market, and the elimination of these obstacles must be the purpose of the measure in question. Another justification could also be the distortion of competition.

However, the consequences of the *Tobacco Judgment* for the Community legislator are not yet clear. In particular, it is not clear with which degree of detail the justification required by the ECJ has to be given. It seems unlikely that the Court would require such a justification for every provision of a possible measure. One might perhaps consider giving such a justification for specific areas of law, or even groups of provisions.

The Communication concludes by asking, with some emphasis, for broad and

---

[40]   See Staudinger (n. 2, 356).
[41]   See Schulte-Nölke (n. 2, 920); Leible (n. 2, 479) and Staudinger (n. 2, 354).
[42]   ECJ, Case C-376/98, 5.10.2000, ECR I–8419.

detailed feedback from the Community institutions, industry and retail business, academics, consumers' associations and legal practitioners. The purpose is to launch a wide-ranging debate.

II. THE POLITICAL AND INSTITUTIONAL CONTEXT OF THE COMMISSION COMMUNICATION

In order to have a complete understanding of this Communication it is necessary to describe the political and institutional context. The Communication has to be seen in the light of *three converging developments*. These are the intentions of the EP for the harmonisation of substantive private law, ongoing and completed academic work in this area, and above all, the momentum given by the European Council.

1. The EP Resolutions

The EP adopted its first resolution on this subject in 1989 and a second in 1994.[43] It stated, among other things, that the harmonisation of certain areas of private law was essential to the completion of the internal market. However, these resolutions were not followed by any significant reactions from the Commission or the Council. The reason for this lack of enthusiasm probably lies in the fact that the political situation was not favourable for such projects. Generally a project of such scope would not be undertaken if it were clear that it would not attract sufficient support in the Council.

Later, the EP launched a major study, the final report on which was submitted in the summer of 1999.[44] This study examined central areas of private law and the necessity for their harmonisation. It could be considered as academic ground-work for a statement in the EP resolution of 16 March 2000 on the Commission's work programme for 2000. The EP stated 'that greater harmonisation of civil law has become essential in the internal market' and called on the Commission to conduct a study in that area.[45] The Commission replied that it would 'present a communication to the other Community institutions and the general public with the aim of launching a detailed and wide-ranging discussion'.

The efforts of the EP became more concrete in November 2000 when the Legal Affairs Committee organised a public hearing on the subject.[46] Following

---

[43] EC OJ C 158, 400 (Resolution A2-157/89); EC OJ C 205, 518 (Resolution A3-0329/94).

[44] European Parliament, Directorate General for Research, Study of the systems of private law in the EU with regard to discrimination and the creation of a European Civil Code (PE 168.511).

[45] EC OJ C 377, 323 (Resolution B5-0228, 0229-0230/2000, 326 at point 28).

[46] See working document of 6.11.2001 of the Legal affairs and Internal Market committee, PE 294.922.

this hearing the committee discussed a draft for a third, more concrete own-initiative EP resolution. This draft was later transformed into a draft EP resolution reacting to the Commission communication and submitted to the EP plenary. On 15 November 2001 the EP Plenary discussed, modified and adopted the resolution by a large majority.

2. Academic Work

The second development is the ongoing and completed academic work. First and foremost there are the Principles of European Contract Law of the Commission on European Contract Law (often referred to as the Lando Commission after its chairman).[47] The Communication also mentions the preliminary draft of a European Contract Code prepared by the Pavia Group[48] and the considerable ongoing work of the Study Group on a European Civil Code. There is the Common Law of Europe casebooks project,[49] and other projects could be mentioned.[50]

This academic work is mentioned as a second development for two reasons. The more obvious reason is that, no matter what decisions may be made on the possibility or desirability of a future European contract law, it is indispensable that any such law should be based on broad and in-depth preparatory academic work. This academic work should include a strong element of comparative legal analysis of the existing legal orders of the Member States. However, going beyond a pure comparative law approach, it is also important to have drafts that offer solutions, based on or developed from models found in national legal orders, for existing problems.

This would not necessarily mean that the Commission or the European legislator would adopt such models wholesale and uncritically. Even for simply political reasons that is improbable. Furthermore, it is only natural that Member States, being convinced of the appropriateness of the solutions found in their own legal orders, will try to put forward models from their own legal regimes. This is not only legitimate, but may be useful. Solutions found in national legislative and judicial practice often have proven value and are accepted by the society in question. Simply from the point of view of the public acceptance of a future European contract law, it would be essential to adopt solutions to legal problems which have been shown by practical experience to be conveniently adapted to existing problems.

---

[47]   O. Lando and H. Beale (eds.), *Principles of European Contract Law*, Parts I and II (2000).
[48]   European Contract Code – Preliminary draft (Academy of European Private Lawyers, Pavia, 2001).
[49]   W. van Gerven (ed.), *Common Law of Europe Casebooks: Contract* (Oxford and Portland, Oregon, 2001).
[50]   See the examples mentioned by Leible (n. 2, 472).

3. The Momentum from the European Council

The third and most important development line is the momentum from the European Council. In October 1999 the European Council of Tampere requested in its conclusions 'as regards substantive law an overall study on the need to approximate Member States' legislation in civil matters'[51] and asked the Council to submit a report by 2001.

These conclusions have considerable political importance. An analysis of the conclusions of the European Council from the first to the most recent,[52] suggests two interesting conclusions. First, all the essential steps within the process of European integration have been launched or decided on by European Councils. Second, almost all the important projects of European integration, which were launched at European Councils, have also been implemented. Seen from such an angle the Tampere conclusions could be the starting point of a political process, which could only be launched by an institution with the political authority of the European Council.[53]

The next step in this process was the European Council of Laeken (Brussels) in December 2001, which was supposed to monitor the follow-up of the work started in Tampere. The Council report was submitted to the European Council; however, it was very much occupied with politically more urgent matters. Therefore there was no clear steering from the European Council on the issue of European contract law. In point 61 of the conclusions, it is only stated that

> 'the European Council took note of the documents and reports submitted to it and the conclusions adopted by the Council which they contain (see Annex IV). It calls upon the institutions to take operational action on them without delay, while taking full account, when appropriate, of the policy guidelines set out in these conclusions'.

Annex IV included the report from the Council on the implementation of the Tampere conclusions, which stated as point III that the work has to continue on the basis of the reflection on the need to approximate Member States' legislation in civil matters and the Council report on this issue. One might also refer to point 45 entitled 'Harmonisation of laws, mutual recognition of judgements and the European arrest warrant'. Here it was mentioned that efforts to surmount the problems arising from differences between legal systems should continue, particularly by encouragement of recognition of judicial decisions,

---

[51] Presidency conclusions, Tampere European Council 15 and 16 October 1999, SI(1999)800 at paragraph 39.

[52] See Reichenbach, Emmerling, Staudenmayer and Schmidt, *Integration: Wanderung über europäische Gipfel* (1st edn, 1999).

[53] See Reichenbach, Emmerling, Staudenmayer and Schmidt (n. 52, 117).

both civil and criminal. However, the context of this paragraph does not suggest that it focuses mainly on European contract law.

III. PROSPECTS OF EUROPEAN CONTRACT LAW IN THE LIGHT OF THE COUNCIL REPORT AND EP RESOLUTION

The Belgian Presidency scheduled a presentation of the Commission Communication to the Internal Market/Consumer Affairs Council for 27 September 2001. The Justice and Home Affairs Council adopted a report on 16 November 2001 for submission to the European Council in Laeken. On the previous day the EP had adopted a resolution on the Commission Communcation.

1. The Council Report

The Council report is characterised by a strong effort to be balanced. The reasons for this are twofold. First, the Council did not yet know the results of the consultation launched by the Commission Communication and did not want to pre-empt it. The second reason for the lack of a clear political position should be seen in the fact that, at the present stage of the political discussion, the Member States internally, and in their relations with each other could not yet agree on future prospects, or on what line to take. One might regret that the Council missed the opportunity to give clear political steering. Indeed, the Council would have had the chance to give further work a political and substantive impetus, which would definitely have influenced future discussions. However, looking realistically at the spectrum of opinions within and among the Member States, a clear position going beyond the existing report was not very likely.

The report of the Council contains in its introduction[54] first a clarification of how the Council interprets the mandate given by the European Council of Tampere. While referring to the EP resolutions, the Commission communication and academic work, the Council emphasises the central role of contract law. Surprisingly, the Council also mentions – with careful formulation – family law as a possible subject for a discussion on the approximation of national private laws.

In the following chapter[55] the Council briefly mentions – similarly to the Commission Communication – the other instruments, i.e. harmonised private international law rules and international instruments on harmonised substantive law. It is worth mentioning that the Council emphasises – again like the Commission Communication – the limits of these approaches. Another interesting point in this context is that Member States, which have not yet ratified

---

[54] Points 1–4.
[55] Points 5–8.

relevant agreements, are encouraged to do so. This is particularly important for the Vienna Convention on the International Sale of Goods (CISG), which has not yet been ratified by the United Kingdom, Ireland or Portugal. The fact that this chapter also refers to the programme of measures for the implementation of the principle of mutual recognition of decisions in civil and commercial matters is not surprising, given that it was the Home and Justice Affairs Council which adopted this report. However, it is new and important that the Council indicates in this context that the necessary degree of confidence could be attained in the future if the convergence of substantive laws is enhanced.

The following part[56] on contract law is, together with the conclusions, the central part of the Council report. One major concern, which is part of the underlying reasoning of the whole chapter, is clearly recognisable. That is the need for the greater coherence and the improvement of the existing *acquis communautaire*, which is emphasised several times. In this context it is also briefly mentioned that the results of harmonisation achieved through directives are sometimes regarded as insufficient, in particular because of the significant variations between national implementing measures. This is worth mentioning because one can conclude from this that there is a growing reflection process on this matter in the Council. It is equally interesting that the Council mentions – like the Commission Communication – the problem of the lack of uniform definitions for general terms and concepts in Community law, which can cause different results in commercial and legal practice.

The Council mentions a number of the most important Community instruments in the area of private law and recognises that these instruments have created a '*ius commune*' in the relevant areas of national law. Besides the demand for better coherence in Community law, the Council report gives priority to a more horizontal approach to harmonisation, aiming at the creation of a European common core of private law if a need for harmonisation is revealed.

Finally, the Council expresses the wish to examine whether the differences in the areas of non-contractual liability and property law constitute barriers to the proper functioning of the internal market. This is the second area of law where the Council report goes beyond the scope of the Commission communication.

The fourth part of the Council report[57] deals with family law and will not be discussed in detail here. It mentions in particular the political declarations of the Council and EP as well as ECJ case law in this area. The purpose is to emphasise the significance of family law for the free movement of services.

The conclusions of the Council report[58] are addressed to the Commission and include what the Commission, according to the Council, should do in the follow-up to its Communication. The most important conclusion is the request

---

[56] Points 9–13.
[57] Points 14–20.
[58] Points 21.

to the Commission to communicate the results of the consultation launched by its Communication and its recommendations in the form of a Green or White Paper to the Community institutions and the public by the end of the year 2002. As far as the contents of this future Green or White Paper is concerned, the Council would want the Commission to examine at least some specific points. It should identify the Community acts to be reviewed and the reasons for such a review. Furthermore, it should point to the areas of law where the diversity of national legislation undermines the proper functioning of the internal market and the uniform application of Community law. The Commission recommendations should also cover the possibility of adopting a more horizontal approach for new legislative initiatives and their impact on the consistency of private law. Another suggestion from the Council concerns regular co-ordination between Member States in the area of private law during the transposition of directives, an approach which is already partially practised. The last point refers to the working methods to be implemented to achieve greater approximation of national laws and to prevent inconsistencies.

In addition to the Green or White Paper, the Council would also like the Commission to launch a study in the areas of non-contractual liability and property law in order to find out whether the differences in Member States legislation constitute obstacles to the functioning of the internal market. In the same context, the Council – specifically referring to the free movement of persons – asks for a study in the area of family law by the end of June 2003.

When summarising the Council report, one can emphasise three major points. First, the scope of the report is considerably larger than that of the Commission Communication because it dedicates considerable attention to family law and the areas of non-contractual liability and property law as potential obstacles to the internal market. The second point to note is the relative absence of political guidance. One clear element of steering is the reference to the improvement of coherence of the existing *acquis communataire*, which can be understood as a reaction to Option III of the Commission communication. The Council makes all further-reaching work conditional on the analysis of the results of the Commission communication. Finally, it gives one clear task to the Commission, the presentation of the Green or White Paper by the end of 2002.

2. The EP Resolution

Compared to the Council report, the EP resolution is much more concrete and contains much clearer and at the same time much more ambitious political guidance. From the recitals, it should be noted that the EP specifically mentions two groups for which the internal market has, to a large extent, not yet brought desirable advantages: small and medium-sized enterprises and consumers.[59] The

---

[59] Recitals H and I.

resolution itself also emphasises the concern for consumer interests in emphasising the aim of equitably balancing the interests of undertakings and consumers as well as the burden placed on consumers and legal representatives.[60] It is important to note that the EP resolution – in agreement with the Council report and Commission Communication – stresses the limits of private international law such as the Rome Convention and internationally harmonised substantive law such as the CISG.[61]

The EP criticises the restriction of the scope of the Commission Communication to contract law. It also mentions – similar to the request of the Council for a study – the areas of non-contractual liability and property law as relevant.[62]

After having listed the main EC instruments in the area of private law the EP simply confirms that the relevant Directives are not well co-ordinated and their implementation poses problems in relation to national private laws. It therefore emphasises that the different rules should be applied more consistently.[63] The EP underlines explicitly the need to pursue the harmonisation of contract law with the aim of facilitating cross-border transactions in the internal market.[64] However, it also includes a reminder of the ECJ case law,[65] which probably refers to the *Tobacco Judgment*.

The core of the EP resolution is the request, addressed to the Commission, for a detailed action plan[66] including very ambitious deadlines. The steps of this action plan can be regrouped in three phases: short-, medium- and long-term measures.

The short-term measures are to be undertaken by the end of 2004 and include the creation of a database in all Community languages, which is to contain national legislation and case law in the area of contract law. On this basis, comparative law research and co-operation are to be promoted with the aim of working towards common legal concepts and solutions and a common terminology for all national legal systems, i.e. Option II of the Commission communication. The EP wants to be regularly informed about the progress of the work and will provide its opinion on it. Parallel to this work on Option II, Option III is also to be pursued and the Commission is requested to put forward legislative proposals aimed at consolidation of existing EC law. At the end of the first phase the Commission is to consider whether further provisions relevant to the internal market are essential, paying particular attention to electronic

---

[60] Point 6.
[61] Recital J.
[62] Points 9 and 13.
[63] Point 7.
[64] Point 6.
[65] Point 10.
[66] Point 14.

commerce, which is growing. In relation to these provisions, the EP suggests the instrument of a regulation, while for specific areas of consumer protection law it still prefers the instrument of the directive.[67]

The second phase, from 2005 on, is to start with the publication of the comparative analysis and common legal concepts and solutions. At the same time the Commission is to promote the dissemination of Community law and the results of Option II in academic training and among legal practitioners. More important for European legislation is the request that all EC institutions apply the common legal concepts, solutions and terminology consistently when involved in the legislative process.

The third, long-term phase is to start with EC legislation implementing the common legal principles and terminology for cross-border and purely national contracts in a way that leaves intact the possibility of parties to choose the applicable law. The practical effects of this legislation are to be evaluated from 2008 on. The results of this evaluation could eventually lead to the establishment and adoption of a body of rules on contract law from 2010 on. In the context of the third phase, it is important to note that the EP would prefer a regulation available for use on an optional basis under private international law.[68] The EP stresses the use of Article 95 as a legal basis here.

IV. CONCLUSION

It is now the moment to wait for the analysis of the contributions received by the Commission during the public consultation launched by the Communication and how the Commission will react to the Council report and the EP resolution. The Council has made a definite request for the submission of a Green or White Paper. It is obvious that a project of such potential significance can only be undertaken in an extremely consultative manner. Only such an approach would ensure the focus on the real problems and ultimately guarantee acceptance by all stakeholders.

Whatever the results of the debate and whatever the selected approach, it is obvious that the present Commission Communication is a major step in the development of European private law. It has launched a political process and – as is often the case – the essential question of this process is not how detailed problems will be solved or what the final result will look like. The essential point is much more that the political discussion and decision-making process has been launched at all.

---

[67] Points 19 and 20.
[68] Point 11.

Part II
Enhancing Contract Law Harmonisation (Option III)

INTRODUCTORY NOTE

Contract law harmonisation is the only option which is already in place. It focuses on contract law regulation (not on facilitative law), i.e. on mandatory law reducing freedom of contract for needs of protection. Its aim is mainly the protection of consumers (mostly in situations of asymmetric information and of undistorted competition in markets). As there is contract law harmonisation already in place, there is also space for evaluation of existing law. This evaluation can, first, take the form of an empirical investigation (see Ch. 3). Second, it can take up certain shortcomings, such as focusing on the remaining more important obstacles to cross-border contracts; enhancing the level of consumer protection (for instance, by creating an independent EC competence); reducing inconsistencies (no uniform concepts, split between consumer and other private law, and remaining discrepancies between national laws) (see for all this Chs. 4, 5 and 6). And third, it can focus on the question whether there are structural changes in the minimum harmonisation approach which would better level the playing field and potentially also adjust consumer protection at a more adequate level (see Ch. 7). However, as contract law harmonisation covers virtually no facilitative law which is traditionally the much larger body of contract law, enhancing contract law harmonisation only would also mean that only the important obstacles are further reduced and that no comprehensive contract law on the Community level is introduced (or at most on an optional basis).

3. Design for an Empirical Data Investigation into the Impact of Existing Contract Law Harmonisation under the White Paper of 1985

*Andreas Schwartze**

I. INTRODUCTION

It is often assumed that differences in national legal rules, especially in the field of contract law, create a negative impact on cross-border trade.[1] This might be supported from an economic perspective: an 'international' business relationship that establishes connections with more than one legal system will normally lead to higher transaction costs than a purely domestic one.[2] These additional costs are mainly expenses for information that are spent by the parties to reduce uncertainties concerning the legal basis of the transaction.[3] To be sure, the transaction is founded on the specific contract between both sides, but statutory law more or less invisibly completes (non-obligatory legal rules) or replaces (mandatory legal rules) the negotiated terms; therefore on the one hand the actors have to know which legal provisions they cannot circumvent and on the other hand the less they arrange in their contract the more they should know about the subsidiary regulations.[4]

---

[*]   Professor of Private and European Private Law at Innsbruck University.

[1]   See for example O. Lando, 'European Contract Law', in: H.-L. Weyers, *Europäisches Vertragsrecht* (Baden-Baden, Nomes, 1997), 81, 98, Chr. Watrin, 'Integration durch Recht', in: J.F. Baur and Chr. Watrin, *Recht und Wirtschaft der Europäischen Union* (Berlin/New York, de Gruyter, 1998), 126 *et seq.*

[2]   Commission of the European Communities, 'Communication on European Contract Law', COM(2001) 398 final, OJ EC 2001 C 255/1, para. 31, see J. Cornides, 'Braucht der Binnenmarkt ein einheitliches Vertragsrecht?', *Wirtschaftsrechtliche Blätter* (2001), 407, 409, S. Leible, 'Die Mitteilung der Kommission zum Europäischen Vertragsrecht', *EWS* (2001), 471, 473 *et seq.* More generally D. Schmidtchen and H.-J. Schmidt-Trenz, 'New Institutional Economics of International Transactions', *Jahrbuch für Neue Politische Ökonomie* 9 (1990), 3, D. Schmidtchen and H.-J. Schmidt-Trenz, 'Private International Trade in the Shadow of Territoriality of Law' (1991) 58 *Southern Economic Journal* 329.

[3]   Chr. Kirchner, 'Europäisches Vertragsrecht', in: Weyers, *Europäisches Vertragsrecht* (Baden-Baden, Nomes, 1997), 103, 117 *et seq.*, H.-J. Schmidt-Trenz, *Außenhandel und Territorialität des Recht* (Baden-Baden, Nomes, 1990), 168–170.

[4]   See A. Schwartze, *Europäische Sachmängelgewährleistung beim Warenkauf* (Tübingen, Mohr, 2000), 5–8.

In cross-border contractual relationships the legal uncertainty is threefold: first, there is the uncertainty about the national set of rules that has to be applied to the contract – this depends on the conflicts of law rule. Secondly, there is the uncertainty about the content of the applicable law – this depends on the strangeness of a legal system for one or both of the parties. And thirdly, there is the uncertainty about the enforceability of claims – this depends on the applicable rules of procedure.

Although there is almost a consensus that these uncertainties are in general raising the transaction costs for the parties, it is debatable if this effect is strong enough to have a significant influence on the behaviour of the actors – in the sense that they are reluctant to enter a contract with someone resident in another country. But this question is of great importance for the future development of contract law within the European Union. The European Community only has the competence to harmonise legal regulations of the Member States which are concerned with the establishment and the functioning of the Internal Market under Article 95(1) EC Treaty if there is more than simply an abstract risk of the impediment of one of the four freedoms, or at least a considerable distortion of competition within the Internal Market.[5] This means that it is not permitted to approximate the contract law of the Member States to strengthen the Internal Market if the influence of different national legal rules for contracts on cross-border trade is only marginal. Or in other words, it makes no sense to bear the costs of harmonisation for the benefit of reducing such a small amount of transaction costs. In this case, any continuation of contract law harmonisation is at least economically doubtful.

Against this background the Commission is asking the economic actors to present 'concrete examples' which could show the hindering effect, especially by increase of costs, of the Member States' divergent legal rules on trade within the Community.[6] However, examples will not be enough. A general calculation of the costs of non-harmonisation of contract law is needed to clarify the legislative agenda. Unfortunately, the amount of transaction costs is very difficult to value, considering the fact that they vary from case to case – in the area of contract law this depends, for instance, on the parties' experience with foreign law. Even the parties themselves would have difficulties in estimating their own transaction costs, which is why a survey on this matter[7] does not seem to be very helpful.

An easier way would be to measure the impact of harmonisation of contract law on the volume of cross-border transactions. If the level of economic activity

---

[5] ECJ 5.10.2000 – case C-376/98 *Federal Republic of Germany/European Parliament and Council*, [2000] ECR I-8419, on the Directive concerning the advertising of tobacco products.

[6] Commission (n. 2 above), para. 72.

[7] Eurobarometer No. 39 of September 1993, cited in COM(95) 520 final, 5, concerning the Draft Directive on the sale of consumer goods.

between the Member States in a legally harmonised area is increasing, the main goal of an approximation of laws (economically called 'trade creation') is reached – although it has to be verified that harmonisation of law has a strong influence on this intended positive effect. In the following I will try to sketch a structure for an empirical study which could shed more light on this question.

II. TWO BASIC ASSUMPTIONS FOR AN EMPIRICAL DATA INVESTIGATION

1. First Hypothesis: Extended transfer of goods and services means extended use of contracts

While it is very difficult, if not impossible, to estimate the number and the importance of contracts concluded between parties from different Member States, even in a particular economic area, there is a long tradition and experience to measure the flow of goods and services from one country to another. If contracts are the basis for import and export transactions, there has to be a strong correlation between the amount of goods traded and of services distributed across the border and the quantity of contracts entered into. Certainly, it is not possible to conclude from a particular level of exchange of goods and services a reciprocal number of contracts, but it seems plausible that a significant rise in product transfer is based on a higher number of exchange contracts. If there is an increase in cross-border transactions compared with the overall economic development, that suggests that this kind of transaction has been made easier for the parties by a reduction of transaction costs.

2. Second Hypothesis: Extended use of contracts means reduced uncertainty concerning contract law

Apart from the legal uncertainty described above, a multiplicity of other factors is unfortunately hampering cross-border transactions. For that reason it is not clear to what extent each of these variables influences the development of product exchange between the Member States. To demonstrate the complexity of the problem I will briefly describe some of the relevant institutional barriers to trade.[8]

First, there are tariffs, quotas and other 'visible' interventions of the national authorities in the flow of goods and services across their borders. However, within the EC these kinds of restrictions have been almost completely removed since the 1970s and therefore are of no relevance for the planned empirical investigation.

The second factor is non-tariff barriers to trade, in the first place technical

---

[8]   Natural trade barriers, like geographical distance or lack of infrastructure, leading to an increase of transportation costs, are left out.

regulations such as product standards and other requirements often imposed by public law, concerning the marketing of goods and services.[9] These provisions should be unified within the Internal Market but this process is still underway, therefore the planned empirical investigation must take into account any such unification measures carried out in the field and within the period under research. Because of their mandatory character, a co-ordination of these non-tariff barriers strongly facilitates the movement of products between the Member States – certainly much more than any harmonisation of contract law.

Thirdly, the different national tax systems create distortions for cross-border transactions – sometimes also classified as non-tariff barriers. Thus any harmonisation in this field intensely influences the level of international economic relations and must therefore be considered in the empirical investigation.

The second and third factor mentioned above, technical and fiscal barriers to trade (together with physical barriers), have been made responsible by the Commission for most of the problems burdening the establishment of an Internal Market in the White Paper of 1985.[10]

Fourthly, there are obstacles for cross-border trade which are not caused by rules or regulations. A prominent example is the changing of preferences of the economic actors. Even if this is normally a rather slow development, it may be stimulated by the differentiation of products.[11] Consequently, the planned empirical investigation has to ensure that the area under research is large enough to minimise these side-effects.

Focusing on contracts and contract law, the investigation cannot be reduced to the main agreements between the parties, because for its performance it is often necessary – especially under international circumstances – for each party to conclude auxiliary contracts with third parties, for example regarding the transportation or the insurance of the goods. Facilitating those contracts also stimulates cross-border transactions. This is even more obvious for arrangements concerning the payment in return for the goods or services. If the process to fulfil monetary obligations is easier, the debtor is more likely to accept such obligations. Since the EC has simplified payments from one Member State to another, not least by stabilising the exchange rates and setting up a single currency, the resulting transaction cost-reducing effects must be taken into account.

Finally, the legal uncertainty in cross-border contractual relationships has to be handled separately following the three elements mentioned above. This is because the uncertainty concerning the national set of rules which is applicable

---

9   See P. Brenton, J. Sheehy and M. Vancauteren, 'Technical Barriers to Trade in the European Union', (2001) 39 *J. of Common Market Studies*, 265.

10   White Paper on the Completion of the Internal Market, COM(85) final, 310.

11   J.U.-M. Nielsen, H. Heinrich and J.O. Hansen, *Economic Analysis of the EC* (Maidenhead, McGraw-Hill, 1992), 57.

to the contract is minimised in the Member States of the EC by the unified private international rules on contractual obligations introduced by the Rome Convention of 1980.[12] Beyond that, the uncertainty related to the enforceability of claims is reduced within the Internal Market by the unified rules on jurisdiction and enforcement of judgments contained in the former Brussels Convention of 1968, now transformed into Regulation 44/2001.[13] In addition to that, the possibility of using arbitration and obtaining a recognised title under the New York Convention[14] exists.

In light of the above, it should be clear that measuring the result of contract law harmonisation is very complicated because various other influences on the usability of contracts in international trade have to be separated. The feasibility of this task depends heavily on the area which will be chosen for the empirical investigation.

III. POSSIBLE AREAS FOR AN EMPIRICAL DATA INVESTIGATION

In view of the many factors that influence international transactions, the planned investigation has to be restricted in its scope. Therefore the sector of harmonised contract law to be analysed should be defined, also where the harmonisation effect could best be observed and the products which are affected by contract law harmonisation. For each of these limitations one can think of several selection criteria.

1. Selection of Legal Sector

To study the effects of legal harmonisation it is necessary to compare a particular set of rules before it is harmonised with the same set of rules after a successful harmonisation. In the field of contract law the areas which could be examined are limited, because until now the EC has approximated only some parts of the contract laws in the Member States.

The main attention is drawn to the harmonisation of consumer protection, which in the early years has only affected methods of concluding contracts with non-professionals (doorstep transactions, distance selling) and special types of consumer contracts (consumer credit, package travel, time-share residence). Later, some harmonisation measures reached the core of contract law (unfair contract clauses, consumer sales). Apart from that, there has been mainly some co-ordination of laws concerning banking, insurance and securities contracts.[15]

---

[12] Consolidated version OJ EC 1999 C 27/34.

[13] OJ EC 2001 L 12/1.

[14] United Nations Convention on the Recognition and Enforcement of Foreign Arbitral Awards of 10.6.1958.

[15] Commission (n. 2 above), Annex 1.

The selection between these 'islands' of harmonisation should be guided by the following considerations:

– 'internationality' of transactions
As long as most of the contracts are made on a national basis, the effect of harmonisation is fairly small and difficult to observe. This is true for consumer contracts – or was true even before harmonisation. Therefore, co-ordination related to contracts with a high proportion of cross border operations is preferable; such as, for instance, the 1997 Directive on cross-border payments.
– period of harmonised law in force
Because the actors must realise the gains of harmonisation and adapt their behaviour, the effects of harmonisation grow over the time the amended rules are in force. This argues in favour of the 'older' contract law approximation. It may be even doubted if the 1993 Directive on Unfair Contract Clauses has been established for long enough in the Member States to serve as a fruitful object of empirical investigation. Consequently, a survey on the influence of the Consumer Sales Directive of 1999 will not make sense before some years of application in the Member States. From this perspective the 1986 Directive on Consumer Credit[16] or the Directives on Life Insurance of 1979, 1990 and 1992 are candidates for selection.
– intensity of influence on contractual behaviour
Nearly all measures to harmonise contract law have been directed at mandatory rules. This type of regulation creates bigger hindrances for the Internal Market than non-obligatory rules.[17] The effects of harmonisation related to mandatory contract law should therefore be more evident than the planned co-ordination of gap-filling contract law. That suggests excluding harmonisation measures regarding non-obligatory regulations.

Taking this into account I would suggest pre-selecting harmonisation measures in the field of consumer credit, life insurance or securities, perhaps also the fairly new Directive on Cross-border Payments for an empirical investigation.

2. Selection of Territorial Scope

To simplify the evaluation, the investigation should be concentrated on the exchange of goods or services between two states at a time. The candidates could generally not only be chosen from the fifteen Member States, but depending on the concrete harmonisation instrument, even from the EFTA Countries or from associated East European nations.

---

[16] Report on the operation of this Directive in COM(95) 117 final.
[17] See for example E.-M. Kieninger, '100 Jahre BGB – Zeit für ein Europäisches Zivilgesetzbuch?', in: *Jahrbuch Junger Zivilrechtswissenschaftler 1996* (1997), 245, 247, 251 *et seq.*

Some criteria to select between the states are:

– intensity of cross-border relations
The more contracts which are concluded between actors of the selected states, the more evident the harmonisation effect, therefore strong economic relations, in the chosen field of research, such as between the EC states, will facilitate the investigation. This is not necessarily concentrating on neighbouring nations. On the other hand, the size of the economy might be of relevance.

Within the EC, Germany, the United Kingdom, France and Italy seem to have the strongest economic relationships with each other.

– extent of differences in contract law
Harmonisation is very effective if there have been large differences between the legal rules of the two selected states before the approximation. That makes it necessary to select members of two different legal families, such as for instance, Germany, belonging to the continental civil law and the United Kingdom belonging to the common law tradition. However, this has to be considered depending on the choice of the legal sectors because in some cases, especially concerning modern regulations, this traditional classification will not be helpful.

I would suggest pre-selecting a combination of Germany, the United Kingdom, France or Italy for the planned investigation.

3. Selection of Objects Traded Across Borders

At the least the survey must be focused on a certain type of product, be it goods or services. That of course, is connected to the decision under (1.) concerning the harmonised set of rules as co-ordination usually catches certain objects only. Again it is the internationality of the selected kind of objects which counts. Another selection criterion could be the absence or minimal influence of the above mentioned (II.2) additional factors hampering cross-border transactions. The suggestion under (1.) – consumer credit, life insurance and securities – is supported by these additional elements.

IV. CONCLUSION

Even if an empirical data investigation concerning the effects of contract law harmonisation is a very difficult task, an attempt should be made as soon as possible, because if the co-ordination of mandatory rules in the past will not show significant results regarding the Internal Market, a co-ordination of non-mandatory contract law in the future is unlikely to have a relevant influence on the transaction costs of the parties. In this case 'prima facie' the economic argument in favour of a harmonisation of contract law based on the Internal

Market would fail. In other words, the goal of harmonisation – to reduce the differences of rules – would not be enough to justify EC activity in the field of contract law, so that the goal of regulation – to create a 'better' or more efficient law – has to be concerned:[18] But this would require a totally different analysis!

Finally, I would like to ask for support, of course, from lawyers – especially from the colleagues participating in this conference – but from economists too (who should be specifically invited to join the SECOLA). This support is needed to refine the rough structure for an empirical data investigation into the impact of contract law harmonisation I have proposed.

---

[18] On this two different functions of approximation of laws see A. Schwartze, *Deutsche Bankenrechnungslegung nach europäischem Recht* (Baden-Baden, Nomes, 1991), 115.

4. Finding the Remaining Traps Instead of Unifying Contract Law

*Hugh Beale**

The case that I wish to make is that we may need more harmonisation of contract law (in the broad sense in which it is referred to in the Commission's Communication) but that we need no more than harmonisation.

Insofar as it rests on barriers to intra-Community trade caused by differences between the laws of Member States, the case for further harmonisation is largely intuitive rather than proven by empirical evidence. In areas of specific contracts that are heavily regulated, certainly differences between the various national laws do create barriers to trade and give local firms an advantage in each national market. There are concrete examples of this in relation to the Smart Car Insurance problem[1] and from Financial Services generally.[2] As we move to less regulated areas, hard evidence is more difficult to find. However even practising solicitors who advise parties to cross-border contracts will admit that it is frequently necessary to take advice even about the law of other Member States.[3] This must add to the cost, even if it is not an absolute barrier to cross-border trade.

Recent directives on consumer protection have been justified in terms of encouraging consumers to have confidence in cross-border shopping and thus developing the single market.[4] I would imagine that differences in substantive law are very marginal in this respect. The problems of language, different cultural arrangements and of legal enforcement are far more likely to influence the consumer's decision. I would imagine that the trouble and expense involved, even if there were no differences in substantive law, would mean that frequent cross-border shopping is relatively unlikely for small purchases, except those

---

[*] Professor of law, University of Warwick; Law Commissioner, Common Law. This paper reflects only the author's personal views.

[1] See the response to the Communication by the Commission on European Contract Law and the Study Group on a European Civil Code, para.16. The responses may be read at http://europa.eu.int/comm/consumers/policy/developments/contract_law/comments/index_en.html.

[2] See the response of the London Investment Bankers Association.

[3] See the response of the Law Society.

[4] e.g. Council Directive 1999/44/EC of 25 May 1999 on certain aspects of the sale of consumer goods and associated guarantees, EC OJ 1999 L 171/12, Recital 4.

S. Grundmann and J. Stuyck (eds.), An Academic Green Paper on European Contract Law, 67–72
© 2002 *Kluwer Law International. Printed in Great Britain.*

which the consumer perceives as entailing very little risk. Larger purchases are more problematic but, for consumers, are likely to be infrequent. In contrast, businesses may make more sizeable purchases much more frequently. They might find the trouble and expense of cross-border shopping more worthwhile but might be deterred by legal differences. Thus it is the costs to businesses on which I think we should concentrate.

Intuitively, I believe that legal differences do add cost to business contracts. Either one party has to submit to the other party's law, and may therefore have to incur cost in finding out what that law is when planning the contract and if a dispute arises; or else the parties will have to choose some neutral law. That is likely to involve a cost to each of them, at least for the first few times that they do so.

We then need to ask which differences in substantive law it is which cause cost. In terms of substantive results, the work of the Commission on European Contract Law has gone a long way to showing that there are really rather few significant differences in the results reached by the different systems. Just how few is not surprising to a comparative lawyer, but has struck many of us who are new to comparative law very forcefully. Obviously, there are different nuances. For example, specific performance is a much more common remedy in continental systems than it is in the common law systems, even when one allows for differences in terminology (specific performance by a third party at the debtor's expense seems to be the functional equivalent of the remedies of termination and damages for the cost of having the work done by another in the common law systems) and what actually happens in practice (I understand that in Germany specific performance is not normally claimed unless a substitute is not readily available from elsewhere).[5] But the really significant differences in outcome between the systems are limited, for example to the existence or not of a duty of disclosure,[6] or are very unlikely to affect most contracts (e.g. revision of the contract for hardship[7]).

When we turn to special contracts, however, the picture begins to look a bit different. Here we begin to find that similar concepts may be applied by the different systems in rather different ways with different outcomes. Thus the common law system on the one hand and the French and German systems on the other all recognise a distinction between obligations to use care and skill and obligations that are stricter, for example obligations 'of result'. But when we look at the area of construction law, we find that these different obligations are applied to different circumstances. In common law, the contractor is under

---

[5]   See K. Zweigert and H. Kötz, *An Introduction to Comparative Law* (3rd English edn., Clarendon Press, Oxford, 1998), 480; O. Lando and H. Beale, *Principles of European Contract Law, Parts I & II* (Kluwer, The Hague, 2000), 398, 402.

[6]   See Lando and Beale, *Principles of European Contract Law* (n. 5 above), arts 4:103 and 4:107.

[7]   Lando and Beale (n. 5 above), art. 6:111.

a strict liability as regards the quality of the materials used,[8] but only an obligation to use reasonable care and skill in the work;[9] and an architect is only liable for reasonable care and skill. In both French and German law, on the other hand, both contractor and architect are responsible for the fitness for purpose of the work, and this is either an obligation of result[10] or 'guarantee liability'.[11] I understand that in German case law this even extends to the supervisory obligations of the architect.[12] This seems to suggest that we may need further harmonisation in these areas.

I think it may be desirable for another reason also. Many of the rules of PECL are very open textured. For example, the provisions on disclosure of information in effect require the employer to disclose information which good faith requires that it should disclose.[13] I suspect that, unless there are some more detailed principles to offer guidance, these provisions will be applied in very different ways by different courts. I would imagine that an English arbitrator is likely to take the line that good faith only requires disclosure of the exceptional, whereas a French arbitrator might start from the opposite presumption.

I also believe that there many other areas that need to be examined to see whether harmonisation is needed. At least, tort and unjust enrichment are also crucial. If we think about construction contracts and the legal barriers to firms bidding across borders to do construction projects, it is not only the law of contract which is going to be important to the bidder. There are also questions such as its potential liability to third parties (pure tort); its liability for defects after completion, when the building may belong to somebody other than the original client (in some systems at least a question of tort law[14]); and questions of work done in anticipation of a contract which never materialises (which is likely to involve restitution and possibly liability for negligent mis-statement). Other areas which need work are those of personal security and security over moveable property.

It is for this reason that I very much welcome the work being done by Professor von Bar's study group on a European Civil Code. Colleagues will know that there are teams working on sales,[15] services (including construction),[16]

---

8   See *Young & Marten* v. *McManus Childs* [1969] 1 AC 454, H.L.

9   Supply of Goods and Services Act 1982, s. 13; a designer may be under an obligation to provide a design that is fit for the purpose but only in exceptional circumstances, see *Greaves & Co (Contractors) Ltd* v. *Baynham, Miekle & Partners* [1975] 1 W.L.R. 1095, C.A.; *Hawkins v. Chrysler (UK) Ltd* (1986) 38 Building L.R. 36, C.A.

10   Arts 1792 and 1792-1 Code civil (*Loi No. 78-12 of 4 January 1978*).

11   BGB §§ 633–637.

12   BGHZ 45, 372; 83, 131; Larenz, *Schuldrecht/II-1*, para. 53 I.

13   See arts 4:103 and 4:107, n. 6 above.

14   e.g. in the UK: see *Murphy v. Brentwood District Council* [1991] 1 AC 398, H.L.

15   In Utrecht, under the leadership of Professor Ewoud Hondius.

16   In Tilburg, under the leadership of Professor Maurits Barendrecht.

franchise and agency contracts,[17] personal security and security over moveables,[18] insurance[19] and financial services[20] as well as tort and unjust enrichment.[21]

Even if the substantive outcomes of contract law in the various member states is pretty similar, it has to be admitted that it is quite difficult to know what the other countries' law is because of the differences in terminology and concepts. This must lead to the question, would it not be better to unify the law so that we all had the same system and use precisely the same concepts and terminology.

I can see that there is a strong argument in favour of unification, but I am not persuaded. First, I think that there is positive value in diversity. Professor Wilhelmsson[22] has made the point much more ably than I can that diversity encourages experimentation and experimentation encourages legal development. I would have some fear that a monolithic contract law would be much less adaptable to new circumstances. But, secondly, I believe that in all aspects of our life, whether it be religion, art or law, we should encourage pluralism. Diversity is one of the things that makes our society interesting to live in and I do not wish to limit pluralism unless it is strictly necessary to do so.

This brings me to my main argument, which is that unification is unnecessary. I believe that for most purposes, differences between our laws of contract are really not very important, subject to one proviso. This is that there should be no major differences between the systems which constitute hidden traps, particularly not differences which might expose parties when they are unlikely to be insured or to be able to take other precautions.

My argument that relatively minor differences between the legal regimes, including differences in concept and terminology, are not particularly important rest on the empirical studies of the use of the law of contract which have been carried out in my country[23] and, by Simon Deakin and his colleagues,[24] on a comparative basis between England, Italy and Germany. Certainly the UK studies suggest that business people (in this case, in the manufacturing industry) make rather little use of the law of contract, not only in settling disputes but

---

[17]   In Amsterdam, under the leadership of Professor Martijn Hesselink.

[18]   In Hamburg, under the leadership of Professor Ulrich Drobnig.

[19]   In Hamburg, under the leadership of Professor Jurgen Basedow, linked to the project led by Professor Fritz Reichert-Facilides, Innsbruck.

[20]   Professor A. Prüm (Luxembourg) and Professor L. Aynès (Paris).

[21]   The last two under the leadership of Professor von Bar in Osnabrück.

[22]   'Private Law in the EU: Harmonised or Fragmented Europeanisation?' (unpublished paper).

[23]   H. Beale and T. Dugdale, 'Contracts between Businessmen' (1975) 2 *British J. Law and Society* 45, which to a large extent replicates the famous study by S. Macaulay, 'Non-contractual Relations in Business' (1963) 28 *American Sociological Review* 55.

[24]   See Deakin, Lane and Wilkinson in: J. Michie and S. Deakin, *Contracts, Co-operation, and Competition: Studies in Economics, Management, and Law* (Oxford University Press, 1997).

also in planning contracts. The parties very seldom refer to the contract even when a dispute does arise; they are far more likely to rely on trust, business understandings or simply the pressure they can exert by threatening loss of future business than they are to rely on legal provisions or even the terms of the contract. They only plan contracts when the risk are relatively high. In other circumstances they are content to rely on rather vague agreements or simply on an exchange of standard forms, the conflicts between which are never sorted out. Even when the parties do go in for a degree of contract planning, typically because the items being sold are 'high risk' (for example, aircraft spares) or because they are dealing with a party with whom they have not dealt before, it is my interpretation that the parties are often much less concerned with reaching legal certainty than they are with ensuring that there is sufficient common understanding of the norm (legal or non-legal) which will govern their relationship for it to be able to work smoothly and to provide some basis for the negotiations of any dispute which might arise.

Certainly, there may be cultural differences between our countries. Simon Deakin's work suggests that there is a significant contrast between attitude of business people to contract law in Germany than the equivalent in England: the Germans are likely to see the contract as a way of building trust whereas in England, contract and trust are seen as being mutually exclusive and reference to the contract is likely to destroy the commercial relationship. However, I do not think that in either case the parties are necessarily concerned with the precise details either of the general law or of the contract. They are more concerned, I suspect, to ensure that there is a broad understanding so as to avoid difficulties of a major kind or very nasty surprises should some dispute arise.

This suggests to me that businesses are unlikely to worry about the details of the law on the other side, providing they can assume with reasonable confidence that the outcome under whichever legal system they are operating is broadly the same. It is only in the case where a dispute arises and the parties are unable to reach a negotiated commercial settlement that it will become necessary to descend into the finer points of law and to work out which law governs the contract and precisely what that implies. This is going to be, in percentage terms, a very small number of cases.

I do not deny that there are some businesses which require much greater certainty than the manufacturers who formed the subject of the studies I have referred to. In particular, where markets fluctuate very much it is very common for the parties to plan the contract in very considerable detail (using standard forms that are signed by both parties) and to use arbitration or litigation as a way of solving disputes. I believe that such parties are likely to have a preference either for a known national law (and of course in many cases that is English law) or for a neutral international system such as the Principles of European Contract Law or the Unidroit Principles of International Commercial Contracts.

My conclusion is that we do not need to unify our laws of contract and that, although having diversity adds something to the costs, there would be significant other costs, in terms of loss of pluralism and possibly loss of flexibility, in surrendering that diversity. However, we do need to ensure, as I said earlier, that there are not major traps in doing business across borders without knowing much detail about the other party's law. For example, an architect should think very carefully before undertaking work in another jurisdiction in case she finds that, on one hand, she is exposed to 'fitness for purpose liability' for a design but, on the other, her professional insurance only covers her for negligence. Equally, it may be desirable for contractors to have a greater understanding of what an employer is required, as a matter of good faith, to disclose about site conditions and so on.[25] Precisely which differences need to be ironed out has to be worked out through studies of the kind being done by Professor von Bar's group. I suspect that some further sectoral harmonisation will prove to be necessary, not only in construction but possibly even in such basic areas as sales law (in other words to extend the protection given by the consumer sales directive to business purchasers). But I would begin and end with harmonisation.

---

[25] See further H. Beale, 'Principles of European Conract Law and Construction Contracts' (1998) *International Construction Law Review* 85, 97–98.

5. European Consumer Law – The Minimal and Maximal Harmonisation Debate and Pro Independent Consumer Law Competence

*Geraint Howells**

The European Commission's *Communication on European Contract Law*[1] outlines at least four options for the development of European contract law – no action, promoting the development of common contract law principles, improving the quality of legislation already in place or adopting new comprehensive legislation at the EC level.[2] The first is unrealistic if it means no further activity in the field of European contract law, but is perhaps best understood as continuing in the present punctual manner. The last is a dream of a European Civil Code which idealists aspire to and no doubt can make out a case for. If this were chosen there would be technical questions about whether there is yet Community competence and whether a Community legal instrument or a Convention is the best way forward. Nevertheless such a dramatic step does not yet seem politically acceptable. One only has to consider the opposition to common rules on contract formation in the narrow area of e-commerce to see how sensitive this topic can be. One might question whether the core values of a European private law are yet sufficiently well established. Further research would need to be undertaken to assess whether the disturbance to national legal systems is worth the gains. The second objective of promoting common contract principles is already happening.[3] Community support to a particular set of principles may encourage their adoption but this is essentially a question for the market.

Improving the quality of legislation in place should of course be an ongoing process and indeed most Directives include provisions for reports and possible revisions. However, this can be understood for a call for something greater. One could imagine a process of taking stock of areas of community activity in EC contract law and producing improved consolidated legislation. My own area of interest, consumer protection, provides one such area that could benefit from

---

* Professor of Law, Faculty of Law, University of Sheffield, UK.
[1] COM(2001) 398.
[2] *Ibid.*, 13–17.
[3] O.Lando and H. Beale, *Principles of European Contract Law* (Deventer, Kluwer, 1999). There have also been various other academic networks.

S. Grundmann and J. Stuyck (eds.), An Academic Green Paper on European Contract Law, 73–80
© 2002 *Kluwer Law International. Printed in Great Britain.*

some rationalisation. Probably one would need to go beyond mere contract law provisions and include private and public law issues, for the real world does not divide up neatly into lawyers' categories. Indeed at a recent conference in Trier Professor Van Gerven called for such actions to be taken using the instrument of regulations so as not excessively to burden national legislators with implementation obligations. Although he did not expressly call for maximal harmonisation, this would seem to be in line with the use of a Regulation and to fit in with current thinking within the Commission.

Its recent discussion document *Ideas for a Consumer Policy Strategy*[4] talks about the need for a high harmonised level of consumer protection across the EU. However, there are subtle differences of language that need to be considered. For instance, there is a world of difference between a highly harmonised level of EU consumer law and maximal harmonisation in the sense of not allowing any additional national rules. Equally, harmonising at a high level can be a separate goal from maximal harmonisation. Does high refer to the quality of the protection or level of harmonisation? The e-commerce Directive adopted an approach consistent with maximal harmonisation. Equally the proposed Regulation concerning sales promotions in the Internal Market[5] can be seen as a potential insight into Commission thinking in that it is both a Regulation and adopts a maximal harmonisation approach with mutual recognition in areas where national rules would otherwise create barriers to trade. This is a break from a trend of adopting minimal harmonisation Directives, and indeed other trends within the Commission's policy strategy such as the Green Paper on fair trading using general standards and co-regulation at least seem to appreciate the need for a more flexible regime.

The maximal approach harkens back to the product liability Directive, which although not expressly said to be a maximal harmonisation Directive and despite some arguments to the contrary, came to be viewed as a maximal harmonisation Directive.[6] Interestingly, that was a Directive proclaimed to be an Internal Market measure with only incidental benefits to consumers. It is clear to see how, from an Internal Market perspective, maximal harmonisation is appealing. However, even if it were possible to harmonise at a level which suited all states' preferences for consumer protection there would still be dangers in it.

For many years consumer lawyers were keen on European activity in their areas. Whilst there might have been some drawbacks because of the quality of the laws produced and hindrance to national initiatives, on the whole the effects were positive in most countries. Issues were agreed upon, which might never have been introduced at the national level – such as product liability reform,

---

4   Available on website of DG-SANCO.
5   COM(2001) 546.
6   See now Cases C-52/00 *Commission v. France*, and C-183/00 *González Sánchez v. Medicina Asturiana SA*.

collective injunctions also spring to mind from a UK perspective, and other consumer rights were protected by virtue of their European origin from deregulatory tendencies. It was true that with the addition of more Nordic countries there were fears that their protective approach might be undermined, at least indirectly, by the EC's narrow view of protection which invoked the image of a rational 'active and critical information-seeking' consumer at the expense of more vulnerable consumers.[7] However, if the EC does switch to a maximal harmonisation approach there will be far more concern.

I. THE CASE FOR MINIMAL HARMONISATION?

The minimal or maximal harmonisation debate is not just a question of whether Europe or Member States can develop the best consumer laws. Although there are clearly concerns to be expressed about the strength of the business lobby in Brussels compared to consumer groups; the weakness of consumer protection within EU policy which is focused on market integration and the need for any European rules to respect national traditions and circumstances. It is fair to say, however, that EC consumer law has no settled philosophy, for whilst some measures clearly start with strong consumer protection aspirations these are often diluted by the need to justify their scope in terms of the Internal Market, and other measures place Internal Market concerns to the fore and seem to pay little attention to the needs of consumers. EC consumer rules have some history but it is a limited history. There has not been enough time for the sediment to rest, to use Tuori's analogy.[8] Thus it is impossible to say what the deeper values of EC consumer policy are, how strong they are and whether they can be viewed as independent of Internal Market policy. Undoubtedly, however, by their very nature they tend towards a one solution fits all approach and this downplays the local traditions, circumstances and needs.

One of the greatest dangers of maximalisation, however, is that it represents a fixing of the goal posts. One thing is certain, that businesses will respond to any regulation by seeking to minimise its impact either by finding strategies to avoid adverse consequences or changing business practices to side-step such rules. They are not to be criticised for this; it is an inevitable feature of how business has to work in a competitive economy.[9] However, it does mean that

---

7   See discussion in Howells and Wilhemsson, *EC Consumer Law* (Aldershot, Dartmouth, 1997), 138.

8   K. Tuori, 'EC Law: An Independent Legal Order or a Post-Modern Jack-in-the-Box?' in: L.D. Eriksson and S. Hurri (eds.), *Dialectic of Law and Reality* (Helsinki, 1999), 397–41: cited in: T. Wilhelmsson, 'Private Law in the EC: Harmonised or Fragmented Europeanisation', [2002] *ERPL*, 77.

9   See, J. Hanson and K, Logue, 'The Costs of Cigarettes: The Economic Case for Ex Post Incentive-Based Regulation' [1998] *Yale L. J.* 1163.

the law needs to be capable of adapting quickly to such problems and the European legislative machinery does not seem appropriate for rapid responses.

There is also a more positive case that can be made out for minimal harmonisation. Member States can act as laboratories, experimenting with practices which if successful can be integrated into EU policy. Consumer credit is a good example of how this might work. The initial consumer credit Directive was modest.[10] The review of the legislation sought to draw on national experiences using the minimal harmonisation clause.[11] Hopefully the Directive will be revised to provide better consumer protection.[12] The next Directive might not be ideal, as some Member States may still hesitate to accept some rules, but that matters little, for experimentation can continue and no existing protection is impaired. It is useful to note that using states as a legal laboratory is seen as a key feature in the US and the role of state Attorney-Generals in consumer protection is not to be underestimated.

II. IS MINIMAL HARMONISATION POSSIBLE?

At one level the *Tobacco Judgment* favoured mutual recognition and maximal harmonisation, for it was clearly concerned that the Internal Market would not be enhanced if, despite complying with a Directive, a product might nevertheless be prevented from circulating within the Community.[13] However, that view might apply less to background private law rules than to rules on advertising that more directly impact on the freedom of goods to circulate within the Community. Moreover, the *Tobacco* case has also taught us that some differences between national laws are so insignificant that they do not justify intervention by the European legislature on the basis that harmonisation is needed for the functioning of the Internal Market. Most of these rules would also seem not capable of acting as barriers to trade, although the relationship between positive and negative harmonisation rules is not completely settled. Therefore one might assume that when a Directive includes a minimal harmonisation clause it leaves the Member States a certain room for manoeuvre. One particular case study suggests otherwise. The misleading advertisement Directive defined misleading

---

[10]   EC OJ 1987 L42/48, as amended.

[11]   Report on the operation of Directive 87/102/EEC for the approximation of the laws, Regulations and administrative provisions of the Member States concerning consumer credit: COM(95) 117.

[12]   A Discussion Paper has been issued.

[13]   Case C-376/98 [2000] ECR I–8419 *Germany v. European Parliament and another (supported by France and others, interveners)* and Case C-74/99 [2000] ECR I–8599 *R v. Secretary of State for Health and Others, ex parte Imperial Tobacco Ltd and others* (2000) All E.R. (EC) 769. This point was made by J. Drexl in his paper to the Secola conference 'Continuing Contract Law Harmonisation under the White Paper of 1985 – Partly with Modifications (see Ch. 7 below)'.

as something that 'deceives or is likely to deceive'.[14] Behind this formalistic definition lay a debate as to whether when controlling advertising one judged the advertisements against the standard of the vulnerable consumer needing the protection of the state not to be misled or whether one intervened only when a rational consumer would be misled. The misleading advertising Directive appeared to leave Member States the autonomy to continue with their own consumer protection policy so long as it satisfied the minimum levels prescribed. However, this was only a chimera of freedom. A combination of two lines of argument has resulted in a severe levelling down of protection in some states. The minimal harmonisation standard in the Directive is fast approaching a maximal harmonisation standard. First, the court interpreted the misleading standard in the Directive against the standard of the rational Internal Market consumer.[15] This was understandable given the context of a decision whose ultimate purpose was to encourage the parallel importation of cars. However, this same demanding standard was applied in the context of free movement case law to challenges to decisions under German unfair competition law which condemned advertisements as misleading once 10–20 per cent of consumers would be misled.[16] One would have imagined that so long as the German meaning of misleading at least contained the European meaning then Germany would be allowed to continue its own policy to protect its citizens. Clearly, however, this was not the case. Why was this? Was it simply that the German application of their rules was so outlandish that the court really only saw them as protective measures in disguise? In other words, the European law was a prompt to modernise German law. Given that the application of the standards rests with the German courts this might be viewed as a result that is not entirely unwelcomed in Germany. Or was it a recognition that even legitimate measures of consumer protection sometimes have to be sacrificed on the altar of Internal Market reasoning? If the latter, what are the implications?

Perhaps it is significant that the type of rules affected by the German controls on advertising affect the presentation of the product and hinder cross-border advertising campaigns and are therefore the sort of measures which continue to be subject to free movement controls after *Keck*.[17] If this is the case, then there may be less impact on the rules of private law which merely provide default rules. Their effect on Internal Market policy might be seen as being less direct.

III. HOW SHOULD EC LAW BE MODERNISED?

To date most consumer protection measures have been adopted through Directives. The choice of a regulation for the proposals on sales promotions

---

[14]   (EC) OJ L 250/17, art. 2(2).

[15]   Case C-373/90, *Criminal proceedings against X* [1992] ECR I–131.

[16]   Case C-210/96, *Gut Springenheide GmbH and Rudolf Tusky v. Oberkreisdirektor des Kreises Steinfurt – Amt fur Lebensmitteluberwachung,* [1998] ECR I–5655.

[17]   Joined Cases C-267 and C-268/91, *Keck and Mithouard* [1993] ECR I–6097.

might be a sign that things are changing. Indeed, Professor van Gerven has suggested the use of a Regulation for the task of consolidation in order to prevent national legislators having to go through the implementation task. A task that is not only time consuming, but which also creates complexities when wording differs from the European Directive or adaptations are made in order to dovetail it into the national framework.

Behind the choice of Directive or Regulation might be thought to lie a debate over harmonisation or uniformity. This is a debate that Europe has never really treated seriously. It in fact involves two interlocking questions: what measures should be addressed at the European level and to what extent need they be harmonised? The former has been clouded by the Internal Market origin of EC consumer law, and the extent of harmonisation has again been judged by Internal Market concerns. This is certainly one dimension, but a regime set up to create consumer confidence would both tackle a wider range of issues and be more concerned with minimum than maximum standards.

In many ways Directives have often come to function like Regulations. Occasionally states put national glosses on implementing measures, especially where they seek to integrate them into existing national regimes, but the experience from the UK is that governments (or at least officials) favour staying close to the European wording. There are some incentives for this built into the system. Infringement proceedings by the Commission are certainly one such incentive, although the chances of being targeted for legal action seems something of a lottery. Equally, state liability under *Francovich*[18] provides a further incentive, although the requirement that a breach be sufficiently serious[19] perhaps protects states where their implementation simply puts a national slant on the Directive's wording. However, the strongest control on national discretion comes from the principle of indirect effect whereby implementing laws are to be interpreted in line with Directives.[20] In one recent important UK High Court decision on the application of strict product liability to contaminated blood products, the judge went so far as simply to ignore the wording of the UK's Consumer Protection Act 1987 in favour of the product liability Directive.[21] This may have been going too far, but it emphasises the uncertainty about the nature of Directives.

If national discretion is to be meaningful, then it seems that the role of the Directive needs to be reinterpreted. Failing that, the Regulation would seem to

---

[18] Cases C-6 and 9/90, *Francovich and Others v. Italy* [1991] ECR I–5357.

[19] Cases C-46 and 48/93, *Brasserie du Pécheur v. Germany* and *R v. Secretary of State for Transport, ex parte Facto tame* [1996] ECR I–1029.

[20] Case 14/83, *Von Colson and Kamaan v. Land NordrheinWestfalen* [1984] ECR 1891 and Case C-106189, *Marleasing SA v. La Comercial International de Alimentación* [1990] ECR I–4135.

[21] *A and Others v. The National Blood Authority and Others* [2001] 3 All ER 289.

be little different from a Directive save that it removes the need for the agonies of the implementation process, which might be viewed as something of a show for domestic consumption. However, national governments might be reluctant to accept Regulations because they would have no chance to ameliorate the poor draftsmanship of EC legislators. One might also suspect that neither the EC nor the states would readily give up the Directive, for it provides a lubricant whereby differences can be compromised and ambiguities in the EC law exploited when enacting national interpretations. There would also need to be some alteration to the style of Regulations and one could imagine that the debate as to whether all Regulations were directly effective as well as directly applicable would be reignited.[22]

IV. WHAT SHOULD BE HARMONISED?

Any attempted codification of EC consumer law should be both broad and deep. Broad in the sense that it does not make sense to limit it to mere codification of private law rules. Consumer protection does not respect any legal categories and includes a wide range of legal techniques that need to be co-ordinated. Depth is required to ensure that consumers are not caught unawares by national peculiarities. This should also increase legal certainty and be to the advantage of business.

One example might illustrate the need for detailed harmonisation. Elsewhere I have argued for a greater harmonisation of the right of withdrawal.[23] This involves co-ordinating as far as possible the various cancellation periods and the date from when they run. Even basic issues like what counts as a day towards the cancellation period are not currently harmonised. However, this needs also to cover the consequences of exercising the right of cancellation in far more detail than is presently the case.

To what extent does the harmonisation of consumer law require a harmonisation of private law? There are certainly some points of private law that need to be harmonised to ensure laws are capable of uniform application across Europe. Most obviously several contract law obligations centre around the conclusion of the contract. In the absence of a grand harmonisation, consideration ought to be given to specifying when specific rules are needed in particular contexts to indicate when contracts have been concluded. E-commerce situations are a prime example of where such rules are needed, for consumers will often not know in which jurisdiction they are contracting. Given that one of the objectives of EC consumer policy is to encourage consumers to shop outside their own state it would seem that a minimum legal certainty about when

---

22 G. Winter, 'Direct Applicability and Direct Effect: Two Distinct and Different Concepts in Community Law' (1972) 9 *CMLRev* 425.
23 'The Right of Withdrawal in European Consumer Law' forthcoming.

contracts are concluded is not unreasonable. The failure to include such rules in the E-commerce Directive is lamentable.

The lack of detail in Directives is now generating uncertainty, which in turn generates litigation, which is of little use to anyone save lawyers. For instance, in the product liability context the European Court said in the *Danish Kidney* case[24] that the damage had to be interpreted in a Community sense. More recently the ECJ has determined that immaterial damages are within the meaning of damage within the Package Travel Directive.[25] Given the present state of EC law the quantum of damages is likely to remain a matter for national law so long as the amounts satisfy the requirements of effectiveness within EC law, but this is just one example where the EC legislator could usefully be more explicit or at least more open where no Community conclusions can be established.

V. A FINAL PLEA

What I am proposing is a major review of the current substantive private law of the EC. Part of this process will be to learn from the implementation process in member states and actual practice. However, I would also argue for a more fundamental revision. Many of the criticisms of EC consumer law result from the Janus-faced nature of EC consumer policy.[26] It claims to be concerned with consumer protection, but only from within the confines of an Internal Market perspective. Internal market ideology can sustain high or low levels of protection. The Community claims to favour a high level of protection, but the need for Internal Market justifications mean that Community laws often only deal with part of the problem. Moreover, the threat of legal challenge – enhanced after the *Tobacco Judgment* – also frequently causes the rules that are introduced to be watered down as a compromise to fend off political opposition. Ideally consumer protection should be an independent legal base, but failing that any consolidation should also be undertaken within a legal regime which provides that once a measure is within the Community's competence then the solution should be the best possible, even if incidentally measures with a less direct impact on the Internal Market are included. This message about the need for a proper legal basis would seem to be a valuable lesson for those who favour a general codification to learn from the consumer lawyer's experience.

---

[24] Case C-203/99, *Henning Veedfald v. Arhus Amtskommune* [2001] ECR I-1169.
[25] Case C-168/00, *Leitner v. TUI Deutschland*.
[26] A phrase used to describe this juxtaposition of values by Norbert Reich in *Europäisches Vervraucherschutzrecht* (Nomos Baden-Baden, 1993), 45.

6. Directives on Consumer Protection as a Suitable Means of Obtaining a (More) Unified European Contract Law?

*Bernard Tilleman and Bart Du Laing**

I. INTRODUCTION

On the occasion of the issuance of the Communication on European Contract Law of 2001[1] from the Commission to the Council and the European Parliament we would like to address the question whether the European Union should continue the (indirect) harmonization of European civil law by means of directives in the field of consumer law. This track has been followed up to now in accordance with the European Commission's 1985 White Paper concerning the completion of the internal market.

The classical plea for a European consumer and contract law is based on the fact that the functioning of the internal market is hindered by disparities between national rules. These disparities would refrain consumers to contract in another Member State, whose legal rules are unfamiliar to them.

II. (OFTEN NEGATIVE) INFLUENCE ON NATIONAL PRIVATE (CONTRACT) LAW

1. Preliminary Remark on the Lack of Internal Coherence of European Directives on Consumer Law

When taking a global look at the various directives on consumer law, one is struck by the lack of internal coherence of European directives. Would it not be wise to adopt uniform notions and wordings of the concepts 'consumer' and 'professional' instead of defining the scope of application of the various directives on a case-by-case basis?[2]

---

*   Professor, K.U. Leuven and Assistant Professor, K.U. Leuven.
[1] COM(2001) 398 final.
[2] Tenreiro, 'Les pratiques commerciales et les contrats: la protection des consommateurs en Europe', *JT DrEur* 1997, 49, 50 *et seq.* Cf. Joustra, 'Consumer Law', in: Hartkamp/Hesselink/Hondius/Joustra/Du Perron, *Towards a European Civil Code – Second Revised and Expanded Edition*, (1998), 133, 143–146; Landy, 'Le consommateur européen: une notion éclatée', in: Osman, *Vers un code européen de la consommation – Codification, unification et harmonisation du droit des Etats-membres de l'Union européenne*, (1998), 57.

S. Grundmann and J. Stuyck (eds.), An Academic Green Paper on European Contract Law, 81–102
© 2002 *Kluwer Law International. Printed in Great Britain.*

Another example concerns the lack of uniformity of the rights of rescission or cancellation which is granted to the consumer by various directives. If one wants to generalize this instrument of consumer protection, it seems evident that one should use a uniform terminology and try to coordinate as far as possible the diverse aspects of this right, such as the cancellation period, as well as the legal consequences of cancellation. However, there exist substantial differences between the various directives with regard to cancellation periods. The legal consequences of this withdrawal are not clearly regulated, so that each national legal system is trying to fill in the blanks by adopting its own national legal concepts.[3] German lawyers consider contracts with a cancellation right to be 'schwebend unwirksam',[4] while Belgian lawyers requalify sales contracts with a right of cancellation as options.

Before aspiring to unify European civil law, one should strive to harmonize, streamline and consolidate the existing set of rules on European consumer law.[5] This could be achieved, for instance, by a general directive adopting a single concept of 'consumer', or defining a uniform notion of cancellation right. It is indeed difficult to speak of harmonization by means of Directives if these Directives themselves are not yet (more or less) 'harmonized' on an internal level.[6] The internal consistency of directives on consumer protection being already relatively small, this inconsistency will not fail to reflect upon the national private (contract) law systems.

2. Fragmentation of National Private (Contract) Law Systems

a) Unjustified Dual Legal Regime of 'Consumer' and 'Non-Consumer' Contracts

In the field of contract law, the relevant directives generally aim at consumer protection. It is the Trojan horse by which the European legislator entered civil

---

[3]   Joustra (n. 2 above) 133, 141; Howells, 'European Consumer Law – The minimal and maximal harmonisation debate' (lecture held at the SECOLA Conference on 'Communication from the Commission on European Contract Law (Harmonisation, Code, Optional Code)', Leuven, 30 November and 1 December 2001), http://www.secola.org/, 8; Staudenmayer, 'Die Mitteilung der Kommission zum Europäischen Vertragsrecht', *EuZW* 2001, 485, 487 *et seq.* Cf. Roth, 'Europäischer Verbraucherschutz und BGB', *JZ* (2001), 475, 480 *et seq.*

[4]   BGH 19 March 1997, *ZIP* 1997, 848.

[5]   Van Gerven, 'Codifying European Private Law' (lecture held at the SECOLA Conference on 'Communication from the Commission on European Contract Law (Harmonisation, Code, Optional Code)', Leuven, 30 November and 1 December 2001), http://www.secola.org/, 16. Cf. Howells (n. 3), 2.

[6]   In this respect, Staudenmayer speaks of EC Law as being 'verhandeltes Recht' (Staudenmayer, *EuZW* (2001), 485, 487).

law.[7] Whereas 'early' directives on consumer law affected civil and contract law only marginally, the more recent directives often affected the aforementioned areas more immediately. This is particularly the case with the Unfair Contract Terms Directive and the Directive on the Sale of Consumer Goods.

Since quite a few national authorities, including the Belgian legislator generally speaking, seem to prefer the adoption of specific legislation on consumer protection to the incorporation of the directives in the existing legislation by extending the scope of application of the consumer directives to non-consumers,[8] one of the main problems constitutes the fragmentation (by way of dissemination) of national contract law. 'Instead of contributing to securing uniformity, these forms of legislation may have the opposite effect, that of legal disintegration.'[9]

With regard to the Belgian transformation of the Directive on Unfair Contract Terms, van Gerven spoke of the 'verkokering van het privaatrecht', by which he meant that the division of *inter alia* contract law between a contract law destined for consumers and 'another' 'general' contract law can lead to unjustifiable differences in the overall framework of the national contract law system.[10]

Yet another example of fragmentation can be found in the Belgian adoption of the Consumer Credit Directive.[11] Whereas in the Belgian Civil Code the loan

---

7   Tichadou, 'Droit privé et droit communautaire: développements récents en législation et en jurisprudence', in: Naome, *Droit européen, actualités et perspectives*, (2001), 225, 241. Cf. Tonner, 'Verbrauchsgüterkauf-Richtlinie und Europäisierung des Zivilrechts', *Betriebs Berater* 1999, 1769, 1769 ('Europäisches bzw. europäisierten Zivilrecht auf der Grundlage von EG-Richtlinien hat sich bislang nur in Sonderbereichen entwickeln können, weil dem europäischen Gesetzgeber eine Kompetenzgrundlage für die Schaffung allgemeinen Zivilrecht fehlt. Das Verbraucherrecht hat sich dabei als das wichtigste Einfallstor in das Zivilrecht der Mitgliedstaaten erwiesen.').

8   Cf. with regard to German law on the possible underlying reasons for this approach Roth, 'Transposing 'Pointillist' EC Guidelines into Systematic National Codes – Problems and Consequences' (lecture held at the SECOLA Conference on 'Sales and Trends in European Contract Law', Rome, 8 and 9 June 2001), *http://www.secola.org/*, 9 *et seq.*; Roth, *JZ* (2001), 475, 484. Cf. also Joustra (n. 2 above) 133, 137 *et seq.* (lack of time; combination of private and public law; detailed character of the rules).

9   Chamboredon, 'The Debate on a European Civil Code: For an "Open Texture"', in: Van Hoecke/Ost, *The Harmonisation of European Private Law* (2000), 63, 65 (with regard to a Community private law based on European regulations and directives).

10   Cf. with regard to German law Tonner, 'Die Rolle des Verbraucherrechts bei der Entwicklung eines europäischen Zivilrechts', *JZ* (1996), 533, 539 ('Die Richtlinie über mißbräuchliche Vertragsklauseln ist eine Verbraucherschutz-Richtlinie. Sie wird vom deutschen Gesetzgeber aber nicht im ohnehin weitgehend europäisierten Sonderprivatrecht Verbraucherrecht umgesetzt, sondern im allgemeinen Zivilrecht und kann dadurch auch dort einen Prozeß der Europäisierung in Gang setzen [...].').

11   Council Directive 87/102/EEC of 22 December 1986 for the approximation of the laws, regulations and administrative provisions of the Member States concerning consumer credit, EC OJ 1987 L 42/48.

agreement is considered to be a real contract (i.e. a contract whose formation supposes the delivery of the object of the agreement as well as the mutual agreements of the parties concerned), a loan agreement within the scope of the Belgian Consumer Credit Law has become a(n obligatorily written) consensual contract (i.e. a contract whose formation only supposes the mutual agreements of the parties concerned). Apart from additional fragmentation of national contract law, this causes a discrepancy in the theoretical framework of Belgian contract law.

When analysing the recent Directive on the Sale of Consumer Goods[12] from a Belgian contract lawyer's point of view, one can only regret the resulting disparity of legal regimes, e.g. as to warranties. Warranties in sales agreements concerning movable goods between consumers and professionals will be governed by the legislation adopted in view of the aforementioned Directive, but warranties in international sales agreements between professionals will often be governed (at least partially) by the (similar regime of the) Vienna Convention on the International Sales of Goods, and general Belgian private sales law will continue to apply to the sales of immovables and electricity, distinguishing between a sale between commercial agents and non-commercial agents.[13] Bearing in mind the European rules concerning unfair terms in so-called 'consumer contracts',[14] the field of application of Belgian national sales law is likely to become very narrow.[15]

One is left wondering whether the seemingly desirable degree of protection could not have been reached within the limits of the existing contractual framework, thus respecting (some of) the individuality of the national legislation. We think that the first question to be asked is whether consumer protection really justifies a separate body of rules. This can certainly be the case. We are not sure, however, whether separate rules concerning legal warranties should exist with respect to consumer contracts. The fact that the German legislator is considering

---

[12] Directive 1999/44/EC of the European Parliament and of the Council of 25 May 1999 on certain aspects of the sale of consumer goods and associated guarantees, EC OJ 1999 L 171/12.

[13] Cf. e.g. with regard to French national sales law Raynard, 'De l'influence communautaire et internationale sur le droit de la vente: quand une proposition de directive s'inspire d'une convention internationale pour compliquer, encore, les recours de l'acheteur', *RTD Civ.* (1997), 1020, 1024.

[14] Roth points out that, '[a]s there is no reference to the unfair terms directive [in the sale of consumer goods directive], it may be presumed that the systematic relationship between both directives has not been really thought through' (Roth (n. 8 above) 5).

[15] Cf. Collins, 'From Liberal Rights to Post-national Private Law Regulation' (lecture held at the SECOLA Conference on 'Sales and Trends in European Contract Law', Rome, 8 and 9 June 2001), *http://www.secola.org/*, 6 ('In the case of consumer sales, for instance, the relevant private law standards are now set even for purely domestic transactions at a European rather than nation state level').

extending the directive on the sale of consumer goods to non-consumers in order to avoid internal inconsistencies in its legal system seems to affirm the inadequacy of separate bodies of rules in this field.

b) Fragmentation of the National Legal System as a Result of the Fragmented Nature of the European Legislation

The fragmentation of the existing national contract law systems can partly be explained by the lack of direction, and hence the fragmented nature, of the measures taken by the European Union, as mentioned above. '[Another] problem to be mentioned is the rather scattered appearance of the measures taken, both in regard to the areas covered and to the rules created.'[16] In this respect, Roth talks of the 'pointillist' nature of the European legislation, that is, 'the fragmentary and somewhat [sic] ad hoc character of Community legislation, and [...] the unsystematic manner in which it has developed up till today'.[17]

Although the explanations for this piecemeal approach are a.o. of a *political* nature, *rather than* a *juridical* one, this inevitably influences the global picture of the national law systems concerned in a way that we do not always approve of, as explained earlier.[18]

---

[16] Muller-Graff, 'EC Directives as a Means of Private Law Unification', in: Hartkamp, Hesselink, Hondius, Joustra and Du Perron, *Towards a European Civil Code – Second Revised and Expanded Edition* (1998), 71, 81.

[17] Roth (n. 8 above) 2.

[18] De Ly, *Europese gemeenschap en privaatrecht*, (1993), 38; Hauschka, 'Grundprobleme der Privatrechtsfortbildung durch die Europäische Wirtschaftsgemeinschaft', *JZ* (1990), 521, 523 *et seq.* ('Eher handelt es sich um in nationale Systeme eingestreute Fragmente rechtlicher Gestaltung, deren Antinomie von Zusammenhanglosigkeit und Detailgenauigkeit die innerstaatliche Rechtsordnung vor erhebliche Probleme stellt.'); Muller-Graff, 'Privatrecht und europäisches Gemeinschaftsrecht', in: Muller-Graff, *Gemeinsames Privatrecht in der Europäischen Gemeinschaft*, (1993), 195, 222 ('Das Angleichungsverfahren vermag überdies die Zerstörung von Einheitlichkeit und Ubersichtlichkeit der nationalen Kodifikationen zusätzlich zu begünstigen.'); Roth (n. 8 above) 7 ('Following an ad hoc- and issue-oriented approach, [Community directives in the field of private law] necessarily become a threat for the consistency of solutions and value judgements reached in the national legal order.'); Roth, *JZ* (2001), 475, 483. Cf. nonetheless *inter alia* Remien, 'Illusion und Realität eines europäischen Privatrechts', *JZ* (1992), 277, 282 ('Der Zerfall der nationalen Kodifikationen wird zwar von Richtlinien – anders als von Ubereinkommen und Verordnungen – weniger vorangetrieben. Dieser Vorteil wird aber nur selten dadurch ausgeschöpft, daß die harmonisierten Regeln dem BGB oder HGB eingegliedert werden, sondern oft durch Erlaß von Spezialgesetzen verschenkt.') (with regard to German law); Sauphanor, *L'influence du droit de la consommation sur le système juridique*, (2000), 364 ('Enfin, la variété des méthodes d'intégration du droit communautaire, qu'il s'agisse de la juxtaposition, de la 'fusion-absorption' ou de la transformation, a permis une incorporation des directives *sans grande perturbation de l'ordre juridique interne*, sauf en matière de clauses abusives.') (with regard to French law) (emphasis added).

c) Fragmentation of Consumer Law due to the Coexistence of National and Europe-inspired Rules

Some Directives create a fragmentation at a second level, namely that of the internal coherence of consumer(-oriented) law itself. In some cases, indeed, consumers are left with a choice between, on the one hand, (general) national rules that already existed before the adoption of the Directive, and, on the other hand, (specific) rules resulting from the implementation of the Directive into national law. Instead of reducing the already denounced complexity, the possibility of combining pre-existing regulations with new ones can thus create even further discrepancies.

This is the case in a number of countries (such as Belgium, France and Germany) with respect to product liability, as far as pre-existing national remedies resulting from, for example, general tort law have been maintained regardless of the diverging remedies adopted in view of the implementation of the Product Liability Directive.[19]

An incoherence may also result from the fact that national legislators do not always adequately seek out the best way of implementing directives, as they sometimes limit themselves to transcribing the directive without confirming whether implementation is really necessary, given the fact that the national legal system already provides solutions imposed by a directive.

An example can be found in the Belgian Consumer Credit Law. Article 38 of the aforementioned law could be considered as a (unnecessary?) repetition of article 1244 Belgian Civil Code. Questions have been raised as to whether and when the consumer can or cannot invoke both provisions (simultaneously). A better thought-out transformation of the Consumer Credit Directive into Belgian law could probably have avoided this incoherency.

One of the underlying reasons for the coexistence of pre-existing national legislation and Europe-inspired legislation in the field of consumer law can be found in the fact that the aforementioned directives often do not correspond with the dogmatic structure, the underlying principles or the socio-economic starting-points of the national legal systems in question.[20]

A perhaps useful observation on the side can nevertheless be obtained from

---

[19]   Ulmer, 'Vom deutschen zum europäischen Privatrecht?', *JZ* (1992), 1, 6.

[20]   Vranken, 'Europees privaatrecht. 'Bridging the gap' tussen wetenschap en praktijk', *TPR* (2000), 3, 4 ('Toch blijven de richtlijnen qua onderwerp tamelijk verspreid. Ook passen ze niet altijd bij de dogmatische structuur, achterliggende beginselen of dragende sociaal-economische uitgangspunten van de nationale rechtsstelsels. Bovendien zijn ze vaak nogal eenzijdig op consumenten gericht en de hierin gereflecteerde waarden hebben in sommige landen geen algemeenheidsaanspraak.'). Cf. Roth, *JZ* (2001), 475, 475 ('Verbraucherschutz [ist] [...] in *rechtspolitischer Perspektive* an die europäischen Vorgaben – also die mit den Richtlinien verfolgten Zwecke – gebunden [...].').

Hommeloff (although it was stated in a different context): 'Der Einfluß, den Richtlinien auf das deutsche Zivilrecht ausüben, könnte in seiner Intensität gedämpft werden, wenn der Europäische Gerichtshof bei der Richtlinien-Auslegung auf das nationale Recht der Mitgliedstaaten und seine Grundsätze zurückgreifen würde.'[21] If at first reading a Directive seems to be in contradiction with the underlying principles of national contract law systems, a more 'conform' interpretation of the Directive could prove useful for avoiding incoherencies. It remains to be seen, however, whether at this moment it is advisable to introduce some kind of obligation to interpret Directives in the light of 'the underlying principles of national contract law systems' (alongside the well-known obligation to interpret national law in the light of the objectives and text of the Directive). It is, to say the least, doubtful.

According to Roth (in his lecture held at the first SECOLA Congress on 'Sales and Trends in European Contract Law'), a good legislator should try to avoid similar discrepancies and/or overlaps by adapting his pre-existing national law to and/or bringing it into conformity with the measures adopted in view of the obligatory transformation of European Directives.

> 'It is to be expected that the [...] alternative [to transform the directive into national law, and to adapt the autonomous private law in order to prevent inconsistent or incoherent solutions] will become the prevailing strategy for the national legislator, the more Community directives penetrate into the realm of national private law. The consequence of this strategy is, of course, that 'pointillist' directives will have a spin-off effect: solutions reached in a directive for a specific problem will be extended to other areas of law that are not covered by the directive. [...] Community directives thus create a driving force for the reform of autonomous national private law – outside the scope of the relevant directive.'[22]

For some legal systems, the future transformation of the dispositions of the Directive on the Sale of Consumer Goods regarding lack of conformity offers a good illustration of this possible difference in approach. With respect to French law, Tournafond distinguishes along the more general lines set out by Roth.

> 'Une première solution serait de se contenter d'une simple transposition *a minima* dans le code de la consommation sans rien toucher aux textes du code civil. [...] L'inconvénient serait évidemment de surajouter encore un nouveau régime de responsabilité à ceux, innombrables, qui existent déjà en la matière. Il est douteux que cette accumulation d'actions en strates successives constitue une bonne politique législative. Elle ne peut qu'accroître le risque d'interférence

---

[21] Hommelhoff, 'Zivilrecht unter dem Einfluß europäischer Rechtsangleichung', *AcP* (1992), 71, 98.

[22] Roth (n. 8 above) 7 *et seq.* and Roth, *JZ* (2001), 475, 487 *et seq.* Cf. Tonner, *JZ* (1996), 533, 539 *et seq.* ('Ausstrahlungswirkung').

et à terme le nombre de litiges.'[23] With regard to the Directive on the Sale of Consumer Goods, Tournafond expresses, not without reason, a preference for an incorporation in and an adjustment of the existing French Civil Code. The first approach will probably be followed by Belgium, the second by Germany.

One of the options exists in taking the consumer-oriented Directive as the overall starting point for the national law concerning the matter regulated by the Directive.[24] Although this will unquestionably create a greater coherence in the national law system, one could argue that the specific provisions with regard to consumers are not necessarily suitable to found a general body of rules for 'consumers' as well as 'non-consumers'.[25]

3. Continuing Discrepancies Between National Private (Contract) Law Systems

A reason for adopting directives in the field of contract law could be found in the fact that a more harmonized law of contract is beneficial to entrepreneurs, since they would no longer be obliged to take into account the different national law systems.[26] However, this is only true with regard to *total* harmonization. Speaking of *minimal* harmonization, as is the case with the current directives,[27] the said entrepreneurs, alongside the (supposedly protected) consumers themselves, will still be left with the often painstaking[28] and costly[29] task of investigating possible differences between national laws since member states are allowed to adopt regulations containing a higher degree of consumer protection.[30]

---

[23] Tournafond, 'Remarques critiques sur la directive européenne du 25 mai 1999 relative à certains aspects de la vente et des garanties des biens de consommation', (Dalloz, 2000), 159, 160.

[24] As seems to be the case in Germany for the Directive on the Sale of Consumer Goods.

[25] Cf. Roth, *JZ* (2001), 475, 482 *et seq.*, 487 and 489 ('Die Einbeziehung des Verbraucherschutzes in das BGB darf nicht dazu führen, daß dem Verbraucherschutz dienende Regeln zum Leitbild des Vertragstyps werden.').

[26] Cf. COM(2001) 398 final, 9 (para. 30).

[27] Howells among others discerns a tendency towards maximal harmonization directives (n. 3 above) 2 *et seq.*

[28] It is e.g. difficult to predict where the rules on a certain topic can be found, in view of the fact that the topic itself can often be related to quite different existing fields of national law (Joustra (n. 2 above) 133, 137). Cf., e.g., with regard to French sales law Raynard, 'Droit communautaire et vente: les enjeux d'une transposition à venir (Directive du 25 mai 1999 sur certains aspects de la vente et des garanties des biens de consommation)', *RTDCiv* (2000), 440, 444 *et seq.*

[29] We will not address the somewhat more economic analyses regarding the costs of (dis)information in relation to the harmonization of legal systems. Other contributions in this book deal thoroughly with these problems.

[30] Hondius, 'De consumentenkoop in Europees perspectief/naar een richtlijn consumentenkoop en consumentengaranties', *Tijdschrift voor Consumentenrecht* (1996), 245, 247 *et seq.* (with regard to the Directive on the Sale of Consumer Goods and Associated Guarantees);

Further in the text, we will nonetheless also point out that many (recent) directives tend to contain a very detailed set of legal rules, which can, but not always necessarily does, somewhat artificially enhance the 'unifying' effect of these measures, at the same time denying their legal specificity.[31]

This problem could be solved (at least partially) by (systematically) making use of minimum *and* maximum provisions.[32] Then, at least, the parties concerned would have some idea of what can (and has to) be expected when contracting abroad.

Consumer directives contain mostly mandatory law and thus limit contractual freedom. It should be stressed that parties involved in cross-border transactions may only be hindered by disparities in mandatory domestic legislation. In cases in which domestic contractual law is non-mandatory, the contracting parties can escape from the law of a member state by making use of their contractual freedom.[33]

4. Regulations as an Alternative to Directives?

It is often suggested that Regulations would be a better means for the unification of member state law than the Directives seemingly preferred up to now. It is indeed true that the use of Regulations instead of Directives would create a uniform set of rules in the given area. This technique is not unproblematic, however. Once 'unified' by means of regulations, the national legislators will be unable to adjust their (contract) law systems with regard to the 'unified' field. This could bring about a possibly undesirable obligation for the member states to opt for the consumer-oriented rules as the basis for national contract law. Moreover, they would become unable to react efficiently if inconsistencies were to appear at a later time.[34]

Joustra (n. 2 above) 133, 141 *et seq.* Cf. De Geest, 'Regulatory Competition and Information Problems: Towards (Extremely Detailed) International Default Codes' (lecture held at the SECOLA Conference on 'Sales and Trends in European Contract Law', Rome, 8 and 9 June 2001), *http://www.secola.org/*, 6; Dougan, 'Minimum Harmonization and the Internal Market', (2000) 37 *CMLRev* 853, 865 *et seq.* ('Observing the considerable extent to which the Member States had taken advantage of this facility to improve on the level and scope of substantive protection guaranteed by the Directive, and the variety of their reactions, the Commission remarked that, as a result, the measure had only a modest impact on the original objective of harmonization.') (with regard to the Consumer Credit Directive).

[31] Cf. Howells (n. 3 above) 7.

[32] Dougan among others seems to imply that the Treaty itself already provides a 'ceiling' (Dougan, (2000) 37 *CMLRev* 853, 855). Be that as it may, the solution proposed here will be able to eliminate a greater amount of controversy.

[33] Cf. ECJ 24.1.1991–case C-339/98, *Alsthom Atlantique SA v. Compagnie de construction mécanique Sulzer SA* [1991] ECR I–107, 124.

[34] 'One of the greatest dangers of maximalisation is [...] that it represents a fixing of the goal posts.' (Howells (n. 3 above) 4 *et seq.*).

III. COMPETENCE OF THE EUROPEAN UNION

1. In General

Leaving aside for the time being the possible negative impact of directives on consumer protection on national private (contract) law, a second important question to address deals with the competence of the European Union to intervene in national private (contract) law in the said manner. One must indeed not forget that the European Union is bound by its founding treaty and subsequent amendments. In other words, if no legal ground to act in a certain field can be found in this treaty, it cannot – in principle – legislate in this area.[35] Strictly speaking, the European Union does not explicitly possess any attributed competence with respect to (private) contract law or (private) law of obligations.[36]

This does not have to mean that it does not have any ability to intervene in this field; it simply means that it cannot realize these interventions in a direct manner. One has to look for adequate legal bases in the treaty that allow the European Union to exert an *indirect* influence on national contract law systems.

Since only some general provisions of the treaty [namely arts. 94, 95, 153 and 308 EC Treaty (former arts. 100, 100A, 129A and 235)] can be considered eligible to fulfil this role, the principle of subsidiarity (art. 5 EC Treaty) inevitably springs to mind.[37] After all, according to the European Commission as reported by Franzen:

'[D]ie Verwirklichung der Grundfreiheiten gehört zur ausschließlichen Zuständigkeit der Gemeinschaft, während flankierende Maßnahmen, welche 'einige als harmonisches Funktionieren des Binnenmarkts bezeichnen', dem Anwendungsbereich des Subsidiaritätsprinzips nicht entzogen werden könnten.'[38]

'[L]es dispositions spécifiques ayant un caractère fragmentaire, force est de se tourner vers les dispositions à vocation générale mais ces dernières s'avèrent d'un maniement délicat compte tenu de leur caractère subsidiaire.'[39]

---

[35] Picod, 'Les fondements juridiques de la politique communautaire de protection des consommateurs', in: Osman, *Vers un code européen de la consommation – Codification, unification et harmonisation du droit des Etats-membres de l'Union européenne* (1998), 73, 75.

[36] Idot, 'Les bases communautaires d'un droit privé européen (traité de Maastricht et traité de Rome)', in: De Vareilles-Sommières, *Le droit privé européen* (1998), 22, 27.

[37] Cf. nevertheless also Muller-Graff (n. 16 above) 71, 73 *et seq.*

[38] Franzen, *Privatrechtsangleichung durch die Europäische Gemeinschaft* (1999), 59.

[39] Idot (n. 36 above) 22, 25.

2. With Regard to the Principle of Subsidiarity

The opinions on the exact meaning and scope of the principle of subsidiarity tend to diverge. More specifically with regard to Directives on Consumer Protection, Sauphanor states the following:

'La subsidiarité peut être perçue de façon *défensive*. Elle apparaît alors comme un frein aux incursions communautaires dans les secteurs de compétences partagées. Son respect doit logiquement provoquer une réduction ou un abandon de l'action communautaire lorsqu'il n'apparaît plus justifié que certains objectifs soient poursuivis à l'échelon de la Communauté.

La subsidiarité peut au contraire, dans une perspective beaucoup plus *positive*, être considérée comme 'un principe instrumental' pour encourager l'intervention de la Communauté selon une évaluation faite en termes d'efficacité. Dans ce cas, elle ne suggère pas une dépossession des compétences de la Communauté mais impose de rechercher une meilleure efficacité de ses interventions.'[40]

We are inclined to adhere to the first reading of the principle of subsidiarity. Unlike, amongst others, Sauphanor, we do not think that a 'minimalist' interpretation of the principle of subsidiarity necessarily influences the development of community legislation in a negative way.[41] We would like to stress the fact that many directives nowadays simply fall below the required level of necessity to found an action on the level of the European Union.

'Alle genannten Gemeinschaftsregelungen lassen weitgehend den Zusammenhang mit den ursprünglichen Aufgaben der Gemeinschaft vermissen. Sie stellen beliebig herausgegriffene Sondermaterien dar, die nach bestimmten Vorstellungen der Kommission in präzise Konturen gefaßt werden, ohne daß hierfür eine Notwendigkeit bestanden hätte oder wesentliche Vorzüge gegenüber bestehenden Lösungen erkennbar wären.'[42]

The second line of thought regards the principle of subsidiarity primarily as a functional notion. This means that it always has to be related to the objectives pursued by the European Union. In view of the fact that most of the Directives (indirectly) addressing national contract law systems are connected with the goal of consumer protection, an action by the European Union would be justified provided that the same level of consumer protection could not have been reached by other means, i.e. by the member states themselves.

'Au regard de la spécificité de l'objectif que doit poursuivre la politique

---

[40]   Sauphanor (n. 18 above) 342 (emphasis added).
[41]   Cf. *ibid.* (n. 18 above) 346.
[42]   Hauschka, *JZ* (1990), 521, 529.

communautaire en faveur des consommateurs, la mise en oeuvre de la subsidi-arité doit se traduire non pas par une déréglementation au plan communau-taire mais par une mise à l'écart des actions qui se révéleraient inefficaces pour atteindre un niveau élevé de protection.'[43]

Although this last reading is in theory not necessarily problematic *as such*, the existing practice shows that it opens the doorway to much strictly speaking 'unnecessary' community legislation.

3. With regard to the White Paper of 1985

Subsequently, we would like to question the conformity of many (recent) direct-ives with the goals set out by the European Commission in its White Paper of 1985 concerning the completion of the Internal Market (COM(85) 310 final, 14 June 1985). Generally speaking, the White Paper of 1985 proclaimed the need for less detailed regulation, favouring legislation that is mainly concerned with the essentials in a given field.

a) With regard to the Goal of the Completion of the Internal Market

In most cases, the European Commission invokes the completion of the Internal Market in support of its proposals for directives on consumer protection. These directives may influence national contract law, and can thus be considered as having a (somewhat) harmonizing *casu quo* unifying effect in this area. This argument, however, not infrequently remains questionable. In fact, although being *formally* adopted on the basis of the completion of the Internal Market, directives on consumer protection often have no other objective than the realis-ation of 'more' consumer protection.[44] The legal ground of the completion of the Internal Market could arguably have been abused in order to (indirectly)[45] harmonize European contract law.[46]

'Since any type of contract might involve a cross-border element once one

---

[43] Sauphanor (n. 18 above) 344.

[44] Cf. Roth, *JZ* (2001), 475, 479 ('Richtlinienvorschläge wurden angestoßen durch die für den Verbraucherschutz zuständige Generaldirektion, nicht durch die Generaldirektion für den Binnenmarkt.').

[45] The addition of the word 'indirectly' depends mainly on whether one approaches the effect on contract law as (politically) intentional or unintended.

[46] Cf. also Dougan, (2000) 37 *CMLRev* 853, 881 *et seq.* and 883 ('It is thus possible to envisage a situation in which a national rule aimed at protecting consumers is challenged as being contrary to a single market directive, but the Member State argues that the directive itself was incorrectly adopted under Article 95 on the single market (with its restricted grounds of justification for the national rule) rather than, say, Article 153 EC on consumer protection (with its more permissive grounds of justification).').

includes the itinerant consumer, and since national laws are always potentially different in their details, the Commission does not appear to have any difficulty in justifying the basis of Directives under the Internal Market provisions of the treaty.'[47]

With regard to the Consumer Credit Directive, Hauschka observes that there is no international market for loans within the limited scope of the said directive. Cross-border transactions are probably not cost effective for small loans. He therefore sees no justifiable reason to adopt a directive that implies a fundamental change of domestic rules governing lending agreements. According to this author, this constitutes another example of the consequences of the lack of a clear division of competences between the member states and the European Union.[48,49]

Another example can be found in the Doorstep Directive.[50] 'Haustürgeschäfte – Gegenstand der EG-Richtlinie betreffend den Verbraucherschutz im Falle von außerhalb von Geschäftsräumen geschlossenen Verträgen – sind gewiß nicht die

---

[47]   Collins (n. 15 above) 9.

[48]   Hauschka, *JZ* (1990), 521, 528. Others point out that the conclusion that there does not exist many cross-border transactions in some areas dealt with in community legislation *is caused by* the existence of diverging national law systems in the fields concerned (Hondius, *Tijdschrift voor Consumentenrecht* (1996), 245, 248 ('Een vierde contra-argument is dat er momenteel weinig grensoverschrijdende consumententransacties worden afgesloten. Zo dit al waar is, rijst de vraag of dit wellicht mede moet worden toegeschreven aan uiteenlopende wetgeving.')). Hence an action by means of a Directive could stimulate the emergence and/or the development of cross-border transactions. In our view, the problem with this kind of argument lies in the fact that it reverses the initial question.

[49]   As early as 1965, Foriers wrote the following considerations on a similar subject:

'Mais on aperçoit immédiatement que l'intrusion de nombreuses normes nouvelles conduit nécessairement à des heurts, à des collisions, qui s'expliquent d'autant mieux que les normes faisant irruption répondent très souvent à une philosophie différente de celle du droit interne concerné, sinon radicalement opposé à celle-ci.

Donc si la quête jurisprudentielle n'est pas encore très fournie soyons persuadés que ce n'est là qu'une situation due à la nouveauté du sujet, non à l'harmonieuse compatibilité des textes communautaires et de droit interne.'

'Les antinomies entre normes communautaires et normes de droit interne sont résolues en fonction des compétences dont les Etats ont entendu se dépouiller ou qu'ils ont voulu se réserver en vertu des traités.

L'analyse des compétences aura pour résultat d'arrêter les effets de la loi interne dans la mesure nécessaire à l'efficacité du droit communautaire.' (Foriers, 'Les antinomies entre dispositions de droit communautaire et dispositions de droit interne', in Perelman, *Les antinomies en droit* (1965), 320, 328 and 335 *et seq.*).

[50]   Council Directive 85/577/EEC of 20 December 1985 to protect the consumer in respect of contracts negotiated away from business premises, EC OJ 1985 L 372/31.

typische Domäne grenzüberschreitender Vertriebsorganisationen.'[51] We cannot resist the urge to quote an already much-quoted phrase spoken during the discussion of this Directive in the European Parliament: 'Well, doorsteps have many qualities, but one of them is that they do not cross frontiers.'[52]

'Il apparaît que certaines directives fondées sur l'article 100 ou 100 A du traité (new art. 94 and 95 EC-Treaty ou certaines de leurs dispositions sont parfois éloignées de l'impératif d'élimination d'entraves, celui-ci pouvant servir de prétexte à l'adoption d'une directive visant principalement à protéger les consommateurs.'[53]

Others, however, seem to believe that the opposite is true. They argue that the need, or since the adoption of article 153 (especially art. 153(3)(a)) EC Treaty (former art. 129A), the ongoing practice[54] to adopt Directives on Consumer Protection on the basis of provisions aiming at the completion of the Internal Market affects the possibilities regarding consumer protection in a negative way, since only national consumerist laws which hinder exchanges would be eligible for harmonization.[55] Looking at this question from a national contract lawyer's point of view, we think that this allegation unduly disregards the need for a demonstrable legal foundation to – even incidentally – intrude upon a legal area for which the European Union has no exclusively attributed competence, such as contract law. Although we are aware of the fact that a more consumerist lawyer will regret the phenomenon described above, one ought not to overlook the fact that the boundaries of consumer protection as it exists nowadays should not be stretched too far beyond its inherent limits.

On the contrary, we dare to propose that the above is in any case not true with regard to the European Union's existing 'policy' concerning contract law,

---

[51] Hommelhoff, *AcP* (1992), 71, 73. Cf. Franzen (n. 38 above) 75 (n. 34 above); Roth, *JZ* (2001), 475, 477 *et seq.*

[52] Quotation taken from Franzen (n. 38 above) 75 (n. 34 above).

[53] Picod (n. 35 above) 73, 78.

[54] The European Union has not made much use of art. 153 up to now (Joustra (n. 2 above) 133, 140; Picod (n. 35 above) 73, 75 *et seq.*; Pizzio, 'L'application du droit primaire', in: Osman, *Vers un code européen de la consommation – Codification, unification et harmonisation du droit des Etats-membres de l'Union européenne* (1998), 87, 95.

[55] *Ibid.* 87, 88 *et seq.* ('L'objectif poursuivi par de telles directives, qui est de supprimer les obstacles à la libre circulation des marchandises et des services créés par la disparité (des législations nationales), conduit le plus souvent à une harmonisation dont la finalité première est de gommer les différences nationales et non d'élever le niveau de protection des consommateurs.'), 92 ('Or, une telle base ne peut faire de la politique de protection des consommateurs qu'un sous-produit de la politique du marché intérieur dans laquelle elle est enfermée.') and 99 ('En définitive, la politique communautaire en faveur des consommateurs semble toujours être l'éternel second, en ce sens qu'elle se situe toujours dans le sillage d'une autre politique.').

which up to now (out of sheer necessity? seems rather to *follow* in the wake of the consumer policy of the European Union.[56] Regarding the Directive on the Sale of Consumer Goods, Grundmann argues, however, that 'the EC legislature, for the first time, so clearly stated two sets of scopes: first, the classical set of two scopes, consumer protection and Internal Market functioning, but also, second, a new set of scopes, now those of internationalising and modernising national laws in Europe'.[57]

b) *With Regard to the Legal Nature of Directives*

Finally, in the White Paper of 1985, a choice was made to opt for minimal harmonization. Notwithstanding this, Muller-Graff rightly points out that the more specific – and thus *de facto* 'binding' – the formulation of a Directive, the less it respects the inherent freedom of the member states to adopt the measures which *they* deem the most suitable to obtain the goals set out in the directive.[58] One could argue that the type of directive which has become popular in recent years in fact denies the nature of this instrument as it was initially conceived. In the words of Muller-Graff: 'While the *objective* is sometimes only laid down in rather vague provisions, often the *result* to be achieved is defined by a set of precise provisions in private law directives.'[59] If the European Union wants to impose a uniform binding set of rules upon its member states, the directive does not seem the most suitable for the purpose,[60] to say the least, and according to some, the Regulation would seem more apt to realize this objective. The conclusion that this last instrument is more difficult to adhere to from a *political*

---

[56] Cf. Joustra (n. 2 above) 133, 140 ('Still, consumer law may be considered as a trendsetter where the creation of a uniform European Civil Code is concerned.') and 141.

[57] Grundmann, 'Consumer Law, Commercial Law, Private Law – how can the Sales Directive and the Sales Convention be so Similar?' (lecture held at the SECOLA Conference on 'Sales and Trends in European Contract Law', Rome, 8 and 9 June 2001), *http://www.secola.org/*, 13.

[58] Muller-Graff (n. 16 above) 71, 74 and 81; (somewhat more balanced) Muller-Graff (n. 18 above) 195, 222 ('*Für* den Angleichungsweg [by way of Directives (BT and BDL)] mag der Legitimationsgewinn durch die Beteiligung der nationalen Parlamente angeführt werden. [...] Aber im Grunde wird die Aushöhlung der nationalen Legislativkompetenz nur kamoufliert. *Börner* spricht nicht zu Unrecht von einem Feigenblatt. Da ein Ziel nur so genau erreicht wird, wie es die Mittel gestatten, und da die Unterscheidung zwischen Ziel und Mittel, wie *Börner* expliziert hat, logisch nicht durchführbar ist, ist die detaillierte Richtlinienfassung (nonetheless) zu Recht oft unvermeidbar [...].'). Cf. De Ly (n. 18 above) 51; Hauschka, *JZ* (1990), 521, 524 *et seq.*; Remien, *JZ* (1992), 277, 281 *et seq.*

[59] Muller-Graff (n. 16 above) 71, 74.

[60] Hayder, 'Privatrechtsvereinheitlichung durch die Europäische Gemeinschaft – Kommentar zum Vortrag von Hans Claudius Taschner', in: Muller-Graff, *Gemeinsames Privatrecht in der Europäischen Gemeinschaft* (1993), 167, 168 *et seq.*

viewpoint, however, partly explains the *juridical* tendency to make use of 'denatured' directives instead.

'So sind z. B. konkrete Fristen oder gar Zinsformeln im Grunde genommen keine Sache des europäischen Richtliniengebers – ganz abgesehen davon, daß die Richtlinie nach Art. 189 Abs. 3 EGV das genuine Mittel zur Rahmenvorgabe ist und nicht zur verbindlichen Detailregelung. Man könnte sogar sagen, die Schaffung immer neuer inhaltlicher Mindestgarantien und Rückabwicklungsmodalitäten, die zu einem Verbraucherschutz-Labyrinth zu entarten drohen, werde dem selbstgesetzten Ziel letztlich nu wenig gerecht. Es scheint an der Zeit, sich im richtliniengestützten Verbraucherschutz wieder mehr auf den wesentlichen Rahmen zu besinnen. Rechtsangleichung bis in jede Einzelheit ist kein Gebot eines vereinten Europas, sondern auf Dauer eher schädlich.'[61]

'Zwar erlaubt die heutige Harmonisierungspraxis den Erlaß derart detaillierter Normvorgaben, so daß die Umsetzung von Richtlinien mitunter nur durch die Verabschiedung entsprechender, sozusagen identischer nationaler Rechtsakte gewährleistet werden kann. Doch ist bei alledem nicht die 'verfassungsmäßige' Definition der Richtlinie im Artikel 189 EWG-Vertrag [new art. 249 EC Treaty] aus dem Auge zu verlieren.'[62]

Not everyone, however, thinks that the above is necessarily a bad evolution, in view of the conclusion that more detailed Directives unquestionably result in a comparatively 'higher' degree of harmonization.[63]

IV. CONCLUSION

Before the European Union aspires to realize the very ambitious project to codify European law as a whole, it should critically reflect on its past achievement. More and more often, national legislators are urged to evaluate the impact

---

[61] Sturner/Bruns, 'Die Umsetzung der Verbraucherschutzrichtlinien und ihre Auswirkungen im nationalen Recht – Bewertung aus der Sicht der deutschen Rechtsprechung', in: Heusel, *Neues europäisches Vertragsrecht und Verbraucherschutz – Regelungskonzepte der Europäischen Union und ihre Auswirkungen auf die nationalen Zivilrechtsordnungen* (1999), 81, 88.

[62] Hayder (n. 60 above), 167, 168 *et seq.*

[63] Cf. Franzen (n. 38 above) 71 ('Wie detailgenau rechtsangleichende, aufgrund von Art. 100 EGV (Art. 94 n.F.) ergangene Maßnahmen sein dürfen, bestimmt sich aus ihrer Funktion zur Herstellung des Gemeinsamen Markts und kann lediglich unter diesem Aspekt Begrenzungen erfahren. Insofern können dem Begriff der Rechtsangleichung allenfalls Präferenzen für ein bestimmtes Instrumentarium – welches jedoch im Rahmen von Art. 100 EGV (Art. 94 n.F.) ohnehin zwingend ist –, nicht aber inhaltliche Direktiven für die Dichte und Intensität der in der innerstaatlichen Rechtsordnung zu erlassenden Regelungen entnommen werden.').

of their legislation *post factum*. It could be a very interesting exercise to carry out such an evaluation with regard to the European legislator on a much more thorough scientific basis than we have done in this rather provocative article. The project of a European civil code can probably not be achieved within the existing legal framework. It would be deplorable that the European Union should therefore choose to continue on the indirect way we described above in view of the fragmentation of the national legal system in which it results. The divergence of some legal rules within the European Union can in some cases even be fruitful, as the competition between different legal solutions may lead to the optimal rule. A codification in certain limited areas has certainly to be the fruit of an extensive and long debate on various conflicting legal solutions. Only such a debate may result in unified rules that are accepted and uniformly applied by the whole European legal community.

SELECTED BIBLIOGRAPHY

Books and Articles in Books

J. BASEDOW (ed.), *Europäische Vertragsrechtsvereinheitlichung und deutsches Recht* (Tübingen, Mohr Siebeck, 2000), 281.

J. BASEDOW, 'Europäische Vertragsvereinheitlichung und deutsches Recht – Einführung', 1–3.

T. BOURGOIGNIE, 'Le principe de subsidiarité et son application à la politique communautaire de protection des consommateurs', in *Liber Amicorum Paul de Vroede* (Antwerpen, Kluwer, 1994), 193–227.

A. CHAMBOREDON, 'The Debate on a European Civil Code: For an 'Open Texture''', in M. VAN HOECKE and F. OST (eds.), *The Harmonisation of European Private Law* (Oxford/Portland Oregon, Hart Publishing), 2000, 63–99.

F. DE LY, *Europese gemeenschap en privaatrecht* (Zwolle, Tjeenk Willink, 1993), 63.R. DENUIT, 'La politique communautaire des consommateurs', in CDVA (ed.), *La promotion des intérêts des consommateurs au sein d'une économie de marchés* (Brussels, Kluwer, 1993), 173–186.

P. FORIERS, 'Les antinomies entre dispositions de droit communautaire et dispositions de droit interne', in C. PERELMAN (ed.), *Les antinomies en droit* (Brussel, Bruylant, 1965), 320–336.

M. FRANZEN, *Privatrechtsangleichung durch die Europäische Gemeinschaft* (Berlin/New York, Walter de Gruyter, 1999), 735.

S. GRUNDMANN (ed.), *Systembildung und Systemlücken in Kerngebieten des Europäischen Privatrechts – Gesellschafts-, Arbeits- und Schuldvertragsrecht* (Tübingen, Mohr Siebeck, 2000), with:

S. GRUNDMANN, 'Das Thema Systembildung im Europäischen Privatrecht – Gesellschafts-, Arbeits- und Schuldvertragsrecht', 1–49.

W. KILIAN, 'Äußeres und inneres System in einem noch fragmentarischen Europäischen Schuldvertragsrecht?', 427–441

C. KIRCHNER, 'Ein Regelungsrahmen für Rechtseinheitlichkeit und Rechtsvielfalt in der Gemeinschaft', 99–113

M. MARTINEK, 'Unsystematische Überregulierung und kontraintentionale Effekte im Europäischen Verbraucherschutzrecht oder: Weniger wäre mehr', 511–557

N. REICH, 'Verbraucherrechte als – unverzichtbare – subjektive Rechte passiver Marktbürger', 481–509

H.-B. SCHAFER, 'Grenzen des Verbraucherschutzes und adverse Effekte des Europäischen Verbraucherrechts', 559–568

U. STEIN, 'Systembildung durch privatautonome Rechtssetzung und ihre Grenzen im Europäischen Binnenmarkt', 669–689.

A. HARTKAMP, M. HESSELINK, E. HONDIUS, C. JOUSTRA and E. DU PERRON (eds.), *Towards a European Civil Code – Second Revised and Expanded Edition* (Nijmegen/Den Haag–London–Boston, Ars Aequi Libri/Kluwer Law International, 1998) 652.

P.-C. MULLER-GRAFF, 'EC Directives as a means of Private Law Unification', 71–89

C. JOUSTRA, 'Consumer Law', 133–148.

J. HUET, 'Les sources communautaires du droit des contrats', in ASSOCIATION HENRI CAPITANT (ed.), *Le renouvellement des sources du droit des obligations* (Paris, L.G.D.J., 1997), 11–27.

L. IDOT, 'Les bases communautaires d'un droit privé européen (traité de Maastricht et traité de Rome)', in P. DE VAREILLES-SOMMIERES (ed.), *Le droit privé européen*, in N. MOLFESSIS (ed.), *Collection Etudes Juridiques*, I (Paris, Economica, 1998), 22–35.

W. HEUSEL (ed.), *Neues europäisches Vertragsrecht und Verbraucherschutz – Regelungskonzepte der Europäischen Union und ihre Auswirkungen auf die nationalen Zivilrechtsordnungen*, in *Schriftenreihe der Europäischen Rechtsakademie Trier*, XXV (Keulen, Bundesanzeiger, 1999) 360.

N. FONTAINE, 'Analyse des techniques de legislation européenne en matière de droit des contrats – Le point de vue du Parlement européen', 51–55.

D. HOFFMANN, 'Analyse der europäischen Rechtssetzungstechniken im Bereich des Vertragsrecht aus der Sicht der Europäischen Kommission', 39–50.

E. HONDIUS, 'Consumer Law and Private Law: the Case for Integration', 19–38.

J. MURRAY, 'Consumer Protection in the EC and Contract Law – Some reflections from the Perspective of Consumer Organisations', 57–59.

R. STURNER and A. BRUNS, 'Die Umsetzung der Verbraucherschutzrichtlinien und ihre Auswirkungen im nationalen Recht – Bewertung aus der Sicht der deutschen Rechtsprechung', 81–90.

P.-C. MULLER-GRAFF (ed.), *Gemeinsames Privatrecht in der Europäischen Gemeinschaft*, in *Schriftenreihe des Arbeitskreises Europäische Integration e.V.*, XXXIII (Baden-Baden, Nomos, 1993), with:

R. HAYDER, 'Privatrechtsvereinheitlichung durch die Europäische Gemeinschaft – Kommentar zum Vortrag von Hans Claudius Taschner', 167–170.

C. JOERGES and G. BRUGGEMEIER, 'Europäisierung des Vertragsrechts und Haftungsrechts', 233–286.

P.-C. MULLER-GRAFF, 'Privatrecht und europäisches Gemeinschaftsrecht', 195–230.

H.C. TASCHNER, 'Privatrechtsentwicklung durch die Europäische Gemeinschaft – Rechtsgrundlagen, Ziele, Sachgebiete, Verfahren', 155–165.

F. OSMAN (ed.), *Vers un code européen de la consommation – Codification, unification et harmonisation du droit des Etats-membres de l'Union européenne* (Brussel, Bruylant, 1998), 421.

A. JEAMMAUD, 'Unification, uniformisation, harmonisation: de quoi s'agit-il?', 35–55.

F. OSMAN, 'Codification, unification, harmonisation du droit en Europe: un rêve en passe de devenir réalité?', 11–34.

F. PICOD, 'Les fondements juridiques de la politique communautaire de protection des consommateurs', 73–85.

J.-P. PIZZIO, 'L'application du droit primaire', 87–99.

N. SAUPHANOR, *L'influence du droit de la consommation sur le système juridique* (Paris, L.G.D.J., 2000), 425.

H. SCHULTE-NOLKE and R. SCHULZE (ed.), *Europäische Rechtsangleichung und nationale Privatrechte*, in R. SCHULZE (ed.), *Europäisches Privatrecht*, IX (Baden-Baden, Nomos, 1999), with:

L.A. DEFLORIAN, 'Consumer Contracts in Italian and Community Law – Patterns of Integration and Disintegration', 119–172.

O. REMIEN, 'Verbraucherrecht oder allgemeines Privatrecht für die Europäische Union?', 107–117.

H. SCHULTE-NOLKE and R. SCHULZE, 'Europäische Rechtsangleichung und nationale Privatrechte – Einführung', 11–20.

D. STAUDENMAYER, 'Die Richtlinien des Verbraucherprivatrechts – Bausteine für ein europäisches Privatrecht?', 63–78.

J. SMITS, *Europees Privaatrecht in wording – Naar een Ius Commune Europaeum als gemengd rechtsstelsel* (Antwerpen/Groningen, Intersentia, 1999), 302.

J. SMITS, 'Introduction: Mixed Legal Systems and European Private Law', in J. SMITS (ed.), *The Contribution of Mixed Legal Systems to European Private Law* (Antwerpen/Groningen, Intersentia, 2001), 1–13.

E. STEINDORFF, *EG-Vertrag und Privatrecht*, in J. SCHWARZE (ed.), *Schriftenreihe Europäisches Recht, Politik und Wirtschaft*, CLXXXV (Baden-Baden, Nomos, 1996), 480.

Articles in Journals

H. COLLINS, 'From Liberal Rights to Post-national Private Law Regulation' (lecture at the SECOLA Conference on 'Sales and Trends in European Contract Law', Rome, 8 and 9 June 2001), *http://www.secola.org/*.

E. DEARDS, 'The Proposed Guarantees Directive: Is It Fit for the Purpose?', *Journal of Consumer Policy* [1998], 99–119.

G. DE GEEST, 'Regulatory Competition and Information Problems: Towards (Extremely Detailed) International Default Codes' (lecture at the SECOLA Conference on 'Sales and Trends in European Contract Law', Rome, 8 and 9 June 2001), *http://www.secola.org/*.

M. DOUGAN, 'Minimum Harmonization and the Internal Market', *CMLRev.* [2000], 853–885.

J. DREXL, 'Continuing Contract Law Harmonisation under the White Paper of 1985–Partly with Modifications' (lecture at the SECOLA Conference on

'Communication from the Commission on European Contract Law (Harmonisation, Code, Optional Code)', Leuven, 30 November and 1 December 2001), *http://www.secola.org/*.

U. DROBNIG, 'A Subsidiary Plea: A European Contract Law for Intra-European Border-Crossing Contracts' (lecture at the SECOLA Conference on 'Communication from the Commission on European Contract Law (Harmonisation, Code, Optional Code)', Leuven, 30 November and 1 December 2001), *http://www.secola.org/*.

S. GRUNDMANN, 'EG-Richtlinie und nationales Privatrecht – Umsetzung und Bedeutung der umgesetzten Richtlinie im nationalen Privatrecht', *JZ* [1996], 274–287.

S. GRUNDMANN, 'Consumer Law, Commercial Law, Private Law – how can the Sales Directive and the Sales Convention be so Similar?' (lecture at the SECOLA Conference on 'Sales and Trends in European Contract Law', Rome, 8 and 9 June 2001), *http://www.secola.org/*.

S. GRUNDMANN and W. KERBER, 'European System of Contract Laws – A Map for Combining the Advantages of Centralised and Decentralised Rulemaking (draft version of 17 November 2001)' (lecture at the SECOLA Conference on 'Communication from the Commission on European Contract Law (Harmonisation, Code, Optional Code)', Leuven, 30 November and 1 December 2001), *http://www.secola.org/*.

C.E. HAUSCHKA, 'Grundprobleme der Privatrechtsfortbildung durch die Europäische Wirtschaftsgemeinschaft', *JZ* [1990], 521–532.

G. HIRSCH, 'European Contract Law – A Challenge for national and international Law, Economy and Sociology' (lecture at the SECOLA Conference on 'Sales and Trends in European Contract Law', Rome, 8 and 9 June 2001), *http://www.secola.org/*.

P. HOMMELHOFF, 'Zivilrecht unter dem Einfluß europäischer Rechtsangleichung', *AcP* [1992], 71–107.

E.H. HONDIUS, 'De consumentenkoop in Europees perspectief/naar een richtlijn consumentenkoop en consumentengaranties', *Tijdschrift voor Consumentenrecht* [1996], 245–255.

G. HOWELLS, 'European Consumer Law – The minimal and maximal harmonisation debate' (lecture at the SECOLA Conference on 'Communication from the Commission on European Contract Law (Harmonisation, Code, Optional Code)', Leuven, 30 November and 1 December 2001), *http://www.secola.org/*.

H.-W. MICKLITZ, 'Ein einheitliches Kaufrecht für Verbraucher in der EG?', *EuZW* [1997], 229–237.

H.-W. MICKLITZ, 'Die Verbrauchsgüterkauf-Richtlinie', *EuZW* [1999], 485–493.

F. PARISI, 'The Harmonization of Legal Warranties in European Law: an Economic Analysis' (lecture at the SECOLA Conference on 'Sales and Trends in European Contract Law', Rome, 8 and 9 June 2001), *http://www.secola.org/*.

J. RAYNARD, 'De l'influence communautaire et internationale sur le droit de la vente: quand une proposition de directive s'inspire d'une convention internationale pour compliquer, encore, les recours de l'acheteur', *Revue Trimestrielle de Droit Civil* [1997], 1020–1024.

J. RAYNARD, 'Droit communautaire et vente: les enjeux d'une transposition à venir (Directive du 25 mai 1999 sur certains aspects de la vente et des garanties des biens de consommation)', *Revue Trimestrielle de Droit Civil* [2000], 440–445.

N. REICH, 'Some critical comments on the Commission Communication of 11.07.2001, Com (2001) 398 final 'On European Contract Law' (lecture at the SECOLA Conference on 'Communication from the Commission on European Contract Law (Harmonisation, Code, Optional Code)', Leuven, 30 November and 1 December 2001), *http://www.secola.org/*.

O. REMIEN, 'Illusion und Realität eines europäischen Privatrechts', *JZ* [1992], 277–284.

W.-H. ROTH, 'Transposing "Pointillist" EC Guidelines into Systematic National Codes – Problems and Consequences' (lecture at the SECOLA Conference on 'Sales and Trends in European Contract Law', Rome, 8 and 9 June 2001), *http://www.secola.org/*.

W.-H. ROTH, 'Europäischer Verbraucherschutz und BGB', *JZ* [2001], 475–490.

A.K. SCHNYDER and R.M. STRAUB, 'Das EG-Grünbuch über Verbrauchsgüter-garantien und Kundendienst – Erster Schritt zu einem einheitlichen EG-Kaufrecht?', *ZEuP* [1996], 8–74.

R. SCHULZE, 'Le droit privé commun européen', *Revue Internationale de Droit Comparé* [1995], 7–32.

R. SCHULZE, 'Auf dem Weg zu einem europäischen Zivilgesetzbuch?', *NJW* [1997], 2742–2743.

J. SMITS, 'Naar een nieuw Europees consumentenkooprecht – Over de Europese richtlijn verkoop van en garanties voor consumentengoederen in het Nederlandse recht', *Nederlands JuristenBlad* [2000], 1825–1830.

J. SMITS, 'Toward a Multi-Layered Contract Law for Europe' (lecture at the SECOLA Conference on 'Communication from the Commission on European Contract Law (Harmonisation, Code, Optional Code)', Leuven, 30 November and 1 December 2001), *http://www.secola.org/*.

D. STAUDENMAYER, 'Die Mitteilung der Kommission zum Europäischen Vertragsrecht', *EuZW* [2001], 485–489.

M. TENREIRO, 'Garanties et services après-vente: brève analyse du Livre Vert présenté par la Commission européenne', *Revue Européenne de Droit de la Consommation* [1994], 326.

M. TENREIRO, 'Les pratiques commerciales et les contrats: la protection des consomma-teurs en Europe', *Journal des Tribunaux Droit Européen* [1997], 49–57.

K. TONNER, 'Die Rolle des Verbraucherrechts bei der Entwicklung eines europäischen Zivilrechts', *JZ* [1996], 533–541.

K. TONNER, 'Verbrauchsgüterkauf-Richtlinie und Europäisierung des Zivilrechts', *Betriebs Berater* [1999], 1769–1774.

O. TOURNAFOND, 'Remarques critiques sur la directive européenne du 25 mai 1999 relative à certains aspects de la vente et des garanties des biens de consommation', *Dalloz* [2000], 159–162

P. ULMER, 'Vom deutschen zum europäischen Privatrecht?', *JZ* [1992], 1–8.

R. VAN DEN BERGH, 'Forced Harmonisation of Contract Law in Europe – Not to be continued' (lecture at the SECOLA Conference on 'Communication from the Commission on European Contract Law (Harmonisation, Code, Optional Code)', Leuven, 30 November and 1 December 2001), *http://www.secola.org/*.

W. VAN GERVEN, 'De beginselen 'subsidiariteit, evenredigheid en samenwerking' in het Europese gemeenschapsrecht', *Rechtskundig Weekblad* [1991–92], 1241–1246.

W. VAN GERVEN, 'Verkokering van het privaatrecht', *Tijdschrift voor Privaatrecht* [1991], 1021–1023.

W. VAN GERVEN, 'Codifying European Private Law' (lecture at the SECOLA Conference on 'Communication from the Commission on European Contract Law

(Harmonisation, Code, Optional Code)', Leuven, 30 November and 1 December 2001), *http://www.secola.org/*.

J.B.M. VRANKEN, 'Europees privaatrecht. 'Bridging the gap' tussen wetenschap en praktijk', *Tijdschrift voor Privaatrecht* [2000], 3–12.

7. Continuing Contract Law Harmonisation under the White Paper of 1985? – Between Minimum Harmonisation, Mutual Recognition, Conflict of Laws, and Uniform Law

*Josef Drexl**

I. INTRODUCTION

These comments on the Commission's Communication on European Contract Law[1] address the past, the present, as well as the future of internal market policy. Historically, the comments will go back to the harmonisation approach of the White Paper of 1985,[2] the so-called 'new approach'. Focusing on the present state of contract law, the comments will discuss the issue of whether the approach of 1985 also works in the field of contract law. Finally, to the extent it proposes possible modifications in the field of contract law, the analysis deals with the future of European internal market legislation.

1. A 'Second New' Approach to Establishing the Internal Market?

In its Communication of 11 July 2001, the Commission questions very openly the hitherto applied approach of harmonising the law of the Member States with respect to contract law. In a non-exhaustive list the Commission mentions four options for further action: (1) no action at all; (2) promoting the elaboration of common principles of contract law; (3) improving the quality of existing Community legal instruments and (4) adoption of new comprehensive legislation at the EC level.

In order to react to the Commission's quest for advice it is necessary to analyse the virtues and deficiencies of the so-called 'new approach' of 1985,[3] designed to establish the Internal Market. By questioning this approach for

---

* Prof. Dr., LL.M. (Berkeley), University of Munich, Institute for European and International Economic Law; Director at the Max Planck Institute for Intellectual Property, Competition and Tax Law (Munich).
[1] Communication from the Commission to the Council and the European Parliament of 11 July 2001 on European Contract Law, COM(2001) 398 final (see also: http://europa.eu.int/comm/off/green/index_en.htm). See Staudenmayer, 'Die Mitteilung der Kommission zum Europäischen Vertragsrecht', *EuZW* [2001], 485.
[2] See, White Paper on the completion of the Internal Market, COM(85) 310 final.
[3] See COM(85) 310 final.

S. Grundmann and J. Stuyck (eds.), An Academic Green Paper on European Contract Law, 103–129
© 2002 *Kluwer Law International. Printed in Great Britain.*

contract law, the communication may well trigger a second move to establishing the Internal Market ('second-new approach').

2. Intentional Ambiguities?

The Commission in its Communication might be blamed for two ambiguities which are probably intentional. The first ambiguity relates to the objective of further action, the second one to the issue of Community power in the field of contract law.

a) Internal Market Orientation of the Communication

The Commission's Communication could easily be misinterpreted as an alignment with initiatives for the introduction of a comprehensive European Civil Code. Advocates of such a code, however, are probably disappointed by a more thorough reading of the Communication which unveils a very traditional understanding of the objectives of European contract law. The Commission makes very clear that its initiative is only designed to optimise the functioning of the Internal Market;[4] the creation of a uniform European contract law is not considered to be an objective in its own right.

This modest approach, nevertheless tending to considerably enlarge action in the field of contract law, reminds us of the very foundation of European contract law which is anchored in the harmonisation of the laws of the Member States with the objective of establishing the Internal Market (Art. 95 EC).

The following analysis is designed to take this Internal Market orientation of European contract law seriously. The question of whether there should be a uniform European contract law for different – more political – ends, for example, for the purpose of building a common European civil society, will not be discussed.

Nevertheless, introducing a uniform European contract law (option 4 mentioned by the Commission) could emerge as the preferred option which would largely amount to some kind of core provisions for a European Civil Code. This is why the Commission's position remains ambiguous as to the issue of such a code.

b) Community Power in the Field of Contract Law

Most surprisingly, the Commission does not discuss the issue of Community powers in the field of contract law. There might be two explanations: first, the Commission probably wants to find the answer to the substantive law question first, without being restricted by the current set of Community powers under

---

[4]   Cf. COM(2001) 398 final, 8 (paras. 23–32).

the EC Treaty. Secondly, new Community powers could be created in the framework of a new revision of the Treaties in the near future.

Nevertheless, the Commission's silence on the issue of Community powers has to attract criticism. Community powers are and always have been objective oriented. As Article 95 EC demonstrates, there is no general power of the Community *for* contract law, but there is power to harmonise contract law *in order to* establish the Internal Market. We may conclude that the Commission is only pretending to avoid the competence issue, but addresses it indirectly in its Communication by sticking to the Internal Market orientation known from Article 95 EC. Thereby, the Commission at least accepts the current framework of the Treaty objectives and competences.

In fact, an evaluation of the current state of contract law cannot leave aside the issue of competence. This is even more important since the ECJ, in the *Tobacco Advertising* case of 2000,[5] has acknowledged core principles of the Community policy on harmonisation. The Communication does not even mention this important decision.

3. Outline of Further Analysis

It is the purpose of these comments to discuss whether there is a need for a 'second-new' approach to implementing the Internal Market with respect to contract law. The analysis will demonstrate that the 'new' approach of 1985, combining minimum harmonisation with the principle of mutual recognition, cannot work in the field of contract law (*infra* II). In order to optimise the Internal Market, the analysis will propose a conflict of laws approach, designed to substitute the principle of mutual recognition (*infra* III). The analysis further proposes a broader approach to European contract law based on a distinction between mandatory and optional contract rules (*infra* IV).

II. THE HARMONISATION APPROACH OF 1985 AND CONTRACT LAW: MINIMUM HARMONISATION DOES NOT WORK

In order to evaluate the quality of the traditional harmonisation approach of 1985 as applied to contract law (*infra* C), it is necessary to explain this approach

---

5   ECJ 5.10.2000–case C-376/98 *Federal Republic of Germany v. European Parliament and Council* [2000] ECR I-8599. See Amtenbrink, 'Harmonisierungsmaßnahmen im Binnenmarkt im Lichte der Entscheidung des Europäischen Gerichtshofs zur Tabakwerberichtlinie', *VuR* [2001], 163; Hervey, 'Up in smoke? Community (anti)-tobacco law and policy', (2001) 26 *ELR* 101; Hilf and Frahm, 'Nichtigerklärung der Richtlinie zum Tabakwerbeverbot: Das letzte Wort?', *RIW* [2001], 128; Reich, 'Rechtsangleichung im Binnenmarkt', *VuR* [2001], 203; Stein, 'Keine Europäische 'Verbots'-Gemeinschaft – das Urteil des EuGH über die Tabakwerbeverbots-Richtlinie', *EWS* [2001], 12.

first (*infra* A) and then to analyse the power of the Community to harmonise the law of Member States (*infra* B).

1. The 'New Approach' of 1985

For the purpose of this analysis, the still-identifiable approach to establishing the Internal Market, developed in the White Paper of 1985 and 'institutionalised' under the Single European Act of 1987,[6] can be characterised by *four elements*: first, the establishment of the Internal Market is largely based on a *policy of harmonisation* of national laws. Secondly, in order to avoid unnecessary harmonisation of substantial law, harmonisation is combined with the principle of *mutual recognition of equivalent domestic standards*. Thirdly, in many fields the European legislator prefers *minimum harmonisation* to total harmonisation,[7] thereby allowing Member States to go beyond Community standards. The fourth element is of a constitutional and political nature. In order to promote the establishment of the Internal Market, the Single European Act changed the voting rule on the Council from unanimity (Art. 94 EC, ex-Art. 100 ECT) to a *qualified majority rule* (Art. 95 EC, ex-Art. 100a ECT).

These four elements must be understood in their entirety and interaction. Under the unanimity rule of ex-Article 100 EEC Treaty (now Art. 94 EC), it had become obvious that the Community would not be able to go very far with the harmonisation of national laws. The qualified majority rule implemented by the Single European Act made adoption of harmonising Community measures more likely. At the same time, the smaller number of Member States needed for approval on the Council favours the adoption of a more intense form of harmonisation.[8] Whereas this constitutional element describes how to adopt a piece of harmonising legislation politically, the other three elements characterise the specific substantive approach to harmonisation.

The concept of harmonisation as such makes clear that Community legislation is not designed to create uniform law.[9] In English legal writing 'harmonisation' is generally used in the same sense as 'approximation' of laws,[10] much better translating the more enlightening French term of '*rapprochement*' and, therefore,

---

[6]   See Dougan, 'Minimum Harmonisation and the Internal Market', (2000) 37 *CMLRev* 853, 855.

[7]   Cf. the understanding by Dougan, *ibid.* 853.

[8]   Only stronger involvement of the Parliament works in the opposite direction. For an economic analysis of the decision making of European legislation, see Cooter and Drexl, 'The Logic of Power in the Emerging European Constitution: Game Theory and the Division of Powers', (1994) 14 *Int'l Rev. L. & Econ.* 307.

[9]   Slot, 'Harmonisation', (1996) 21 *ELR* 378, 379; Vignes, 'The Harmonisation of National Legislation and the EEC', (1990) 15 *ELR* 358.

[10]   In this very sense Slot, (1996) 21 *ELR* 378 (at n. 9).

more commonly used in the English version of the Treaty, especially in Article 95 EC. The objective of this provision consists in the establishment of the Internal Market rather than a uniform Union-wide legal system. Equally, in other provisions on harmonisation, the Treaty applies harmonisation as a means to attain a particular objective of integration, whereas legal integration is not a valid objective in its own right. The harmonisation approach goes along with the application of the instrument of directives (Art. 249 EC), although Article 95 EC would not exclude other forms of Community action. Directives are addressed to the Member States which then have to implement the directive by changing their own domestic law. Harmonisation thereby leads to a kind of 'co-legislation' of the Community and the domestic legislators. In general, harmonisation is more acceptable to the Member States and consequently a more successful approach than adoption of uniform law.

In 1985, it was clear that total harmonisation of the law of Member States would be difficult to achieve. In order to promote the establishment of the Internal Market, the Community, to a large extent, preferred an approach of minimum harmonisation, according to which Member States only have an obligation to respect the European standard, but are allowed to introduce more stringent or advanced protection of the interests involved. Accordingly, minimum harmonisation is identified as the very feature of Community harmonisation in the post-Single European Act era, whereas the previous approach was based on full – or total – harmonisation.[11] However, especially in the field of consumer contract law, minimum harmonisation has been an accepted approach from its very beginning.[12]

In respect to the establishment of the Internal Market, minimum harmonisation alone is a very problematic approach. Legal requirements under national laws continue to differ largely. Under the *Cassis de Dijon* formula,[13] the application of the more protective law of the country where the product is sold may be justified by mandatory requirements such as considerations of consumer protection. In order to guarantee the free movement of goods, services, persons and capital, the Community legislator largely relied on the principle of mutual recognition. This principle creates an obligation of Member States to accept the equivalency of the legal standards of the country of origin. The liberating advantages of mutual recognition are enormous. The fundamental freedoms are put fully into action as long as the law of the *country of origin* is respected. It is

---

[11] See Sauter and Vos, 'Harmonisation under Community Law: The comitology issue', in: Craig and Harlow, *Lawmaking in the European Union* (London, Kluwer, 1998), 169, 171 *et seq.*

[12] See Micklitz and Weatherill, 'Consumer Policy in the European Community: Before and After Maastricht', (1993) 16 *J. Consumer Pol'y* 285, 301–303.

[13] See ECJ 20.02.1979 – Case 120/78 *Rewe-Zentral AG v. Bundesmonpolverwaltung für Branntwein* [1979] ECR 649, 662 (para. 8).

no surprise that this very concept can be found as an element in harmonising directives adopted under Article 95 EC which are especially designed to promote and facilitate cross-border trade, most recently and prominently in the Electronic Commerce Directive of June 2000.[14] According to the principle of the country of origin, as included in this directive, the standards of the country of origin apply even in sectors where harmonising measures have not been adopted yet.[15]

Minimum harmonisation and mutual recognition must be seen in conjunction with each other. Minimum harmonisation can only guarantee the Internal Market if complemented by a principle of mutual recognition. Otherwise, Member States might be allowed to enforce their higher standards of protection, thereby creating obstacles to the exercise of the fundamental freedoms. On the other hand, mutual recognition is only acceptable to the necessary number of Member States on the Council if a minimum of protection can be guaranteed by substantive harmonisation throughout the European Union.

2. Power of the Community to Harmonise the Law of the Member States

The principles of the 'new approach' set out so far were underlined by the European Court of Justice in the *Tobacco Advertising* case of 2000.[16]

Of course, the ECJ decision is most important in defining the limits of the Community's legislative power.[17] Thereby, the Court held that, under Article 95 EC, a measure adopted 'genuinely must have as its object the improvement of the conditions for the establishment and functioning of the Internal Market'. A 'mere finding of disparities between national rules and the abstract risk of obstacles to the exercise of fundamental freedoms or of distortions to competition' would be insufficient to justify the choice of Article 95 EC as a legal basis for harmonisation.[18]

However, there is a second reading which is equally important. Though more implicitly, the Court also identified principles which have to be respected in order to promote the Internal Market by harmonising measures. In the case of the Tobacco Advertising Directive, the Court admitted that there are disparities between national laws that might cause barriers to trade in goods and services and distort competition. In addition, the Court was not opposed to the minimum

---

[14] Directive 2000/31/EC of 8 June 2000 on certain legal aspects of information society services, in particular electronic commerce, in the Internal Market (Directive on electronic commerce), EC OJ 2000 L 178/1. See, in general, Pearce and Platten, 'Promoting the Information Society: The EU Directive on Electronic Commerce', (2000) 6 *ELJ* 363.

[15] According to Art. 2(h) of the Electronic Commerce Directive, it is not necessary that the domestic law was especially drafted for the purposes to regulate electronic commerce.

[16] *Supra* n. 5.

[17] See also Amtenbrink, *VuR* [2001], 163, 170 *et seq.*

[18] Para. 84. .

harmonisation approach as such,[19] but it criticised that the directive did not contain any additional rule guaranteeing the free movement of products that conform to the substantive minimum requirements of the directive.[20] This holding contradicts former views[21] according to which minimum harmonisation, especially in the field of consumer contracts, was thought to be in line with the Internal Market concept.

The conclusion can be stated as follows: The mere adoption of measures that pursue a form of minimum harmonisation are insufficient to guarantee the Internal Market. Minimum harmonisation must be combined with a second device. In the *Tobacco Advertising* case this device would have been the principle of mutual recognition.

3. Deficiencies of the Harmonisation Approach in the field of Contract Law

The *Tobacco Advertising* decision does not deal with contract law. Nevertheless, it does prove to be extremely important for it since the approach of minimum harmonisation is frequently applied especially in the field of consumer protection.[22]

a) The Problem with Harmonisation of Contract Law

As we can conclude from the Commission's Communication, concerns about the insufficiency of European contract law do not just stem from minimum harmonisation, but from the very concept of harmonisation and the instruments of directives.[23] However, this might only be a problem of scale rather than of substance. If it turns out that, in fact, harmonisation has not gone far enough to establish the Internal Market, it will have to be intensified. Harmonisation of contract law, then, may also include the definition of general concepts of contract law, like the one of damages and concepts of unjust enrichment, and, perhaps more important, contractual remedies.

It is true that, according to the general principle of *effet utile*, harmonisation

---

[19]   Similarly, Reich, *VuR* [2001], 203, 205 *et seq.*

[20]   Para. 104.

[21]   See, for example, Hoffmann, 'Gerechtigkeitsprinzipien im Europäischen Verbraucher-vertragsrecht – Fortschreitende Privatrechtskodifikation als Teil des sozialen Europas', in: Krämer, Micklitz and Tonner, *Law and Diffuse Interest in the European Legal Order, Liber amicorum Norbert Reich* (Baden-Baden, Nomos, 1997), 291, 302 *et seq.*

[22]   See, for example, Art. 8 Council Directive 93/13 of 5 April 1993 on Unfair Terms in Consumer Contracts, EC OJ 1993 L 95/29.

[23]   Cf. also the concerns expressed by Müller-Graff, 'EC Directives as a Means of Private Law Unification', in: Hartkamp, Hesselink, Hondius, Joustra and du Perron (eds.), *Towards a European Civil Code* (Nijmegen, Ars Aequi Libri and The Hague/London/Boston, Kluwer, 1998), 71, 80–82.

would rather leave the choice of enforcement measures relating to contractual obligations to the Member States (Art. 10(1) EC). However, the concept of directives would not *per se* exclude harmonisation of contractual remedies. On the other hand, a more advanced form of harmonisation – including remedies – would largely pre-empt the power of the Member States to take into account their own policy considerations in the process of transposition. Nevertheless, the Consumer Sales Directive[24] clearly demonstrates that the Community legislator is willing to harmonise the legal consequences (the famous *Rechtsfolgen* in German terminology) by granting particular individual rights to the consumer. In fact, the line to be drawn between issues to be dealt with under European contract law and those left to the national legislator is not defined by European law, in particular the EC Treaty, but is rather a matter of the decision-making process of European legislation. For instance, the right of revocation contained in European consumer contract law not only defines contractual obligations, it provides for a right of the consumer to withdraw from the contract. In this particular case, European law deals with the remedy issue. Nonetheless, the national legislator retains some flexibility for integrating the consumer's right of revocation within the domestic private law system. The issue of whether the consumer is legally bound before the end of the term of revocation might not have been decided by the particular directive; neither does European law solve the issue of restitution in cases where the contract was performed before the consumer's withdrawal.

These very few ideas demonstrate that, from a conceptual perspective, harmonisation in the field of contract law turns out to be much more complicated than in the field of technical standards. In the latter field, a clear distinction can usually be made between the European standard to be respected and the enforcement measures to be defined by the Member States, whereas in the field of contracts, issues of obligations, rights of the parties to the contract, additional issues relating to legal consequences, such as restitution issues, and fundamental legal concepts of the law of obligations, such as the concept of fault and damages, are closely intertwined. The dichotomy of minimum and total harmonisation is very insufficiently suited to fully describe the complexity of the problems of harmonisation in the field of contract law. Hence, in order to consider the effectiveness of the European harmonisation approach to contract law, not only minimum harmonisation deserves a critical analysis, but the harmonisation approach as such and as compared to a more comprehensive approach of drafting uniform contract law.

In fact, there are clear indications that especially leaving the definitions of

---

[24] Directive 1999/44/EC of the European Parliament and the Council of 25 May 1999 on certain aspects of the sale of consumer goods and associated guarantees, EC OJ 1999 L 171/12. See Staudenmayer, 'The Directive on the Sale of Consumer Goods and Associated Guarantees – a Milestone in the European Consumer and Private Law', (2000) 4 *ERPL* 547.

contractual remedies to the Member States may well turn out to fail to establish the Internal Market. An enlightening example may be provided by the implementation of the Electronic Commerce Directive.[25] The directive includes several provisions on contractual obligations in Article 9 to 11 without defining the remedies available in case of a breach of those obligations.[26] Here, Member States may either decide – most ambitiously – to partially change their rules on contract formation,[27] or – in a very ambiguous way – to create an additional set of contractual or pre-contractual obligations that do not affect the conclusion of the contract as such,[28] or – maybe insufficiently in the light of the *effet utile* principle – to leave enforcement to business or consumer associations or the consumer ombudsman in a system of unfair competition law or market law.[29]

For very good reason the European legislator did not adopt an approach of minimum harmonisation in this case. In order to guarantee the functioning of electronic commerce, Member States are not permitted to go beyond the level of protection for consumers set out in the directive, but the directive still does not harmonise all issues at stake. Thereby, harmonisation remains incomplete with persisting and arguably even more obstacles to the free movement of goods and services. However, taking into account the resistance of Member States to agree on more advanced European rules of contract formation, it is not the Community to be blamed, but the attitude of Member States to defend their domestic private law systems.

The critique on harmonisation as such would argue for a 'second new'

---

[25] *Supra* n. 14.

[26] Cf. Hultmark Ramberg, 'The E-Commerce Directive and formation of contract in a comparative perspective', (2001) 26 *ELR* 429 *et seq.*, criticising that the directive does not harmonise the legal effects of input errors.

[27] It is interesting to see that, under Sec. 214 of the US Uniform Computer Information Transactions Act (UCITA), in a case in which the service provider fails to provide to a consumer methods to detect and to correct input errors (cf. Art. 11 (2) of the Directive on electronic commerce), the consumer can rely on the error in order to withdraw from the contract. The text of UCITA can be found under http://www.ucitaonline.com. By 8 October 2001, UCITA has been adopted under state law by seven US states and the District of Columbia. On the Act, see Nimmer, 'UCITA: A Commercial Contract Code', (2000) 17/5 *The Computer Lawyer* 3. Both UCITA and the obligation of the directive are influenced by the OECD Guidelines on consumer protection on the Internet; see: Recommendation of the Council in respect of the Guidelines on the protection of consumers in the context of electronic commerce, adopted on 9 December 1999 (http://www.oecd.org/dsti/sti/it/consumer/prod/Guidelines_final_en.pdf).

[28] This is the approach of the newly adopted Sec. 214e of the German Civil Code (Bürgerliches Gesetzbuch); on the earlier draft, see Drexl, 'Verbraucherschutz und Electronic Commerce in Europa', in: Lehmann, *Electronic Business in Europa* (Munich, Beck, 2002), 473, n. 89–96.

[29] This seems to be the approach adopted in Sweden. .

approach, preferring regulations to be adopted under Article 308 EC to harmonising directives. However, given the unanimity rule of Article 308 EC and the reluctance of Member States to defend there national systems of contract law, decision making would be particularly difficult.

b) Minimum Harmonisation, Mutual Recognition, and Contract Law

The difference between minimum harmonisation and the concept of harmonisation in general, at least in the field of contract law, is rather one of degree than substance. Harmonisation by its very nature only reduces the disparities between national legal systems, without excluding them. On the other hand, the establishment of the Internal Market does not necessarily require uniform law. As the analysis has already demonstrated, minimum harmonisation may contribute to the establishment of the Internal Market provided that it is combined with additional legal techniques guaranteeing the exercise of the fundamental freedoms.

Consequently, our attention turns to the application to the principle of mutual recognition. According to this principle, the Community would prefer an obligation of Member States to accept domestic standards of other Member States in cross-border cases to an approach of advanced harmonisation of substantive standards.

Mutual recognition has its main scope of application in the field of technical standards.[30] With respect to private law, it might be applied to tort law. For instance, a service provider situated in the European Community, who makes available certain information on a website, may only be considered to have committed a tort according to the principles of the country of establishment. In fact, this is the situation which now exists under the principle of the country of origin provided for in the Electronic Commerce Directive.[31]

In the field of contract law, however, mutual recognition would not work for a very simple reason: it is up to the general rules of private international law (conflict of laws) to define the applicable law.[32] According to international private

---

[30] See Burrows, 'Harmonisation of Technical Standards', (1990) 53 *MLR* 597. See also Pelkmans, 'The New Approach to Technical Harmonization and Standardization', (1987) 25 *J. of Common Market Studies* 249.

[31] See *supra* n. 14.

[32] It is very much in dispute whether the principle of the country of origin, as included in the Electronic Commerce Directive, constitutes a rule of private international law; in the sense of a rule of conflict: Mankowski, 'Das Herkunftslandprinzip als Internationales Privatrecht der e-commerce-Richtlinie', *Zeitschrift für vergleichende Rechtswissenschaft* 100 (2001), 137; rejecting the idea of a rule of conflict: Ahrens, 'Das Herkunftslandprinzip in der E-Commerce-Richtlinie', *CR* [2000], 835, 837 *et seq.* Article 1(4) of the Directive states that the Directive does not establish additional rules on international private law nor does it deal with the jurisdiction of Courts.

law, based on the idea of freedom of contract, the parties to a contract can generally decide which law governs the formation of the contract and the rights and obligations flowing from their contractual relationship. Consequently, the Electronic Commerce Directive expressly excludes the application of the principle of the country of origin with respect to the freedom of contract and consumer contract law.[33]

We may conclude: Minimum harmonisation and even harmonisation as such are insufficient techniques to the establishment of the Internal Market. Whereas, in many other fields, the 'new approach' of 1985, combining minimum harmonisation with mutual recognition, can guarantee the free movement of goods and services, this approach does not work in the field of contract law. The European legislator has to rely on private international law rather than mutual recognition.

III. PRIVATE INTERNATIONAL LAW AND THE INTERNAL MARKET

Rules of private international law can be found as an integral part of the body of European law, and, in some cases, national rules of private international law are the object of harmonisation. So far, however, private international law has not received sufficient attention as a technique towards the establishment of the Internal Market.[34]

1. Freedom to Choose the Proper Law Applicable to the Contract

According to international private law, based on the idea of freedom of contract, the parties can generally decide which law governs the formation of the contract and the rights and obligations flowing from their contractual relationship. Under this rule of free choice of the proper law, the parties to a contract can escape from the law of a Member State that would otherwise restrict the fundamental freedoms. Accordingly, the ECJ, in the *Alsthom* case of 1989, rejected the idea that a rule of national contract law would be inconsistent with ex-Article 30 ECT (now Art. 28 EC) in a case in which private international law allowed the

---

[33] Article 3(3) of the Directive to be read together with the Annex.

[34] See, however, Grundmann, 'Binnenmarktkollisionsrecht', *RabelsZ* 64 (2000), 457. Grundmann (especially at 460) argues that, in the framework of the provisions on the fundamental freedoms, the principle of the country of origin has to be understood as a conflict of laws rule. In general, the fundamental freedoms are not considered to have an implication for conflict of laws; see Kreuzer and Wagner, 'Europäisches Internationales Privatrecht', in: Dauses (ed.), *Handbuch des EU-Wirtschaftsrechts*, 2nd Vol. (Munich, Beck, 2001), R note 102.

parties to escape from the application of the national rule by opting for its non-application.[35] Consequently, within the scope of party autonomy to decide on the proper law applicable to their contract, there is a strong argument against any need to harmonise contract law.

However, disparities between legal orders adversely affect the conclusion of cross-border contracts. Professionals and consumers might abstain from concluding such a contract because they are unfamiliar with the law of the other Member State. Knowledge is necessary in order to make an informed decision on the comparative advantages of different national laws.

This very information problem has become a prominent argument in European consumer contract law. For instance, the preamble to the Consumer Sales Directive argues for a European minimum standard of protection in order to increase consumer confidence in and to protect legitimate expectations of consumers as to the level of protection abroad, with the objective to convince the consumer to shop in other states.[36] However, the information problem is not just one which consumers have to face. It also provides a valid argument for the supplier who has to consider a multitude of different legal requirements in the Member States. It is interesting to see that now, the Commission in its Communication also takes into consideration the supplier's perspective.[37] Suppliers of goods and services might easily abstain from cross-border transactions because of not being familiar with foreign consumer contract law.

Although, under the freedom of choice principle, legal disparities do not work as obstacles to the exercise of the fundamental freedoms, the problem with general contract law remains fourfold: (1) disparities between national rules increase transaction costs for cross-border contracts as compared to 'internal' contracts. (2) Information between competitors might be distributed unequally. Usually some firms have more international business experience and, hence, are more familiar with the law of different Member States. At the same time, other firms, which in the past used to operate only on a national level, encounter problems of acceding to foreign markets. (3) The situation for domestic and foreign firms is different. Whereas a foreign firm may be able to escape to a more favourable foreign law, a domestic competitor has to deal with the application of the national rules, although possibly the domestic rules are more favourable. Then, the domestic competitor has the competitive advantage of knowing the law, whereas the foreign competitor, unfamiliar with the domestic law, has

---

[35] ECJ, 24.01.1991. Case C-339/89, *Alsthom Atlantique SA v. Compagnie de construction mécanique Sulzer SA*, [1991] ECR I–107, 124 (note 15), dealing with strict liability of the vendor for defective products under French law which, however, can be excluded by agreement.

[36] Para. 4 *et seq.* of the preamble to the Consumer Sales Directive (n. 24 above).

[37] Para. 30 of the Communication.

to face an information and discovery problem. (4) Information might be distributed differently between the parties of the contract. This is a problem especially for consumers who, in contrast to the supplier, do not conclude similar cross-border contracts on a daily basis.[38] The supplier might propose the application of the law with less consumer protection, and the consumer would not be aware of the comparative disadvantages.

The first problem, namely the mere existence of additional transaction costs for cross-border contracts would probably not justify harmonisation under Article 95 EC. Transaction costs neither create obstacles to the exercise of the fundamental freedoms, nor distortions of competition. However, there might be a case for a set of opt-in uniform contract rules to be adopted under Article 308 EC. The situation is different as to the latter three arguments. Though differing national laws do not constitute obstacles to the exercise of the fundamental freedoms, there are appreciable distortions of competition. Harmonisation could further the readiness of smaller and medium-sized firms to engage in cross-border business. However, as we have seen above, harmonisation as such, and not just minimum harmonisation, has particular drawbacks. Information problems will continue to exist as long as harmonisation remains incomplete. Even the applicability of harmonised foreign rules fixed in a foreign language might cause economic actors to abstain from cross-border contracts. Consequently, adoption of opt-in contract rules under Article 308 EC seems to be the more effective approach.

We can conclude that to the extent parties are free to choose the proper law applicable to their contract, there are no obstacles to the exercise of the fundamental freedoms. However, disparities between national laws and the arising information problems therefrom may prevent economic actors – especially consumers and small and medium-sized firms – from concluding cross-border contracts. The information problem causes appreciable distortions to trade which can be reduced by harmonisation under Article 95 EC.

Nevertheless, adoption of an opt-in set of contract rules under Article 308 EC should be preferred.[39] However, the approach under Article 308 EC has the considerable institutional drawback of requiring unanimity of the Member States on the Council; but, given the largely diverging traditions in the European Union, this is probably the politically most appropriate institutional arrangement. A minority of Member States should not be outvoted on the sensitive issue of contract law. In order to guarantee the success of the project, it would be recommendable, similarly to the European Currency Union, to leave it to

---

[38] Cf. Hoffmann (n. 21 above) 295 *et seq.* (arguing that transaction costs prevent the consumer from evaluating the advantages of competition between legal systems in Europe).

[39] With a similar conclusion, taking harmonisation only as the second-best solution for a common private law, Müller-Graff (n. 23 above) 82.

the Member States whether they accept this opt-in set of contract rules for their nationals.

2. Mandatory Contract Rules, especially on Consumer Contracts

The situation is different in cases in which mandatory rules of domestic contract law come into play. The freedom of choice principle, in general, also allows escaping from mandatory national contract rules. This is true in particular with respect to the rules relating to contract formation.[40] In other fields, however, the international private law of the individual Member State is likely to ensure the applicability of domestic mandatory contract rules also in cross-border situations in order to fully enforce the policy of its legislation. This is especially true in the case of mandatory consumer contract law for which Article 5(1) of the European Convention on the Law Applicable to Contractual Obligations, the so-called Rome Convention,[41] under certain criteria, guarantees the application of the mandatory domestic law of the country of the consumer's domicile. Outside the field of consumer contract law, domestic private international law may enforce particular mandatory rules under a doctrine of *loi de police*[42] or of public order (*ordre public*).[43]

Consequently, there is an obvious Internal Market justification for the Community legislator to legislate in the field of consumer contracts and, beyond, on mandatory contract rules in general. Consumer law, in fact, provides an interesting field of research, given the considerable body of European harmonisation already existing. For very good reason, the Commission's Communication mentions it at the first and most prominent place on its list of the *acquis communautaire* in the field of private law.[44]

---

[40] However, with respect to pre-contractual obligations, the situation is quite unclear. The German rule on *culpa in contrahendo* might well be qualified as a tort rule, so that parties cannot decide on the applicable law. The ECJ did not discuss this issue in: ECJ 13.10.1993 – case C-93/92 *CMC Motorradcenter GmbH/Baskiciogullari* ECR I–5009. In fact, it was irrelevant, because, in the underlying case, the Court had to deal with a consumer contract for which Art. 5(1) of the Rome Convention on the Law Applicable to Contractual Obligations provides for the application of the mandatory law of the country of the consumer's domicile. Consequently, German law was the applicable law in the case irrespective of the qualification of precontractual obligations.

[41] Convention of 19 June 1980; see Morse, 'The EEC Convention on the Law Applicable to Contractual Obligations', (1982) *Yearbook of European Law* 107; Williams, 'The EEC Convention on the law applicable to contractual obligations', (1986) 35 *ICLQ* 1. See also Grundmann, *Europäisches Schuldvertragsrecht* (Berlin, New York, De Gruyter, 1999), 148–188.

[42] Under certain conditions, Art. 7 of the Rome Convention allows such a rule.

[43] See Art. 16 of the Rome Convention.

[44] See the Annex to the Communication.

In the field of consumer contracts, Community legislation is characterised by the minimum approach to harmonisation. This approach seems to find an obvious justification in the Treaty provisions of Article 95(3) and 153(1) EC with the obligation of the Community legislature to pursue a high level of consumer protection. However, as the analysis demonstrates so far, minimum harmonisation alone cannot guarantee the establishment of the Internal Market, and, in addition, mutual recognition is not a device to be found in consumer contract directives, nor would this principle be a suitable device in the specific field.

In order to identify a 'substitute device' for mutual recognition, our attention turns to private international law. However, a closer analysis reveals that at the present state of legal development, the private international law system in the European Union is even counter-productive with respect to the objective of establishing the Internal Market.

In more recent consumer contract directives, we find the general rule of conflict of laws according to which the law of the directive has to be applied provided that the case has a close connection with the territory of at least one Member State.[45] This rule is clearly designed to enforce the Community legislature's policy decision to protect the European consumer against the application of the law of a third country which does not meet the Community minimum requirements of protection.[46] It does not respond to the issue of diverging national standards within the European Union, still permitted under the minimum approach to harmonisation.

This latter issue is predominantly dealt with under Article 5(2) of the Rome Convention, applicable in all Member States. In some other directives, especially in the field of insurance contracts,[47] the Community legislator has opted for a similar formula, protecting the consumer against the application of the unknown foreign law.[48]

From this point of view, European harmonisation may even be deemed to

---

[45]   See, for example, Art. 6(2) of Council Directive 93/13/EC of 5 April 1993 on Unfair Terms in Consumer Contracts, EC OJ 1993 L 95/29; Art. 12(1) of Directive 97/7 of the European Parliament and of the Council of 20 May 1997 on the Protection of Consumers in Respect of Distance Contracts, EC OJ 1997 L 144/19.

[46]   See Kreuzer and Wagner (n. 34 above) R note 38.

[47]   Article 7 of Second Council Directive 88/357/EEC of 22 June 1988 on the coordination of laws, regulations and administrative provisions relating to direct insurance other than life assurance and laying down provisions to facilitate the effective exercise of freedom to provide services and amending directive 73/239/EC, EC OJ 1988 L 172/1; Art. 4 of Second Council Directive 90/619/EEC of 8 November 1990 on the coordination of laws, regulations and administrative provisions relating to direct life assurance and laying down provisions to facilitate the effective exercise of freedom to provide services and amending directive 79/267/EC. See Kreuzer and Wagner (n. 34 above) R note 265. .

[48]   See Grundmann (n. 41 above), 863–865.

reinforce difficulties for the exercise of the fundamental freedoms,[49] especially by introducing obligations of the party to inform the consumer about his or her rights according to the applicable law in the country of the consumer's domicile. A very drastic and obvious example can be drawn from the implementation of the Directive on Distance Contracts[50] which provides for a right of the consumer to withdraw from the contract within a period of no less than seven working days (Art. 6). In 2000, Germany implemented a general revocation term of 14 days. In addition to what the Directive on Distant Contracts requires, this period will only start to run, according to the new German law which came into force on 1 January 2002, when the supplier provides for the information required by the Electronic Commerce Directive. It is obvious that a supplier also wanting to use the Internet in order to sell to consumers will hardly be able to meet the requirements of more than one domestic law. Even for specialist lawyers, it has become extremely difficult to give sufficient advice on how to correctly design a commercial website even according to one domestic law. This holds true even more so when it comes to cross-border electronic commerce. Obviously, differences in mandatory contract law create obstacles to the fundamental freedoms.[51]

This obvious preference given to the protection of the consumer contradicts the traditional approach of a combination of minimum harmonisation and mutual recognition. The mutual recognition approach would argue for a different conflict of laws rule, namely allowing the supplier to agree with the consumer on the application of the law of the country of the supplier's settlement. According to this analysis, there is a strong case for a revision of or a deviation from Article 5(2) of the Rome Convention for cross-border consumer contracts between contracting parties located in different Member States and the adoption of the free choice principle. This proposal does not *per se* contradict consumer protection under European legislation. Article 5(2) of the Rome Convention dates from a time (1980) when European consumer contract protection was non-existent and harmonisation was difficult to achieve under the unanimity

---

[49] With a similar critique on Art. 5(2) of the Rome Convention: Grundmann, 'Europäisches Schuldvertragsrecht', *NJW* [2000], 14, 16.

[50] Directive 97/7 of the European Parliament and of the Council of 20 May 1997 on the Protection of Consumers in Respect of Distance Contracts, EC OJ 1997 L 144/19.

[51] However, there is the question whether the Keck decision of the ECJ would argue against obstacles to the fundamental freedoms; see ECJ 24.11.1993 – joint cases C-267 and 268/91 *Keck and Mithouard* [1993] ECR I–6097. The analysis demonstrates that mandatory rules of contract law, applied to cross-border transactions can considerably prevent suppliers of goods and services from concluding cross-border contracts and, therefore, restrict access to the domestic market. With an identical result: Stuyck, 'Patterns of Justice in the European Constitutional Charter: Minimum Harmonisation in the Field of Consumer Law', in: Krämer, Micklitz and Tonner, *Law and Diffuse Interest in the European Legal Order, Liber amicorum Norbert Reich* (Baden-Baden, Nomos, 1997), 279, 285 *et seq.*, arguing that *Keck* only applies to internal situations.

rule of ex-Article 100 EEC Treaty (new Art. 94 EC). Today, there is no sufficient reason why domestic contractual protection meeting the requirements of the directives should not be accepted as substantially equivalent to domestic protection.

The only valid counter-argument against the application of the free choice principle would be an institutional one. The European level of consumer protection, in some instances, might still be considered to be too low because the Member States remained unable to agree on a more advanced level of protection; nevertheless, minimum harmonisation should be preferred to a complete abstention from harmonisation. Such situations are more likely to be found in cases of older legislation when unanimity was needed on the Council under ex-Article 100 EC Treaty (Art. 94 EC). Arguably, such a situation exists in the field of consumer credit law. There, Member States have largely decided to go beyond the European level of consumer protection the Community directive.[52] However, application of the free choice principle would be the appropriate approach with respect to the harmonisation of the rules on doorstep selling, distance selling, package travel arrangements, timesharing contracts, and consumer sales. The qualified majority rule under Article 95 EC, in general, guarantees that Member States and the Parliament can agree on an appropriate Community level of protection.

Beyond already harmonised issues, the free choice principle should also be accepted as a general rule for electronic contracts in order to promote and facilitate electronic commerce. With a similar objective, the Community legislator has extended the principle of the country of origin even to areas not yet harmonised under Community law and, thereby, generalised the principle of mutual recognition.[53] There is no reason why the consumer on the internet has to live according to the legal standards of foreign advertising law, but should still be able to rely on national consumer contract law.

Outside the area of already harmonised consumer contract law and the special field of electronic commerce, there is no justification for abandoning the approach of Article 5(2) of the Rome Convention. Of course, the Community legislator may react under Article 95 EC whenever consumer protection turns out to be insufficient, but, under a generally applicable free choice rule, the national legislator would lose its authority to define the most appropriate contractual protection of consumers in cross-border cases. Again, the mutual recognition analogy may bring us to the most adequate approach. Outside the sphere of

---

[52] Council Directive 87/102/EEC of 22 December 1986 for the approximation of the laws, regulations and administrative provisions of the Member States concerning consumer credit, EC OJ 1987 L 42/48. See also the 2001 Discussion paper on the amendment of Directive 87/102/EEC concerning consumer credit: http://www.europa.eu.int/comm/consumers/policy/developments/cons_cred/cons_cred1a_en.pdf.

[53] Cf. *supra* n. 14.

harmonised issues and the Internet, the application of national law should only be tested according to the principles of the fundamental freedoms which do not *per se* exclude a justification of national law.[54] We may conclude that the free choice principle should only be applied to the extent Community law has already harmonised consumer contract law and, in addition, to Internet-related cases.

In addition, the legislator would also have to decide on the proper law when the parties fail to agree on the applicable law (objective choice of law). In Article 5(3), under certain criteria, the Rome Convention prefers the law of the country of the consumer. This rule seems appropriate even within the scope of already harmonised law and on the Internet. As we have seen above,[55] the consumer, who does not conclude similar cross-border contracts on a daily basis, has to face a particular information problem. The rule of conflict of Article 5(3) reduces the information problem. The supplier has to convince the consumer to agree on the applicability of a different domestic law and, thereby, signals the deviation from the possibly more protective law of the country of the consumer's residence.

In general, the private international law approach proposed above, based on party autonomy, fulfilling the functions of the mutual recognition principle to establish the Internal Market in the field of contract law, has the considerable advantage that minimum harmonisation can be continued. Minimum harmonisation does not have to be replaced by an approach of total and complete harmonisation of the law of the Member States.

In addition, mandatory contract law, especially consumer contract law, can and should be part of the proposed set of opt-in contract rules to be adopted under Article 308 EC. Following the different speed approach, such rules would create a level playing field for competition between the legal orders of the Member States and European contract law. If the European rules prove to be acceptable for the business community and consumers, the Community legislator can later proceed to harmonising the national law accordingly.

3. Conclusion: Free Choice Principle, Minimum Harmonisation and Opt-In Community Contract Rules

These comments try to take private international law seriously and argue against a necessary tension between mandatory contract law and the free choice principle. Since the Community has power to harmonise national contract law, there is no need, at least to the extent harmonisation effectively takes place, for free choice of the applicable contract law not to be the leading star of Internal

---

[54] Conflicts between national mandatory contract rules and the fundamental freedoms do not arise frequently. An example, however, can be found in the *Motorradcenter* case, *supra* n. 40.

[55] See *supra* III.A.

Market legislation even with respect to mandatory law. At the same time, the free choice approach does not question Community legislation on mandatory contract law. Rather, it argues for its reinforcement. The Member States and the Parliament, under Article 95 EC, will only accept the free choice principle if the domestic contract law of all Member States meets certain quality standards, especially with respect to the protection of consumers.

In line with the free choice principle, adoption of an opt-in and more comprehensive set of European contract rules on the basis of Article 308 EC, including optional rules as well as mandatory ones, would considerably contribute to the smooth functioning of the Internal Market by offering an alternative legal system acceptable to contracting parties from different Member States. This Community set of contract law would avoid the costs of a sudden introduction of a uniform European contract law and, on an everyday basis, would have to prove its quality in competition with the domestic law of the Member States. Thus, the opt-in approach combines the advantages of legal diversity with the needs of the Internal Market.

IV. DEFINING THE BORDERLINE BETWEEN OPTIONAL AND MANDATORY CONTRACT RULES

The analysis so far has demonstrated that there is a stronger Internal Market justification for harmonisation of mandatory contract rules than of optional rules. In order to respond to the problems caused by conflicting domestic optional rules, adoption of an opt-in set of contract rules turns out to be sufficient and should be preferred to a harmonisation approach. The fundamental distinction between optional rules and mandatory rules, therefore, has to be considered to be fundamental for the future development of European contract law. The issue of how to draw the line between optional and mandatory rules deserves closer consideration.

1. The Need for an Active Role of the European Legislature – Towards a Market-Oriented Concept of Contract Law

Contract law, at least in market societies, starts from the very assumption that contractual relations should be governed in principle by party autonomy. Nevertheless, all private law systems recognise mandatory contract rules, designed to limit the scope of party autonomy. Within the European Union, obstacles to the exercise of the fundamental freedoms stem from the fact that particular Member States introduce mandatory rules in contractual situations which are left to party autonomy by the law of other Member States. Even if the law of several Member States provides for mandatory rules in particular situations, the individual rules and methods of regulation may differ greatly.

A pragmatic approach to harmonisation of mandatory contract rules would consist, in a first step, in identifying such situations of diverging regulatory approaches in the Member States. The result of this approach is obvious: the very existence of mandatory contract rules in some Member States will be the argument to extend this kind of market regulation by private law to other Member States. In general, though not always, the former will be very reluctant to give up their earlier policy considerations and to move back to the principle of party autonomy. In addition, the institutional framework of European Community works in this very direction by acknowledging particular objectives and creating regulatory power of the European legislature to protect particular interests, especially consumer interests, justifying a deviation from the principle of party autonomy. As an overall result, the body of mandatory European contract law would expand.

A remarkable example for such an expansion of mandatory contract rules can be found in the case of harmonising the law on consumer sales leading to mandatory contract rules throughout the European Union, whereas only a number of Member States had introduced such consumer protection before.[56] The preamble to the Consumer Sales Directive does not reveal any market justification for the introduction of mandatory rules. It refers only to the need to protect the consumer without explaining why the consumer should not be able to waive the retailer's liability.[57]

The objective of establishing the Internal Market justifies harmonisation by Community law. Though there is a particular Internal Market justification for taking harmonising action, disparities between domestic laws do not afford a

---

[56] On the situation in individual Member States see Arnokouros, 'The transposition of the Consumer Sales Directive into the Greek legal system', (2001) *ERPL* 259; Bird, 'Directive 99/44/EC on certain aspects of the sale of consumer goods and associated guarantees: its impact on existing Irish sale of goods law', (2001) *ERPL* 279; Bruun Nielsen, 'Directive 1999/44/EC of the European Parliament and the Council on certain aspects of the sale of consumer goods and associated guarantees and its influence on Danish law', (2001) *ERPL* 189; Elvinger, 'La Directive 99/44 du 25 Mai 1999 et le droit luxembourgeois, (2001) *ERPL* 309; Grundmann, 'European sales law – reform and adoption of international models in German sales law', (2001) *ERPL* 239; Hogg, 'Scottish law and the European Consumer Sales Directive', (2001) *ERPL* 337; Hondius/Schelhaas, 'In conformity with the Conumer Sales Directive? Some remarks on transposition into Dutch law', (2001) *ERPL* 327; Jeloschek, 'The Transposition of Directive 99/44/EC into Austrian Law', (2001) *ERPL* 163; Lete, 'The Impact on Spanish contract law of the EC Directive on the Sale of Consumer Goods and Associated Guarantees', (2001) *ERPL* 351; Pinna, 'La transposition en droit français', (2001) *ERPL* 223; Scotton, 'Directive 99/44/EC on certain aspects of the sale of consumer goods and associated guarantees', (2001) *ERPL* 297 (on Italian law); Watterson, 'Consumer Sales Directive 1999/44/EC – The impact on English law', (2001) *ERPL* 197.

[57] The only reference to the issue can be found in para. 22 of the preamble. It reads: '[T]he parties may not, by common consent, restrict or waive the rights granted to the consumer, since otherwise the legal protection afforded would be thwarted.'.

particular Internal Market justification for introducing mandatory contract rules. This kind of very *reactive harmonisation* takes care of the needs of the Internal Market. Nevertheless, it does not necessarily guarantee the adoption of high-quality European contract law.

A different approach would consist in the development of a proper European contract law theory which integrates, as its most important objective, the identification of situations in which particular action is needed in order to guarantee the smooth functioning of the contract law and market system. Expressed in different words, the issue to be considered is not so much whether national contract rules differ, but rather whether, in the context of the Internal Market, there is a need to respond to particular market and contract failures by the adoption of mandatory contract law. Mere existence of mandatory contract law in some Member States may only indicate, without providing for sufficient evidence, that, in a given situation there is in fact a market justification for the introduction of mandatory law.

This analysis does not argue for a reduction and limitation for the introduction of European mandatory law. Rather, it supports an active role of the European legislature in the design of contract law in the European Union, being an important part of the regulatory framework of the Internal Market and the market economy in the Union. Actually, in some areas, the European legislature has passed largely consistent rules for the regulation of particular sectors. Particularly the Community directives on doorstep selling, distance contracts and electronic contracts in their entirety nowadays appear as a rather comprehensive and consistent approach to protect one contracting party, namely the consumer, against the disadvantages of particular methods of distribution.[58] Thereby, European law by the very introduction of mandatory law achieves a balance of the overall economic and competitive benefits with the need to adequately protect one contracting party against inherent risks of the particular distribution system. It is no surprise that the Commission is now considering merging the different directives in one single directive on distribution systems.[59]

2. Reconsidering European Consumer Contract Law

European consumer contract law constitutes the most important field where we encounter mandatory European contract rules. The question to be answered

---

[58] Micklitz, 'Vertragsschlussmodalitäten im Diskussionsentwurf eines Schuldrechtsmodern-isierungsgesetzes', *VuR* [2001], 71.

[59] The European Commission initiated a study on the reform of the existing regulatory system. See, Institut für Europäisches Wirtschafts- und Verbraucherrecht e.V. (VIEW), 'Door to Door Selling – Pyramid Selling – Multi-Level Marketing. Contract No. AO/7050/98/000156. A Study commissioned by the European Commission. Final Report', http://www.europa.eu.int/comm/dgs/health_consumer/library/surveys/sur10_02.pdf. See also Brammsen, 'Auf dem Weg zu einer europäischen Direktvertriebsrichtlinie?', *EWS* [2001], 312.

remains whether the above mentioned active role of the European legislature as to European contract law, amounting to a market-oriented approach to it, is compatible with the Treaty concept of consumer protection and how this concept will be implemented and with what consequences.

a) Compatibility of the Market-Oriented Concept with the EC Treaty

The market-oriented concept seems to collide with Article 95(3) and Article 153(1) EC. Both provisions stipulate an obligation on Community institutions and especially the European legislature to pursue 'a high level of consumer protection'. Both provisions are clearly based on the idea that consumer protection can easily be measured and compared. The idea of different levels of protection also signals that there could always be a higher level of consumer protection. Still, a more ideal world can be imagined. Consequently, the Member States, in the sense of minimum harmonisation, are left to go beyond the European level and to raise the level of protection in the interests of consumers.

According to the market-oriented approach, different levels of protection are not the correct understanding of consumer protection. The issue would rather be whether there is a need and a justification for the legislature to intervene in the interplay of the free forces of the market and to deviate from party autonomy by adopting mandatory contract rules. Whereas Article 95(3) and Article 153(1) EC are rather to be read in the sense of a *maximisation of consumer protection*, the approach submitted above argues for an *optimisation of contract law*, whereby market failures are accepted phenomena and need to be responded to by adopting mandatory contract rules.

Nevertheless, the submitted approach can be reconciled with the provisions of the Treaty. A policy designed to 'promote consumer interests' and to 'ensure a high level of consumer protection', as laid down in Article 95(3) and 153 EC, deserves to be supported, but, in the context of contract law, has to be understood in a particular way. The principles of freedom of contract and a working and competitive market are not directed against the consumer as such.[60] Rather, both elements enable the consumer to pursue his or her autonomously defined economic preferences in the Internal Market. This concept of the active and informed consumer is well established under the existing Community legal system. It is part of the case law on the interpretation of the fundamental freedoms as well as of special consumer contract legislation which is designed

---

[60] This is a concept that gradually gains more support, cf. for example Stuyck (n. 51 above) 279, arguing that there is no justification for consumer protection that goes beyond market rationality. See also Stuyck, 'European Consumer Law After the Treaty of Amsterdam: Consumer Policy in or Beyond the Internal Market?', (2000) 37 *CMLRev* 367. However, against a purely competition-oriented approach to European contract law, Hoffmann (n. 21 above) 306–309.

to promote consumer confidence in the quality of legal standards in other Member States. At the same time, it is also true that there are contractual situations in which the consumer has to confront particular disadvantages. That is why European consumer law largely deals with specific marketing methods that may easily disadvantage the consumer, as well as complex types of contracts. On the other hand, however, consumer contract law should refrain from going beyond what is necessary to respond to the identified failures of the contract law system. An overall introduction of mandatory contract rules would centralise the decision making in the market and violate the self-determination of consumers. 'Maximum' consumer protection would patronise consumers and contradict their interests.

To give an example of possibly perverted consumer protection, it is worthwhile to mention the liability of the seller for used products according to the European Consumer Sales Directive. Such liability is mandatory, although the seller might be unable to measure the risk of such liability correctly and, therefore, ask for a considerably higher price. The purchasing consumer, who is unable to afford a new product in the first place, might rather want to pay a lower price and accept the risks of buying a defective product. Hence, European consumer protection turns out overprotective and may even destroy a market for used products.

For the correct understanding of the Treaty provisions, the consequences are clear: Article 95(3) and Article 153(1) EC have to be understood in the sense of *optimising contract law* by the introduction of mandatory provisions on consumer protection. This understanding does not preclude that, in some instances, the 'level of European consumer protection' is still too low and should be raised, since the already existing instruments of consumer protection are only insufficiently responding to the existing market failure. In such cases, possibly in the case of consumer credit law,[61] consumer protection appears 'sub-optimal' and should be put on a 'higher level'. However, as we were able to see, consumer protection can also go too far.

b) Defining Failures of the Market Mechanisms and the Contractual System

According to the market-oriented understanding of consumer protection, it is the most important task of the European legislature to identify relevant failures of the market mechanisms and the contractual system and to respond to these failures appropriately with legal instruments – for instance, with obligations of the other party to inform and a possible right of the consumer to withdraw from the contract.

It is not the purpose of these comments to expand too much on this concept of consumer protection which was developed in a former publication under the

---

[61]   Cf. *supra* n. 52.

catchword of *economic self-determination of the consumer*.[62] Obviously, methods to determine situations of such failures are not restricted. Arguments coming from economic analysis can be as convincing as daily court practice and common sense. More importantly, the European legislator should be aware of the need to justify the adoption of mandatory contract law in the preamble to the directives. Recognition of this requirement, at least, would have triggered much more thoughtfulness and discussion about the need for mandatory contract rules in the case of consumer sales.[63]

In view of the approach of harmonisation to be taken, the market-oriented approach meets three objectives: (1) it would guarantee the smooth functioning of the Internal Market; (2) it would adequately balance the protective and the enabling aspects of consumer contract law; and (3) it would integrate consumer contract law in general contract law. In particular, this last aspect could further the integration of such European harmonisation in the domestic legal system.

c) Taking off the Straitjacket of Consumer Contract Law

The market-oriented approach to mandatory law has particular virtues. Up to now, the European legislature has always been obsessed with the idea of consumer protection since a proper Community consumer policy came into existence in the 1970s and has been recognised under Article 95(3) and 153 EC. In reaction to the Commission's Communication of July 2001, the European Consumer Law Group even wants to reinforce this particular emphasis on consumer law, to continue with minimum harmonisation and to develop a 'true European Code on Consumer Law'.[64] According to the analysis undertaken in the framework of these comments, this approach is both dangerous and modest.

---

[62] Drexl, *Die wirtschaftliche Selbstbestimmung des Verbrauchers* (Tübingen, Mohr/Siebeck, 1998); See also Drexl, 'Verbraucherrecht – Allgemeines Privatrecht – Handelsrecht', paper presented at the 2001 conference of the Ernst-von-Caemmerer-Gedächtnisstiftung (September 2001), about to be published.

[63] Only recently, quite a bit of criticism was expressed on the adoption of mandatory contract rules in the field of consumer sales law; see Canaris, 'Wandlungen des Schuldvertragsrechts – Tendenzen zu seiner Materialisierung', *AcP* 200 (2000), 273, 362 f. (arguing in the sense of a violation of the German Constitution and the EC Treaty); Martinek, 'Überregulierung im Europäischen Verbraucherschutzrecht', in: Grundmann (ed.), *Systembildung und Systemlücken in Kerngebieten des Europäischen Privatrechts* (Tübingen, Mohr and Siebeck, 2000), 511, 535–541. It is no surprise that such criticism comes primarily from Germany where consumer sales were governed by party autonomy until the implementation of the directive.

[64] See, European Consumer Law Group, 'Response to the Communication on European Contract Law', Doc. ECLG/343/2001 of 15 October 2001, especially concluding note III. 5 (http://www.europa.eu.int/comm/consumers/policy/developments/contract_law/comments/3.3.pdf).

The dangerous aspect of continuing with the obsession with consumer protection is obvious and has already been made clear by the comments in the discussion of the market-oriented approach of mandatory contract law. In particular, it would separate consumer contract law from general private law without a convincing justification, whereas the market-oriented approach integrates consumer protection as an example of dealing with market and contract failures, simply as a general problem of private law.[65]

However, the consumer obsession of European contract law is also too modest for the very simple reason that market failures do not occur to the disadvantage of consumers only. Market failures constitute a general phenomenon. European contract law has largely neglected to address market failures to the disadvantage of non-consumers, although this group of persons traditionally engages much more in cross-border transactions than consumers. Therefore, the European legislator should give more recognition to the issue of whether particular instruments of consumer protection do respond to a general problem of contract law and should consequently also be extended to non-consumers.[66] Such an extension would make sense, for example, with respect to the control of non-negotiated general contract terms. In principle, German law, since the introduction of the Act on General Contract Terms (*Gesetz über allgemeine Geschäftsbedingungen*, AGB-Gesetz) in 1976, for very good reasons, has always afforded protection not only to consumers but also to undertakings, whereas the Community Directive on Unfair Contract Terms[67] is limited in scope to consumer contracts. In fact, the justification for intervention does not consist in the economically or intellectually disadvantaged position of the consumer vis-à-vis a commercial or professional actor, but in the inherent risks of agreeing to a set of contract terms that were drafted, thought over and unilaterally introduced by the other contracting party.

In general, the market-oriented approach broadens the perspective of legislating on mandatory contract rules and frees consumer contract law from its straitjacket. On the other hand, especially in the case of regulating particular marketing practices, limiting the scope of mandatory law to consumers makes sense since protection is needed only for persons who are not sufficiently familiar

---

[65] See also Hondius, 'Consumer Law and Private Law: Where the Twains Shall Meet', in: Krämerm, Micklitz and Tonner, *Law and Diffuse Interest in the European Legal Order, Liber amicorum Norbert Reich* (Baden-Baden, Nomos, 1997), 311, 327, arguing for a concept of consumer contract law as part of private law.

[66] With a similar conclusion Tenreiro, 'Un code de la consommation ou un code autour du consommateur? Quelques réflexions critiques sur la codification et la notion du consommateur', in: Krämer, Micklitz and Tonner, *Law and Diffuse Interest in the European Legal Order, Liber amicorum Norbert Reich* (Baden-Baden, Nomos, 1997), 339, 355 *et seq.*

[67] Council Directive 93/13/EC of 5 April 1993 on Unfair Terms in Consumer Contracts, EC OJ 1993 L 95/29.

with the inherent risks of the particular practice and who are not confronted with such practice on an everyday basis.[68]

V. CONCLUSIONS

In the field of contract law, the 'new approach' to harmonisation of the White Paper of 1985 turns out to be very ineffective. Harmonisation as such and minimum harmonisation in particular allows disparities to persist between the domestic law of the Member States, adversely affecting the smooth functioning of the Internal Market, whereas especially in the field of technical standards, the mutual recognition principle guarantees the exercise of the fundamental freedoms, mutual recognition is not a principle to be found in European contract law. It is rather up to conflict of laws rules to determine the proper law applicable to the contract.

As to the significance for fundamental freedoms and the legal devices designed to contribute to the establishment of the Internal Market in the field of contract law, a clear distinction has to be made between optional and mandatory rules. Domestic optional rules do not create barriers to trade. However, the existence of different private law systems in Europe cause information costs, thereby increase transaction costs and give rise to considerable distortions of competition. Consumers and smaller and medium-sized firms, for lack of familiarity with the foreign law, might be reluctant to engage in cross-border transactions. In order to respond to these problems, however, adoption of opt-in contract rules under Article 308 EC should be preferred to the harmonisation under Article 95 EC or even the introduction of a uniform European contract law. The opt-in approach combines the advantages of legal diversity with the needs of the Internal Market.

In the field of mandatory contract law, the situation is similar to the extent that private international law follows the free choice principle (principle of party autonomy) to determine the proper law applicable to the contract. However, private international law very often deviates from party autonomy in order to safeguard the enforcement of the underlying policy consideration of national

---

[68]   On the other hand, limiting European consumer contract law in its application to business actors contracting with consumers does not justify a qualification of European consumer contract law as 'business contract law' ('Recht der Unternehmensgeschäfte'); see, however, Grundmann, *NJW* [2000], 14, 15 *et seq.*, on the basis of a quantified analysis of European directives rejecting the very concept of a European consumer contract law in favour of a European business contract law. Instead, the correct definition of the scope of application should always start with the analysis of the individual market failure which may only exist to the disadvantage of the consumer. At the same time, the application of the law is limited to business actors in order not to impose the contractual obligations of European consumer protection, especially the obligation to inform the consumer, on privately acting persons.

legislation. This is especially true with respect to Article 5(2) of the Rome Convention on the Law Applicable to Contractual Obligations which, under certain criteria, provides for the application of the mandatory law of the country of the consumer's domicile. Due to this rule of law, which is also applicable in the area of harmonised consumer contract law, a supplier settled in one Member State and marketing products in other countries has to respect a multitude of domestic rules. Consequently, even after harmonisation, domestic consumer contract law continues to constitute barriers to the exercise of the fundamental freedoms. Seen in the light of the recent decision of the ECJ on the Tobacco Advertising Directive, the existing approach to harmonising consumer contract law seems insufficient to establish the Internal Market.

A 'second-new approach' would consist in the application of the free choice principle. Application of this principle should be limited to situations harmonised by European law and to electronic contracts. Outside this scope, national consumer contract law should only be controlled according to the principles of the fundamental freedoms. In order to establish the Internal Market, the free choice principle would fulfil the functions of the mutual recognition principle.

In addition, the 'second-new approach' argues for a broader approach to European contract law legislation. Instead of maximising contractual consumer protection, European legislation should optimise contract law with the objective of guaranteeing the smooth functioning of the Internal Market. In light of this market-oriented approach, the European legislator, in any instance, should thoroughly consider whether there is a market justification for the introduction of mandatory contract rules. Since market failures constitute a general phenomenon of contract law not limited to consumers, the European legislator should also consider whether certain instruments of contractual consumer protection can be extended to the protection of non-consumers.

Returning to the options considered by the Commission for further action,[69] the above comments advocate a combination of options 3 and 4. As to existing Community legal instruments, action for improving their quality is needed (option 3) and, as it was possible to see, can also be accomplished. In addition, adoption of an opt-in set of contract rules would amount to new comprehensive legislation at EC level (option 4). Such legislation, as the future may show, may turn out as a first step towards a comprehensive European Civil Code. However, the establishment of the Internal Market does not require such a Code.

---

[69] *Supra* I. A.

Part III

A European Code Replacing National Laws (Option IVa)

INTRODUCTORY NOTE

In part III, the pros and cons of the idea of a European Code substituting national laws (option IVa of the Commission's Communication) is discussed. The part which brings together the proponents of a European Code which would substitute national laws is not easy to summarise. First, not all authors really favour such a code, most have at least certain reservations although perhaps less explicit than the clear opponents. Second, the style of the papers is very different, ranging from papers almost philosophically inspired to those which are clearly draft-oriented, from papers heavily influenced by modern regulation theory to those based on classical private autonomy contract law theory.

After Bianca's pragmatic plea for a progressive codification of European Private Law (Ch. 8) in which he also gives clear examples, von Bar (Ch. 9) makes a plea for drafting the Code now, mainly by scholars, and extending it to other areas. Basedow (Ch. 10) sees a sound comparative law basis only in contract law and therefore advocates a European Code only in this area and even there potentially only in some decades. Bussani and Hesselink (Chs. 11 and 12) speak about the policies behind the Codification Process – who could win, perhaps scholars who regain prestige, and which philosophy could be furthered, a more liberal one? They are therefore not clearly proponents of a Code, Hesselink even quite the contrary. Gandolfi and Lando (Chs. 13 and 14) clearly advocate a continuation of what they have already elaborated with the Principles or Draft Code. Mattei (Ch. 15) is in favour of a European Code, but only a slim Code with mainly mandatory rules because the lack of such unification only favours business. Schwintowski (Ch. 16) on the other hand rather advocates a framework code only – besides national laws – and thus almost transcends already the borderline to the opponents of a European Code substituting national contract laws.

Opposition, in the case of Van den Bergh (Ch. 17), is very much based on findings which are virtually undisputed in economics, i.e. that decentralised rule-making has important advantages as well. Van den Bergh even rates the advantages of centralised rule-making as minimal and the disadvantages as considerable. Collins (Ch. 18) sees advantages of unification only if uniformity is reached and even then there may be strong opposing interests, principally that of quality of the law which is paramount. Reich (Ch. 19) criticises the Communication as not addressing the core issues: there is no competence for a European Code substituting national laws, one should do the homework first and codify what is already there in the area of consumer law.

8. Progressive Codification of European Private Law

*C. Massimo Bianca**

1. Although it is not my intention to trespass upon the 'yes–no to codification' debate, I want to briefly make clear that in my opinion the European Union needs a Code throughout Europe governing private legal relations in the fields of human rights, contracts, ownership, torts, and so on.

A Code means a systematic and unitary body of rules expressing the *law* to which private parties are subject, and which the courts are bound to apply. The European Union needs a single Civil Code because there cannot be real equality under different private laws and because different private laws are an objective obstacle to free cross-border trade transactions of goods and services.

To realize this aim the formulation of 'principles' is not sufficient. Principles are important for the elaboration of the theoretical structure and foundations of the rules of law, but principles which are not legally binding cannot achieve uniformity of law.

Arbitrators may settle disputes relative to international contracts availing themselves of principles not belonging to a certain legislation. Such principles may be chosen by the parties to be applied to their contracts. However, these eventualities affect only a small percentage of the trade experience and are not sufficient to allow us to presume the existence of a system of law: a system of law exists when there are rules which grant rights recognized and enforced under a public or private judicial authority.

At the moment, national courts and arbitrators are called to administer the law of the State to which they belong or the law of the State which, according to the rules concerning conflict of laws, governs the case. No Italian court would decide a case applying 'principles' proposed by academics or anyone else instead of applying Italian law or the law that the Italian private international law no. 218 of 1995 prescribes.

2. Though Europe needs a single Civil Code, it is unlikely that the target will be reached in a short time. Some continental civil codes are seen not only as a body of rules, but rather as the expression of cultural inheritance, symbols of national pride, means of political influence of the State. We can apply similar

---

*   Professor of Civil Law, University of Rome, 'La Sapienza'.

S. Grundmann and J. Stuyck (eds.), An Academic Green Paper on European Contract Law, 133–136
© 2002 *Kluwer Law International. Printed in Great Britain.*

considerations to the Common Law. That is why it is very difficult for some Member States to give up their legal tradition and conform their domestic Private Law to a foreign code.

These difficulties must not dissuade us from working hard for a European Civil Code and, most importantly, for a European Contract Code (as the Gandolfi Commission is doing). But if the realization *ex abrupto* of a European Code is out of sight for the time being, it seems reasonable in the meantime to try the alternative of a progressive codification, that is a codification carried on step by step through the regulation of single institutes of Private Law.

The idea of a progressive codification could encounter the objection – already voiced – that the single institutes are inserted in a frame of general rules which integrate their regulation, and that a uniform law cannot be achieved without those rules having been laid down.

This objection is not decisive because, first, the general rules of private law usually result from the rules originally governing single contracts, or single torts or facts. In reality, it is the regulation of single institutes that opens the way to the formation of general rules.

3. Secondly, it must be considered that a sort of progressive codification of European Civil Law is already going on, whereas the need for uniform rules is more urgent. Through the not entirely advisable way of Directives, the Member States have been called to conform important institutes of private law to certain European patterns. This has been possible because, however important the single institutes may be, the acceptance of a uniform regulation has not, for the Member States, implied the renunciation of the national identity of their private law. In this perspective the necessity for fixing similar rules with regard to companies, consumer protection, privacy, e-commerce, etc., is overwhelming.

4. Generally the Directives contain gaps which every Member State is allowed to fill. That leads to divergent applications of them. Furthermore, the possibility of different national rules in matters governed by the Directives may arise from different interpretations of the Directives proposed by the lawyers of the Member States. Hence the demand for a uniform interpretation of the acts of the European Union to the furthest possible extent.

The Society of European Contract Law (SECOLA) is willing to operate in this direction. In fact, it was founded with the precise aim of favouring the promotion of European contract law. SECOLA has already taken a first positive step by fostering a 'European' Comment on the 1999/44/EC Directive, which is carried out by scholars and lawyers from various European areas. This initiative is intended to further an interpretation of the Directive, not influenced by the single contexts of national legislations. The Comment has been edited by Bianca and Grundmann and is currently issued by four European publishers.

5. The goal of a Uniform European Private Law cannot be reached solely by means of Directives. The divergent applications allowed by the same Directives inevitably lead to different rules. Directives can only assure similar rules whereas Europe must try to reach not similar, but *common* rules. A progressive codification, I believe, is the way to acquire in a reasonable time, common European private law rules.

Such codification may start from those areas which appear ripe for receiving uniform regulation and which are available to become cornerstones of the future Code. For example, we can first look at monetary obligations. The introduction of a European currency (the Euro) now makes it particularly urgent to develop a uniform regulation of those obligations. Uniform regulation of monetary obligations should fix a single legal rate of interest for delayed payments. The provision of a single rate of payment could not be achieved by CISG owing to the different monetary systems involved. However, the introduction of a common currency, subject to the same devaluation index, opens the way to a common interest rate. The need for such an interest rate has been pointed out by Directive 2000/35/CE of 29 June 2000, which acknowledges that different rules regarding money payments obstruct the smooth functioning of the Internal Market (see recital n. 9 thereof). The Directive, however, offers only a partial solution to the problem, as it only fixes a minimum interest rate and this minimum only governs trade transactions.

Other provisions concern recover costs, unfair agreements regarding the effect of performance delay, speed of recovery proceedings, etc. But we are far from a complete body of rules regarding monetary obligations, which should take in account trade transactions, but also trade relations, though the different nature of the obligations justifies different interest rates (see the Gandolfi Avant Project). It should also take into account not only cases of delayed payments, but all the cases of utilization of money without a contract clause fixing the interest rate (the principle known in Italy as natural fruitfulness of money).

Furthermore, a uniform statute of monetary obligations should deal with the means of payment, how a debtor may discharge himself of his obligations in case of a creditor's delay in receiving payment, the form of a valid tender, the payments made by a third person (a possibility freely allowed in some legislations but not in others: the Lando Principles limits it in spite of my efforts to introduce therein a permissive principle), and so on.

6. Finally, we can point to the contract of sale and other main contracts. A remarkable step has been made by issuing Directive 1999/44/EC of 25 May 1999 on certain aspects of the sale of consumer goods and associated guarantees. This Directive has shown that a uniform European regulation of the contract of sale may be at hand. The Gandolfi Commission has already undertaken the task of studying a project of a European sale, taking into account the Vienna Convention

on International Sale, the above mentioned Directive and all the models of European legislations.

With the cooperation of SECOLA I believe it could quite soon be possible to offer to the EU a scheme of a modern law of sale, as the first positive piece of the European Civil Code.

9. Paving the Way Forward with Principles of European Private Law

*Christian von Bar**

In this brief paper I would like to make the following (interrelated) points: We should not always merely concentrate on whether or not the enactment of a European Civil Code is a desirable final goal. For reasons which I will explain later, I have no doubt that it is, but before we can run we have to learn to walk. The political case for a pan-European codification of private law is best tested against the background of a potential legislative text drafted with the benefit of and from the standpoint of legal science. My second point is this: A successful drafting of principles of European private law is the eye of the needle through which we must all pass. We should, therefore, do the utmost to co-operate in this respect, in mutual trust and support, but without eliciting more competition amongst academics than is really necessary. Even law professors must learn to play in teams, otherwise we will weaken our cause. New groups are good, a common roof for all of us would be better. This brings me to my third point: Based on the foundations laid down by the Commission on European Contract Law we now have to do the utmost to come up with a properly drafted and structured Restatement (or perhaps better: Statement) of at least the major parts of patrimonial law, including consumer protection and the *acquis communautaire* already achieved in that regard. Such a (re)statement must, of course, leave room for later developments, for instance in family law (in respect of which a new Commission on European Family Law has just announced its foundation). Foremost, however, the restatement must tackle the right issues and offer acceptable solutions in the law of obligations and in essential parts of property law as well. Finally, I do think that we will need a legally binding text. But that does not necessarily imply that we should stop thinking about intermediate steps, and neither does it imply that we exclude the possibility of some countries proceeding at a faster speed of legal approximation than others. All jurisdictions will have to make their own cost/benefit analysis, and the result of that need not necessarily be the same everywhere at the same time.

---

*   Dr.jur.; Professor of Law and Director of the Institute of Private International and Comparative Law at the University of Osnabrück (Germany); Bencher (Hons.) of Gray's Inn; FBA.

S. Grundmann and J. Stuyck (eds.), An Academic Green Paper on European Contract Law, 137–145
© 2002 *Kluwer Law International. Printed in Great Britain.*

EUROPEAN CODE REPLACING NATIONAL LAWS

I. INTRODUCTION

For all of us engaged in the process of the Europeanisation of private law these are exciting days: there is the EU Commission's communication on contract law taking up the conclusions of the Tampere Summit of 1999, another (although surprisingly unconnected) Communication by the EU Commission on consumer protection, the official support of the first national government (Italy) backing the idea of a European Civil Code, a new resolution of the EU Parliament pointing in the same direction and most probably the impending return of harmonisation of private and commercial law to the agenda of a Council summit. One conference follows on the coat-tails of the last, newspapers busily report on developments that have been unfolding for a long while behind the scenes, sometimes not even noticed, let alone taken seriously by colleagues in the academic world. National legislators for the first time in European history have come to rely heavily on principles drafted by trans-European commissions. National Parliaments and national councils of lawyers organise meetings entitled 'towards a European Civil Code', and Council Presidencies do the same, the former Swedish Presidency even officially taking up and submitting to the other national governments the idea of establishing a European Law Institute and a European Law Academy. These are the riggings of a ship which is about to set sail.

In this climate I am grateful to the organisers of this conference for the opportunity to reflect on where we stand and how we should make use of this extraordinary readiness to mould a sustainable common future. In this brief paper I would like to make the following (interrelated) points: We should not always concentrate *only* on whether or not the enactment of a European Civil Code is a desirable final goal. For reasons which I will explain later, I have no doubt that it is. But before we can run we have to learn to walk. The political case for a pan-European codification of private law is best tested against the background of a potential legislative text drafted with the benefit of and from the standpoint of legal science. My second point is this: A successful drafting of principles of European private law is the eye of the needle through which we must all pass. We should, therefore, do the utmost to co-operate in this respect, in mutual trust and support, but without eliciting more competition amongst academics than is really necessary. Even law professors must learn to play in teams; otherwise we will weaken our cause. New groups are good, a common roof for all of us would be better. This brings me to my third point: Based on the foundations laid down by the Commission on European Contract Law we now have to do the utmost to come up with a properly drafted and structured Restatement (or perhaps better: Statement) of at least the major parts of patrimonial law, including consumer protection and the *acquis communautaire* already achieved in that regard. Such a (re)statement must, of course, leave room for later developments, for instance in family law (in respect of which a new

Commission on European Family Law has just announced its foundation). Foremost, however, the restatement must tackle the right issues and offer acceptable solutions in the law of obligations and in essential parts of property law as well. Finally I do think, as said before, that we will need a legally binding text. But that does not necessarily imply that we should stop thinking about intermediate steps, and it does not imply either that we exclude the possibility of some countries proceeding at a faster speed of legal approximation than others. All jurisdictions will have to make their own cost/benefit analysis, and the result of that need not necessarily be the same everywhere at the same time.

II. CONTENTS OF THE RESTATEMENT

My impression from the responses which I have seen so far to the EU Commission's communication is that by far the dominant view accepts that the drafting of a (Re)statement or a set of structured Principles of European Law is a good and sensible thing to do. I would even go one step further and say that such a Restatement is the *conditio sine qua non* for all further progress. Allow me to repeat what we, in the Commission on European Contract Law and its successor, the Study Group on a European Civil Code, think it should cover. We believe in particular that the Restatement should not be restricted to contract law alone. At least as far as the Restatement is concerned we need a broader approach, enabling the academic as well as the law-making world to acquire a full picture not just of the general part of contract law, and not only the most important specific contracts too, but also the law of extra-contractual obligations and the parts of moveable property law which are highly relevant from a practical aspect. True, our perspective deviates a bit from the EU Commission's communication, but a closer look quickly reveals that the differences are much smaller than one might at first think. And we feel that we not only have some important backing from the Tampere Summit (which did not narrow down the work to be done to contract law). The European Parliament has in mind exactly the same scope of work to be done as we have.

The Study Group has not yet decided about the final structure of our Restatement. Professor Johnny Herre from Stockholm University will present some first ideas to the Oxford meeting of our group next month. Those proposals clearly acknowledge the difficulty of this matter, and they also demonstrate some lacunae which still need to be filled. Professor Herre is proposing, for the time being, six 'books' (or parts): Book 1: General Provisions of the Code (e.g. aims, scope, territorial application and terminology); Book 2: Contracts (in general), including formation, validity and interpretation; Book 3: Obligations in General (amongst other topics: performance, remedies, prescription, plurality of parties, substitution of debtors and set-off); Book 4: Specific Contracts and Extra-Contractual Obligations (sales, services, leases, agency, distribution and franchising agreements, loans, personal securities, insurance contracts, negotiorum gestio and unjustified enrichment, and tort law); Book 5: Property Law (transfer of ownership in moveables, securities in moveables, assignment of claims, trust law); and Book 6: Consumer Protection.

Whatever the Co-ordinating Group makes of this first and very preliminary draft, the following seems obvious to me. We in the Study Group have our basis in the Principles of European Contract Law (PECL), which were drafted by the Commission on European Contract Law. It has assigned to us in the Study Group the right to make use of the PECL in a way that fits with the needs of a sensible structure of the whole Restatement (and of course with attribution of the source from which the articles, comments and notes are taken). That includes the chapters prepared by the third commission which will be published in 2002. A future Restatement of patrimonial law with the contents we have in mind, however, cannot leave the PECL completely untouched. It may well be that we will have to arrange the chapters of the PECL in a different sequence and to enlarge some of them to cover not only contractual but also extra-contractual obligations. In other areas individual rules might have to be moved or even deleted in favour of a more elaborate set of rules dealing with that specific issue. For example, should we agree to have an independent separate chapter on unjustified enrichment law covering the *condictio indebiti* (or the *répétition de l'indu*) as well, then no doubt certain black-letter rules within the PECL, in particular those on the consequences of an avoidance of the contract and on the effects of illegality, will need revision. Furthermore, there are rules in the PECL in regard to which we might have to ask ourselves whether (and, if so, how) they should be brought into line with our tort law principles. One thinks, for example, of the provisions on damages or on the definition of intention which, according to the PECL, includes recklessness. That latter solution is one which might cause some severe problems within tort law unless a narrow understanding of recklessness is employed. One should not forget that one of the core aims of writing a European Restatement is to achieve a common terminology, and one prerequisite for that is the development of a common terminology for at least the whole of the law of obligations.

I think it needs no explanation here why the Study Group has not confined its work to the law of contracts. A vision of the content and structure of the adjacent areas of the law is essential and indispensable to avoid contradictions, gaps and disequilibria of laying down obstacles to further developments which could only be eradicated in the future with exorbitant effort. We have always to keep in view the fact that contract law forms an organic whole with all economically relevant branches of private law which must be developed in tandem. Without such an approach it would be difficult, if not impossible, to envisage first legislative texts within contract law or even a European Code of Contract Law, for, what we first need is some agreement on what contract law as an entity should cover and at the present time we are still rather far away from that. Besides this, it seems obvious that the EU Commission itself wishes to proceed with the approximation of other areas of the law as well. Liability for defective services and even more so liability for defective products are illustrative examples. The EU Commission has most recently invited tenders for a closer analysis of the possibility to harmonise negligence-based product liability as well, be it in contract or in tort. It seems apparent to me, however, that there can be no isolated solutions in the regime of liability in tort for negligence. That is because there is obviously no reason for supposing that the liability of a producer for negligence in relation to bodily injury and damage to property can follow different rules from those determining the liability for negligence for other tortfeasors. In the joint response of the Commission on European Contract Law and the Study Group on a European Civil Code we have given a whole series of other examples as evidence for the fact that contractual and extra-contractual obligations are so closely linked with each other that we would run into very serious trouble were we to cut off the latter from our deliberations.

A third observation that immediately springs to mind when starting to think about a more detailed structure of the European Restatement and its possible function in serving as a basis for a Code is the sheer amount of work to be done. The Study Group has so far made an astoundingly speedy progress, but there are still some non-negligible gaps and for the time being, due to organisational and financial constraints, we have to live with these. In some of those areas which we cover colleagues have just started their investigations; in others some major problems still need to be resolved, quite apart from the substantial amount of detail that has to be addressed. Another difficulty that I had underestimated when we started is the problem of translation. Our working language is English, but it sometimes turns out to be impossible to translate the texts into all our languages without producing awkward-sounding results. That in turn may compel a change in the English text, even though we have already achieved agreement on its wording. The alternative – i.e. to say that only the English text is authoritative – does not 'sound right' in a European context. I am not pouring water into the wine, but I must say that the Restatement cannot be realised without an ongoing constant effort of all involved or prepared to get involved and acceptance of a full-time responsibility.

Within the general framework of this conference there is, however, one even more important point: consumer protection. It seems clear to me that the future Restatement will need a coherent set of rules in this area of private law, and this not only for obvious political reasons. Given the fact, mentioned earlier, that the EU Commission has issued two independent communications, one on contract law and the other on consumer protection, one might doubt whether the EU Commission itself is fully aware of the fact that we are really talking here about one and the same project. There can be no doubt that we must not repeat the mistakes committed by the draftsmen of the Civil Codes of the twentieth century, and there can be no doubt either that today consumer protection belongs to the common and truly European heritage of the Member States. The question, therefore, is not whether to include specific rules on consumer protection, but rather which, and perhaps even more importantly, how. If one agrees that an independent Code on Consumer Protection would be the worst possible solution, fundamentally affecting the quality of our private law systems, then there remain three alternatives. One would be to draft a separate part (or book) of the Restatement entitled 'consumer protection', as Professor Herre seems to have in mind. The advantage of that approach would be in having all relevant consumer protection rules assembled in one place, creating a reference point here for all future EU legislation in this field and enabling work on this part with a view to option III of the EU Commission's communication, which contemplates a strategic improvement of the existing EU legislation in this field. There are also, however, severe disadvantages. Quite apart from the political point often made by representatives from industry, that a two-track private law system for professionals on the one hand and consumers on the other is undesirable, there are substantial technical difficulties involved in that approach. Are we really sufficiently clear about the question which rules belong to the world of consumer protection and which do not? For instance, to give just one example, what about the negligence-based product liability I mentioned earlier? I do not yet wish to express a firm view on these matters, but it might be better to draft rules on consumer protection directly within the context where they are needed, within the rules on formation of contracts, for instance, within sales and services, within personal securities, and so forth. The same approach would then apply to extra-contractual obligations as well, to tort law too, of course, but also to unjustified enrichment law. Article 9 of the Distance Sales Directive 97/7 EC (which excludes the enriched party's liability in respect of unsolicited services and goods) furnishes a good example. It is, incidentally, an interesting illustration for quite another reason as well, because taken literally it would ruin more than fifty per cent of the whole sphere of negotiorum gestio in one stroke! That is because unsolicited services are at the heart of negotiorum gestio. Once again this shows the enormous dangers inherent in the present piecemeal approach of EU legislation in the field of private law.

Consumer protection, by the way, is a very fine example for a point I made in the beginning. Generalists of contract law and specialists in the field of consumer protection should find a proper mode of co-operation here instead of going on working in separate, unco-ordinated groups. Not only will both benefit from each other's expertise: it is the end result that matters, and its quality depends on a joint effort.

III. BEYOND THE RESTATEMENT

How should we proceed? What are we aiming at in concrete terms? I am well aware that discussions will go on for some time and that any forecast is bound to overlook certain aspects of this very complex movement. Everything seems still possible. It may well be that our project goes off like a rocket, and it may be that nothing or very little will happen beyond the Restatement. With this uncertainty in mind I would like to stress two points which in my view are of fundamental importance. First, it is appropriate that the notion of a European Civil Code be taken seriously as one possible end goal, even if it should later emerge that its implementation does not command sufficient majority support. Further work can only be conducted at the requisite level if this potential final goal is not ruled out. Secondly, it could easily turn out to be fatal if one restricts the range of possible solutions right from the beginning to a black and white approach, that is to say by pressing the simple alternative of a 'yes' or 'no' to a European Civil Code, be it a contract code or a wider-ranging code on patrimonial law. We have many more options at our disposal. What should be done is to create an intellectual and a psychological atmosphere in which the next stages recommend themselves as a natural solution, step by step and without undue pressure on those countries which think they need more time to accommodate themselves to a renewed *jus commune europaeum*.

A Restatement is clearly not a legislative text. The former contains observations and proposals, while the latter is binding. A text without any binding authority, without any official stamp, will remain the result of a 'private enterprise' and disappear in the book shelves. Practitioners will not pay any serious regard to it, universities will not teach it. Law is only what is made binding; fine arts are the discipline of other faculties. What is more, a European Restatement is something fundamentally different from the American Restatement. We should, perhaps, not use the word 'Restatement' at all and employ rather the notion of European Principles throughout. That is because hardly any set of principles can be drafted without some deviation from some existing private law systems within the EU, be it in substance, in structure or in style. It is the very purpose of drafting commented and annotated principles to allow for the first time a common view of legal problems that we share. That is our difficulty, but it is also our challenge and our chance.

Against this background we in the Commission on European Contract Law and the Study Group on a European Civil Code have proposed to the EU Commission a gradual programme, which of course can be criticised in detail but whose substance I still believe is correct. So far it seems that we have at least managed to convince the European Parliament of these ideas.

Stage 'zero', so to speak, is the drafting of commented and annotated principles. It may be premature to assume that the PECL and the principles emerging from within the Study Group on a European Civil Code will find the approval of those within the European institutions who have the political legitimacy to express an official view on them, but for the time being let us start from that assumption. The question as to which is a 'better' restatement, in other words *the* Restatement, will only need an answer if there is more than one, and up to now the question does not arise. However, it is exactly because of this background that in the not too distant future we should come back to the idea of establishing a European Law Institute and a European Law Academy. The first practical steps in that direction have been initiated.

The next stage should be measures for the promotion of the Restatement. By that we mean measures to promote university study of the Restatement as an integral part of national legal education. Furthermore, we envisage recommendations to the European courts and to superior national courts to have regard to the Principles where there is doubt as to the existence of a common European rule of law or to the correct application of national law in matters falling within the scope of the principles. Another very important and perhaps decisive step would be achieved if the Community institutions would accept that subsequent Community legislation affecting private law should be formulated in terminology consistent with the Principles, making appropriate use of their concepts and explaining the relationship of the Community legislation to the Principles. What is needed here are express references to the Principles in the recitals that always introduce a new legislative text as a sort of *Motive*.

We further recommend making the Principles 'partially' binding in this first and perhaps still somewhat experimental phase by their use by Community institutions and national public bodies when inviting tenders and concluding contracts with private law subjects.

By these means the Principles will receive a widespread attention. Practitioners, law makers and, above all, the jurists of a new generation will become acquainted with them. The Principles will have time to penetrate the minds of jurists and to attract commentators in order to identify where the texts need improvements. From the outset, however, one general idea behind the Principles and the Code should be that the articles leave sufficient room for flexibility in order to enable courts to adapt them to their local or regional needs. Uniform Principles will not necessarily always lead to results which are one hundred per cent identical everywhere, and I am not concerned about that at all. I would not even endorse the idea, at a later stage, of leaving the final authority of binding interpretation of a given rule to one single European court.

'Phase one' should probably end with a careful evaluation of the results so far achieved. From that point in time onwards one will be in a position to discuss afresh the political case for a European Civil Code and its scope of application, and it is very hard to foresee the options which will then present themselves in a realistic way. One possible 'intermediate scenario' that *today* springs to mind is a legislative measure that would allow parties to voluntarily give effect to the Principles as the law governing their relationships, whether or not cross-border, and whether or not today within a field of law in which the existing choice of law instruments allow for party autonomy. Depending on the then predominant view, one would reverse the order in the following phase: at least as far as cross-border legal relationships are concerned the Principles would apply as a matter of law, unless the parties 'opt out'. Again, it is somewhat premature to come up with more detailed plans or ideas, because it could well be that some countries at least, or even the Community as such, would like to combine these phases or that they even think that the time has come to unite under a shared binding text. We have no means to foresee that. We have no means either to foresee the impact which the Euro will have on our sense of the rights and wrongs of such a programme, and we have no means to foresee whether or not a new generation will really be reluctant to turn into a joint Code what they have learned at university. Even the distinction which we all make today between cross-border and purely domestic cases might well have disappeared for many purposes in a market that describes itself as a single Internal Market.

In lieu of a summary I would like to finish by saying: *Carpe diem.* Let us be optimistic and go ahead. The Study Group on a European Civil Code is not a closed shop. It is prepared to co-operate with everyone, prepared to learn from everyone and open to constructive criticisms. Let us build a new common law for our old continent, and let us do it together.

10. The Case for a European Contract Act

*Jürgen Basedow**

According to the programme of the conference, the following contribution should expose 'the core arguments in favour of a code substituting national laws'. The reference to codification and to the abrogation of national law certainly has an electrifying effect on some participants and helps to put life into academic debates, but when it comes to the drafting of legal policies, moderation, precision and responsibility are more important than the liveliness of discussions. The Commission communication to the Council and the European Parliament on European contract law,[1] therefore requires a more accurate description of the present policy options (infra 1.). In accordance with the structure of the Commission communication I shall then explain to what extent divergent contract law can actually impair the operation of the internal market (infra 2.) and why a European Contract Act would favour the functioning of the Single European Market (infra 3.).

Althouth the resulting proposal for an open-ended European Contract Act appears to be cautious and circumspect against the background of the ongoing discussions, it will certainly meet the criticism of those who deny the legislative competence of the Community for any kind of comprehensive legislation in the field of private law; some concluding remarks must therefore be devoted to this issue (infra 4.).

I. WHAT KIND OF ACT?

In the first place it is necessary to cut back the idea of a European Civil Code. While some authors prefer this long-term perspective and have even set up a European research project dedicated to a European Civil Code, realism requires an acknowledgement that present research and discussions are by no means

---

* Professor Dr. iur., LL.M. (Harvard Univ.). Director of the Max-Planck Institute for Foreign Private and Private International Law, Hamburg and Professor of Law, Hamburg. Slightly revised version of a paper published in the *Journal of Business Law* 2001, 569 *seq.* The author gratefully acknowledges the kind permission of Sweet & Maxwell for a second publication of the text. See moreover, for more details: J. Basedow, (1996) *CMLRev*, 1069 *et seq.* (for section II, introduction). J. Basedow, 21 (1998) *Transportrecht*, 58 *et seq.* (for section II.2.); J. Basedow, (1997) *ZEuP*, 615 *et seq.* (for section II.4.).
[1]   COM(2001) 398 final.

S. Grundmann and J. Stuyck (eds.), An Academic Green Paper on European Contract Law, 147–154
© 2002 *Kluwer Law International. Printed in Great Britain.*

directed towards such a target. A European Civil Code which would follow the model of various continental codes would at least include a comprehensive regulation of the law of persons and succession, of family relations and of property. The major parts of the existing civil codes deal with these matters. Moreover, some more recent civil codes, such as those of Italy and The Netherlands, equally cover additional areas such as company law, labour relations or shipping. All this is far beyond the reach of present aspirations of European scholars.

The work of legal scholars all over Europe is in fact confined to the harmonisation of various aspects of contract law including securities in movables, and to related obligations such as torts and restitution. While there appears to be some reflection on a European regime for a matrimonial property contract which would be regarded as valid in all Member States, other aspects of family law do not seem to be the object of harmonisation efforts. The same holds true for succession and for the law of property. In these areas, too, European regulations to be adopted, on the basis of article 308 EC on a European will or a European mortgage might be useful, but such projects would create additional legal institutions and obviously have nothing in common with a progressive harmonisation or unification of the existing national laws of succession or property. While company law has been the object of harmonisation efforts for more than 30 years, this work is not related to the present movement towards a European Civil Code; at present it is conducted with a view to the operation of capital markets rather than in the light of the progressive harmonisation of private law.

Even within the limits of the law of obligations, modesty is recommended. Comparative research is advanced and has brought about several attempts at unification in the field of contract law, but it lags behind with regard to other obligations. A realistic policy would therefore focus on the law of contracts, including securities in movables, and could be extended, at a later stage, to other obligations.

Even with regard to contract law we should not expect a comprehensive regulation dealing with all possible issues and aspects. For reasons relating to the different progress made in comparative research one could at present envisage the adoption of an act on general contract law covering issues which are not linked to specific types of contract. It should also be possible to put into effect a unified regime for certain types of contract such as the sale of goods, construction, insurance, transport of goods by road, commercial agency, factoring and financial leasing, licensing, etc. But the variety of contract regulation is great among the Member States. There are certain types of contract which are subject to specific legislation in some Member States while they are entirely left to case law in others. Moreover, commercial life gives rise to new types of transactions every year. Some of these novelties are confined to single Member States or regions of the Community; it is only there that legislators see a need for regulation. It follows that a European contract act dealing with specific types of contract should be open not only for contractual innovations but also for national legislation dealing with new types of contract. Thus, a European contract act would by necessity be incomplete. Yet the Community should advance in that direction for reasons of economic and social integration.

II. DIVERGENCIES OF CONTRACT LAW AS IMPAIRMENT OF THE INTERNAL MARKET

It is a widespread belief that the legislative powers conferred upon the Community by virtue of article 95 EC do not allow for a comprehensive legislation of contract law. As explained on other occasions, this view overly narrows the concept of the establishment and functioning of the internal market. Legislation which pursues this objective is not limited to the removal of national restrictions of the basic freedoms; it would suffice that such legislation helps to overcome psychological barriers such as those which are undoubtedly created by different legal frameworks of transnational business. However, even on the basis of a narrow interpretation the Community would be empowered and also obliged to continue its policy of harmonisation with regard to those areas and issues of contract law which are subject to different mandatory regulations at the national level. Some of them will be outlined here.

1. Insurance Contract Law

When the European Commission conceived its Single Market Programme for the insurance industry some 20 years ago, it also proposed a directive on the harmonisation of insurance contract law. This harmonisation turned out to be extremely difficult and was finally held to be less urgent and less significant than economic regulations of the insurance sector dealing with premiums, investment policy and administrative supervision. When agreement had been reached on the latter points the Community institutions decided to give up the idea of a harmonisation of substantive law and adopted a conflict of laws solution in the second and third directives. This solution basically provides that the parties to an insurance contract covering a 'big risk' are free to choose the applicable law. With regard to 'small risks', in particular consumer insurance, the choice of law is excluded; the contract is governed by the law of the policyholder.

As a consequence, insurance companies are unable to offer coverage in all Member States on the basis of one and the same policy as far as small risks are concerned. At an academic conference, a member of the staff of an important Swiss insurer reported that a car manufacturer had asked for the drafting of a European motor insurance policy which was to be sold together with the car in all Member States. After extensive research the project was abandoned because the national insurance contract laws which are mandatory in most Member

States very often contradict each other and do not allow for an all-European policy.

2. Contracts for the Carriage of Goods

International transport in Europe is essentially carried out on the basis of international conventions which have been ratified by all or most Member States. Thus, international road transport is subject to the 1956 Convention on the contract for the international carriage of goods by road (CMR). While all Member States are contracting parties to that convention, it is by no means applied in a uniform way in all Member States. In particular, it is considered to be absolutely mandatory in all Member States except Italy where the *Corte di Cassazione* has repeatedly held that the convention will be applied only if incorporated into the consignment note by an appropriate reference clause.

The disparities are even greater with regard to the so-called cabotage transport carried out within a Member State by a carrier established in another Member State. In accordance with the relevant Community regulations, some Member States such as Germany explicitly exclude the free choice of law and prescribe the application of German law with regard to cabotage transport in Germany. Other Member States also insist upon the application of their respective national provisions. As a consequence, the European road haulage industry has to cope with very different liability regimes with regard to transport operations within the internal market which comes down to unnecessarily high premiums for liability insurance.

3. Securities in Goods

Under the general rules of private international law, ownership and other rights *in rem* are governed by the lex situs. It follows that retention of title clauses contained in contracts for the international sale of goods have to be assessed in the light of different national laws governing the issue in the course of an export transaction. It is a common occurrence that a retention of title clause stipulated by a German exporter loses its effect once the goods are imported into countries like Italy or Spain, whose laws require a costly registration of such clauses in order to be valid. Under a 'market solution' conceived by the exporting industry, a bank guarantee is used as a substitute, but it is obvious that this solution generates additional costs which are absent in intra-state commerce. While article 4 of Directive 2000/35 provides for the validity of retention of title clauses, it does not appear to cope with the extinction of rights *in rem* caused by the cross-border transfer of the goods; nor does it deal with further disparities existing with regard to the extension of title retention to the proceeds derived from the sale of the goods, etc.

4. Factoring

The laws of the Member States differ considerably with regard to the assignment of receivables, which is an important instrument for the financing of export transactions. In particular, some Member States restrict the assignment of future receivables or the bulk assignment of receivables while others take a very liberal stand in these matters. As a consequence, the factoring industry meets serious obstacles in Member States of the former type, whereas factoring is favoured by laws of the latter type. Similar differences exist with regard to the validity of clauses contained in sales or services contracts which prohibit the assignment of any claims arising from those contracts. The divergences between the national laws have attracted little attention so far under the aspect of the internal market, since factoring contracts are usually concluded between a seller and a factoring company established in the same country; therefore the factoring contract usually does not contain a transfrontier element. From an internal market perspective factoring companies should, however, be able to offer their services outside the Member State of their establishment throughout the whole Community. At present, this would require a very careful analysis of 15 different national laws relating to the assignment of receivables. As in the insurance sector they would not be able to use one and the same type of contract throughout the Community. A 1988 Unidroit Convention on international factoring could provide a solution, but has only been ratified by three Member States so far.

5. Standard Forms

The law relating to unfair contract terms contained in standard forms has been harmonised with regard to consumer transactions. Outside the scope of Directive 93/13 national laws differ considerably. Some Member States such as Germany or the Scandinavian countries subject all kinds of contract clauses to a broad judicial control irrespective of their use in consumer or commercial contracts. Others provide for a limited control by way of interpretation or only allow the striking down of specific contract clauses contained in commercial contracts. In the light of Directive 93/13 the French *Cour de Cassation* has restricted its control even further. The disparities are enhanced if we look at the practical application of the respective laws. While the judicial control of standard conditions of contract appears to be an exception in most Member States, the German courts have been eager to purge standard forms in all sectors of the economy of clauses which they hold to be unfair; there is a decision of the *Bundesgerichtshof* in these matters almost every week. The list of clauses which have been invalidated in commercial transactions is long: certain penalty clauses, the exclusion of set-off, clauses which shorten limitation periods, the reference of disputes to arbitration panels which are not properly manned, the extent of personal and real securities and the like. Thus, German courts have developed a very dense control of standard conditions contained in insurance contracts. As soon as Germans make use of the Internet to buy coverage in England, more often than not the German Courts will grant the same protection to German policyholders in such international contracts. While, in Britain, insurance contracts are regarded as being essentially outside the scope of judicial control of Directive 93/13, English insurers will have difficulties with the practice of German courts.

6. Direct Marketing in Consumer Transactions

Directive 85/577 relating to the protection of consumers in respect of contracts negotiated away from business premises has introduced the consumer's right to withdraw from certain contracts within a period of not less than seven days after receipt of a notice which contains the information on the right of withdrawal. The directive has been implemented in very different ways. An inquiry into the details of that implementation has shown that neither the sellers and suppliers nor the consumers can trust in any meaningful core regulation which is contained in their home law and which they may equally expect abroad. The national laws relating to the content of the said notice, to the calculation of the time limits, to the extinction of the right of withdrawal where the relevant information is not given, to the consequences of withdrawal, etc., show a wide variety of solutions.[2] If there was a need for harmonisation in 1985, that need is still unsatisfied.

The examples given above display very different characteristics. Some of them may be cured by an insulated measure of the Community while others rather call for the adoption of general rules on contract law. Thus, it is difficult to assume that the deficits of the Doorstep Selling Directive can be remedied by a Community Act which deals only with the calculation of time limits or the restitution of goods in consumer contracts made outside business premises. Rather, the need for Community rules of a general scope appears obvious.

III. THE CASE FOR A EUROPEAN ACT ON GENERAL CONTRACT LAW

As explained above general contract law has to supplement specific acts lest the achieved uniformity in specific areas falls apart. Nevertheless, the link between general contract law and the functioning of the internal market may appear too weak in order to allow for Community legislation based upon article 95 EC in this field. As pointed out before, that view appears to be based on an overly narrow interpretation of article 95. That Treaty provision would allow for the adoption of a European Act on general contract law. Nevertheless, there are additional reasons for Community action in this field, reasons of a cultural and

---

[2] J. Basedow, [1997] *ZEuP*, 1075–1121.

political nature which may be outside the scope of article 95 EC. These reasons relate to legal education and to the professional consciousness of lawyers.

1. A European Contract Act and Legal Education

A European Contract Act would be of fundamental use in creating a common conception of civil law on the part of jurists, and above all on the part of students of law. If the study of law in the Member States at the present time is looked at, the observation would have to be made that these students are marked by a nationalism which is unknown in other sectors of higher education. While young Europeans at secondary school level must learn at least one foreign language and often two, these studies seem to prove themselves completely unnecessary for students of law once they have completed their second-level studies. The subjects which they must study in the first and second year of law are almost everywhere essentially national: constitutional law and administrative law, criminal law and several private law subjects, above all the law of contracts. The non-national disciplines (be they comparative law or Community law, public international law or the conflict of laws) normally form the subject of third- or fourth-year studies – by which time the student has already learned the false lesson that the essence of law is national and when he or she has already forgotten some of the former knowledge of foreign languages.

Moreover, after two years the student has begun to recognise structure in what had appeared to him or her at the beginning to be a chaos made up of legal provisions. He or she becomes conscious of the system which characterises the relevant national code and which facilitates the mystery of the civil law. The structures of this code are like a lifeboat in an apparently limitless ocean. The English student, although he or she does not study a codified law, goes through the same psychological development. For him or her, the structures furnished by the principles and by the leading cases are equivalent to this lifeboat – which is like an attractive-looking cruise ship for somebody who had initially been close to drowning. It is at this stage of legal studies that the student is confronted with Community law, fragmentary, pointillist and structured by a system which is totally diverse from the national legal system. For the student, the 'beauty' of the national system is disturbed by this poorly systematised body of law full of clumsy provisions. In brief, the present legal education tends to promote an attitude on the part of lawyers which is rather hostile to Community law.

In view of the essential role which lawyers and law play in the process of European integration, this anti-European effect of the teaching of law seems utterly unacceptable. It would facilitate the taking root of the Community's cultural basis in the consciousness of lawyers if legal studies began with a European subject. It would be more reasonable if young lawyers learned first what is common to all of Europe so that they could then continue with the study of their national laws. It follows that at least one of the subjects taught in the first year should be European. Contract law seems to lend itself more readily to this objective than do criminal law or constitutional law, which are subjects more directly linked to the existence of the Member States and to the habits and the particular values of individual nations.

2. A European Contract Act and the Professional Consciousness of Lawyers

Another important objective of the codification of contract law at Community level would be the creation of a common point of reference for the practising lawyers and legal scholars of the various countries. Indeed, a European Contract Act would offer a point of crystallisation for the professional community of European lawyers and for its common consciousness – which has tended to develop poorly on a diet of agricultural policy regulations, and of directives governing the substances which may be used in the manufacture of toys, or the additives which are permitted in drinks. Given that the European Community is in the first place a community of law, consciousness on the part of lawyers from various countries that they are forming part of the same professional group is of essential importance for the purposes of subsequent integration. The identification with European law which is so important for students is so also for practitioners.

The cultural effect which is to be expected from the adoption of a European act of general contract law is similar to that which is brought about by the use of the same notes, bars and keys in music or by the same grammatical structure in languages. While the music composed by a Finnish composer, influenced by his national environment, may differ from that of a Spanish musician, they both use the same categories to think and note down their ideas, which in turn allows them to hear and understand each other's music even if they are deaf. The same holds true for the study of a foreign language. The first step to comprehension is the understanding of its grammar and syntax, and it is well known that it is particularly difficult to learn languages which have different structures. What we need in contract law above all is a common grammar as a kind of common background to the various national laws and to the specific Community acts.

IV. THE LEGISLATIVE COMPETENCE OF THE COMMUNITY

The legislative competence of the European Community to adopt a comprehensive act dealing with the general part of European contract law is in dispute.[3] I have argued in a different context that the EEC should be regarded as enabled, under article 95 EC to enact 'a common contract law for the common market'.[4]

---

[3]   See *Tilmann and van Gerven* in European Parliament, doc. PE 168.511 of June 1999, p. 183 *seq.*

[4]   J. Basedow, (1996) *CMLRev.*, 1069 *et seq.*

I do not intend to reiterate on those discussions here. But the opponents of Community legislation in this field believe to have found additional support for their views in a recent decision of the European Court of Justice which merits some commentary at this stage.

In its judgment of 5 October 2000 in case C-376/98 (*Federal Republic of Germany v. European Parliament and Council of the European Union*)[5] the Court of Justice has in fact favoured what may be called a narrow interpretation of article 100a (now: article 95) EC. In the words of the Court, 'to construe that article as meaning that it vests in the Community legislature a general power to regulate the internal market would not only be contrary to the express wording of the provisions cited above but would also be incompatible with the principle embodied in article 3b of the EC Treaty (now article 5 EC) that the powers of the Community are limited to those specifically conferred on it (recital 83) ... If a mere finding of disparities between national rules and of the abstract risk of obstacles to the exercise of fundamental freedoms or of distortions of competition liable to result therefrom were sufficient to justify the choice of article 100a as a legal basis, judicial review of compliance with the proper legal basis might be rendered nugatory. The Court would then be prevented from discharging the function entrusted to it by article 164 of the EC Treaty (now: article 220 EC) of ensuring that the law is observed in the interpretation and application of the Treaty (recital 84).' The former Advocate General Professor van Gerven has in fact concluded from these words that the European Community lacks the legislative competence for the adoption of a European Civil Code, even if that is limited to business matters such as the law of obligations and of property.[6]

With all respect for the learned author I regret to say that I cannot agree with these conclusions. It is true that legal opinion is divided as to whether article 95 EC requires a specific legislative need to remove certain restrictions to the operation of the internal market or whether that provision also allows the adoption of Community legislation on the basis of an abstract reasoning that the proposed act is liable to improve the operation of the internal market. But the judgment cited above does not take a stand in that dispute. For court decisions have to be read 'on the facts', i.e. in the light of the case decided. It should be borne in mind, that the Court of Justice, in that case, had to deal with the legal basis of a directive prohibiting the advertising of tobacco products. At closer sight the directive under scrutiny was an impairment of the internal market itself. For the prohibition of advertising effectively prevents the integration of national markets, in particular in those Member States which used to have national tobacco monopolies until recently. In such countries the respective state-owned companies have of course maintained their market power even after

---

5   [2000] ECR, I-8419.
6   (2001) *Tijdschrift voor Privaatrecht*, 261, 271.

the deregulation of the state monopolies, and the prohibition of tobacco advertising protects them against new market entrants. It is against this factual background that the above-cited considerations of the Court of Justice have to be read. They refer to Community measures which do not only tend to petrify the market structure of the European tobacco markets but which would also deprive the European advertising industry of its most significant source of income. In my view, it cannot be inferred from the tobacco judgment that the Court of Justice rejects the abstract approach to internal market legislation without qualifications; this view is underpinned by the very recital 83 which points out 'that the measures referred to in article 100a(1) of the Treaty are intended to improve the conditions for the establishment and functioning of the internal market.' While the tobacco advertising directive did not meet that requirement, a European contract act would do so.

The preceding assessment is confirmed by the recent opinion of the Court of Justice of 9 October 2001 in the case concerning the anullment of the directive on the legal protection of biotechnological inventions (case C-377/98, *Netherlands v. European Parliament and Council of the European Union*).[7] In that case the plaintiff alleged that the mere differences in the laws and practices of the Member States relating to the protection of biotechnological inventions and the likelihood of their becoming greater did either not exist or only concerned secondary issues which do not justify harmonisation. With regard to that assertion the court pointed out that recourse to article 100a (now: article 95) EC as a legal basis is possible 'if the aim is to prevent the emergence of future obstacles to trade resulting from multifarious development of national laws provided that the emergence of such obstacles is likely, and the measure in question is designed to prevent them.' (recital 15). In order to justify the need for the directive, the defendant Parliament and Council had referred to various provisions of the national laws of the Member States which were taken from the Convention on the Grant of European Patents of 1973 which were said to be open to differing interpretations as regards the patentability of biotechnological inventions. To put it more clearly, the argument related to national provisions which had already been the object of international harmonisation and even unification. Nevertheless, the court points out that the possibility of differing interpretations suffices to establish a risk of 'divergences of practise and case law prejudicial to the proper operation of the internal market.' It therefore concludes that the directive 'was correctly adopted on the basis of article 100a of the Treaty.' (recital 29).

At the present stage it appears to follow from the case law of the European Court of Justice that the European Community is effectively empowered to adopt measures which favour the operation of the internal market even if they are only designed to foreclose different interpretations of existing uniform laws.

---

[7]   [2001] ECR, I-7079.

Thus, the Court of justice seems to be inclined towards what was called the abstract interpretation of article 95 EC before. This would include the legislative competence to enact a European contract act. The least that can be said is that nobody should feel discouraged to cooperate in the harmonisation of European contract law for the mere pretension that the Community is not enabled to legislate in that field. Quite to the contrary, the odds are rather in favour of such competence.

11. The Contract Law Codification Process in Europe: Policies, Targets and Time Dimensions

Mauro Bussani*

I. INTRODUCTION

This contribution addresses the issues implied by the following questions: (a) What is the contract law to be codified? (b) What is the possible impact of a European Contract Law Codification upon the other private law fields? (c) Which are the driving forces behind and ahead of the European codification process?

The paper approaches these issues by focusing *sub (II)* on the fragmentation in different layers of European Contract Law within and across national frontiers, and on the bearing that this 'stratification' can have on the choice of adopting a code with either a 'regional' or a world-wide scope. In the perspective pursued by the Conference, *sub (III)* I will emphasize a true borderline subject such as the recoverability of pure economic loss in European law. This is particularly meant to stress the kind of awareness required by the debate when dealing with a piecemeal codification effort. *Sub (IV)* the paper tackles some issues implied by – and not always made explicit within – the discussions about the European codification: the alleged parallelism between economic and legal integration, the role of scholarship within the European legal stage, the 'pride and prejudice' aspects of the legal uniformity v. legal diversity debate.

II. THE CONTRACT LAW TO BE CODIFIED

1. A Broken Glass

a) Coherence in Contract Law?

In approaching this subject I do not aim to tackle the technical aspects of each field of contract law.[1] I will rather point up a general feature of the domain,

---

*   Professor of Law, University of Trieste, Italy.
[1]   I will not focus either on other crucial problems for the would-be Code, i.e. the linguistic choice and appropriate semantic level to be attained by its wording. On the latter problems see e.g. A. di Robilant & U. Mattei, in 'The Art and Science of Critical Scholarship', (2001) 75 *Tulane Law R.*, 1053; K. Kerameus, 'Problems of drafting a European Civil Code', (1997) 5 *ERPL*, 475, 482. As far as the feasibility of a code is concerned, there is no doubt that a great deal depends on the quality and the semantic level chosen by its drafters, on its capacity to codify common understandings, and on its ability to reflect the diversity of

which runs across technicalities and, nonetheless, seems to be of critical importance in view of whatever 'harmonizing', not to mention 'codifying', purpose.

One can easily realize that in the contract law field not everything is as clear or plainly readable as the common legal discourse would expect it to be. Looking at this area of the law from a domestic standpoint, national contract law everywhere appears far from being compact, namely far from showing an inner and coherent logic that corresponds to the features of what the municipal lawyers regard as a 'system'. Observing the same area from the comparative law point of view one finds that there exists not only a differentiation across legal concepts and languages – it is well known, for instance, that contract, *Vertrag* and *contrat* are not synonyms[2] – but also a stratification affecting legal rules.[3] I will dwell on the latter phenomenon.

b) Contract Law Layers

European contract law systems are deeply and increasingly characterized by an evident fragmentation.

(aa) First, we have consumer contracts – a consumer being 'a natural person who is acting for purposes which are outside his trade, business or profession': to comply with the definition of article 2(b) of the Directive on Unfair Terms in Consumer Contracts of 5 April 1993. These are contracts whose one remarkable feature is the attenuation of the widespread dogma of consensualism, namely the idea according to which the whole of the effects of a contract descend from the meeting of wills fixed at the moment of its formation. Indeed, suffice to recall that the consumer, regardless of any different

---

the legal cultures that operate in Europe today. See A. Gambaro, 'Codice Civile', in: *Digesto IV, Civile, II* [1988], 442. Moreover, a European Civil Code would not meet, in and of itself, the need for a European interpretative community: the former and the latter, a common code and a common culture, call for each other. See *infra*; nn. 5, 7 and 9.

2   R. Sacco, 'Formation of Contracts', in: A. Hartkamp, M. Hesselink, E. Hondius, C. Joustra, E. du Perron (eds.), *Towards a European Civil Code* (Ars Aequi Libri, Nijmegen, 1998), 191 *et seq.*

3   Cf. H. Kötz and A. Flessner, *European Contract Law. Vol. I: Formation, Validity, and Content of Contracts; Contract and Third Parties* (trans. T. Weir), (Oxford, Clarendon Press, 1997), 11 *et seq.* (see also 124 *et seq.*). For a broader, though still in progress, presentation of the stratification issue across the whole of private law relationships, see M. Bussani, '"Integrative" Comparative Law Enterprises and the Inner Stratification of Legal Systems', in: S. Feiden and C.U. Schmid (eds.), *Evolutionary Perspectives and Projects on Harmonisation of Private Law in the EU*, in: EUI Working Papers, Law No. 99/7 (Badia Fiesolana-San Domenico, Firenze. 1999), 57 *et seq.*; published also, in a lightly different version, in (2000) 8 *ERPL* 83 *et seq.*

clause s/he has subscribed to, can usually withdraw his/her offer, can rescind the contract, or can terminate it.[4]

(bb) Secondly, we find the special and very important niche of employment contracts, which are still quite strictly controlled by national collective agreements and specific legislative rules across the continent.[5]

(cc) Then, we have the so-called business contracts, where the parties are both entrepreneurs. These contracts, even though they are not always impervious to review in terms of inequality of bargaining power, are out of reach of EU consumer law and only in some fields (e.g., technology transfers, franchising, late payments in commercial transactions, payment and security settlement systems) are they subject to pieces of EU legislation. Moreover, business contracts – particularly when international and involving large corporations[6] – usually either self-regulate the choice of both forum and applicable law, or (most of the time) get possible disputes out of ordinary jurisdictions by resorting to arbitral awards made by private arbitrators.

(dd) Finally, we have the large body of what we could call, by default, 'civil' or, as some may prefer, 'ordinary' contracts. This is the layer, together with that of the consumer's, to which the current European codification debate usually refers.

2. The Business Practice

On this stratification some further remarks must be added. The first concerns the 'business layer', the second will deal with the 'ordinary' contracts.

A distinctive feature of most business contracts, especially when international, is that they consist to a significant extent of the actual contracting practices of lawyers and their clients, including what they say to one another at the negotiation stage.[7] All this flows into the written contract and for this reason contract

---

[4] See W. van Gerven, 'A Common Law For Europe: The Future Meeting The Past?', (2001) 9 *ERPL*, 485 *et seq.*; R. Sacco, 'Formation of Contracts', in: A. Hartkamp *et al.* (eds.), *Towards a European Civil Code*, at 191 *et seq.*; C. Joustra, 'Consumer Law', *ibidem*, at 133 *et seq.*

[5] For a general survey, R. Blanpain, *European Labour Law*, 7th edn. (The Hague, London, Boston, 2000); B. Bercusson, 'Freedom of Association and Fundamental Trade Union Rights', in: ETUI (ed.), *A Legal Framework for European Industrial Relations* (Brussels, June 1999), 7 *et seq.*; S. Sciarra, 'From Strasbourg to Amsterdam. Prospects for the Convergence of European Social Rights Policy', in: P. Alston (ed.), *EU and the Human Rights* (Oxford UP, Oxford, 1999), 488 *et seq.*

[6] Especially when these are international contracts they entrust their legal regime to the kind of customary law commonly known as lex mercatoria. On the critical choice of whether or not to include these contracts within the Code, see K.D. Kerameus, 'Problems of drafting a European Civil Code', (1997) 5 *ERPL*, 475 and *infra* n. 5.

[7] On this and what follows see M. Shapiro, 'The Common Core – Some Outside Comments', in: M. Bussani and U. Mattei (eds.), *Making European Law. Essays on the*

practice has since long been and still is moving from short to long contracts. But the foregoing also implies that specific national law may come to matter increasingly less as contracting parties and their counsel write increasingly more of their own law.

This occurrence is worth stressing especially when one notes that most of the written private parties' contract law is specifically designed to amend or evade specific national legal provisions, or to substitute specific agreements between the parties for generally applicable rules or principles.[8] To be sure, some of the most extreme of these evasions or substitutions would not be enforced by courts if litigated.[9] Indeed, many contract terms that would not be enforced by courts at the time when they were written are not submitted to courts, and when one party challenges them, the other usually settles.[10] This is why some contract terms may be written in contracts for years without being subject to judicial veto. The longer they survive, and the more prevalent in practice, the more likely they are to eventually be approved by courts as long-standing business practices when they are finally challenged. Hence, certain contract terms that 'good lawyers' are convinced are not judicially enforceable are precisely those that will constitute future contract law.[11] In any event, contract practice may be changing the substance of contract law far more rapidly than national legislation, international legislation or academic law-making.[12]

Another highly relevant feature in contract practice is now reaching huge proportions across the business law community.[13] This involves American-style long contracts, English as the language of contracts, large American and English law firms as the writers of contracts, the choice of US or English law as the substantive law of the contract, and the choice of the United States or England as the jurisdiction for litigation concerning the contract. It may well be that common lawyers are obtaining more of the business because they are more adept at giving clients what they want and less prone than civil lawyers to tell

---

'*Common Core' Project* (Quaderni del Dipartimento di Scienze Giuridiche, Trento, 2000), 123 *et seq.*

[8] Shapiro (n. 7), 128–129.

[9] Shapiro (n. 7), 129.

[10] See e.g. the field research done by H. Beale and T. Dugdale, 'Contracts between Businessmen: Planning and the Use of Contractual Remedies', (1975) 2(1) *British J. Law and Society*, 45, 51 *et seq.*, 59 *et seq.*

[11] Shapiro (n. 7), 129.

[12] Shapiro (n. 7), 129.

[13] In view of the possible inclusion of the latter community within the paradigm of the 'artificial societies', see B. Schäfer and Z. Bankowski, 'Mistaken Identities: The Integrative Forces of Private Law', in: M. van Hoecke and F. Ost (eds.), *The Harmonization of European Private Law* (Hart: Oxford, Portland, Oreg., 2000) 21, 30 *et seq.*

the clients that what they want the law forbids.[14] But still the point is that business contract law in practice is becoming more and more the law set out in long contracts written by American and English lawyers in the English language and arbitrated or litigated under American or English law. Thus the real risk is that – without both the technical awareness and the strategic vision that I seek to outline later – any European codification effort in this field may end up as a mere rhetorical exercise.

3. The 'Ordinary' Layer

Taking seriously what has been said so far, and in spite of the Lando Commission's wishes, 'ordinary' contracts are bound to represent the main area that can actually be targeted by (or seen within the scope of) the 'Principles of European Contract Law'. Even within this limited perspective, however, what has to be stressed is that European law-makers, legal professionals and ultimate law-users could expect a much more neat and clear approach than the one so far embraced by the pioneering Commission. Let me set forth two simple, but in my view decisive, remarks.

First and foremost the draft fails to meet a basic requirement that seems an indispensable condition for fostering the adoption, and then the implementation or simply the use, of a European Contract Code. Indeed, what is missing is a precise notion of the 'contract' that the Project intends to codify.

It is true that in almost every system we find a category which includes all the agreements acting as sources of obligations between the parties and implying a reward to the promisor: the category that is named *contrat*, contract, *Vertrag*, *contratto* and so forth. It is also true, however, that these various labels are not mutually overlapping.[15] The working language of the Lando Commission being English, one can wonder whether or not the 'contract' codified therein includes gratuitous agreements such as gifts or gratuitous deposits. As is well known, in France and Italy a gift is a contract and a gratuitous deposit is a contract; in England neither of them is included in the notion of contract.

Besides, one may wonder whether the discipline of contract under review would apply only to agreements intended to be a source of obligations or whether it would *per se* be sufficient to create a real security (such as a pledge or a mortgage), whether it would *per se* be sufficient to the transfer of movable property, or whether it would *per se* be sufficient to the transfer of property in land. If the answer to the last three questions is negative, one could ask about the further element to be coupled with the consent of the parties (or of the party concerned). Should we need, according to circumstances, an *Auflassung*, an

---

14 Shapiro (n. 7), 130; H. Kötz, 'The Trento Project and Its Contribution to the Europeanization of Private Law', in: M. Bussani and U. Mattei (eds.), (n. 7), 118.

15 See Sacco, 'Formation of Contracts' (n. 2), 191 *et seq.*

inscription, a *trascrizione*, a registration – i.e. a series of further formal requirements? Should we need, according to circumstances, the *Übergabe*, the *consegna*, the *livraison*, that is to say the delivery of the object of the transfer?[16]

The second remark is less technical but perhaps even more important, because it entails the role of contract law codification within the overall European legal harmonization process. I refer to the awareness which is needed of the possible outcomes stemming from the reference to such notions as, for example, 'good faith' in a transnational context (see, e.g., arts. 1:106(1) and 1:201 of the Lando Principles).

For sure, such a rule can be of much help – for instance, in overcoming the obstacles which are interposed in many systems by local lawyers, judges and scholars to the repression of unfair behaviour which ends up by affecting the contractual relationship.[17] On the other hand, there is always a risk, which must be neutrally assessed, because exposure to it implies the answer to the question about the costs one intends to reduce through the codification. The risk is that through notions such as 'good faith', national courts recycle the (after the codification) repealed national rules – or interpretations of the new rules built upon the old mentality.[18]

At the very least, this makes it straighforwardly clear how strictly connected to and necessary by a supranational code is the establishment of a supranational Supreme Court charged with the task of assuring the attainment of an acceptable threshold of uniformity in the interpretation of the legal rules.

---

[16] See Sacco (n. 2) 191 *et seq*. On all this, one must add, little if any assistance comes from other texts that have been conceived in a transnational perspective. No assistance comes from the Vienna Sales Convention, which does not deal with gratuitous agreements and even states its disregard (art. 4, b) about the issue of the 'effect which the contract may have on the property in the goods sold'. Not even the Unidroit Principles are of much help in this respect, because they cover only commercial contracts (though in the light of these Principles it is not completely clear what a commercial contract is precisely, apart from the exclusion of consumer contracts), they do not deal with gratuitous agreements nor do they deal with transfer of property.

[17] Cf. R. Zimmermann and S. Whittaker, *Good Faith in European Contract Law*, in: *Cambridge Studies in International and Comparative Law. The Common Core of European Private Law* (Cambridge, UK, 2000), 655 *et seq*., 660 *et seq*.

[18] See Sacco, 'Formation of Contracts' (n. 2), 198 *et seq*.; H. Kötz and Flessner (n. 3), 117. Consider a German plaintiff who brings an action in France against a French entrepreneur, his contractual counterpart, claiming that the latter breached the duty of good faith (in terms of *Schutzpflicht*) – say because, while the defendant was performing his contractual obligation of delivering a good he damaged a different interest of the plaintiff. There is no doubt that such a lawsuit could end up being a waste of time and money – under no matter what provision imposing good faith – whenever the French judge argues that the duty upon the defendant has to be seen just as 'une obligation de sécurité de moyens'. On the scope of the latter category see G. Viney, *Introduction à la responsabilité* (Paris, L.G.D.J., 1995), 284 *et seq*.

4. Layers and Lessons

Whatever target is pursued as regards European legal integration, if such integration is to be effective and not merely wishful thinking, the above remarks seem worthy of consideration.

In particular, the need to take account of contract law stratification appears enhanced if we are to be fully cognizant of the legal relationships that we want to bring about and which are likely to be created by a code or by any other authoritative regulation. More specifically, such analysis seems necessary in order to understand (i) what kind and what level of integration to pursue, (ii) for what areas of contract law,[19] (iii) what is the correct balance to strike between the widely shared goal of reducing transaction costs on the one hand,[20] and on the other, envisioning options grounded on the maintenance of the status quo, the enactment of a few directives, the adoption of a Code, the drafting of a sort of Restatement, and so forth.[21]

5. The Geo-Political Role of a Contract Law Code

All the foregoing seems to me to lead straight to another problem that any European code drafter should tackle. The question is the geo-political purport of the would-be European Code, i.e., the role we want to make this code play in the world-wide legal arena.

Because this problem lies beyond the scope of this paper, I will restrict myself to two simple questions. Is this contract code meant to be the by-product of a Euro-European debate, focusing on the needs of European law-users and tying the chances of its possible circulation outside the continent to its inner technical features, or to the EU's political prestige? Should this European code, on the contrary, be thought of since its very conception as a possible leading pattern in the ongoing worldwide competition among legal models?

This is a kind of problem that classical nineteenth- and twentieth-century national codes could, and actually did, overlook. Yet it seems to me that the ongoing current situation of political and economic affairs around the globe is

---

[19] See S. Grundmann, 'The Structure of European Contract Law', (2001) 9 *ERPL*, 505 *et seq.*

[20] On this subject see U. Mattei, 'The Issue of European Civil Codification and Legal Scholarship. Biases, Strategies and Developments', (1998) 21 *Hastings Int'l & Comp. L. Rev.*, 883, and *ibidem* further references.

[21] The costs connected with the status quo are easy to specify: they take mainly the form of information costs. In a context where several legal systems may be involved in any particular legal transaction, diversity creates unpredictability and requires a specialized bar. As a consequence, a significant proportion of business resources must be devoted to paying specialized practitioners to give transactional and litigation assistance, rather than being invested in wealth maximizing activities. On these points see U. Mattei (n. 20). See also *supra*, n. 7.

urging the 'European codification' debate to pay more attention to the issue than the latter has received so far.

To outline what the object of this 'attention' should be, let me highlight the following. At stake here is a clear option to be taken. The kind of choice scholars and legislators should make is whether to adopt a single-level or a double-level Contract code.

a) The Double-level Code

Such a code could consist, on the one hand, of a set of provisions dealing with consumer contracts and ordinary contracts (including or excluding from its scope employment contracts, according to the social and economic policies we wish to enforce through the code). Its redactors could take as a starting point EU consumer law and the drafts prepared by the Lando and Gandolfi Commissions and elaborate on those rules: the text should be conceived and written with a view to coordinating what is worthwhile of EU law in force and to gather those notions, techniques and remedies which are as common as possible to the European legal cultures. This is a task that, as far as I know, is not so distant in nature and scope from what is currently being pursued by Professor von Bar's Study Group and its decentralized contract law units.

The second codification aim could be the production of a sort of Business Contracts Code. This should both restate, whenever useful, EU business law and 'Europeanize', whenever and if necessary, the rules actually adopted in international commercial transactions. To be sure, some could see this twofold code as a transnational updating of the domestic dichotomy between commercial and civil codes. The point is, however, that the dissociation outlined here could usefully lend itself to meeting the needs of the transnational perspective that must be adopted by any European code drafter. Furthermore, the planning of the second layer could easily start with hardening the 'soft-law' approach of the UNIDROIT Principles of International Commercial Contracts and adapting what is worth keeping from United States UCC and other international instruments such as the Vienna Convention on International Sale of Goods. This second layer could mainly draw its strength from its clarity and its orderly embodiment of what is dispersed across EU law as well as across long contracts practice and commercial customs around the world. Yet all that would possibly allow this 'part' of the code (and European contract law professionals) to enter the competition for 'applicable law' leadership in the transnational business arena. Lastly, and politically speaking, in view of the preparation of both texts, the drafters should force themselves to decide whether to bear the burden of a time-consuming mediation between continental and English and Irish legal cultures (I stress 'cultures' and not 'rules')[22] or simply to leave the European

---

[22] See also *infra* n. 27 and corresponding text.

common law countries with the option of following the continental, its own or the former colony's model.

b) The Single-level Code

This, in its turn, would be an all-inclusive classical contract code, akin to the one being drafted by the Lando Commission, merging rules which are conceived as fitting both civil and commercial contracts. This kind of code, in and of itself, may possibly not withstand competition in the business arena as I hinted before, but its drafters could make another choice. The latter should have both a technical and a political meaning. This code should be aware of its non-business vocation and, with all due respect to the legal traditions, represent a sort of counter-power option, the European way to a fair balance of weight between counterparts, to the repression of any form of discrimination,[23] to the protection of human rights values[24] and to a cost-saving technical clarity.[25] All these features could make this

---

[23] Among the most recent works, cf. B.S. Markesinis, 'Our Debt to Europe: Past, Present and Future', in: B.S. Markesinis (ed.), *The Coming Together of the Common Law and the Civil Law* (Hart, Oxford, Portland, Oreg., 2000), 37, 51 *et seq.*; G.C. Rodriguez Iglesias, 'Judicial Protection of the Citizen under European Law', in *ibidem*, 195, 204 *et seq.*; L. Wildhaber, 'Some Reflections on the First Year of Operation of the 'New' European Court of Human Rights', in *ibidem*, 215 *et seq.*; C. Mirabelli, 'Preliminary Reflections on Fundamental Rights as the Basis of a Common European Law', in *ibidem*, 225 *et seq.*; J.G. Añon, 'Current Problems of Legal Dogmatics in European Regulation: The Principle of Equality and the Policies of Affirmative Action', in: M. van Hoecke and F. Ost (eds.), *The Harmonization of European Private Law* (n. 13), 189 *et seq.*; M. Elósegui, 'The Kalanke Case and the Marschall Case in the Court of Justice of the European Communities. The Women's Quota and Alexy's Principles Theory', in *ibidem*, 207 *et seq.*

[24] Cf. H.P. Glenn, *Legal Traditions of the World: Sustainable Diversity in Law* (Oxford, OUP, 2001), 116 *et seq.* See values and rules embodied in the Council Directive 2000/43/EC of 29 June 2000 implementing the principle of equal treatment between persons irrespective of racial or ethnic origin, in EC OJ 2000 L 180/22; esp. art. 3, 1st paragraph, litt. h (as to the application of the Directive to 'access to and supply of goods and services which are available to the public, including housing') and art. 14 ('Member States shall take the necessary measures to ensure that: (a) any laws, regulations and administrative provisions contrary to the principle of equal treatment are abolished; (b) any provisions contrary to the principle of equal treatment which are included in individual or collective contracts or agreements, internal rules of undertakings, rules governing profit-making or non-profit-making associations, and rules governing the independent professions and workers' and employers' organisations, are or may be declared, null and void or are amended.').

[25] This is an option to be also left open to the 'ordinary and consumer contracts' leg of the double-level code. However, as soon as one takes into consideration a) actual European need of entering the competition for the legal pattern leadership, b) time, cultural and technical mediation costs as driving factors of any codification effort, one easily realizes that the competitive 'value added' of such a double-level code has to be found much more and much more consistently in its business contracts part than in its Euro-European not

code what Europeans should expect their code to be, that is, a code which encompasses the most advanced values and rules of Western legal civilization.

The code-drafting task should not, however, be carried out overlooking the possible geo-political role of such a code. Again leaving aside the common law countries with the option of following either western models, the codification process should take into account, and possibly include in the process itself, scholars and practitioners coming not only from eastern Europe, but also from Latin America, Africa and all the other areas of the world where the continental 'patrimonial' law has had and still has a deep sway over the legal tradition, over the civil codes and the other private law rules concerned.[26]

Both above choices take for granted the need of having a code – a necessity on which this paper will dwell later – and none of them, of course, settle either the problem of the actual implementation and enforcement of such a code, or the related issue concerning the establishment of a (single or double, for 'civil' and 'commercial' matters) uniformity-driven Supreme Court. Both the above choices may do away with the rhetoric of a convergence between common and civil law, leaving this 'coming together' to its own dimension, which is the factual, relentless and competitive dimension of the day-by-day making of the law within and across national boundaries, cultures and market opportunities.[27] But both above choices could allow the continental legal tradition not to miss the opportunity that the European current situation and ongoing codification process offer. The chance is to reinstate itself in the role and within a perspective which have long been its own and which can represent its own future, as soon as its scholars and legislators become aware of what is at stake and how to deal with it.[28]

---

for business contract rules. A still different issue regards the possible choice for a business contracts code limited in its scope to international transactions. On this point see the contribution of U. Drobnig in this volume: 'A Subsidiary Plea: A European Code for Intra-European Border-Crossing Contracts', Ch. 21 below.

[26] For the sake of statistics one could recall that of every 100 Euro of marchandise export of the EU, 10.6 go to North America (US and Canada) and 9.7 to a selected sample of civilian countries including Eastern European and Latin American countries, Egypt, Morocco, Tunisia and Turkey. See the WTO Report, *International Trade Statistics 2001*, Table III.39, in http://www.wto.org/english/res_e/statis_e/its2001_e/chp_3_e.pdf.

[27] Outside the boundaries of historical and cultural debate on the 'Western Legal Tradition' (see A. Gambaro and R. Sacco, *Sistemi Giuridici comparati* (Torino, 1996), 41 *et seq.*), one can grasp the mainstream of the discussions concerning the merging of common and civil law technicalities in the perspective of a European legal harmonization, in R. Zimmermann, *Roman Law, Contemporary Law, European Law* (Oxford, OUP, 2001), esp. 107 *et seq.*; B. Markesinis (ed.), *The Gradual Convergence* (Oxford, Clarendon Press, 1994); *id.* (ed.), *The Coming Together of the Common Law and the Civil Law* (Oxford, Portland, Hart, Oreg., 2000).

[28] See H.P. Glenn, *Legal Traditions of the World* (n. 24), 116 *et seq.* The author emphasizes, among other aspects, the profound relation of the civilian codes 'to the value of the human person, and the need for extricating the human person from much of the social fabric which had come to envelop the human person', 130.

III. IN THE NEIGHBORHOOD OF CONTRACT

1. Insights into the Case of Tort Law

The need for a uniformity-driven European Supreme Court mentioned above also comes to the fore when one approaches the legal borderlines which surround contract law. Within this perspective, a straighforward example may be given by tort law. Indeed, a glance at the European law of torts confirms how deeply conscious the code drafters will need to be about the overall implications of remoulding private law.

The kind of awareness that is required in legal debate can be simply illustrated. Suffice to recall, for instance, the problems raised by the catalogue of notions which straddle the tort and contract law fields, such as 'standard of conduct',[29] causation,[30] foreseeability,[31] 'protected interest'[32] and so forth. Other examples come from the flexible boundaries that comparative analysis enables us to draw as to so-called 'consequential' economic loss (i.e. an economic loss connected to even the slightest damage to the person or property of the plaintiff), as well as from the great reliance of certain regimes upon contract rules to handle issues that in other regimes are straightforwardly governed by tort law.

The same point concerning the interdependence between legal domains can be stressed choosing the opposite standpoint, i.e. highlighting how any attempt at codifying tort law would be closely dependent on the solutions which the same Code intends to offer in the other fields of private law, mainly with regard to contract and property.

To give further evidence of what I mean, let me draw on the in-depth study that Vernon V. Palmer and myself have conducted over the last 5 years on the recoverability of pure economic loss in thirteen legal regimes of Europe. What this study makes clear, in the perspective of my contribution to this seminar, can be summarized as follows:

---

[29] Cf. e.g. M. Bussani, *La colpa soggettiva. Modelli di valutazione della condotta nella responsabilità extracontrattuale* (Padova, Cedam, 1991), 131 *et seq.*; *id., As peculiaridades da noção de culpa: um estudo de direito comparado* (Porto Alegre, Livraria do Advogado, 2000), 32 *et seq.*

[30] Cf. T. Weir, 'The Staggering March of Negligence', in P. Cane and J. Stapleton (eds.), *The Law of Obligations. Essays in Celebration of John Fleming* (Oxford, Clarendon Press, 1998), 97, 124 *et seq.*

[31] Cf. J. Gordley, 'Responsibility in Crime, Tort, and Contract for the Unforeseeable Consequences of an Intentional Wrong: A Once and Future Rule?', in: P. Cane and J. Stapleton (eds.), *The Law of Obligations. Essays in Celebration of John Fleming* (n. 30), 175, 198 *et seq.*

[32] Cf. C. von Bar, *The Common European Law of Torts* (Oxford, Clarendon Press, 1998), 464 *et seq.*, 485 *et seq.*

(i)   If possession is included in the framework of property rights, or if it is at any rate protected by proprietary remedies, any infringement of possession will permit recovery of the economic loss, regardless of whether it is called consequential or pure. If possession is not included in the property framework, however, or if the power of control over the thing is not sufficient in and of itself for the holder to be deemed a possessor, then the recoverability of the economic loss caused to the holder (by interference with the thing itself) becomes an issue to be settled.

(ii) If the right to electricity (but the same could apply to hertzian or other electromagnetic waves)[33] is deemed a right in rem whose transfer from the supplier to the user is completed as of the date of the agreement, any damage to the system supplying that energy (such as the cutting of power cables) will be considered an infringement of property rights and therefore will raise no problems in any of the legal systems investigated here.

(iii) If the manner in which Germany and Austria apply the notions of *'culpa in contrahendo'* or the 'contract with protective effect to third parties',[34] is adopted as a model for a European Code, it is beyond doubt that many of the issues raised in 'pure economic loss' cases will be settled by contract principles, with little need to resort to tort law rules.

(iv) The Code's infrastructure regarding transfer of ownership would clearly have manifold effects in any 'Double Sale' case. Indeed, the right of the first buyer (*solo consensu*) to obtain compensation depends on a variety of factors, the role of which is actually to define who has the property right in the thing. These factors include the presence of good or bad faith, the completion of delivery (for movables), compliance with formalities like registration and recording (for immovables) and the effects assigned to the registration itself.

---

[33]   For the debate on the legal nature of these entities, see U. Mattei, *Basic Principles of Property Law. A Comparative Legal and Economic Introduction* (Greenwood Press, Westport, Central London, 2000), 76 *et seq.*, 153 *et seq.*

[34]   The same could be said for such notions as the French concept of *'chaîne de contrats'*. This refers to a series of contracts which, though distinct in law, form part of an economic complex. An example can be found in the chain which links a site owner to the contractor, the contractor to the sub-contractor and the latter to the supplier of the building materials. See H. Kötz and A. Flessner, *European Contract Law*, I (trans. T. Weir) (Oxford, OUP, 1997), 255 *et seq.* As to this technical notion and its actual impact on the recovery of pure economic losses, see G. Viney, *Introduction à la responsabilité* (Paris, LGDJ, 1995), 338 *et seq.*; W. van Gerven, J. Lever and P. Larouche, *Tort Law* (Oxford, Hart, 2000), 32 *et seq.*, 236 *et seq.*

2. Policies and Interpreters

The above simple remarks only hint at the web of relationships which link the tort and contract law fields. Even when all the above (and possibly other)[35] boundary issues have been clearly settled, the scope and structure of remedies at the disposal of tort and contract law users will still depend on other critical choices – and first among these come the major political choices that need to be made at a more general level about the whole of European patrimonial law.[36]

Any choices made by the drafters and codifiers are indeed the surrogate political acts of the legislator (whether the latter's approval of their work is one of default, rubber stamp or close consultation). Thus, any decision by the redactors to decrease, enlarge or simply maintain the existing unequal levels of protection for loss-bearers across Europe, is first and foremost a political question that must be answered. To be sure, the substantive decision necessarily has implications for the draft methodology to be adopted. To cite the simplest example, it may be that if the decision is to protect loss-bearers as broadly as possible, rather than in highly specific 'privileged loss-type' situations, then a general clause will be the legal instrument to implement it, rather than a formula grounded on a list of protected interests.

---

[35] For instance, our issue would certainly be affected, both theoretically and operationally, by any decision to allow or forbid the concurrence of tortious and contractual actions. As mentioned, the second alternative is better known as the French 'règle du non-cumul'. This rule clearly has a particular bearing because, if the European Code embraces it, we would predict that some cases on pure economic loss would disappear from tort law only to reappear as contract law questions. See G. Viney, *Introduction à la responsabilité* (Paris, L.G.D.J., 1995), 413 *et seq.*; C. von Bar, *The Common European Law of Torts* I (Oxford, Clarendon Press, 1998), 449 *et seq.*; T. Weir, *Complex Liabilities*, No. 52, Vol. XI, (Oxfor, IECL, 1976); P. Schlechtriem, 'The Borderland of Tort and Contract – Opening a New Frontier?', (1988) 21 *Cornell Int'l Law J.*, 467 *et seq.*

[36] Undoubtedly political choices have to match technical needs. The latter are substantial and most of them are raised by the fact that the very structure of private law compels any integrative effort to vary the approach according to the needs of the different domains on which it focuses. For example, it is one matter to deal with certain subjects (such as the statute of limitations) in which a combination of legislative data, a glance at the case law and, when necessary, some reference to both recent and distant history promise at the outset to be crucial to solving the problems; it is quite another to have to deal with topics in which any integration-concerned jurist must have an enormous variety of instruments and data at his disposal. This is particularly so, e.g., for topics such as administrative law, with respect to certain areas of property law, particularly as regards immovables. Similarly, the functioning of local Stock Exchanges and financial markets must be considered with reference to the areas of corporation law, financial law, and security interests. Fiscal law and contractual practices must be taken into account when considering new or 'modern' contracts, and so forth. On all this, see M. Bussani, 'Choix et défis de l'herméneutique juridique. Notes minimes', in (1998) 3 *Revue internationale de droit comparé*, 735 *et seq.*

Yet, one should have no illusions that even the clearest policies, whether stated in general clauses or protected interest formulas, will be translated into the 'law in action' without undergoing interpretative modification by judges and scholars. This is especially true, as said, in the absence of a European Supreme Court endowed with the authority to ensure the uniformity of interpretations and applications of legal rules. But it goes without saying that such a Court, like any other Court, will never be able to prevent developments, refinements and qualifications in the interpretation of the same rules whenever, over time, these changes will be felt appropriate by the interpretive community.[37]

IV. THE DRIVING FORCES BEHIND AND AHEAD OF THE EUROPEAN CODIFICATION PROCESS

1. Market, Currency, Law and the Time Factor

All of these could appear as a cry in the dark if compared to the dazzling path traced by the bulk of prominent European scholars aiming at nothing but the (single-minded) civil code.

One of the reasons that this goal is pursued lies in the argument that ongoing business relationships among the Member States, and monetary union, urgently required approaches tailored to the needs of facilitating the integration of legal and economic markets in (at least) the euro area within a relatively short period of time. To be sure, the motto *'one market, one currency'* justified the plans that

---

[37] See e.g. A. Watson, 'Comparative Law and Legal Change', (1978) 37 *Cambridge L. J.*, 313; P.G. Monateri, ' "Everybody's Talking": The Future of Comparative Law', in (1998) 21 *Hastings Int'l & Comp. L. Rev.*, 825; and cf. W. Ewald, 'Comparative Jurisprudence (I): What Was It Like to Try a Rat?', in (1995) 143 *U. Pa. L. Rev.*, 1889; *id.*, 'Comparative Jurisprudence (II): The Logic of Legal Transplants', in (1995) 43 *Am. J. Comp. L.*, 489. Indeed, even on the morrow of the adoption of whatever code, the law will not be given. What will be given is the existence and survival of specific interpretative practices worked out by the jurists and the other legal actors, with the contribution of the law-users. In other terms, the real issue affecting the legal discourse, as well as the implementation of any code, is (what Hegel called *Sittlichkeit*, and a whole tradition before him, *sensus communis*, i.e., to our purposes) the concrete life of a legal culture, the 'web' of beliefs rooted in an historically situated legal community. To be sure, the finite and contextual character of a community's common heritage opens up the possibility of and the need for continuous control by an 'uninhibited, robust, and wide-open' debate – to use (out of context) the celebrated phrase of J. Brennan in *N.Y. Times Co. v. Sullivan*, 376 *U.S.* 254 (1964), at 270. But under every methodological choice there necessarily lies a question of values and of ends among which the jurist must choose, though keeping in mind that whenever we deal with 'law', we deal with something which cannot be grasped by referring to principles, rulings and provisions stated once and for ever. See M. Bussani, 'Choix et défis de l'herméneutique juridique. Notes minimes', 50 *Reve internationale droit comparé*, 1998, 735 and *supra* n. 10.

led to the single currency. The achievement of the latter has given a new dimension to the internal market, bringing economic actors closer together and increasing and intensifying legal relationships across the euro area. One could question, however, whether the parallelism between economic and monetary integration, on the one hand, and legal codification on the other, withstands comparison with the lessons of history. In view of this question, let us consider some European examples, not so distant in time and all of them drawn from inside the age of codifications.[38]

Following the political unification of Germany in 1871,[39] a new national monetary unit based on the gold standard, the Reichsmark, was introduced in 1875–6 to replace nine different monetary systems.[40] An internal market with free movement of goods already existed because of the customs union (*Zollverein*) effective from 1834. In spite of this internal market, the linguistic uniformity and the introduction of a common currency, several private law regimes persisted (the Prussian and Bavarian codes, the Napoleonic code, Roman and Canon law, etc.) for the period of almost 30 years.[41]

---

[38] Outside Europe, the case of the United States of America could also be of interest. Indeed, one of the aims of the integration of European markets is to create an area that compares itself with the economic might of the United States of America. Whilst in terms of population the European Union exceeds the USA, in macro-economic terms Europe lags well behind. The USA is a federal union of fifty states, each with its own legislative and political powers, but it is, however, a single market. Of course sharing not only a currency, but also a common language and a federal central government and legislature is of the essence for such singleness. Europe has just started with one of the three: a single currency. The Community is no more than an embryo of a federal authority, with limited powers that are moreover subject to the principle of subsidiarity. Furthermore, private and contract law belongs, in the USA, not to the federal level but to the state level. And in this a certain comparison with Europe may be made: the USA has a single market in spite of the fifty state laws on contract. To be sure, a decision, say, of a New York court dealing with a sophisticated financial dispute would have legal authority for local courts throughout the USA, but this is far from the situation in Europe, where private law disputes are still adjudicated at national level with no, or only occasional, cross-border authority. See A. Sánz de Vicuña (n. 39).

[39] On what follows see A. Sáinz de Vicuña, 'Legal Consequences of the Single Currency', General Report to the F.I.D.E. Congress – Helsinki 2000, summary in G.O. Zacharias Sundström and Matti R. Kauppi (eds.), XIX F.I.D.E. Congress, IV, Helsinki (2000), 76 *et seq.*

[40] Cf. S. Homer and R. Sylla, *A History of Interest Rates*, 3rd edn. (New Brunswick, London, Rutgers UP, 1991), trans. R. Villani: *Storia dei tassi di interesse* (Milano e Bari-Roma, 1995), Ch. III, 351 *et seq.*

[41] It is worth recalling that prior to the German unification, the law of negotiable instruments (*Wechselordnung*) and General German Commercial Code (ADHGB) had only been gradually adopted by the States of the Deutscher Bund. Cf. K. Zweigert and H. Kötz, *Introduction to Comparative Law* 3rd edn. (T. Weir trans.) (Oxford, Clarendon Press, 1998), 141.

In Switzerland, the Constitution of 1848 provided for a single market and a single currency, but not for a unified private law system, which was kept within the domain of the cantons. This state of affairs led in 1874 to a revision of the Constitution which allowed for codification. The 'Code des Obligations' was only adopted in 1881 and came into force in 1883.

As to the United Kingdom, it is worth stressing that monetary union among England, Wales and Scotland in the early eighteenth century did not lead to any systematic harmonisation of civil and commercial law. Moreover, Article 18 of the Act of Union stated that 'no alteration may be made in laws which concern private right'. In the domain of the law of contract, many differences still exist between English and Scottish law.[42]

The historical example of Sweden, Denmark and Norway may be added to the above. Those countries agreed in 1871 on a Scandinavian monetary union that lasted until 1914, and from which the three countries took a common name for their respective, now separate, currencies, the 'krone'. Though a proper common codification has always been outside the scope of Nordic ambition and tradition,[43] these countries – whose languages are closely cognate – did harmonise their legislation, inclusive of legislation on real property, on commercial and maritime matters. At present, a common law on contracts is shared by the three countries although they lack a common currency and political unity.[44]

One is tempted to conclude that the above historical examples support the idea that there is no automatic overlap between economic and legal integration. In particular, one may infer that the combination of an internal market with a single currency in territories with different laws is not necessarily tied to – nor does it inevitably engender, at least in the short run – the unification of the rules applying within that market. Germany, Switzerland, the UK, and to a lesser extent the Nordic countries, are evidence of this.

To be sure the same facts could be seen the other way round, so that 'most of the time', in the short or in the long run, legal uniformation ends up being unavoidable if the same area (enjoys a common – not limited to the elite – linguistic ground, and) has been affected by a deep economic integration.

Either way, the point to be stressed concerns the relevance of the time factor. This cannot be understimated because its mature use enables us to gauge and proportionate the harmonization measures we have in mind. They could be taken and scaled according to the growth, in the legal professionals' community,

---

[42] An up-to-date survey in the reports *Scotland*, by E. Reid and R. Leslie, in V.V. Palmer, *Mixed Jurisdictions Worldwide, The Third Legal Family* (Cambridge, Cambridge UP, UK, 2001), respectively at 201 *et seq.*, 221 *et seq.*, 227, 231 *et seq.*, 235 and 247 *et seq.*, 252 *et seq.*

[43] See L. Sevón, 'Statutory Lawmaking: A Nordic Perspective', in *De Lege, Towards Universal Law* (Uppsala, 1995), 179 *et seq.*; A. Sánz de Vicuña (n. 39).

[44] See K. Zweigert and H. Kötz, *Introduction to Comparative Law* 3rd edn. (T. Weir trans.), (Oxford, Clarendon Press, 1998), 280 *et seq.*

of the necessary awareness of the need for that harmonization or unification, of the most appropriate tools to achieve it, of the size and the impact of the compromises to be made in view of a European legal unity, of the need of a radical change in university curricula and of the overcoming of a foreign – not to mention comparative law – blindness in domestic scholarship. It may be that all this will take less than fifty or a hundred years. But the span of time that is necessary to attain this 'cultural revolution' is by no means a factor that can be overlooked if any Code, and its implementation, is to escape a grim doomsday.

2. In Defence of European Scholarship

The codification idea and the widespread success it enjoys seem to me, nonetheless, grounded on some socio-cultural reasons which are worth mentioning and are possibly enhanced by the above mentioned European law fragmentation. In the Western legal tradition it is well known that continental legal scholars and common law judges have always perceived themselves as an organ of a body called Law, a body with both an origin and a destiny that is perennial, not contingent.

As guardian of those origins and executor of that destiny, the jurist has always had some sophisticated technical apparatus at his disposal. This machinery varies according to the historical and geographical conditions in which the jurist happens to find himself. But this apparatus has invariably served to maintain the priestlike quality of the jurist and of the *corpus juris* whose messenger and artisan he is; a *corpus juris* which can, in its turn, appear under various names, including Roman Law, Natural Law and/or Rational Law, *ius commune*, Common Law, *Code Civil*, *usus modernus pandectarum*, and so on. The jurist no longer seems to live in this cultural setting.

Nowadays national and European legislators – reinforcing and broadening the existent multi-level legal framework – have increasingly assumed the role of a breathless oracle intervening in whatsoever field in order to satisfy the requests addressed by any politically relevant pressure group. This state of things feeds the well known phenomenon of micro-legislation, often affected by bureaucratic contents and wording. Interpretation and enforcement of this law are usually entrusted to mediation councils, technical committees, agencies, the so-called independent authorities, or other new or old-fashioned administrative bodies.

The final outcome of this phenomenon is easy to understand, at least as far as continental Europe is concerned. It is the weakening of the role of the scholars and their traditional machinery, as both of them are compelled to come to terms with provisions whose nature and contents are increasingly indifferent to the given legal tradition and to the inner consistency of the given legal system.

Transplanted into the 'European codification debate', this situation can lead to (or back the promoters of) the conclusion that legal systems presently diverge too much, that the time, in other words, is not ripe to enact a Restatement or

Civil Code; a defence of the *status quo* that, as everybody knows, fits perfectly with the need of the professional élite to keep the leadership over national and transnational legal affairs. Professional élite is a label to be understood in its variety ranging from the European practitioners and judges to the continental (mostly municipal) academics.[45]

This is why one of the fundamental reasons which supports the idea of, and the debate about, a European Civil code seems to be the self-comprehension of (most) comparative law scholars of their own role and of the dangers to which the latter is exposed; dangers that come from the bureaucratic turn of the national and European legislators as well as from the more and more scattered, fragmentary, out-of-control (both substantive and linguistic) texture of legal rules.

Thus, the relationship between the codification process and European scholarship can be understood in a perspective which goes further than the classical *Savigny v. Thibaut* quarrel. Indeed, we cannot suppose that the bureaucratic and piecemeal attitude of the law-makers stops or decreases its yield, nor that (culturally) parochial lawyers relinquish their attitude and give up their self-interests. Consequently, one of the real and most important risks that 'pro-European legal integration' scholarship has to face appears to be, eventually, not the enactment of the European Code but rather its absence. Indeed, the preparation and interpretation of a Code would again provide legal scholarship with social prestige and technical indispensability, reinstating scholars in their traditional role of artisans and messengers of the law.

It is in this perspective that one may understand and support the idea of the codification and the effort made by a passionate legal scholarship not to give up its role.

3. 'Pride and Prejudice'

The way that the private law unification process is currently managed, however, shows a critical disadvantage: the idea that the unification has to be attained through a Code, that is, an act of a legislature. It is not a matter of 'democracy deficit' I want to address – that issue can be settled through political actions

---

[45] But see also the position taken by a prominent English scholar: B.S. Markesinis, 'Why a code is not the best way to advance the cause of European Legal Unity', (1997) 5 *ERPL*, 519. According to this author, rather than towards a codification the efforts should aim to train an élite of truly European practitioners. However, since this élite bar would charge high fees to clients – fees which are likely to be a significant cost for each legal transaction – this expensive advice will not be affordable by everybody. This would create (*rectius*: maintain) both very high transaction costs and an unfair advantage for large business as against the rest of the law-users. See also n. 21.

and agreements whose review lies beyond the scope of this paper.[46] Herein the focus is different.

As long as the ultimate source of the law is the will of the people affected by it – as it is, for instance, with regard to national or international commercial customs – any new rule is grounded on widespread agreement, with no traumatic rupture of the pre-existent law. A new code, by a new statute, may not have the same *souplesse*. It goes without saying that whenever a code is national it mirrors domestic lawyers' language and views, it makes use of techniques and notions that are rooted in the local practice, it gives solutions for well-known and widely distributed social and economic requests. On the contrary, codes and statutes drafted with a view to setting up a transnational uniformity necessarily have to choose among different models and rules. They erase some rules belonging to a model and substitute for them other rules from other languages and different legal cultures, languages and cultures which can be more or less unknown by the other law-users in the other legal systems concerned by the law reform.[47]

Doubtless, what forces legal integration can either be an act taken by mutual consent by two or more States, or an act taken by a pre-eminent authority.[48]

---

[46]   On the topic see, e multis, W. van Gerven (n. 4), 495 *et seq.*; G. Alpa, 'European Community legislation and the Codification of "Private Law"', (2000) 8 *ERPL* 321 *et seq.*; J. Basedow, 'Codification of Private Law in the European Union: the making of a hybrid', (2001) 9 *ERPL*, 35, 43 *et seq.*

[47]   'Sans variations, nous n'aurions pas de progrès, car le progrès est la variation. Si nous voulons le progrès, nous voulons la variation; et si nous acceptons la variation, nous acceptons la diversité': R. Sacro, 'La diversité des droits', in *Mélanges en l'honneur de C.A. Cannata* (Bâle, 1999), 411 *et seq.* On the same tune, A.T. von Mehren, 'The U.S. Legal System: Between the Common Law and Civil Law Traditions', in: (2000) 40 *Centro di studi e ricerche di diritto comparato e straniero. Saggi e conferenze*, Roma. The author stresses, at 17, that 'Until such times as the institutions, values, and circumstances that shape law are homogeneous, diversity will ensure significant differences in legal practices, institutions, and values'.

[48]   R. Sacro, 'Diversity and Uniformity in the Law', 49 *A. J. Comp. L.* 171, 177 *et seq.* (2001). Referring again to the US experience, one can note that the market pressures in favour of legal certainty set up the factual conditions under which the American Law Institute, in 1923, created the technique of *Restatements:* a permanent effort after systematization of case law. But it was only in 1940 that the National Conference of Commissioners on Uniform State Laws (which adopted in 1896 the Uniform Negotiable Instruments Law, in 1906 the uniform laws on Sales and on Warehouse Receipts, and half a dozen more uniform laws) decided to embark on the project of a Uniform Commercial Code (UCC) that would update and replace the existing set of uniform laws. It was then in 1952 that a first draft of the UCC saw light; but after a round of discussions with state legislators the first official text was adopted only in 1957 and the text was revised and updated on several occasions. The UCC, however, and as is well known, is not a civilian code. (i) It is a flexible tool: it is not mandatory *per se* and requires endorsement by state legislators, who can select parts of the code and not all its provisions, and who can modify or supplement its content. (ii) It is foreseen as an on-going project, and not a finalized code. (iii) It will add articles as

The latter happened, for example, in Italy, France and Germany when private law was unified. Nevertheless, the same feeling which praises the values of legal unification may sometimes play the opposite role, making a new unification difficult. There is little doubt that current resistance raised by, say, Italian, French and German lawyers to the adoption of a European Civil Code (besides the weight of the dependence on professional routine) is most of the time caused by the pride related to the traditional image and rhetoric of the national codes.

What is worth stressing is that at the very core of this resistance, one can easily find the will to keep timeless a legal solution – the national code(s) – in the name of history. History, though, involves becoming. It can create nothing eternal and nothing invariable.[49] It seems meaningless, then, to side with differences in the name of a self-deceptive invariability. In other words, one can stand up for diversity but upon condition that this is not done in the name of invariability.

Social and economic reality, moreover, constantly ask the law to renew itself to meet new needs, and each innovation always competes with the previous, or a different, solution. It is this competition which usually makes the simplest and the most cost-effective rule to obtain. One of the occurrences which can slow down this self-innovating process is precisely the legal integration dictated by a supranational authority. The law imposed in this way deprives the legal systems of the possibility of remodelling themselves through internal changes. Yet 'change' is what is always requested of the law by ever-moving social and economic phenomena, first and foremost the market. What is likely to occur, instead, in the aftermath of such a 'top down' forced integration, is that any legal innovation will turn out to be dependent on the working of an array of devices which, in a multilingual and multicultural context like the European one, prove to be belated and consequently ineffective – implying the setting up of international conferences, new preliminary drafting, large majority decisions, and so forth. The easiest outcome to predict all this is a material delay in the law's development.

In any case – and in conclusion – reducing the amount of legal models in force means limiting the number of possible starting points for further progress and future evolutions. Even worse, such reduction curbs the profits usually deriving from the competition among legal models. To be sure, whenever this competition turns out to be mostly due to academic distinctions about concepts

---

needs demand: it is subject to the revisions that time may require – and a Permanent Editorial Board is entrusted with the out-of-court interpretation of its provisions, and may submit *amicus curiae* briefs to judicial courts where interpretative questions are to be solved. See e.g. J.J. White and R.S. Summers, *Uniform Commercial Code* 5th edn. (West, St. Paul, Minn., 2000), 1–25.

[49] R. Sacro (n. 48), 176 *et seq.* Cf. A. Chamboredon, 'The Debate on a European Civil Code: For an "Open Texture"', in: M. van Hoecke and F. Ost (eds.), *The Harmonization of European Private Law* (n. 10), 63, 68 *et seq.* and *ibidem* further references.

or explanations (while operative rules do not lie so far from each other), it could disappear with no regret, replaced by some 'better' solution. But what we need to keep in mind is that the choice for or against erasing differences must be adopted with full awareness of how deeply the ideas of change and development are embedded in the relentless mutation of reality and of law – 'change *is* the tradition'.[50] This is why scholars, and most of all comparativists, cannot leave alone those supranational legislators who are pursuing the knowledge and the governance of complexity.

---

[50] H.P. Glenn, *supra* n. 24, at 117 (emphasis in original); M. van Hoecke, 'The Harmonization of Private Law in Europe: Some Misunderstandings', in: M. van Hoecke and F. Ost (eds.), *The Harmonization of European Private Law* (n. 13), at 1, 5 *et seq.*

12. The Politics of European Contract Law: Who has an Interest in what Kind of Contract Law for Europe?

*Martijn W. Hesselink**

I. INTRODUCTION

I come to this debate as a Dutch scholar with (moderate) left-wing ideological sympathies. With many of my compatriots I share a faith, admittedly sometimes somewhat naïve, in international and European ideals and organisations. Like most legal scholars I have a particular interest in the structure of the law. And like most social-democrats I have limited faith in markets and a belief in the need to regulate them in order to achieve social aims. I am telling you this not because I think these facts could in themselves be of any interest to you, but because they may be relevant when appreciating what I am going to say in this paper.

The subject assigned to me for the conference was: 'The political stakes in the European contract law debate'.[1] In particular, I will focus on the question who

---

* Martijn W. Hesselink is Professor of Private Law at the Universiteit van Amsterdam and Director of the Amsterdam Institute for Private Law.

[1] On the politics of contract law see generally: D. Kennedy, 'Form and Substance in Private Law Adjudication', 89 *Harv. L. Rev.* 1685, 1713–24 and D. Kennedy, *A Critique of Adjudication (fin de siècle)*, (Cambridge, Mass., 1997). With a focus on European contract law see U. Mattei, 'The Issue of Civil Codification and Legal scholarship: Biases, Strategies and Developments', 21 *Hastings Int'l & Comp. L. Rev.* (1998) 883; D. Caruso, 'The Missing View of the Cathedral: The Private Law Paradigm of European Legal Integration', 3 *ELJ* (1997), 3–32; M.W. Hesselink, 'The Principles of European Contract Law: Some Choices Made by the Lando Commission', in: M.W. Hesselink and G.J.P. De Vries, *Principles of European Contract Law; Preadviezen uitgebracht voor de Vereniging voor Burgerlijk Recht* (Deventer, 2001) and the contributions to the special issue of the *European Review of Private Law* (2002:1) dedicated to the Amsterdam seminar on 'Critical Legal Theory and European Private Law': D. Kennedy, 'The Political Stakes in 'Merely Technical' Issues of Contract Law', U. Mattei and A. di Robilant, 'The Art and Science of Critical Scholarship: Post Modernism and International Style in the Legal Architecture of Europe'; P. Legrand, 'On the Unbearable Localness of the Law: Academic Fallacies and Unseasonable Observations'; E. McKendrick, 'Traditional Concepts and Contemporary Values'; T. Wilhelmsson, 'Private Law in the EU: Harmonised or Fragmented Europeanisation?'; C.W.M. van Sandelingenambacht, 'Legal Postism and the End of European Private Law'; M.W. Hesselink 'Editorial'.

S. Grundmann and J. Stuyck (eds.), An Academic Green Paper on European Contract Law, 181–191
© 2002 *Kluwer Law International. Printed in Great Britain.*

has an interest in what kind of European contract law? I will discuss three political dimensions of the European contract law debate: II) empowerment, III) national traditions and IV) ideology.

II. EMPOWERMENT

The various possible outcomes of the present debate would have different consequences for the power which different (groups of) actors exercise with regard to contract law. This may frequently explain their position in the debate.

1. Academics

Academics specialise in rationality, objectivity, abstraction and system. They are therefore often critical of the present state European contract law is in.[2] In particular, many scholars lament the patch-work approach which the European Union has adopted with its directives, and many of them would even be prepared to abandon their national civil code in favour of a European code in order to restore order and system into private law. One of the alternative solutions suggested by the European Commission (EC) in its Communication (the second one), is the promotion of principles:[3] the EC could promote comparative law research aimed at finding common principles. This option has received a warm welcome from the academic world. Not only from those who would immediately benefit from such a course of action, i.e. the Lando Commission and the Von Bar Group,[4] who have actually been drafting such principles,[5] but also from

---

[2] See e.g. O. Lando and H. Beale *Principles of European Contract Law, Parts I and II, Prepared by The Commission on European Contract Law* (Kluwer, The Hague, 2000), xxii, and H. Kötz, 'Comparative Law in Germany Today', *RIDC* [1999], 753 *et seq.* Compare P.C. Müller-Graff, 'EC Directives as a Means of Private Law Unification', in: A.S. Hartkamp *et al.* (eds.), *Towards a European Civil Code*, (2nd ed. Nijmegen and The Hague, London/Boston), 71 *et seq.*, at 82, Ch. Joerges, 'The Impact of European Integration on Private Law: Reductionist Perceptions, True Conflicts and a New Constitutional Perspective', *ELJ* [1997], 378–406, D. Caruso (n. 1), 14, O. Remien, 'Einheit, Mehrstufigheit und Flexibilität im europäischen Privat- und Wirtschaftsrecht', 62 *RabelsZ* (1998), 627, 639; V. Zeno-Zencovich, 'The 'European Civil Code', European Legal Traditions and Neo-positivism', in: G. Alpa and E.N. Buccico (eds.), *Il codice civile europeo: Materiali dei seminari 1999–2000* (Milano 2001), 375, 378; M. Hesselink, *De redelijkheid en billijkheid in het Europese privaatrecht* (Deventer 1999), 20, all with further references.

[3] Communication from the Commission to the Council and the European Parliament, COM(2001) 398 final, No. 52.

[4] See for example the *Joint Response* that the Commission on European Contract Law and the Study Group on a European Civil Code sent to the European Commission in reply to its Communication.

[5] See O. Lando and H. Beale (eds.), n. 2.

other academics.[6] This is not surprising, since with that option the future of European contract law would largely be in the hands of academics.[7]

Academics may also welcome the more far-reaching fourth-suggested solution, i.e. some kind of formal enactment, possibly within a European Code of Contracts or even a European Civil Code. However, the prospect of handing the project over to politicians also worries them. Politicians are not experts in contract law, at least not to the extent that academics are, and politicians tend to compromise and enter into political deals which may seriously endanger the quality of the end-product.[8]

2. The Legislators

The legislator's claim to have a say in the future of European contract law is obviously based on its democratic authority, although in the case of the European legislator the democratic basis is rather slim. The European Parliament has called for a European civil code on several occasions, most recently in late 2001. [9] However, as everybody knows, the power of the European Parliament is still

---

[6] Of course their is no unity among academics. This became very clear at the 1997 Scheveningen conference where every scholar promoted his own project. See the contributions published in *ERPL* [1997], especially M. Joachim Bonell, 'The Need and Possibilities of a Codified European Contract Law', 505 *et seq.*; U. Drobnig, 'Scope and General Rules of a European Civil Code', 489 *et seq.*; W. van Gerven, 'Coherence and National Laws: Is There a Legal Basis for a European Civil Code?', 465 *et seq.*; O. Lando, 'Why Codify the European Law of Contract?', 525 *et seq.*, B.S. Markesinis, 'Why a Code is Not the Best Way to Advance the Cause of European Legal Unity', 519 *et seq.*; U. Mattei, 'A Transaction Costs Approach to the European Code', 537 *et seq.*

[7] This would restore the tradition in many European countries. In Germany especially there is a long-standing tradition from the drafting of the BGB through the recent *Schuldrechtreform* (among the members of the *Kommission zur Überarbeitung des Schuldrechts* who presented its proposals in 1992 were H. Kötz, D. Medicus, and P. Schlechtriem). And in the Netherlands Meijers and most of his successors who drafted the 1992 Civil Code were academics. Also, in Great Britain many statutes and law reforms are prepared by the Law Commissions, which also (but not exclusively) include academics (e.g. at this moment Hugh Beale, a prominent member of the Lando Commission and the Von Bar group). And in France much private law legislation in many areas, like family law (Carbonnier), traffic liability (Tunc) and product liability (Ghestin) has been prepared by academics. This tradition has been disturbed by recent activism in the field of contract law by the European Union, especially by its many directives.

[8] An example that is frequently referred to is the Vienna Sales Convention (United Nations Convention on Contracts for the International Sale of Goods) which contains many compromises, some of which even contradict each other. Compare E. Hondius, 'Weens koopen verdragenrecht', (1996) *WPNR* 6233, 567 *et seq.*

[9] Resolution of 26 May 1989, EC OJ No. C 158/401, Resolution of 6 May 1994, EC OJ No. C 205 519, and Resolution 15 November 2001, COM(2001) 398 – C5-0471/2001 – 2001/2187 (COS).

rather limited. The real political power in the European Union lies with the Council of Ministers and with the European Commission. The Council of Ministers tends to mainly follow national interests, which I will come back to in a moment. What stake does the Commission have in the debate? From which option would the Commission gain most in terms of empowerment?

Clearly, for the Commission things only become interesting in the options which involve some kind of formal enactment (Options 3 and 4).[10] Therefore, from the perspective of the EC the first option it mentions (leave everything to market forces) would do no good. And clearly, for the EC the more extensive the field of action would be, the better. This may explain the broad definition which the EC gives in its Communication on contract law.[11]

However, there may be a problem: why should the European Union be allowed to take action in the field of contract law at all? Do any of the European treaties give the EC the necessary power to interfere with contract law? The strategy which the EC has adopted is to focus on the Internal Market, which has always been the EC's trump card for empowerment. Contract law is a central institution of a market and the differences between the contract laws of the various member states amount to obstacles to the proper functioning of the common market. Therefore, if the European systems of contract law differ, and if this obstructs the market, then the EC should take action in order to remove these obstacles.[12] Another obstacle which the EC will have to deal with is existing doubts as to whether it is up to the job. The specific competence of civil servants with regard to (comparative) contract law has especially been doubted.[13] Are the best contract lawyers to be found in Brussels? This may explain the suggestion by the EC that academic 'experts' could carry out the preparatory work of establishing common principles which could provide a legitimate basis for the EC's actions.

---

[10] However, option 2 may be strategically preferable for the Commission. The Commission would thus give a good impression of its faithfulness to the subsidiarity principle. And at a later stage they could propose to formally enact what will then in substance have become a common European contract law.

[11] In the view of the EC 'contract law' includes large parts of what is regarded in most European countries as the general law of obligations, tort law and property law (securities in movables). See Communication, No. 13.

[12] In a moment I will come back to the question whether the only imaginable function of contract law is to facilitate the smooth functioning of the Internal Market.

[13] V. Zeno-Zencovich (n. 2), 377–378, 'Legrand's doubts, expressed in a manner that could be even more forthright, as to the legal skills of the EU bureaucracy should be entirely supported. [...] with obvious exceptions, this group does not have at its disposal great legal skills. This is because of its background, its methods of recruitment, the cultural differences amongst its members, and the lack of a profound knowledge of the legal traditions of member states. [...] It is therefore perfectly justifiable to be severely critical of the EU legislation, both as regards its content and the mentality it expresses.'; P. Legrand (n. 1); O. Remien (n. 2), 627, 646.

Until now I have spoken of the EC as one monolithic player in the overall power game. However, within the EC internal struggles for empowerment have been going on. Therefore, the Directorate-General for Health and Consumer Protection may be better off with a Consumer Code. A first step in that direction would be the enactment, for example by regulation, of a consolidated version of the *acquis communautaire* in the field of consumer law. This approach is indeed suggested by the EC as the third option in its Communication. On the other hand, the option of integrating European consumer law into a European code of contracts risks jeopardising the strong grip on European contract law which this D-G has had to date.[14]

3. Courts

Courts are active in the business of resolving conflicts. That is, they apply the law. However, it has been long recognised in all European countries that in practice courts also play an important role in further developing the law. European law is ultimately developed by the European Court of Justice (ECJ). The power which the ECJ currently yields would be immensely enhanced if it were also to be the final instance in all contract or even all private law cases in Europe, as a result of the enactment of either a Contracts Code or a Consumer Code or regulation (options 3 and 4).[15] This would especially be the case if the code were to be as abstract, general and open-textured as the Principles of European Contract Law.[16] These principles only provide starting points for decision-making and give rise to many specific questions that courts would have to resolve. Therefore, if some degree of uniform application is aspired to, then the ECJ will have to play a very active role from the beginning. If, however, the interpretation of the Code were to be left entirely to national courts, as is the case for CISG, the uniforming effect would be much smaller. Therefore, it seems likely that the strongest empowerment effect of enacting a European Code of Contract Law would be very much in favour of the ECJ. It would not only become the ultimate authority in Europe in cases concerning contract law, but it would also be its task to further develop it.[17]

---

[14] Consumer law is frequently referred to as the engine of European contract law. However, there are also examples of directives in the field of contract law which do not apply to consumers. See e.g. Council Directive 86/653/EEC of 18 December 1986 on self-employed commercial agents (OJ L 31.12.1986, 17)) and Directive 2000/35/EC of the European Parliament and the Council of 29 June 2000 on combating late payment in commercial transactions (OJ L 210, 8.8.2000, 35).

[15] The drawback of course, would be the resulting tremendous workload.

[16] See M.W. Hesselink (n. 1), 39.

[17] In the case of preliminary rulings (art. 234 (former 177) EC) the ECJ's power is shared with the national courts.

4. Local Actors

Obviously, national academics, practitioners, courts and legislators are the ones who share a clear common interest in the first option mentioned in the EC's Communication: no EC action. In all the other options they would only lose power: they will either have to share or even completely give up the power which they have invested in. Today, scholars are the exclusive specialists with regard to their respective national laws. They do not have to fear any competition from foreigners. Even the opinion of the most eminent foreign scholar will not be regarded as a higher authority on Dutch law than a Dutch commentary. Similarly, Dutch practitioners share a monopoly in advising their clients on Dutch law and in representing them in Dutch courts. If Dutch contract law were to be replaced by European contract law, this would be different. Dutch scholars and practitioners would have to compete with their colleagues from other member states. Of course, competition in itself would not necessarily render them worse off. On the contrary, they might even be able to increase their market share. However, that would require a significant new investment, whereas the investment, they have made so far in specific expertise in Dutch national law would become largely worthless. National courts of last instance would undergo a decline in status since in private (or contract) law cases they would no longer be the highest authority. Moreover, if the EU were to adopt a similar judiciary system to the US, then 'federal' cases would be administered by a network of European federal courts spread all over the Union, which would also reduce the power of the lower national (i.e. non-'federal') courts. As to national legislators, they have never been very active in general contract law; nevertheless, it is (at least formally) the national legislator who enacts civil codes[18] and law reforms.[19] In the case of the adoption of one of the courses of action suggested by the EC as the fourth option they would partially or completely lose that power with regard to contract law.

III. NATIONAL TRADITIONS

Of course, there are also important national interests at stake. All European countries are proud of their own national legal tradition. Austria has one of the oldest codes, The Netherlands has the newest. The French with their *Code civil* and the Germans with their *BGB* are each the godfather of powerful legal families. And England, Wales and Ireland share a tradition of their own which is characterised by a case-to-case approach instead of general solutions, such as a code. Therefore, were the EC to enact a European contracts code, it would

---

[18] See e.g. the global or partial recodifications in Italy (1942), Greece (1946), Portugal (1967), The Netherlands (1992) and Germany (2002).
[19] See, as a recent example, in England the Contracts (Rights of Third Parties) Act 1999.

find itself before *l'embarras du choix*. Which national system should be the model? The Italian code, says the Gandolfi Group.[20] None of them, reposts the Lando Commission: we should adopt new concepts and new terminology.[21] However, it is of course neither possible nor indeed desirable to create a new European contract law that bears no similarity at all to the contract law of any of the member states (that would be somewhat similar to the buildings which figure on the euro banknotes). Of course, it would be rather odd to leave a possible solution unused merely because is has been successfully adopted in one or more member states. Therefore, it seems much more appropriate to borrow from all the European systems.[22] However, that raises the question of how much and what should be borrowed from which country. Any proposal for a European code of contracts is likely to be scrutinised for its cultural ingredients: is my national tradition sufficiently represented?

Some concerns have already been expressed.[23] Some scholars warn against German cultural imperialism.[24] Others point out that enacting a European code would effectively mean replacing in England, Wales and Ireland a minority tradition (common law[25]) with the tradition shared by the majority of EU member states (civil law).[26] And still others see risks of a north/south divide.[27] Clearly, this debate is merely a specific contract law variant of a general debate that European politicians have been only too familiar with.

IV. IDEOLOGY

I will address three ideological questions raised by the Commission's Communication: a) the functions of contract law; b) the ideological basis of contract law; and c) the ideological implications of the structure of contract law. Thereby, I will mainly concentrate on the political distinction between the left

---

20 See G. Gandolfi, 'Pour un code européen des contrats', *RTD Civ.* [1991], 707 *et seq.*; G. Gandolfi (ed.), *Code Européen des contrats – Avant projet* (Milano, 2001).

21 PECL, Introduction, xxv.

22 That is what the Lando Commission claims to have done. See for a cultural analysis of the PECL (n. 1), 67 *et seq.*

23 See generally H. Collins, 'European Private Law and Cultural Identity of States', *ERPL* [1995], 353–365, and T. Weir, 'Die Sprachen des europäischen Rechts; Eine skeptische Betrachtung', *ZeuP* [1995], 368 *et seq.*

24 U. Mattei, 'The Issue of Civil Codification and Legal scholarship: Biases, Strategies and Developments', 21 *Hastings Int'l & Comp. L. Rev.* 883; P.G. Monateri, 'Black Gaius; A Quest for the Multicultural Origins of the "Western Legal Tradition"', 51 *Hastings Law J.* (2000), 479–555.

25 In Europe; outside Europe many countries share the common law tradition including the US, Canada, Australia and New Zealand.

26 See especially P. Legrand, 'Against a European Civil Code', 60 *MLR* (1997), 44–62.

27 M.W. Hesselink, *The New European Legal Culture* (Deventer 2001), 71.

(social-democrat) and the right (liberal, conservative) which for more than a century has been the main ideological opposition in most European countries.[28]

1. Functions of Contract Law

What functions does contract law perform in our society? When reading the Commission's communication one would think that contract law has only one role to fulfil: to facilitate the proper functioning of the Internal Market. Contracts and contract law are crucial market institutions which should ensure efficient exchange. The ideology underlying the Communication is clearly a market ideology. The only reason which it suggests for possible EC activity is the possible market impediments stemming from differences between the contract laws of the member states and from transaction costs resulting from a lack of information with regard to the presence of such differences. The underlying assumption seems to be, on the one hand, that if there are no important divergences or if the market can function with such divergences, then the EC should not interfere, whereas, on the other hand, the mere fact that divergent national rules impede the Internal Market may be a sufficient reason for an intervention of some kind by the EC. Such action would obviously consist of removing the impediment.

However, obstructing the proper functioning of the common market is not the only role these diverging rules of contract law (especially the mandatory ones) play. Most rules other than the general principles of freedom of contract and binding force of promises protect one party against the other in order to avoid what is perceived as injustice. Therefore, unless EC action would categorically consist of adopting the highest standard of protection, replacing national laws by European law would not only lead to a gain (enhancing the functioning of the market), but would also entail a loss (at least in the perception of those who benefit from the diverging national rule): a loss of protection for those groups of citizens who are currently protected by this diverging rule.

2. The ideological basis of contract law: autonomy and solidarity

Clearly, such a market-oriented approach to contract law which is based on an ideological choice which is closely related to classical liberal *laissez-faire* ideology,

---

[28] The idea of a third way merely begs the question: where does the third way exactly lie between the path of autonomy and the route of solidarity? There is no right answer; choices (including choices for compromises) have to be made. See the scholars mentioned in n. 1. On the future of the political distinction between the left and the right, see N. Bobbio, *Destra e sinistra; Ragioni e significati di una distinzione politica* (Rome, 1999); contrast R. Dworkin, *Sovereign Virtue: The Theory and Practice of Equality* (Cambridge, Massachusetts, London, 2000).

also has important consequences for the question of what the uniform law should look like. If the only or the main function of contract law is to facilitate efficient exchange, then the best contract law is clearly a contract law that is based on freedom of contract[29] and which places as few limits as possible on the enforceability of contracts. At best, we would need some uniform mandatory rules in order to remedy market deficiencies (especially information deficiencies), and some default rules in order to reduce transaction costs.

However, if it is accepted that contract law also performs other functions, for example, distributionist and other social functions, the picture becomes completely different. The history of contract law in the twentieth century shows that there is no reason to have such excessive confidence in the market. If the case law on contracts has demonstrated one thing, then it is that many contracting parties (not only consumers) are not 'rational agents' as most market models assume. Abundant European case law shows that players on the market frequently make decisions that do not best serve their interests, even if they have been given all the relevant information they need in order to make a 'rational' decision. Therefore, since the beginning of the last century, the courts have in many cases protected such parties. In most European countries the courts have felt the need to impose all kinds of duties and to place innumerable limits on (the exercise of) all kinds of rights. They did so frequently in the guise of mystifying doctrines like good faith and abuse of right which formally uphold the principle of freedom of contract.[30] The courts in particular have imposed many altruistic duties to take the interests of the other party into account (duties of care, duties to co-operate, duties to inform, duties of loyalty) which do not fit well in a market model which is based on self-reliance. It is important to note that most of these protective interventions were not limited to consumers and other categories of presumed weaker parties. On the contrary, in many countries they were developed in highly commercial settings, where, however, one party had ended up in serious trouble and where the courts thought it to be inappropriate under the circumstance to stick to the principles of the freedom and the binding force of contract. These court interventions are usually inspired by social interventionist and other paternalistic concerns. Thus, protection of parties that made wrong decisions, even while having all the relevant information, is a fully legitimate concern of contract law which is inspired by social-democrat and christian-democrat ideology.

A nineteenth-century code, exclusively or primarily based on the principle of

---

[29] See explicitly the Communication, n. 27.

[30] See my *De redelijkheid en billijkheid in het Europese privaatrecht* (Deventer, 1999) (n. 2), where I examine nearly a thousand cases from various European jurisdictions in which the courts 'apply the doctrine of good faith'. For a brief account in English see my 'Good Faith', in: Hartkamp *et al.* (eds.), *Towards a European Civil Code*, 2nd. edn. (Nijmegen and Den Haag/London/Boston 1998) 285 *et seq.*

party autonomy, would be wholly unacceptable from a social-democrat political perspective. It would bring us back to a *laissez-faire* conception of the economy which the courts and the legislators in all European countries successfully overcame during the course of the twentieth century. For the twenty-first century we need a Code which contains these important social achievements.[31] Today, one can no longer claim that private law is essentially based on autonomy and tuck all the so-called exceptions away in a correction device like good faith or abuse of right. A European code of general contract law should be based on both (conflicting) principles which underlie contemporary politics and private law: autonomy and solidarity.

3. 'General contract law' and regulation

For the same reason, a European code which would merely contain non-mandatory general contract law would (at least from a (moderate) left-wing perspective) itself be politically unacceptable. A European code of contracts should not merely contain rules that parties can freely deviate from (party autonomy) but also those rules which protect consumers, tenants, workers, small businesses, etcetera, which mandatorily apply to their transaction. A code which only contains general contract law without including protective regulation would seem excessively liberal and would really be of little use to most European citizens. Or, to put it in more explicitly political terms: from a left-wing perspective most of the important law (most of the political achievements in the twentieth century) would be missing. As far as protective rules of an EU origin are concerned, the third option mentioned by the EC would be a logical first step. Annex III to the Communication provides an interesting starting point. A next step might be the extension of the field of application of some of these rules.

V. FINAL REMARKS

When discussing the political agendas of the participants to the debate on the future of European contract law, I do not mean to accuse anybody of doing anything indecent. There is nothing indecent (at least in my view) in standing

---

[31]   In the same sense T. Wilhelmsson, *Social Contract Law and European Integration* (Dartmouth, Aldershot, 1995); B. Lurger, *Vertragliche Solidarität, Entwicklungschancen für das allgemeine Vertragsrecht in Österreich und in der Europäischen Union* (Baden-Baden, 1998); J.B.M. Vranken, 'Over partijautonomie, contractsvrijheid en de grondslag van gebondenheid in het verbintenissenrecht' in: J.M. Barendrecht, M.A.B. Chao-Duivis and H.A.W. Vermeulen (eds.), *Beginselen van contractenrecht: Opstellen aangeboden aan B.W.M. Nieskens-Isphording* (Deventer, 2000); C. Jamin, 'Plaidoyer pour le solidarisme contractuel', in: G. Goubeaux *et al.* (eds.), *Études offertes à Jacques Ghestin; Le contrat au début du XXIe siècle* (Paris, 2001).

up for one's own interests, values and ideologies to prevail, especially if one does so with transparency. I wanted only to point out that these interests, values and ideologies do not necessarily coincide. Rather, they are frequently diametrically opposed. In other words, the questions which are on the table are far from being politically neutral, and there are many stakeholders in the debate. Moreover, there is no 'right answer' to these questions: the future of European contract law will depend on political choices.

What choice would I make? From what I said at the beginning you will have guessed. As a European idealist I believe in some benefits from European unity, although I fully appreciate the value of plurality which, if anything, has been the main characteristic of Europe. Therefore, I would favour a European code or restatement with a sufficiently open and flexible structure in order to take all these varying interests and ideologies into account. It should provide a framework for debate, a common European language. Moreover, I would only favour European action if it would mean social progress.

Therefore, in terms of the Communication, today I would favour a combination of the second, third and fourth approaches: on the one hand a consolidated version of European regulation ('mandatory law'), especially in the field of consumer law, as a firm basis for further development of harmonised protective regulation in other fields (protection of employees, tenants, small businesses etcetera), combined, on the other hand, with a set of principles of European contract law either as a restatement or as fall-back provisions of general contract law, which apply when the parties have made another choice (in the same way as CISG), as suggested by the EC, provided that they are truly based on both (contradicting) ideas underlying contemporary contract law in Europe, i.e. autonomy and solidarity.[32]

---

[32] The PECL provide a good starting point. They are much more social than most European codes (but case law in many countries is more social). However, adding the principle of solidarity to the principle of freedom of contract in art. 1:102 PECL would be indispensable. See further M.W. Hesselink (n. 1), especially 48 *et seq.*

13. Un Code Européen des Contrats: pourquoi et comment

*Giuseppe Gandolfi**

1. La voie 'législative' telle qu'elle figure dans l'Acte qui a institué la Communauté

Le Traité de Rome de 1957 indiqua la voie que les organes communautaires doivent emprunter pour assurer l'efficience du 'marché intérieur' et en particulier pour éliminer les barrières constituées par la pluralité des droits. L'harmonisation des dispositions législatives, réglementaires et administratives des Etats membres fut prévue, devant être mise en oeuvre par le truchement de réglementations et directives. Dans le Traité fut donc choisie la voie, c'est à dire l'instrument, de la loi: il fut prévu que soient émanées des dispositions communautaires pour harmoniser, et donc modifier, les dispositions nationales.

Mais cette voie prévue par le Traité apparaît plus claire encore dans l'usage que les organes communautaires ont fait, en plus des réglementations, également des directives. J'ai parlé d'harmonisation. Le Traité mentionnait quant à lui l'expression «rapprochement». Mais comment en réalité ce concept doit être désormais compris résulte de l'application qui en a été faite au cours des décennies successives, moyennant l'émanation des directives, au terme toutefois d'un brève période d'incertitude.

Je ne veux en effet aucunement ignorer que celles-ci furent tout d'abord considérées comme un moyen apte à atteindre les objectifs prévus par le Traité en permettant aux Etats-membres de bénéficier d'une certaine marge discrétionnaire dans leur application: une marge qui devait confirmer l'indépendance et l'autonomie des Etats, évitant ainsi d'arriver à une véritable unification du droit. Il était en effet prévu que la directive n'engage l'Etat que pour ce qui concerne le résultat à atteindre, confiant à celui-ci la compétence relative à la forme et aux moyens à adopter pour son application. Et on peut également observer qu'à ce propos certaines incertitudes se manifestèrent déjà lorsque le concept de 'résultat' fut rendu en allemand par le mot *Ziel*, en lieu et place du mot *Ergebnis:* ceci conduisait à supposer qu'une compétence législative plutôt étendue avait été reconnue aux Etats. Davantage de poids eurent par la suite,

*   Professeur de droit privé et droit privé européen à l'université de Pavie, président de l'Académie des Privatistes Européens.

S. Grundmann and J. Stuyck (eds.), An Academic Green Paper on European Contract Law, 193–205
© 2002 *Kluwer Law International. Printed in Great Britain.*

en 1965, les remontrances de Maurice Couve de Murville eu égard au fait, qu'à son avis, des directives trop détaillées et précises étaient émises. Un remède fut trouvé dans l'engagement à observer l'unanimité, avec le compromis du Luxembourg. Et ce jusqu'à ce que, *re melius perpensa*, la situation évolue, à la lumière également du fameux arrêt de la Cour de Justice de 1973, selon lequel il faut considérer qu'avec le Traité de Rome les Etats-membres ont renoncé, vis-à-vis de la Communauté, bien que dans certains secteurs seulement, à leur souveraineté. C'est ainsi que le problème des directives trop détaillées sembla surmonté; aucune plainte ne fut en effet plus soulevée par les Etats, et aucune censure ne fut émise par la Cour de Justice. Se fit au contraire jour la conviction que la Communauté n'était en rien tenue à reconnaître un pouvoir de décision aux Etats pour la mise en oeuvre des directives. Il s'ensuivit la déduction que les directives, lorsqu'elles sont précises et détaillées, et ne laissent aucune marge de manœuvre – par exemple dans le sens d'aggraver certaines sanctions – doivent être mises en œuvre par ceux-ci: la procédure d'infraction en cas de défaut d'application ou de mise en oeuvre imparfaite est en effet prévue.

Donc – et ici, après ce bref *excursus* rétrospectif, je me rattache à ce que j'observais auparavant – l'application due des directives précises et détaillées comporte nécessairement non pas un simple 'rapprochement', mais bien l'uni-formité, l'unification. Et l'unification implique sans le moindre doute que les dispositions, c'est à dire les lois en vigueur dans les différents Etats déchoient, et qu'elles sont remplacées par les dispositions communautaires.

Telle est donc la voie pour assurer l'efficience du 'marché intérieur' qui fut prévue par les pactes communautaires, puis ensuite validée par leur application. Elle doit donc être empruntée pour affronter le problème de la pluralité des systèmes juridiques, sous une forme appropriée qui permette de mettre en œuvre une unification effective; et ceci – dois-je ajouter – non seulement parce que cette voie a son fondement dans les pactes communautaires, mais également en raison des avantages importants et spécifiques qu'elle offre, au-delà du fait que les autres solutions, auxquelles certains se réfèrent, ne permettraient pas de résoudre d'une manière idoine les problèmes actuels du marché intérieur.

Je ferai brièvement allusion aux inconvénients auxquels nous exposeraient les autres solutions qui sont proposées; mais cela au terme d'une nécessaire digres-sion, toujours en matière de choix de méthode comme ceux pris en compte dans la perspective de l'intégration communautaire.

2. L'hypothèse que puissent être empruntées d'autres voies, différentes de la loi

On a avancé avec autorité l'idée, toujours objet de considération, que l'harmonis-ation puisse se faire en Europe par d'autres voies, comme la jurisprudence, la doctrine, les ententes entre les organisations d'entrepreneurs. On doit sans aucun doute reconnaître l'indispensable fonction, également créative, que ces sources exercent; mais ceux qui les considèrent en mesure d'opérer aussi pour l'unification du droit, doivent admettre que les pactes communautaires n'y ont pas fait référence, optant au contraire pour l'instrument de la loi; ainsi toute dispute à cet égard doit être considérée comme purement académique et nullement actuelle.

On a également avancé l'hypothèse que la pratique mercantile, avec le concours des organisations d'entrepreneurs, puisse mettre en oeuvre une évolution convergente qui finisse par aboutir à l'harmonisation. Mais attribuer un semblable rôle aux usages mercantiles, malgré l'importance indéniable que ceux-ci revêtent dans la vie des trafics, revient à cultiver une idée illusoire. Ces usages, comme les règles basées sur l'habitude, possèdent en effet un caractère fragmentaire et sectoriel, et se révèlent globalement lacunaires. L'expérience importante du 'droit coutumier' est à cet égard significative. Lorsque Charles VII, connu comme le roi de Bourges, en disposa en 1454 le recueil officiel, il fut nécessaire de les intégrer avec de nombreux inserts, les ainsi dites interpolations tirées du droit écrit. Et le problème de l'unification du droit en France fut résolu seulement avec l'émanation du Code Napoléon. Quant aux déductions que l'on peut en tirer, il peut sans doute être utile de remarquer qu'au lendemain de la signature du traité de Rome on put constater qu'il ne prenait pas en considération l'harmonisation des usages, des différentes pratiques, des standards techniques, qui jouent pourtant un rôle significatif dans les affaires internationales; et l'on observa encore que les règlements et les directives ont comme uniques destinataires les Etats membres, ce qui n'était pas prévu pour les recommandations dans le précédent Traité CECA. Le Traité de Rome de 1957 se prononça en somme nettement pour la solution législative. Sans aucun doute ce choix fut effectué par les six Pays fondateurs de la Communauté, à savoir les Etats de l'Europe continentale appartenant à l'aire de *civil law*. Mais il fut ensuite partagé par les Pays de l'aire de *common law* avec leur adhésion successive au Traité. Et d'autre part le Royaume-Uni lui aussi, se proposant l'harmonisation des droits anglais et écossais, mit sur pied la *Law Commission* qui choisit pour la réaliser, en ce qui concerne le domaine contractuel, la voie de la loi, et précisément la rédaction d'un code.

Le Traité de Rome lui aussi – reprenant le flambeau après les nécessaires divagations intervenues – a choisi la voie de la loi pour éliminer les barrières constituées par la pluralité des droits qui empêchent l'efficience du 'marché intérieur'. Et la loi doit donc réaliser l'unification du droit des contrats, qui sont les instruments grâce auxquels se déroulent les rapports dans le marché. Mais, pour être effective, l'unification doit être réalisée par l'émanation d'un corpus de règles organique et exhaustif, c'est à dire avec un 'code européen des contrats'.

Cette voie est aussi recommandée – comme je le disais – à cause des inconvénients qui dériveraient des autres solutions qui sont parfois suggérées, et que je prends à présent en considération.

3. La proposition visant à procéder avec l'harmonisation «minimum», l'intensifiant

Certains suggèrent, la réputant la solution idoine, l'idée de poursuivre l'harmonisation (dite «minimum») actuellement en oeuvre en l'augmentant, mais en accordant pour des situations déterminées une certaine marge de manœuvre aux Etats-membres, et en consacrant une attention particulière aux contrats conclus par les consommateurs.

Il faut avant tout reconnaître, à ce propos, que l'émanation de nombreuses et importantes directives a marqué dans le secteur des contrats un progrès décisif tant sous l'aspect économique et social que technico-juridique, et certes pas seulement pour ce qui concerne les rapports dans lesquels interviennent les consommateurs. Certaines bases ont été constituées qui marqueront le futur droit privé européen.

Mais à côté de cette constatation se profile un autre et délicat problème, qui se révèle dans l'interrogation suivante: en fonction de la meilleure efficience du marché intérieur, le système des directives est-il suffisant pour affronter globalement le problème de la réalisation d'un droit européen des contrats? Il ne semble pas que l'on puisse apporter à cette interrogation une réponse affirmative si l'on tient compte des nombreuses orientations apparues dans la doctrine, où ont été prises en considération tant la nature intrinsèque que la manière dont la 'directive' a pu être employée et ensuite fonctionner. Et il faut admettre en effet que le système des directives a donné et donne lieu à divers inconvénients, et pas seulement en raison du retard dans leur application de la part des Etats-membres. Comme on a pu en effet l'observer dans la littérature traitant des directives en matière contractuelle, des inconvénients importants peuvent ressortir de leur langage, de leur contenu, de même que de leur caractère fragmentaire.

Avant tout, et pour ce qui concerne le langage: l'emploi d'expressions abstraites, en l'absence de définitions ou d'indications, peut comporter, avec la traduction dans le langage juridique propre aux différents Etats, des applications différentes de partie de celles-ci: on fait allusion dans la 'Communication de la Commission européenne' du 11 juillet 2001 aux concepts de 'dommage' et surtout de 'dommage moral'; mais que l'on songe aussi à la notion de 'bonne foi'. On pourrait multiplier à l'envi les exemples.

En deuxième lieu, et eu égard au contenu, il convient d'observer que d'importantes différences lors de l'application des directives de la part des Etats-membres peuvent découler du fait que chacune d'entre elles se base naturellement sur des présupposés conceptuels donnés, présupposés qui peuvent toutefois être absents de certains systèmes juridiques. Ceci peut entraîner alternativement le double inconvénient suivant: si les termes de la directive sont traduits littéralement, et donc reçues d'une manière quasiment inaltérée, peut naître un conflit entre les règles reçues et les divers principes de base du système juridique, avec d'évidentes difficultés dans leur coordination et leur application par le juge et surtout pour les particuliers. Si en revanche les termes de la directive sont modifiés pour les conformer aux principes de base d'un système juridique, il se produit alors une différence eu égard aux normes des autres Pays. Et il convient d'ajouter que ces inconvénients peuvent survenir plus fréquemment avec des directives particulièrement précises: leur intégration dans les systèmes juridiques des Etats peut alors parfois se révéler problématique.

En troisième lieu, et pour ce qui touche au caractère fragmentaire des direct-ives, il faut dire que celles-ci, si elles concernent la matière contractuelle, peuvent parfois mal se conformer au droit privé des Etats dont les systèmes juridiques proviennent – et c'est le cas pour la majorité d'entre eux – de structures sys-tématiques qui trouvent leur coordination dans des codifications intrinsèquement coordonnées. Mais de ce caractère fragmentaire peut parfois aussi découler un défaut de coordination entre les règles des différentes directives: ce défaut est sensible surtout si celles-ci concernent des matières analogues, ou bien des matières différentes mais qui dans la variété des relations d'affaires exigent une application conjointe. A ce propos, la susdite 'Communication de la Commission européenne' fait allusion aux directives concernant respectivement le démarchage à domicile et l'utilisation à temps partiel de biens immobiliers, et l'on remarque entre elles un conflit pour ce qui touche au droit de rétractation. On peut ajouter que des lacunes analogues ont été révélées par la doctrine dans les directives sur les contrats *à* distance (9717/CE) et sur certains aspects de la vente des biens de consommation (99/44/CE). Il s'agit du très ancien problème des 'antinomies' entre différents textes juridiques, qui se manifestaient déjà dans l'antiquité justini-enne pour le Digeste et le Code, c'est à dire pour des règles contenues dans des fragments et des lois remontant à des périodes ou à des sources différentes. Il est superflu ici de rappeler les énormes incertitudes qui en dérivèrent dans les siècles postérieurs, et quel fatras babélien d'opinions divergentes une semblable situation donna lieu. En 1518 François Ier de Valois affirma que le droit alors en vigueur en France était «un labyrinthe tortueux et obscur d'où semble exclus l'entrée du plus grand nombre de sujets et où également les hommes les plus doués se perdent». Ce fut là l'une des nombreuses, soucieuses et réitérées dénonci-ations d'une condition problématique, qui poussa la Constituante à adopter en 1791 l'unanime délibération précisant «qu'il sera fait un code de bis civil commun à tout le royaume»; douze ans plus tard était promulgué le Code Napoléon. En somme, le problème attaché au caractère fragmentaire du *Corpus iuris iustini-aneum* ne trouva sa solution définitive qu'avec les codifications du dix-neuvi-ème siècle.

Ajoutons encore ceci sur le thème du contenu: il peut arriver qu'il détermine une difformité au niveau de l'application. Par exemple: la directive sur les clauses abusives (93/13/CEE) ne considère pas comme telles les clauses qui corres-pondent *à* des dispositions nationales impératives: ainsi cette même clause peut-elle être considérée abusive dans un Etat-membre et dans un autre non. Au lieu de l'harmonisation, demeure la difformité des différents systèmes juridiques et la concurrence est alors inévitablement faussée.

Toujours en matière de clauses abusives, et à propos de la réception de la directive les concernant, l'expérience italienne apparaît symptomatique, surtout si on la confronte avec celle d'autres Etats-membres. On a discuté pour savoir s'il fallait que les dispositions soient contenues dans une loi '*ad hoc*', insérées dans la 'loi communautaire' globale, ou bien dans le code civil, et dans quel livre, puisqu'en Italie n'existe plus désormais un code du commerce. Et tout ceci non sans se demander si de semblables dispositions devaient constituer un *ius singulare* pour les consommateurs ou si elles pouvaient avoir une incidence, et de quelle manière, sur le droit commun. Cette interrogation a entraîné une réaction différente dans les divers Etats-membres eu égard au choix de leur positionnement dans les textes juridiques qui devaient les accueillir, tandis que dans l'aire de *common law* l'interprétation judiciaire a revêtu un rôle décisif. Ces divergences se traduisent – mais pas uniquement pour ce qui concerne les clauses abusives – en autant de difficultés pour l'avocat (et bien entendu pour l'homme d'affaires) qui doit s'assurer de savoir quelles sont les règles effectivement applicables et surtout si et où les dispositions de la directive pertinente ont été reçues, et comment.

Donc le système des directives communautaires jusqu'à présent suivi a sans doute tracé, dans le cadre du droit européen des contrats, d'importants parcours que la future législation européenne devra suivre. Toutefois il faut désormais considérer que, de par son caractère fragmentaire et sectoriel et les inconvénients qui peuvent en découler – toutes choses que la doctrine a relevé – ce système n'est plus à l'heure actuelle un instrument suffisant pour résoudre globalement et d'une manière adéquate le problème de la réalisation d'un droit des contrats au sein de l'Union européenne. Le temps est désormais venu qu'une telle réalisation soit mise en œuvre d'une manière globale et organique, grâce à l'instrument du «règlement».

Eu plus particulièrement égard à l'attention que l'on recommande d'avoir envers la situation des consommateurs, il convient d'observer que leur protection – conformément du reste à une tendance qui se manifeste depuis quelques décennies – est indéniablement méritoire, et pas seulement sous son aspect social. Il est certes vrai que sous leur aspect quantitatif les contrats des consommateurs constituent vraisemblablement une large majorité des contrats globalement stipulés. Mais les consommateurs se trouvent seulement d'un côté dans la dynamique du marché; ils occupent, et partiellement, le côté de la «demande»; et le marché vit de la demande et de l'offre, et se réalise à travers la production et l'échange de biens et services, surtout pour les matières premières, la production industrielle, manufacturière, etc. Et puis les consommateurs sont protégés non seulement par les règles que l'on émane en leur faveur, mais surtout en assurant la liberté de la concurrence et la pluralité de l'offre, réduisant ainsi les prix au détail. D'autre part, il est inadmissible de considérer les consommateurs comme une enclave, un groupe isolé: les dispositions qui les protègent doivent être coordonnées avec la discipline générale du contrat et se fondre avec les autres règles le concernant.

C'est en revanche dans un système juridique communiste que les consommateurs revêtent un rôle essentiel: la où en somme le code civil – comme le fut le «*Zivilgesetzbuch*», de la République démocratique allemande – est un «*Versorgungsrecht*», est un droit voué à l'approvisionnement des consommateurs car il n'y n'existe ni initiative privée, ni libre concurrence et que la production et l'offre dépendent uniquement des entreprises d'Etat. Dans l'Union européenne – mais il est oiseux de le préciser – la situation est radicalement différente. Le «Livre blanc» de la Commission européenne du mois de juin 1985 a proclamé l'exigence d'un renforcement du tissu industriel et commercial du marché intérieur. C'est donc ce problème qu'il faut affronter: assurer l'efficience du marché intérieur, garantissant l'expansion de la production et des trafics en situation de libre concurrence. Prendre en considération attentive le problème des consommateurs est juste, même plus que fondé, mais demeure insuffisant pour assurer l'efficience du marché intérieur européen.

4. L'idée de mettre en oeuvre une codification progressive

A ceux qui se prononcent en faveur d'une codification progressive, c'est à dire graduelle, il est spontané de demander à quels modes et à quels délais ils entendent se référer. Sans doute le point de vue que le Professeur Bianca a avancé dans sa contribution mérite-t-il d'être écouté, car penser aujourd'hui à une codification globale sur le droit privé pour l'aire européo-communautaire revient à mettre en avant un vague projet que l'on peut considérer pour le moment irréalisable; et ce d'autant plus si l'on tient compte du prévisible élargissement de l'Union européenne. Mais dans l'Europe des quinze aussi unifier le droit privé, qui contient le droit de la famille et des successions, est une entreprise au succès fort incertain. Que l'on songe à ce que le testament est en Italie et au contraire en Allemagne, et aux sujets qui peuvent être héritiers en Italie et en revanche en France. D'autre part les droits de la famille et des successions concernent des rapports personnels qui n'ont rien à voir avec le fonctionnement du marché intérieur européen, en vue duquel ont été conclus les pactes communautaires. Pour l'heure, pour le fonctionnement du marché intérieur, une codification de la matière des contrats et de la responsabilité extracontractuelle est nécessaire et suffisante.

On ne saurait en revanche ignorer, et celle-ci existe dans de nombreuses constitutions, que dans certaines conventions internationales, fut prévue la possibilité d'effectuer des révisions quelques années après leur entrée en fonction dans les différents Etats. Ceci se produisit, par exemple, dans la Convention de Genève de 1930 sur la lettre de change: sur demande d'au moins six Etats la Société des Nations pouvait convoquer une conférence pour y introduire des amendements. Et une récente directive (n° 44 de 1999) prévoit elle aussi un réexamen de ses dispositions quelques années après leur application afin d'y apporter des modifications ou des intégrations. Penser à une codification par degrés peut dans ce sens être considéré raisonnable. Tonte règle dans le monde occidental est considérée comme susceptible de modification à la lumière de l'expérience.

Mais il y a aussi les partisans de l'idée d'une harmonisation progressive à effectuer «par étapes», par le truchement d'une sorte de '*restatement*', et ceci en partant du repérage des dispositions communes à divers Etats-membres, pour ensuite les divulguer, dans l'intention de réaliser, sur leur base, une plus complète réglementation commune. Il s'agit cependant d'une idée stérile, qui ne saurait être partagée.

On parle fréquemment d'un *ius commune europaeum* dû à l'apport de la science juridique, qui existait jusqu'au XIXe siècle, mais qui a disparu avec les codifications nationales. Aujourd'hui, dans l'Union européenne, n'existent pas de dispositions qui soient communes à tous les Etats-membres: il y en a de communes à certains Etats mais pas à d'autres. Et ceci dès le niveau des notions fondamentales. Des exemples significatifs nous viennent en aide. Dans certains Etats le contrat est un simple accord, dans d'autres il exige une '*consideration*'; dans certains Etats il peut avoir des effets réels, dans d'autres seulement obligatoires; dans certains Etats il est interprété conformément à la volonté des sujets, dans d'autres suivant la signification littérale des mots employés; et, en cas d'inexécution, dans certains Etats le débiteur répond seulement s'il a été négligent, dans d'autres sa responsabilité est de nature objective. D'aucuns objectent tout de même qu'au moins certaines idées de base, qui sont communes, existent. Par exemple – remarque-t-on – lorsqu'un contrat est contraire à la loi il est nul et ne produit pas d'effets; et si un contractant n'exécute pas l'obligation qui lui incombe, la contrepartie peut résilier le contrat. Mais il s'agit là d'idées empiriques, inexactes ou incomplètes, car dans certains Etats le contrat nul peut produire des effets en vertu d'un traitement de régularisation, et dans d'autres non; et si un contractant n'exécute pas, il est prévu qu'il puisse, dans certains Etats, bénéficier d'une prorogation pour exécuter, et dans d'autres non. En somme, l'idée de recourir à un '*restatement*' en fonction propédeutique, en vue de l'objectif à atteindre, est donc sans conteste à refuser. Les rédacteurs de la Convention de Vienne de 1980 sur la vente internationale s'en sont rendus compte et nous ne pouvons l'ignorer: le Prof. André Tunc, qui participa à sa rédaction, en parla à plusieurs reprises, lorsqu'il fut Président de l'Académie des Privatistes Européens.

Il est en revanche indubitablement nécessaire – mais il s'agit de toute autre chose – d'opérer un examen comparatif des sources, directes et indirectes, des différents Etats en fonction de la rédaction d'un corpus de règles qui soient globalement destinées au marché intérieur européen. Et c'est ce qu'a fait et continue à faire cette Académie.

5. La suggestion d'émettre des règles 'optionnelles'

Au préjugé voulant que la discipline législative du marché intérieur ne doive pas dépendre d'une imposition venue d'en haut, mais doive constituer le résultat d'un choix conscient des destinataires des règles, est en partie due la suggestion de proposer un code des contrats seulement 'optionnel'. J'ai parlé de préjugé, parce qu'on ne saurait certes ignorer – mais il s'agit là d'une notion absolument élémentaire – que le droit est de toute manière un ensemble de règles hétéronomes, n'étant autonomes que les seuls préceptes moraux. Le fait de laisser le plus large espace possible à l'autonomie privée, limitant les normes impératives aux situations qui l'exigent réellement, constitue un tout autre problème.

Quant à l'hypothèse d'un code optionnel, on en conçoit deux différentes idées. Certains envisagent une option qui concernerait chaque Etat membre, qui pourrait accueillir ou ne pas accueillir un tel code. Il est certain que si un quelconque Etat le refuse, alors l'harmonisation ne peut se faire, et le problème demeure. D'aucuns pensent-ils peut-être qu'a été introduit de cette manière aux Etats-Unis l' «*Uniform Commercial Code*»? Il s'agit alors de faire remarquer qu'en Amérique on ne pouvait faire autrement: l'organe fédéral n'aurait pu discipliner la matière du contrat que pour les rapports inter-Etats, puisque la compétence à légiférer incombe aux Etats pour les rapports intérieurs. Et l'on notera que des conséquences négatives sont par la suite apparues, car certains Etats, sur la base de leur compétence, ont apporté des modifications, l'harmonisation venant alors à faire défaut. Ce n'est en somme pas une voie à emprunter.

D'autres pensent à la faculté concédée aux différents contractants d'accueillir ou non un tel code optionnel lorsqu'ils concluent leur contrat. Et il faut dire qu'il s'agit là encore d'une idée inadéquate, comme on peut le déduire de deux faits significatifs. Une telle faculté fut justement concédée aux particuliers du Royaume Uni pour la Convention de La Haye de 1964 sur la vente internationale. Et avec quel résultat? Aucun d'entre eux ne se prévalut d'une telle possibilité. En outre – et il s'agit là du deuxième fait significatif – un semblable système a été exclu pour son inutilité lors de la rédaction de la déjà citée Convention de Vienne de 1980.

Une solution dans un certain sens semblable, et dont on entend aussi parler, est celle d'un ensemble de principes ou de dispositions optionnelles, élaborées en doctrine, et dont l'application pourrait être suggérée aux juges ou aux arbitres lorsque les règles nationales manqueraient ou bien se révéleraient insuffisantes pour décider de la controverse. Cette solution est à déconseiller car elle comporte un risque fort grave. Divers systèmes juridiques indiquent en effet la manière de se comporter en cas de lacunes législatives: il faut recourir aux ressources offertes par l'herméneutique ou à l'analogie. L'application, donc, de ces dispositions optionnelles entraîne l'appel ou le recours et l'annulation des sentences pour violation de la loi. Et en rapport avec cette idée d'un semblable recueil de 'lignes directrices' il convient sans doute de rappeler un fait célèbre, à savoir le destin que connut un recueil analogue, le deuxième projet Cambacérès: présenté à la Convention de 1794, il ne fut pas même examiné et fut liquidé au motif que pour l'unification du droit français il fallait un code de règles contenant des solutions et certes pas une simple 'table de matière'.

6. Evaluation de quelques idées insidieuses

Je disais que militent en faveur d'un code des contrats, qui se substitue aux règles nationales, tant les inconvénients causés par les autres solutions auxquelles j'ai fait allusion que les grands avantages qu'un tel code peut offrir.

Mais avant de faire allusion aux avantages, je dois infirmer certaines idées affleurantes, d'autant plus insidieuses qu'elles sont avancées avec autorité, idées selon lesquelles un code créerait un nivellement, un aplatissement des riches cultures nationales et en bloquerait l'évolution; et que, de toute façon, l'abrogation des règles nationales d'un Pays et leur substitution par d'autres règles de matrice non nationales serait sans doute combattue, voire refusée, par les citoyens européens des différents Etats, non seulement pour les graves difficultés d'adaptation qu'elle entraînerait, mais aussi pour des motifs de dignité nationales. Pour ces raisons aussi ne serait tout au plus concevable qu'un code qui réglât les rapports transfrontaliers et non également ceux se déroulant à l'intérieur du territoire des Etats-membres; et si jamais la décision commune de lancer un code se faisait jour, sa rédaction ne pourrait se prévaloir d'un 'modèle' national; ce schéma de travail, étant nécessaire, devrait être esquissé par les rédacteurs sur la base de leur expérience actualisée et à la lumière des valeurs formant la culture juridique européenne actuelle.

En bref. Qu'un code, et plus généralement la loi, puissent paralyser l'évolution du droit est un argument rassis, qui fut déjà avancé il y a deux siècles, et qui a aujourd'hui fait son temps. Savigny surtout en fut d'abord un partisan convaincu avant de changer d'avis et de proposer en sa qualité de ministre de la justice la rédaction d'une ordonnance sur la lettre de change. Dans le monde occidental, comme on l'a observé, la succession des lois au fil du temps est un phénomène fréquent, mais l'interprétation évolutive elle-même y prend part. L'histoire du droit infirme l'idée qu'un code destiné à être commun à plusieurs peuples puisse en aplatir, en les nivelant, leurs différentes cultures, mais aussi celle voulant que la substitution des règles nationales par d'autres règles de matrice non nationale détermine de fortes réactions et créent de toute manière de grandes difficultés d'adaptation. Cette même histoire du droit nous enseigne les effets positifs de l'application à des peuples dotés de cultures fort différentes du code général autrichien pendant plus d'un siècle, et qu'en Europe l'ABGB toujours, le Code Napoléon, le BGB, le code civil italien, etc. ont été à diverses époques élargis à des citoyens d'autres nations sans pour autant créer des difficultés notables d'application.

L'idée de réglementer avec un nouveau code les seuls rapports transfrontaliers, et non ceux se déroulant à l'intérieur des Etats-membres, a fait également l'objet d'une attention particulière lors des colloques qu'a tenu l'Académie des Privatistes Européens: le collègue Dieter Medicus s'y consacra particulièrement. Mais une telle idée a été écartée, tant pour les difficultés qu'elle créerait déjà au

niveau didactique, étant donné le besoin de mettre en place un double enseigne-
ment avec les contaminations qui pourraient en dériver, que pour les incertitudes
que la phénoménologie pourrait engendrer dans l'application des diverses règles.
Et on affirme justement que ce sont de semblables risques qui ont conduit à
déconseiller une telle solution ces dernières décennies passées aux Etats Unis.

Et même l'idée – dont me fit part en son temps un collègue du Nord de
l'Europe – de rédiger un code sans adopter le moindre modèle, pas même comme
schéma de base, ne saurait être acceptée. Pour le juriste, tenir compte des
précédents, même pour s'en écarter, est indispensable. Il existe un précédent fort
significatif sur lequel il convient de réfléchir. En 1874 la première commission
chargée de la rédaction du code allemand (le futur BGB) décida de n'adopter
comme modèle ni un code en vigueur ni un projet précédent. Mais elle dut
ensuite revenir sur sa décision; et eu égard à la matière des obligations et des
contrats elle recourut au projet de Dresde remontant à 1866. Dans le cas d'un
code européen des contrats l'adoption d'un modèle apte, et j'insiste sur le mot
«apte», même sous la forme d'un simple schéma de base, se révèle également
indispensable surtout pour deux raisons: avant tout parce qu'un tel code doit
s'accorder avec les cultures juridiques européennes; et en outre parce que seule
l'adoption d'un modèle de base permet de recueillir des propositions, provenant
de juristes de différente formation et différentes cultures, propositions qui s'avèrent alors homogènes même si elles diffèrent dans leur contenu, et de les coor-
donner en vue de la rédaction des normes; autrement dit, si les rédacteurs ne
sont pas assistés dans leur tâche par une trace de base leurs propositions courent
le risque de n'être pas coordonnées entre elles et donc de ne pouvoir être
employées avec profit.

Le code italien a été choisi comme l'un des deux schémas de base, avec le
contract code de McGregor, sur suggestion de juristes parmi les plus éminents
en Europe; et ceci pour sa position médiatrice entre les expériences française
et allemande et parce qu'il est plus proche que ces derniers de l'expérience
anglaise; et ce choix a été apprécié par les juristes anglais de l'Académie des
Privatistes Européens, qui ont opté pour de nombreuses solutions contenues
dans le code italien.

7. Avantages spécifiques qu'un 'code des contrats' apporterait au marché intérieur

Et, enfin, je ferai allusion aux avantages que peut offrir un 'code européen des
contrats' qui se substitue aux dispositions nationales. Ce code élimine effectivement tous les obstacles au fonctionnement du marché intérieur relevant de la
multiplicité des droits. Les entrepreneurs et les consommateurs se sentent encour-
agés à instaurer des rapports avec des personnes ou des organismes d'autres
Etats membres, car un tel code permet de savoir avec certitude quelles sont leurs
obligations et quels sont leurs droits, et ceci permet en outre d'exclure que des
personnes sans scrupules puissent exploiter à leur profit les différences existant

entre les différents systèmes juridiques. Tant de manière préventive qu'en cas d'anormalité survenue, leurs avocats sont en mesure de les conseiller et de leur prêter assistance sachant qu'ils peuvent computer sur une certitude raisonnable du droit. Et les juges sont ainsi mis en mesure de résoudre les controverses sur la base de règles certaines et d'immédiate consultation, sans tomber dans les incertitudes qui dérivent de l'application de la Convention de Rome de 1980 portant sur le droit applicable.

Mais ceci aux conditions suivantes, conditions facilement réalisables: que le code soit traduit dans toutes les langues des Etats membre; qu'il réglemente de manière véritablement exhaustive la matière contractuelle, évitant les vides juridiques qui compromettraient l'unification et créerait de dangereuses incertitudes ou des retours fatals à l'application des droits nationaux; qu'il soit constitué de règles claires et simples qui contiennent des solutions raisonnables et acceptables dans tous les Pays de l'Union européenne, à savoir qu'il ménage un espace adéquat à l'autonomie privée avec des règles impératives uniquement pour les situations véritablement nécessaires, facilite du mieux qu'il peut la bonne fin des rapports contractuels sans rigidités et exclusions absurdes, permette l'emploi alternatif de formes et de modalités pratiquées habituellement dans les différents systèmes, favorise les compositions extrajudiciaires des controverses en évitant le plus souvent possible le recours au juge, affronte également ces problèmes vitaux dont la solution a été réclamée dans la société européenne depuis des dizaines d'années.

J'ai dit qu'il s'agit là de conditions qui peuvent facilement se réaliser puisque celles-ci, et ce n'est pas là seulement mon avis, se trouvent en effet réunies dans le projet de l'Académie des Privatistes Européens.

Mais, avant de conclure, je voudrais adresser quelques mots à tous ceux qui nourrissent des perplexités, manifestent leur scepticisme face à une innovation qui pourrait sans conteste revêtir une vaste portée.

Toutes les idées neuves, comme l'est celle d'un 'code européen des contrats', peuvent certes susciter des réserves; mais s'il s'avère nécessaire de les imposer, on ne pourra alors faire autrement que de les accueillir.

Que l'on pense à ce que dit Napoléon lorsqu'on lui fit voir l'invention de Stephenson, la locomotive; il déclara: «C'est une chose trop dangereuse; l'humanité ne pourra l'accepter». Et nous sommes en revanche arrivés jusque sur la lune! Exactement comme il y a soixante ans on considérait comme utopique une Union européenne et qu'à présent on pree de l'entrée en son sein de la Russie, et que nous avons déjà la monnaie européenne.

Il faut considérer l'avenir avec prévoyance et avec cet optimisme qui est le propre de l'homme de loi, surtout si son expérience ne s'est pas uniquement formée sur les ouvrages de doctrine, mais aussi dans les salles des tribunaux. Plus encore que pour les chercheurs, le droit est fait pour les hommes d'affaires et les consommateurs. Il faut en être conscients, et penser sur cette longueur d'onde, avec le sens du futur et du concret.

Et je conclus, me référant à ce que l'on a déclaré avec autorité à propos d'un semblable code: qu'il servirait à construire l'Europe, à renforcer son unité politique, c'est à dire à favoriser la formation d'une conscience européenne et d'une culture juridique européenne; ce serait, là encore, un important pas en avant pour le progrès socio-économique et politique de notre Europe.

14.   Why Does Europe Need a Civil Code?

*Ole Lando**

I. IS A UNIFICATION OF EUROPEAN CONTRACT LAW NEEDED? IS IT FEASIBLE?

The Union of today is an economic community. Its purpose is the free flow of goods, persons, services and capital. The idea is that the more freely and abundantly these can move across the frontiers the wealthier and happier we will get. It should therefore be made easier to conclude contracts and to calculate contract risks. Anyone doing business abroad knows that a foreign law will govern some of his contracts with foreign partners. The unknown law of the foreign countries is one of his risks. They are often difficult for him and his local lawyer to get to know and to understand. They make him feel insecure. A supplier of goods and services can only use his standard terms in his own country. He will not know how to plan his sales strategy abroad and this may keep him away from foreign markets. The electronic commerce has promoted and will to an increasing extent promote international trade and the experience already is that the different laws of contract are a problem for those who engage in that trade. Different contract laws have always been an impediment to world trade. In Europe the existing variety of contract laws is a non-tariff barrier to the inter-Union trade. It is the aim of the Union to do away with restrictions of trade within the Communities, and therefore the differences of law that restrict this trade should be abolished.

1.   The Legal Integration is Lagging Behind

In the last decades there have been some developments of what may be called EU contract law. Most important, perhaps, are the directives providing protection for the consumer as a contracting party: Directive on the Self-employed Agent of 18 Dec 1986 contains mandatory rules, most of which protect the agent. The Union legislation has provided some Europeanisation of contract

---

* Professor dr. dr. h.c. mult., Copenhagen Business School, Chairman of the Commission on European Contract Law. This contribution is a summary of articles published elsewhere, see notably: O. Lando, 'Why Codify the European Law of Contract?', ERPL (1997) 525; O. Lando, 'The Harmonization of European Contract Law through a Restatement of Principles', Oxford 1997; O. Lando, 'Some Features of the Law of Contract in the Third Millennium' (2000) 40 Scandinavian Studies in Law, 343.

S. Grundmann and J. Stuyck (eds.), An Academic Green Paper on European Contract Law, 207–213
© 2002 *Kluwer Law International. Printed in Great Britain.*

law. However, it is only a fragmentary harmonisation. It is not well co-ordinated, and, since the national laws of contract are different, it causes problems when they are to be adjusted to the various national laws. There is no uniform European law of contract to support these specific measures.

2. Is the Europeanisation of Contract Law Feasible?

Can the fifteen or more States agree on a unified contract law? European lawyers are divided by different legal methods and rules and by different legal languages. The greatest divergence is between the legal method and language of the civil law countries of the European Continent and the common law countries of the British Isles.

However, there are also similarities between the legal systems, the most striking being one of ideology and results. In spite of differences in the social, political and intellectual history of the various countries, and in spite of the fact that the law makers, be they legislators or courts, have pursued their policies through very different legal techniques we see that the legal values are basically the same. This, it is submitted, has several causes.

a) Judges have a common ideology and behaviour. The environment in which a judge was raised and now lives creates a species of mankind, the case deciding man *(homo judicans)*. Most of the guardians of our law and justice grew up in well-to-do bourgeois homes with moral traditions. In school and at university the judge *in spe* was a good and relatively virtuous student with strong ties to his home. Most judges have a strong sense of responsibility. They face people who are often in a critical situation, and they feel that they must do justice. These features may explain some of their common habits.

b) The second factor is the common roots of the laws of Europe as in other countries whose laws have a European origin. Everywhere there has been the strong impact of Roman law, Christian ethics, the great European moralists, in modern times the democratic institutions, and in Europe the unified and harmonised laws of the European Union.

Today there is a European law and it is growing. It has and will establish a considerable uniformity of legal thinking. In the rest of the world the mass and importance of harmonised or unified law is also increasing. In commercial law the flagship is the United Nations Convention on the Contract for the International Sale of Goods (hereinafter CISG). It has already had an influence on the domestic sales law of several member states. This growing mass of unified law increases the common core.

c) A third factor is the similarity of economic and social conditions in the countries of the Union, the market economy and the industrial states. Many other countries outside the Union share this similarity. In these societies the legal problems that arise are similar, as are the answers which economic consideration give to the problems. The agents of the market need safety and predictability; they also wish rules which make the conclusion of contracts swift and inexpensive.

The ideas of how the rules should be have always travelled. From early times legislators have borrowed from foreign sources, and today they do so to an increasing extent. Modern mass media make it easy for political ideas to gain ground. For instance, when some leading nations have provided protection of the consumer this idea spreads all over the world.

In the UNIDROIT Working Group which drafted the *Principles of International Commercial Contracts* and in the *Commission on European Contract Law* the participants often found the common core in the positive law. There were admittedly differences of opinion. Most of them, however, did not reflect national attitudes but rather the political attitude of the individual members, notably on how much freedom of contract the parties should have. By and large, the members of the two groups nourished the same legal values. We discovered that there was less convergence among the legal systems than consensus among us about which rules should be adopted as fair and appropriate.

The Court of Justice of the European Communities has judges from all the member countries and some of these judges have told me about a similar experience. There is often agreement about the outcome of a case, although the reasons for the decision may vary considerably. This attitude makes it likely that the courts in Europe will give a unified European contract law a uniform application.

II. IS THERE A WILL TO EUROPEANISE?

One must realise that today many lawyers in Europe do not wish a Europeanisation of contract law. Some consider the national law to be part of the nation's cultural heritage. It reflects the spirit of the people. The law of a nation is based on its entire past. The law must develop, but a people should not cut off its historical roots. They are innate in the people. The present law cannot be understood in isolation; it is tied to the past from which it has emerged. In each epoch the nation should reasonably take cognition of, rejuvenate and keep its laws fresh. What is true for the lawyers of one state may be false for the lawyers of another. The truth about contract law, they argue, is not the same for a Swede as for an Italian, for an Englishman as for a German.

To introduce a new contract law in Europe will admittedly cost sweat, tears, and money, and many lawyers will hate to see all that which they themselves have learned and practised disappear and the need to learn a new contract law. No doubt the emotional wish to preserve the peculiar character of each national law will prove to be a serious political obstacle to unification, but it is one which must be overcome if the European Union is to function satisfactorily. Contract law and commercial law is not folklore, and who today in Paris mourns for '*Les coutumes de Paris*', or in Prussia for '*Das allgemeine Landrecht für die preussischen Staaten*'?

III. HOW SHOULD THE EUROPEANISATION OF THE CONTRACT LAW BE BROUGHT ABOUT?

1. 'Creeping' or Codified European Contract Law?

Should the Europeanisation be done 'from above' so that the European Parliament or the State Legislatures enact a Civil Code? Or should it develop 'from below', the spirit of the people and the endeavours of the doctors being the engines that propels it? This question was also discussed in Germany in the early nineteenth century. In 1814 the Heidelberg professor Anton Friedrich Justus Thibaut advocated the enactment of a civil code in Germany. In the same year the Berlin professor Friedrich Carl von Savigny published a manifesto opposing Thibaut's idea and glorifying the Common Roman Law, *Das gemeine Recht*, which was then applied in most of the German States. I will hereinafter call those who wish a codification in Europe the 'Thibauts' and the antagonists of this idea the 'Savignys'. To use the names of Thibaut and Savigny for the two schools of thought is, I must admit, a poetic licence. The situation in Germany in 1814 was different from that of Europe today. However, much of the discussion in 1814 reflects current problems.

Both the Savignys and the Thibauts agree that European contract law should be harmonised or unified. The Savignys, however, imagine a common law being developed through fertile debates in the European universities, in law reviews, and in books. A European Contract Law, the Savignys say, should grow organically and slowly in the people, led by the academics. This new European law should be taught to the students who, when they become judges, will apply it in their decisions. The Savignys wish the new European law to 'creep' into the minds of the Europeans. They refer to the proud tradition of Roman Law, which spread in Europe from the time of the glossators of the eleventh century, and which reigned in Continental Europe until it was replaced by the great codifications of the nineteenth century.

There is, it should be added, agreement between the Thibauts and the Savignys on several issues. They agree on how the European Private Law should be prepared. Even if you decide to codify you must till the ground first, and the methods advocated by the Savignys may also be useful for the Thibauts.

Provided that the Principles of European Contract Law are not codified, the Savignys do not object to the drafting of principles. Like the American Restatements of the law, such as the Restatement of the Law of Contracts, they might provide solutions for national courts in cases where their own law is silent or where their law is in need of reform, and such reform may be brought about by the courts. The Court of Justice of the European Communities could consider the Principles which, when deciding issues in contract, wishes to apply a contract law common to the laws of the Member States. Furthermore, arbitrators often apply general principles of law (the *lex mercatoria*), a 'neutral' set of rules instead of national law, to international commercial disputes, and they might wish to apply the Principles. Those who, when drafting international standard form contracts for European or world use, are in need of balanced terms which consider both parties' interests, may wish to use or to refer to such principles.

The European Union has promoted a European regime of academic lawyers whose platform is no longer their own country, but Europe, and whose writings and debates are concerned with the future European law. This regime is also necessary for the Thibauts who wish a European Contract Code. They too need European Contract Law to be discussed among academics and to be taught in the classroom before and after it has been codified.

That which divides the Savignys and the Thibauts is the question whether the law should be Europeanised by way of the 'creeping' method or by codification (legislation). The Savignys prefer the 'creeping' harmonisation. They see the universities as the main platform for the debates on the future civil law of Europe. They imagine that the writings of learned scholars and Socratic seminars under the palm trees of academia will distil the *ultima ratio* and establish a European Contract Law. However, it is questionable whether the writings of the academics of a new regime and their discussions suffice to bring about a Europeanisation of contract law.

First, it will be very difficult to establish a system of simple and clear rules. A law based on academic debates tends to become complicated. It is likely that confusion will come to reign if the European doctors are given the task of establishing a European contract law. Although a regime is emerging, European lawyers are still divided by different legal languages and methods. When Roman law reigned in Europe its many and contradictory sources created a great amount of insecurity. This mess was to some extent cleared when the French Civil Code was introduced in a number of European countries. In comparison with the former law the Code was clear and succinct, forceful in its language and free from detailed digressions.

Even if the professors were to agree on the principles of a European contract law one cannot expect that the courts would adopt this law as the Savignys imagine. Today neither on the Continent nor in the British Isles can the courts free themselves of the fetters of the law laid down in the national codes, statutes or precedents. A unified law can only be applied fully by the courts of Europe if the legislator tells the courts that they must. A European Civil Code has to be prepared, passed and promulgated. It will not provide detailed rules and will therefore allow for a certain polycentrism, but there will be certainty about the main principles. Together with the practising lawyers and the judges, the doctors will work them out, but they have to be passed, either by the legislatures of the Union Countries or by the Council and the Parliament of the European Union.

But is there not a danger that when negotiated by the government delegates the future Code of obligations will become a step backward and that the result will be a host of poor compromises? Some of the EC and Union Directives are such ailing issues. However, if carefully structured and prepared by academic scholars, as was the CISG, the Code may become a great step forward. CISG was proof that governments can co-operate to make good rules. Its success seems to show that.

2, The Commission on European Contract Law

These considerations have guided the Commission on European Contract Law. Since 1982 it has been working to establish Principles of European Contract Law (hereinafter PECL). It has drafted articles which, like the American Restatements, are supplied with comments which explain the operation of the articles. In these comments there are illustrations, ultra-short cases which show how the rules are to operate in practice. There are also notes which tell of the sources of the rules. Part 1 of the Principles dealing with performance, non-performance and remedies was published in 1995. A new edition of the Principles which includes a revised version of Part 1, in addition deals with the formation, validity, interpretation and contents of contracts and the authority of an agent to bind his principal. It was published in 1999, and is hereinafter referred to as PECL I and II. In 1997 the Third Commission began to prepare rules on conditions and the effect of illegality, and rules on subjects which are common to contracts, torts and unjust enrichment, such as plurality of creditors and debtors, assignment of debts and claims, set-off, and prescription. PECL III will appear soon.

With a few exceptions, the members of the Commission of European Contract Law have been academics, but many of them are also practising lawyers. The Members have not been representatives of specific political or governmental interests, and they have all pursued the same objective, to draft the most appropriate contract rules for Europe.

The main purpose of the Principles is to serve as a first draft of a part of a European Civil Code. However, before they are enacted, and in transactions between parties where one is in the Union and the other outside the Union and between parties both of whom are outside the Union, the Principles may also be applied as part of the *lex mercatoria*.

The Principles may be compared with the American Restatement of the Law of Contract, mentioned above, which was published in its second edition in 1981. The Restatement purports to state the Common Law of contracts of the United States. In the European Union where a common law cannot be claimed to exist, a more radical process must establish the Principles. No legal system has been made the basis of the Principles. We have not based the Principles on one legal system such as Italian, French or German law. The Commission has paid attention to all of the systems of the Member States, but not every one of them has had influence on every issue dealt with. The rules of the legal systems outside the Communities have been considered. Some of the Principles reflect ideas which have not yet materialised in the law of any state. In short, on a comparative basis the Commission has tried to establish those principles which it believed to be best, having regard to the economic and social conditions in Europe.

An attempt has been made to draft short rules which are easily understood by the prospective users of the Principles, such as practising lawyers and business people. The Commission has made an effort to deal with those issues in contract which face business life of today and which may advance trade, especially international trade. However, the Principles are not intended to apply exclusively to international transactions.

3. The Future European Law of Contract May Take Several Avenues

One such avenue is a continuation of the fragmented Union legislation and continued debates between members of a growing European academia on the principles of contract law In this way an unwritten European *jus commune* may emerge. This is what the Savignys hope for. It will be somewhat diffuse and polycentric, but it may eventually straighten out some of the differences between the national laws. It will probably take a long time to achieve it, as is shown by the experience of the United Kingdom. For almost 300 years the English and the Scots have lived together in a Union. They have basically the same culture and speak the same language. A major part of their law has been unwritten. Most of the uniform law they have has been brought about by legislation, but since this legislation has not touched upon the basic principles of private law the two members of the United Kingdom still have two systems of law. The Union of today has at least 16 legal systems and 11 languages. If no legislative measure is taken, the peoples of the Union will probably continue to have different contract rules. Those who will establish a European Contract Law by way of a natural outgrowth must arm themselves with great patience.

Another avenue is a European Civil Code covering the law of contracts. This is what the Thibauts want, and, as you can guess, I am one of them. One must expect that an intensive trade will create a need for the greater amount of legal certainty which a Code will provide. World trade has grown very fast, and this brought CISG into existence. In the countries of the European Union where, since the Common Market was established in 1958, inter-Union trade has increased even more than world trade, unification of the law of contract will become more urgent the more trade and communication grow.

15. Hard Minimal Code Now – A Critique of 'Softness' and a Plea for Responsibility in the European Debate over Codification

*Ugo Mattei**

This paper advocates the immediate commencement of a genuine, pluralistic political process leading to a binding codification of European Private Law. It is a critique of what I characterize as the postmodernist 'soft' discourse of current European private law. This soft ideology stays behind proposals of 'restatement' of European law; notions of 'model' European codes; assertions of the sufficiency of European legal science as an alternative to codification; theories of competition between national legal systems as an efficient pattern of private law integration; notions of facilitating, optional 'default law' as an efficient alternative to mandatory binding legal rules. My claim is that such soft rhetoric is yet another pattern of reception of American legal categories, poorly fitting the present fabric of the European legal scenario, and yielding to a variety of political consequences that should be spelled out rather than remain implicit.

The new European Code should be hard, minimal, not limited to contracts, and process-oriented. It should aim to reflect the social fabric of European capitalism. The European codification process should look beyond the frontiers of Fortress Europe and locate itself in the global dynamic of law-making.

I. POSTMODERN CONDITION AND THE DEBATE OVER THE CODE

Postmodernism is the logic of late capitalism.[1] It is the domain of the weak, the mild, the soft, the relative, the unprincipled, the random, and the rhizome.[2] Postmodernist legal discourse gives up claims of universality, objectivity and

* The author is Alfred and Hanna Fromm Professor of International and Comparative Law at UC Hastings and is Professore Ordinario di diritto civile nell' Università di Torino. The author wishes to thank Nili Cohen, Laura Nader, Mauro Bussani, Luisa Antoniolli Deflorian and Anna di Robilant for helpful contributions in its conception and unfolding.
1   See F. Jameson, *Postmodernism: or the Cultural Logic of Late Capitalism* (1991); D. Harvey, *The Condition of Postmodernity: An Inquiry into the Origins of Cultural Change* (1990).
2   See G. Deleuze and F. Guattari, *Mille Plateaux* (1980).

monism.[3] The nation state blurs; sovereignty is decentralized; and legal propositions cannot be legitimized in terms of right or wrong. Justice becomes relative, and efficiency becomes expediency, pragmatism and strategy.[4]

In a postmodernist environment, 'avant garde' jurists have discovered pluralism.[5] They have abated hierarchy, and they have claimed that the law is the domain of professionalism, culture, and technique.[6] Jurists have finally eliminated positivism, state-centrism, and dogmatism in legal reasoning. Legal style has become a pastiche of different modes of thought – many times borrowed from experiences of different domains of knowledge or of different legal experiences.[7] Political legitimacy is the last of concerns. If legal reasoning is a technique of argumentation, a battle of hired weapons, there is no space for the myth of political representation. People no longer believe that the law is the will of the community as expressed by the political process. Such mode of thinking has characterized American legal thought from the last decade of the twentieth century,[8] and it has, in due course, been received in Europe.[9]

A strong, dominant position of legal scholarship among the sources of law has been the background in which, at least on the Continent, postmodernist legal discourse has been received.[10] The domain of the law has long been the domain of jurists in Europe, an elite of sophisticated intellectuals, traditionally legitimized by knowledge and scholarship.[11] Too high is the degree of complexity of the postmodernist market place to be understood, let alone regulated, by politicians. Let politicians be busy with dismantling the welfare state, deciding immigration policies, and negotiating tariffs and quotas. Let them deal with the problems arising from the unification of the currency and the issue of European defence. Let them deal with the enlargement. Let them keep their hands off private law. They can do no good in this area.[12]

---

[3]   See U. Mattei and A. di Robilant, 'The Art and Science of Critical Scholarship: Postmodernism and International Style in the Legal Architecture of Europe', (2001) 75 *Tulane L. Rev.*

[4]   See N. Mercuro and S.G. Medema, *Economics and the Law: From Posner to Postmodernism* (1997); see also R. Posner, *Frontiers of Legal Theory* (2001).

[5]   Pluralism, in the European context is fully accounted for by M. Bussani, '"Integrative" Comparative Law Enterprises and the Inner Stratification of Legal Systems', (2000) 8 *ERPL*, 85.

[6]   See G. Teubner, *Law as an Authopoietic System* (1993).

[7]   See G. Minda, *Postmodern Legal Movements* (1995).

[8]   See Feldman, *American Legal Thought from Premodernism to Postmodernism* (2000).

[9]   See M.W. Hesselink, *The New European Legal Culture* (2001).

[10] Mattei and di Robilant, n. 4.

[11] See A. Gambaro, 'Western Legal Tradition', in P. Newman (ed.), *The New Palgrave: A Dictionary of Economics and the Law* (1998).

[12] See R. Zimmermann, 'Civil Code and Civil Law. The 'Europeanization' of Private Law within the European Community and the Re-Emergence of a European Legal Science', (1995) 1 *CJEL*, 63.

II. THE WHETHER AND THE HOW IN EUROPEAN PRIVATE LAW

The issue of the new European Private Law has been unfolding in three phases. The first, beginning in the early 1980s, dealt with the *whether*: is there such a thing as European private law? The answer is found in the facts. Legislative, judicial and scholarly development at the European level has characterized even the core areas of private law. Resistance from more conservative, domestic lawyers has been ineffective – at least at the theoretical level. Consent on the *existence* of a subject matter called European private law is now practically unanimous.[13]

European private lawyers have also been remarkably quick in reaching consent on claiming a professional monopoly on the construction of the legal framework of the market. The academic jihad against Brussels bureaucrats, launched early in the 1990s, has also been successful. The Europeanisation of private law has to be seen as a professional project.[14]

Naturally, some divisions were bound to happen when it comes to the question of who are the members of the professional groups involved in the project. The question was never really on the table for an open discussion, but we can easily see a couple of opposite trends. We could name such trends as *the elitists* against *the democrats*. Both the elitists and the democrats share English as a sort of lingua franca, despite the attempts, particularly on the German side, to maintain some presence of the language.[15] The fact that the debate on European private law is happening mostly in English has dramatically changed the hierarchies of academic prestige.

Those active in the European private law movement tend to be a younger generation of academics who are fluent in English and are neither the mainstream comparativists nor the leading scholars within the national legal systems. Of course, there are exceptions, but this sociological shaking seems to be quite clear. Within this sociological background, nevertheless, there are major differences. 'Elitists' tends to refer to self-selected small groups of well-connected and known scholars that, as a consequence, tend to be male members of the leading European jurisdictions, grounding their prestige on a more or less open claim

---

[13] See, among many, the essays in M. Bussani and U. Mattei (eds.), *Making European Law: Essays on the Common Core Project* (2001).

[14] See, for example, R. Zimmermann, n. 13. See H. Kotz, 'A Common Private Law for Europe: Perspectives for the Reform of European Legal Education', in: B. De Witte and C. Forder (eds.), *The Common Law of Europe and the Future of Legal Education* (1992).

[15] One scholarly periodical expressly devoted to European Private Law, *Zeup*, is published mostly in German. There are also two Italian periodicals *Europa e Diritto Privato* and *Contratto e Impresa Europa* that are expressly devoted to the subject matter. Neither *Zeup* nor these Italian journals, however, significantly overcome local readership or specialized circles.

of law as science.[16] More democratic projects tend to involve a younger generation of academics, with more equal gender and jurisdiction-based constituency. 'Democrats' are usually more open in the political nature of the projects in which they find themselves involved and, in particular, more open to the idea that some dialogue with the European legislator is unavoidable.[17]

The second phase of the ongoing project of Europeanisation has been much more divisive. Let us call it the phase of the *how*: how should the community of European private lawyers (however selected) use its monopoly?

The divisions on the issue of the *how* have been polarized around a few basic questions. Should European private law be codified?[18] Should it be restated? Should it be left to legal science within a revival known as *usus hodiernus pandectarum*?[19] Should it be developed around some 'core' special statutes such as those guaranteeing consumers' protection? Should there be attempts to bridge the distinction between common law and civil law by efforts of harmonisation, or should this 'cultural' difference be preserved?[20] Should such legislation be in the nature of directives (letting leeway to state jurisdictions into the domain of implementation), or should it be in the nature of directly binding regulation?[21]

---

[16] See, for example, H. Kotz, 'Comparative Legal Research and its Function in the Development of Harmonized Law: The European Perspective', in: *De Lege, Towards Universal Law* (Uppsala, 1995). An interesting discussion of the roots of such approach with particular attention to the legacy of E. Rabel can be found in D. Gerber, 'Sculpting the agenda of Comparative Law. Ernst Rabel and the Façade of Language', in: A. Riles (ed.), *Rethinking the Masters of Comparative Law* (2001). Leading elitist projects is the so called Lando Commission. See O. Lando and H. Beale (eds.), *Principles of European Contract Law*, Parts I and II, (2000). For a discussion see M. Hesselink, 'The Principles of European Contract Law. Some Choices made by the Lando Commission', in (2001) 1 *Global Jurist Frontiers*, at www.bepress.com.

[17] See for more detail U. Mattei, 'The Issue of European Codification and Legal Scholarship. Biases, Strategies and Perspectives' (1998) 21 *Hastings Int'l & Comp. Law Rev.* 883; see also D. Caruso, 'The Missing View of the Cathedral: The Private Law Paradigm of European Legal Integration', (1997) 3 *ELJ*, 3; C. Joerges and O. Gernstenberg, *Private Governance, Democratic Constitutionalism and Supranationalism* (1998). A Democratic Project is, in the intention of its editors, the Common Core of European Private Law. See M. Bussani and U. Mattei, 'The Common Core Approach to European Private Law', (1997) 3 *CJEL*, 339.

[18] See M.J. Bonell, 'The Need and Possibilities of a Codified European Contract Law', (1997) 5 *ERPL*, 505; B. Markesinis, 'Why a Code is Not the Best Way to Advance the Cause of European Unity', (1997) 5 *ERPL*, 519.

[19] See R. Zimmermann, *Roman Law, Contemporary Law, European Law. The Civilian Tradition Today* (2001).

[20] See for example, H. Collins, 'European Private Law and the Cultural Identity of States', (1995) 3 *ERPL*, 353.

[21] See, for recent collection of essays, M. Van Hoecke and F. Ost, *The Harmonization of European Private Law* (2000); V. Heiskanen and K. Kulovesi, *Function and Future of European Law* (1999).

Should codification be comprehensive or piecemeal?[22] In this paper, I will not directly approach any of such questions, but will only tackle those that are directly connected with my subject matter, i.e. codification.[23]

As early as 1989, when the Strasbourg Parliament, the only democratically representative institution of the European Union, for the first time recommended action in the domain of civil codification, the scholarly reaction has been luke-warm. Such attitude is shared today by a variety of scholars, who have expressed severe critiques to the recent, quite detailed discussion of the subject matter offered by the Direction General 24.[24] Some have suspected an attempt by the 'Brussels bureaucrats' to claim an even larger role in the making of private law. Others have dismissed the recommendations as the action of a weak political actor, not to be taken too seriously. Yet others have denied that the EU would have any jurisdiction on a civil code.[25]

True, some proposals have been advanced by self-appointed groups of scholars, and some of this activity (such as that of the Lando Commission) has indeed been successful in seizing the stage of European private law. Nevertheless, perhaps because of a more rooted positivistic imprint in European legal scholar-ship, the issue of legitimacy quickly arose and even such self-appointed groups, lacking any political legitimisation whatsoever, have made it clear that their product had little in common with the traditional idea of codification.[26]

The traditional idea of codification, which is the product of nineteenth-century modernist *grand style* and is supported by a transcendent idea of sovereignty vested in the State, is a comprehensive, territorial, systematic body of private law rules claming quasi-constitutional status in the edification of the bourgeois legal order.[27] Codes are to be applied and enforced by other, subordinate institutions of the legal order.[28]

---

22 See T. Wilhelmsson, 'Private Law in the EU: Harmonised or Fragmented Europeanisation?', *ERPL* (2002) forthcoming.

23 A variety of views can also be found in A.S. Hartkamp and others, *Towards a European Civil Code* (2nd edn., 1998).

24 Between the more articulate critiques one should remember those expressed by H. Collins at the Recent Leuven Conference (30 Nov., 2001) organized by the Society for European Contract Law. Of this author is worth reading at least H. Collins, 'Formalism and Efficiency: Designing European Commercial Contract Law', in (2000) *ERPL*, 211.

25 For a discussion thoroughly referring to the literature of many countries, see O. Remien, 'Denationalisierung des Privatsrechts in der Europaishen Union? Legislative und Gerichtliche Wege', 35 *Zeitschrift fur Rechtsvergleichung* (1995), 119 *et seq.*

26 See for example O. Lando and H. Beale, 'Principles of European Contract Law', n. 17. See also, for the views of another of such groups, G. Gandolfi, 'Pour un Code Européen des contrats', *RTD Civ.* [1991], 707. The first significant results of the Pavia Group are set out in G. Gandolfi (ed.), *Code Europeen des Contrats – Avant Project* (2001).

27 See J.L. Halperin, *Histoire du droit privé francais depuis 1804* (1996).

28 See A. Gambaro, 'Codice Civile', in: *Digesto IV Discipline Privatistiche Civile* (1988).

Present day codification proposals are much more cautious and less ambitious.[29] They are limited in scope, as today we are reduced to discussing whether contract law should be codified.[30] They are presented – borrowing from US style even in such a traditionally civilian area of expertise – as 'model codes' or 'restatements'. Notions such as 'soft law', 'creeping codification', 'open texture', and 'bottom up' are used.[31] Such proposals are to be, 'interpreted', 'discussed', 'considered', and 'harmonized' by a variety of other *sources of law*.[32]

III. SURRENDER TO THE ACTORS OF MARKET GLOBALISATION?

What is behind such paradigm shift? In this paper, I claim that what we are witnessing is a real change in the relationship between the law and the market. The soft cultural attitude, typical of postmodernist scepticism, irony and loss of faith, is functional to a new legal and economic order in which the market governs the law rather than the other way round.[33] European private lawyers, in a mood of revolt against the positivistic attitude of state-centric twentieth-century positivism, have thrown away the baby with the bathwater. They have failed to seize the tremendous opportunity of renovation and critique stemming from the codification of private law at the European level.[34]

What is going on is the European counterpart of what anthropologist Laura Nader, linguist Noam Chomsky and other critical thinkers have significantly portrayed as an anti-law movement unfolding in present day American Law.[35] It is the final assault of Empire on all such institutions of the nation state that do not fit its profile of economic hegemony and global corporate governance.[36]

---

[29] See V. Zeno-Zencovich, '"The European Civil Code", European Legal Traditions and Neo Positivism', in: G. Alpa and N. Bucicco, (eds.), *Il codice civile europeo: Materiali dei seminari* (2001), 375 *et seq.*

[30] See W. Van Gerven, 'L'harmonization du droit des contrats en Europe: Rapport introductif', in: C. Jamin and D. Mazeaud (eds.), *L'harmonization du droit des contrats en Europe* (2001).

[31] See C.U. Schmid, '"Bottom Up" Harmonization of European Private Law: Ius Commune and Restatement', in: *Function and Future of European Law* (n. 22).

[32] See for example K.P. Berger, *The Creeping Codification of the Lex Mercatoria* (1997); A. Chamboredon, 'The Debate on A European Civil Code, For an Open Texture' in: *The Harmonization of European Private Law* (n. 22).

[33] See A. Stephanson, *Manifest Destiny. American Expansionism and the Empire of Right* (1995); S. Sassen, *Losing Control? Sovereignty in the Age of Globalization* (1996).

[34] See for the most blunt critique of codification rooted in such postmodernist mood, P. Legrand, 'Against a European Civil Code', (1997) 60 *MLR* 44.

[35] See L. Nader, *Law in Motion. Anthropological Projects* (2002), forthcoming; N. Chomsky, *Rough States* (2001).

[36] The idea of Globalization as Empire has been advanced by M. Hardt and A. Negri, *Empire* (2000). The competing but complementary one, that of globalization as Americanization is interestingly discussed in S. Strange, *The Retreat of the State* (1996).

Scholars have detected this phenomenon in a variety of areas of US law, such as the so-called tort law reform, by which powerful corporate defendants try to emasculate the plaintiff's bar for fear of class actions and punitive damages. The shift towards compulsory ADR and the tremendous pressure to settle aims at silencing victims of abuse in the workplace or in the family. An episode of oppression by means of 'harmony ideology' then offers another important example.[37] More generally a similar trend is visible in the creation of a strong and prestigious conservative scholarly critique of the politically legitimate sources of law within the US legal academy. Such critique, in order to show the efficiency of the common law process, has accused legislatures of being captured by lobby money.[38] This idea is orthodoxy in those US law and economics circles that have been able to gain major influence in framing the international financial institutions' development plans for the Third World. In Europe, the conservative notion that European contract law should serve efficiency because of its value-neutral and technical content, and that the Code in this perspective should only be facilitative rather than binding, is now gaining acceptance.[39] Such attitude that considers 'legal science' as neutral and insulated from capture is similar to the classic law and economics attitude that considers the 'common law process' similarly insulated. But such idea is no more robust (or less arbitrary) in the old continent than it is in the US. The high degree of insulation of US courts of law that should shield them from any risk of capture is only accepted as an article of faith by mainstream American legal culture (the prestige of art. 3 of the US Constitution is tremendous). There is no empirical testing whatsoever of the effectiveness of the insulation devices provided by article 3 of the US Constitution for the members of the Federal judiciary (tenure of office and guaranteed salary). Moreover, some scholars who certainly cannot be considered radicals, are now beginning to question the neutrality and technocracy of private legislatures and independent authorities. The day in which we realize that outright corruption is not the only danger in the present complex political setting, we will end up questioning the bias in favour of the common law process developed in American scholarship.[40] Similarly, the 'neutrality' of the new European private law scholars

---

37 See L. Nader, *Law in Motion* (n. 36). On the notion of Harmony Ideology as a controlling process see L. Nader, *Harmony Ideology* (1990).

38 See for a critical discussion of the politically conservative background of law and economics D. Kennedy, 'Law and Economics from the Perspective of Critical Legal Studies', in: P. Newman (ed.), *The New Palgrave. A Dictionary of Economics and the Law* (1998).

39 Such position is taken by a variety of scholars. At the Leuven Conference it was taken by C. Kirchner, R. Van Den Bergh and H.Collins. But such normative use of a biased version of law and economics is even more dangerous in the European legal landscape than in the US. See D. Kennedy, 'The Political Stakes' in: '"Merely Technical" Issues of Contract Law', *ERPL* [2002].

40 See, for example, A. Schwartz and E.R. Scott, 'The Political Economy of Private Legislatures', (1995) 143 *University of Pennsylvania Law Review*, 595.

as builders of (soft and technical) codification proposals should at least be questioned rather than being taken for granted, mirroring in front of the traditionally most prestigious between the civilian 'oracles of the law' the same idolatry that in the US is granted to the judiciary.[41]

In this cultural context, one might wonder if the strong emphasis of private law default rules being efficient as proxies of what parties would have agreed upon is not itself, proposed by conservative law and economics scholars, yet another strategy to justify and grant legitimation to rapacious and self-serving corporate behaviour.[42] Indeed, the idea of default law, *ius dispositivum* as we know it in the civil law tradition, is at the very root of the recent but already well-established notion that in Europe civil codification, in one way or another, should be soft. It is, however, important to stress that parties should be left free to make their options only once the legal system has been able to establish, by binding and effective law, its control against opportunistic behaviour.[43] Soft law is not at all fit for this purpose. As postmodernism and extreme relativism, it only fits the logic of Empire.

In other words, the legal scholar who resists giving up his or her critical function in the face of any proposal of soft law should ask a fundamental, perhaps naïve question. Soft for who? If the law is soft with aggressive and opportunistic market actors who, under the shield of soft legality, succeed in transferring costs to society rather than facing the real social cost of their market activity, it is much better to have it hard.

IV. SOFT RHETORIC FOR HARD PRACTICES

Soft law is often advertised as more efficient because it respects the differences in preferences of market actors. Similar arguments are voiced by many of such scholars who use American-inspired ideas of competition between legal systems as arguments against the codification of private law at the European level.[44] Indeed, cultural relativism fosters this ideology because incorrect default law can still be changed by making a deal; whereas incorrect hard law introduces negative and incurable incentives.[45] If it is impossible to make any prediction in terms of

---

[41] This faith on the value of a 'scientific' Code is behind the Von Bar project, which is rumoured to be reflected in the last and very recent European Parliament position on the issue. See the contribution of Ch. Von Bar in this volume.

[42] I discuss the issue of default rules in U. Mattei, 'Efficiency and Equal Protection in the New European Contract Law. Mandatory, Default and Enforcement Rules', (1999) 39 *Virginia J. Int. Law*, 537.

[43] See R. Cooter and T. Ulen, *Law & Economics* (3rd edn., 2000) I discuss the issue in U. Mattei (n. 43).

[44] At the Leuven conference, this approach has been defended in the contribution by long-time President of the European Law and Economics Association, R. Van Den Bergh.

[45] See R. Cooter and T. Ulen (n. 43).

right and wrong, then it is better to proceed tentatively, leaving ground for corrections. Similar concerns are behind favouring standards on rules, favouring Directives on Regulation, and favouring restatements over codification, because the normative language of even a Model Code makes it harder than the 'merely descriptive' suggestions contained in a Restatement.[46] Scholars from a variety of perspectives have demonstrated that the Restatement is by no means a merely descriptive exercise (even assuming the possibility of such distinction between fact and value in the law).[47] It is consequently unacceptable that such a claim of neutrality is maintained in Europe in front of a legal scenario in which we simply do not know yet how to answer the fundamental question 'Is there a European private law to restate?'.[48]

Similarly, talking about creeping codification is also a soft strategy, because it conveys an idea of factual condition of the being (a sort of evolutionary necessity), and not of outright choice, as in the case of a codification project.[49] It is as if the present state of the European legal landscape in the domain of private law, were not the aggregate of a number of political choices determined by a clear hegemony of the German legal community within the Brussels political process. Rather, the relationship of power that determines the unfolding of the law is 'neutralized' and the outcome can only, naturally, be today's status quo of soft contract law. Such naturalization of the political process has to be denounced as a conservative strategy because it hides the power relationship behind it.[50] Similarly, talking about 'harmonization' of law transmits a signal of tolerance for diversity that is absent in the notion of 'unification'. It is, however, almost too easy to show that harmony is itself an ideology very soft only as a façade.[51] Indeed, it is very hard with the weak side of the power relationship (in this case less-prestigious European legal systems) and it does not openly face the responsibility stemming from choices.

The truth of the matter is, however, that social conflicts such as those happening in the distribution of cooperative surplus, or in deciding the of shares of

---

[46] See the classic A. Rosett, 'Unification, Harmonization, Restatement, Codification, and reform in International Commercial Law', (1992) 40 *Am J. Comp. Law* 683.

[47] I devote to this issue some thoughts in U. Mattei, 'Fatto e valore. Il paradosso ermeneutico dell'analisi economica del diritto', in: J. Derida and G.Vattimo (eds.), *Diritto, giustizia e interpretazione* (Coord. M. Bussani, 1998).

[48] It is even doubtful if such a question could be posed at all even when long-range efforts such as the Trento 'Common Core Project' will be completed. For a critical discussion see D. Kennedy, 'The Politics and Methods of Comparative Law', in: M. Bussani and U. Mattei, *Making European Law. Essays on the Common Core Project* (2nd edn., 2002), forthcoming.

[49] See Berger (n. 32).

[50] See L. Nader (n. 35).

[51] See L. Nader (n. 35).

common resources, are mediated and solved by institutions.[52] Such institutions might take the shape of formal or informal law attempting to create rules for the market (e.g. rules fostering fair market practices), or might simply take the shape of the market buying out the law. What is not covered and determined by law is covered and determined by market forces that, by definition, either are regulated (of course we are talking here of private law regulation) or are left rough. Consequently, strong market actors naturally prefer soft law because in the absence of any regulatory force by the legal system, they are able to make the rules of the very same game in which they are playing.[53]

The critical observer should not be fooled by the appealing and delicate nature of soft arguments: respectful of differences, aware of cultural specificities, concerned with gaining efficiency from flexibility, and refusing the arrogance of decision making in the name of cultural relativism.[54] This is exactly the postmodern logic serving corporate rapacity.[55]

It is easy to observe the change of rhetoric in present day US political discourse, which is the intellectual humus in which cultural models for present days European debates originate. 'No smoking!' becomes 'Thank you for not smoking'; 'please do not disturb'! becomes 'privacy please'! 'Go away'! becomes 'you are kindly invited to leave', and so on. Orders become invitations. The clear-cut assumption of leadership and responsibility, with an active and a passive subject, takes the façade of a cooperative game. There is nothing soft in this change of rhetoric except the rhetoric itself. Smokers cannot decline to be kind enough not to smoke in all public buildings. Harsh fines are still enforced. Minimum wage workers in large five-star hotel chains are still fired if a client complains about having been disturbed in his privacy. If 'asked to leave' a public or private facility because your behaviour does not conform with the rules set by the management and you decline to do so, they will still call the police whose handcuffs are not soft.

Law, as well as language, can present itself in a large variety of semantic clothing. There is not much soft in its nature, nevertheless, because there is not much that is soft in the economic transactions and in the power relationship that connects individuals to each other in the market place. In a sort of zero sum game, at least one institutional setting is to be hard. Either the law is hard keeping economic transactions under control (and potentially making them soft), or the economic relationship is hard and keeps soft law under its thumb, determining its form as well as its substance.[56] Adapting Althusser's intuition,

---

[52]   See D. North, *Institutions Institutional Change and Economic Performance* (1991).

[53]   Such analysis stems from basic public choice theory. See for an accessible and critical discussion, Mercuro and Medema (n. 5).

[54]   See for a collection of such attitudes P. Legrand, *Fragments of Law as Culture* (1999).

[55]   See M. Hardt and A. Negri (n. 36); L. Nader (n. 35).

[56]   See, with emphasis on ideology, D. North, *Structure and Change in Economic History* (1982).

either the law is a coactive apparatus of the state, that arguably might even sometimes serve the interests of the weak, or (dressing soft clothing) it is a coactive apparatus of the global market, stronger and harsher even than Leviathan. In this case, however, the only interest it can serve is certainly that of the stronger.[57]

If this is the scenario, any discussion about the 'how' of making private law European has to keep it in mind. Soft metaphors hide harsh power relationships. The stakes need to be clear; the cards need to be on the table. Postmodernist irony should not hide the truth. As social historian Barrington Moore once said:

> 'In any society the dominant groups are the ones with the most to hide about the way society works. Very often, therefore, truthful analyses are bound to have a critical ring, to seem like exposures rather than objective statements. ... For all students of human society sympathy for the victims of historical processes and scepticism about the victor's claim provide essential safeguards against being taken in by the dominant mythology. A scholar who tries to be objective needs these feelings as part of his working equipment.'[58]

V. IN DEFENCE OF HARD LAW AS A EUROPEAN NECESSITY

In order to be successful, legal institutions competing with strong economic actors need to be strong and highly effective. The stronger the actors, the stronger the institutions must be if individual selfishness and interest is to be channelled for the welfare of everybody.[59] The rhetoric about the efficiency of soft law has to be exposed in order to achieve informed guesses on what the impact of the Europeanisation of private law carried on by alternative means is going to be.[60] I submit that emphasis on softness in the making of European private law is likely to mean lawlessness and a free battleground for exploitative business interests.

Someone has suggested, in one of the few thoroughly insightful papers on European codification, that the United States model should be kept present.[61] To be sure, because soft law is an American metaphor, we need to place it in context. Scholars have trained us to understand that transplants of legal institutions, formal or informal, are not like exports of commodities.[62] Both the context

---

[57] See L. Althusser, *Sur la reproduction* (1995).

[58] B. Moore, *Social Origins of Dictatorship and Democracy: Lord and Peasant in the Making of the Modern World* (1966) 523.

[59] See C.L. Schultze, *The Public Use of Private Interest* (1977).

[60] Such predictive function is crucial to the comparative legal and economic analysis, see U. Mattei and A. Monti, 'Comparative Law and Economics. Borrowing and Resistance', (2001) 1 *Global Jurist Frontiers* 2 at www.bepress.com.

[61] M. Reimann, xxxx *Tulane Law Rev.* xx.

[62] See, for example, E. Grande, *Imitazione e diritto. Ipotesi sulla circolazione dei modelli* (2001); see also, in our context A. Watson 'Legal Transplants and European Private Law', (2000) 4.4 *Electronic Journal Of Comparative Law*, at http://law.kub.nl/ejcl/44/44-2.html.

of reception and that of origin are highly relevant in order to make a prediction on what is likely to happen. Present day European context cannot be more different that the context of US law, where Restatements and Model Codes were suggested and developed as soft law alternatives to hard law from the 1930s of the past century.[63] The United States of the twentieth century was indeed the institutional system with the strongest judiciary that has ever been produced in the history of humankind – strongest not only in terms of power, but also of prestige. Restatements were suggesting rules to this kind of judiciary – a professional group of people given so-called inherent power to pursue public policy in the solution of individual conflicts. The decisions of the US judiciary, reinforced by *stare decisis*, have never been perceived as soft.[64] The American judiciary's role in the process of making the general rules of the game has always proved stronger than the role of legislators. Statutory law, in fact, could never do much more than suggest piecemeal changes.[65] As to the Model Codes, the dialogue was only apparently with State legislatures that were free to maintain or modify them. Indeed, the dialogue was still with these courts, whether state or federal did not matter, given the substantial cultural uniformity of US law. Strong institutional actors and scholars were trying to 'persuade' by using a normative semantic level like that of the UCC or the Model Penal Code.[66] It is no surprise that such famous examples of soft legislation are deeply connected with two individual scholars, Professors Llewellyn and Wechsler, respectively. In other words, soft law in the US never undermined, either rhetorically or in substance, the really strong actors of the legal system who are the legitimated forces of control of the public sphere on the economic behaviour of market actors.[67] Nor could default law, as free choice of contractual rules, dangerously affect the principle that courts are still in charge. When they wish to do so, courts have full inherent equitable power to control, amend, and modify even the most clearly expressed choice of the parties. They have the power to do so, both in the interest of one of the parties to the contract or of third parties.[68]

In Europe, such a background scenario of strong self-legitimized institutional actors with inherent powers to channel individual economic self interest in

---

[63] See, for the classic discussion, G. Gilmore, *The Ages of American Law* (1977).

[64] See, for a classic discussion H.M. Hart and A.M. Saks, *The Legal Process* (1994).

[65] See, from the early ages, J.N. Pomeroy, 'The True Method of Interpreting the Civil Code', (1884) 4 *West Coast Rep* 585; see also, for more of a recent account, G. Calabresi, *A Common Law for the Age of Statutes* (1982).

[66] On the first, W. Twining, *Karl Llewellyn and the Realist Movement* (1973); on the last, E. Grande, 'Comparazione dinamica e sistema giuridico statunitense: analisi di una circolazione incrociata di modelli', (2001) 29 *Quaderni Fiorentini*, 173 *et seq.*

[67] See, for a discussion of the use of such power by US courts, D. Kennedy, *A Critique of Adjudication* (1997).

[68] See M. Trebilcock, *The Limits of Freedom of Contract* (1993).

directions compatible with the public welfare is simply absent.[69] National courts of law have never performed that function in the civilian continent. True, Europe is not only the civilian continent, but the sensitivity of British courts with public policy issues has always been much weaker than in the US. Moreover, the issue of uniformity makes the European institutional scenario even weaker and potentially carefree for large transnational business interests than does that of the US. In Europe, in the absence of a European judiciary both formally (there are no European Courts of general jurisdiction) and culturally (national judiciaries are not uniform, either sociologically or culturally), there are simply not any institutional actors capable of monitoring the everyday bread and butter economic abusive behaviour. A soft Europeanisation of private law lowers responsibility for national legal systems, persuaded, as they are, of the existence of another level of the legal system 'better located', according to subsidiary discourse, to monitor global transactions.[70] The softness discourse at the European level undermines the prestige of national civil codes that are considered obsolete and out of fashion exactly because they are hard.[71] However, such national civil codes are the only source of principled legitimacy of judicial power in present day Europe. Thus their cultural undermining is a blank cheque to corporate rapacity.

Put simply, given the available institutional background, a hard European civil Code seems a prerequisite for the development of an effective set of rules of the game capable to keep economic activity under control. A *balcanized* system of private law allows the kind of forum shopping that makes large global market actors irresponsible of the social costs that they produce. To be sure, I am not arguing here that a hard code would be all that is needed for an effective European system of private law. Elsewhere, I argued, in papers devoted to contract law and trust law respectively,[72] that a system of European courts of general jurisdiction is also a necessity at this point. Nevertheless I believe that given the European legal path such a code would be a necessary if not sufficient condition to make Europe a genuine legal system capable of controlling the behaviour of international corporate capital. Such institutional effectiveness is in turn necessary for Europe to effectively compete with the United States in the international legal arena.[73]

Is this a nostalgic and backwards-looking idea? Is it a return to old-fashioned

---

[69] See materials in H. Jacob, E. Blankenburg, H. Kritzer, D.M. Provine and J. Sanders, *Courts Law and Politics in Comparative Perspective* (1996).

[70] See, in general, L. Antoniolli-Deflorian, *La struttura istituzionale del nuovo diritto privato europeo* (1996).

[71] See examples in the papers by Samuel and Chamboredon (n. 33).

[72] See U. Mattei (n. 43); U. Mattei, 'Basic Issues of Private Law codification in Europe: Trust', 1 *Global Jurist Frontiers*, 1 at www.bepress.com.

[73] See Bordieau, xxxx.

positivism? I believe that it is neither, but rather that it is only the realistic taking into account that Europe and the United States have travelled different paths in the law. If there is a desire to merge the path, moving European institutions strait in the American shadow, this shift away from the European structure of legitimacy should be part of a conscious political choice. It should not happen as some creeping phenomenon, presented as a technically more advanced step in the development of private law.

VI. THE ISSUE OF CONTENTS: *WHAT'S IN* THE CODE?

European capitalism has been characterized by a much more social flavour than its US counterpart.[74] Whether the hard European Code will be an old-fashioned replica of previous codifications will depend on the content of the Code: the third phase – that of the *what's in* – of European private law. I submit that the new European Code should be able to capture and reflect in the rules of the game it sets forward, some of the values of the European social model of capitalism. If capable of doing so, it might impose itself as a model capable of competing with US hegemony. By helping to do so, European scholarship might interrupt the trend of Europe being reduced to yet another province of US-led corporate Empire.[75]

As to this last point, I will pose here only a few questions for discussion, some of the preliminary issues that the scholarly debate should clarify to make political choices possible. Institutions, and consequently codes as institutions, should serve a purpose. Proposed reforms and changes should create advantages and benefits for the community they serve. The first question to pose is, consequently, whose interests does the European private law system have to serve? Is the European civil code only to serve the interests of the Europeans? Alternatively, is Europe a sufficiently strong world power (both in terms of economy and of culture) that its legal system can influence global developments in the present moment of high uncertainty about what path we should walk in the future of world capitalism?[76] I submit that European private lawyers should take full advantage of the cosmopolitan perspective stemming from their comparative law background, (which has proved to be a necessity rather than a choice in present day Europe), to think worldly, that is, to imagine a legal structure of the European market capable of working as a model and consequently serve the global community and not merely the European interests.

Arguing for a hard cod does not mean taking a legalistic attitude or underestimating the beneficial potentials of the market as an institution of resource

---

[74] See M. Albert, *Capitalismo e Controcapitalismo*; See also G. Gros Pietro and E. Reviglio and A. Torrisi, *Assetti proprietari e mercati finanziari europei* (2001).

[75] See G. Arrighi and B.J. Silver, *Chaos and Governance in the Modern World System* (1999).

[76] See D. Harvey, *The Limits to Capital* (1999).

allocation and wealth production. Indeed, disregarding such potentials of the market and the incapability of handling tools of interdisciplinary analysis has imposed a dear price to the present state of the debate on European private law.[77] Put simply, European lawyers, if paralleled with their US counterparts, have been good comparativists but very poor economists and social scientists. The lack of knowledge in other social sciences has, for a long period of time, closed European lawyers (common lawyers as well as civilians) into a useless black letter style of legal positivistic analysis that has made them completely disregard the social and economic impact of their legal constructions.[78] Once the costs of legalism have been understood, at least by some avant-garde (mostly of comparativists) in a relatively recent past, the poor condition of background understanding has not ceased to play a negative role.[79] In the efforts of their *kempf* against positivism and in the late and hasty discovery of the existence and virtues of the market, European lawyers (as well as a large number of policy makers throughout the political spectrum) have trusted the virtues of an unregulated market much more than what it is in order. Rather than limiting and trimming regulation where wasteful, European legal culture has participated in surrendering the political process and its legitimated production of binding rules of behaviour to unrestricted market practices only softly regulated, when regulated at all. This trend is based on bad economics and even worse law and economics.[80]

The market is healthy when in open competition with other institutions, most significantly the legal system and the political process.[81] The market should neither be ignored nor made the object of idolatry. It should be regulated to the extent necessary to make all the actors pay for their social costs. Such regulation, short of coming only from public law and *ex ante* government authorization, should be rooted in substantive private law.[82]

I suggest that the European hard code should be minimal, in the sense of containing only those fundamental principles that can readily be used by courts to force market actors to internalise social costs.[83] Nevertheless, a minimal hard

---

[77] See U. Mattei, *Comparative Law and Economics* (1997).

[78] See M. Hesselink (n. 10).

[79] See, for a classic critique of black letter positivism, R. Sacco, 'Legal Formants. A Dynamic Approach to Comparative Law', (1991) 39 *Am. J. Comp. Law*, 1.

[80] A critique of uncritical reception of law and economics in Europe can be found in U. Mattei (n. 78).

[81] See D. North (n. 53).

[82] See R. Cooter and T. Ulen (n. 44).

[83] Attempting to regulate details is futile. See P.B. Stephan, 'The Futility of Unification and Harmonization in International Commercial Law', (1999) 39 *Virginia Journal of International Law*, 743. See the contribution of G. De Geest to this volume, in favour of a very detailed Code.

civil code should by no means be limited to the law of contracts.[84] Seen from the perspective of social sciences, economics in particular, private law is an integrated body of fundamental rules of the game.[85] The laws of contracts, torts, property, restitutions and corporations, in this perspective, play a very similar role. They integrate and complete each other as private law rules introducing correct sets of incentives for a fair and open market. Variations in form might be substantial. They are, however, the resultant of historical accidents (sometimes referred to as legal culture) that do not change the fundamental substance. The truth of the matter is that taxonomy in the law must only serve the purpose of organizing knowledge and should never be seen as something that determines the substantive solution to social problems. For too many years, European lawyers (again in the Continent as well as in the common law) have been victims of the illusion that deducting, or inducing, rules from taxonomy could be seen as a scientific exercise. Such formalistic exercise has only been a waste of time and has many times guided ill-considered decisions.[86] For some years now, I have been busy coordinating the painstaking efforts of many colleagues to try understanding as much as possible how things really are in European private law.[87] Our efforts have been conscious of the many difficulties and epistemological objections that we were facing. Nevertheless, our experience has been that taxonomy is bound to become a cage if any attempt is made to use it beyond the its very minimal (but so important at the same time) task of organizing materials.

As long as the hard Code contains a regime comprehensive enough to force internalization of costs, any taxonomy works. A good suggestion, based on an information costs reduction rationale, would be to use the one that at the moment is more widely understood.[88] Contract law is poorly equipped to take care of externalities imposed on third parties. Tort law is poorly equipped to allow idiosyncratic preferences to unfold. Property law tends to be less flexible than the previous two, and its deep connection with land law places a large part of it arguably outside the European jurisdiction.[89] In corporation law the necessity to make clear what is default law and what is mandatory is perhaps the

---

[84] A number of distinguished European scholars are now pointing at contract law as the only target of codification. See recently, J. Basedow, *ERPL* [2001] and his contribution to this volume.

[85] See R. Cooter, *Towards a Unified Theory of contract Property and Tort. The Model of Precautions.*

[86] See P. Grossi, 'Historical Models and Present Plans in the Formation of a Future European Law', in: A. Gambaro and A.M. Rabello (eds.), *Towards a New European Ius Commune* (1999).

[87] See M. Bussani and U. Mattei (n. 18).

[88] See U. Mattei, 'A Transaction Costs Approach to the European Civil Code', (1997) *ERPL*, 537 and the contribution of H. Collins to this volume.

[89] See A. Gambaro, 'Toward a Codification of the European Law of Property', in: A. Gambaro and M. Rabello (eds.), (n. 87), at 89 *et seq.*

most crucial problem.[90] The law of restitution might make good some shortcomings of the traditionally poor European tort process. What is mandatory in all these areas should be spelled out in the hard European Code.

This is not the paper to attempt to discuss further details. On top of everything, it would be arrogant. However, let me spell out one final point that I consider highly relevant for this preliminary discussion. I believe that the political choice to make a hard code would be courageous because of the many criticisms that it will receive from the more conservative and influential part of the lawyer's profession. I do not believe, however, that this choice should belong to lawyers, nor that the effort would prove to be futile. True, in Europe today major symbolic choices (and the civil code would certainly qualify as one)[91] are carried on by technocrats and imposed on the people. Possibly the euro is the most important of those. Nevertheless, the deficit of democracy that is plaguing Europe should not be seized by influential professional guilds to claim privileges and powers that clearly do not belong to them. The euro should not have been the decisions of bankers. The Code should not be the decision of lawyers.

European policy makers, in charge of deciding this issue, should not underestimate the potential major impact of such an important piece of legislation in the current lawless global corporate marketplace.[92] Many people in the world (including in the United States the many discontents of the World Bank and the IMF as global law-makers) would welcome a truly responsible piece of economic legislation, something that Europe owes to humankind to make good its less than respectable exploitative past.[93] A European civil code, prestigious because of the strengths still enjoyed by the culture behind it, could become, in the global world, a true piece of model legislation.[94] If a leading jurisdiction such as Europe begins to change its attitude towards lawless capital globalisation in favour of a more social model of economic development, this could be a first move of counter-trend away from global hegemony and exploitation.[95]

How to do that? In this paper, I wish only to offer some insights on the basic issues that should be thoroughly discussed by scholars and policy makers in deciding the legal framework for an efficient European market. One important lesson that we can learn from social sciences and from the most advanced

---

[90] Suffice to think about the major debate provoked by F. Easterbrook and D. Fishel, *The Economic Structure of Corporate Law* (1991); see C. Marchetti, *La Nexus of Contracts theory* (2000).

[91] On the important of such aesthetic dimension in the competitive success of a source of law, see A. Robilant, 'The Aesthetics of Law', 1 *Global Jurist Advances*, 2 at www.bepress.com.

[92] See S. Sassen, *Globalization and its Discontents* (1998).

[93] See A. Loomba, *Colonialism/Postcolonialism* (1998); E. Said, *Culture and Imperialism* (1994).

[94] See the contribution of M. Bussani to this volume.

[95] S. R. Gill and D. Law, 'Global Hegemony and the Structural Power of Capital', (1989) 33 Int. Studies Quarterly, 475.

approaches to legal scholarship is the importance of the dynamic process, in the production of institutions as well as of technology and products. The processes, not only the outcomes, should attract attention of scholars as well as of legislators.[96]

Most of the externalities, most of the social costs dumped in the backyard of our weaker neighbours of the south of the world, *are created during the process of production* of commodities that are consumed by the more than 200 million people who make up the European market.[97] Such process of production is traditionally ignored by private law, concerned as it is only with the final outcomes. In economic terms, this simply introduces an alternative. Either European consumers pay too little for their commodities because their prices do not reflect the true social costs of production (environment, labour exploitation, etc.) and European capitalism is once again subsidized by former colonies,[98] or multinational corporate logo-lords (mostly European, Japanese and North American) make unfair profits pocketing the value of such social costs.[99] In both cases, such economic reality should be a concern for the European policy maker drafting the rules of the game. Today we know that a large number of successful market competitors on the European market offer an inefficiently high number of products at an artificially low price. Such multinational competitors push smaller market actors out of business. Smaller market actors do not externalize costs of production on people in the south of the world. Usually by acting locally, such weaker actors have to comply with European standards of labour conditions and environmental protection and, as a consequence, cannot supply as many commodities at such low prices.

Producer's liability, one of the frontier advances in private law, only covers social costs imposed by the outcome of productive process in the consumer's market. Indeed, this is a small fraction of the externality problems, which a system of private law should tackle in approaching problems globally.

This basic change of perspective – from the outcome to the process – is bound to lead to important insights, cutting across significant sections of the substantive rules of the game. This perspective, more than any other, might cure the presently existing gap between substantive rules, remedies and procedures: a plague with which the civilian dogmatic attitude should not infect the European legal process. Focusing on processes rather than on outcomes is likely to allow scholars, policymakers, (and perhaps even the people!) to perceive the importance of the

---

[96] See, in the domain of comparative law, D. Gerber, 'System Dynamics: Toward a Language of Comparative Law?', (1998) 46 *Am. J. Comp. Law*, 719. Among legal anthropologists, L. Nader (n. 36).

[97] See for a fascinating discussion of such process of externalization, N. Klein, *No Logo* (2000).

[98] See A. Loomba (n. 93).

[99] This is the fundamental thesis of N. Klein (n. 97) and of many other critiques of corporate globalisation. See, e.g., Arrighi and Silver (n. 75); Hardt and Negri (n. 36).

stakes that are on the table. Codifying private law in this sense is the true process of creation of an economic constitution for Europe. Because the economy is not disconnected from culture, ideology and society, this is a constitutional moment that should be perceived and evaluated as such.[100] It is a daunting task and a tremendous opportunity that cannot be wasted.[101] Approaching the issue of European Codification as a technical exercise, involving only a small *nomenklatura* of well-known legal scholars, unduly tables the moment of choices. Suggesting soft solutions only confirms Europe as a periphery of the economic Empire.

---

[100] See, on the notion of constitutional moment, B.A. Ackerman, *We The People* (1991). In the European institutional context see J. Weiler, 'The Transformation of Europe', (1991) 100 *Yale Law Journal*, 2043.

[101] See, for scepticism on the possibilities of legal culture seizing this opportunity, A. Negri, 'Postmodern Global Governance and the Critical Legal Project', (2001) 1 *Global Jurist Advances* 3 at www.bepress.com.

16.   The European Civil Code: A Framework Code Only

*Hans-Peter Schwintowski**

I. GROUNDWORK AND EVOLUTION

Europe is moving towards a European Civil Code. The European Parliament began calling for a European Civil Code and a European Commercial Code as early as 1989.[1] A great deal of academic and practical groundwork has already been done – for instance, the Lando principles[2] and the draft for a European Contract Code proposed by the Academy of European Lawyers.[3] Other preparatory developments include the investigations of the Study Group on a European Civil Code[4] and those of the Tilburg Group.[5] In October 1999, the Tampere European Council requested an overall study on the need to approximate Member States' legislation in civil matters. The Commission responded on 11 July 2001 with the presentation of a *Communication on European contract law*[6] and encouraged both academic experts and legal practitioners to express their comments on the proposal. In particular, the Commission is seeking concrete examples of cases where civil law differences between the Member States make intra-Community trade more onerous and lead to higher costs.[7] Thus it would

---

*   Professor for Civil Law, Commercial – Business – and European Law at Humboldt University, Berlin.
[1] (EC) OJ [1994] C 158/400; also (EC) OJ [2001] C 205/518; 3rd resolution in October 2001.
[2] Lando and Beale (eds.), *Principles of European Contract Law, Parts I and II* (The Hague, Kluwer, 2000); the third part – general issues of contract law – should be completed by the end of 2001.
[3] Sonnenberger, *RIW* (2001), 409, he refers to: Academy of European Lawyers (ed.), *European Contract Law – Preliminary Draft* (Universita di Pavia, 2001).
[4] On this topic, cf. von Bar, 'Die Study Group on a European Civil Code', in: Gottwald, Jayme and Schwab (eds.), *Festschrift Henrich* (Bielefeld, Gieseking, 2000), p. 1 *et seq.*
[5] On this topic, cf. Spier and Haazen, 'The European Group on Tort Law', *ZEuP* [1999], 469.
[6] COM(2001) 398 final; on this topic, cf. Grundmann, 'Europäisches Schuldvertragsrecht' *NJW* 2001, p. 14ff.; Schulte-Nölke, 'Ein Vertragsgesetzbuch für Europa', *JZ* 2001, p. 917ff.; Staudenmayer, 'Die Mitteilung der Kommission zum Europäischen Vertragsrecht', *EuZW* 2001, p. 485ff.
[7] According to the European Court of Justice, harmonisation pursuant to Article 95 EC Treaty requires more than the abstract danger of limitation of inter-state trade. The first quota is a decision of the European Court of Justice, therefore there is no title for this article, *EuGH NJW* [2000], 3701 *Tobacco Advertising Directive*; on this topic, cf. Amtenbrink, 'Harmonisierungsmaßnahmen in Binnenmarkt im Lichte der Entscheidung

S. Grundmann and J. Stuyck (eds.), An Academic Green Paper on European Contract Law, 235–248
© 2002 *Kluwer Law International. Printed in Great Britain.*

be the *concept of the internal market* itself that would constitute the basic legitimation of a future European Civil Code. Europe could, of course, approach the objective of an internal market through continued and increased *harmonisation*, but this would not be tangibly observable by the citizens of Europe, because implementing directives into the national law of the Member States would rob these directives of their explicitness of provenance. Besides – and this is an even more convincing argument – it cannot be guaranteed that legal instruments passed by the Community are consistent with each other and that no deficits will arise from their implementation within national systems.

II. ANTECEDENTS AND MODELS[8]

1. The Code of Hammurabi

The search for the oldest law codes leads us far away and long ago to ancient Mesopotamia, modern-day Iraq. The Akkadian king Hammurabi united the land between the rivers into a mighty empire, marking the start of what we know as Babylonian history. It is during this time that the Code of Hammurabi (*c.* 1729–1687 BC) was drawn up.[9] The famous stele inscribed with its 282 rules is kept in the Louvre; a copy can be seen in the Pergamon Museum in Berlin.[10] The prevailing opinion, first expressed by Koschaker, assumes that Hammurabi structured his code on the basis of existing Sumerian law and expanded it with Akkadian supplements and amendments.[11] This would not seem at all inept, as

---

des Europäischen Gerichtshofs zur Tabak Werberichtlinie', *VuR* 2001, p. 163; Reich, 'Rechtsangleichung im Binnenmarkt – Marktöffnung oder Soziälschutz', *VuR* 2001, p. 203ff.; Roth, 'Die Schuldrechtsreform im Kontext des Europarechts', in: Ernst and Zimmermann (eds.), *Zivilrechtswissenschaft und Schuldrechtsreform* (Tübingen, Mohr Siebeck, 2001), 225, 232 *et seq.*

[8] An overview of major codes of law: around 1700 BC, Code of Hammurabi, Babylon; *c.* 1200 BC, The Decalogue of Moses, Israel; *c.* 600 BC, Draconian Laws and Solon, Athens; *c.* 449 BC, Law of the Twelve Tables, Rome; *c.* AD 535, *Corpus Juris Civilis*, Emperor Justinian, Byzance; *c.* 1140, *Corpus Juris Canonici*; *c.* 1230, Sachsenspiegel (Saxon Mirror) (Eike von Repgow); *c.* 1532, *Carolina, Peinliche Halsgerichtsordnung* (Penal Code), Emperor Charles V; *c.* 1756, *Codex Maximilianeus Bavaricus Civilis*, Kreittmayr; *c.* 1794, *Preussisches Allgemeines Landrecht* (General Prussian State Law), Suarez; *c.* 1804, *Code Civil* (Code Napoléon}; *c.* 1811, *Österreichisches Allgemeines Bürgerliches Gesetzbuch* (Austrian Civil Code); *c.* 1896, Bürgerliches Gesetzbuch (German Civil Code).

[9] Seidl, *Römische Rechtsgeschichte* (Köln, Berlin, Bonn, München, Carl Heymanns Verlag, 1963), 25; Hans Fehr, *Hammurabi und das saalische Recht* (Bonn, A. Marcus & E. Weber's Verlag, 1910); Paul Koschaker, *Rechtsvergleichende Studien zur Gesetzgebung Hammurapis* (Leipzig, Veit, 1917).

[10] For more detail, cf. Rudolf Gmür, *Rechtswirkungsdenken in der Privatrechtsgeschichte* (1981), 241 *et seq.*

[11] Seidl (n. 9), 25 *et seq.*

Hammurabi's aim was to consolidate the multinational state he had created. What could have been more natural for him but to build his system for maintaining order and solving conflicts by drawing upon his peoples' shared roots and modernising them, thereby creating a common denominator that would be convincing for all.

2. The *Corpus Juris Civilis*

Without a doubt, history's most significant body of legislation is the work of the Roman Emperor Justinian. Justinian ascended the East Roman imperial throne in AD 527, long after the western parts of the Empire had fallen to Germanic tribes (AD 476). In AD 530, Justinian appointed a commission to draw up the *Digesta*, a selection of writings by classical jurists (e.g. Ulpian and Papinian) adapted for modern practical use. Justinian's code acquired the force of law on 30 December 533; it consisted of the *Institutiones*, the *Digesta* and the *Codex*, which was promulgated on 29 December 534. Since then, the collection has been known under the name *Corpus Juris Civilis*. The *Institutiones* are considered the definitive textbook on Roman law. Between the high Middle Ages and the late nineteenth century they were the alpha and omega of law courses at European universities.[12] Starting around the late thirteenth century, the *Corpus Juris Civilis* was adopted as *jus commune* in nearly all of continental Europe. From Europe, it spread to the whole world; nearly all legal systems have been moulded by it and by its method. In the German Reich, it was not until the entry into force of the *Bürgerliches Gesetzbuch* on 1 January 1900 that the last vestiges of Roman law disappeared. Until then, it had still applied directly as *gemeines Recht*, a form of common law developed and modified by centuries of practice, for nearly 17 million people – one quarter of the Reich population at the time.

Roman law has left a deep impression on modern law: both the basic values and individual provisions of the world's various civil law systems and the terminology, system and method of law codes bear traces of its influence. Justinian's ambitious plan of creating a code of law *for all times* did not succeed, as we know.[13] His code was amended for the first time as early as AD 535 – in fact, during his own reign. Nevertheless, the Code of Justinian did indeed prevail for nearly 1400 years. When, in 1814, Friedrich Carl von Savigny spoke against a codification of civil law, it was not so much because he thought the Code of Justinian was the best: it was because he believed that laws were mostly the product of *legal custom*, in other words that law was 'first developed by custom and popular faith, next by jurisprudence – everywhere, therefore, by internal

---

12   Behrends, Knütel, Kubisch and Seiler, *Corpus Iuris Civilis, Die Institutionen, utb* (1993).

13   Constitutio Tanta, Section 23: 'and it shall be valid henceforth and for all times'.

silently operating powers, not by the arbitrary will of a law-giver'.[14] Furthermore, Savigny believed that time was not yet ripe for a *good code,*[15] as Germans did not yet possess the language 'in which a code could be composed'.[16] Savigny was therefore vehemently opposed to the ideas expressed by Thibaut in *On the Need for a General Civil Law for Germany,* which had also been published in 1814.[17]

3. The Allgemeines Preussisches Landrecht, or General Prussian State Law

Savigny felt that his opposition to codification was confirmed by the composition of the General State Law for the Prussian States, the *Allgemeines Landrecht für die preussischen Staaten.* This impressive codex came into force in 1794. It is one of the codifications of natural law undertaken in the later phase of absolutism, the only one that contains a truly comprehensive order based on the system developed more than one hundred years earlier by Samuel Pufendorf in *De Jure Naturae et Gentium.*[18] The Landrecht was meant to be based on Justinian law. Frederick II wanted it to be in the highest degree simple, popular, and, at the same time, complete, 'so that the business of the judge might consist in a kind of mechanical application of the law'.[19] In fact, the history of the Landrecht after 1794 is actually the history of its progressive erosion, a process which began as soon as it had come into force. A profusion of royal decrees, rescripts and cabinet orders encroached on the freshly published code. The first major upheaval began with the Stein-Hardenberg reforms: the abolition of the corporative system, the introduction of freedom of trade, municipal self-government, the elimination of hereditary servitude – all of these were changes that brought about amendments to the text of the Landrecht. As early as 1826, the king gave the order for a comprehensive legal reform, and after 1871, the German Empire assumed legislative competence in matters of civil law, so that only the sections of the Landrecht that dealt with public law retained any practical significance.[20] Nevertheless, Savigny mentions one major advantage of the Landrecht, namely

---

[14]   Friedrich Carl von Savigny, *Of the Vocation of our Age for Legislation and Jurisprudence* (Translated from the German by Abraham Hayward), (New York, Arno Press, 1975), 30.
[15]   Friedrich Carl von Savigny (n. 14), 66.
[16]   Friedrich Carl von Savigny (n. 14), 68.
[17]   Anton Friedrich Justus Thibaut, *Über die Notwendigkeit eines allgemeinen bürgerlichen Rechts in Deutschland* (Heidelberg, Mohr und Zimmer Verlag, 1814, reprinted in 1997).
[18]   Friedrich Carl von Savigny (n. 14), 102; Uwe Wesel, *Geschichte des Rechts* (München, Beck, 1997), 400 *et seq.*
[19]   Friedrich Carl von Savigny (n. 14), 106, with reference to the Cabinetsordre of 1780.
[20]   *Allgemeines Landrecht für die preussischen Staaten von 1794, Textausgabe mit einer Einführung von Hans Hattenhauer,* 1970.

'the relation which it bears to the local sources of law. It was introduced merely as a subsidiary law in the place of ... Roman ... common law'.[21]

Still, the *Landrecht* had not been developed in vain. A wonderful testimony to the code's merit was provided by the Prussian nobleman Achim von Arnim in a letter to his brother-in-law Savigny in 1814:

> 'And I should verily wish to know how it could otherwise have been achieved that in Prussia even the peasant should no longer regard the law ... as a mysterious conjuration of spirits or a game of chance, but indeed as something true, honest and highly dignified, that [this same peasant] enjoys being shown citations in the Landrecht and thus lets himself be kept from engaging in foolish litigation ... From a legal point of view, the Landrecht was for our nation as important as Luther's translation of the Bible'.[22]

4. The Concept of Codification

To be precise, the modern concept of codification is a relatively late development in the history of jurisprudence, one that did not exist prior to the eighteenth century.[23] Justinian's *Corpus Juris* is not a code of law in the modern sense: it is a collection of loosely structured legal material dating from various epochs. The principles of the new legal form were developed in the context of a legislation theory.[24] An in-depth study of the conceptual history of legislation was published in 1960 by Sten Gagnér.[25] According to Gagnér, the modern concept of codifying laws is the outcome of changes in continental European scholasticism. The common characteristic of the codification concept, he says, is a positivistic attitude, an acceptance of the status quo.[26] The formal prerequisites of a good *codification* can be summarised as follows:

(1) Codified law should be comprehensive and stable. A code should not contain casual rules enacted only for specific, temporary conditions.

(2) In terms of its content, a code of law should be an implementation of the

---

[21] Friedrich Carl von Savigny (n. 14), 101.

[22] Quoted by Hattenhauer (n. 20).

[23] Helmut Coing, *Europäisches Privatrecht*, Vol. II (München, Beck, 1989), 7 *et seq.*

[24] Franz Wieacker, *Das Sozialmodell der klassischen Privatgesetzbücher und die Entwicklung der modernen Gesellschaft* (Karlsruhe, Karlsruher Forum, 1953), reprinted in: *Industriegesellschaft und Privatrechtsordnung* (Karlsruhe, Karlsruher Forum, 1975), 9 *et seq.*; Helmut Coing, 'Zur Vorgeschichte der Kodifikation: die Diskussion um die Kodifikation im 17. und 18. Jh.', in: *La formazione storica del diritto moderno in Europa* (Atti del terzo Congresso internazionale della società Italiana di Storia del Diritto, Firenze, 1977), II, 797–818.

[25] *Studien zur Ideengeschichte der Gesetzgebung* (1960).

[26] For more detail cf. Wolfgang Fikentscher, *Methoden des Rechts in vergleichender Darstellung*, Vol. I (Tübingen, Mohr, 1975), 413 *et seq.*

social contract. It should be designed for a society of free and equal individuals, and it should protect liberty, equality and ownership.

(3) As to form, the code should be a list of rules, not a catalogue of case decisions. The rules should be clear and simple in their formulation. The idea is that, because every citizen should know his rights and their limitations, he should be able to understand the code. In Locke's words, the code should be a 'standing rule to live by' for the individual.

(4) A good code of law must have a systematic, clearly arranged logical structure.

(5) It must also be written so as to leave the judge little discretion in individual cases. The law should rule, not the judge.

The conflict of objectives inherent in these requirements had already been recognised in the eighteenth century. Jeremy Bentham suggested that the dilemma could be solved by supplementing the simple rules of law with an official commentary that would be binding for the judge.[27]

In the United States, the idea of drawing up a comprehensive code of civil law has often been discussed. In 1811, Jeremy Bentham wrote to President Madison, eloquently describing the advantages of such a codification and offering to take on the task himself. His offer was politely but firmly turned down.[28] Moves to codify American commercial law were more successful. Around 1940, the American Law Institute and the National Conference of Commissioners realised that restatements and uniform laws could not standardise commercial law to the extent that would have been necessary to make commercial operations safe and predictable enough. Both organisations concluded that commercial law should be codified, and ultimately a unified commercial code, the *United States Uniform Commercial Code* (UCC), was drawn up.[29] One of the jurists who played an outstanding role in the codification of the UCC was Karl Llewellyn, who had studied European and American law as well as sociology and anthropology. He had first-hand knowledge of German law, spoke and read German fluently and was the author of a study on precedent law published in German. Llewellyn had also studied in Paris and Lausanne, and he was aware of the chaos that uniform laws and the separate development of case law in the individual states had wrought on the American legal system Out of consideration for common-law traditions, the UCC includes a *reservation clause* which gives the courts wide discretion to draw on earlier case law unless it has been expressly replaced by the Code itself.[30] Important areas such as insolvency, the doctrine of estoppel,

---

[27] Coing (n. 23), 9.

[28] Zweigert and Kötz, *Einführung in die Rechtsvergleichung* (Tübingen, Mohr, ed. 3, 1996), 236 *et seq.*; Herman, 'Schicksal und Zukunft der Kodifikationsidee in Amerika', in: Zimmermann (ed.), *Amerikanische Rechtskultur und europäisches Privatrecht* (Tübingen, Mohr, 1995), 45.

[29] Herman (n. 28), 73.

[30] Herman (n. 28), 85.

agency, and defective intention are explicitly not covered by the UCC. The style of the UCC is more long-winded than that of European codes of law. Nevertheless, codification of commercial law guarantees at least that everyone is working with the same book.[31]

However, the competence of individual states in the core areas of private law remains undiminished. Any one of the 50 states may enact its own legislation in the areas of family law, succession, contract, tort, corporate law, property, insurance and securities, and judge-made law may diverge from state to state.[32] The resulting diversity of rules is mitigated by the theory of *implied powers* and the *commerce clause*, two regulations that give the federal authorities the competence and the right to enact laws when this is *necessary and proper*. All the same, the famous words of Supreme Court Judge Oliver Wendell Holmes that 'general propositions do not decide concrete cases' are, even today, hardly contested in the United States.[33] And Roscoe Pound is said to have advocated that laws should be repealed every 30 years, because a later generation cannot reasonably be expected to execute the laws of an earlier one.

III. THE LOGIC OF THE EUROPEAN CIVIL CODE

There are without a doubt many noteworthy reasons that speak against a European Civil Code. The strongest argument seems to be the United States, which, to this day, treats itself to one of the most complicated legal systems in the world. Competition between the systems seems to pervade the American legal markets. Of course there is in fact no such competition, as individual states do not allow their citizens *free choice of law*. Americans are far from the principle of *reciprocal recognition* of the supposedly competing legal entities: indeed, the red tape involved in enforcing and upholding relatively simple contracts – leases, employment contracts or loan agreements – is immense. Americans have become accustomed to the fact that they do not understand their legal system. It is quite normal for them to seek legal counsel, even in situations that Europeans could normally assess and deal with on their own. The unusually high number of attorneys per capita speaks volumes.[34]

The cost pressure resulting from a legal system of this kind is enormous, and the cost-cutting, economic theory of law now favoured by American economists

---

[31] Herman (n. 28), 85.

[32] Zweigert and Kötz (n. 28), 245.

[33] *Lochner v. New York*, 198 U.S. 45, 76; for more detail cf. Mathias Reimann, 'Amerikanisches Privatrecht und europäische Rechtseinheit' in: Zimmermann (ed.), *Amerikanische Rechtskultur und europäisches Privatrecht* (n. 28), (1996), 132, 152.

[34] According to estimates, there is one lawyer per 500 Americans; in Europe the ratio is estimated at approx. 1:4000.

and jurists is as academic as Hermann Hesse's glass bead game.[35] But above all – and this should be food for thought – legal orders are first and foremost, as the name says, *orders* regulating socially adequate behaviour; only in second place, though this is just as important, are they a means of conflict-solving, or, more precisely, of *legal peace*. Such orders include systems of rules covering, for instance, road traffic, property matters, credit security, product liability or the conclusion and enforcement of contracts. Then there is the huge bulk of public law with commercial or construction or food regulations, and finally criminal law, which of course – even in countries with a common-law tradition – is codified, albeit with varying exigencies and legal consequences. The concept of a legal order provides the impetus for the systematic establishment of a legal framework, because this is the only way order can legally realistically be created. The decisive issue is not so much the exact content of the order: it is the fact that the order is binding for all, and that it therefore creates a consistent guide to behaviour – in other words, legal certainty.

1. The Logic of Harmonisation

In this context, it is particularly significant for Europe that the Treaty of Rome, which came into force on 1 January 1958, formulated the concept of a common market from the start. In the current version of the Treaty, this concept can be described as the *internal market objective* (Art. 14 EC). At issue here is an area without internal frontiers in which the free movement of goods, persons, services and capital is ensured (Art. 14 para. 2 EC), an area where the European Council, acting by a qualified majority on a proposal from the Commission, determines the guidelines and conditions necessary to ensure balanced progress in all the sectors concerned (Art. 14 para. 3 EC). The internal market idea is complemented by a comprehensive list of objectives laid down in Article 3 of the Treaty. It is not only a question of banning customs duties and dismantling trade obstacles, not only a question of developing common commercial, agricultural and transport policies or uniform social or health policies, or of encouraging the establishment and development of trans-European networks: the idea is to establish a system that will ensure that competition within the internal market is not distorted, and finally to approximate the laws of Member States to the extent required for the functioning of the common market (Art. 3 para. 1(h) EC).

In other words, approximating the laws of Member States is one of the basic objectives that the European Union set itself back in 1958. On the basis of this objective, the European Council, the Commission and the European Parliament have passed hundreds of directives and dozens of regulations that have meanwhile been implemented in the legal systems of the Member States. Europe is

---

[35] Schwintowski, 'Ökonomische Theorie des Rechts', (1998) *JZ*, 581–588; Idem, 'An Economic Theory of Law', *The Journal of Interdisciplinary Economics* (2000) (Vol. 12), 1–16.

above all a *community of law*, and it has chosen to make harmonisation of the laws of the Member States one of its principal aims. This harmonisation process, which was given a major impulse by Jacques Delors and the 1985 white paper on the internal market, and later, once the internal market concept had been perfected by the Treaty of Maastricht in 1992, driven ahead by the Treaty of Amsterdam and the Nice European Council, is irreversible.

European contract law already exists, as recently demonstrated by Stefan Grundmann in his opus magnum.[36] The extent to which contract law in Europe has been harmonised is also documented by the Communication from the European Commission of 11 July 2001. Annex 1 of this paper contains an excellent description of the *acquis communautaire* in this area: harmonised laws in the areas of consumer contracts, unfair competition, package holidays, consumer credit, distance contracts, timesharing, commercial agents, employment, liability for defective products, e-commerce, electronic signatures, securities and insurance services, protection of personal data, copyright, media or public procurement. These are but examples showing how much progress has already been made on the way to harmonising European private law. Also worthy of mention are the sale of consumer goods, the directive on unfair terms in consumer contracts and the directive on comparative advertising.[37] These many efforts to harmonise private and contract law are supported by a multitude of directives dealing with corporate and accounting law.

Europeanisation has therefore been taking place at a steady but gradually increasing pace since January 1958 – in other words, for more than forty years. It is a process which has affected a great number of fields including, of course, private and commercial law. Many areas of private law have already been Europeanised, for instance – and particularly so – information regulations for financial services or the sale of consumer goods.[38] This means that Europe is already well into the discussion process called for by Savigny as a prerequisite for the creation of a *good code*. At this point it would be absurd for Europe to stop in its tracks and abandon the project of actually realising the harmonisation idea in the form of a common European Civil Code. This would be tantamount to throwing away everything that harmonisation has achieved so far and that has long since become reality in the Member States. The true logic of harmonisation entails not only safeguarding what has been achieved at the end of a long discussion process among the Member States of the European Union, but also presenting it to the citizens of Europe in a new quality and in a manner which, for the first time, also shows that Europe's community of law exists not only in

---

[36] Grundmann, 'Europäisches Schuldvertragsrecht', *ZGR-Sonderheft* (1999).

[37] For more detail cf. Schwintowski, 'Vertragsschluss für Waren- und Dienstleistungen im europäischen Verbraucherrecht: Form und Inhaltsbindungen kontra Privatautonomie', *EWS* [2001], 201–208.

[38] Grundmann, 'Privatautonomie im Binnenmarkt', *JZ* [2000], 1133, 1135 *et seq.*

the minds of Brussels bureaucrats but also as a code which is truly meaningful for every individual in the world's largest economic entity. And because Europeans are finding it so difficult to develop and feel something of a *European identity*, it is up to the Member States of the Community to take advantage of this unique opportunity and do what has already so often brought peace and unity to individual nations: create a common, a European code of civil law.

The logic of harmonisation, which will ultimately lead to a common European Civil Code, has also long been perceptible in the judicial decisions of the European Court of Justice. Two epoch-making rulings of the European Court of Justice – the *Dassonville*[39] and *Cassis de Dijon* cases in 1979[40] brought about a decisive breakthrough for the fundamental concept of *mutual recognition* in Europe. Goods offered for sale lawfully according to the laws of one Member State must be accepted by its European neighbours even though the importing country may have laws to the contrary – unless these conflicting provisions are based on *compelling public interests*. This principle was reaffirmed by the ECJ in the subsequent *Keck* decision.[41] As it stipulates that the standards for goods and services in all EU Member States are to be recognised as mutually equivalent as long as they do not affect compelling public interests, the principle of *mutual recognition* in effect harmonised broad segments of national law almost at one go. Further harmonisation is necessary only where compelling public interests are affected – in all other cases European individuals and companies are free to choose among the legal provisions of the various Member States. Meanwhile the ECJ, in the *Centros* decision, has clarified that the principle of *mutual recognition* applies not only at the level of the four freedoms of the EC Treaty but also in corporate law.[42]

European law has long permeated the legal systems of the individual Member States to a significant extent, linking them to each other and offering manifold options. But none of this is visible from the outside, because there is no symbol to help Europeans understand and grasp this legal unity. The European Civil Code already exists: its fundamental principles have been laid down. All that is left to do is to clothe this harmonisation *oeuvre* in the fitting garment: to launch the *European Civil Code* as the logical conclusion of European harmonisation.

---

[39] Slg. 1974, 837.

[40] Slg. 1979, 649.

[41] Slg. 1993, I–6097; on this topic, cf. Schwintowski, 'Freier Warenverkehr im europäischen Binnenmarkt', *RabelsZ* [2000], 38–59; Jutta Kessler, *Das System der Warenverkehrsfreiheit im Gemeinschaftsrecht* (1997).

[42] *ECJ*, 9.3.1999, *JZ* [1999], 669 and *EuZW* [1999], 216; on this topic cf. Grundmann (n. 38), 1139 with further supporting references. This is the judgment of the European Court of Justice (from the 9.3.1999 = RS (212/97), therefore there is no title of the article.

2. European Linguistic Diversity

There is another reason why Europe should not shirk the *logic of harmonisation*. In contrast to the United States, Europeans have so far failed to agree on a uniform language, at least in the areas of science and commerce. Efforts made in this direction have barely been noticed: there is no political will for a pan-European language. Europe is thus forgoing one of the most important factors of economic and cultural integration. If communication is impossible or difficult, it becomes harder to overcome mutual feelings of strangeness: people distance themselves from one another and tend to define themselves on the basis of their own linguistic group.

When he calls himself an *American*, a citizen of the United States expresses the fact that he is part of a single, large nation, no matter how diverse and varied it may be. The word *European*, on the other hand, has not yet acquired this unifying character for the citizens of countries of the European Union. People in Europe are French, Spanish, Italian, British or German, but in no way *European*. Alone, the idea that a *European* could feel equally at home in Rome, Paris, Athens or Stockholm is likely to be met with general disapproval. At best, Europe is seen as a centuries-old *cultural space*,[43] not as a single political or economic national structure, and not even as a common home shared by a variety of peoples with different languages. In other words, Europe has not yet managed to forge common bonds that might draw its Member States together in the same manner that India or China, for instance, have united the many linguistic and ethnic groups within their population.

One of the likely reasons why Europe is not finding its way into the hearts of its citizens is that it has so few tangible external symbols. Indeed, the introduction of the euro will be one of the first major steps towards Europe. It took a long time for Europeans to understand the enormous strength of the dollar as a symbol of being an American. But Americans have more than only a common currency: they also share a common language, and of course also the concept of personal freedom, which transcends the nation and has its foundation deep in the history of the US. In addition to these three extraordinarily strong unifying roots, Americans also have a highly regarded constitution and, in the field of commercial and economic law, the Uniform Commercial Code (UCC). From an American perspective, this wealth of unifying symbols may make it seem quite unnecessary to create a civil code which, like the UCC, would apply uniformly in all the states. We should also not forget that the US basically follows the English common-law system, and that this is done in a virtually uniform manner across the country. The identifying effect of this type of country-wide legal system is obvious. An American knows that justice is administered according to the same method in every state. This identity of methods and

---

[43]   Paul Koschaker, *Europa und das römische Recht* (München, Beck, 1966), 2 *et seq.*

systems has a stabilising effect on the nation – and a civil code may not only be unnecessary, it could even prove to be an alien element.

Things are totally different in Europe. Instead of a single language we speak many, very different languages, a linguistic diversity that will increase as Europe expands to the east. A single European constitution may have developed, and it may be perceptible in the judicial decisions of the European Court of Justice, but just like a European Civil Code, it has yet to be launched. And of course, in a continent where English common law competes with the civil-law tradition, there can be no question of a uniform legal system. Nor is there yet a single, unifying European Commercial Code. As Europe's first unifying symbol, only the euro is to Europe what the dollar is to America. All of this shows how urgently Europe needs symbols that will create a sense of community. A European Civil Code would thus be a superb opportunity to give the European idea another visible and meaningful symbol. This is an opportunity which we should not gamble away carelessly.

IV. A EUROPEAN CIVIL CODE MODEL

If a European Civil Code is to become reality, the first question to be answered should be what the objectives and purposes of such a code should be, in other words, what it should be able to achieve. One thing needs to be stated clearly from the start: a European Civil Code is not intended as a replacement for national civil codes. Europe is the concept and expression of a multinational federation with a strong, nation-based legal culture. All the harmonisation efforts of the last forty years of Community history have not changed this in any way, and it is a notion that must be respected by a future European Civil Code.

A European Civil Code should thus reflect the general basic principles of civil and contract law in Europe. On the one hand, these are principles that have linked the nations of Europe to each other since the days of Roman law anyway, the same notions that show up as Standards and Principles in textbooks of English Common Law. The European Civil Code should therefore, first and foremost, formulate rules that are already practised uniformly by all, for instance in the areas of conclusion of contract, formation of intention, rescission on the ground of mistake, or assignment of claims and rights. In addition, it should codify a few binding rules that are or should be of fundamental importance in regulating the private-law aspects of the lives of the citizens of Europe. These are above all *information rules*, rules that ensure transparency in formation of intention and thus provide for a certain balance of powers.[44]

If the European Civil Code was to be limited to essentials, its provisions could be formulated in such a manner as to be clear, simple and comprehensible for all Europeans. People should be able to take this code of law and, having read

---

[44] For more detail cf. Grundmann (n. 38), 1137 *et seq.*; Schwintowski (n. 37), 203 *et seq.*

it, know what to do and not to do. Yet if it is to be more than mere case law, thereby falling back into the legislative methods of the Ancients, the European Civil Code must also help implement a judicial *system*.

Limitation to essentials as a prerequisite for a first European Civil Code forces us to carefully consider what material such a code should actually contain. It would seem almost self-evident that a European Civil Code should not cover family law or law of succession. However, it may indeed be conceivable that, even in these fields, the basic principles that are already shared Europe-wide should be codified as well. The option of marriage under family law and the principle of universal succession are fundamental values that are shared across Europe – so why should they not be named? Nevertheless, the European Civil Code should avoid going into details.

Whether this should also apply to property law is something that would have to be discussed at greater depth. One of the main impediments to European unification is that so far we have no uniform European law for securing loans by mortgage. It is therefore virtually impossible to use a property located in another European state as collateral for a loan in one's own country. This creates massive obstacles to trade, so it would be at least a good idea to consider the inclusion of a new European mortgage law in the new European Civil Code – perhaps as an option. The concepts of ownership and possession should also be included and defined. Whether detailed rules for transfer of ownership and possession and for bona fide acquisition should be included as well is an arguable point. As I see it, these areas should not necessarily be components of a European Civil Code. Essentially, the European Civil Code would therefore focus on contract law. The German tradition of dividing the legal material into a *General Section* and a separate *Law of Obligations* would not be a likely model for a European Civil Code. The areas to be resolved would be legal capacity and the ensuing protection of minors, the principles of declaration of intention and of conclusion of contract as well as the principles of rescission and invalidity of legal transactions for other reasons. Breaches of contract and their legal consequences would have to be defined, and it would perhaps also be useful to mention the issues of limitation and forfeiture of actions. A few particularly important types of contracts, for instance sales contracts, credit agreements, or building, travel and Internet contracts, should at least be outlined. The same applies to product liability and liability in tort.

What is decisive in all of these cases is, once again, that only common European roots, supplemented with a few further indispensable rules, should be codified. The national laws of the Member States would exist parallel to the European Civil Code. National codes would provide the details needed to fill in the European legal framework and ensure that Europe's variety of legal cultures is retained. Europe should also put into place a court system allowing its citizens to raise fundamental common aspects of private and commercial law at a European level. The European Court of Justice and the first-instance court are already functioning institutions. They would have to be expanded, strengthened and given the jurisdiction over the application and interpretation of a future European Civil Code.

V. SUMMARY OF THE MAIN RESULTS

1. The creation of a European Civil Code is based on the logic of harmonisation of civil law in Europe.
2. This is underscored by the principle of mutual recognition.
3. In contrast to the United States, Europe has not developed any great number of unifying symbols. Indeed, the first true such symbol is the euro. A European Civil Code could become a second building block on the way to a better internalisation of the European concept in the hearts of the citizens of Europe.
4. A European Civil Code, because of the unifying effect it would have, has become particularly desirable and urgent in view of the upcoming expansion of Europe towards the east.
5. The European Civil Code will be a supplement – not a replacement – for national codes of civil law.
6. The European Civil Code will be restricted to essential matters. Its form will be clear, simple and comprehensible. It will reflect those rules of civil law which today are generally accepted as common across Europe, and it will supplement these with a small number of other important, indispensable rules. Most of these additions will be rules concerning information and transparency requirements.
7. The future European Civil Code will not deal with family law or with the law of succession. In this respect, only a few basic rules that are already accepted across Europe will be included in the Code. The same applies to property law.
8. The core of the European Civil Code will be European contract law. Here as well, the scope of the Code will be restricted to essential aspects.
9. The details and the actual implementation of the basic rules set out in the European Civil Code will be handled by each country's national laws.

17. Forced Harmonisation of Contract Law in Europe: Not to be Continued

*Roger Van den Bergh**

I. INTRODUCTION

In its Resolution of 16 March 2000 the European Parliament stated 'that greater harmonisation of civil law has become essential in the internal market'.[1] Harmonisation of private law, in particular contract law, is also favoured by many prominent comparative lawyers. They equally infer the need for a European private law from the interests of trade in the internal market: legal diversity means costs and risks, whereas harmonisation of law increases legal certainty and facilitates cross-border trade.[2] In its Communication of 11 July 2001 on European Contract Law the European Commission launched a detailed and wide-ranging discussion on the desirability of new legislation in the field of contract law.[3] The Communication presents a non-exhaustive list of four possible options: no EC action, to promote the development of non-binding common contract law principles, to review and improve existing EC legislation and to adopt new comprehensive legislation at EC level. This article argues against the latter option and favours, under certain conditions, more limited legislative interventions.

At the outset, it should be stressed that any measure at the EC level must be in accordance with the principles of subsidiarity and proportionality (Art. 5 EC Treaty). Both principles embody mechanisms to avoid overregulation. The subsidiarity principle has introduced a presumption in favour of member state regulation. Since this presumption is a legal requirement in the European Union, the primary focus should be on justifications for Community action, rather than on

---

* Professor of Law and Economics, Erasmus University Rotterdam, e-mail: r.vandenbergh@law.eur.nl.
1 (EC) [2000] OJ C 377/323 (Resolution B5-0228, 0229–0230/ 2000, 326 at point 28). In 1989 and 1994 the European Parliament adopted Resolutions expressing the desire for a harmonisation of European private law. See: (EC) [1989] OJ C 158/400 and [1994] OJ C205/518.
2 O. Lando, 'Die Regeln des Europäischen Vertragsrechts', in: P.-C. Müller-Graff (ed.), *Gemeinsames Privatrecht in der Europäischen Gemeinschaft* (Nomos, 1993), 473–474.
3 Communication from the Commission to the Council and the European Parliament on European Contract Law, 11.07.2001, COM(2001) 398 final.

S. Grundmann and J. Stuyck (eds.), An Academic Green Paper on European Contract Law, 249–268
© 2002 *Kluwer Law International. Printed in Great Britain.*

justifications for action at lower levels of government. The formulation of the subsidiarity principle[4] clearly invites economic analysis: decentralisation is to be preferred to centralisation as long as the benefit–cost ratio of the former is more advantageous than the benefit–cost ratio of the latter. Hence, the question whether one should favour harmonisation of laws, brought about by action at the central level, to competition between legal orders achieved by decentralisation, should be answered by looking at the benefits and costs of both options. Not only the subsidiarity principle, but also the proportionality principle invites a full economic analysis. The requirement that measures should not go beyond what is necessary to achieve the required end (Art. 5 EC Treaty) can be reformulated in economic terms. If there are different instruments to reach a certain goal, the most cost-effective method should be chosen. Costly legal solutions should give way to cheaper instruments.

A second important introductory remark relates to the present state of the harmonisation process in the field of contract law. The European legislator has taken a piecemeal approach to harmonisation. This implies that there are no uniform broad principles of contract law, relating to such issues as the formation, validity and interpretation of contracts. The great bulk of harmonisation measures so far have been inspired by the wish to correct inequalities in economic strength and to protect the so-called weaker party from manipulations and abuses by the other economically superior party. Many directives have been enacted in the field of consumer law with the aim of conferring protection on buyers assumed to be disadvantaged by processes of free bargaining. As a consequence, EC law making exhibits a strong interventionist character. A large set of legal rules is not 'facilitative' in the sense that they provide mechanisms for ensuring mutually beneficial outcomes, but 'interventionist' since they supersede voluntary transactions.[5] Interventionist law creates winners (those who benefit from the protection) and losers (those who are the subject of legal obligations). Since the desirability of harmonisation of laws is also dependent on the characteristics of legal rules, the analysis below will take the differences between facilitative and interventionist rules into full consideration.

In this article, economic analysis will be used to assess both the costs and the

---

[4]   Article 5(2) EC Treaty reads as follows: 'In areas which do not fall within its exclusive competence, the Community shall take action, in accordance with the principle of subsidiarity, only if and in so far as the objectives of the proposed action cannot be sufficiently achieved by the Member States and can, therefore, by reason of the scale or effects of the proposed action, be better achieved by the Community'. The reference to scale economies and the emphasis put on the effects of the action invites economic analysis, since law on its own has no tools to predict and evaluate the effects of regulatory intervention at different levels of government.

[5]   See the distinction made by A. Ogus, 'Competition between national legal systems: a contribution of economic analysis to comparative law', (1999) *ICLQ*, 412–413.

benefits of harmonisation of contract law. The structure of the article is as follows. First, a critical look will be taken at the arguments favouring harmonis-ation of contract law, brought forward mainly by comparative lawyers. It will be shown that these arguments do not allow final decisions as to whether and, if so, how contract law should be harmonised. Second, attention will be paid to the possible disadvantages of harmonising rules of contract law. Third, economic criteria for harmonisation will be presented. It will be shown that these arguments are not strong in the context of contract law. Fourth, it will be argued that in the absence of forced harmonisation rules of contract law may still tend to be uniform. This is the case when preferences of citizens are homogeneous with respect to cost-minimising rules of facilitative law or the degree of minimum protection guaranteed by interventionist law. Finally, in response to the questions posed in the Commission's Communication a proposal will be made in favour of competition between legal rules and, therefore, non-binding rules of con-tract law.

II. COSTS AND BENEFITS OF HARMONISATION

1. Traditional Arguments in Favour of Harmonisation of Laws: Market Integration and Legal Certainty

A most prominent argument in favour of harmonisation of law is that diversity of legal rules can create non-tariff barriers to international trade and thus impede fair competition. It seems obvious that harmonisation of contract law generates advantages in the context of international trade. Those engaged in international transactions will incur reduced costs in acquiring information about the gov-erning legal principles and eventually also about the enforcement of rights and obligations. It is argued that both market integration and legal certainty will be favoured. From this perspective, it can be easily understood why European policy-makers as well as many comparative lawyers advocate harmonisation of law. However, the ready appreciation of the advantages of harmonisation often blinds the proponents of harmonisation to the costs which it will generate. Before focusing on the latter, some criticisms of the market integration goal will be presented. The argument about legal certainty is discussed below: even though it may be a valid justification for harmonisation, its scope should be limited to the correct proportions (see 3.2 below).

a) Market integration versus allocative efficiency

In the ongoing debate market integration is presented as a goal in itself. It should not be forgotten that market integration is an instrument to reach the economic and social objectives of the EC Treaty. Article 2 mentions, among other goals, a harmonious and balanced development of economic activities and a high degree of competitiveness; according to Article 3 market integration is an instrument to reach these goals. If market integration is no longer seen as a goal in itself, it becomes possible to focus attention also on the possible costs of an overzealous elimination of trade barriers. The conflict between market integration and the goal of allocative efficiency is well documented in the literature on competition law. Classical examples are the efficiency losses caused by the absolute ban on territorial protection for dealers and a too-strict prohibition of price discrimination.[6] The possible conflict between market integration and efficiency goals is not limited to competition law. Harmonisation of laws for reasons of market integration may also cause efficiency losses.

Allocative efficiency implies that European citizens can satisfy their preferences at competitive prices. In the field of contract law, many Directives include mandatory provisions to cure problems caused by a disparity between the positions of the contracting parties. European consumer policy aims at a 'high level of protection' (Art. 153(1) EC Treaty); as a consequence rules of contract law of the member states are harmonised in order to protect so-called weaker parties (consumers) from manipulations and abuses by producers and traders who are seen as intellectually and economically superior. The European Directives may be criticised for not having chosen efficient remedies to the said problems (see below at 3.5). At this point, another criticism is addressed. Consumer law is interventionist law: consumers are 'protected' at the expense of producers and traders who can pass on the costs of this 'protection' via higher resale prices.[7] Harmonising law may surpass preferences of consumers in a certain jurisdiction. Preferences of consumers in different countries with respect to the priority they accord to consumer protection relative to other concerns are likely to differ systematically. Preferences will vary depending on levels of income and alternative economic opportunities. A high level of consumer protection will cause a rise in prices; consumers willing to buy low-quality goods at lower prices may no longer be able to do so. An argument in favour of harmonisation might be that the consumer laws in some member states do not reflect the real preferences of the consumers in that state. It is, however, far from clear why the more remote European legislator is in a better position to assess what consumers in a particular member state really want. European law is no guarantee that political failures will be avoided. If the consequence of harmonisation is that consumer preferences are no longer satisfied at competitive prices, allocative efficiency is offered on the altar of the internal market.

---

[6] See R. Van den Bergh and P. Camesasca, *European Competition Law and Economics. A Comparative Perspective* (Antwerpen, 2001), 248–251 and 267–270.

[7] The precise amount of costs passed on to consumers depends on the degree of demand elasticity.

b) The 'level playing field' argument

The argument in favour of harmonisation also takes a different form: if countries are permitted to maintain lax policies, this will confer a competitive advantage on domestic industries and it will place pressure on governments in other countries to relax their policies in order to maintain the competitiveness of their own producers and traders. In the words of the Commission, harmonisation of law is needed to create a level playing field for industry in Europe.[8] There are several problems with this line of reasoning. The argument is distributional, rather than economic and harmonisation of laws is not necessarily an adequate response to the problem of unequal competitive conditions in the European market.

First, it is not necessarily illegitimate to exploit differences in legal rules. International trade is based on comparative advantages. International trade occurs when nations can exploit their differences (not similarities). Comparative advantage is not exclusively exogenously determined, but is significantly shaped by endogenous government policies, including law.[9] Refusing to exploit differences in government policies seems to be in contradiction with the essence of international trade itself. If competitive conditions were totally equal, there would also be no trade. The argument in favour of a level playing field appears to be distributional rather than economic.[10] If legal rules confer a competitive advantage on firms in a particular member state, the consequence will be that prices for consumer goods in the international market will be reduced with welfare gains to consumers who previously had to pay higher prices. Some losses will be incurred by industries previously complying with stricter laws, but gains will flow to other industries offering cheaper products. The aggregate welfare consequences for the entire market are likely be beneficial. Competition between states may be rejected only if it would cause a 'race to the bottom', so that the overall quality of the legal system would be too low. This claim is discussed below. At this point, it should already be noted that harmonisation for this reason is without convincing empirical evidence and that international trade may also stimulate the opposite tendency, i.e. a 'race to the top'.

Second, harmonisation of a particular field of law is not necessarily an appropriate remedy to create a level playing field for industry in Europe. The problem with a partial centralisation plan is that it does not equalise all costs. The costs of complying with a particular set of regulations are only one component of the total costs of production. Harmonising one type of regulation (e.g. consumer

---

[8]   See, for example, the considerations of the Directive on unfair contract terms ((EC) [1993] OJ L 95/29) and the Directive on product liability ((EC) [1985] OJ L 210/29).

[9]   Other important factors in the competition between states are collective investments in infrastructure, education, research and development and healthcare.

[10] In this sense also: A. Ogus (n. 5), 417 .

law) will leave 'competitive distortions' intact in other fields of regulation (e.g. environmental law). Furthermore, the goal of creating a level playing field will not be reached, since industries in some countries will keep an advantage in terms of infrastructure, wages, labour productivity, and so on. Countries that perform well on the non-harmonised components of costs will thus keep competitive benefits. The ultimate answer is to eliminate the possibility of competition over any of the costs mentioned, including both costs of complying with regulations and other production costs. Such a comprehensive Community intervention would equal an outright rejection of the subsidiarity principle.

2. Costs of Harmonisation

Easy-to-understand arguments with respect to market integration blind the European regulator (and many comparative lawyers) to the substantial costs of harmonisation. Obviously, harmonisation of laws brings benefits. As stated by the Commission, disparate national rules lead to higher transaction costs, especially information and possible litigation costs for enterprises in general and small and medium-sized firms and consumers in particular.[11] However, the precise amount of the savings remains hidden, since quantitative data are lacking. In addition, the analysis is very partial because it totally neglects the benefits of diversity. Differences in legal rules allow satisfaction of a greater number of preferences and allow for learning processes.[12] To the costs caused by the loss of these advantages must be added the administrative costs of harmonisation, which may also be substantial.

The transaction cost savings stressed by the Commission may be outweighed by the costs of formulating uniform principles, reaching agreement on common principles, formulating new rules in accordance with these principles and subsequently adapting national legal systems. The latter costs should not be underestimated, since private law is deeply entrenched in national legal culture: the legal language, the conceptual structure and procedures may vary significantly across jurisdictions.[13] The time spent by legal experts (comparative lawyers) and government officials on preparing and effectuating changes brought about by forced harmonisation could be calculated and expressed in monetary terms; the transaction cost savings could also be calculated. If this exercise was carried out, the desirability of harmonisation could be better assessed.

On top of the quantifiable costs, there are other losses that should be taken into account in a full cost-benefit analysis. The full costs of harmonisation can

---

[11] Communication (n. 3 above) at point 31.

[12] See for an elaboration of this point: R. Van den Bergh, 'Towards an institutional legal framework for regulatory competition in Europe', *Kyklos* [2000], 437–444.

[13] See P. Legrand, 'The impossibility of legal transplants', (1997) *Maastricht J. of Eur. and Comp. L*, 111.

only partly be calculated. However, the fact that some components of these costs cannot be expressed in quantitative terms should not distract from the risk that they might be substantial. The lack of diversity (no competition between legal orders) resulting in fewer satisfied preferences should again be mentioned. It should be added that competition between legislators also generates the advantages of a learning process. Differences in rules allow for different experiences and may improve an understanding of the effects of alternative legal solutions to similar problems. This advantage relates both to the formulation of the substantive rules and their enforcement. Reference can be made to Justice Brandeis' famous description of federal systems as laboratories of law reform.[14] Finally, information advantages at lower levels of government may be lost. Decentralisation is more efficient the more valuable local information is for appropriate rule making and enforcement. The European Commission seems to realise the importance of this argument (and the resulting cost savings) in the field of law enforcement,[15] but it is also a valid concern at the stage of the formulation of substantive rules. Not only can one assume that national legislators are better aware of local preferences; they can also better appreciate whether new rules fit in the existing legal framework and what would be the costs of their mandatory enactment.

3. Arguments in Favour of Harmonisation of Contract Law

a) General insights

The preceding paragraphs should not give the wrong impression that harmonisation of law cannot be justified by economic reasons. Taking allocative efficiency rather than an unqualified market integration approach as the goal of policy making, it is possible to advance four reasons why legislative action at the EC level, including harmonisation of laws, may be appropriate: (1) to profit from scale economies, (2) to internalise interstate externalities, (3) to prevent a race to the bottom, and (4) to cure inefficient state law.[16] The first three reasons in favour of centralised rule making and harmonisation of laws can be easily understood by drawing a parallel between competition on the markets for ordinary goods and competition between laws. The fourth reason builds on

---

[14] *New State Ice Corp. v. Liebmann,* 285 US 262, 311 (1932).

[15] A clear example is the White Paper ((EC) [1999] OJ C 132/1), which advocates decentralised enforcement of the EC competition rules by national competition authorities and courts.

[16] Distributional goals (e.g. a more equitable distribution of income between producers/traders and consumers) are not discussed here, since it is obvious that rules of private law are not effective instruments to redistribute income in contractual relations (H. Demsetz, 'Wealth distribution and the ownership of rights', (1972) *Journal of Legal Studies,* 223–232).

Public Choice theory: the political process in the member states may be deficient so that centralisation is needed to improve upon the outcomes of the decision-making. To avoid misunderstandings, it should be added that arguments in favour of central rules do not automatically imply that (full or partial) harmonisation is necessary. Here the proportionality principle warns against over-regulation.

If laws are not harmonised, there is scope for competition between legislators. Generally, more legislators are better than one. A monopoly on the markets for legislation may cause inefficiencies similar to the losses in terms of productive and dynamic inefficiency on ordinary goods markets. Since he faces no competition, the centralist rule-maker has no incentive to reduce the costs of the legal system (productive inefficiency) or to develop new forms of legal protection (dynamic inefficiency). However, reducing the number of legislators may be efficient if there are important scale economies to be obtained. Markets for legislation may exhibit characteristics of natural monopolies: it cannot be excluded that important cost savings can be achieved by a centralised gathering of the information needed to design efficient laws. In addition, markets for legislation may fail in the same way as ordinary markets for goods or services do not generate efficient outcomes because of market imperfections. A major market imperfection is the problem of externalities, which in the regulatory context occur if a state externalises the costs of legal rules to other jurisdictions, while keeping the benefits within the state borders. Consequently, the need to cope with externalities between legal orders is a major argument in favour of centralised decision-making. Another argument is known as the risk of a 'race to the bottom'. This argument posits that states, in an effort to induce geographically mobile firms to locate within their jurisdiction, will offer them suboptimally lax rules (e.g. lenient environmental standards, corporate law-favouring managers and so on) in order to benefit from additional jobs and tax revenues. If there is support for this prediction, the danger of destructive competition between legislators may justify centralisation. Apart from these arguments, centralised rule making may be necessary because the political processes at the member states level lead to an underprotection of interests. The Public Choice rationale maintains that centralist rules cure inefficient outcomes at lower levels of government.

These arguments are analytically distinct and should not be confused. The danger of interstate externalities exists even in the absence of a race to the bottom. The Public Choice rationale does not focus on the existence of interstate externalities or the risk of a race to the bottom, but on the inability of states to maximise welfare. It should be obvious that the strength of the arguments in favour of centralised law making differs across different fields of law. For example, the externalities argument is valid only if legal rules affect transactions with interstate repercussions. In the remainder it will be investigated whether the above reasons may support harmonisation of contract law.

b) Scale economies and transaction cost savings

From an efficiency viewpoint, centralisation may be defended because of scale economies or transaction cost savings. If scale economies are important, central rule making may be required. An example is the production of the information needed to formulate legal rules. Some information relevant to the entire European Community can be most efficiently provided by Community institutions; decentralisation would cause substantial costs of duplication. In the legal literature, great emphasis is put on the need for legal certainty. If rules are harmonised, uncertainty as to the precise contents of the law decreases and – so it is argued – case law will tend to be more predictable. In economic terms, transaction costs, in particular costs of information, negotiation and enforcement, decline.

It must be stressed that the importance of the scale economies argument will vary across different fields of law. Scale economies may be important for the design of efficient rules of public law such as safety regulation, but negligible in other fields of law, such as private law. Transaction cost savings can be substantial in the field of interventionist law but will be lower when parties choose from facilitative rules. It must be added that the legal certainty argument tends to be overstated. Information costs decrease when only one and not several legal systems must be analysed, but legal uncertainty may also be a feature of common rules. Common rules are only really uniform if they are also interpreted in the same way. The use of vague notions in EC legislation and legal language differences across member states will remain a hindrance to the achievement of full legal certainty.

It is remarkable that the threshold for harmonisation measures in the field of contract law has always been low. There is no requirement that lack of harmonisation has a substantial effect[17] on interstate trade and, as a consequence, there is a danger that European law will pre-empt fields of private law, where the harm to market integration is outweighed by efficiency savings. With respect to contract law, the Commission would now at last 'like to find out if the co-existence of national contract laws in the Member States directly or indirectly obstructs to the functioning of the internal market, and if so to what extent'.[18] This quotation shows that there are no hard data available on savings, which could be achieved by harmonising contract law. It is unclear if, and if so, to what extent the lack of uniform rules of contract law reduces the willingness to do cross-border business. Impediments to trade are more likely in the field of

---

[17] The ruling of the European Court in the *Tobacco* judgment that 'mere finding of disparities between national rules and the abstract risk of obstacles to the exercise of fundamental freedoms or distortions of competition' (ECJ 5.10.2000, Case C-376/98, *Federal Republic of Germany v. European Parliament and Council*, not yet officially reported) is insufficient raises the threshold for Community intervention but may still be deficient from an economic perspective.

[18] Communication (n. 3 above), at point 23.

interventionist law; in the area of facilitative law the parties concerned may draft their own rules which probably would be better adapted to the problems encountered. Even when transaction cost savings can be shown, it must again be taken into account that market integration is not a goal in itself. The savings achieved must be set off against the benefits of diversity.

c) Interstate externalities

In diverging policy fields member states' laws may cause adverse externalities for other Community members. If allocative efficiency is to be reached in a federal state, preferences for inefficient national rules in any field of law may be satisfied only to the extent that costs are borne by the population preferring such rules.[19] To internalise across-the-border externalities, centralisation may be necessary. This insight is relevant to explain Community action in many fields. Air pollution is an obvious example.[20] In addition, the negative effects of a merger on prices in different countries may require control by a central antitrust agency.[21] However, before jumping to the conclusion that centralist solutions (including harmonisation) are needed, it should be investigated whether bilateral agreements between the member states involved are not superior to full centralisation, given the availability of information and the negotiation and enforcement costs at different regulatory levels. In the law and economics literature the first alternative is known as Coasian bargaining.[22] The Coase theorem tells us that if there are well-specified property rights, full information and low transaction costs, the efficient solution will result through bargaining between the Member States without any need for further Community intervention. Hence, an important task for the EC is to provide an institutional framework in which Coasian bargaining is possible. If the number of member states affected by the externalities is too large or reaching agreements is impeded by opportunistic behaviour, harmonisation of laws may be needed.

At first sight, the externalities argument does not seem convincing in the field of contract law. Generally, contracts do not cause effects for third parties because

---

[19]   In the literature on federalism this is known as the principle of fiscal equivalence (W. Oates, *Fiscal Federalism* (New York, Harcourt Brace Jovanovich, 1972)).

[20]   See R.J. Van den Bergh, M. Faure and J. Lefevere, 'The subsidiarity principle in European environmental law: an economic analysis', in: E. Eide and R. Van den Bergh (eds.), *Law and Economics of the Environment* (Oslo, Juridisk Forlag, 1996), 121–166.

[21]   R. Van den Bergh, 'Economic Criteria for Applying the Subsidiarity Principle in the European Community: The Case of Competition Policy', (1996) *International Review of Law and Economics*, 363–383.

[22]   Named after Nobel Prize Winner Prof. R.H. Coase, who is generally considered a founding father of New Law and Economics, in which economic insights are used outside the field of antitrust, such as private law. The Coase theorem was developed in: R. Coase, 'The problem of social cost', 3 (1960) *Journal of Law and Economics*, 1 .

of the principle of privity: the rights and obligations agreed upon only concern the contracting partners. In addition, EC Directives also contain rules applying to domestic trade, where cross-border effects are clearly absent. This does not imply, however, that the externalities problem is entirely irrelevant. It is indeed possible that a network of contracts generates externalities. Decisions as to quality and price taken by a trader may have both positive and negative effects on downstream or upstream salespersons of the same distribution chain. For example, a decision to lower quality to achieve higher profits may bring short-term benefits to a single retailer, but will harm the distribution network at large. Under EC competition law, not all devices to cope with this problem are allowed: whereas it is legal to exclude non-qualified distributors in open and accessible markets, a direct solution of the problem by imposing minimum prices is out-lawed.[23] This excursion into a different field of law shows that the externalities problem is not a major concern of the European legislator. Also in the area of contract law, the Directives do a poor job in curing externalities. In the Directive on sales contracts and consumer guarantees, this important matter is curiously left out of the harmonisation project.[24] Upstream liability of producers and wholesale sellers is necessary to ensure that proper incentives to ensure quality are given to parties with actual control of the likelihood of product defects. However, the availability of a right of redress is left to national law. Given the interstate externalities that an absence of upstream liability may cause, it is astonishing that the Directive does not regulate this issue. Obviously, it must be added that a showing of externalities is in itself no sufficient reason to justify harmonisation of laws. It must be impossible to internalise the externalities by applying national rules of contract law: for example, because contract remedies are made unavailable by technical reasons of national law. The task of European law is to fill the gaps when performance or compensation claims and, therefore, full internalisation of cross-border externalities is impossible.

The externalities problem can also be analysed from another perspective. Differences in consumer law do not cause technological externalities. However, to justify harmonisation, the concept of externalities can be given a different meaning, including also psychic spillovers.[25] Such an argument has already been advanced in other contexts, including environmental law. People living in country A who prefer a high level of environmental protection may be willing to pay for measures protecting endangered species in country B. Similarly, European citizens preferring a high level of consumer protection could suffer if this level is not guaranteed in another member state, even though it may be compensated by economic savings. It is, however, extremely difficult to determine the disutility

---

[23] Van den Bergh and Camesasca (n. 6), 247–248.

[24] See consideration 9.

[25] W. Wils, 'Subsidiarity and EC environmental policy: taking people's concerns seriously', (1994) *Journal of Environmental Law*, 85–91.

function of foreign consumers. For this reason, harmonisation of laws to correct psychic externalities cannot easily be justified.

d) Race to the bottom?

Law-makers may be motivated to attract firms from other jurisdictions since that should entail increased investment, demand for labour and tax revenue. The theoretical basis for this fear is the existence of prisoners' dilemmas between member states. When the European Commission proposes harmonisation of laws, it usually refers to the need to prevent inequality of competitive conditions across the member states. This fear may be rephrased in economic terms as the danger of prisoners' dilemmas. States may operate, not in a market-like setting, but in a prisoners' dilemma game. When legislators can be analogised to firms selling in a competitive market, decentralised rules may be preferable. In contrast, when states compete under prisoners' dilemma conditions, national rules will produce a result that is worse than a federal rule.[26] Regulatory laxness may occur when substantive rules have to be enacted, and also at the implementation stage. A state will only gain in the struggle to attract business by choosing in favour of laxness, when other states do not act in the same way. However, if all other states follow, only the businesses will gain. The result of this prisoners' dilemma is a race for the bottom and centralisation will then be required to generate efficient outcomes.

However, it should be obvious that there will be many variables operating on decisions as to location and that the contents of legal rules (and the connected costs) may have only a minor impact, if at all. Even in areas of law where one might expect a substantial impact, theoretical and empirical research shows that there is no convincing proof for a race to the bottom and that, by contrast, a race for the top may take place. For example, there is no support for the claim of a race to the bottom in environmental law: neither theoretically nor empirically.[27]

It seems highly unlikely that firms will relocate plants to profit from lenient contract law. It should be added that states might not only acquire benefits in case of physical migration, but also by charging fees for using legal constructions. For example, 16 per cent of the total tax revenue of Delaware is derived from incorporation fees.[28] However, it does not seem feasible to charge fees for using contract doctrines developed in a single jurisdiction.

---

[26] S. Rose-Ackerman, *Rethinking the Progressive Agenda* (New York, Free Press, 1992), 167.

[27] See R. Revesz, 'Rehabilitating interstate competition: rethinking the "race to the bottom" rationale for federal environmental regulation', (1992) *New York University Law Review*, 1210 with further references.

[28] R. Romano, *The Genius of American Corporate Law* (Washington, DC, AEI Press, 1993), 8–9.

e) The Public Choice rationale

To justify harmonisation of contract law it could be argued that states do not have the competence or are not willing to enact 'good' contract law. Such a claim is more difficult to support with respect to facilitative law, since parties involved may draft their own sets of rules. The argument would mainly apply to interventionist law: national states would not always be inclined or able to enact welfare enhancing rules protecting weak contract parties, in particular consumers. On the one hand, it must be admitted that consumer law is not a well-developed area in all member states. On the other hand, a low degree of regulatory intervention may indicate that citizens are not willing to pay the price for mandatory consumer protection. It should be added that there might be a minimum level of protection, on which all consumers would agree, even if it results in higher consumer prices. Political failure in some member states may deprive consumers from this protection. However, there is no guarantee that regulatory failures can be avoided at EC level. The rule of a qualified majority (Arts. 95–96 EC Treaty) is deficient in this respect; only when the need for regulation and the regulatory tools used are almost unanimously consented in the fifteen Member States can EC regulatory failure be avoided.

A critical look at EC Directives immediately shows that several rules of consumer protection may cause inefficiencies rather than curing them. EC Directives often also exhibit a lack of understanding of the basic economic insights and thus fall a long way short of providing efficient rules. A major problem is that the protection is often mandatory: consumers preferring a lower degree of protection cannot put aside their protection in exchange for a lower price. Generally, legal measures drafted in the Internal Market Directorate interfere less with contractual freedom than Directives enacted by the Consumer Protection Directorate General. The latter remains heavily influenced by out-dated views on consumer protection. Legal rules are supposed to cure economic inequality. This approach is deficient for two reasons. First, since reasons for the supposed inequality are not made explicit, it is impossible to target legal solutions at the causes of market failure. Second, real life effects of the granted protection should not be ignored: it must be acknowledged that consumer protection raises prices and may cause adverse effects.[29] Against this background, the claim that European law is needed to 'modernise' state law[30] can thus hardly be supported. Consumer law is in great need of a new paradigm: instead of trying to cure inequality attention should be shifted to the problems caused by information asymmetries and opportunistic bargaining. Within the confines of this article three examples should suffice to illustrate the relevant economic

---

[29]   R. Van den Bergh, *Averechts recht* (Antwerpen, Intersentia, 1999).
[30]   Green Paper, COM(93) 509, 105.

insights: the regulation of unfair contract terms, the provision of cooling-off periods and the Sales Contract Directive.

A first example is the EC Directive on unfair contract terms[31] which is based on the outdated view that the consumer is economically inferior and should be protected by invalidating unfair clauses. Contractual terms that have not been individually negotiated are regarded as unfair if they cause 'a significant imbalance in the parties' rights and obligations arising under the contract, to the detriment of the consumer'.[32] This view focuses on a distributional problem and neglects the central economic cause of quality deterioriation on consumer markets. Standard terms will be inefficient when consumers are not able to judge the experience qualities of clauses in standard form contracts. An efficient response to this problem does not consist of information remedies (such as the one provided by Art. 5 of the Directive[33]) since only rational fools would be willing to spend resources on reading and comparing contract clauses. Since information disclosure cannot cure the problem of adverse selection, quality regulation prohibiting contract terms which rational, well-informed consumers would not voluntarily accept, is needed. The Directive contains a general clause, but no binding list of specified unfair terms. An efficiency assessment of the regulation of standard form contracts involves an unavoidable trade-off between higher prices and more favourable terms. From this perspective, a black list has considerable advantages. Not only does a clear *ex ante* prohibition reduce uncertainty; it also enables markets to adjust prices. Blacklists allow learning processes. If market data show that the price for the better quality is too high, the law can be changed, yielding to the evidence of the revealed consumers' preferences.[34] Compared to national legislation,[35] which blacklists a number of contractual terms in consumer contracts, the EC Directive does a poor job in increasing overall consumer welfare.

A second example is the regulation of cooling-off periods. Although cooling-off periods can be seen as potential remedies for problems of irrational behaviour, situational monopoly and informational asymmetry, the current rules fail to cure the mentioned inefficiencies in all situations. These shortcomings may again be attributed to the fact that the rule-makers wanted to correct a problem of unequal bargaining power yet neglected the relevant economic insights. Cooling-off periods are not always sufficiently long to cure the informational asymmetries;

---

[31] Council Directive 93/13 EEC of 5 April 1993 on unfair terms in consumer contracts, (EC) [1993] OJ L 95/29 .

[32] Article 3, Directive 93/13.

[33] 'In the case of contracts where all or certain terms offered to the consumer are in writing, these terms must always be drafted in plain, intelligible language'.

[34] See also R. Pardolesi and A. Pacces, 'Clausole vessatorie e analisi economica del diritto: note in margine alle ragioni (ed alle incongruenze) della nuova disciplina', *Diritto Privato 1996* (Milano, Cedam, 1997), 377–426.

[35] Examples include the German, Dutch and Belgian laws.

they neither cope with problems of moral hazard on the part of the consumer nor prevent adverse effects.[36] Taking these problems into account, it is reassuring that rules on cooling-off periods differ across member states; these differences allow for learning processes which should be aided and not stopped by mandatory EC rules.

Finally, the Sales Contract Directive also seems to neglect the relevant economic insights. It harmonises the purchaser's rights in case of defective goods. Which goods are defective is decided upon reasonable expectations about the normal use of the good and especially declarations before the formation of the contract. In economic terms the Directive provides a mandatory legal warranty for a minimum period of two years. Only the need to ensure that obligations resulting from sales contracts are performed seems to have been the concern of the European legislator. Under such an approach the different economic functions of warranties are neglected. Warranties do not only provide incentives to the seller to perform his contract duties; they also allocate risk between parties and function as signalling mechanisms. A full warranty is only efficient if the following conditions are simultaneously met: the buyer is risk averse, the seller has private information and the latter also controls the risk of product defects.[37] In the cases where sellers, too, are risk averse, buyers have private information and bilateral precaution reduces risk, partial warranties are economically superior. This explains why commercial warranties are often of shorter duration. By compelling a mandatory coverage of two years, the Directive may force contracting parties to accept solutions reducing their well-being.

It must be concluded that the Public Choice rationale cannot provide convincing arguments to justify broad-ranging harmonisation of contract law in Europe. The redistributive goal of EC consumer law cannot be achieved. Since the rules are not targeted at the relevant problems of informational asymmetries and opportunistic behaviour, current EC law has shown itself unable to cure existing inefficiencies in consumer markets. In addition, asserted shortcomings of member states' law must be set off against the risk of political distortions at the EC level. There are serious doubts as to whether a remote legislator is able to correctly assess consumer preferences.

4. The Alternative: Competition Between Rules and Spontaneous Harmonisation

The preceding section of this paper has shown that there are no convincing economic reasons for harmonisation of contract law. Lack of harmonisation

---

[36] P. Rekaiti and R. Van den Bergh, 'Cooling-off periods in the consumer laws of the EC Member States. A comparative Law and Economics approach', (2000) *J. Consumer Pol'y*, 371–407.

[37] F. Parisi, 'The harmonization of legal warranties in European law: an economic analysis', *George Mason University Law and Economics Working Paper Series*, http://papers.ssrn.com/abstract = 276993.

measures does not imply that rules of contract law will greatly differ. Member states may decide to amend their codes in response to legal solutions adopted in another Member State. Competition between legislators and legal uniformity is not mutually exclusive. Whereas harmonisation by means of central rules (EC Regulations and Directives) implies forced co-ordination of legislative provisions in the member states, dynamic competitive processes may produce voluntary harmonisation. The result of this process of innovation and subsequent amendment may be a substantial uniformity across the states.[38] If one is willing to take competitive processes seriously, the answer to the question whether harmonisation is needed must be left to the process itself.

Spontaneous harmonisation may be expected when preferences across countries are homogeneous. Such homogeneity will be rare when legal rules are of an interventionist type, creating benefits for some citizens but imposing costs on others. Diversity of interests will lead to heterogeneous preferences and impede spontaneous harmonisation. In contrast, when legal rules are facilitative, all involved parties may realise gains from cost-reducing measures. Hence, they will all prefer the least costly legal solution and competition between jurisdictions will be won by the 'cheapest' rule. Cost-reducing changes in legal systems often emerge as the consequence of international competition. Ogus mentions two examples: the restriction of the doctrine of state immunity by English judges and the attenuation of the requirement that defaulting promisors must be given a formal notice by French judges.[39]

Another example of spontaneous ongoing harmonisation is the evolution of contract remedies.[40] The principal remedy for breach of contract in Anglo-American law is an award of monetary damages. By contrast, in civil law countries a promisee is entitled to require the breaching party to perform according to the contract. In practice, however, the differences between common law and civil law are smaller than the contradictory rules seem to suggest. On the one hand, under Anglo-American law specific performance may be required if it can be shown that damages are an inadequate remedy. Traditionally, judges ordered specific performance when the breaching party was a seller who had agreed to sell a unique good (for example immovable property or artworks). On the other hand, in civil law countries the right of the promisee to request specific performance is not absolute. Recently the Dutch Supreme Court ruled that the

---

[38] The scope of such a voluntary harmonisation may be larger than the degree of uniformity brought about by centralisation. Directives, for example, often contain escape clauses or grant the Member States a number of options to choose between, that may endanger the goal of full harmonisation.

[39] A. Ogus (n. 5).

[40] See generally, from a law and economics perspective: P.G. Mahoney, 'Contract Remedies: General', in: B. Bouckaert and G. De Geest (eds.), Encyclopedia of Law and Economics (Vol. III, Cheltenham, Edward Elgar, 2000), 117–140.

promisee has no free choice between damages and specific performance, but that this choice is limited by requirements of reasonableness and fairness and that the justified interests of the breaching party should be taken into account.[41] This formulation has opened the door for arguing an efficient breach of contract. Law and Economics scholars have argued that a contract would require performance in all circumstances except those in which non-performance would result in greater joint wealth.[42] Allowing efficient breach of contract is a prime example of a cost-minimising rule. It is noteworthy that this theory is now accepted in both common law and (some) civil law jurisdictions. This spontaneous harmonisation occurred in the absence of compelling EC Directives.

In the field of interventionist law spontaneous harmonisation is less likely but not excluded. Cooling-off periods were designed in the context of self-regulation. Given their ability to cope with problems of information asymmetry, mail order businesses introduced them to signal quality. Consumers who found themselves unhappy with a given purchase were given the right to cancel the contract within a seven-day period. The legislator thus copied a rule that initially emerged within the self-regulatory framework of distance selling.[43] When the EC Directive was finally enacted in 1997, the right of a cooling-off period was already widely guaranteed by self-regulation and national consumer protection legislation.

5. The Role of European Law

European law does not fully profit from the lessons from economic theory. If the European regulator took the benefits of competition between legal orders seriously, he would in the first place organise competition between the member states' laws and would enact rules of substantive European law only if and where such competition cannot lead to efficient outcomes. Competition among rules of law is related to the sovereignty of the Member States. Therefore, the creation of a legal framework for competition between legal orders is a matter of constitutional design. At present, there is no European constitution, which creates sufficient scope for diverging legal rules and spells out rules of conduct for the competing legislators. At best, the current text of the Treaties may be qualified as a quasi-constitutional framework, which contains the first building blocks of a European Constitution. It should be improved upon to become a general legal framework (*'Ordnungsrahmen'*) safeguarding the beneficial effects of competition between legal systems, whilst at the same time coping with economic distortions on markets for legislation if the latter may be expected to occur.

---

[41] HR, 5 January 2001, NJ, 2001, 79. See for a comment: M. Veldman, 'Grenzen aan het recht op nakoming', *WPNR* [2001], 727–738.

[42] S. Shavell, 'Damage measures for breach of contract', (1980) 11 *Bell Journal of Economics*, 466–490.

[43] See Rekaiti and Van den Bergh (n. 36), 381.

Competition between sellers of laws requires that buyers are informed about contents and effects of alternative rules, and can freely choose the set of laws best adapted to their preferences. If the European legislator took competitive processes seriously, European law would take a dramatically different form: instead of programmes of harmonisation, one would rather see measures to strengthen competitive pressures and improve information flows. In the first place, competition requires a sufficient number of legislators to make sure that varying preferences can be satisfied. To start with, the European legislator could stimulate competition by offering European rules as a sixteenth[44] choice (as a complement to the fifteen legal systems of the member states) for firms and citizens. Offering additional choices, rather than harmonising immediately certain rules of substantive law, will also preserve the benefits of competition as a dynamic process. Competition between the EU lawmaker and national law-makers may enhance spontaneous harmonisation. From a dynamic perspective this outcome is preferable to forced harmonisation by means of binding rules of European law. Unfortunately, rules of European law often simply replace rules of national law and thus restrict choices rather than increasing them. A clear hostile view on competition can be seen in the Directive on consumer guarantees. The rule that the seller is liable during a period of two years for having delivered goods that are not in conformity with the contract is mandatory (no competition from legal rules enacted inside the EC) and the consumer's protection may not be undermined by applying legal rules of non-member states to the contract (no competition from outside the EC).[45]

In addition to increasing competitive pressures, measures to improve information flows should be taken. On this point too EC law is defective. Currently there is no common terminology in the laws of the member states; the common law uses a language that is not easily understandable to civil lawyers (for example, notions such as privity of contract or estoppel). Comparison of the strengths and weaknesses of different legal solutions concerning issues such as the formation and validity of contracts and remedies for non-performance is difficult because of information deficiencies caused by a non-uniform terminology. Standardisation would be extremely helpful to make competition on the market for legislation work. Of course, this suggestion supposes that differences in language do not reflect different preferences but are merely pointless incompatibilities.

Although the presumption should remain that member states are able to achieve the relevant policy goals, corrective measures may be needed when interjurisdictional competition leads to suboptimal outcomes. A system of concurrent powers perfectly meets this need. In such a system states retain the right to enact legislation as long as the Community institutions do not make use of

---

[44]   Or a seventeenth choice if Scots law is seen as a mixed legal system.
[45]   Directive 1999/44, Art. 7.

their power to achieve Community objectives. The next step, then, is to make sure that the response of the European regulator is adequately targeted at the problem at hand and does not go further than necessary to reach the goals of the Treaty. From this perspective, the proportionality principle enshrined in Article 5(3) EC Treaty may be seen as an important element of the quasi-constitutional framework safeguarding competition between legislators. The proportionality principle requires that Community acts must be appropriate to the aim to be achieved and may not go beyond what is necessary for that purpose. In cases of total harmonisation such competition is ruled out entirely. It will be difficult to reconcile this far-reaching intervention by the European legislator with the proportionality principle.

If one takes the proportionality principle seriously, costs and benefits of alternative solutions, ranking from legislative action representing a low degree of interference to highly interventionist measures, must be compared. A full comparative institutional approach necessitates comparing the strengths and weaknesses of either leaving the issue to be the member states ('doing nothing') or regulation at the Community level, including a comparative analysis of varying legal instruments. In the field of consumer law information rules should generally be preferred to imposing mandatory solutions. Only when information measures are unable to correct market failures (or when problems arise from opportunistic behaviour of sellers) should farther-reaching regulatory intervention be considered.

III. CONCLUSION

Harmonisation of contract law is often favoured because it would reduce information costs and increase interstate trade. This easy-to-understand argument should not be too readily accepted, however. On the one hand, the relevant economic savings (reduced transaction costs) have not yet been quantified. On the other hand, the costs of harmonisation largely go unnoticed. The latter include the administrative costs of legal changes and the disadvantages flowing from reduced diversity. The advantages of competition between legal rules must not be underestimated: if rules differ, more preferences can be satisfied and learning processes remain possible. It is remarkable that the EC harmonisation measures concern rules of interventionist law, where preferences may be supposed to diverge most strongly. From an economic perspective, it is equally deplorable that EC law does not fully cover situations of cross-border externalities, where the argument in favour of harmonised rules is most convincing.

From an economic perspective there is no strong case in favour of harmonisation of rules of contract law. Hence, the role for EC law seems to be limited. Detrimental cross-border effects could justify a limited regulatory intervention in cases where member states' laws are unable to internalise across-the-border externalities. In addition, rules of European law could strengthen competition between legal rules (and the resulting benefits) by providing non-binding rules as an additional choice. Competition between rules does not imply that the degree of legal uniformity will necessarily be lower than under a regime of forced harmonisation. As far as facilitative law is concerned, the competition will be won by the least costly rules. Spontaneous harmonisation may also occur in areas of interventionist law if preferences are homogeneous with respect to a minimum level of legal protection. In addition to strengthening competitive processes, the European legislator should review and improve the existing legislation to prevent welfare losses. This review must also include the possibility of repatriating competencies back to the member states if the latter have a competitive advantage over the EC in enacting efficient rules of contract law.

18. Transaction Costs and Subsidiarity in European Contract Law

*Hugh Collins**

My comment on the Green Paper on European Contract Law[1] implies a criticism of its starting point. The Green Paper describes a broad range of possible options with respect to the legal regulation of transactions in the European Community. The options range from doing nothing to the introduction of something equivalent to the private law codes that apply within most Member States. In between these extremes, the Commission notes as possible choices the development of optional uniform rules, more specific measures aimed at regulating particular kinds of transactions, and many other variations. To choose between the options, we need to establish clearly what might be the intended gains. Indeed, given the potential expense and complexity of most of the options, we require some persuasive arguments that doing nothing is either costly or undesirable for some other reason. Thus I shall focus on the potential reasons for a European initiative with respect to transnational contact law. What does the Green Paper assume are the problems that any initiative should address? Once we are clearer about the problems to be solved, we may be able to pick a more sure-footed way through the range of options presented for our consideration.

The central question that the Commission in the Green Paper poses is whether EC regulation of contracts is required in order to remove direct or indirect obstacles to cross-border trade caused by divergent regulatory regimes. The Commission asks for evidence as to whether the proper functioning of the Internal Market is hindered by problems in relation to the conclusion, interpretation and application of cross-border contracts. I shall argue that the search for non-tariff barriers to the free movement of goods and services presented by general contract law is likely to prove fruitless and sets an unhelpful agenda. A better question is whether transnational regulation of some type can contribute to the overall reduction of transaction costs in commercial cross-border transactions. But I shall argue that the most important question about proposals for harmonisation of contract law remains a political debate rather than an economic one. The fundamental issue is whether some form of harmonisation of contract law can contribute to a form of better economic integration that nevertheless respects an appropriate degree of political sovereignty for nation states.

---

* Professor of English Law, London School of Economics.
[1] COM(2001) 398 final.

S. Grundmann and J. Stuyck (eds.), An Academic Green Paper on European Contract Law, 269–281
© 2002 *Kluwer Law International. Printed in Great Britain.*

My paper is mostly devoted to an explanation of why questions about trans-action costs and political integration are the important ones, and why the Commission's question about obstacles to the internal market is misconceived. I am not necessarily suggesting either that the Commission is unaware that it is asking the wrong question or that it disagrees that my questions are the relevant ones. The Green Paper is for public consumption and its authors may not want to broach even more controversial questions. It is no doubt necessary for the Commission to tie its initiatives securely within the competence of the European Union, and so the emphasis on the operation of the Internal Market is the obvious lifeline on which to hang this initiative. The section of the Green Paper entitled 'Implications for the Internal Market' (part 3.2) thus contains the core justifications for considering the options listed in the report. But this constraint on the ambit of discussion does not apply so forcefully to this paper, though eventually we must consider the appropriate scope of EC legislative competence.

I. LEGAL DIVERSITY AS AN OBSTACLE TO TRADE

The Commission asks for specific examples where divergences in contract law in relation to formation, interpretation, and enforcement between Member States directly or indirectly obstruct cross-border contracts. It is often assumed that variations in contract laws do create obstacles to cross-border transactions. Hence the Commission asks for evidence of obstructions rather than asking whether legal diversity could, even in theory, constitute a non-tariff barrier. Yet the basis for this assumption about the effect of legal diversity is unclear.

It is important to distinguish between obstacles to trade and transaction costs. Obstacles to trade or non-tariff barriers prevent cross-border trade, because suppliers are unable to comply with the national law. Trade barriers prevent a business from selling its normal product or from selling it in the customary way. Such laws are certainly appropriate targets for dismantling or harmonisation on the ground of promoting the internal market. In contrast, transaction costs, viewed narrowly, are the costs of entering contracts. Like other costs such as manufacture and transport, these costs feed into the cost of the product to a consumer. Transaction costs may make cross-border trade less competitive, because consumers are unwilling to pay the higher price for an equivalent foreign product. But transaction costs are no more a barrier to trade than the additional costs of transport over greater distances. The question to be considered first is whether variations in contract laws between Member States create obstacles to trade, not merely greater transaction costs.

For most contracts for the supply of goods and services, diversity in contract laws presents no obstacle to cross-border trade. The goods and services can be supplied as usual, the only difference being that the cross-border element raises a question of the choice of law. The parties to the contract therefore have to incur the additional expense of determining which law should govern the transaction. In some instances, such as contracts with consumers and employees, the Rome Convention of 1980 in effect determines the applicable law,[2] so that choice does not have to be made. It is true, of course, that a business may not be able to use its customary standard form contract in cross-border trade. The applicable law may render that contract unworkable or invalid. The business will have to incur the expense of constructing new contracts to suit the legal requirements of the applicable law. The business may need to generate as many as sixteen types of standard form contract in order to be able to do business throughout the European Community. But this expense is a transaction cost rather than an obstacle to trade.

The position may be different where the contract itself represents the product being sold. In the case of insurance, for instance, the standard form contract or insurance policy is the product that is being sold. Diversity in national laws applicable to insurance no doubt renders it extremely difficult or impossible to market the same insurance policy throughout the European Community. This problem of an obstacle to trade seems likely to occur whenever the contract is the product itself, rather than a device for conferring entitlements to other products or services.

Diversity in contract law can also impose an obstacle to trade when the law regulates permissible marketing techniques. If a business is unable to use its established and successful marketing techniques in another country, that may effectively prevent its extension across borders. For example, if a business uses a format franchising technique for its retail outlets, and if that technique is forbidden or is restricted in some countries, the opportunity for cross-border trade in the sense of business expansion into new markets is inhibited.

These two instances of genuine barriers to trade – contracts that constitute the product and marketing techniques – are certainly cases where the European Community needs to act in order to eliminate obstructions to cross-border trade. Several Directives address these problems, albeit not always comprehensively and successfully. In addition, the ECJ has used competition law to invalidate unjustified impediments to marketing techniques.[3]

Would any harmonisation of general contract law contribute to the solution of these genuine barriers to cross-border trade? It is hard to see what advantage could be gained because the problems are so specific. Special contract laws rather than general principles govern contracts that constitute the product such as insurance, and it is those special contract laws that create the obstacle to trade. Similarly, with respect to the regulation of marketing techniques, it is not

---

[2] Consolidated version (EC) OJ C 27, 26.1.1998, p. 34, Articles 5, 6.

[3] E.g. ECJ 16.5.93 – Case C-126/91 *Schutzverband gegen Unwesen in der Wirtschaft v. Y. Rocher GmbH* [1993] ECR I–2361; ECJ 10.5.95 – Case C-384/93 *Alpine Investments v. Minister van Financien* [1995] ECR I–1141.

the general law of contract but particular regulation of fair trading that causes the problem. In both cases the obstacles to trade can be addressed by specific Directives that harmonise laws, and any further harmonisation of general contract law would not alleviate the barriers to cross-border trade.

1. Legal Risk

Despite these elementary observations about the irrelevance of the diversity of national contract laws to the issue of non-tariff barriers to trade, it remains a popular view that somehow this diversity creates a barrier. In the absence of tangible examples, the barrier is described as psychological, that is, a matter of perception. It is claimed that businesses are dissuaded from cross-border trade by the knowledge that the laws may differ. In other words, there is a perception of enhanced legal risk, which discourages cross-border transactions.

Legal risk is the risk that the content of the law and its effects will not prove to be what one or both parties to the contract expect. This risk is always present in transactions, because there is a chance that the law may be interpreted in an unforeseen way by a court. Legal risk can be minimised by various techniques, such as use of standard form contracts, explicit detailed agreements, and the use of arbitration or some other familiar dispute resolution mechanism. These arrangements are usually adequate to prevent unforeseen legal consequences of transactions.

Does a cross-border element change the size of legal risk in transactions? In principle, there should be no change in legal risk arising from the law of contract. Once the parties have made an explicit choice of applicable law, the normal level of legal risk associated with that legal system will apply to a contract. What does augment legal risk in cross-border transactions is the uncertainty caused by private international law. In other words, legal risk is increased because the additional variable of another branch of law becomes involved. The size of the additional risk depends upon the extent that national laws place restrictions on express choice of law clauses. Whenever that express choice has uncertain validity, as in consumer and employment contexts under the Rome Convention, legal risk increases owing to the presence of a cross-border element. This additional legal risk can be reduced either by placing no restrictions on express choice of law clauses or by harmonising those areas of law where choice of law is restricted. Professor Grundmann has argued persuasively that most of the current Directives relating to contract law fit into the latter category, that is mandatory consumer laws that cannot be avoided by choice of law clauses.[4]

Yet we need to question whether enhanced legal risk in cross-border transactions of these types where choice of law is restricted really amounts to an obstacle to trade. Foreign businesses can comply with local regulations when selling

---

[4]   S. Grundmann, 'The Structure of European Contract Law' (2001) 4 *ERPL* 505.

across borders. In this respect they are in the same position as domestic sellers with no cross-border element in the transaction. No doubt the cross-border trader will have to become informed about local laws, particularly those dealing with consumer protection. Is this requirement for a trader to become informed an obstacle to cross-border trade? The laws are hardly secret and apply routinely to purely domestic traders. Unless we regard all mandatory rules of consumer protection as an obstacle to trade, there does not appear to be any special obstacle to cross-border transactions as compared to purely domestic transactions. These mandatory rules, however, generally serve the purpose of protecting competitive markets as well as protecting consumers, so they should not normally be regarded as an obstacle to trade. There are transaction costs in discovering the local regulations, but those costs do not amount to a barrier to trade and they apply equally to domestic businesses.

2. Risk and Trust

The internal market may not be working as well as its sponsors had hoped, but it seems unlikely that legal risk is responsible for non-tariff barriers of any significance. If legal risk cannot explain the widespread assumption that there are obstacles to cross-border trade caused by diversity in contract law, is there some other ground for explaining the psychological perception that cross-border trade is somehow more difficult? We should look elsewhere for the causes of the lack of competitive pressures arising from cross-border trade. We should remember in this context that contracting is an inherently risky activity.

One can never guard completely against the general risks of disappointment and betrayal.[5] For this reason most contracts are made between parties who know each other through previous transactions which have proven reliable. The consumer tends to shop at the same supermarkets and stores, a construction company uses a small group of subcontractors, and a manufacturer tends to acquire its supplies from a small group of familiar suppliers. It is this understandable pattern of choosing contracting partners from those with whom one has a prior history of successful dealings that presents the greatest obstacle to the formation of perfectly competitive markets. No legal system, whether national or transnational, can significantly challenge this obstacle to perfectly competitive markets. When entering contracts, the parties will always wish to minimise the risks, and one easy way to do this is to confine the choice of contracting party to a person who has proven reliable in the past.

These general risks of disappointment and betrayal are in my view the greatest obstacles to trade. These risks may be accentuated in instances of cross-border trade, not because of the international character of the transaction, but simply because the major source of trust, a history of prior successful dealings, is absent.

---

[5]   H. Collins, *Regulating Contracts* (Oxford: Oxford University Press, 1999) Chapter 5.

The central problem for the completion of the Internal Market is therefore merely a generalised version of the problem in all contracting: to improve trust, so that parties are willing to take the risk of entering contracts with relative strangers.

It is a conceit of lawyers that the law of contract and other types of regulation of markets can significantly improve trust, thereby encouraging individuals and businesses to take the risk of entering contracts with strangers. There is little empirical evidence to support this belief. If at all possible, no-one relies entirely on the possible legal sanction for breach of contract to protect themselves against disappointment and betrayal. Instead they seek to protect themselves by other methods. Buyers refuse to pay for goods and services until they have been received and inspected. Sellers refuse to deliver goods unless they are paid in advance, receive a bank guarantee of payment, or they retain some kind of proprietary security right. No-one wants to rely exclusively on the normal sanctions provided by the courts for breach of contract such as an award of compensation. The law therefore provides little support for trust. Its most important role lies in facilitating other methods of self-help such as enforcing bank guarantees and security rights.

In the absence of a history of prior dealings between the parties, which forms the basis of trust, the most important substitutes that encourage trust are likely to be found in acceptance of common social and trading norms. These conventional standards of behaviour emerge as interactional norms of trading according to standards of fairness and honesty. The norms may be given institutional endorsement through trade associations or other private organisations that set standards. The norms may also have indirect legal effect in the sense that their standards may be used to concretise the general principles of private law such as a requirement of good faith or of reasonable care. The Commission in its Green Paper notes the significance of these informal standards on the content of standard form contracts: 'certain clauses in contracts may result from common practice in a given member state ... It may be hard to agree a contract containing terms and conditions different from those generally applied in a particular member state.'[6] What may be the most important obstacle to cross-border trade is the absence of these conventional norms between the parties, in the sense that they are unsure whether or not the other shares the same norms of fair dealing. It is not the diversity of national laws that appears significant, but rather the perceived absence of a shared set of understandings about how business should be conducted.

Within the risky activity of entering contracts, therefore, the legal risk presented about the content and effects of the law of contract is likely to figure as a relatively minor risk that influences behaviour in the sense of determining whether trade takes place. Failures to consummate cross-border transactions

---

[6] COM(2001) 398 final, 9 (para. 29).

will be generally accounted for by reference to other kinds of risk, mostly a low level of trust that the other party will prove reliable. An awareness of legal risk may contribute to these failures to trade, but it is unlikely to be determinative in itself, because ultimately it can be resolved by an increase in transaction costs. The real problem is rather the weakness of the substitutes for trust formed on the basis of prior dealing, such as conventional standards for doing business. Changes to the law, at least with respect to the general rules of private law, will not overcome this problem of the lack of interactional norms on which to establish trust.

It follows from this analysis that the Commission's request for examples where cross-border trade has been impeded by legal risk is likely to produce scant empirical evidence of problems. Legal risk may prove a contributory factor, but other risk considerations are more likely to prove determinative. Even where legal risk is a contributory factor, it will almost always be the case that with additional legal expense the risk can be significantly reduced. Thus legal risk should usually be no more than an additional transaction cost, which, when added other transaction costs, will discourage parties from entering the contract for cost/benefit reasons. Legal risk as a non-tariff barrier to trade is therefore a very slender thread on which to hang a juggernaut like a code of European contract law.

II. Transaction Costs

If we define transaction costs narrowly as the costs of entering contracts, it is possible to argue that cross-border transactions incur on average higher trans-action costs, which tends to discourage such trade. The cross-border element introduces the additional dimension of the legal risk in coping with potential differences between legal systems.

Transaction costs with respect to coping with legal risk are provoked by uncertainty and ignorance. The uncertainty lies in the prediction of legal out-comes. This uncertainty is an inherent feature of law, though some legal systems are no doubt more predictable than others. The problem of ignorance arises from lack of knowledge of law, and is a matter of degree. Ignorance is likely to be greater with respect to foreign legal systems. In any cross-border transaction, this problem of ignorance is likely to be greater than in a purely domestic transaction simply because knowledge of two legal systems is required.

Transaction costs are incurred in coping with both these sources of legal risk. Uncertainty can be reduced by means of elaborate written contracts and through careful investigation of the rules of the relevant legal system. Ignorance can be reduced by legal research. All these remedies involve the use of lawyers and thus add to transaction costs. We can therefore assume with reasonable confidence that transaction costs will be higher in cross-border transactions. Lawyers have to be paid to sort out the additional legal risk of differences between legal systems. It is not possible for a business to use its standard trading conditions with the same confidence as in the case of purely domestic transactions.

But the presence of higher transaction costs in cross-border trade establishes nothing in itself. There are many additional costs in cross-border trade, such as the higher cost of transport and additional bank expenses. The important question is rather whether transnational legal regulation of contracts can help to reduce these transaction costs.

With respect to ignorance, there can be little doubt that uniform laws applicable throughout Europe would, after a period of transition, reduce the problem of ignorance considerably. Lawyers would know the law applicable in all Member States because it would be uniform and the same as domestic law. This advantage in saving on transaction costs provoked by ignorance is also true of the perhaps more manageable option of introducing uniform laws to govern particular transaction types, such as sales, commercial leases, security arrangements, etc.

With respect to uncertainty, there is no clear advantage of transnational law over national law. The problem of predictability has to be addressed at any level of regulation, and it is controversial how that best may be achieved. Some believe codes produce certainty; others maintain that common law systems of precedent produce greater predictability. My own view is that legal systems that try to understand the expectations and understandings of the parties to the contract and implement them have the edge on questions of predictability and the reduction of transaction costs.[7]

Transnational regulation carries with it the risk of diminished certainty in one respect. The problem will be to secure a uniform interpretation of the law in each Member State. Common uniform rules will not on their own guarantee such a result.[8] The normal legal technique for ensuring such a result is to establish a hierarchy of courts with the task of ensuring uniformity within the jurisdiction by means of regulating inferior courts' decisions on appeals. This expensive, but tried and trusted, method for securing uniformity of interpretation implies a much greater significance for a system of European Community civil law courts.[9] This problem of securing a uniform interpretation of the law applies whether the legislative instrument of the Community were to be a Regulation or a Directive.

The transaction cost analysis does not seem to provide a compelling case for uniform laws. Uniform laws will not necessarily increase certainty or predictability. That outcome depends not on their transnational character but on the

---

[7] H. Collins, 'Formalism and Efficiency' (2000) 8 *ERPL* 211.

[8] G. Teubner, 'Legal Irritants: Good Faith in British Law or How Unifying Law Ends Up in New Divergences' (1998) 61 *MLR* 11.

[9] H. Collins, 'Transnational Private Law Regulation of Markets' (1998) 4 *Europa E Diritto Privato* 967.

regulatory techniques employed. Uniform laws may in fact reduce certainty, unless some method for uniform interpretation is achieved, with the effect of thereby increasing transaction costs. Uniform laws may, however, reduce the costs of overcoming ignorance of the law in the sense that, if there is only one law to discover and examine, the costs of so doing will be reduced. A uniform law would be an improvement over a choice of law approach in that the latter normally requires from lawyers a knowledge of two legal systems.

What does this transaction cost approach suggest should be the route forward for EC regulation in the field of contract law? With respect to the creation of an optional set of rules that could be chosen by the parties, the transaction cost approach cannot point to any advantages. The creation of a seventeenth system of law, which the parties may select as their choice of law, neither reduces uncertainty nor ignorance. It has no benefits from a transaction cost point of view. Indeed, as is the case with any transnational and novel law, it is likely in fact to increase uncertainty, at least in the medium term, so that it would provoke increased transaction costs.

With respect to the option of providing a uniform code of contract law as the default rule in the event that the parties fail to make an explicit choice of law, the transaction cost approach does not point to such an unequivocal conclusion. Default rules only save on transaction costs if they are the rules that the parties would normally choose themselves. If the default rule is unsatisfactory to the parties, they will have to incur the transaction cost of avoiding it through contractual agreement. Default rules therefore save on transaction costs only if they are the rules that would in the majority of cases be chosen in any event. Given that no European contract code exists at present, we cannot say whether or not parties to contracts would choose this legal system as the relevant rules for their transaction in the majority of cases. We can only speculate that for the majority of transactions the parties would continue to prefer their own domestic laws, in order to reduce their transaction costs in minimising legal risk. If this speculation is correct, a default rule of a EC code of contract law would probably increase transaction costs.

With respect to the option of compulsory code of contract law, we have observed that this proposal must in the long term reduce transaction costs provoked by ignorance of legal risk, but the reduction of transaction costs with respect to certainty depends upon the content or form of the regulation, not its transnational character. I think that the production of regulation of contracts that achieves maximum certainty is an extremely difficult task and it makes sense to approach it in an incremental or trial and error approach. It follows that a transaction cost approach probably favours the development of uniform laws for particular types of contract rather than the extremely ambitious option of regulating all types of contract at once.

Even if the transaction costs argument is persuasive to encourage transnational regulation of contracts, we need to pause to consider whether or not the argument falls within the competence of the EC. Does the EC have a general power to seek to reduce transaction costs in order to improve the competitiveness of the internal market? Such a power would be extremely wide, though perhaps it might be permitted under a unanimous vote procedure. The argument for action to approximate laws for this purpose of the reduction of transaction costs could be strengthened by reference to the idea of the competitiveness of Europe in world markets.

The reason why transaction costs matter is fundamentally that they create a competitive disadvantage for an economic system. At first sight the absence of a uniform law does not affect competitiveness between economic blocs. A German company selling to the USA has the same choice of law problem as an US company selling to Germany. But this mirror image does not apply to complex or assembled products. A typical product such as a car is produced by an assembly company from parts supplied by numerous suppliers. Often these suppliers come from other Member States in the EC. Thus a German car may contain components purchased from France, Italy, or the UK. Similarly, a US car will be assembled from parts typically derived from other US producers. The transaction costs surrounding these component supply contracts feed into the eventual cost of the product. There is a competitive advantage for economic blocs if these transaction costs in component supply contracts can be minimised. A similar argument can be made with respect to services that feed into the costs of a final product. Transaction costs provoked by choice of law problems thus have a bearing on the competitive advantage of economic blocs such as the USA and the EC. To the extent that legal risk provokes transaction costs, this places an economic bloc at a competitive disadvantage.

It is therefore possible to argue on the basis of the competitiveness of the EC in global markets that we should seek to minimise transaction costs arising from legal risk. This policy of enhancing the competitiveness of the EC is surely within the competence of the EC and does not provoke strong objections based on subsidiarity. In structure, it is the same argument that provided partial support for the development of a single currency: the transaction costs of changing currency in cross-border trade presented a competitive disadvantage compared to other trading blocs with a single currency. Yet, as this analogy suggests, the reduction of transaction costs by the provision of a common currency or a uniform law of contract is not the most important consideration. Just as a single currency raises deep questions about the relation between national sovereignty and economic integration, so too does a proposal for a uniform law of contract.

III. SUBSIDIARITY

There is a striking contrast in the preceding discussion between the technical nature of the debate about transaction costs and the lofty ambition of a European Code of Private Law. The great European Codes were ostensibly introduced not just to reduce transaction costs but rather as a political statement of the values of a liberal society and as a technique or affirmation of nation-building. What is striking about the Green Paper is the absence of similar kinds of justifications. We do not find a justification in terms of the need to protect and respect the rights of European citizens to enjoy their property and contractual rights at a high uniform level. Nor do we find assertions of the need to build a sense of identity for Europe as a political entity. No doubt the explanation for this silence can be credited largely to the principle of subsidiarity.

The effect of the principle of subsidiarity is to drive the conversation about European contract law towards areas of established competence of the EC, such as obstacles to cross-border trade. The conversation can either take the form of the reduction of obstacles to trade, or it can take the form of improvements to existing regulation. This latter policy is also presented in the Green Paper under the general theme of better regulation. Better regulation is, however, fairly narrowly conceived. It is described as the removal of inconsistencies and the reduction of unnecessary complexity. Personally I regret the absence of any broader political discussion. I see a parallel between the introduction of a single currency and a single contract law. They have equal symbolic political significance in my mind, representing the transition from nation states towards a transnational political and economic order.

Even if the EC has no appetite for such potentially divisive issues, I regret the absence of discussion of lower level political and legal reforms. For example, the creation of European Contract law actually creates the opportunity for member States to improve their commercial laws. Most countries are complacent about the strengths of their legal systems to support and promote commercial activity, but I doubt whether this confidence can be based upon any rigorous empirical enquiry. When the US embarked upon the project of a Uniform Commercial Code, there were two objectives: uniformity to reduce transaction costs provoked by legal risk, and improvement of the law. It is no doubt controversial whether the latter objective of improvement of the law was successful, but my point is that the opportunity was taken to try to make the law better. It would be a pity in my view if we concentrated solely on the issues surrounding uniformity and did not consider simultaneously the potential to improve commercial law.

But the most fundamental question still seems to me to be the question of the political or symbolic significance of a European civil law. Is this a goal to which Europe should aspire? Some may reject this proposal as a step towards federal government, a matter to be resisted in principle as a dilution of the sovereignty of nation states. Among those who are committed to greater European integration, there must also be disagreement about this goal. A European civil code might be regarded as an attempt to put beyond further political discussion some of the basic principles of private law that received their apogee in the nineteenth century. These principles that accord great respect to private autonomy and private property rights, though historically essential elements in the formation of market societies, have not proven acceptable in modern societies without substantial modifications such as labour law and consumer law. It is possible, of course, that a new European Code could embrace modern principles that reflected contemporary values about fairness and fair dealing. But in order to achieve this differentiation in contract law, all countries have had to introduce more particularistic regulation for different kinds of transactions. The centrifugal tendencies of modern contract law cast doubt on the possibility of reinventing general principles applicable to all contracts except at the most abstract level.

It is at this point in the debate that we encounter a conflict between theories of legal reasoning. Traditional or dogmatic jurists insist that it is only possible to bind particularistic regulation of contracts into an integrated and consistent whole body of law by enacting general abstract principles in the form of a general code of private law. Without these general principles, it is argued, there will be no foundations on which to build consistent interpretations of the particularistic regulation of contracts. From a more 'realist' perspective, however, any reliance upon abstract concepts and principles to bring coherence and predictability to law is an illusion. Moreover, it is a dangerous illusion, because it suppresses open debate about the purposes or policy objectives of the law. From a realist perspective, the law would be more transparent and serve its functions better if we could dispense with misleading generalisations and stick to the problems of regulating concrete issues.[10]

Most legal scholars are familiar with this debate and know where they stand within it. For my part, I find it almost surprising that the debate persists and has resurfaced again in the clamours for a European civil code. I had thought that the influence of realist approaches was too profound to leave much credibility to the view that abstract concepts and principles serve any useful purpose in society. Plainly my perception of the state of legal scholarship in Europe was misguided or overly optimistic. That is not to say that I disagree with the ambition to provide more comprehensive regulation of particular kinds of contracts. The detailed regulation of particular issues arising in particular kinds of contracts, such as sellers' warranties in contracts of sale to consumers, will inevitably create the problems of gaps and unpredictable boundaries as this new regulation is fitted into national legal systems. These problems can be tackled by more comprehensive regulation of particular types of transactions. But I doubt whether the enactment of general principles of contract law or private law as a whole will assist in solving these typical problems of modern regulation.

IV. CONCLUSIONS

My comment on the Green Paper commenced with the uncontroversial proposition that it is important to ask the right questions when considering the options

---

[10] For a broad-ranging discussion of this debate, see M.W. Hesselink, *The New European Legal Culture* (Deurne, Kluwer, 2001).

for further EC initiatives in the realm of contract law. I have argued that the Green Paper assumes without adequate foundation that diversity in national contract laws can create barriers to cross-border trade. Though such barriers may exist, I have suggested that the source of these barriers is primarily to be discovered in the diversity of social rather than legal norms, so that legal intervention is unlikely to prove productive. I have also argued that the Green Paper eschews many of the important and interesting questions posed by integration of commercial law, though no doubt there are good reasons for so doing.

The Green Paper does discuss briefly the relevant question of increased transaction costs in cross-border trade. But I have argued that the key issue is whether transnational regulation can reduce transaction costs in commercial transactions. The answer to this question seems to me to be reasonably clear. Transnational regulation can reduce transaction costs in commercial transactions only by becoming a compulsory uniform law, but the real benefits only emerge if the transnational regulation becomes reasonably certain or predictable. My view is that this goal can probably only be achieved by tackling regulation on a case by case basis, that is dealing with one type of transaction at a time. The unification of EC contract law also offers the opportunity of improvement in legal regulation, an opportunity that I hope will not be lost.

19. Critical Comments on the Commission Communication 'On European Contract Law'

Norbert Reich*

I. SOME SURPRISES

The long awaited Commission communication[1] requested by the Council and the European Parliament comes as a surprise. 'Der Berg kreiste ein Mäuschen'. Not by what the Commission is addressing, but by what it is omitting (*infra* II). Its methodological shortcomings are even more surprising (III). Conclusions should instead be drawn from existing Community 'Sonderprivatrechte' (IV). The proposed options should be fleshed out more than the Commission has done (V). The future of European contract lies in combining different options (VI), but common effort may shape them into a master plan: 'Kleine Ursache – große Wirkung'?

Before giving evidence for our critique, some questions should be raised about the structure of Annex I, which seems to be the basis of the Communication. This is a jumbled mixture of Community directives having some (not always clear) relationship to private, not necessarily contract, law. Directive 2000/35/EC of the EP and the Council of 29 June 2000 on combating late payment in commercial transactions,[2] where fundamental problems of the law of obligations and securities are touched upon, is mentioned under 'systems of payment', while Directive 2000/31/EC of the EP and the Council of 8 June 2000 on e-commerce[3] is put under the obvious heading 'E-commerce' without stressing its importance for contract formation. The heading of financial services lists, rather haphazardly,

---

*   Rector, Riga Graduate School of Law, e-mail norbert.reich@rgsl.edu.lv; an earlier version had been submitted to the Commission in asking for comments on the Communication.

[1]   COM(2001) 398 final, for a quasi-official explanation see the article of the head of the working party, D. Staudenmayer, 'Die Mitteilung der Kommission zum Europäischen Vertragsrecht', *EuZW* [2001], 485; for a discussion St. Leible, 'Die Miteilung der Kommission zum Europäischen Vertragsrecht – Startschuss für ein Europäisches Vertragsgesetzbuch?', *EWS* [2001], 471; Chr. v. Bar, 'Die Mitteilung der Kommission zum Europäischen Vertragsrecht', *ZEuP* [2001], 799; B. Lurger, 'Grundfragen der Vereinheitlichung der Vertragsrechts in der EU (Wein, New York, Springer, 2002).

[2]   (EC) OJ [2000] L 178/1.

[3]   (EC) OJ [2000] L 200/35.

S. Grundmann and J. Stuyck (eds.), An Academic Green Paper on European Contract Law, 283–291
© 2002 *Kluwer Law International. Printed in Great Britain.*

certain directives but without extracting their contract law specificities; surprisingly enough, the Commission seems to imply that a right of cancellation exists only for life insurance contracts which the consumer entered upon his own initiative, not, as Article 30 of the Third Life Assurance Directive 92/96/EC of the Council of 10 November 1992[4] expressly rules, for *any* life insurance contract. One wonders why such special areas as data protection, intellectual property and public procurement are listed under the heading 'private law'. At least some explanation should be given.

Annex III 'Structure of the acquis and relevant binding instruments' is somewhat more helpful as it tries to mention such central elements in contract law as the principles of transparency and fairness (1.1), information requirements (2.1.1), cancellation (3.1) and compensation (3.3). It is surprising, however, that the emerging case law of the ECJ is not even mentioned, whereas an analysis of this could serve to develop some Community principles of contract law, at least in certain areas of 'Sonderprivatrecht' (special area of private law, see infra IV).

II. SOME OMISSIONS

One would have expected the Commission to say something about *competence* in enacting contract law legislation. The communication talks at length about subsidiarity and proportionality (paras. 42 *et seq.*), but this need only be mentioned at all if there is a basis for Community action. The Commission seems to accept this rather casually by saying that where impediments to the functioning of the internal market for cross-border transactions can be shown through its inquiry, 'a horizontal measure providing for comprehensive harmonisation of contract law rules could be envisaged at EC level' (para. 41). The article by Staudenmayer[5] justifies this absence with the open character of the communication inquiring into the need for action without proposing it, and with a possible revision of the EC Treaty in 2004 in mind, but even in this case the principle of attributed (Art. 5(1) EC) competences of the Community should at least be mentioned and caution against hasty proposals.

Until now, the directives cited in the communciation with relation to contract law owe their life to different enactments, for example, on the internal market, freedom to supply services, harmonisation, social policy, and so on. Article 65 may in the future be used for action in areas of contractual conflicts. Is there any basis for a *general competence on contract law*, or is the EC limited to certain areas where contract law may have a specific impact on other EC policies, e.g. the internal market, competition, consumer protection, social policy? I submit – without going into detail – that the second alternative is correct and that therefore no genuine legislative 'horizontal' competence in contract law exists

---

[4]   (EC) OJ [1992] L 360/1.
[5]   *EuZW* [2001] 485, 489.

for the Community. The 'piecemeal' approach of Community contract law (para. 35) is a structural one and cannot be avoided under the present system of attributed competences under Article 5(1) EC.

In paragraphs 23 *et seq.* the Commission is trying to address these problems, albeit in a very vague way. It wants to find out 'if the co-existence of national contract laws in the Member states directly or indirectly obstructs the functioning of the internal market, and if so to what extent'. The Commission recognises the principle of freedom of contracts, but fears that mandatory rules of one country may be an impediment (para. 28). Why, then, not harmonise these mandatory rules rather than contract law in general? The reference to consumer and SME ignorance of contract law of other member states (para. 30) may again justify the harmonisation of consumer law or of certain commercial activities, for example, as has already been done via directives 86/653/EEC of the Council of 18 December 1986[6] on the coordination of the law of the Member States relating to self-employed commercial agents and 2000/35 on late payments.[7] A third and very popular argument is the existence of higher transaction costs in non-harmonised areas (paras. 31–32), but this will not be substantially diminished even if the EC undertakes harmonisation of contract law – national laws will continue to exist, and different regimes have to be coordinated by conflict of laws rules.

Another important question is hardly mentioned in the Communication: What is the relationship between private international law as enshrined in the Rome Convention of 1980 to which all member states adhere, and harmonisation of contract law? Paragraphs 16–17 avoid discussing these problems. However, this question has already been raised in academic writings, where some authors have held that the Community has no competence to legislate, for example in consumer law, because protection by conflict of laws rules under Article 5 of the Rome Convention should be sufficient.[8] Personally, I do not share this opinion. The ECJ has certainly not regarded protective rules in international private law as a substitute for harmonisation, as its judgment against the Netherlands[9] concerning the transparency principle of Directive 93/13/EC of the Council of 5 April 1993 on unfair terms in consumer contracts[10] clearly shows. But what has been said with regard to consumer contracts may not necessarily be true for contract law in general, especially in cross-border commercial transactions.

On the other hand, one must wonder why the Commission does not even

---

6   (EC) OJ [1986] L 382/17.

7   n. 4.

8   For a discussion of the different options in contract law harmonisation cf. the paper by Drexl, ch. 7 above in this volume.

9   ECJ 10.5.2001, case C-144/99, *Commission v. Netherlands* [2001] ECR I–3541.

10   (EC) OJ [1993] L 95/29.

mention the consequences of the Tobacco Judgment[11] for harmonsiation measures based on the internal market competence of the Community. Should not at least a more thorough study of this controversial subject matter be undertaken by independent experts? Staudenmayer[12] seems to imply that once the Commission obtains information on an eventual malfunctioning of the internal market due to absence of contract harmonisation, this may be a justification for Community action. But what are the methodological criteria for determining the relevance of this information?

Outside special areas such as consumer, commercial agency and labour law, one might indeed doubt whether there is any legal basis for contract law harmonisation at all, given that co-ordination is already possible by applying the basic principles of the Rome Convention, especially the guarantee of contractual freedom both with regard to applicable law and content of contracts. In this already existing and seemingly functioning legal framework, where should the place of a possible 'Community code of obligations' or other similar instrument be? Finally, it is submitted that the remarkable bulk of international uniform law which the Commission Communication cites in its Annex II is an argument against Community harmonisation. Globalisation, not regionalisation, seems to be the direction in which international commercial transactions are developing.

There may be some justification for proposing harmonisation of contract law rules in areas not strictly covered by Articles 5 and 6 of the Rome Convention, but where a Community interest is still involved, e.g., in the field of standard contract terms beyond the sphere of application of Directive 93/13, with regard to principles of good faith and effective legal protection, which so far are only haphazardly built into consumer and discrimination protection directives, in relation to the development of 'contorts' (e.g. violation of pre-contracutal obligations, *culpa in contrahendo*). But differences in these areas do not as such justify a Community initiative. The principle of minimum harmonisation authorises Member States to extend their consumer, commercial agency and worker protection legislation to persons not coming under the classical definitions of consumer, commercial agent or worker (SME, franchisees, etc.), and Article 7 of the Rome Convention allows an extension of mandatory protective rules if there is a public,

---

[11] ECJ 5.10.2000, case C-376/98, *Germany v. EP and Council* [2000] ECR I–8419; cf. also recently ECJ 9.10.2001, case C-377/98, *Netherlands v. EP and Council* [2001] ECR I–0000 concerning the legality of Dir. 98/44/EC of the EP and the Council of 6.7.1998 on the legal protection of biotechnological inventions, (EC) OJ [1998] L 211/13, where the Court upheld Community competence because the directive aims at 'preventing damage to the unity of the internal market which might result from Member States deciding unilaterally to grant or refuse such protection' (para. 18).

[12] *EuZW* [2001], 485, 486.

non-discriminatory interest behind them which the ECJ seems to be ready to accept or even require according to its *Ingmar* Judgment.[13]

III. SHORTCOMINGS – IN CONTRACT LAW THEORY

The *methodological shortcomings* of the Communication are revealed by the mere fact that the increase in directives is used as an argument for a possible horizontal involvement of the Community in contract law. How can the Commission prove that quantity is miraculously changing into quality?

One is therefore surprised to read phrases in paragraph 12:

'Contract law encompasses several areas (1) of law. These are linked to different cultural and legal traditions, but most Member States' (2) legal regimes have similar concepts and rules (3). Contract law constitutes the principal body of law regulating (4) cross-border transactions (5) and some Community legislation regulating contract law (6) already exists, although (7) this legislation has taken a sector-by-sector approach.'

This raises the following issues:

1. It is not clear whether the Commission is referring to general principles of contract law or to specific contracts. All Member State jurisdictions differentiate between general contract law and rules for specific contracts (sales, services, credit, etc.).
2. There may be different contractual regimes in one Member State like the UK – England and Wales v. Scotland.
3. There is a considerable debate on whether the legal regimes of Member States are converging via similar concepts or are not converging by maintaining their divergent principles. The academic work undertaken by several groups of European jurists is exactly trying to 'synthesise' these common rules or to propose an academic 'harmonisation' via the development of common principles (like good faith) out of sometimes conflicting rules in codified and case law.
4. Where does contract law have a 'regulating', where an enabling function? This must be distinguished more clearly. The will of the parties, taking into account public interests as well as legitimate interests of weaker parties, are the determining elements of contract law!
5. Contract law does not regulate cross-border situations, but first and foremost internal ones. Cross-border situations are governed by conflict rules, e.g., the

---

[13] ECJ 9.11.2000, case C-381/98 *Ingmar GB/Eaton Leonard Technologies*, [2000] ECR I–9305; comment N. Reich, *EuZW* [2001], 52; L. Bernardeau *JCP G* [2001], I, 328; S. Freitag/ST. Leible, *RIW* [2001], 133.

Rome Convention, which as a result determines applicable (national or international) contract law, or by uniform law such as the Vienna Convention on International Sales (CISG).
6. Community contract law exists in the form of directives which – due to the absence of horizontal direct effect – only work through national contract law.
7. So far Community contract law by necessity has had to take a sector-by-sector approach.

IV. 'SONDERPRIVATRECHTE' – IMPROVEMENT AND CODIFICATION IS NEEDED

Community contract law has developed several distinct *'Sonderprivatrechte'*, for example consumer law, non-discrimination provisions in labour relations, rules protecting the commercial agent. Even if this theory has never been explicitly pronounced, either by the Community legislator or by the ECJ, it does explain why the Community has, on the one hand, legislated extensively in the area of contract law, but why on the other, it has taken (and had to take) a piecemeal approach. Contract law, in the eyes of the Community, does not exist as a body of law *per se*, but as an instrument to attain specific goals written in the EC Treaty (to improve the conditions for cross-border transactions to avoid distortions of competition, to guarantee minimal protection of consumers, workers, and commercial agents, to enable competitive bidding and awarding processes in public procurement, etc.). The instrument of contract law can be employed with or without other instruments, e.g. collective actions (which usually refer to civil procedure, not to contract law), or administrative action where appropriate.

If Community contract law has developed through different 'Sonderprivatrechte', the aim of a European Contract Law today should be to realign these to a great extent unco-ordinated bodies of law and to try to develop general principles in order to systematise them. Therefore, a *codification of Community consumer law* would be, *inter alia*, a first step where some of the basic principles[14] could be distilled out of the existing directives, such as:

- concept of consumer and professional,
- extension of protection to SME,
- basic duties of pre-contractual and contractual information,
- uniform rights of rescission,
- duties to inform about these rights and consequences of non-information,
- specificities of electronic contracts,
- duty relating to specific performance,

---

[14] A comprehensive account of the development of European consumer law has recently been given by H.-W. Micklitz, 'Verbraucherschutz West v. Ost – Kompatibilisierungs-möglichkeiten in der EG', in: H. Heiss (ed.), *Brückenschlag zwischen den Rechtskulturen des Ostseeraums* (Tübingen, Mohr Siebeck, 2001), 137–181.

• remedies in case of non-performance.

Some other areas could probably also be singled out for codification, for example on public procurement contracts, and on contracts for the licensing of intellectual property (with reference to Commission Regulation 240/96).[15] But in the different areas of 'Sonderprivatrecht', the focus would not lie on contract law, but on the regulation of marketing practices where contracts have to play a certain (not exclusive) role.[16]

V. FLESH OUT THE OPTIONS

It is to be welcomed that in recent papers on Community policy the Commission is not simply pursuing its own course of action, but that it summons the input of 'civil society' via formulating certain options on which it asks for comments. While in general we support this more transparent and democratic approach, we think the Commission missed its point in this Communication in proposing only four options in the area of European Contract Law, even if these may be combined (para. 47):

• *Option I: No EC action.* This is not really an option unless the EC had a mandate for action – and this is itself the question (supra II). Since there is contractual freedom anyhow, it is up to the parties to agree to what they want (within the limits of the law).
• *Option II: Promote the development of common contract law principles leading to greater convergence of national laws.* This is again not an option available to the Community; it is already happening in academic and business activities. The Community comes into place as an actor, e.g., when an exemption for a model standard contract having an impact on competition is necessary. But this reflects already existing law. Whether this may become customary law (para. 54) is not for the Community to decide. The same is true with standard contracts (para. 56). A 'restatement' of contract law[17] may be an option for the Community. Ongoing academic initiatives to elaborate, e.g., 'Principles of European Contract Law'[18] or a 'European Contract Code' as mentioned in footnotes 7–9 should probably suffice to bring about a 'soft law harmonisation'

---

15 (EC) OJ [1996] L 31/2; for a disucssion of its importance for European private law cf. N. Reich, 'Innovationssteuerung im europäischen Privatrecht', in: W. Hoffmann-Riem and P. Schneider (eds.), *Rechtswissenschaftliche Innovationsforschung* (Baden-Baden, Nomos, 1997), 330, 337–340.

16 N. Reich, 'From Contract to Trade Practices Law: Protection of Consumers' Economic Interests by the EC', in: Th. Wilhelmsson (ed.), *Perspectives of Critical Contract Law* (Dartmouth, Aldershot, 1993), 55.

17 Cf. Staudenmayer *EuZW* [2001], 485, 488.

18 H. Beale and O. Lando (eds.), *Principles of European Contract Law*, I and II (The Hague, Kluwer, 2000); cf. also Hartkamp *et al.* (eds.), *Towards a European Civil Code* (1998).

as a first step which combines flexibility with contractual freedom and respect for some fundamental values. If the parties to a commercial contract want it, they can choose the 'Principles' to apply to their litigation, or instruct a potential arbitrator to make use of them. The best legal order for contracts would then be determined by the market, not by regulation or harmonisation – a solution already existing in commercial cross-border transactions today, whether in the European or on a globalised market. Competition of legal orders, rather than harmonisation, might be a solution to the problems raised by the communication![19] The Community could support this process by issuing a recommendation and the 'persuasive force' of the principles to resolve contract writing and dispute settlement in cross-border transactions beyond the scope of application of the CISG. According to Article 259(5) EC, recommendations do not have the binding force of law and therefore do not raise questions of competence, but, according to the case law of the ECJ,[20] courts of law 'are bound to take recommendations into consideration in order to decide disputes submitted to them, in particular where they cast light on the interpretation of national measures adopted in order to implement them or where they are designed to supplement binding Community provisions'.

- *Option III: Improve the quality of legislation already in place.* This is again not an option but a requirement. It should be everyday practice with any piece of Community legislation. On the other hand, a codification of 'Sonderprivatrechte' may be advisable (*supra* IV) for the sake of clarity and consistency. The Commission may eventually choose the instrument of a binding regulation to guarantee greater cohesion in the implementation of its legislation, as has recently been proposed with regard to sales promotions.[21]
- *Option IV: Adopt new comprehensive legislation at EC level.* This is only an option when there is competence. It is not (yet) clear whether the material to be collected through this inquiry will suffice to establish a need for harmonisation. Only then would it make sense to discuss the adequate instrument, e.g., directives (which so far have been the preferred instrument in the piecemeal approach), regulations or non-binding recommendations. On the present state of information, a mere transaction cost analysis based on the differences of Member State contract legislation does not suffice to enable the Community to establish non-binding or optional contract law rules. Whether new competences will be transferred to the Community under the 'Post-Nizza-process' remains to be seen.

---

[19] For a discussion of this paradigm, cf. Reich, 'Competition between legal orders', [1992] *CMLRev* 861.

[20] ECJ 13.12.1989, Case [1989] ECR I–4407, 4421 para. 19; for an overall discussion cf. Reich, 'Bankentgelte für die Euro-Umstellung', FS Schimansky, [1999], 241 at 247–249.

[21] Cf. Commission proposal of 2.10.2001, COM(2001) 546 final.

VI. THE FUTURE: COMBINE OPTIONS II AND III

A more thorough discussion would show that the path to a 'European contract law' lies in *combining options II and III*. Options I and IV can be ruled out because they mark radically opposite positions which do not take into account the existing *acquis* or go beyond existing Community competences. Option II would consist of supporting the already ongoing initiatives by academic study groups and extend them through the participation of practitioners, e.g. from the Bar, the judiciary, interested business groups and NGOs. In order to become Community recommendations in the sense of Article 249(5) EC, the Community institutions could install some sort of a 'European Contract Law Commission' which reviews the existing proposals and fleshes out general principles of European contract law which may then be guidelines for interpretation. It could even be envisaged that these principles are recommended to the Member States to be taken over into their legal systems as 'voluntary harmonisation measures' – a procedure which would overcome the democratic deficit of a European contract law by using the traditional competences of harmonisation.[22]

Secondly, if Option III resulted in a codification of 'Sonderprivatrechte' (cf. above IV), a mixture of non-binding, in the words of Grundmann/Kerber,[23] 'default rules', and mandatory consumer protection, labour law, commercial agent provisions, would highlight *a multilevel Community approach to general contract law*. It would guarantee, on the one hand, freedom of contract as a fundamental element of the internal market and, on the other hand, the creation of harmonised and non-discriminatory subjective rights and duties of citizens working or living in the EU.[24]

---

[22] The need for a democratic procedure has been correctly stressed in the chapters by Van Gerven and Wilhelmsson, in this volume.

[23] In this volume.

[24] Cf. my attempt to conceptualise citizenship beyond mere nationality, N. Reich, *Union citizenship – yesterday, today and tomorow*, RGSL Working papers Nr. 3, 2001.

Part IV

An Optional European Code Supplementing, Not Substituting National Laws (Option IVb)

INTRODUCTORY NOTE

In part IV, the idea of an optional European Code supplementing, not substituting national laws (option IVb of the Commission's Communication) is discussed.

Grundmann and Kerber (chapter 20) set up a map of the potential design alternatives. The Communication does not really elaborate this point; there are many more design possibilities than named there: States or parties may have the option, the option may be missing, restricted or full in certain areas and not in others, the situation may be different with respect to mandatory substantive rules, to mandatory information rules and to information rules. The two authors, both from a legal and an economic perspective, also give basic features of evaluation of the different situations.

Particular designs are then discussed by four authors. For the time being, Drobnig proposes a European Code for cross-border situations only, drawing on the experience of the UN Sales Convention, and thus testing a European Contract Law Code. Wilhelmsson proposes to continue harmonisation only for real hard obstacles and favours a mere restatement which is precise, uses easily understandable, not abstract language and concepts, is often changed, full of welfarist values and serves mainly as a tool of standardisation which allows easier communication about diverging solutions. De Geest proposes a European Code with a system of options and with an extremely high number of detailed rules from which states, judges or parties can opt out and each of which indicates who is allowed to make the choice for this very rule. Smits proposes a multi-layered contract law for Europe with detailed rules and the right of option given to the parties.

Kirchner's paper is concerned with the most important argument against a system of various laws, i.e. that choosing between them rationally is conditioned by the processing of information about the different laws and that parties are typically not capable of such processing. He finds a strikingly simple answer to the problem.

Finally, van Gerven gives a schedule of how to proceed, drawing attention to several institutional and political framework conditions.

20. European System of Contract Laws – a Map for Combining the Advantages of Centralised and Decentralised Rule-making

*Stefan Grundmann and Wolfgang Kerber**

I. INTRODUCTION

The EC Commission's Communication on European Contract Law puts the question of how much harmonisation or uniform codification of contract law is needed in the European Union on the political agenda. It proposes four options, three of which are rather evident: first there is the possibility to legislate or not on the European level. The second is the other side of the medal; leaving integration to the market (Option I)[1] and leaving the drafting of European contract law restatements to groups of scholars (Option II)[2] is equivalent to not legislating – even if sponsorship is given. Markets and groups of scholars will step in anyway; and even improving existing EC legislation (Option III) – although really an option – is only the other side of the medal of introducing a new instrument at the EU level. This latter is the last option – Option IV.[3] The Communication is very short on this. It proposes to draft a European Contract Law Code which either substitutes national contract laws or leaves them intact and provides simply a further option. Such an optional European Code – from which states could opt out, according to the Commission's view – is one possibility. This certainly does not exhaust the potential of an optional Code; there are many more variants. This paper concerns Option IV, but also implicitly considers Option III as a model.

The paper takes an overwhelmingly majoritarian view in economics as its starting point: in economic theory, it is virtually undisputed that centralised rule-making has advantages and disadvantages; decentralised rule-making has important advantages and disadvantages as well. Any more centralised tool than

---

S. Grundmann and J. Stuyck (eds.), An Academic Green Paper on European Contract Law, 295–342

an optional European Code would all too easily give up all advantages of decentralised rule-making – mainly the potential of innovation which is certainly paramount in quickly changing times and the potential to serve individual preferences more adequately which is also certainly paramount in a time when democracy and economic theory are based on normative individualism.

The paper therefore investigates the different potential designs of options with respect to a legislative tool on the central level (European Code). It also provides first elements of evaluation of the different parts of this map. Full evaluation is a task for the future which constitutes a whole research programme and requires broad, careful and ongoing discussion. And the map of an optional European Code and the two-level system introduced by it will have a name: we call it the mixed *European System of Contract Laws*, in the plural. By this, we do not only mean that several jurisdictions interplay; we also mean that this is a system, not a transitional solution only. The system should be designed (and core elements are presented here) for keeping flexibility intact in a long-term perspective and to procure standardisation tools (through unification). The ultimate scope is to have the framework for a high quality contract law. In this, transaction costs and the ease of cross-border transactions is only one parameter. High quality contract law is more important.

II. EUROPEAN SYSTEM OF CONTRACT LAWS: BASIC IDEA AND THEORETICAL FOUNDATIONS

1. The Aim: A Two-Level System of Contract Laws

Legal rules can be interpreted as instruments for solving conflicts and facilitating cooperation between individuals in human societies.[4] From an economic point of view, a market economy with an appropriate institutional framework is particularly capable for inducing wealth and economic growth, because market competition leads to the efficient allocation of resources and economic and technical progress. This is also the economic credo of the EC Treaty. Since

---

[4] For the characterisation of legal rules as 'general purpose tools' that are adapted to the 'solution of recurring problem situations', see F.A. Hayek, *Law, Legislation, and Liberty, Vol. 2: The Mirage of Social Justice* (London, Routledge & Kegan Paul, 1976), 21. For a good introduction into New Institutional Economics and Law and Economics as the relevant theoretical foundations for the economic analysis of legal rules see, e.g., E.G. Furubotn and R. Richter, *Institutions and Economic Theory* (Ann Arbor, University of Michigan Press, 1998); R.D. Cooter and T. Ulen, *Law and Economics* (2nd edn., Reading, Addison-Wesley, 1997); H.-B. Schäfer and C. Ott, *Lehrbuch der ökonomischen Analyse des Zivilrechts* (3rd edn., Berlin, Springer, 2000). In economics the ultimate normative orientation are the preferences of the individuals of the society. See from the perspective of constitutional economics, G. Brennan and J.M. Buchanan, *The Reason of Rules* (Cambridge, Cambridge University Press, 1985).

private property and freedom of contract are the core institutions for market economies, an appropriate *contract law* is one of the most important preconditions for the effectiveness of market economies.

Within contract law it is necessary to differentiate between mandatory law and facilitative law. *Mandatory law* limits the freedom of contract of the individuals and therefore has to be seen as *regulations*. There is no doubt from an economic point of view that markets need an institutional framework in the form of mandatory rules in order to ensure the efficient working of markets.[5] But there is much discussion to what extent mandatory rules are necessary and helpful for solving problems of market failure or for attaining additional aims (beyond economic efficiency). That is the difficult problem of 'regulation' versus 'deregulation'. *Facilitative law* encompasses two different groups of functions, which both help to save transaction costs: (1) One group encompasses the functions of the legal order that help the parties to *enforce contracts* ('pacta sunt servanda'; including the services of the court system).[6] (2) The second group consists of supplying *legal standard solutions* ('default rules') for typical transaction or cooperation problems. If the legal order is capable of offering good legal standard solutions for many different typical problems, the parties can save bargaining (and therefore transaction) costs by using those standard solutions instead of writing thick contracts.[7] Therefore a flourishing market economy presupposes the existence of a high-quality contract law, which consists both of appropriate mandatory rules and of transaction cost-saving facilitative law.

If we ask for the appropriate perspective of the evolution of contract law within the EU, we have to consider two important aspects:

(1) In each of the fifteen Member States of the EU a well-established contract law already exists. Therefore we have no situation in which we can design a contract law from scratch. The users of these national contract laws are familiar with it, that is – speaking economically – much specific human capital has already been invested. And it can be presumed that the differences between the national contract laws can at least partly be explained by different problems and preferences. Therefore, different groups of individuals might need different regulations and different standard solutions (default rules).

(2) Furthermore, it is crucial to accept the insight that we cannot assume that we already know the best legal rules for solving problems of transaction and cooperation. On the contrary, we should start systematically from the assumption that the best contract law – and this refers both to mandatory

---

5   See W. Eucken, *Grundsätze der Wirtschaftspolitik* (Tübingen, Mohr, 1952).
6   E.g. see for the problem of optimal remedies in the case of breach of contract, R.D. Cooter and T. Ulen (n. 4), 214 *et seq.*
7   For the saving of transaction costs by offering efficient default rules see Cooter and Ulen (n. 4), 180 *et seq.*

and facilitative law – has not been discovered yet.[8] Therefore innovative improvements of the existing rules are possible and desirable. Additional to that, we have to take into account that the European economy has to thrive in a very dynamic world, in which through technological, economical and social change new problems are emerging, which lead to new possibilities but also problems of transaction and cooperation between individuals (e.g. e-commerce). Another possibility that has to be considered is the change of preferences. Therefore it is necessary that the legal rules of a society (including contract law) have to adapt to these ever-changing circumstances. Both the problem of our limited knowledge of the best legal rules and the necessity to continuously adapt the legal solutions to changing problems implies that a high capacity of adapting and innovating legal rules, both on the level of regulations and the level of legal standard solutions, is an important precondition for the long-term success of a European contract law.[9]

The main thesis of our article is that the aim of ensuring an efficient and adaptable contract law within the EU can best be attained by establishing a consistent two-level system of contract laws in the European Union. In such a *European System of Contract Laws* both national contract laws and a European contract law would be integrated in a systematic way.[10] Since – as we show in the following section – there are considerable advantages and disadvantages

---

[8]   For a thorough analysis of the fundamental knowledge problem that all policy makers (including legislators) need to cope with, see particularly F.A. v. Hayek, 'The Errors of Constructivism', in: F.A. v. Hayek (ed.), *New Studies in Philosophy, Politics, Economics and the History of Ideas* (London/Henley, Routledge & Kegan Paul), 3.

[9]   For a more detailed analysis of the necessity of legal innovations in a dynamic world, see W. Kerber, 'Rechtseinheitlichkeit und Rechtsvielfalt aus ökonomischer Sicht', in: S. Grundmann (ed.), *Systembildung und Systemlücken in Kerngebieten des Europäischen Privatrechts – Gesellschaftsrecht, Arbeitsrecht, Schuldvertragsrecht* (Tübingen, Mohr, 2000), 67.

[10]   The idea of a European two-level system of contract laws can be seen as a special case of a more general concept, in which the idea of federalism is consequently applied both to the European Union in general and to the European legal order in particular. The general problem of centralisation and decentralisation of the European Union can be analysed and solved from the perspective of the economic theory of competitive federalism (which integrates interjurisdictional competition into the traditional economic theory of federalism). For such a perspective see C. Kirchner, 'The Principle of Subsidiarity in the Treaty on European Union: A Critique from the Perspective of Constitutional Economics', (1998) 6 *Tulane Journal of International and Comparative Law* 291; W. Kerber, 'Interjurisdictional Competition within the European Union', (2000) 23 *Fordham International Law Journal*, 217; W. Kerber, 'Wettbewerbsföderalismus als Integrationskonzept für die Europäische Union', *Perspektiven der Wirtschaftspolitik*, [2002] (forthcoming); see also the so-called 'FOCJ' concept in B.S. Frey and R. Eichenberger, *The New Democratic Federalism for Europe: Functional, Overlapping and Competing Jurisdictions* (Cheltenham, Edward Elgar, 1999).

both for a centralised and a decentralised contract law, we claim that the desirable solution for the contract law in the EU is neither an entirely decentralised nor an entirely centralised (and uniform) contract law. Rather we claim that the optimal solution is one skilfully designed combination of European and national contract law rules, both for mandatory and facilitative law. Therefore the problem of the future contract law in the EU should not be discussed in the dichotomy of a centralised, uniform European law versus decentralised, heterogeneous national contract laws. Rather, the discussion should start on the basis of a *concept of an integrated European two-level system of contract laws* and focus on the question, what kind of mandatory rules and legal standard solutions should be established on the European and national levels and what additional rules (including rules for choice of law) are necessary for rendering such a system of contract laws coherent and workable? An entirely centralised law (in the form of a uniform code) or an entirely decentralised law can be seen as the two extreme solutions within the design possibilities such a two-level concept of law offers for the discussion. But our suggestion is that we should look for the optimal mix of centralisation and decentralisation within such a two-level system of contract laws.

2. Advantages and Disadvantages of Centralised and Decentralised Rule-making

For a better substantiation of our main idea of searching for an appropriate combination of the advantages of centralised and decentralised contract law, we will briefly summarise the main arguments for and against centralised and decentralised rule-making.[11]

---

[11] For the discussion about the advantages and disadvantages of uniformity and heterogeneity of legal rules and therefore also about the advantages and disadvantages of centralised and decentralised making of legal rules, see, e.g., P. Behrens, 'Voraussetzungen und Grenzen der Rechtsfortbildung durch Rechtsvereinheitlichung', *RabelsZ* 50, (1986), 19; H. Kötz, 'Rechtsvereinheitlichung – Nutzen, Kosten, Methoden, Ziele', *RabelsZ* 50, 1986, 1; J. Basedow, 'Über Privatrechtsvereinheitlichung und Marktintegration', in: *Festschrift for E.-J. Mestmäcker* (1996), 347; C. Kirchner, 'Europäisches Vertragsrecht', in: H.-L. Weyers (ed.), *Europäisches Vertragsrecht* (Baden-Baden, Nomos, 1997), 118 *et seq.*; F. Parisi and L.E. Ribstein, 'Choice of Law', in: P. Newman (ed.), *The New Palgrave Dictionary of Economics and the Law*, vol. 1 (1998), 236; R. Van den Bergh, 'Subsidiarity as a Demarcation Principle and the Emergence of European Private Law', (1989) 5 *Maastricht Journal of European and Comparative Law* 129; W. Kerber (n. 9), 81 *et seq.*; see for the following arguments also particulary W. Kerber and K. Heine, 'Zur Gestaltung von Mehr – Ebenen – Rechtssystemen aus ökonomischer Sicht', in: C. Ott and H.-B. Schäfer (eds.), VIII. Travemünder Symposium zur ökonomischen Analyse des Rechts, Vereinheitlichung des Zivilrechts in transnationalen Wirtschaftsräumen – Beiträge zur Evolution von Recht und zentraler Rechtsetzung, (Tübingen, Mohr Siebeck, 2002) (forthcoming) and the contribution by R. Van den Bergh, ch. 17 in this volume.

Static and dynamic economies of scale: An important argument for centralised rule-making can be derived from static economies of scale effects, which might arise in the production and application of law. The drafting of laws, the decision processes of the legislators and the implementation of laws can cause considerable costs, which can be interpreted as fixed costs (set-up costs). These costs can be reduced if within one territory such as the EU, only one set of uniform legal rules are established instead of many different ones. Those fixed costs exist both for mandatory and facilitative law. Beyond that, dynamic economies of scale might also be important. If it is true that the quality of a law depends on the number of cases which have been decided within this law, and therefore on the cumulative experience, then from the economic point of view dynamic economies of scale exist. If we have only one set of contract law rules in the EU, more experiences can be accumulated within this law and therefore its quality may be higher in the long run than if different contract laws exist simultaneously.[12]

Transaction costs: The advantage of a centralised set of legal rules is that the information costs about the relevant legal situation for the *users* of the legal rules (firms and consumers) might be considerably lower than in a decentralised system, in which, for example, fifteen different sets of legal rules exist (as within the EU). This is an important argument for centralised rule-making, but it is clear that the argument is only relevant for cross-border transactions, and not for domestic ones. If we take into account also *political transaction costs* in the form of political bargaining processes of agreeing to a set of legal rules,[13] the result of the advantages of centralised and decentralised rule-making are mixed. On one hand, political transaction costs can be reduced by centralised rule-making through saving parallel political processes. On the other hand, it can be suggested that the bargaining costs can be much higher in the case of centralised rule-making, because due to more heterogeneous preferences and interests the consent costs can be much higher than in political processes in national legislations.

Heterogenous preferences and problems: If the preferences, and transaction and cooperation problems are different in the Member States of the EU, then it would be efficient to develop different legal rules for fulfilling these different preferences. This is true both for mandatory and facilitative law. If the preferences

---

[12] Dynamic economies of scale can lead to path dependence effects in legal evolution and therefore also to lock-in effects, which might have to be critically assessed. For an analysis of the perhaps problematic effects of those path dependence effects in the corporate law evolution within the EU after the *Centros* decision of the ECJ see K. Heine and W. Kerber, 'European Corporate Laws, Regulatory Competition, and Path Dependence' (2002), 13 *European J. of Law and Economics*, 47.

[13] For the concept of political transaction costs, see Furubotn and Richter (n. 4), 47 *et seq.*

in regard to the extent of consumer protection are different between the Member States of the EU, any uniform regulation has to be an unsatisfactory average solution. In those cases different mandatory rules might be the superior answer (perhaps combined with establishing uniform minimum or maximum standards for solving other problems). This argument is still more important in the case of facilitative law. If the typical transaction and cooperation problems are different in the various countries, then different legal standard solutions (default rules) should also be offered for reducing the transaction costs of the parties. The existence of heterogenous preferences and problems is an important argument in favour of a greater decentralisation of rule-making.

Externalities: The above mentioned problem that an average solution for the whole EU has negative effects on the fulfilment of differentiated preferences can also be interpreted as a problem of external costs, which many individuals have to bear due to legal solutions that do not correspond to their preferences. In that case decentralised decisions would help to reduce these externalities; but decentralised rule-making can also lead to an externality problem. If the decision of one Member State for legal rules (especially mandatory rules) does lead to certain kinds of negative external effects in other Member States, then decentralised rule-making can lead to noninternalised negative external effects, and therefore to an overall inefficient rule-making within the EU. In a centralised system of rule-making such external effects cannot emerge, but the problem might also be solved satisfactorily by establishing EU minimum/maximum standards (as in the case of fundamental freedoms) which restrict the scope of decentralised rule-making for avoiding those external effects.

Barriers of trade and distortions of competition: Different mandatory legal rules (regulations) or perhaps also different legal standard solutions (facilitative law) are often interpreted as (non-tariff) barriers of trade or as distorting competition within the Internal Market. One can argue that within a centralised legal system with uniform legal rules no such problems can arise for the Internal Market, because all market participants throughout the whole EU act under the same set of legal rules ('level playing field' argument). Within a more decentralised system of legal rules it is necessary to distinguish very carefully, which kinds of differences in the legal rules can lead to unreasonable impediments for the Internal Market.[14] If we have a high mobility of goods, services, factors, firms and individuals within the EU and/or extensive choice of law through the parties, then the problem of distortions of competition through different legal rules in the Member States vanishes, because the mobility allows firms and individuals to use those sets of rules which they deem best for solving their problems. But

---

[14]   For a thorough critique of the 'level playing field' argument see ch. 17 by R. Van den Bergh in this volume.

in any case, the problem of potential barriers to trade and distortion of competition may be greater in a decentralised system of law than in a centralised legal system.

Consistency of a legal order: One important characteristic of a good legal order is its consistency or coherence. Within a system of legal rules there should be neither unresolved conflicts between different (subsets of) rules (i.e. that different rules contradict each other), nor large gaps, for which no rules exist at all. Both problems can lead to serious failures for the working of the legal order. It seems clear that in a centralised, uniform legal system it is easier to attain this aim of consistency and to avoid incompatibilities and conflicts between legal rules. Therefore in a more decentralised system of law, in which rules are enacted by different legislators, problems of incompatibility of legal rules or gaps of regulation can be a much greater problem. For tackling this problem of complementarities between legal rules a more decentralised system of law needs rules and procedures for solving these problems.[15]

Knowledge problem: Two different, but closely related arguments in regard to knowledge problems, can be distinguished. As mentioned above, we should not assume that the knowledge about the optimal legal rules for solving transaction and cooperation problems (both for mandatory and facilitative law) already exist. Legal scholars (and perhaps also economists) might know much about good legal rules, but it would be a 'pretension of knowledge' (Hayek) to assume that it is not possible to discover even better ones. Therefore it is important to establish a legal system that has a large capability for improving their legal solutions. We come back to this argument in the next paragraph. The other kind of knowledge problem is that the knowledge of which legal rules are appropriate for solving the transaction and cooperation problems of the citizens might be widely dispersed and cannot be centralised. This is an application of Hayek's famous argument of the impossibility of centralisation of the dispersed knowledge in a society to the making of legal rules.[16] If local knowledge about the specific problems and preferences in certain regions or Member States exists, then a decentralised system of rule-making is much more suitable for using this local knowledge about the suitability of legal rules for solving transaction and cooperation problems. This may be relevant both for mandatory and facilitative law. Please note that this argument differs from the problem of heterogenous preferences and legal problems.

---

[15] For an analysis of this problem with regard to corporate law, see Heine and Kerber (n. 12).

[16] See F.A. v. Hayek, 'The Use of Knowledge in Society', 35 *American Economic Review* 519. For a critique of the idea of an omniscient central planner in the economic theory of federalism, see A. Breton, *Competitive Governments: An Economic Theory of Politics and Public Finance* (Cambridge, Cambridge University Press, 1996), 185.

Adaptability and innovativeness: Decentralisation can also be positive for the innovative improvement of legal rules and their adaptability to new problems.[17] In contrast to a centralised legal system, a decentralised system allows for decentralised experimentation and therefore parallel experimentation processes with the possibility of mutual learning (through imitation). Therefore a much greater amount of different legal solutions can be generated and tested by the users of law. So much more experience can be accumulated and it is much easier to select superior legal solutions than in a centralised system. Due to the long and tiresome political decision processes on the central level (with its cumbersome procedures of finding broadly acceptable compromises) we cannot expect that in the case of centralised rule-making a high responsiveness to newly emerging problems is possible in the long run. In a largely decentralised system, however, the probability that some jurisdictions enact new and better legal solutions, which can spread by imitation through other jurisdictions, is much higher. In a similar way, it is also much easier in a decentralised system of law to correct wrong decisions about appropriate legal rules (or to reduce the negative effects of wrong decisions) than in a centralised system. So if we think that the optimal legal solutions are not already found and known or presume that we have to expect also for the future the emergence of many new problems due to dynamic change, then the adaptability and innovativeness of the legal system (dynamic efficiency) is very important, leading to a powerful argument in favour of a more decentralised system of law.

Competition among legal rules: The concept of a decentralised system of law can additionally be combined with the idea of competition among legal rules or regulatory competition. If individuals or firms are mobile between jurisdictions, they are able to migrate to that jurisdiction in which the whole body of public goods, legal rules and taxes are most suitable for solving their problems. Consequently, competition processes between jurisdictions for attracting individuals, firms and investments emerge and additional incentives exist for the jurisdictions to improve their legal rules. This kind of regulatory competition, which can refer both to mandatory law and to facilitative law, can be considerably intensified if individuals and firms are granted the right to choose directly between legal rules (choice of law), e.g. between the different contract laws of the Member States. In the theory of regulatory competition there is much

---

[17]   See for the following argument in more detail, Kerber (n. 9), 69 *et seq.* For the general argument that decentralisation in a federal system can lead to more experimentation and mutual learning, see also W.E. Oates, 'An Essay on Fiscal Federalism', 37 *Journal of Economic Literature* 1132 *et seq.*, who characterises federalism as 'laboratory federalism'.

discussion about the workability of competition processes among legal rules.[18] There are both specific arguments of potential failures (as, e.g., 'race to the bottom' arguments) and arguments why competition can increase the advantages of decentralised systems of law. Whereas a centralised system of law excludes the possibility of competition among legal rules, a decentralised system offers the additional opportunity of using the advantages of competition among legal rules. In that case, however, an appropriate institutional framework has to be established for ensuring the workability of competition among legal rules.[19]

Rent seeking problems: Mandatory legal rules (regulations) can be misused for protecting special interest groups (rent seeking behaviour). In the theory of regulatory competition, one argument in favour of decentralised systems of law and regulatory competition is that the mobility of individuals, firms and factors between different jurisdictions or different sets of rules limits the extent of rent seeking behaviour through regulation. Consequently, a decentralised system of law with regulatory competition would lead to a lower level of rent seeking than a centralised system, in which firms, individuals and factors have no possibility to avoid the effects of the rent seeking activities on the central level.

Status quo-situation in the EU: Within the EU we do not start from scratch in respect of contract law. In all Member States a well-established contract law with both mandatory rules and legal standard solutions exists. This implies that

---

[18]   For contributions to the theory of regulatory competition see e.g. H. Siebert and M.J. Koop, 'Institutional Competition. A Concept for Europe?', 45 *Aussenwirtschaft* 1990, 439; V. Vanberg and W. Kerber, 'Institutional Competition among Jurisdictions: An Evolutionary Approach' (1994) 5 *Constitutional Political Economy*, 193; J.-M. Sun and J. Pelkmans, 'Regulatory Competition in the Single Market' (1995) 33 *J. of Common Market Studies*, 67; M.E. Streit and W. Mussler, 'Wettbewerb der Systeme und das Binnenmarktprogramm der Europäischen Union', in: L. Gerken (ed.), *Europa zwischen Ordnungswettbewerb und Harmonisierung* (Berlin, Springer, 1995), 75; H.-W. Sinn, 'The Selection Principle and Market Failure in Systems Competition' (1997) 88 *J. of Public Economics*, 247; K. Gatsios and P. Holmes, 'Regulatory Competition', in: P. Newman (ed.), *The New Palgrave Dictionary of Economics and the Law*, vol. 3 (1998), 271; A. Ogus, 'Competition between National Legal Systems: A Contribution of Economic Analysis to Comparative Law', (1999) 48 *ICLQ*, 405; W. Kerber (n. 9), 67; R. Van den Bergh, 'Towards an Institutional Legal Framework for Regulatory Competition in Europe' (2000) *Kyklos*, 435; J.P. Trachtman, 'Regulatory Competition and Regulatory Jurisdiction' (2000) 3 *J. of Int. Economic Law*, 331; K. Heine and W. Kerber (2002) (n. 12). For a recent monograph about the problem of the feasibility of regulatory competition in regard to corporate law, see K. Heine, *Regulierungswettbewerb im Gesellschaftsrecht. Zur Funktionsfähigkeit eines Wettbewerbs der Rechtsordnungen im europäischen Gesellschaftsrecht* (Berlin, Duncker & Humblot, 2002) (forthcoming).
[19]   See W. Kerber, 'Zum Problem einer Wettbewerbsordnung für den Systemwettbewerb', 17 *Jahrbuch für Neue Politische Ökonomie* [1998], 199; and R. Van den Bergh (n. 18), 435.

the set-up costs for these national laws and many information costs (including specific human capital) by the present users are already made (sunk costs); also, many positive effects of dynamic economies of scale through accumulating much experience in the national contract laws have already been realised. Therefore many costs of a decentralised system, which would have to be taken into account, if we were in a situation without any contract law, are no more relevant for our present problem of developing a perspective for the future contract law in the EU. So the existing huge investments in national contract laws constitute an important argument in favour of a more decentralised system of contract laws.

3. Cumulating the Advantages and Reducing the Disadvantages – Searching for an Optimal European System of Contract Laws

This analysis of the advantages and disadvantages of centralised and decentralised rule-making has made clear that there are many good arguments both for and against centralised and decentralised rule-making. Consequently, the problem of the further development of contract law in the EU is a very complex one. If we take into account (1) the present situation with its well-established national contract laws and also the many already existing EU rules within contract law, and (2) the considerable disadvantages, which are linked to a purely centralised or decentralised solution, it seems reasonable to search for the solution within our above-mentioned two-level system of contract laws with both national and European contract law rules. So the main idea that we want to suggest in this article is, how can we establish a European system of contract laws in which the particular advantages of centralised and decentralised rule-making can be cumulated and the corresponding disadvantages be avoided as far as possible? This can also be seen as an application of the subsidiarity principle. As an example for this idea, consider the possibility that the EU offers additional legal standard solutions to those of the Member States (facilitative law). This might reduce the transaction costs for cross-border transactions and increase the variety of standard solutions offered to the parties, without reducing the innovativeness of the whole system of contract laws due to the maintenance of the competences of the Member States in offering facilitative law.

What does a European system of contract laws mean? It has to be seen as a consistent two-level system of contract law rules, which encompasses both legal rules on the EU level and legal rules on the level of the Member States. These legal rules can consist of mandatory rules and facilitative law, particularly default rules. An additional group of (meta–)rules will be necessary for determining, to what extent the EU and the Member States have the competence to enact mandatory rules or offer legal standard solutions in contract law and to what extent the parties are allowed to choose between these different legal rules (choice of law).[20] Additionally, the contract law rules on these two levels have to be interpreted as a system, because the decisive criterion is its workability as a whole, i.e. whether this European system of contract laws is able to offer efficient solutions for transaction and information problems for the citizens of the EU in the long run.

So the perspective of the development of the future contract law in the EU is not the transition from national contract laws to one European contract law, but the transition from national contract laws to one European two-level system of contract laws sustainable in the long run, within which the specific legal contract law rules (mandatory and facilitative law) can evolve and adapt to the current transaction and cooperation problems. This can also be seen as the attempt to apply the concept of federalism to the legal system ('legal federalism'). Consequently, the central question is, how should the rules for such a European system of contract laws be designed so that on the one hand enough consistency and uniformity can be maintained with the positive effects of reducing transaction costs, avoiding problems of conflict of legal rules and removing obstacles from trade, without on the other hand eliminating the advantages of decentralisation with its positive effects of fulfilling heterogenous preferences, using local knowledge and innovativeness and adaptability due to parallel processes of experimentation? Or, what is the optimal mixture between centralisation and decentralisation? As we have indicated in the last section, economics can help to answer these questions by providing a set of arguments and criteria.

In the following sections a mapping of the design options for such a European two-level system of contract laws will be developed. After presenting in the next section III the main design dimensions of such a system, the most important different design options, i.e. combinations of the dimensions, will be presented and analysed in section IV.

III. DESIGN DIMENSIONS IN A EUROPEAN SYSTEM OF CONTRACT LAWS

The main design dimensions for an optional European Code are concerned with two questions: (1) how binding is the contract law rule, and (2) who decides whether the centralised or the decentralised rule should apply and to what extent? A third question sometimes discussed is less important. It is about how detailed the rules are.[21]

---

[20]   If we include the idea of competition among legal rules (regulatory competition) in this European two-level system of contract laws, those meta-rules can also be interpreted as the institutional framework, which ensures the workability of regulatory competition. Consquently, we can speak of a competitive order ('Wettbewerbsordnung'). See, e.g., W. Kerber (n. 19); Van den Bergh (n. 18), 435.

[21]   There can be principles or detailed rules; both are contained in O. Lando and H. Beale (eds.), *Principles of European Contract Law, Part I and II*, (The Hague, Kluwer, 2000); Unidroit, *Principles of International Commercial Contracts* (Rome, Unidroit, 1994) (although the titles do not necessarily indicate this). Another question related to this topic

1. Facilitative Law (mainly Default Rules) and Regulation (mainly Mandatory Law)

There is a long standing tradition to distinguish non-mandatory law (default rules) and mandatory law.[22] The parties can deviate from the former. Traditionally these rules form the vast majority of contract law.

a) The distinction

aa) Default rules are typically justified as a standard contract offered to the parties which helps them to save transaction costs because they do not have to formulate rules for every eventuality ('Reservevertragsordnung'). In this line of ideas, the legislator should investigate and follow what are the typical wishes of the parties (and not judge them). However, the following explanations also apply if default rules are seen as a set of rules by which the legislator wants to maximise overall wealth, but from which he allows the ultimate cost bearers, the parties, to deviate. Default rules are part of facilitative law (but not synonym). Facilitative law is all law which helps parties to use their freedom of entering into agreements and contains two basic sets of rules. One is about enforcing such agreements (containing rules about *pacta sunt servanda* but also rules about court proceedings, for instance their maximum duration, and about remedies like specific performance as opposed to only damages). The other set consists of the – already named – default rules which form the 'standard contract' or 'Reservevertragsordnung'. The latter is by far the more important. For simplicity's sake we will refer only to this second set in our explanations.

bb) Mandatory law is not primarily concerned with enabling party agreement, but with regulating cases where freedom of contract itself produces sub-optimal results. The problem about mandatory law is that, for regulatory purposes, it forbids or prescribes solutions or conditions excluding them or the other ones

---

is whether to use directives or regulations (COM(2001) 398 final, 20 (para. 63 seq.)) although directives are normally detailed as well. The need has been felt to modify principled rules into detailed rules: see, for instance, and from quite different perspectives: Ch. v. Bar, 'Die Study group on a European Civil Code', *Festschrift for D. Henrich* (2000), 1; J. Smits, 'The future of European Contract Law: on diversity and the temptation of elegance', in: *Towards a European Jus Commune in Legal Education and Research* (Maastricht, forthcoming).

Both in the case of principles and detailed rules, which are unanimously accepted, potential for innovation and for serving different preferences is important. These are the core advantages of decentralised rule-making. On the other hand, at least in the long run, it should be possible (for the ECJ) to also work principles on Community level into a workable set of rules and thus achieve the advantages of centralised rule-making, i.e. standardisation.

[22] See COM(2001) 398 final, p. 2, 10 seq. (para. 27).

from the possible range of solutions or conditions. The restricted range can serve the range of needs or preferences of the parties possibly less completely.[23] Moreover, the solutions excluded can no longer be tested.

Mandatory law is bound to become an issue in the discussion of a European Code if consumer law is to be included. It is mainly mandatory. Not to include consumer law, on the other hand, would mean that the *acquis communautaire* is questioned,[24] that the historic development of European contract law is neglected (in which consumer contract law was a strong driving force)[25] and it would run counter to more general and fundamental ideas about the role of consumer law within private law and the need of integrating these areas.[26] The *acquis communautaire* is so important, particularly in the area of mandatory law, because it is precisely mandatory contract law which is harmonised very substantially and even in almost all questions,[27] although often only at a minimum level.[28] For a

---

[23] See above section II2.

[24] Which the Commission is firmly opposed to: see COM(2001) 398 final, p. 19.

[25] Characteristic is E. Hondius, 'Kaufen ohne Risiko: Der europäische Richtlinienentwurf zum Verbraucherkauf und zur Verbrauchergarantie' [1997], *Zeitschrift für Europäisches Privatrecht (ZEuP)*, 130, 131: 'Insbesondere die Verbraucherschutzrichtlinien haben dazu beigetragen, ein europäisches Privatrecht zu gestalten.' Moreover, in a comparative law perspective, one has to note that all modern codes are integrated codes, namely the Dutch Code, the English Sale and Supply of Goods Act and also the Nordic Codes: E. Hondius, *Consumer Guarantees – Towards a European Sale of Goods Act* (Rome, Unidroit 18, 1996), 7 (for Italy and the Netherlands); in favour of integration: S. Grundmann, 'Generalreferat: Internationalisierung und Reform des deutschen Kaufrechts', in: S. Grundmann, D. Medicus and W. Rolland (eds.), *Europäisches Kaufgewährleistungsrecht – Reform und Internationalisierung des deutschen Schuldrechts* (Cologne, Heymanns, 2000), 281, 282–288; E. Hondius, 'Niederländisches Verbraucherrecht – vom Sonderrecht zum integrierten Zivilrecht', *VuR* [1996], 295, 295; see also the references in n. 26.

[26] See S. Grundmann, 'Consumer Law, Commercial Law, Private Law – How can the Sales Directive and the Sales Convention be so similar?', presentation SECOLA-Conference in Rome, www.secola.org (German version) (2002) *AcP* 202, 40; A. Schwartz, 'Legal implications of imperfect information in consumer markets', (1995) 151 *JITE* 31, esp. 35–46; also, however, for different reasons: E. Hondius, 'Consumer Law and Private Law – the case for integration', in: W. Heusel (ed.), *Neues Europäisches Vertragsrecht und Verbraucherschutz – Regelungskonzepte der Europäischen Union und ihre Auswirkungen auf die nationalen Zivilrechtsordnungen – New European Contract Law and Consumer Protection – the concepts involved in Community regulations and their consequences for domestic civil law – Le nouveau droit des contrats et la protection des consommateurs – concepts de la réglementation communautaire et leurs conséquences pour le droit civil national* (Cologne, Bundesanzeiger, 1999), 19.

[27] See in more detail S. Grundmann, 'The Structure of European Contract Law', (2001) *ERPL* 505, 517–521; and commentaries referred to in n. 42 below.

[28] For this approach and its importance see n. 48 et seqs.

European Code including consumer law, one must ask the question of how to treat rules in a two-level system both for non-mandatory and for mandatory law.

cc) For the design of an optional European Code, the major problem with this distinction is that *default can become mandatory (and vice versa) depending on the situation.* In the following, we mean by mandatory or default, what is mandatory or default in the particular situation. Default rules can become mandatory at least in standard contract terms cases – and this is the vast majority of cases. As far as *unfair contract terms law* applies, the deviation from default rules in standard contract terms must typically remain within narrow limits. In all Member States this is true, at least for consumer contracts, in some also for pure commercial contracts.[29] Thus default rules in standard contract terms cases turn into rules which set a rather narrow corridor of allowed solutions in a mandatory way. Thus many, in some Member States even most contracts in practice, are subject to mandatory law, at least in that only a corridor of solutions is allowed. In these situations, whatever is true in the interplay of centralised mandatory regulation and decentralised mandatory regulation is true also for default rules – although only in an indirect way (via unfair contract terms law) and in an attenuated form (a corridor is left). There is a second situation – also of some importance – in which there is the danger in the future that more law is mandatory law.[30]

b) The additional distinction between mandatory substantive law and mandatory information rules

Mandatory rules typically have restrictive effects on the range of solutions or conditions. Parties can possibly not tailor the contract conditions or solutions to serve best their individual preferences. Parallel experimentation is reduced. There are, however, mandatory rules which do not share this core characteristic

---

[29] See for Art. 3 of the Council Directive 93/13/EEC of 5 April 1993 on unfair terms in consumer contracts, (EC) OJ [1993] L 95/29: ECJ 27.6.2000 – case C-240–244/98 *Océano grupo editorial* [2000] ECR I–4941, 4972 *et seq.*; and, for instance, for German Unfair Contract Terms Law, sec. 307 (2) Civil Code and M. Wolf, in: M. Wolf, N. Horn and W. Lindacher, *AGB-Gesetz – Kommentar* (4th edn., Munich, Beck, 1999), § 9 para. 76. Germany is one of those states where this applies also to pure commercial contracts (see sections 1, 9 and 24 of the German Unfair Contract Terms Code, now integrated into the Civil Code as sections 305 (1), 307, 310 (1) and (2)).

[30] This is so if a European Code substitutes national laws and thus renders all cases within the Community purely domestic cases. Then those rules become absolutely mandatory which today are mandatory only in domestic cases, but are not in cross-border cases under art. 3 of the Rome Convention on the law applicable to contracts (see consolidated version (EC) OJ [1998] C 27/34). This refers to all mandatory rules not concerned with labour law, consumer protection and public good protection.

– and potential disadvantage – of (other) mandatory rules. In this respect, mandatory substantive rules and mandatory information rules are fundamentally different.[31] Mandatory information rules only prescribe the disclosure of information, then leave the freedom to tailor the contract substance to the parties (freedom of contract).[32] Their scope is to enhance the conditions for an optimal use of freedom of contract: they are meant to increase the possibility of rational, i.e. also informed choice, by both parties, bringing the contract solution as close as possible to the real preferences of both parties.[33] As restricting this freedom is the core effect of normal mandatory law also influencing the capacity of innovation in a market, mandatory substantive rules and mandatory information rules are fundamentally different in nature and therefore should and will be distinguished.

2. Choice between Different Sets of Rules

a) Union, States or Parties

Union, states and parties are the three potential decision makers. They will decide about preferences and innovation quite differently. This criterion is not concerned with who offers the rules, but with who ultimately decides on the question, which of the rules which are in the market is applied to a particular problem in the particular case. The Union can decide to have only its law applied to a problem. It may leave an option to the states to choose whether Union law or state law applies. More practical so far is the situation in which the Union decides to apply its law as a minimum standard (directives) or as a maximum standard (mainly fundamental freedoms) and to allow the states to regulate above or below these minimum and maximum standards. Leaving the choice to parties may mean both that they can choose between different solutions offered by the Union and one or more or all states, and that they can choose between different solutions offered by different states, potentially again all states.

---

[31]   See for the following: S. Grundmann, W. Kerber and S. Weatherill (eds.), *Party Autonomy and the Role of Information in the Internal Market* (Berlin/New York, de Gruyter, 2001); S. Grundmann, 'Information, Party Autonomy and Economic Agents in European Contract Law', (2002) 39 *CMLRev.* 269.

[32]   Normally other issues than that of passing on information are the core issues of the contract. In most contracts, the giving of information is only an ancillary duty, often a prerequisite for a 'good' contract.

[33]   Too little information can lead to adverse selection: see A. Schwartz, (1995) 151 *JITE* 31, 46; S. Strassner, *Verbraucherinformationsrecht – rechtliche Grundlagen und rechtsökonomische Aspekte* (Saarbrücken, ÖR-Verlag, 1992), 133–136; Th. Wein, 'Consumer information problems – causes and consequences', in: Grundmann, Kerber and Weatherill (n. 31), 80, 91–96.

It can, however, also mean that parties can choose party-made rules as well, sets of standard terms or individual agreements (traditional freedom of contract).

b) Modalities – Opt In and Opt Out

The most important modality of choice is that of opt in or opt out. As typically there are alternatives, choosing an opt-in design for the one means choosing an opt-out design for the other. The law from which the decision maker has to opt out has certainly a cost advantage or even other advantages. If the state is the decision maker, the burden of political action is on the other alternative; if it is the parties, agreement has to be reached for the other alternative and moreover the party for which the other alternative may be favourable has to be active enough to raise the question at all. In many cases the parties in question do not even want to incur the costs of investigating whether the other alternative might be more favourable. Therefore, if the European Code is applied on an opt-out basis, the evaluation will come closer to that of a solution where the European Code completely replaces the national contract laws. This is one question where distinguishing between cross-border or domestic cases may well seem important: it may be advisable to ask parties to opt out of the European Code in cross-border cases and to opt in in domestic cases (subject otherwise to national law). This is so because in cross-border cases, there is at least one additional argument in favour of the application of a European Code which does not have its equivalent in purely domestic cases: whereas applying one national law gives an advantage to one party in cross-border cases, applying the European Code means eliminating this inequality in access to the law, and potentially also courts.

c) Cross-Border Contracts only?

The cross-border character of a transaction can already be important with respect to the question whether a rule is ultimately binding or not.[34] The cross-border character of the transaction is, however, also important in another respect in the discussion about a European Contract Law Code: a potential design could be to *draft a European Code only for cross-border contracts* first.[35] This is the approach already taken in the (Vienna) Convention on the International

---

[34]   For this aspect, see above n. 30.

[35]   See more extensively the proposal by Drobnig which is expressed in his contribution to this volume; and S. Leible, 'Die Mitteilung der Kommision zum Europäischen Vertragsrecht – Startschuss für ein Europäisches Vertragsgesetzbuch?', *EWS* [2001], 471, 480 *et seq.*

Sale of Goods (CISG),[36] the most prominent piece of international uniform law. Cross-border transactions amount typically to about 20 per cent of all transactions in the bigger Member States (only). For default rules, this solution would come close to the opt-in and opt-out design considered above: it is accepted in principle also for the CISG that even in purely domestic cases parties can choose this Convention to apply (opt-in).[37] In cross-border cases, they have to opt out (Art. 6 CISG).

For mandatory rules, however, a restriction to pure cross-border cases would mean cutting back on the *acquis communautaire*. Only in one case, the payments directive,[38] mandatory EU law applied only to cross-border cases and this meant giving the Member States the freedom to opt in for purely domestic cases (but also to leave it). For mandatory rules, it is particularly important that the options can be given to states or parties.

There may be theoretical[39] and practical concerns[40] with a European Code applying to cross-border cases only. For a map of potential designs, however,

---

[36] Art. 1 *et seq.* of the (Vienna) UN Convention on Contracts for the International Sale of Goods of 11 April 1980, United Nations, Official Records, 1981, 178 (German O.J.) BGBl. 1989 II, 586 (English, French, German); for the states adhering to the Convention (altogether 58 at the end of 2000) see annex B to (German O.J.) BGBl. 2000 II, 595 or J. Honnold, *Uniform Law for International Sales* 3rd edn. (The Hague, Kluwer, 1999), 577 (53 in June 1998).

[37] F. Ferrari, in: P. Schlechtriem (ed.), *Kommentar zum Einheitlichen UN-Kaufrecht – das Übereinkommen der Vereinten Nationen über Verträge über den internationalen Warenkauf-CISG* (3rd edn., Munich, Beck, 2000), Art. 6 paras. 39–43.

[38] European Parliament and Council Directive 97/5/EC of 27 January 1997 on cross-border credit transfers, (EC) OJ [1997] L 43/25.

[39] In one integrated market, where different laws, states laws and EU law, are offered as solutions, and if fundamental freedoms and economic arguments speak in favour of doing so, also in domestic cases, the distinction between cross-border and domestic is bound to fade away. Integration is about diminishing borders, but adjusts very well with the idea of offering different legal solutions as options.

[40] The problem with Conventions applying only to cross-border cases is that there is too little case law (and legal security) building up because of small numbers. Even the UN Sales Convention (n. 36) was only moderately successful, despite its good reputation: see J. Lindbach, *Rechtswahl im Einheitsrecht – am Beispiel des Wiener UN-Kaufrechts* (Aachen, Shaker, 1996), 349; the Convention is not very important in practice according to K. Tonner, 'Die Rolle des Verbraucherrechts bei der Entwicklung eines europäischen Zivilrechts', *JZ* [1996], 541. This is so although, among the international Conventions, the UN Sales Convention is probably still the most successful. M.R. Will, *International Sales Law under CISG – the UN Convention on Contracts for the International Sale of Goods (1980) – the first 555 or so Decisions* (Geneva, Univ. de Genève, 1999) reproduces the case law on the Convention, about 200 cases in Germany. This means that only about 15–20 cases are decided worldwide each year (outside Germany), in most cases by lower courts.

this proposal does not create particular problems. If the European Code covered cross-border cases only, then cases of European law only or of state option would simply be less numerous with respect to mandatory substantive and mandatory information rules. Therefore the advantages and disadvantages named below for these case patterns would remain the same, but apply to a reduced number of cases. For its default rules, even a European Code restricted to cross-border cases could also be chosen within the domestic freedom of contract in domestic cases (as is the case with the UN Sales Convention).

IV. A MAP OF POTENTIAL DESIGNS IN A EUROPEAN SYSTEM OF CONTRACT Laws

1. A Map of Dimensions

From the two core dimensions the following map can be derived which will be taken as the basis for sections 2–4. Within this map, opt-in and opt-out solutions will be taken into account in that the standard from which the decision maker has to opt out is favoured (at least in cost aspects) by the legislator. Therefore the opt-out solution comes closer in policy questions to the next more binding variant of this standard than an opt-in solution.

Choice made by	Mandatory Substantive Rules	Mandatory Information Rules	Facilitative Law
(a) Union			
(b) States having part choice			
(c) States having full choice			
(d) Parties having some choice between			

2. Mandatory Substantive Rules

a) Characterisation and Importance

Mandatory substantive rules in European Contract Law exist or could exist mainly in *two areas*: in *consumer contract law*, potentially also in (contract related) *competition law in the large sense*. Indeed, currently there are two scopes which inspire mandatory law and regulation of the formation, content and termination of contracts. They are protecting the weaker party (mainly inferiority situations as to information)[41] and protecting free competition in markets.[42]

b) EU law only

aa) This solution is the simplest and can be *described* as follows. The Union would prescribe that only its mandatory substantive law applies. There would be no options for states or private parties as to consumer (and potentially also competition) law standards imposed by EU law, for instance termination rights, nullity of diverging solutions, quality standards imposed or also possibly imposed maximum prices.

bb) As *practical examples,* one would have to name legal measures in European Contract Law which prescribe a minimum and at the same time a maximum standard. The only example so far in contract law is not yet in force, the Commission proposed such standards for distance contracts in financial services.[43] Maximum standards are problematic under subsidiarity aspects.[44] Even EC competition law which could be named here applies only to situations with

---

[41] Consumer law is convincingly explained mainly as a law curing information asymmetries. See R.R. Kerton and R. Bodell, 'Quality, choice and the economics of concealment – the marketing of lemons', (1995) 29 *Journal of Consumer Affairs* 1, esp. 20–24; H.-B. Schäfer, 'Grenzen des Verbraucherschutzes und adverse Effekte des Europäischen Verbraucherrechts', in: S. Grundmann (ed.), *Systembildung und Systemlücken in Kerngebieten des Europäischen Privatrechts – Gesellschaftsrecht, Arbeitsrecht, Schuldvertragsrecht* (Tübingen, Mohr, 2000), 559, 559–564; A. Schwartz, (1995) 151 *JITE* 31, esp. 35–46; S. Strassner (n. 33) 126–136; and monographically for information asymmetries: H. Fleischer, *Informationsasymmetrie im Vertragsrecht* (Munich, Beck, 2001).

[42] This is true mainly for the prohibition of cartels, block exemptions, public procurement rules and some rules in intellectual property law (see decompilation of computer programs, etc.); commentary for these areas and more extensive on these areas under the competition law approach: S. Grundmann, *Europäisches Schuldvertragsrecht* (Berlin/New York, de Gruyter, 1999), 905–1171; *id.*, (2001) *ERPL* 505, 515 seq. and 518 *et seq.*; C. Quigley, *EC Contract Law* (London et al., Kluwer, 1997), 81–112.

[43] Proposal for a Directive of the European Parliament and of the Council concerning the distance marketing of consumer financial services and amending Council Directive 90/619/EEC and Directives 97/7/EC and 98/27/EC, (EC) OJ [1998] C 385/10, COM(1998) 468 final; Common Standpoint (EC) of [2002] C 58 E/32.

[44] See ECJ 19.11.1996 – case C-42/95 *Siemens/Nold* [1996] ECR I–6017, 6034–6036 (invoking mainly the scope of the directive); H. Merkt, 'Europäische Rechtsetzung und strengeres autonomes Recht – zur Auslegung von Gemeinschaftsnormen als Mindeststandards', *RabelsZ* 61 (1997) 647, esp. 669–684; for company law M. Lutter, 'Die Auslegung angeglichenen Rechts', *JZ* [1992], 593, 606; for environmental law H. Jarass, 'Binnenmarktrichtlinien und Umweltschutzrichtlinien – zur Abgrenzung des Anwendungsfeldes und zu den Möglichkeiten nationalen Abweichens', *EuZW* [1991], 530, 532.

cross-border implications (and is perhaps not core contract law). A third and the most important example could be a European Code to come comprising consumer contract law. From the aforesaid follows, however, that this would be a fundamentally new approach. Not even competition law, which was so important from the founding days of a European Community, is EU law only.

cc) Basic features of evaluation would include those named in pure form.[45] There would be serious inroads into the capacity of the law to serve and allow the serving of heterogeneous preferences, into the capacity of law to adapt to new needs in a highly dynamic world and into the capacity of law to use multiple sources for learning about better solutions and not to stay in tendency once and for all at one level of knowledge (already imperfect at the time of its use in the legislative process). On the other hand, the typical advantages of centralised rule making may well be not very strong in this situation: standardisation as a device (saving of transaction costs) is important mainly for mass transactions and parties which consciously plan transactions, i.e. for the side of supply, possibly not so much for the consumer. For the side of supply, however, standardisation can also be reached in a minimum harmonisation situation. A potential race to the bottom may well be reduced by EU law only but, again, it can be reduced also by minimum harmonisation.[46]

c) States having part decision power (maximum/minimum fixed by EU)

aa) This solution can be *described* as the now predominant in European Contract Law (in domestic cases). The Union prescribes a uniform mandatory substantive standard to be applied, but only as a minimum or a maximum. Neither states nor parties may deviate from it. Above this level or below this level, however, national law may regulate contracts by its own mandatory substantive standards. In this case, national law would impose its standard, insofar that parties would not have the choice.

bb) The *practical example* for a minimum level fixed by centralised rule making, i.e. Community law, is the law contained in directives which in contract law allow more stringent national law in all cases but one.[47] In purely domestic cases, Member States can certainly apply their more stringent law in a mandatory

---

[45] See above text accompanying n. 8 et seqs.
[46] For both statements about effects of minimum harmonisation see below text accompanying n. 48 et seqs.
[47] This is the Council Directive 86/653/EEC of 18 December 1986 on the coordination of the laws of the Member States relating to self-employed commercial agents, (EC) OJ [1986] L 382/17; see S. Grundmann, *Europäisches Schuldvertragsrecht* (Berlin/New York, de Gruyter, 1999), 77–79 for a list of articles in the other directives which explicitly allow more stringent national law.

way. Conversely, in cross-border cases, Community law probably obliges them to leave some (restricted) choice to the parties: more stringent law cannot be opposed to supply from abroad using its home country law.[48] Thus, for questions of more stringent state law, parties can choose between domestic supply under domestic mandatory law and supply from abroad under other state laws. In the future, there could also be EU model rules for more stringent standards besides the state laws. The rest of the mechanism would not change. An opt-out solution would come close to such options opened in directives, for instance that of reducing the cut-off period contained in article 5(1) of the Sales Directive from two years to one in the case of used goods.[49]

The example for a maximum level set by Community law is fundamental freedoms. They apply only to mandatory state law[50] and forbid a higher level of state regulation (mandatory substantive law) than needed according to EC standards. These standards are quite demanding: national mandatory law has to be justified by mandatory reasons of public good; it has to be carried through

---

[48] This is disputed. See for the position which holds that harmonisation consumes the justification by mandatory public good standards because it defines what is strictly indispensable: A. Bleckmann, 'Probleme der Auslegung europäischer Richtlinien', *Zeitschrift für Gesellschaftsrecht* [1992], 364, 373; S. Grundmann, 'Binnenmarktkollisionsrecht – vom klassischen IPR zur Integrationsordnung', *RabelsZ* 64 (2000) 457, 471–476; E. Steindorff, *Grenzen der EG-Kompetenzen*, (Heidelberg, Recht & Wirtschaft, 1990), 84; and rather uniform in this sense, the Italian doctrine, see P. Mengozzi, 'La seconda direttiva bancaria, il mutuo riconoscimento e la tutela dell'interesse generale degli Stati Membri', *Riv. dir.europ.* [1994], 447, 459 *et seq.* The opponents hold that domestic law can still apply if there are mandatory reasons of public good for doing so. See mainly W.-H. Roth, in: Grundmann, Medicus and Rolland (n. 25), 113, 123–126; and A. Baumert, *Europäischer ordre public und Sonderanknüpfung zur Durchsetzung von EG-Recht*, (Frankfurt, Lang, 1994), 232–234; B. Smulders and P. Glazener, 'Harmonization in the Field of Insurance Law through the Introduction of Community Rules of Conflict', (1992) 19 *CMLRev.* 775, 797.

[49] Directive 1999/44/EC of the European Parliament and of the Council of 25 May 1999 on certain aspects of the sale of consumer goods and associated guarantees, (EC) OJ [1999] L 171/12; for this directive see M. Bianca and S. Grundmann (eds.), *EU Sales Directive – Commentary* (Antwerp-Oxford, Intersentia-Hart, 2002).

[50] Indeed, the ECJ does not submit to a fundamental freedoms scrutiny national rules from which parties can opt out in cross-border cases under art. 3 Rome Convention (n. 30): ECJ 24.1.1991 – case C-339/89 *Alsthom Atlantique* [1991] ECR I-107, 124; some authors criticise this rule invoking additional information costs for one party: J. Basedow, 'A Common Contract Law for the Common Market', (1996) 33 *CMLRev.* 1169, 1174–1178; P. v. Wilmowsky, 'EG-Freiheiten und Vertragsrecht', *JZ* [1996], 590, 595 *et seq.*; and E. Steindorff, *EG-Vertrag und Privatrecht* (Baden-Baden, Nomos, 1996), 78 *et seq.* (without, however, even referring to the decision). A justification of the Court's position is given by S. Grundmann, 'Europäisches Handelsrecht – vom Handelsrecht des laissez faire im Kodex des 19. Jahrhunderts zum Handelsrecht der sozialen Verantwortung', *Zeitschrift für das gesamte Handelsrecht (ZHR)* 163 (1999) 635, 656–659.

in a fully consistent and in the least intrusive way possible (principle of proportionality); this means also that state legislators have to prefer mandatory information rules to substantive mandatory rules whenever sufficient for the protective purpose.[51]

If the *acquis communautaire* is to be maintained[52] the minimum standards on a centralised level would not be questioned. What is important is that, so far, most EU contract law minimum standards contain only information rules and therefore fall into another category (see 3 below).[53] Conversely, maximum standards fixed by the EU typically focus on mandatory substantive rules. As mentioned, they even prescribe that priority has to be given to mere (mandatory) information rules if ever possible.

cc) Basic features of evaluation would include a balancing of the danger of market failure – which mandatory substantive regulation should fight in order to be justified – and the danger of state failure which nowadays is accepted to exist as well. The danger of state failure, i.e. the failure to judge market failure correctly and to react to it by the appropriate regulation (potentially also by no regulation), is due mainly to two facts: states may have knowledge problems (distance from the relevant problems; impossibility of full knowledge; rapidly changing knowledge); and they may have incentive problems (rent seeking, lobbyism, public choice).[54]

It may well be that one solution only is not appropriate in the same way to all contract law regulation rules. One should, however, make further investigations in the following direction: both types of regulation possible – regulation on the Community level and regulation on national level – can be too weak or too heavy. They can be exposed to more or less pressure though and thus respond to these concerns in a different way. Regulation on the national level may have a problem of under-regulation. This risk (potential race to the bottom) may well justify minimum regulation on the Community level – a traditional justification given in harmonisation theory. Thus, the risk of under-regulation is reduced by the imminence of harmonisation. The more competition is distorted by under-regulation on the national level the more the pressure for harmonisation increases. Moreover, if there is under-regulation on the Community level, states can still regulate on a higher level and if they do so efficiently the scenario

---

51 See the standard commentaries for all these maximum standards set by EC Treaty Law; for the supremacy of information rules see references below n. 66.

52 See above n. 24.

53 See Grundmann, Kerber and Weatherill (n. 31).

54 For this risk, discussed under the term of public choice, see most prominently: J.M. Buchanan and G. Tullock, *The Calculus of Consent – Logical Foundations of Constitutional Democracy* (Ann Arbor, Univ. of Michigan Press, 1962); J.M. Buchanan, *The Limits of Liberty – between Anarchy and Leviathan* (Chicago, Chicago Univ. Press, 1975); J.M. Buchanan, *Liberty, Market, and State* (New York, New York Univ. Press, 1986).

of rise to the top becomes likely. Thus the main problem in a two-level system is over-regulation.[55] In this respect state regulation can have a real advantage which then speaks in favour of a solution which consciously reserves to state regulation any experimentation with cases and rules where regulation might potentially be too heavy. Over-regulation on the Community level may still be more of a problem because it is typically less put to a test. It may therefore be helpful if the Community regulates only where the need and the tools used are almost unanimously consented. Thus, the need of consent in almost 15 states can serve as a mechanism against state failure. The Commission should deduce from this that regulation should be envisaged only if the consensus in expert (and benevolent) circles is broad and not where the risk of error is considerable. These cases should then be left to state regulation. In order to make this mechanism work smoothly state regulation would, however, have to be put to a test. This test already exists in current EU law: fixing a maximum level means that national regulations are checked against a principle of proportionality and compared against foreign laws which might reach the protection looked for with less intrusive methods. A second test is that of the market. Then not the European Court of Justice would compare solutions, but the side of demand.[56]

d) States having full decision power

aa) This solution can be *described* as one where not even an EU minimum (or maximum) standard is imposed on Member States. The *practical example* would be that of an EU Model Code including those rules which typically are mandatory even in cross-border cases, i.e. also including consumer protection rules. Member States could opt out of this or would have to opt in. Politically, this solution is not likely, because it would mean cutting back on the *acquis communautaire.*

bb) Discussing *basic features of evaluation* means comparison: the split competence solution described (section c above) may be apt to contain the risk of under-regulation without, however, running serious risks of over-regulation. Giving the option to the states to apply their regulation not only for the more stringent rules but generally, may well not have any advantage over this solution. As long as the choice by the parties was not opened up (see section e below), there would be no additional structural mechanism which could help to reduce the risk of over-regulation.[57] Conversely, the powerful mechanism containing the risk of

---

[55]   In this sense also the contribution by R. van den Bergh in this volume. This author, however, would also do away with minimum harmonisation.

[56]   This scenario exists; it falls, however, into another category. See below section e (text accompanying n. 58 *et seq.*).

[57]   If the EU could not even set the maximum level (via fundamental freedoms) the risk of over-regulation would even be increased.

under-regulation which exists in the minimum harmonisation approach would be eliminated. Therefore, the full state option model discussed here could well only have an advantage over the minimum harmonisation model if the regulation on the central level developed in a way where it can often be asked whether this central regulation is not heavy regulation and potentially over-regulation. The advantage would be reduced or even absent, however, if, for mandatory rules (here mandatory substantive rules), the Community legislator followed the above stated counsel and keep central (minimum) regulation at the level which meets virtually unanimous acceptance.

e) Parties having a choice

aa) Already in European Contract Law, there is quite some degree of party choice for internationally mandatory rules.[58] Choice can be given also only as to parts of the solution, for instance for the more stringent rules. Choice in case of mandatory rules never means that parties can completely opt out; they can do so only in combination with opting into another set of mandatory rules. In the following, *three quite representative combinations are discussed.*

bb) The first is represented by current European Contract Law, the *acquis communautaire*. Here, a *minimum set by the Union is not open to party options.* This set is, however, combined with a freedom of choice between different state laws *as to more stringent regulation. The freedom of choice is restricted.* Under current fundamental freedoms doctrine, suppliers from abroad can act under their home country rule.[59] Therefore the side of demand can choose between different sets of more stringent state laws (also state laws with zero more stringent rules). These sets can, however, only be chosen in combination with a supplier having its origin in the country whose law should be chosen. As the more stringent law follows the origin of supply, there is no opt-in and opt-out problem so far.

cc) In the second situation, *choice could be broadened as to the more stringent rules.* The minimum would remain firm. There are three particularly prominent designs. They start from what is well established as home country principle: any supplier can design his conditions taking into account only the rules of his home country (including the more stringent which go beyond the EU minimum standard). In the three designs, the origin of supply would gradually become less

---

[58] This is due to the dual fact that most mandatory EU Contract Law consists of information rules only and that above that minimum, in principle, host countries may not impose their standards on foreign offers (the latter is disputed). See references above nn. 53 and 48 and more in detail S. Grundmann, (2002) 39 *CMLRev.*

[59] For dispute about this, see above n. 48. For a potential right to also opt for the host country standard, see n. 61.

important.[60] A first step would be (1) that the supplier from abroad can alternatively choose the host country's (more stringent) rules.[61] Choice would be more extended if (2) any supplier had to make an offer under his home country rules but was allowed also to make alternative offers under any other law. In this case, in any country the standard of this country would still be offered (home country rule of the domestic supply). Choice would still be broader if (3) any supplier could choose the law under which he wants to make his offers. This would no longer guarantee that the host country standard is offered at all. If the suppliers do not make a choice there would have to be a default solution. This could be either the law of the home country of the supplier or that of the host country. There would certainly be a prerequisite of transparency (otherwise the host country standard should apply).

dd) In the third situation, the parties would have a *choice also as to the minimum itself*, between EU law and one or more state laws. This would mean cutting back on the *acquis communautaire*. Such a solution would only be realistic if it meant that EU law really sets only the scope to be aimed at and that EU and states give a model of how they would accomplish this task with more detailed rules. The parties could then choose.

ee) Basic features of evaluation have to build on the aforesaid: if in fact a split competencies approach could well be structurally superior to a full state option whenever the EU minimum really is restricted to what is basically consented, one should investigate broadening choice primarily with respect to the more stringent rules.

Here, one could investigate in the following direction. Freedom of choice in this area may potentially create a danger for those who cannot inform themselves or understand the differences. This speaks in favour of having one fall-back position where the local regulator – which is particularly responsive to the needs in this market, i.e. the client's home – sets the measure of regulation. This solution is certainly offered, if in purely domestic cases (i.e. between local customers and local supply), domestic law is applied. Any customer can choose to buy home, under his law. This fall-back position would be maintained if suppliers

---

[60]   For an in-principle critique see Kerber (n. 9), 67, 88–96; see furthermore the EC law evaluation of this approach by G. Koenig, J. Braun and R. Capito, 'Europäisches Systemwettbewerb durch Wahl der Rechtsregeln in einem Binnenmarkt für mitgliedstaatliche Regulierungen?', *EWS* [1999], 401.

[61]   Most favourable law principle, advocated under current fundamental freedoms doctrine by W.-H. Roth, 'Der Einfluß des Europäischen Gemeinschaftsrechts auf das Internationale Privatrecht', *RabelsZ* 55 (1991), 623, 645–662; also J. v. Hein, *Das Günstigkeitsprinzip im Internationalen Deliktsrecht* (Tübingen, Mohr, 1999), 423–433; U. Höpping, *Auswirkungen der Warenverkehrsfreiheit auf das IPR – unter besonderer Berücksichtigung des Internationalen Produkthaftungsrechts und des Internationalen Vertragsrechts* (Frankfurt, Lang, 1997), esp. 169–178.

were at least asked to also make an offer under their law, but were given the option to make alternative offers under a foreign law. Giving foreign suppliers the freedom to make offers under their laws does not take away this fall-back position. Any customer in the Union should be able to learn that foreign offers may deviate in law and that they are risky in this sense. If he is not sure, he may buy in a conservative way. Otherwise he has to invest in advice, leave it, or take a risk. Conversely, giving at least some freedom of choice may increase advantages for other customers. They may have their preferences better served. If they cannot judge on this a market for information intermediaries may evolve[62] if information really can be used to take options. Moreover there is more potential of innovation and experimentation. This speaks in favour of offering even local supply the possibility to design offers, at least as an alternative under foreign laws. This also speaks in favour of offering supply from abroad the possibility to design their offers under any national law if only this is made transparent.

3. Mandatory Information Rules

a) Characterisation and importance

Mandatory information rules are the dominant regulatory tool in current European Contract Law.[63] They are hybrid in nature in that they are mandatory in legal construction; as to the capacity of the parties, however, to design the contract and the capacity of the substantive law to evolve, they are basically facilitative or enabling. They leave this design to the parties and are fundamentally aimed at helping them in choosing better designs.

Mandatory information rules are mainly those which prescribe the giving of information and the sanctions if the information is incorrect or incomplete. For the first group of rules, centralised rule making is strong already, for the second, it is weak.

b) EU law only

aa) This situation can be *described* as one in which the question how much information has to be passed from one party to the other is completely fixed by

---

[62] See Th. Gehrig, 'Intermediation in search markets', (1993) 2 *Journal of Economics and Management Strategy* 97; S. Grundmann and W. Kerber, 'Information Intermediaries and Extending the Area of Informed Party Autonomy – as in Capital Markets and in the Insurance Business', in: Grundmann, Kerber and Weatherill (n. 31), 264; F. Rose, *The economics, concept, and design of information intermediaries* (Heidelberg, Physica, 1999); A. Yava, 'Search and Trading in Intermediated Markets', (1996) 5 *Journal of Economics and Management Strategy* 195.

[63] See Grundmann, Kerber and Weatherill (n. 31).

(mandatory) EU law or in which the question of liability for incorrect or incomplete information is completely decided on by EU law.

bb) The *practical example* could be a future European Code if it replaced the national regimes on information. Another example could be directives which fix the minimum level and at the same time also the maximum level. A closer look at current EU law shows that this situation already partly exists. Contrary to what is the case for mandatory substantive rules, information rules are numerous in current European Contract Law and they can often be understood as more than minimum rules. They prescribe exact amounts of content (as minimum) which, however, may not be extended or only moderately, by the Member States. This is the case with all rules which prescribe that all material information be given but at the same time that it be given in a clear and understandable way. Thus, information overkill will be avoided, the information has to be kept at a level which can easily be digested. The corridor left to Member States is thus narrow, if not reduced to one optimal solution. This type of information rule is to be found in article 11 Investment Services Directive for all transactions in securities markets,[64] but also in directives which describe the items about which information has to be given in an enumerative way. There may even be a general principle in this sense inherent to all European information rules.[65]

cc) Basic features of evaluation have to do with the nature of mandatory information rules as opposed to mandatory substantive rules. The evaluation structure is not the same. An EU law only solution has, first, less adverse effects, because the particular shortcomings of centralised rule making are weaker. Mandatory information rules are less intrusive than mandatory substantive rules and even have a liberalising effect: they are an alternative to mandatory substantive rules already on Community level and push back this type of rule on this level; moreover they have their effect also on mandatory substantive rules on the state level. Fundamental freedoms prescribe that national legislators choose mere

---

[64] Council Directive 93/22/EEC of 10 May 1993 on investment services in the securities field, (EC) OJ [1993] L 141/27; amended in (EC) OJ [1995] L 168/7. Article 11(1) reads: '... must be applied in such a way as to take account of the professional nature of the person for whom the service is provided [and] ... that the investment firm ... makes adequate disclosure of relevant material information in its dealings with its clients ...' The text is so open because the information to be given depends so much on the individual situation and the needs are difficult to standardise (professionality, investment scopes, etc.). The rule is even designed such that the intermediary should transpose standardised primary securities markets information (prospectuses, etc.) to the individual needs of the individual investor in each case. See Grundmann and Kerber (n. 62), 264; S. Grundmann, in: C. Ebenroth, K. Boujong and D. Joost, *Handelsgesetzbuch* (Munich, Vahlen, 2001), Bankrecht para. VI 31; S. Heinze, *Europäisches Kapitalmarktrecht – Recht des Primärmarktes* (Munich, Beck, 1999), 376–386.

[65] In this sense now, even the Commission, see COM(2001) 398 final, pp. 59, 61.

information rules where this is sufficient protection.[66] This means that one of the two types of market failure which are really important in contract law – and even the one which is still more core contract law – is mainly solved by information rules leaving all advantages of potential variety in substance intact. EU law only in mandatory information rules may be problematic as to the question how much information should be given.[67] It does not, however, restrict the variety of solutions for different preferences and the capacity of law for innovation in substantive law questions. In the case of information rules, EU law only is, second, also a stronger option on the side of advantages of centralised rule making. Standardisation advantages of an EU law only solution may well not be so important in the case of substantive mandatory rules. The side of demand often does not know the law and does not consider it to be so important. And for the side of supply, standardisation advantages can also be reached in a split competencies solution.[68] Conversely, standardisation seems to be important for the side of demand as well in the case of information rules. These rules are more about the product itself even though they may also inform about the law.[69] For a comparison of products, it is certainly helpful exactly for the side of demand that information be standardised and thus easier to compare.

c) States having decision power partly (maximum/minimum fixed by EU)

aa) This situation can be *described* parallel to the one in which mandatory information rules are fixed partly by the Union, but only at a minimum level or a maximum level.

---

[66] ECJ 20.2.1979 – case 120/78 *Cassis de Dijon* [1979] ECR 649, 664; 22.6.1982 – case 220/81 *Robertson* [1982] ECR 2349, 2361 *et seq.*; 11.7.1984 – case 51/83 *Commission v. Italy* [1984] ECR 2793, 2805 *et seq.*; and also for the freedom of establishment: ECJ 9.3.1999 – case C-212/97 *Centros* [1999] ECR I–1459, 1495.

[67] Here there can be over-regulation and – less likely – too little regulation. Typically, it is rather information overkill which is feared with respect to Community law: see, for instance M. Martinek, 'Unsystematische Überregulierung und kontraintentionale Effekte im Europäischen Verbraucherschutzrecht oder: Weniger wäre mehr', in: S. Grundmann (ed.), *Systembildung und Systemlücken in Kerngebieten des Europäischen Privatrechts – Gesellschaftsrecht, Arbeitsrecht, Schuldvertragsrecht* (Tübingen, Mohr, 2000), 511, passim (for huge parts of consumer contract law); H.-D. Assmann, 'Die Regelung der Primärmärkte für Kapitalanlagen mittels Publizität im Recht der Europäischen Gemeinschaft', *AG* [1993], 549, 560; *id.*, 'Die rechtliche Ordnung des europäischen Kapitalmarkts – Defizite des EG-Konzepts einer Kapitalmarktintegration durch Rechtsvereinheitlichung "von oben"', *ORDO* 1993, 87, 103 (for capital market law).

[68] See above, text accompanying n. 48.

[69] Examples are to be found in virtually all directives, for instance, the Package Travel Directive, the Distance Selling Directive and also in art. 6 of the Sales Directive (reference above n. 49). For this latter example, see explanation in: E. Hondius, *Consumer Guarantees – towards a European Sale of Goods Act* (Rome, Unidroit 18, 1996), 17 *et seq.*

bb) The *practical examples* diverge – first for fundamental freedoms (maximum level). These do not play an important role for mandatory information rules.[70] Mostly fundamental freedoms even impose the use of information rules on national legislators (supremacy of information rules).[71] The picture diverges, second, also with respect to minimum standards, again in various aspects: mandatory information rules in European Contract Law are more numerous than mandatory substantive rules. At the same time the proportion of minimum rules and minimum/maximum rules is changed. Among these numerous information rules there are many which also fix a maximum standard (see section b above) so that the (remaining) mere minimum rules may not even be information rules in majority.[72]

cc) Basic features of evaluation are concerned with the fact that in EC contract law information rules are more numerous than mandatory substantive rules and that they more often also fix maximum standards. Thus the EU law only solution is more predominant. As fundamental freedoms are not so important for information rules we need not discuss EU law fixing a maximum, but compare EU law only with EU law fixing a minimum standard.

In this case, the basic potential advantage of a split competences solution for substantive mandatory rules was seen in that the EU can avoid over-regulation and that at the same time there is no serious risk of under-regulation because Member States can react. The evaluation is not completely the same in the case of mandatory information rules. If information allows comparison in markets, the case for standardisation is stronger. At the same time, over-regulation is less of a problem if the setting of the standard is left to the segments of the markets concerned to a certain extent. This is the effect of a transparency rule which says that all material information has to be given in a way which is clear and understandable to the client. Then the segment itself decides to a certain extent what are the contents needed (material) and allowed (not abundant and therefore

---

[70] Different only where information may lead to discrimination of foreign offers, mainly with respect to language requirements. See, for instance, ECJ 3.6.1999 – case C-33/97 *Colim v. Bigg's Continent Noord* [1999] ECR I–3175; in detail: Usher, 'Disclosure rules (information) as a primary tool in the doctrine on measures having an equivalent effect', in: Grundmann, Kerber and Weatherill (n. 31), 152, 160–164.

[71] See references in n. 66.

[72] One example is the Council Directive 84/450/EEC of 10 September 1984 relating to the approximation of the laws, regulations and administrative provisions of the Member States concerning misleading advertising, (EC) OJ [1984] L 250/17; amended in (EC) OJ [1997] L 290/18 (now including comparative advertising, but not strictly contract law). Another example could be the Unfair Contract Terms Directive (n. 29) where little is said about the handing over of the standard terms themselves or about information on them. Different, for instance, sec. 2 of the German Unfair Contract Terms Code, now sec. 305 (2) of the German Civil Code as of 1 January 2002.

reducing transparency). Thus the EU law only solution has more advantages than the split competences approach and less disadvantages in the area of mandatory information rules than in that of mandatory substantive rules. The evaluation is not so clear in favour of a split competences approach. In fact, the contrary seems plausible in many cases.

d) States having full decision power

This situation is difficult to imagine (EU law as a mere model code). The solution seems at least as unlikely politically than in the case of mandatory substantive rules (*acquis communautaire*). As its structural inferioriority to a split competences solution has been shown to be plausible and as standardisation is even more important for mandatory information rules than for mandatory substantive rules this solution does not seem very attractive theoretically either. For these two reasons, it should not be discussed at length.

e) Parties having a choice

aa) As in the case of substantive mandatory rules,[73] giving parties a choice can mean only that they have the choice between two or more mandatory information regimes, not that they can opt out completely (default rule). Again the choice may be split, for instance different for the minimum standard and for the more stringent rules.

bb) The first – *lex lata* – example would again be that the *minimum is set by the Union and not open to party options* and that there is *restricted freedom of choice as to more stringent national information rules* – if they are admitted at all, which is less universally the case with mandatory information rules.[74] If admitted at all, these more stringent information rules may in principle not be imposed on suppliers from abroad if the rules are burdensome and thus constitute an obstacle to their offers.[75]

cc) Broadening the choice of parties as to more stringent information rules could mean that suppliers can choose to act under their home country rule but also under the host country rules.[76] It could also mean, second, that any supplier has to comply with his home country rules (his 'origin'), but in addition may design an offer under a set of information rules which he chooses (his chosen 'origin'). This would be similar to offering alternative sets of standard terms at

---

[73] See above, text accompanying n. 58.
[74] See above, text accompanying n. 64.
[75] See above, n. 48.
[76] See references in n. 61.

different prices.[77] Broadening the choice of parties as to more stringent information rules can go still further. Then, yes, there would be a default rule (for instance home country or host country) but suppliers could opt out of it (without making any offer under it) and choose another set of national information rules, potentially also one which did not have any rule going beyond the Community law minimum. One could also imagine that opting out has to be accompanied by an explanation of what are the main differences between the chosen regime and the default regime.[78] In this last solution, the default standard would not necessarily be offered at all.

dd) Again, making the *minimum really optional* is politically not very likely and probably not to be wished for.[79]

ee) Basic features of evaluation of these three situations would include: the problems centralised rule-making raises are less important in the case of mandatory information rules. In contract law this is so, first, because freedom of design remains intact and, second, because in contract law (perhaps contrary to company law), the best producer and supplier of information as to the product is virtually always the side of supply. Thus information rules prescribing the disclosure of all material product related information in contract law do not seem to raise considerable doubt. Experimentation is less needed. Conversely, the problems of decentralised rule-making, i.e. mainly complexity, are more important in the case of information rules. Complexity is potentially more detrimental here because the very feature of information is comparability. This seems to indicate that for information rules a cautious approach by the Community legislator would allow an EU law only solution to be acceptable in virtually all cases of contract law.

4. Facilitative Law (including Default Rules)

a) Characterisation and importance

Facilitative law consists mainly of *default rules*.[80] Individual drafting of the contract would be possible in all solutions named below at b–e – with one

---

[77] See for the (very positive) German view about this kind of contract drafting: H. Brandner, in: P. Ulmer, H. Brandner, H.-D. Hensen and H. Schmidt, *AGB-Gesetz – Kommentar* (9th edn., Cologne, Schmidt, 2001), § 9 para. 112; M. Wolf, 'Freizeichnungsverbote für leichte Fahrlässigkeit in Allgemeinen Geschäftsbedingungen', *NJW* [1980], 2433, 2439.

[78] Traces of such an approach can be found in the Community law on stock exchange prospectuses, see arts. 38 *et seq.* of Directive 2001/34/EC of the European Parliament and of the Council of 28 May 2001 on the admission of securities to official stock exchange listing and on information to be published on those securities, (EC) OJ [2001] L 184/1.

[79] See above, text at n. 56.

[80] For the different groups of facilitative law and examples see above, text at n. 22.

important exception: as far as *standard term contracts are used* unfair contract terms law renders default rules partly mandatory, i.e. sets a narrow corridor, because only minor divergence from the default solution is allowed.

b) *EU law only*

aa) This solution can be *described* as one in which the Union is the only statal body which has the competence to supply parties with the standard default rules. Within the Union (i.e. EU 'domestic' cases) this would be the law from which parties cannot opt out by genuine choice of law (art. 3(3) of the Rome Convention on the law applicable to contracts of 1980).[81] There could be the choice of foreign law rules (also sets of rules) only within internal EU law freedom of contract and the limits which EU law would set. The narrow corridor for standard contract terms is probably the most important of the limits.

bb) The *practical example* is the European Code which replaces national contract laws.[82] This Code would decide both on the default rules and – as second branch of facilitative law – on the enforceability of the contract. The latter cannot be EU law only. For instance, a European court system is utopic today, there could only be minimum rules, for instance on duration of court proceedings. In the following, the focus is on default rules. One second example is those – not very frequent – cases in which rules contained in directives are not really mandatory, but default rules. The outstanding example is article 2 of the Sales Directive. Here, the standard of the quality owed is that of the average – the normal aptitude for use and other qualities normally expected. This standard is, however, subject to changing by party agreement – above and also below average if the deviation is made sufficiently transparent.[83] So-called general principles of con-

---

[81] See reference above at n. 30. This solution is already so universal (at least there are no more liberal conflicts rules abroad) that it is taken as given.

[82] One of the alternatives in option IV according to COM(2001) 398 final, p. 21 (para. 67).

[83] S. Grundmann, in: M. Bianca and S. Grundmann (eds.), *EU Sales Directive – Commentary* (Antwerp-Oxford, Intersentia-Hart, 2002), Art. 2 paras. 8–10; M. Lehmann, 'Informationsverantwortung und Gewährleistung für Werbeangaben beim Verbrauchsgüterkauf', *JZ* [2000], 280, 283; P. Romana Lodolini, 'La direttiva 1999/44/CE del Parlamento europeo e del Consiglio su taluni aspetti della vendita e delle garanzie dei beni di consumo – prime osservazioni', *Europa e diritto privato* [1999], 1275, 1284; not entirely clear: M. Tenreiro and S. Gomez, 'La directive 1999/44/CE sur certains aspects de la vente et des garanties des biens de consommation', *REDC* [2000], 5, 14; opposite view in: H. Beale and G. Howells, 'EC Harmonisation of Consumer Sales Law – a Missed Opportunity?', (1997) 12 *Journal of Contract Law* 21, 28; G. de Cristofaro, *Difetto di conformità al contratto e diritti del consumatore – l'ordinamento italiano e la direttiva 99/44/CE sulla vendita e le garanzie dei beni di consumo* (Padova, Cedam, 2000), 76–79; H.-W. Micklitz, 'Die Verbrauchsgüterkauf-Richtlinie', *EuZW* [1999], 485, 492; D. Staudenmayer, 'Die EG-Richtlinie über den Verbrauchsgüterkauf', *NJW* [1999], 2393, 2397; see also the subtle

tract law are not a third example, because outside areas of exclusive EU compet-ence they are not binding law.[84]

cc) Basic features of evaluation are, first, about measurable[85] advantages of a European set of default rules. Such a set furthers the scope which default rules have more generally – reduction of transaction costs.[86] A European set would add to this scope at least in the situation of cross-border transactions, because only in the case of a European set of default rules do parties have easy and equal access to the set of default rules. This helps reduce transaction costs at least for one side (not having to inform itself about a completely foreign law), possibly for both sides if they do not yet know which law will be chosen or applied. Otherwise, in cross-border cases one party has to accept a set of default rules typically better known to the other – an old problem of unfair contract terms law – and more accessible in case of dispute. It is, however, disputed how high these gains are.

There are also disadvantages of a European Code only. Sets of standard terms provided by a legislator have advantages over sets of standard terms provided by other bodies. Parties often think of them as being less biased, and they typically cover more broadly all problems. Having only one set of standard terms with statal origin means that only one type of preference structure is served, only for one type all the cost advantages of a set of default rules are given. Offering more statal default solutions gives a broader range of preference structures in the population the possibility to use one supposedly balanced set of default rules. EU law only could raise a second problem whenever parties want to deviate by using standard contract terms. And this may be the case in the overwhelming majority of contracts today.[87] In these cases, the default rules

---

analysis by W. van Gerven and S. Stijns, in: Bianca and Grundmann (this n.) Art. 7 paras. 23–26.

[84] See S. Grundmann, 'General Principles of Private Law and Ius Commune Modernum as Applicable Law?', *Festschrift for R. Buxbaum* (2000), 213; an example may be *pacta sunt servanda*: see W. Lorenz, 'General Principles of Law: their Elaboration in the Court of Justice of the European Commmunities', (1964) 13 *Am. J. Comp. L.* 1, 11 *et seq.* (general yes, but not detailed enough in concrete cases).

[85] We do not discuss whether 'the' Code would be a political symbol important for the Union. Possibly lawyers take their perspective too absolutely and therefore might overrate the symbolic importance of such a Code in the public at large.

[86] See above section II 2.

[87] Especially if unfair contract terms law also applies to pure commercial contracts as in Germany. Besides the problem raised here, there are good theoretical arguments for such an approach. See M. Adams, 'Ökonomische Begründung des AGB-Gesetzes – Verträge bei asymmetrischer Information', *Betriebsberater (BB)* [1989], 781, 787; J. Köndgen, 'Grund und Grenzen des Transparenzgebots im AGB-Recht – Bemerkungen zum "Hypothekenzins-" und zum "Wertstellungs-Urteil" des BGH', *NJW* [1989], 943, 946 *et seq.*; I. Koller, 'Das Transparenzgebot als Kontrollmaßstab Allgemeiner

define the legal paradigm from which parties may no longer deviate considerably. Therefore, the problems of having only one set of default rules in nowaday's world – which uses and must use standard contract terms in the large majority of cases – are more or less the same as having only one set of mandatory (substantive) rules: There would be serious inroads into the capacity of law to serve heterogeneous preferences, to adapt to new needs in a highly dynamic world and to use multiple sources for learning about better solutions. The latter two disadvantages would not be eliminated even if the EU chose to offer different sets of default rules itself (for serving different preferences).

c) States having part decision power (maximum/minimum fixed by EU)

aa) In *this situation,* default rules are fixed partly by the Union, but only at a minimum level or a maximum level. This is not so easy to conceive, if party wishes are the main guiding line and not protection of one party or third parties. There can be more protection, but a more for one party typically can deviate more from the wishes of the other party.

bb) The *practical examples* in the Union are only minimum standards. Fundamental freedoms do not apply to default rules and thus do not impose maximum levels for them.[88] Minimum standards are at least on the agenda. The Communication raises the question whether differing default rules do not create different practices in different countries from which parties of that country cannot easily deviate.[89] The same is true for diverging interpretation or diverging transposition of Community law. One could therefore imagine that European law would set standards in a uniform way from which national legislators can not deviate (minimum), but leave it to national legislators to decide on other aspects of the same question. Community law could say, for instance, that there is a right to rescind any contract of a certain type after ten years and leave it to national law to fix shorter terms. It is still easier to imagine that not all questions are subject to a default rule in the European Code – as is already the case, for instance, in the Sales Directive: there may be a duty to deliver goods in conformity with the contract, but the question of after-sale services may be left open. Theoretically, one could again imagine that the European Code treats only the questions where a concurring will of both parties is very much beyond doubt and that other questions are again left to national laws.

cc) Basic features of evaluation have to do with the advantage of the split named in mandatory substantive law. There the interplay reduced the danger of under-

---

Geschäftsbedingungen', *Festschrift for E. Steindorff* (1990), 667, 669 *et seq.*; and from an economist's perspective: Schäfer and Ott (n. 4), 420–422.

[88] See references at n. 49.

[89] COM(2001) 398 final, p. 11 *et seq.* (paras. 29–32).

and of over-regulation equally. This is not a danger in facilitative law unless it becomes mandatory and has to be judged accordingly. On the other hand, the solution is complex and thus does not fulfil the cost reduction function of default rules ('*Reservevertragsordnung*') ideally. A full set of EU law, not reduced only to minimum rules, seems preferable in this respect. Moreover, the advantages of innovation and experimentation are less well used under a split competences solution where there is only one solution (EU) for one part than if there is full party choice between different sets of rules offered.

d) States having full decision power

aa) In *this situation* states could fully opt out of European default rules. They would not even be obliged to keep a core of it. The choice would not be left to the parties.

bb) Practical examples are likely in two forms (so far not in directives). A European Code could be drafted only as a model code – like the Uniform Commercial Code in the United States. States would be free to opt in. Basically this can be achieved by recommendations.[90] If, after having opted in, states may not opt out again, the solution is afterwards that of EU law only. States could also be asked to opt out, otherwise the European Code applies. In practical outcome, this solution would come close to that of EU law only again. A European Code could also cover only cross-border cases as the only model (EU law only), but also domestic transactions if states do not opt out of it or opt into it. The latter would always be possible. The former would again come close to an EU law only solution in practice also for the domestic cases. Under the CISG which certainly offers this possibility as well signatory states did not opt in so far. The combination described here is one of EU law only in some cases (the cross-border cases, less numerous) and states having full decision power in others (the domestic cases).

cc) Basic features of evaluation would have to be developed by comparing this situation with that of full party choice. In case of full party choice, the decision how to best serve individual preferences is with the party concerned. This solution probably also gives more incentives for experimentation and innovation. However, the state could opt for more uniformity in that he opts into the European Code abolishing his own law (and nevertheless serve as an innovator of last resort if EU law does not develop). This reduces complexity as compared

---

[90] For instance, Recommendation 97/489/EC of the Commission of 30 July 1997 on trans-actions via electronic payment instruments (in particular as to the relationship between issuers and holders of such instruments), (EC) OJ [1997] L 208/52; see, however, 'Communication from the Commission to the Council and the European Parliament – electronic commerce and financial services', COM(2001) 66 final, 18 *et seq.*

to a party choice solution. The amount of complexity seems, however, not to be enormous, and therefore the advantages named of the party choice solution could easily be higher.

e) Parties having a choice

aa) Parties may have the choice of the set of default rules, first, in *cross-border cases*. This means simply extending the solution contained in article 3 of the Rome Convention on the law applicable to contracts:[91] a European Code would then be optional, i.e. it would constitute one more option (not EU law only). Then, in cross-border situations it would be likely that the European Code would be the default set of rules from which parties would have to opt out – as in the case of the UN Sales Convention. This would give parties equal access to the law from the beginning.

bb) A choice could be given also in *domestic cases*. Even without an optional European Code, there would be a further development also if other states' laws could be chosen without the limitations of article 3(3) of the Rome Convention on the law applicable to contracts. If there was an optional European Code the choice could either be given between this Code and internal state law or between the optional European Code and several or all state laws. The default set of rules, however, could only be the European Code or the internal law in both cases.

cc) Basic features of evaluation can best be given for a solution in which the European Code is the default rule in cross-border cases and the national set of rules in domestic cases. Minimum protection of third parties or of one party is not a dominant issue in facilitative law, nor is under- and over-regulation. This speaks for reducing complexity – because the cost saving aspect is paramount – and having several full sets of rules available for diverging preferences, thus also fostering innovation and experimentation. National rule making is legitimate if at all because the national legislator is closer to potentially diverging preferences. Moreover, having national law as the default solution in domestic cases helps to keep these sets alive. Having full sets (not split competences) both on EU and on the national level thus seems to be preferable for facilitative law. There is one tough question. This is whether full choice of law should also be given with respect to other national laws in purely domestic cases. Even for this choice, there are good reasons: in an integrated system of laws, cross-border cases where such choice would certainly be possible become 'normal' day-to-day life. Thus, parties should be prepared for options in each case. One would have to see whether such a solution (all states' laws can always be chosen) would go beyond

---

[91] See reference above at n. 30. This solution is already so universal (at least there are no more liberal conflicts rules abroad) that it is taken as given.

the capacity of court systems. An option between domestic law and the European Code should not.

V. SOME CONCLUSIONS AND EVALUATIONS

1. Designing European Contract Law as a Two-level System of Contract Laws

In section II we suggested that the problem of the future design of contract law in the EU should be conceived within a two-level system of contract laws, with both European and national contract law rules. In section III the main design dimensions of such a European system of contract laws were elaborated. By combining these different design dimensions many potential design options can be deduced. In section IV the most important of these design options have been analysed. Each of these design options were described and illustrated by legal examples, which already exist or are discussed. It was also given a short evaluation in form of the advantages and disadvantages of these options in comparison with other options. But these evaluations should not be seen as complete and exhaustive. An all-encompassing evaluation would have implied the assessment of these options in regard to all advantages and disadvantages that have been presented in section II. This is neither possible in one article nor was that the intention of this paper. The main intention was (1) to illustrate that the concept of a European two-level system of contract laws is very suitable to discuss the problem of centralised and/or decentralised contract laws in Europe in a productive way, and (2) to elaborate the most important design options of such a Europan system of contract laws – in the form of a mapping. Our, to some extent, preliminary evaluations of the design options in section IV should show how the criteria of section II can be used for the evaluation of these design options. But much more research is necessary before a well-considered proposal for the design of a whole European system of contract laws can be presented. However, we think that our analyses in section IV allow for two well-founded conclusions that we present in the following.

2. European Mandatory Law – Mainly Information Rules

Two mechanisms may well keep regulation at a balanced level between over- and under-regulation, considering also the risk of state failure. Mandatory substantive rules and mandatory information rules have to be distinguished.

a) Minimum on EU level, competition for more stringent rules

The first mechanism consists of properly allocating legislative powers. Regulation on the Community level and regulation on a national level are exposed to different degrees of pressure. The former needs to win in the discussion among the 15 Member States, but it is exposed to less pressure. There is more competition if the players can move capital, products or other factors more easily. Certainly within an internal market this is easier than on a global level. Therefore regulation on the national level is under more pressure: in harmonised areas this is market pressure already within the Community because – as far as it reaches beyond the directive – it must not be imposed onto suppliers from abroad.[92] In the remaining areas not harmonised (the exception in contract law) there is at least justification or scrutiny pressure: regulation has to be justified by mandatory reasons of public good and this has to be ascertained by the Court of Justice as an independent body.[93]

For the question how to allocate legislative powers for regulating market failure, the line of arguments could be:[94] states (and supranational Communities) are at risk not to ascertain the risks of market failure correctly or to regulate it poorly or both. There is limited knowledge in both questions. And decision makers can be guided by other concerns than to find the most efficient solution (personal advantages, e.g. in elections).[95] Therefore, the risk of market failure has to be set off against the risk of state failure.

Having regulation on Community level only where the need and the tools used are almost unanimously consented in 15 states can serve as a mechanism against state failure. The Commission should deduce from this that regulation should be envisaged only if the consensus in expert (and benevolent) circles is broad. It should not propose regulation where the risk of error is considerable. This is so because there is still the possibility of regulation on national level. And on this level the risk of state failure is considerably reduced by the types of pressure named.

To sum up: regulation on the national level is subject to market and justification pressure to an extent which in the long run should efficiently do away with gross over-regulation. The risk of under-regulation (potential race to the bottom) remains and may justify regulation on the Community level. Thus, on the state level, although only the risk of over-regulation is subject to market and justification pressure the risk of under-regulation is reduced by the imminence of harmonisation. The more competition is distorted by under-regulation on the

---

[92]   See text accompanying n. 48.
[93]   See text accompanying n. 51.
[94]   More in detail for the particular case of the European Community (discussing the role which the fundamental freedoms with the home country principle, the minimum harmonisation concept and the legislative procedure in the Community play for the concept of jurisdictional competition): see S. Grundmann, 'Wettbewerb der Regelgeber im Europäischen Gesellschaftsrecht – jedes Marktsegment hat seine Struktur', *Zeitschrift für Gesellschafts- und Unternehmensrecht (ZGR)* [2001] 783; W. Kerber, (2000) 23 *Fordham Int'l Law J.* S217, S228–S248.
[95]   See references above at n. 54.

national level the more the pressure for harmonisation increases. On the Community level the mechanism against over-regulation is weaker (reduced market and justification pressure). A real risk of under-regulation is minor as the states can regulate on a higher level and if they do so efficiently the scenario of rise to the top becomes likely. If the risk of over-regulation on Community level is really the one least taken care of by countervailing market or scrutiny pressure, the decision makers should be aware of it. Lean solutions should deliberately be preferred here.

b) Minimum on EU level typically information rules

The second mechanism is concerned with substance. According to the case law of the European Court of Justice, information rules have to be preferred to substantive mandatory rules whenever they grant sufficient protection.[96] This approach is very much also taken by the Community legislator. This is precisely targeted regulation which at the same time leaves space in substance for individual preferences, innovation and experimentation.

3. European Facilitative Law Supplementing, not Substituting National Facilitative Law

a) Advantages

European facilitative law supplementing, not substituting national facilitative law would largely serve the aims of uniform facilitative law, including the gains in transaction costs because of decreases in information costs, etc. At the same time, the core advantages of decentralised rule making would largely remain. These are, first, a serving of different preferences with different sets of default rules which are in the market and which are developed by bodies which have high potential in needs like thorough investigation, transparency to an interested public, high-quality personnel participating in the process. These are, second, that more experimentation takes place and thus more solutions are tested, reducing knowledge problems which any rule-making encounters because of the complexity of questions treated. And these are, third, the potential of innovation which is higher in a competitive situation – and be it only competition in prestige and in indirect and slowly developing advantages.[97]

---

[96] See references above, n. 66.

[97] Indeed these factors seem to suffice. At least in company law, also under the seat theory, most reforms were apparently driven by concerns about competitiveness: see for the three big Member States and their last company law reforms C.P. Claussen, 'Aktienrechtsreform 1997', *AG* [1996], 481; P. Hommelhoff and D. Mattheus, 'Corporate Governance nach dem KonTraG', *AG* [1998], 249; J. Zätzsch and M. Gröning, 'Neue Medien im deutschen Aktienrecht – zum RefE des NaStraG', *Neue Zeitschrift für Gesellschaftsrecht (NZG)* 2000, 393; *Modern Company Law – For a Competitive Economy – The Strategic Framework – A*

The one difficult question, therefore, is whether more freedom should be given to the parties even in domestic cases.

b) Comparison with EU facilitative law only and/or with state law only

aa) A solution *EU law only* in facilitative law would considerably reduce some of these advantages. Even if the national laws were not used so often any longer they would still be there as an alternative – comparable to the considerable advantages of potential competition. In an EU law only situation, the potential of innovation, of testing different sets of knowledge embedded in different sets of rules and of serving heterogeneous preferences would be reduced. This is still more important (and the above reasoning, section 2, applies) whenever default rules become mandatory to a certain extent such as namely in the case of standard terms contracts (potentially only in consumer contracts).

Certainly, even if there was EU only high potential private law subjects could step in and procure the public with additional sets of default rules. These could be chosen under the freedom of contract offered by EU facilitative law. There is one concern though (irrespective of potentially stricter limits to freedom of contract). Such an initiative is not likely to come. The incentive for an international group such as the Lando Group would be reduced after the entering into force of a European Code. And even with the incentive given today, the group took decades for the drafts. Moreover, such drafts would have to build up case law and a potential of knowledge, now existing for national laws. This need is potentially too high an entry barrier. Thus probably no alternative set of default rules would successfully develop – excepting certain particular contracts by a legislator, such as the International Chamber of Commerce, which is perhaps less accepted generally (representation!) and declining in importance.

These advantages of a solution with national sets of default rules continuing to exist and with party choice have to be set off against certain disadvantages of such a two-level system. The main disadvantage is that of higher complexity, of having more knowledge to administer. This argument, however, never led anyone to propose that the alternative of different types of limited liability companies should be abolished and that one set of rules would be sufficient.[98] Moreover, the problems of complexity can considerably be reduced by the particular design of the choice (see section c below). Therefore, efforts should rather be invested in optimising the design of choice.

Consultation Document from the Company Law Review Steering Group (2/1999), passim; Y. Guyon, 'Présentation générale de la société par action simplifiée', *Revue des Sociétés* [1994], 207, 209.

[98] And this is the other huge field of the law in a market economy: see R.H. Coase, *The Firm, the Market, and the Law* (Chicago, Univ. of Chicago Press, 1988). Contract is the core tool of market.

bb) The reasons named against an EU law only solution apply partly also to solutions in which *states could decide that their facilitative law applies* instead of EU facilitative law.[99] This solution would be weaker than party choice solutions for the advantages of decentralised rule making. Other sets of rules could either be chosen under national freedom of contract – then, the solution would partly be that of party choice, but only private party rule setters would step in. Or the choice would be reduced in internal law – then different preferences would less be served, parallel experimentation and innovation would be reduced. Moreover and perhaps even more important, a state option solution would not even guarantee the advantages of centralised rule making either (which a party choice solution does in principle).

c) Opt in and opt out as refinement tools

The choice of opt in or opt out can influence complexity and also the question which advantage is stressed still a bit more.

Using EU facilitative law as the default rule in cross-border cases helps to build up case law and expertise for the EU set of rules. This is needed for having the advantages of centralised rule making. Moreover, both parties would be treated equally as to transaction costs. Complexity would not be higher than in an EU law only situation. There, standard terms would have to evolve for serving deviating preferences. It should be even easier to apply foreign statal default rules – typically only a few of them – than evolving (at best international) sets of standard terms.

In domestic situations, national facilitative law could be the default solution. This would keep the alternative lively and with it the potential of innovation and of parallel experimentation. The arguments named in favour of centralised rule making do not apply here. Parties would have equal access to the law, transaction costs would not be very high. And if there are differences in preferences, the local default rule has better chances to mirror the regional preferences. The only costs are those of administering two sets of default rules in each member state. Even if other national facilitative laws can be chosen, they are not default solutions and thus do not add much complexity.

VI. SUMMARY

1. a) This paper is concerned with option IV of the EC Commission's Communication on European Contract Law. Indeed, there is only the option either to keep the status quo (improving it gradually) or to introduce another kind of instrument. Among the options in Option IV, that of an optional

---

[99] Solutions in sections IV 4 c and d. The solution is in fact closer to EU law only if states have to opt out.

European Code, i.e. of leaving national contract laws to run parallel, is discussed in more detail. The idea is that in economic theory, it is virtually universally agreed that centralised rule making has advantages and decentralised rule making also has important advantages. Why, then, not combine both by establishing a certain mix. The *mix would be that of a European System of Contract Laws* – in the plural. It is a system, not a solution for transition. The system should be designed (and core elements are presented here) for keeping flexibility intact in a long-term perspective and to procure standardisation tools (through unification) nevertheless.

b) An efficient contract law that helps parties to solve transaction and cooperation problems and that contributes to the avoidance of market failures is an essential precondition for the workability of market economies. Contract law consists both of mandatory rules, which primarily have the task of reducing potential market failures, and of facilitative law, which should help the parties to enforce their contracts (*pacta sunt servanda*) and to reduce transaction costs by offering legal standard solutions (default rules).

c) For the future contract law evolution in Europe it is necessary to take into account (1) that in the EU already fifteen well-established national contract laws exist, and (2) that it is necessary that the contract law in Europe has the capacity to adapt to the ever-changing transaction and cooperation problems, i.e. that within the European contract law system the possibility of legal evolution by legal innovations is of great importance. From this perspective we want to suggest that the aim of ensuring an efficient and adaptable contract law within the EU can best be attained by establishing a *consistent two-level system of contract laws* in the European Union. Since both an entirely decentralised and an entirely centralised contract law system suffers from serious disadvantages, the basic idea is to design a European system of contract laws in such a way that the advantages of centralised and decentralised rule-making are cumulated and the disadvantages avoided as far as possible. This two-level system would encompass both mandatory and facilitative law. An important implication is that the future perspective of contract law in the EU should not be seen as the transition from national contract laws to one European contract law, but to one in the long run stable European two-level system of contract laws, within which the specific legal contract law rules can evolve.

d) As an analytical basis for assessing different design options for such a European system of contract laws, the most important *advantages and disadvantages of centralised and decentralised* rule-making are summarised. Static and dynamic economies of scale favour centralised rule-making. The same is true for the aim of reducing transactions costs. The heterogeneity of preferences and transaction and cooperation problems in different countries is a powerful argument for decentralisation. The emergence of externalities and inconsistencies within a legal order is less likely in a centralised system. The serious knowledge problems about the best legal rules (including problems of local knowledge) and the necessity of adapting legal rules to changing problems are strong arguments for a decentralised system of legal rules, in which the capacity for legal innovations is larger due to the possibilities of decentralised experimentation and mutual learning. This argument is strengthened if a workable regulatory competition can be established within a decentralised system of law. Also, rent seeking problems might be solved better in a decentralised legal order. But in a centralised legal system there will be less problems of obstacles of trade and distortions of competition. Finally, the status quo situation in the EU with its well-established national contract laws has to be seen as a strong argument for a more decentralised system.

2. There are *two core design dimensions*. The first is how binding a contract rule is. There are default rules, mandatory substantive rules and also mandatory information rules. The latter are mandatory but leave the parties the possibility to design the content nevertheless. They therefore do not share the core characteristic of mandatory substantive rules which reduce the design possibilities to a small range or even to one solution only. In many cases, unfair contract terms law may render default rules mandatory to a certain extent. The second dimension is which body decides on the question which set of mandatory substantive, mandatory information or default rules applies to the particular case. It can be the Union (European Code substituting national laws), the states which have an option to make their law applicable (instead of EU law, Optional European Code), possibly also only above or below a minimum or a maximum level set by the Community (fundamental freedoms and directives or again an Optional European Code) or also the parties. The latter is yet another design of an Optional European Code. Within these dimensions, one can also place the distinctions cross-border cases only or also purely internal cases and opt in/ opt out.

3. For all three kinds of rules one can distinguish four situations: a) EU law only, b) and c) an option for the states to opt into or out of EU law, possibly only above or below a minimum or maximum level set by the EU, and d) different types of party autonomy. In case of *mandatory substantive law*, this concerns mainly the minimum or the more stringent rules.

a) EU law only would be introduced with a European Code containing, for instance, mandatory substantive consumer protection. This would be basically new in Community law. Even in competition law, there is no EU law only approach. The disadvantages would be that of a restricted range of solutions and thus a restricted potential to serve diverging preferences, a restricted potential of innovation and of experimentation. The standardisation advantages of centralised rule making can be reached for the side of supply also by different means and are less important for the side of demand with respect to substantive mandatory law.

b) EU maximum standards for national laws is the scenario of fundamental freedoms, minimum standards that of directives which allow more stringent national rules (in domestic cases). A full opt-out solution for states (section c below) would cut back on the *acquis communautaire*. Fundamental freedoms prescribe that states may not enact mandatory substantive rules whenever information rules would do. Conversely, there are not many substantive mandatory rules in contract law directives so far. Minimum regulation on EU level reduces the risk of under-regulation (by states and in the whole two-level system). If at the same time it concentrates on cases of market failure and rules reducing market failure which are undisputed, the risk of over-regulation is also considerably reduced in the whole system. Therefore, supermajority prerequisites and a careful comparative law discussion within the legislative process are welcome. Above the level universally consented, regulation is disputed. Now, in cases of knowledge problems competition is particularly important, here between the different states and their proposals for more stringent rules.

c) States laws substituting EU mandatory substantive rules is a solution which is not very likely. Core advantages of the split competences approach (section b above) would be given up. If indeed EU law regulation is restricted to rules universally consented the split competences approach could be structurally superior.

d) Party autonomy with respect to mandatory substantive rules can only mean choice between different sets of mandatory law. Three situations are of particular importance. As to more stringent rules, parties can choose under current fundamental freedoms doctrine between domestic supply under domestic law and foreign supply under the supplier's home country rules. The freedom would be extended if suppliers could tell under which law they want to act, perhaps imposing on them to offer also the alternative of their home country law. Indeed, those other laws can be offered in the market anyway already under current law by suppliers based in those other jurisdictions. It is less likely that a choice will be given also for the minimum set by the EU (or all rules). Those who can not or do not want to exercise their autonomy in a meaningful way enjoy enough protection if the domestic law standard is offered at all. For this purpose, local suppliers may need to remain forced to offer this standard for domestic supply. There is no need, however, that they may not offer in addition also under another national law. Other customers, potentially using information intermediaries, should have the option to choose foreign supply and foreign standards. Diverging preferences can better be served, the competitive pressure for innovation and experimentation is higher. The customer in need of conservative protection does not lose, the other customers can win. Therefore, one should allow supply from abroad to act under his home country rule but also under a chosen rule of another Member State if this is made transparent.

4. *Mandatory information rules* are also mandatory, but very different in function. So far, most mandatory rules in European contract law are information rules.

a) EU law only would be introduced with a Code containing rules which prescribe the giving of information and the sanctions if the information is incorrect or incomplete. Already today, many rules in EU directives do not prescribe a minimum level only ('all material information' or certain items) but also a maximum level. This can well be, if information has to be given in a 'clear and understandable' way. EU law only in information rules does not have the same negative effects on the matching of diverging preferences, on the potential of innovation and experimentation, as the substance of the contract (law) is still open to choice. On the other hand, a uniform rule is here more important also for the side of demand, as information is given about the whole product now (clients being more interested in information about the product than about the law) and standardisation helps to compare.

b) That EU laws set a maximum level for national mandatory information is a very atypical situation. More important are more stringent national information rules. However, the proportion of mandatory minimum information rules (as compared to all mandatory information rules) is much lower than that of mandatory minimum substantive rules. The split competences solution is much better to defend for mandatory substantive law: there it is a tool to avoid over-regulation; information rules, however, are already rather lean and focused regulation (directly curing the information asymmetry). And on the other hand, in the case of mandatory substantive rules, standardisation was not so important for the side of demand and can be reached for the side of supply by other means. In information rules, standardisation is important also for the side of demand and can be reached only by uniform rules.

c) States laws substituting EU mandatory information rules is still more unlikely and – because of the reasons given above in a and b – probably not to be preferred as a solution.

d) Giving parties a freedom of choice as to mandatory information rules can again only mean that they can choose between different sets. Again the first choice is that under current fundamental freedoms doctrine parties can choose supply from domestic suppliers under the more stringent rules of domestic law or from foreign suppliers under the more stringent rules of the supplier's home country rules. The only reservation to be made is that more stringent information rules are not so often allowed at all. The other two options would again be parallel to those named for mandatory substantive rules (summary section 3d above). For two reasons, these options are less important than for mandatory substantive rules: first, the freedom to design the content is left untouched, anyway – and with it the higher possibility of serving a large range of preferences and the higher potential of innovation and experimentation; second, prescribing disclosure of relevant product related information in contract law constitutes an almost universally accepted rule. Conversely, two-level complexity appears to be more problematic because comparability is a core quality of information which is better served by standardisation.

5. *Facilitative rules* (mainly default rules) allow in principle diverging party agreement which, however, does not profit from the cost advantages of the use of the default rules. Moreover, unfair contract terms law may render them quasi-mandatory.

a) This renders an EU law only solution questionable even in the case of facilitative law. The practical example would be a European Contract Law Code which substitutes national contract laws completely. In cross-border cases, an EU set of default rules helps at least one party to reduce information costs – in the long run it is cheaper to know one international set of default rules than many different foreign laws. Moreover it guarantees equal access. However, having only one set of default rules with statal origin means that only one type of preference structure is served, i.e. is given the cost advantages. Moreover, experimentation and innovation would no longer be carried forward for default rules by different statal – i.e. typically neutral and well equipped – legislators. If default rules are in fact mandatory (because of standard contract terms law), the considerations on EU law only in mandatory substantive law apply.

b) States having partial options is conceivable only in combination with EU minimum standards (fundamental freedoms do not apply to default rules). For default rules, even the split with minimum standards is difficult to conceive. Split competences are good in that they may equally reduce the risk of over- and of under-regulation. This is, however, no risk in facilitative law. Then the solution is too complex and thus not ideal for the (predominant) cost-saving function; moreover it does not have the advantages of full choice (see section d below).

c) States would have full options if an EU contract law code was enacted only as a model code. This solution could be chosen only for one part of the transactions (for instance the purely domestic cases) and be combined with an EU law only solution for other cases (those concerned with cross-border transactions). This solution is inferior to the party choice solution in that it is not the party concerned who decides about his preferences and potentially also with respect to experimentation and innovation incentives. If the state opts into the EU Code and abolishes his own state law, this may, however, reduce complexity.

d) If parties are given a choice, in cross-border cases this would be between the different states' laws (already happening today) and an optional European Code.

This latter would be default if one wanted to guarantee equal access to the parties and inspire life into such Code. In domestic cases national law would potentially remain the default rule and at least opting for the European Code should probably be possible. This solution allows for better serving of diverging individual preferences and maintains the potential of innovation and experimentation. Moreover, it is less complex than split solutions and thus better serves the cost-saving function of facilitative law.

21.   A Subsidiary Plea: A European Contract Law for Intra-European Border-Crossing Contracts

*U. Drobnig**

I. THE ISSUE

All commentators agree that, practically speaking, the diversities of national contract regimes most strongly affect intra-European cross-border transactions in general and cross-border trade in particular. The uncertainties about the contract law of other member states clearly increase transaction costs: such costs must either be incurred in paying for information about the legal system of those member states where commercial customers are located, or they tend to increase prices for the increased legal risk which is involved in these cases if the exporter does not obtain the necessary information and therefore is exposed to an unknown legal regime.[1]

It is obvious that this increased financial burden on cross-border intra-European commercial exchanges disadvantages suppliers of goods and services from other member countries as against domestic suppliers of the same or equivalent goods and services. This commercial disadvantage of foreign as against domestic suppliers clearly hinders the full realisation of the internal market which postulates, *inter alia*, the free exchange of goods between member states.[2]

II. REMEDIES

How can the aforementioned obstacle to a fully developed internal market be overcome?

1. A Completely Unified Regime for All Transactions

The focus of almost all proposals and also of Alternative no. IV in the Communication of the EC Commission has been to create a unified regime for

---

*   Professor, emeritus Director at the Max-Planck-Institute for Foreign Private and Private International Law, Hamburg.
[1]   For an extensive analysis of these transaction costs, see the contribution of H. Collins.
[2]   Art. 3(1)(c) EC Treaty.

S. Grundmann and J. Stuyck (eds.), An Academic Green Paper on European Contract Law, 343–351
© 2002 *Kluwer Law International. Printed in Great Britain.*

transactions, whether of a purely domestic character or involving an intra-European cross-border element. Such full unification, or at least harmonization of contract law (and related legal fields), would be the ideal solution: a single, unified contract law would govern in all member states.

However, the idea of a European contract law (or law of obligations or even of a patrimonial law) which would replace the corresponding branches of the member states' domestic legal systems, is rather novel. In many member states it is hardly known and, therefore, has not yet been much discussed. It is therefore, to put it mildly, at least doubtful whether there is a realistic chance that in the near future a completely unified European contract law would be accepted by all member states. For this reason, an alternative model is offered here for discussion.

2. A European Contract Law for Intra-European Cross-Border Transactions

A compromise between an as yet possibly unrealistic ideal and present-day realities could be achieved by limiting, for the time being, the geographical scope of application of the future European contract law to intra-European cross-border transactions. Most international unified law uses a similar approach by limiting its application to 'international', i.e. cross-border transactions.[3]

a) The Principle

As on the international level, this solution would fill the most glaring gap in the civil law regime of the present European internal market. Today, in most intra-European cross-border transactions, at least one of the parties is disadvantaged because it is charged with the burdens and costs of having to ascertain the terms of the – foreign – law governing the contract of the parties. True, the relevant conflicts rules are unified by the Rome Convention of the member states of 1980.[4] However, these rules have merely unified the rules determining which national contract law is applicable; usually it is the law of one of the parties.[5] This means that the *other* party has to shoulder:

- the risk of being exposed to surprising and disadvantageous terms of that law; or
- the cost and risk of having to ascertain the contents of that contract law; and
- in litigation, the costs of experts familiar with that law.

A great political advantage of the subsidiary solution advocated here is that, for

---

[3]   Cf. J. Kropholler, *Internationales Einheitsrecht* (Tübingen, Mohr Siebeck, 1975), 167–169.
[4]   Convention on the law applicable to contractual obligations of 19 June 1980, (EC) OJ [1980] L 266/1.
[5]   Cf. arts. 3 and 4.

the time being, the national contract laws would remain unaffected and continue to govern domestic transactions occurring within the various member states. At the same time the legislative jurisdiction of the European Community for such an instrument is clearly offered by EC Treaty article 95. The subsidiarity requirement of article 5 para. 2 EC Treaty is also fulfilled, since the member states do not dispose of sufficient means to achieve the necessary uniformity of law for cross-border transactions and only the Community can ensure by legislative action a uniform regime for them.

In fixing the criteria for a cross-border transaction, at least in the field of contracts proper, use can be made of the practical experience with the UN Convention on International Sale of Goods (CISG) of 1980. Article 1 para. 1 CISG fixes criteria for 'international' sales, and this provision may serve as a model for establishing and interpreting a corresponding rule for intra-European cross-border contracts.

b) Possible Objections

It is sometimes said that the parties can settle the issue of the applicable law by agreeing upon a choice of law clause. Such clauses, however, are usually proposed by the stronger party and usually contain a choice of its own legal system. This means that the aforementioned burdens resulting from unfamiliarity with the applicable foreign law, and the costs involved in overcoming this, are typically imposed upon the weaker party; by this, I mean the weaker *commercial* party, since consumers already enjoy special protection (*infra* c). This result certainly does not commend itself in an internal market.

Another objection is the complaint that a unified regime for cross-border contracts would introduce a new complexity since it would increase the existing 15 or rather (with Scots law) 16 contract systems by adding one more. This argument, however, is untenable. On the contrary, as far as it goes, for all cross-border transactions the uniform contract regime would replace the 15 or 16 existing national contract laws. No party would be preferred any longer by choosing its own national law for the contract. Rather, the parties would be on a par with respect to the law governing their contract.

Related to the foregoing is the objection that it is absurd to envisage a system which turns on the criterion of crossing *borders* in a Europe where borders are being eliminated.[6] This argument begs the question. True, economically and politically the intra-European borders become less and less relevant. However, for the unharmonised fields of law, legal frontiers still exist. As I said before, I wish they would disappear for contracts, or obligations, or patrimonial law (*supra* II 1). This paper contains, as its title clearly indicates, merely a *subsidiary* proposal where the desired unification cannot be achieved (*supra* II 2). In this

---

6   Cf. the contribution of S. Grundmann and Kerber, Ch. 20.

case, the legal frontiers will remain; rules intending to overcome them would be better than the present full diversities.

c) Exclusions

Two fields of contract law would have to be exempted from a uniform law for cross-border contracts because existing Community rules specifically decree reservations for national law. I am referring to the 1980 Rome Convention on the Law Applicable to Contracts, articles 5 and 6. According to these provisions, generally speaking, the mandatory rules in force at the consumer's habitual residence and at an employee's regular place of work have preference over a foreign legal system that may be applicable by the parties' choice or by virtue of objective criteria. Such preference, however, only takes place if and insofar as the law at the 'weaker' person's place of residence or work is more favourable to him than the law chosen by the parties or applying by virtue of objective criteria. Those strong preferences for specific rules of national legal systems established by Community law must of course, in the interest of consistency, also be respected here.

d) Options of the Parties

In accordance with widely followed international practice with respect to unifying conventions on 'ordinary' contract law, the parties should have the possibility both of opting out of the European regime and of opting into it.

For opting out, CISG article 6 offers a model clause. Opting out may consist either of completely excluding the European law or of doing so partially, including the power to deviate from the terms of the European law, except where it is mandatory.

For opting in, no formulas seem to have been established as yet. Two situations should be envisaged: first, purely domestic contracts rooted in a member state or even in a third state should be covered. In particular, for domestic contracts linked to a transborder import or export transaction the European contract law should be attractive in order to harmonise the law governing such a chain of contracts. Also for the transactions of the European Communities themselves, the present practice of choosing a member state's law may be replaced by agreeing on the new European regime. Second, European contract law should also be open for transactions of a party residing in a member state with a party residing in a third country, respectively, if the parties so agree.

In order to remove doubts about the admissibility of these various types of opting in, a specific clause should be inserted into the Rome Convention on the Law Applicable to Contracts or into the European Contract Law itself.

III. PROSPECTS FOR THE FUTURE

For the proponents of a European Contract Law or a Code of Patrimonial Law, the subsidiary solution briefly sketched here is only an interim solution. Opponents may be willing to regard it as an acceptable but definitive solution. This issue can be settled later.

If public opinion in the member states has become more enlightened and the legislative jurisdiction of the European Community has been broadened, further steps extending the scope of application of the European contract law may be envisaged. It is not unlikely that not all member states would be willing to move forward at the same speed; such flexibility is possible and must be accepted. If the time has come to take further steps, experiences gathered in applying the new European law in practice may bring to light deficiencies which can then be repaired.[7]

It would seem that in a step-by-step approach, as advocated by a number of commentators,[8] the application of a European contract law to intra-European cross-border transactions is an important and realistic first step.

IV. APPENDIX: SECURITY RIGHTS IN A EUROPEAN CONTEXT

The Communication by the EC Commission and most of the replies to it concentrate on the diversities of the national regimes of *contract* law; neighbouring fields of patrimonial law are only marginally touched upon.

I would like to draw attention to one such adjacent field, that is, security rights in movable assets. In this special field, while we are basically confronted with the same types of problems as in contract law, these problems are much more serious and therefore more difficult to solve.

1. The Importance and Diversity of Security Rights

It is generally known that a good supply of credit is indispensable for the smooth running and a successful growth of the highly developed European economies. The cost of credit and therefore also the access to, and quantity of credit, depend on the risk that the debtor may default on his obligation to repay the credit when due.

---

[7] Cf. S. Leible, 'Die Mitteilung der Europäischen Kommission zum Europäischen Vertragsrecht – Startschuß für ein Europäisches Vertragsgesetzbuch?', *Europäisches Wirtschafts- und Steuerrecht* [2001], 471, 479.

[8] Apart from Leible (n. 7) 478–479; J. Wuermeling and A. v. Graevenitz, 'Europäisches Privatrecht: Wider den Oktroi der Uniformität', *Europarecht* [2001], 631, 642; C. Schmid, 'Legitimitätsbedingungen eines Europäischen Zivilgesetzbuchs', *Juristen-Zeitung* [2001], 674, 680. See also the contribution of J. Drexl, Ch. 7 and of J. Smits, Ch. 24.

This risk may be decisively reduced if the debtor (or a third person) can furnish good security under a legal regime that allows:

– the taking of present and future assets as security;
– charging assets that can be left in the debtor's possession so that he can use them as equipment or to produce new goods; and
– selling them in order to obtain the proceeds with which to repay the initial credit.

Comparative studies of relevant legislation, case law and practices have shown that those basic goals of a 'good' regime of security can be reached only to very different degrees in the various member states. In fact, there are remarkable differences, especially between the big member countries and some smaller ones, but to some degree even between the big ones.

2. Two Major Issues

Similar to those in the field of contracts, but in a much more aggravated form, two issues arise:

First: In view of the diversity of national regimes for security rights, there is no level playing field for debtors as well as creditors. Since the comparative risks for creditors differ from member country to member country, the corresponding costs which debtors have to pay to creditors, as reflected by the interest rates for credit, differ correspondingly.

Second: Equally, if not more aggravating, is the risk of securing credit on assets that are moved across borders from one member country into another. Typically, these are export goods, on the one hand, and means of transport, such as lorries which may be highly equipped for refrigeration, but also ships and aircraft, on the other.

According to an almost universally accepted conflicts rule, the creation and effects of property rights are subject to the law where the relevant tangible assets are located. Technically expressed, property rights are governed by the *lex rei sitae*. If there is a change of *situs*, upon crossing a national border, the property regime changes too. It depends upon the new *lex situs* whether and if so, with what effects it will recognise a security right validly created in another member state.

Application of this rule has led to very different results, due to the differences of the respective substantive security regimes. Security rights created in other member countries have usually been recognised in countries with a very liberal, creditor-friendly regime. By contrast, security rights created in these countries have often not been recognised in member countries with a narrower regime, such as France or Italy.

It goes without saying that these consequences of diverse security regimes are incompatible with an internal market which postulates, inter alia, the free movement of goods and capital.

3. Possible Solutions

As in the field of contract law, two major solutions can be envisaged.

a) Uniform Regime for Movable Property

The most radical solution would be a European unified regime for rights in movable property. Such a regime would have to deal, at a minimum, with all aspects of ownership, possession and security rights, probably including their treatment in executions and bankruptcy.

This is a major task, the more so since in this area much less preparatory comparative work than in contracts has so far been undertaken. Also, resistance would probably be even stronger than in the field of contracts because property in general is thought to be more closely bound up with 'basics' of each country; this, however, applies to the regime of immovable property rather than that of movables.

b) Uniform Regime for Transborder Movement of Assets Charged With Security Rights

Whatever the position taken for the domestic property regimes of movables, experience on the international level shows that states are willing to accept unified regimes covering the transborder movement of assets that are charged with security rights.

(i) International Approaches

Roughly speaking, without going into details, one can distinguish a conflicts approach and one aiming at substantive uniformity.

(a) The *conflicts approach* calls for the recognition of security rights validly created according to a fixed legal system. The most successful instrument using this approach is the 1948 Geneva Convention on the International Recognition of Rights in Aircraft, which is binding today upon about 90 states. According to article 1 of this Convention, property rights, including inter alia non-possessory security rights such as mortgages and hypothecs, must be recognised by all Contracting States, under two provisos. First, the property rights must have been validly created according to the law of the Contracting State in which the aircraft had been registered at the time of creation; and second, the property rights must have been validly registered in a public register of that state. Similar, although less detailed rules have been agreed upon for security rights in ships, both those used on the high seas and in inland navigation.

The weakness of the conflicts approach is that it cannot overcome its own limits: it can merely indicate which legal system is to be applied, but it has no direct influence on the relevant substantive rules. Without the help of additional substantive rules it cannot provide for an adequate conversion of the foreign security right into a domestic right which may require substantive and formal adaptations, such as a new registration with retroactive effect, and so on. These problems do not usually affect means of transport which, by definition, quickly pass from one jurisdiction to another since they are intended to be in 'permanent transit'. Only in cases of an international sale may problems arise but these are usually solved by repayment of existing loans and creation of new ones; the transfer of security rights to a foreign regime is thus avoided.

(b) The most advanced and promising *approach to substantive uniformity* is presently undertaken in the framework of the UNIDROIT convention relating to security rights in highly mobile equipment. This project is very advanced; on 16 November 2001 it was finalised by a Diplomatic Conference convened in Cape Town. This instrument, although limited to a narrow field, demonstrates the feasibility of achieving international consensus on substantive rules for security rights.

Both the desirability and the basic feasibility of international agreement on substantive uniformity for security rights are confirmed on the regional level by relevant uniform instruments adopted in 1997 by the OHADA (*Organisation pour l'Harmonisation en Afrique du Droit des Affaires*) for 14 Francophonic countries in central and western Africa as well as the draft rules presently being discussed by the Organization of American States (OAS). Admittedly, though, agreement on uniform rules in parts of Francophone Africa was facilitated by the fact that the participating countries disposed of a common basis, namely French law. While there is no comparable uniform basis in Latin America, at least there is a common general legal framework and a common desire to modernise the (sometimes antiquated) national laws, inspired by the modern approach of article 9 of the American Uniform Commercial Code.

(ii) European Approaches

The two typical approaches to the transborder effects of security rights can also be observed at the European level – although, amazingly, so far partly only in vague outline and partly only for a narrow special field.

(a) The *conflicts approach* can be illustrated by article 4(1) of the Directive on Delayed Payments in Commercial Transactions of 29 June 2000.[9] This provision

---

9   (EC) OJ [2000] L 200/35.

merely says that the seller 'according to the applicable national rules, as determined by private international law' retains ownership in sold goods until full payment, provided that before delivery of the goods the retention of title had been expressly agreed between seller and buyer. The meaning of this provision is uncertain and controversial since it is the result of a compromise between very diverging proposals of the Commission and the European Parliament on the one hand and the Council on the other. It is therefore unfortunately very doubtful whether article 4(1) promotes transborder effects of retentions of title in any way.

(b) *Unification of substantive law*, especially of security rights, is pursued by a Draft Directive on financial security rights. This Draft is part of a sustained effort to promote a uniform European financial market and has a correspondingly narrow and extremely specialised scope of application.

But the Statement of Reasons is generally relevant. It underlines (no. 1.2) that creditors who intend to reduce their credit risks by demanding security have to take into account 15 different legal system on security and on insolvency. Also, the risk that a security is invalid is higher in cross-border transactions than in domestic ones. Therefore, a uniform minimal standard is necessary.

The subject-matter scope of the proposed Directive is extremely narrow and highly specialized. Thus, the institutions which may act as security givers and as secured creditors are restricted to a few major players in the financial markets, such as central banks, publicly supervised finance institutions or legal entities with a minimum capital of at least 100 million EUR. Also, the assets which may serve as security are very restricted: only money accounts or securities, either in bearer form or those that can be transferred by book entries on securities accounts.

Whatever one may think about the privileged treatment of security rights in the special financial assets covered by the Draft Directive, it confirms, if confirmation were still required, two essential points:

First, the grave obstacles to which creditors who seek to obtain reliable Europe-wide security rights are exposed. Second, the Draft also confirms that a European uniform substantive regime for security rights is not a professorial illusion, but can be achieved.

4. Conclusion

My conclusion is brief. Both the need for an intra-European cross-border system of security rights and the basic feasibility of such a system have been demonstrated. What remains to be done is difficult enough: to elaborate, on the basis of thorough comparative research, a uniform set of rules for security rights in movables.

22. The Design of an Optional (Re)statement of European Contract Law – Real Life Instead of Dead Concepts

*Thomas Wilhelmsson**

I. REASSESS CONCEPTS AND STRUCTURES!

Few of the American TV series have been running as long as the debate on unification or harmonisation of European private law and contract law. This continuing story of Europeanisation of private law has been on the agenda for decades, and the players are still in good shape. As in other series, when the story seems to become dull a new hero is introduced. For a long time the main participants in the play have been enrolled from the academic community[1] and from the European Parliament,[2] but now the Commission, which earlier has performed only side-roles preparing specific and fragmented enactments especially in the area of consumer law, finally has tried to enter the scene in a more prominent position. In July 2001, it published the Communication from the Commission to the Council and the European Parliament on European Contract Law.[3]

---

*   Professor of Civil and Commercial Law, Vice-Rector, University of Helsinki.

[1]   This discussion is so well known that sources really need not be mentioned. A. Hartkamp *et al.*, *Towards a European Civil Code*, (2nd edn., The Hague, Kluwer, 1998) (with comprehensive references) is often used as a standardised reference in this context. Journals like *ERPL* and *ZEuP* keep the series running. The most ambitious 'restatement' works are, of course, made by the Lando Commission, see O. Lando and H. Beale (eds.), *Principles of European Contract Law*, Parts I and II (The Hague, Kluwer, 2000) and Christian von Bar's 'Study Group on a European Civil Code'. The 'Trento project' in its turn is searching for 'The Common Core of European Private Law'.

[2]   See Parliament Resolution on action to bring the private law of the Member States into line, (EC) OJ [1989] C 158/400 as well as Resolution on the harmonisation of certain sectors of private law of the Member States, (EC) OJ [1994] C 205/518. See also the resolution on the work programme of the Commission in the year 2000, where the Parliament stated that 'greater harmonisation of civil law has become essential in the internal market', (EC) OJ [2000] C 377/323, 326. The Parliament has also commissioned a study 'The private law systems in the EU: discrimination on grounds of nationality and the need for a European Civil Code' (PE 168.511) (can be read on the address http://www.europarl.eu.int/workingpapers/juri/pdf/103_en.pdf).

[3]   COM (2001) 398 final. In its Resolution on the Communication 15.11.2001 the European Parliament again appears as very harmonisation friendly, advocating the establishment of a common body of law.

S. Grundmann and J. Stuyck (eds.), An Academic Green Paper on European Contract Law, 353–372
© 2002 *Kluwer Law International. Printed in Great Britain.*

In this context there is no need for a description of the content of the Communication. Neither shall I attempt to review it. Sufficiently many have already voiced their disappointment with the performance of the new actor. After such a long period of academic discussion one would have hoped for a document with much more content and reflection concerning the arguments which already have been put forward by many. Anyway, the Commission, even though it cannot be said to have started a discussion (which has been going on for years!), probably has succeeded in bringing in a lot of new players on the scene. In spite of its shortcomings the Communication may therefore lead to a deeper analysis of the situation, bringing in more arguments also from other actors – for example from the political, business life and civil society spheres – than from the comparative law community which has very much dominated the discussion so far.

The focal point of the previous discussion has been the question whether Europe needs a common Civil Code or Contract Code or whether other measures are sufficient to overcome the problems which the strong legal variations in Europe are perceived to create. The Communication mainly focuses on this issue. Personally I have elsewhere defended a sceptical view on a European codification, proposing a more pluralist approach: an *experimental European law* based on a *free movement of legal ideas and doctrines.*[4] As the most important *pros* and *cons* concerning the codification issue certainly have been put on the table many times before in the discussion, I will not repeat my arguments at length in this context. I will only – in Section 2 of the paper – shortly mention the basic arguments, as they are also relevant for the issue I will deal with in this paper, that is the dynamic and structure of a possible European 'restatement' of contract law.

As is well known, the Commission in its Communication as one option mentions the promotion of the work on common principles of European contract law. What is sought for is academic and practical comparative work along the lines of the Lando Commission and the Study Group. Some have even used the word 'restatement', although one should then bear in mind that such work in the European context must be considerably more choosing and developing than restating in the American sense – it is rather a 'statement' than a 'restatement'.[5] I have much less problems with the promotion of such restatement work than with the idea of a 'real' European code. Under certain circumstances I could even foresee that such a restatement could function and be recognised as a kind of optional contract code to be chosen by the parties as their law. In order to clarify my basic position, in Section 3 of the paper I will shortly discuss some

---

[4]   In the paper 'Private Law in the EU: Harmonised or Fragmented Europeanisation?'. The paper, based on lectures given in the year 2000, is published in (2002) *ERPL*, 77.

[5]   Despite this fact, I will here speak about 'restatements'. The reason for this is given in Section 3.

of these prerequisites, connected with the need for safeguarding the dynamic nature of the norm production. The restatement should continuously stay open for influence from the dynamics of 'real life'.

However, I believe that focusing the discussion only on the question of the normative status of the European material and the ways in which the norms are produced is not sufficient. In this paper I will therefore also look at the *conceptual structure* of the possible restatement(s). My thesis is the following: in developing the European restatement(s) we have to some extent to detach ourselves from the abstract legal–technical language which is typical for the national codifications and partially also for the common law (I specify this criticism of the traditional concept structure in Section 4). Instead we have to use a legal language which *to a greater extent takes into account the real-life circumstances* giving rise to the legal problem (Section 5). Such a development is not only based on a normative wish to promote a realistic legal engineering within an experimental European legal sphere. The need for conceptual creativity also reflects changes in the role of law in late modern society.

II. NO CODE!

The proponents of a European Civil Code or a European Contract Code have defended this idea with a variety of arguments. The *economic–practical arguments* are, quite naturally, at the forefront in the Communication from the Commission. The first aim of the Communication is to start a collection of information concerning problems which result from divergences in contract law. The Commission wants to know, whether these divergences between the Member States hinder the proper functioning of the Internal Market and whether they 'discourage or increase the costs of cross-border transactions'.[6]

Some academic writers stress the practical and economic arguments for a European Civil or Contract Code. According to this view, without a common European private law, cross-border transactions are more difficult and the transaction costs for such transactions are much higher. The Lando Commission and the Study Group in their response to the Commission Communication[7] also underline this argument, referring to the substantial costs connected with the diversity of national contract laws. However, the empirical evidence of the cost effects is scarce. Of course, obviously in some cases some negative cost effects occur as a consequence of the diversity of laws, and in some cases this may even have a hindering effect on cross-border transactions. Personally I believe, as long as empirical evidence to the contrary is not produced, that these cost effects

---

6 COM (2001) 398 final, 2.

7 *Communication on European Contract Law, Joint Response of the Commission on European Contract Law and the Study Group on a European Civil Code*, 30.09.01 (hereinafter *Joint Response*).

in general are not very substantive. The stressing of the cost effects rather seems to be in line with lawyers' usual tendency to overemphasise the role of law and of legal certainty[8] in commercial transactions. However, as Stewart Macauley showed a long time ago in his classical study on businessmen's contractual behaviour, the law plays a very minor role in comparison with other business considerations.[9] As this is often true both for the stage of making and performing the contract as well as for negotiations concerning problems in contractual relations, considerable costs related to the divergences in contract law often occur only in the relatively rare – in comparison with all contractual relations on the market – situations when there is a dispute and this dispute has become juridified.

Anyway, for commercial partners which have the opportunity to use choice of law clauses – the need for mandatory consumer protection, etc., is a different issue – it is often a sufficient solution to have a European 'restatement' (like the Lando Principles of European Contract Law), to refer to.[10] As there is some uncertainty whether principles of this kind when chosen by the parties can be applied by courts as a kind of autonomous partial legal order,[11] and not only as contractual clauses to be applied on the basis of a national law, such a role could be acknowledged through a European legislative act. In addition, in most EU countries the UN Convention on Contracts for the International Sale of Goods (CISG) is in force as a common background legislation for cross-border sales. Therefore, there does not seem to exist any pressing need for a European codification of general contract law.

There are undoubtedly practical, and sometimes costly problems connected, for example, with the great variations in the rules on secured transactions, including retention clauses, and with differing mandatory rules in specific areas, such as insurance. Problems of this kind can, however, be relieved through targeted, problem-oriented harmonisation measures, as have been done in consumer and labour law so far. I can also foresee focused harmonisation concerning limited questions of general contract law where the differences between the national rules can produce very unfair results; for example concerning the rules on the effect of change of circumstances. A general codification is hardly needed

---

[8] The fact that many important issues of contract law are unsolved in national legal systems does not seem to be any great obstacle to national transactions. As just one such example one could refer to the very practical problem of 'the battle of the forms', which in many countries has not been clearly solved.

[9] S. Macauley, 'Elegant Models, Empirical Pictures and the Complexities of Contract', (1997) *Law & Society Review*, 505.

[10] As foreseen by the Principles Art. 1:101(2).

[11] See Lando and Beale (n. 1), 98 *et seq*. See also, e.g., D. Busch and E. Hondius, 'Ein neues Vertragsrecht für Europa: Die Principles of European Contract Law aus niederländischer Sicht', *ZEuP* [2001], 223, 225–228.

in order to achieve sufficient harmony concerning issues where harmony is practically important, even though some friction between such targeted measures and the national laws can be foreseen in individual cases.

Instead, several arguments may be advanced *against* a European Civil Code or even a European Contract Code. As I have elaborated my scepticism in more detail elsewhere, I will only very briefly mention my three main arguments here.[12]

1. A general codification of European contract law would very likely imply a *stronger emphasis on traditional liberal values* in contract law.[13] The great codifications on the Continent are mostly a product of the *Rechtsstaat* of the nineteenth century, and it is not easy to include in such codifications the often rather varying elements of consumer protection and other rules on protection of the weaker party which are so typical for the Welfare State. The more general parts especially are difficult to build on a materia which is based on very contradictory values. For example, the idea of a 'general part of the law of obligations' is closely connected with traditional subjective contract law and does not suit the more status-oriented contract law of today.[14] The Principles of European Contract Law, made by the Lando Commission, offer a good example of the difficulties to include welfarist thinking in a general 'codification': although in principle thought to be applicable to all kinds of contracts, including for example consumer contracts, they do not contain very many signs of welfarist thinking. The solution offered in the Principles, to expel the welfarist elements to what the Germans use to call a *'Sonderprivatrecht'* outside of the 'general' private law,[15] would not represent a welfarist solution, as it clearly would ideologically emphasise the values of the 'general' private law as a kind of main starting point.

2. Christian von Bar has stressed that a Civil Code obtains its dignity because 'it is not so freely amended like some statute for consumer or tenant protection'.[16] This citation not only offers a good illustration of my first argument against codification, it also states the object of my second criticism, concerning the *static character* of a codification. A general Civil or Contract Code would be relatively

---

[12] As to more references and a more broad presentation of my arguments, see my above-mentioned (n. 4) paper in (2002) *ERPL*, 77.

[13] Some even see this as an important reason for supporting European codification; see, e.g., W. Tilmann, 'Das gewerbliche Rechtsschutz vor den Konturen eines europäischen Privatrechts', *GRUR Int.* [1993], 275, 278.

[14] Thus, based on a thorough analysis, J. Schovsbo, *Immaterialretsaftaler* (Copenhagen, Jurist-og Ökonomforbundets Forlag, 2001), 373–375.

[15] See Lando and Beale (n. 1.) xxv.

[16] C. von Bar, 'The Study Group on a European Civil Code', *Tidskrift, utgiven av Juridiska Föreningen i Finland* [2000], 323, 333.

immune against various kinds of needs of changes.[17] This is true both for market-oriented pressures based on changes in commercial reality and for democratically founded demands for more regulation of the welfarist type. The fact that there has been a 'succesful enactment of new civil codes' in the Netherlands and a variety of post-socialist countries does not as such contradict this claim,[18] as these enactments either were prepared for a long time or were the result of thorough societal upheavals. The dynamic of commercial life as well as the varying welfarist demands generate needs for changes also in a shorter time-perspective and in more stable general social structures.

As the national codifications are already relatively static in comparison with other national norm production, this feature would most certainly be even more emphasised if the codification were to be made on European level. The complicated European legislative machinery would make it almost impossible to make changes to a European Civil Code. At the same time such a Code would remove important parts of private law from the legislative competence of the Member States.

3. Some proponents of a European Code have related the work to a perceived need for building a European identity. In such a view the role of law as a factor shaping identity is (over?)emphasised. A common legal system is seen as contributing to a common identity. However, the striving for a common European law on this ground seems to be based on a false or at least problematic interpretation of what the European identity is and what it could be. It is in fact easy to defend a claim that the essence of the European identity lies precisely in the plurality of languages and cultures (including commercial cultures!) and therefore also in a pluralist law. A European codification would therefore *rather weaken than strengthen the prevailing European identity*. In addition, in a legal engineering perspective, the European pluralism need not be seen only as a weakness. It can also be considered a resource. The strength of Europe lies in a fruitful interplay between the similarities and the variations. This applies to legal thinking as well. Precisely the variations between the legal orders, combined with a more or less common understanding of the essence of law, make possible an experimental and learning European law. On this approach I have based my proposal for a free movement of legal ideas and doctrines as an alternative to codification.

The battle between those who favour a European Code and those who are against it is sometimes described as a clash between forward-looking 'Europeanists' or 'internationalists' on the one hand and narrow-minded, conservative 'nationalists' on the other hand.[19] In view of my arguments, especially the

---

[17] Compare the more dynamic idea of a framework directive put forward in the Green Paper on European Union Consumer Protection, COM (2001) 531 final, 11 *et seq.*

[18] Cf. J. Basedow, 'Codification of Private Law in the European Union: the making of a Hybrid', (2001) *ERPL*, 35, 40 *et seq.*

[19] See also Lando in the above-mentioned (n. 2) study commissioned by the Parliament, Document PE 168.511, 125, who hints not only at the reluctance to learn new things, but also at the fear of giving up local monopolies. I will not here pursue the analysis of possible

third one, it should be obvious that I cannot accept this way of describing the positions. It is perfectly possible to be forward-looking and European-minded without defending the idea of a European Civil Code (one could even claim that the proponents of the nineteenth-century idea of a large codification are the backward-looking ones). The development I favour, and which I have previously outlined in more detail, is a free movement of legal ideas and doctrines, which implies a radical lowering of the national legal borders. Such a free movement requires a thorough openness – promoted through legal research and education, contacts between lawyers and judges across the borders, etc. – towards impulses and 'irritants'[20] both from Brussels and directly from other Member States. These irritants can and should be used to break down such outdated national legal structures which cannot be defended by any other arguments than references to tradition. For example, both the Unfair Contract Terms Directive and the Consumer Sales Directive have performed important tasks in this respect in many Member States.[21] Even the German *Schuldrechtsreform* needed the impetus from EC law in order to become reality.

My criticism against the idea of a European Civil Code, in other words, is to a large extent a criticism of the use of the technique of a general codification. This technique, which in today's social and legal environment is problematic as such, would to my mind be especially unfortunate when used at European level.

The criticism of the codification technique would not necessarily hit a collection of norms of the 'restatement'-type as hard as a real Code. In the following I will analyse more closely, in the light of my codification critique, why and under what circumstances I find a European 'restatement' acceptable.

III. A DYNAMIC (RE)STATEMENT?

One of the key elements of my criticism against a European Code concerns its necessarily static nature which would not only make it too immune against the influence of new commercial and social needs, but also would reduce the possibilities of making continuous use of national experiences when developing the law. The same problems would not necessarily be connected with various kinds of

---

self-interests of codification sceptics, only mention that there may of course be self interests involved in the camp of proponents as well as, for example, C. von Bar, *A Common European Law of Torts* (Roma, Centro di studi e ricerche di diritto comparato e straniero, Saggi, conferenze e seminari 19, 1996), 2 has noted, the new tasks connected with European harmonisation 'could lend jurisprudence a new splendour and attraction to the intellectual élite which has come to abandon it'.

[20] See G. Teubner, 'Legal Irritants: Good Faith in British Law or How Unifying Law Ends Up in New Divergences', (1988) *MLR*, 11.

[21] See, e.g., the special issue on the implementation of the former Directive (1997) 2 *ERPL* and on the implementation of the latter (2001) 2–3 *ERPL*.

soft law – for example, academically produced common 'principles' – which the Commission in its Communication regards as one alternative. Such soft law can be deemed useful in various respects, even in case one does not accept the Commission's emphasis that the main task of this kind of principles would be to bring about more convergence of national laws.[22] The Lando Commission and the Study Group – the most important creators of such principles so far – in their joint response to the Commission Communication therefore also analyse in a positive light the need to develop and promote 'restatements' and to create new working methods for such a work.[23]

As mentioned earlier such restatements can be used as reference point for commercial partners wanting an equal playing field which is known to both of them. Through some kind of European legislation one could even confirm the possibility of an arrangement where a restatement in a cross-border transaction would form a kind of autonomous norm collection to be applied in its own context without any reference to national law.[24] This could be combined with some form of official European acknowledgement of 'good restatements', which would both strengthen the position of these restatements in law teaching and make them more known among business people and business lawyers as well as among judges and arbitrators.[25] Through such an acknowledgement procedure the need for safeguarding a sufficient degree of mandatory protective rules could perhaps be met as well. This could in other words be an answer to the well-founded criticism against the restatement method, put forward by some 'codifiers', that it is too soft to fulfil the protective functions of welfarist private law and that it means a 'Surrender to the Actors of Market Globalization'.[26] This answer implies both a somewhat new approach to the materials on which the restatements are built, as I will note more in detail below, and to the democratic legitimation of the procedures in which the restatements are made and acknowledged.[27]

---

[22] COM (2001) 598 final, the heading of Option II.

[23] *Joint Response* (n. 7), 61–80.

[24] Such a 'sixteenth model' would, according to Basedow, (2001) *ERPL*, 35, 44, 'be doomed to insignificance'. However, this depends to some extent on the position of the model in the development of law teaching in Europe. And if it would prove insignificant also in spite of more emphasis in teaching, then this shows that the practical problems connected with differing national laws obviously are not so large as the proponents of a harmonisation use to claim.

[25] So far empirical studies show that the judges' knowledge of the projects is 'almost non-existent', K.P. Berger, 'The Principles of European Contract Law and the concept of the "Creeping Codification" of law', (2001) *ERPL* , 21, 29.

[26] U. Mattei, 'Hard Code Now! A Critique of "Softness" and a Plea for Responsibility in the European debate over Codification', paper read at the SECOLA conference in Leuven 30.11.–1.12.2001.

[27] It should be mentioned that the Lando Commission and the Study Group in their *Joint Response* (n. 7) 80, propose the establishment of a European Law Academy, in the work of which also representatives of the European Parliament would take part.

Not only could restatements of this kind be useful for commercial parties. They could also contribute to the dynamic nature of the European legal culture. The restatements could, by taking part in the creation of a *'common legal language'* facilititate the free movement of legal ideas and doctrines in Europe.[28] Without such a common denominator the use of national experiences across the borders is much more difficult. A project like the Lando Commission is useful as a participant in the creation of such a language for the European contract law discourse. In this way it contributes to 'a fruitful discourse culture'.[29] As long as this and other similar projects produce 'soft law' and 'soft legal knowledge', they facilitate the movement of legal ideas within the EU rather than hamper it, as a petrified code would do. They may also function as a kind of softly codified experience to be used in the local legal development[30] as well as a tool for criticism of national law.[31] The use of the European Principles of Contract Law as one of the sources, when developing the law in the post-socialist countries is a good example of a soft law influence on national law.[32]

As mentioned in the introduction, an academic 'restatement' in Europe would in many questions rather mean creating new rules than finding common rules. However, I have preferred to use the term 'restatement' precisely to underline the necessary link between the restatements and the existing and future national legal experience. An efficient use of various national ideas and legal experiments implies a readiness to let well-founded ideas and successful experiments influence new versions of the restatements.

---

[28] As M. van Hoecke and M. Warrington, 'Legal Cultures, Legal Paradigms and Legal Doctrine: Towards a New Model for Comparative Law', (1998) *ICLQ*, 495, 525 *et seq.* have noted, the development of 'some conceptual legal meta-language' is a 'necessary condition for a real development of comparative law'.

[29] K. Riedl, 'The Work of the Lando-Commission from an Alternative Viewpoint', (2000) *ERPL*, 71, 83. In his commentary to the UNIDROIT Principles of International Commercial Contracts Bonell also emphasises their role as a framework for discourse, see M.J. Bonell, *An International Restatement of Contract Law* (Irvington, Transnational Juris Publications, 1994), 2–5. In M.J. Bonell, 'The need and possibilities of a codified European contract law', (1997) *ERPL*, 505 the author expressly defends the idea of non-binding instruments as against a formal Code.

[30] The analysis of the possible influence of international contract law principles on Norwegian law by L.M. Heggberget and E. Nyland, 'Formuleringen av internasjonale kontraktsrettslige grunnprinsipper og betydningen for norsk rett', *Tidsskrift for Rettsvitenskap* (2000), 251 is illustrative.

[31] See, e.g., de Vries in M.W. Hesselink and G.J.P. de Vries, *Principles of European Contract Law* (The Hague, Kluwer, 2001), 185 *et seq.*, who enumerates several points on which he considers the Principles to be better than the new Dutch Civil Code.

[32] See, e.g., on Estonia, P. Varul, 'Legal Policy Decisions and Choices in the Creation of New Private Law in Estonia', *Juridica International* [2000], 104, 114; I. Kull, 'Legal Remedies Provided in the Estonian Draft Law of Obligations Act for Breach of Contractual Obligations', *Juridica International* [1999], 147.

If by the choice of the restatement technique one seeks to avoid the problems of a static codification and to make a continuous use of new national experience, one should accept the ongoing nature of the restatement work.[33] The restatements should be redrafted from time to time. In their Joint Response to the European Commission the Lando Commission and the Study Group therefore also propose some institutional arrangements to take care of this work.[34] If the restatements were to be given some kind of official acknowledgement, it should be discussed whether this acknowledgement should be given only for a certain period of time, after which a new assessment of the restatement would take place.

As the function of the restatement should be to offer parties the best possible collection of rules for their purposes as well as to facilitate the use of experience from various places when developing the law, I would also not necessarily rule out the possibility of several competing restatements being accepted on the scene.[35] However, the need for developing a common legal language requires some strictness in this respect. From this perspective it would seem a better solution as far as possible to integrate in the restatements alternative solutions – to be chosen by the parties – on points where this seems feasible, than to have several different restatements on the same subject. It also goes without saying that the level of mandatory protection should not be subject to the choice of the parties.

In a common law context one easily sees a restatement primarily as a dialogue between academics and the judiciary. In the Joint Response to the European Commission the Lando Commission and the Study Group foresee 'a process of continual restatement where the evolving jurisprudence of the courts in the development of the restatement is integrated, along with academic treatment ...'[36] Certainly court practice is one important aspect of the continuing discourses which produce the raw materials for the restatements. In fact, I believe that case-bound experience of this kind also in the Continental setting will receive greater importance than before in the fragmented, technologically as well as ethically unforeseeable late modern society.[37] For example, even from a German perspective, tort law of today has been called *'eine transnationale Falljurisprudenz'*.[38] Not only national courts, but also the EC Court of Justice[39] can in this context play a role as producers of new legal experience for the restatements.

---

[33] For similar views on what he calls 'Creeping Codification', see Berger, (2001) *ERPL*, 21, 24.

[34] *Joint Response* (n. 7), 78–80.

[35] Cf. *Joint Response* (n. 7), 78.

[36] *Joint Response* (n. 7), 96.

[37] See references below, in Section 5 of the paper.

[38] G. Brüggemeier, 'Haftungsrecht – eine transnationale Falljurisprudenz? Ein Beitrag zur Europäisierung des Privatrechts', in: L. Krämer, H.-W. Micklitz and K.Tonner, *Law and Diffuse Interests in the European Legal Order* (Baden-Baden, Nomos, 1997), 657.

[39] The readiness of the EC Court to change its practices in the face of new societal needs and the possibility of the national courts taking an active position in asking for changes is well analysed by T. Ojanen, 'Between Precedent and the Present', *Turku Law J.* [2001], 105.

However, a restatement arising only from the dialogue between the judiciary and the academics would most obviously be too narrowly founded. It would emphasise the thought of law as a more or less closed autonomous sphere of society which can be developed solely by legal experts. It would ignore the role of law as a political instrument,[40] and thereby exclude the democratic element from the developing of the law. To my mind, many of the most interesting legal experiments are today effected not by judgments of the courts, but by legislative measures. Most of the welfarist elements in private law, related to consumer protection, tenant protection, labour law etc., have been introduced through legislation (although they later may have affected court practice also in unregulated areas). So, a restatement which purports to make use of all the various legal experience produced in the Member States should look not only at court practice, but also at national legislation. In this way the direct democratic influence on national law would imply an indirect democratic effect on the European restatements as well. In addition, the ever more important global elements of law, introduced through conventions and similar measures, can be taken into account.

One of the advantages of a restatement before a Code is precisely that it leaves the legislature a freedom to act when commercial or social needs so require. Even though the existence of an officially acknowledged restatement certainly would restrain the eagerness of the national legislature to develop new solutions, this road would stay open for motivated reactions and experiments.[41] If such actions are considered well founded, it should not be impossible to take them into account when restatements are revised. This is the same both for national legislation as well as for legislative measures on European level. I have elsewhere tried to show how such European measures can be used for developing certain general principles of European contract law.[42] And, as I mentioned before, I certainly do not oppose targeted European measures where a real need of harmonisation is perceived. As experience from many directives, for example the Product Liability Directive, shows, it is not impossible to amend such

---

[40] S. Banakas, 'Liability for Incorrect Financial Information: Theory and Practice in a General Clause System and in a Protected Interests System', (1999) *ERPL*, 261, 284 *et seq.* rightly emphasises that a European tort law cannot be only a comparative law compromise, but has to 'emerge from real European social policy'.

[41] Compare, for example, the recent development of Nordic insurance law. Although there existed almost an identical insurance contracts legislation in the Nordic countries for more than half a century (almost identical Insurance Contract Acts were adopted in Sweden in 1927, in Denmark and Norway in 1930 and in Finland in 1933), new ideas of consumer protection and the development of the insurance sector prompted national reactions, which to a large extent destroyed the Nordic unity in the field. In the 1980s and 1990s different legislation was introduced in the different countries, replacing the unified acts. Sticking to the unity would, however, have been too big an obstacle against the needed development.

[42] In my book *Social Contract Law and European Integration* (Aldershot, Dartmouth, 1995).

measures when this is deemed appropriate. They do not become as static as a Code would.

So, this kind of dynamic restatements, which even could be offered as a kind of optional denationalised reference points for contracting parties, would to my mind be good tools for structuring the pluralist European law, without unduly restricting its opportunity for experimental development. However, in order to safeguard such an inherent dynamic in European law one should not only focus on the method of norm production. The *structure and concepts* of the restatements are also relevant in this context. Both the opportunity to make best possible use of the problem-solving capacity of European law related to the free movement of legal ideas and doctrines as well as the aim to allow some democratic influence over the development of the law require a detachment from an abstract legal–technical concept structure of the law. In the following Sections I will focus my paper on this issue.

IV. AGAINST THE ABSTRACT CONCEPTUALITY OF A CODE

All existing Codes use to a certain extent what one could call an abstract legal language. Such a language is not unknown to common law either, even though common law often applaudes itself for having a more practical approach than the Continental Codes; normative structures like the doctrine of consideration have a rather distant connection to real life.[43] Some problems in incorporating EC directives in national legal structures are obviously connected with the fact that directives are often structured on the basis of real commercial situations like distance selling or timesharing, while national private laws are based on more general and in this sense more abstract legal concepts.

To some extent this is both sound and unavoidable. Legal thinking based on preset norms requires a certain degree of abstraction. Any discussion concerning whether the law should be built on 'abstract' or 'concrete' concepts, counterposed in this way, would be absurd. My question rather concerns the optimal level of abstraction and the keys for the abstraction process. It is not a question of 'either–or' but of a gradual shifting of centres of gravity in the legal concept structure.

My criticism of the idea of codification in Section 2 above is in certain ways connected with the perceived and probably necessary conceptual structure of a general code. Both the references to traditional values and to the static character of the code are partially related to the abstract legal concepts to be used in building a code. I will in what follows try to explain through some examples what I mean when I speak about a problematically abstract character of the concepts of a code.

---

[43] M.W. Hesselink, *The New European Legal Culture* (Deventer, Kluwer, 2001), 21 *et seq.* rightly equals the formalism of English common law and of Continental law.

First, a conceptual method of thinking which makes impossible (unthinkable) legal solutions which do not fit into the conceptual structure of the code, even though the solutions would be practically valuable, certainly underlines both the static and conservative character of the law. It is hard to say, to what extent such thinking still prevails. Usually the claim is made that *Begriffsjurisprudenz* is dead, and should be so. Outdated beliefs in a conceptual method for applying codes should not be used as arguments against a codification. On the other hand, in practice, reasoning bound to certain conceptual ideas certainly is alive and well. And even in the preparation of legislation it is possible that an abstract legal approach can sometimes form an obstacle for good rules.

I will only mention one, to my mind, very good example from the experience of developing EC consumer law. In the Green Paper on guarantees for consumer goods and after-sales services, which was the starting point for the preparation of the Consumer Sales Directive, the Commission strongly advocated the inclusion of provisions on the manufacturer's liability for the legal guarantee towards the buyer of the goods.[44] Such rules, which can be found in several national legal orders, would not only improve the position of the consumer and bring it more in touch with a reality where most defects result from the activities of the manufacturer. They would also have been one of the most important steps in improving the function of the internal market by increasing consumer confidence in transactions made abroad, as it would obviously be easier in many cases for the consumer to turn to a perhaps well-known producer than to a small retail outlet in another Member State. However, although good substantive reasons could be produced for such a solution, it was not included in the adopted Directive. One important argument against such rules, which I personally heard several times from persons engaged in the drafting work in various ways, was the difficulty in accepting such a solution in the light of traditional private law systematics. As there was no direct contractual relation between the manufacturer and the buyer of the goods (where no explicit commercial guarantee was given) and as the claim of the buyer was related to his contractual expectations and therefore could not be classified as a tort claim, it was hard to find 'a legal basis' for the liability of the manufacturer. Of course, I cannot tell whether this argument was decisive, and it is not necessary to make any such assessment in this context. I just mention this example to show how the abstract concept structure of a code (or the equally abstract doctrine of privity of contract in common law) can be used as an argument against practically sound solutions.

Secondly, and this is probably more important, the very abstract character, especially of provisions which can be found in the general parts of the Codes, in itself makes it hard to see, when such provisions are prepared, whether they represent a good regulation of all or even most of the cases they are intended to cover. The *language of real life*, in the commercial world or in the citizen's

---

[44]   COM(93) 509 final, 86–88.

world, has to be translated into another language, the *language of the legal world*, and the further away these languages are from each other, the more likely it is that serious translation errors will occur. An abstract text is usually produced with some examples in mind, and it is not self-evident that the reasons connected with such examples are good ones when confronted with other examples covered by the abstract norm. In the application of the code such an abstract rule does not always offer very good results; the results might also be rather unforeseeable, as the rule might have to be twisted or avoided in order to cope with the problem at hand in an acceptable manner.

These problems would be still more acute in the context of a European codification. The experiences of national abstract rules which have materialised in court practice steer the understanding of the similar European rules to be prepared. The leading cases from one's own jurisdiction offer the practical examples needed to understand the proposed norm, which in another jurisdiction may be read in another practical context due to the cases which in that jurisdiction happen to have reached the courts.

In their Joint Response the Lando Commission and the Study Group mention some very good examples on how similar general concepts can meet very different understandings in different national systems, by referring, *inter alia*, to the law of unjustified enrichments and the law of *negotiorum gestio*. A European codification trying to harmonise such abstract concepts would most certainly run into difficulties of deep misunderstandings and unforeseeable results. And what is more problematic: such general notions may even be used as tools for critique against well-founded practical solutions which do not fit into the scheme. In the Joint Response it is mentioned as a problem that the Directive on distance contracts, according to which the consumer has no obligation to give compensation for unsolicited goods or services, 'obviously makes a deep impact on the law of unjustified enrichments as well as the law of *negotiorum gestio*'.[45]

This experience of problems related to the use of a very abstract approach has to some extent plagued the third stage of the work of the Lando Commission, dealing with rules which are traditionally thought of as rules of the general law of obligations.[46] The discussions on the rules on several creditors and several debtors, for example, which are formulated in a very general mode, were certainly somewhat chaotic because of very different understandings of the practical situations involved. Self-evidently, there is less certainty on the quality of the results in such a situation than when the actual problem to be regulated is clear in the mind of the regulators.

Even if one rejects the idea of a European Civil Code and settles for a dynamic

---

[45]   *Joint Response* (n. 7), 38.

[46]   The Lando Commission has finished its work on these provisions and the result is due to be published in the near future. Personally, I participated as a member of the Commission during the last part of the second stage and during the third stage of its work.

and flexible restatement strategy such as the one I outlined in the previous Section, much of this criticism of an abstract conceptual structure retains its force. Also, in the latter context, a legal structure and language which is too far away from the language of reality may prove counterproductive when one seeks the best practical solutions to legal problems. In addition, if one likes to emphasise the free movement of legal ideas and doctrines as one of the basic fuels for the development of restatements, a very abstract conceptual structure can be considered problematic, as it can become an obstacle against such a movement. This is the case especially if one focuses – as I think to some extent one should – on the need for sharing experiences concerning the solution of evolving practical problems. The concepts of a restatement should not form an obstacle to using practical experience.

The almost paradigmatical example on how practical experience can and should be taken into account without regard to the prevailing abstract legal structure is the well-known English case *White v. Jones*, where the House of Lords (Lord Goff) made extensive use of arguments from German law ('the German experience') when deciding an issue concerning the liability of a solicitor in relation to the intended beneficiary of a will.[47] In this case Lord Goff let 'practical justice' related to the concrete issue outweigh traditional systematics, when the German arguments were borrowed. He did not find it crucial that the solutions to the problem at hand with regard to traditional legal systematics would be placed in different boxes in England and in Germany in the dichotomy contract/delict. Such concrete sharing of experience and a comparable use of the experience in the development of a restatement should not be made too difficult by a rigid conceptual structure of the restatement.

In the light of what I have said so far, the greatest problems in the conceptual structure of a restatement seem to lie in what is vaguely called its *'general parts'*.[48] Both the traditional general part of the whole civil law as well as what Continentals call the general part of the law of obligations contain many concepts and structural solutions that have the strongly abstract character I referred to above. In fact, it is precisely the idea of such general parts to provide rules which are abstracted from more concrete situational rules. Therefore, I would prefer a restatement work focusing rather on more narrow fields than on the private law structure or the structure of the law of obligations as a whole.

Although general contract law[49] can be fairly abstract, a restatement of general contract law is probably acceptable, if it is made sufficiently flexible and supplemented by restatements concerning specific important contract types. In other

---

[47]   [1995] All ER 691, 705–707.

[48]   See also concerning the necessary conservatism of the general part of the law of obligations, Schovsbo (n. 14), 373–375 mentioned above.

[49]   Understood as covering the themes of the First and Second Lando Commission, see Lando and Beale (n. 1), but not necessarily the Third Commission.

words, the shift of emphasis towards the concrete problems to be regulated in the area of contract law implies an acknowledgement of the fact that various contract types and contracting situations on practical grounds can be regulated in different ways. Not all rules necessarily have to be squeezed in under a consequently structured general contract law or be dogmatically bound to a certain concept of contract. In fact, the picture of international contract law very much has this fragmented appearance today. We accept, without great difficulty, that some contract types (for example related to financial services or transportation) are governed in practice by many specific rules typical for the line of business, some with roots in common law and others in national or international usages. Other contract types again are more clearly geared towards traditional domestic values. It would probably be more wise to accept the situation and see the merits of it, rather than deplore the evolving 'Wild West development of law'[50] and the 'hamburger, nasigoreng and pommes legal culture'.[51] This does not, of course, rule out conceptual simplifications and harmonisations between different instruments, when this makes the bulk of rules more understandable.

In this context one also encounters the problem whether one should have the regulation of consumer and business contracts included in the same general restatement(s) or make different restatements for both areas. Various arguments can be given in favour of both solutions. The need for concrete and situation-specific rules, which do not hide the actual situations behind an abstract language, speaks strongly in favour of different restatements. On this ground I would rather prefer this solution.[52] However, a case can be made for more comprehensive restatements as well: they would allow the consumer law experiences to influence contract law more broadly and give the welfarist elements a broader scope.[53] If the latter alternative is chosen, the consumer interest should, of course, be adequately reflected in the organisation preparing the restatement and in the method by which the restatement is acknowledged. The worst solution is a restatement which purports to be general, but does not fully cover the problems of consumer contracts and other weaker party situations. For reasons

---

[50] Tilmann, *GRUR Int.* [1993], 275, 278. This and the following metaphor concern the effects of EC law on private law.

[51] U.H. Schneider, 'Europäische und internationale Harmonisierung des Bankvertragsrechts', *NJW* [1991], 1985, 1993.

[52] The European Consumer Law Group in its Response to the Communication on European Contract Law advocates the elaboration of (minimum) European Principles of Consumer Law and offers itself as a body performing this task. Personally I find this idea worthwhile pursuing.

[53] My view on the separation/integration of consumer law, partially accepting the latter argument as well, is spelt out in somewhat more detail in my paper *Is There a European Consumer Law – and Should There Be One?* (Roma, Centro di studi e ricerche di diritto comparato e straniero, Saggi, conferenze e seminari 41, 2000), 3–9.

I mentioned earlier these problems should not be pushed aside to some kind of specialised '*Sonderprivatrecht*'.

In order to demonstrate why I do not see the thought of a restatement of general contract law as incompatible with a free movement of practical legal ideas, I will conclude this Section by mentioning an example of a harmonised general legal concept which can both offer a new and more understandable inroad into the various rules of contractual liability and which can at the same time in this way facilitate the free movement of legal ideas. I refer here to the definition of what some have called '*control–liability*' as the basis of liability in contract law. This definition, according to which a party can escape liability for breach of contract if he proves that the failure was due to an impediment beyond his control and that he could not reasonably be expected to have taken the impediment into account at the time of the conclusion of the contract or to have avoided or overcome it or its consequences, as well known, has been introduced through the CISG (Art. 79) and has later been adopted not only in some national legal reforms, but also in the European Principles of Contract Law as a general basis of contractual liability.[54] One sees here the development of a harmonised concept based on a compromise between a more strict common law approach and some Continental approaches, which, in spite of some variations in the way it is understood in different national contexts, offers a common frame of reference when discussing contract law experiences from different legal orders. The fact that a restatement would contain such a general starting point should not, however, be an obstacle against using and developing – nationally and Europe-wide – other liability rules for cases where the control–liability seems less suitable.[55] The common language of the general restatement should not be a straitjacket against developing good practical rules for different situations, but in such cases function only as a 'legal meta-language'[56] to which the various rules can be related. It makes the free movement of ideas easier, as the communication of national experiences concerning various forms of liability can be related to the commonly understood control–liability. One may add that the concept of control–liability – like the concept of negligence – is itself flexible enough to allow for a concrete assessment of the placement of various risks, in which assessment one can also take into account national peculiarities and experiences. The definition of control–liability therefore not only offers a common

---

[54]   Art. 8:108, see Lando and Beale (n. 1) 379–384. The same solution is also adopted in the *UNIDROIT Principles* Art. 7.1.7.

[55]   In Finland, for example, there have been doubts about the general suitability of the control liability for situations of defects (as opposed to delay); see, e.g., H. Saxén, *Skadestånd vid avtalsbrott – HD praxis i Finland* (Stockholm, Juristförlaget, 1995), 64, and the liability for defects in consumer sales has been made strict, see the Consumer Protection Act Ch. 5, Sec. 20.

[56]   See the reference to van Hoecke and Warrington above (n. 28).

language to which one can relate the communication concerning other forms of liability, but also, on the micro level, a common language for the discussion concerning how risks have been and should be distributed between the parties. In this way it offers a bridge to the 'real-life circumstances' which I will emphasise in what follows.

V. STARTING FROM REAL-LIFE CIRCUMSTANCES

The promotion of an extensive sharing of experiences in a continuously changing environment not only warrants scepticism towards such general concepts as are used in the general parts of the codifications. I think one may go even further. I believe that more generally, there are good reasons for moving the focus of legal language somewhat in the direction of what one might call various real-life circumstances at the expense of traditional more abstract categories. One may even claim that there is a certain societal call for such a move. Again I should underline that this move means rather subtle changes of the legal language, not substituting the present concept structure with a radically new language.

As *White v. Jones* showed, there seems to be a need for departing from abstract concepts like contractual and delictual liability and discussing in more concrete terms the issue at hand, namely the liability of solicitors failing to draw up wills. A free movement of good legal solutions seems to function best in such a conceptual structure. What we expect from an experimental European legal sphere is really that it is able to develop the optimal solutions to various kinds of societal problems. A borrowing of arguments is easier, the closer to the real problems the legal concepts are. If, for example, one wishes to discuss various solutions concerning the problem of liability for incorrect financial advice with reference to experiences from various national legal orders, one should be able to directly compare the solutions offered, instead of taking the rather cumbersome detour through the differing conceptual structures behind the various national solutions.[57]

The need for structuring a European work to a greater extent on the problems rather than on traditional legal categories is to some extent acknowledged in the academic work which has already been done. The Trento Project, applying the Cornell method, searches for the 'common core' with the help of descriptions of factual situations. Also in the projects aiming at creating new principles there is a certain recognition of the desirability of a more fact-oriented approach. According to Ole Lando, the authors of the Principles of European Contract

---

[57] Banakas, (1999) *ERPL*, 261 in an interesting study has compared the liability for incorrect financial information in French, English and German law. In spite of the very different conceptual starting points he notes 'an interesting convergence' between the three legal orders on this point (283).

Law at least 'tried to avoid legal concepts and used a factual language, which is easier to translate'.[58] The Lando Commission attempted to draft the principles in a language which would be understood both by practising lawyers and business people.[59] It is also interesting to note Christian von Bar's analysis of European tort law where he expressly claims that 'modern tort law's specific instances are ... defined not by legal categories but in terms of real-life circumstances which form the bases of the causes of action'.[60] One might hope that this insight concerning tort law could have some influence on the work of the Study Group more generally.

There are in fact two types of arguments for such a shift of focus towards a greater emphasis on real-life circumstances in the conceptual world of the law. I have here emphasised normative reasons connected with the wish for an experimental law based on the free movement of legal ideas and doctrines. However, I think there also exists a societal pressure or call for modifications of the legal language in this direction.[61] To some extent, internationalisation and Europeanisation of the law, connected with internationalisation of markets, risks and information/communication, more or less inevitably undermine abstract national legal notions. Internationally needed commercial instruments will be developed in a partially commercial language to some extent autonomously from differing national legal terminology. Information concerning adequate legal reactions to actual risks will also be shared in a way which overlaps national conceptual structures. To mention a very topical example from tort law, the experiences from tobacco litigation are communicated and used over the world, despite differences in the conceptual structures of national tort laws.

Not only do internationalisation and Europeanisation produce such pressures. Even at national level, at least in some Member States, new societal phenomena call for a legal decision-making which is less hidden behind abstract legal concepts. The growing interest of mass media in legal decision-making and in discussing the merits of important decisions makes it more and more important for the courts to be able to present their decisions in a language which is understandable to the public (or rather to the journalists presenting the decisions

---

58 O. Lando, 'The Structure and the Salient Features of the Principles of European Contract Law', *Juridica International* [2001], 4, 5.

59 *Joint Response* (n. 7) at 65.

60 von Bar (n. 19) 13. Here I have borrowed the term 'real-life circumstances' from von Bar's paper.

61 I have analysed these pressures closely in my recent book *Senmodern ansvarsrätt. Privaträtt som redskap för mikropolitik* (Helsingfors, Kauppakaari and Uppsala, Iustus, 2001). For references to the large bulk of multidisciplinary research and discussion concerning these issues I have to refer to this book. I have previously published a relatively short sketch in English: 'Private Law 2000: Small Stories on Morality Through Liability', in: T. Wilhelmsson and S. Hurri, *From Dissonance to Sense: Welfare State Expectations, Privatisation and Private Law* (Aldershot, Ashgate, 1999), 221.

to the public). One may even say that there is a growing democratic demand for understandable legal language. The use both of legal procedure and focused legislation for dealing with typically concrete and fragmented demands for reform in late modernity adds to the pressure on the abstract legal concept structure.

In the area of contract law, the call for a legal language which reflects 'real-life circumstances' does not have precisely the same consequence as in the sphere of tort law. Only when speaking about rules on consumer rights, the emphasis can and should be on real life as experienced by the ordinary citizen. The need for a legal language which can be understood directly by the consumers, without interpretation by a lawyer, is often stressed in this context.[62] In a purely commercial context, however, 'real life' would mean rather the realities of commercial life expressed in a language which the actors of this sector can understand. This should not be read as a plea for substituting one expert language, the abstract language of the law, with another expert language, the language of business. I only recognise that a process of intrusion of business language into the legal language is clearly taking place, and to some extent probably has to be accepted. Of course, all specialised expert languages pose certain problems for democratic decision-making.

A legal order which strives to make an open account for the arguments used in solving concrete legal problems in a language which the media, the public and the commercial world can understand should not be locked into a very abstract and self-referential legal language. If the lawyers want to continue to play a role in discussing the real problems of society they have to leave, or at least open the doors to, their conceptual ivory towers. In a world where the belief in large homogeneous ethical systems has vanished, the idea of a Homogeneous Grand System of Law, based on a system of concepts mainly built on its internal logic, cannot be very convincing. A society which has lost its belief in the possibility of a complete and perfect Utopian world does not continue to dream of a complete and perfect legal order.

---

[62] Recently in the Green Paper on European Union Consumer Protection, COM (2001) 531 final, 15 the Commission suggests that 'provision could be made for non-binding practical guidance to be developed in user-friendly language'. Of course, this task is much easier if the rules and legal structure themselves are as far as possible written in a user-friendly language.

23. Information Problems Caused by Regulatory Competition, and Their Solution: International Standard Codes

*Gerrit De Geest**

I. INTRODUCTION

In the past few years, a lively debate has taken place on the desirability of further legal harmonization in Europe. This debate was triggered by the publication of the first version of *Principles of European Contract Law* by the Lando Commission,[1] and has been intensified by the recent Green Book.[2] This debate, however, has not led to a consensus.

The main argument for harmonization is the reduction of transaction costs. These 'transaction costs' are the legal information costs generated by the diversity of legal systems. Proponents of European codes basically argue that law harmonization would reduce these legal information costs and hence facilitate cross-border trade within Europe. The main argument of opponents is that law harmonization would eliminate the competition between legal systems. Without such competition, the incentives to make good law could be undermined, and – even more importantly – valuable experiments would no longer take place, and thus it would become much harder to learn what the best legal rules are. In addition, it is argued, legal diversity can reflect different preferences of citizens.

The lack of consensus as to whether harmonization is desirable is largely due to a different weighing of both problems (reduction of transaction costs versus destruction of regulatory diversity).

In this article, it is argued that it is possible to achieve the best of both worlds if a new type of codification were to be used – international standard codes – and legislators would be put under a number of informational duties. I define

---

* Professor of Law and Economics, Economic Institute/CIAV, Utrecht University, and School of Law, Ghent University.

1 Lando and Beale (eds.), *The Principles of European Contract Law. Part I: Performance, Non-Performance and Remedies*, (Dordrecht, Martinus Nijhoff, 1995); Lando and Beale (eds.), *Principles of European Contract Law, Part I and II*, (The Hague, Kluwer Law International, 2000).

2 Communication from the Commission to the Council and the European Parliament on European Contract Law, 11.07.2001, COM(2001) 398 final.

S. Grundmann and J. Stuyck (eds.), An Academic Green Paper on European Contract Law, 373–385 'international standard codes' as codes containing detailed rules that are declared to be valid in all countries unless a country explicitly drafts an alternative rule. Standard codes define standard settings for legislators and other rule makers, just as suppletive rules are standard settings for contract drafters.

I also argue that the enormous legal information costs European citizens are currently faced with are no unavoidable side-effect of legal diversity. These huge legal information costs are the result of the way in which legal information is organized. They indicate that there is such a thing as a 'market failure' on the market for legal rules. This market failure should be no surprise, given the fact that until now the market for legal rules has not been regulated.

This article is organized as follows. In section 2 I briefly explain what the proposal to elaborate 'international standard codes' involves, why standard codes have to be extremely detailed, and briefly discuss a number of technical issues raised by this new type of codes. International standard codes are only one part of the proposal. The second part is the introduction of information prescriptions for law-makers. Nowadays, law-makers (legislators, courts) are free to make any new rules they want but are not obliged to provide citizens with accessible information on these rules. I argue that rules that deviate from the international standard rules should only be allowed if law-makers clearly indicate to what extent they differ. In section 3 I briefly describe these informational duties: law-makers should indicate for every rule (a) for which standard rule the rule is an alternative (in other words they should locate their rule in the extremely detailed international classification system); (b) precisely describe the rule; (c) in English; (d) in electronic form, according to well-specified information technology standards.

Sections 4 to 7 focus on the core of this article: the economics of the imperfectly functioning market for legal rules. I identify three major market failures that cause the insufficient provision of legal information and hence undermine regulatory competition. The first market failure is discussed in section 4: the absence of proper incentives for law-makers to provide full information on their rules to their clients. The second market failure is analysed in section 5: insufficient standardization. Information costs can be substantially reduced if information is organized according to a detailed standardized classification system and according to standardized information technology norms. On unregulated markets (like the market for regulators) standardization typically takes place too little and too late. In section 6 I argue that law-makers as a group would benefit from a form of public good provision: international standard codes. Since many, if not most, legal rules do not differ substantially among legal systems, law-makers would save an enormous amount of costs if 'standard settings' were drafted, so that they would have to draft the diverting rules only. Such a public good provision takes place on the market-for-contracts. Suppletive goods, produced by the national law-makers and thus financed by all contract drafters, allow contract drafters to save money by having to focus solely on diverting clauses.

In section 7 I analyse whether the failures on the market for legal rules can be corrected by the market for legal services. Little is to be expected from the market for legal services, given the difficulties for actors on that market to fully internalize the benefits of their investments in information.

Finally, section 8 focuses on the role Europe could play in this respect. Instead of delivering new directives or investing in vague tip-of-the-iceberg codifications, European institutions might consider working with extremely detailed European standard codes that may evolve into world standard codes at a later stage.

II. Solution: Extremely Detailed International Standard Codes

Recently I have proposed a new type of codification that would allow regulatory competition while keeping the legal information problems to a minimum: international standard codes.[3] These codes are sets of detailed rules that are to be considered as standard settings for all legal systems; that is, they are presumed to apply in all countries, unless (and to the extent that) a country clearly declares its intent to deviate from one or more articles. For practical reasons, the international standard code (covering the whole body of law) *can consist of several (hundreds of) smaller standard codes* (e.g. one on product liability, one on servitudes, etc.).

The fact that individual states have the right to deviate from the rules of the international standard code does not imply that the international standard rules are inherently suppletive to parties. International standard codes create default settings for law-makers, but this should not be confused with 'default rules'. The latter (also called 'suppletive rules') are rules that are binding to contracting parties only if they do not explicitly agree to deviating clauses in the contracts ('default rules' or 'suppletive rules' are, then, opposed to imperative rules or 'regulation' which are mandatory to parties).

The rules of international standard codes can be imperative. They can state, for instance, that some types of clauses are void, yet the philosophy behind international standard rules is somewhat similar to the philosophy behind suppletive rules. The former save costs to legislators, in that they only have to draft deviating rules; the latter save costs to contract parties, in that they only have to draft deviating clauses. States can opt out of every rule of the standard code. In that respect, international standard codes are also international 'opt-out

---

3   This section is based on De Geest, 'Towards Extremely Detailed International Standard Codes', Working Paper (Utrecht University, Economic Institute/CIAV, 2001), in which the technical aspects of international standard codes are discussed in more detail.

codes'. However, they should not be confused with the idea of 'optional codes' (Green Book)[4] which give contracting parties an additional choice of law.

There are two arguments why an international standard code should be *extremely detailed*. The first is that current law is extremely detailed. Over time, legal rules have been articulated for hundreds of thousands of practical problems. For citizens it is important to have easy access to them all. To put it differently, possible clients of the legal system have to be able to know the product they buy (by living in a state or choosing a state's contract law). Providing full information is a matter of good information management. An international standard code (covering one particular branch of the law) may well consist of more than 100,000 rules. A code with so many rules may look unrealistically detailed, but one should not forget that modern legal systems are as detailed. Most of these detailed rules cannot be found in traditional civil or commercial codes (which give a tip-of-the-iceberg view only), but in other legislative acts, administrative acts, published cases and doctrinal writings, spread over thousands of publications. The idea of having extremely detailed codes is no more than the idea that codes have to retrieve one of their original functions: providing the citizen with information on the existing legal rules.

This first argument for extremely detailed codes applies to codes in general. The second argument applies to international standard codes in particular: not all states have legal rules for the same issues. It is possible that state 1 has a legal rule for problem A and B but not for C, while state 2 has a legal rule for B and C but not for A. A code that defines default settings for law-makers and attempts to be complete should have a rule for A, B and C.

In addition, it is possible that the source of rule B is a legislative act in state 1, while its source is case law in state 2. Therefore, international standard codes should not be limited to one source of law – legislation. This does not mean, however, that rules from case law should attain legislative status once they have been incorporated in the code. For each rule, an *authority-to-change-the-rule* field needs to be completed. This is the institution (e.g. the parliament, the government, the supreme court, or even 'any court') that is competent to change the rule. (Though the international default code should also have default settings as to who can change a specific article, states should have the freedom to have deviating change settings. For instance, the Belgian legal system might agree with the international rules on penalty clauses, but might determine that these rules can be changed only by the parliament, while the default setting might be 'changeable by the supreme court of every country for every country'.) The authority-to-change field also defines whether private parties can change the rules for their own contracts. In other words, whether the rules are suppletive or mandatory.

---

4   Communication from the Commission to the Council and the European Parliament on European Contract Law, 11.07.2001, COM(2001) 398 final, sub 4.4.

The lack of an *authority-to-change* field is the major shortcoming of codifications up to now. Codes normally have two effects, one of which is unintended. The first, intended effect is that legal information is structured. The second, unintended effect is that rules from all legal sources (case law, customary law, doctrine) are transformed into legislation. Since changing a legislative rule is much more difficult and expensive than creating a precedent, this transformation hinders further legal development. The authors of some modern codes were aware of this problem, and tried to prevent legal stagnation by incorporating mainly general principles and leaving details out of the codes. This solution comes at a price: the informational function of codes was nearly lost. Is it not simpler to incorporate detailed rules into codes and declare in an authority-to-change field that these detailed rules can later be modified by courts?

Standard codes do not yet exist. Even extremely detailed rules codes would be more or less a novelty. International classification systems exist, though for law the usual classification indexes are not detailed enough. Is it possible to describe the law with such a level of detail? Yes it is, because it is already described with such a level of detail. The problem is that these descriptions are currently spread over many thousands of publications.

Though the default code should be as detailed as possible, it can never be complete. Therefore, for each element in the classification system (e.g. penalty clauses), it should have a *'fill up gaps' field*. This would allow gap fillers (like courts) to add new detailed rules without having to pretend they just interpreted an existing rule.

To describe detailed rules, you need concepts, and to structure detailed rules, you need a classification system (a structure). Therefore, international standard codes inevitably need to work with standardized concepts and a standardized structure. Yet, classification systems and legal concepts are just scientific tools. There is no reason to freeze science. Scientific innovation and competition should be allowed. It is important to stress that the classification system is just one of many. Every legal scholar is free to order the rules in an alternative way. From an IT viewpoint, proposing a new classification system is the equivalent of programming a new interface to the database. Since the international standard codes and the deviating national rules are organized in a strict way, it will be easier for legal scientists to try out alternative classification systems. In that respect, the international standard codes foster scientific competition with respect to structures.

A final practical issue is the choice of the standard rules. Suppose that some countries use rule A while others rule B. On the basis of what criteria should the international standard rule be chosen? Law and economics literature suggests two solutions.[5] One is to use a majoritarian criterion: simply choose the rule

---

[5]   Craswell, 'Contract Law: General Theories', in Bouckaert and De Geest, *Encyclopaedia of Law and Economics, Vol. III*, (Cheltenham, Edward Elgar, 2000), nr. 4000; De Geest, *Economische analyse van het contracten- en quasi-contractenrecht: een onderzoek naar de wetenschappelijke waarde van de rechtseconomie*, (Antwerpen, Maklu, 1994), Ch. 7.

that is valid in most states. This means that fewer states will have to incur the costs of announcing and formulating an alternative rule (transaction cost saving argument). A second criterion could the optimal rule criterion: simply choose the best rule. 'Best' should refer to the content (result) as well as to the best technical solution to reach the result.

III. SOLUTION: INFORMATION PRESCRIPTIONS FOR LAW-MAKERS

International standard codes are only one part of our proposal. The second part is the introduction of information prescriptions for law-makers. Nowadays, law-makers (legislators, courts) are free to make any new rules they want, but are not obliged to provide the citizen with accessible information on these rules. As the next sections will show, an unregulated market-for-legal-rules leads to an underprovision of information. To remedy this underprovision, four *information duties* for law-makers need to be introduced.

The first prescription is that rules that deviate from the international standard rules should only be allowed if law-makers clearly indicate to what extent they differ. The alternative rule needs to be described in a non-vague way. To give rule-makers an incentive to do so, their rules will be interpreted, in case of doubt, in favour of the international standard law. This is the equivalent of the rule in contract law according to which unclear contract clauses are construed against the drafter.[6] To describe the differing rules, either the international standard terminology is to be used or other legal terms that are properly defined.

The second prescription is that differing rules should be classified according to the classification system of the international standard codes (besides, every law-maker can structure its legal rules also using other classification systems).

The third prescription is that the rules are also described in English. In addition, law-makers are free to use other languages. The basic idea is that all world citizens should be able to know the legal rule. There should be no requirement to study the language of the national law-maker first.

The fourth prescription is that these rules are published in electronic form, on the Internet, according to the information technology prescriptions of the standard code. (In addition, every law-maker can publish its rules also in other ways.)

This duty holds for all legal rules, whether its source is legislation, case law, or another source of law. This implies, for instance, that when a court creates a precedent it is also obliged to formulate the new rule in a clear way.

These four information duties allow people from all over the world to check

---

[6] As for Belgian law, for instance, art. 1162 of the Civil Code states that contract clauses have to be construed against the party that benefited from the clause. There is a tendency in Belgian case law to read this sentence as construed against the *drafter* (Kruithof, Bocken, De Ly and De Temmerman, 'Overzicht van rechtspraak (1981–1992) Verbintenissen', 31 *Tijdschrift voor Privaatrecht* [1994], 171–721, at 452).

easily, for instance, whether Greece follows the normal rules with respect to penalty clauses, and if not, what the Greek rules are.

IV. MARKET FAILURE 1: LACK OF INCENTIVE OF NATIONAL LAW-MAKERS TO PROVIDE INFORMATION TO NON-CITIZENS

Everyday life experience tells us that acquiring information on specific rules from another European system is a nightmare. If you are not fluent in Italian, German or Greek, it is simply impossible to find out how Italian, German or Greek law solves a specific legal problem. Even if you are fluent in the national language, it may take years before you are able to find your way in the chaotic library called the Italian, German, or Greek 'legal system'. Even for trained local lawyers, it is quite time consuming to find the legal answer and quite easy to overlook the relevant legislature or relevant cases. So if there is such a thing as 'regulatory competition' within Europe, it is like a market for cars where consumers cannot even get a picture of the cars that are offered in that market.

Before starting our analysis we have to spend a few lines on categorizing the current system. Is it correct to describe the current system within Europe as a form of 'regulatory competition'? Notwithstanding all informational problems, it is correct to state that rule-making in Europe is essentially decentralized. The subsidiarity principle, according to which the European rules are considered as an exception, is still central. One of the cornerstones since the White Paper of 1985[7] is the obligation for member states to recognize equivalent standards of the member state of origin. This is much more than a practical solution for sectors where European rules have not yet been elaborated. The core idea is that national rules are the principle, and European harmonization an exception. Harmonization normally has the form of minimum harmonization, still leaving some room for diversity, though only in one direction. With respect to suppletive contract law, there is even more regulatory competition for two reasons. First, the freedom of states to makes their own rules is hardly restricted here. Second, international private law allows contracting parties to freely choose any legal system – a choice that is restricted for imperative rules. In summary, the current European system is in essence one of diversity.

The economic literature has emphasized the similarities between legal systems competition and normal market competition. Two authors laid the foundations: Hayek and Tiebout. Hayek developed an evolutionary view on the rise and fall of institutions. According to Hayek, in the long run the fittest institution survives. Tiebout bridged the gap between collective good-producing units (like states) and markets. According to Tiebout, states have no perfect monopoly, since citizens are free to move to another state. This voting-by-feet[8] creates an incentive

---

[7]   White Paper on the Completion of the Internal Market by 1985, COM(85) 310.
[8]   Tiebout, 'A pure theory of local expenditures', (1956) 64 *Journal of Political Economy*, 416–424.

for states to provide the optimal set of (collective) services and goods. It also allows individuals with similar tastes to group together in a collective unit that provides public goods that best fits their preferences. In such a model, differences between states reflect different preferences of their citizens. The general ideas of Tiebout and Hayek have been applied to jurisdictional competition in numerous papers.[9] It has been applied to antitrust law,[10] environmental law,[11] and corporate law[12] in particular.

Frey and Eichenberger proposed an extreme model of regulatory competition: 'functional, overlapping competing jurisdictions' (FOCJ), where citizens can choose between different legal systems for every governmental function separately.[13] Van den Bergh applied the regulatory competition idea to European law. He reinterpreted the subsidiarity principle as a presumption in favour of regulatory competition.[14]

In my opinion, the economic literature has not fully analysed the analogies between markets for legal rules and markets for other goods and services. For the latter, it is generally accepted that there is such a thing as 'market failures'. One of the major market failures is asymmetric information. It is generally accepted that markets need some degree of regulation to function properly.

The high information costs on legal rules, surprisingly, are not considered as signs of a market failure. Most authors do not pay attention to legal information

---

[9]   E.g. Padoa-Schioppa, *Efficiency, Stability and Equity* (Oxford, Oxford University Press, 1987); Siebert, 'The Harmonization Process in Europe: Prior Agreement or a Competitive Process?' in Siebert, *The Competition of the Internal Market* (Tübingen, J.C.B. Mohr, 1990); Vanberg and Kerber, 'Institutional Competition among Jurisdictions: An Evolutionary Approach', (1994) 5 *Constitutional Political Economy*, 193–219; Ogus, 'Competition between National Legal Systems. A Contribution of Economic Analysis to Comparative Law', (1999) 48 *ICLQ*, 405–418.

[10] Easterbrook, 'Antitrust and the Economics of Federalism', (1983) 26 *Journal of Law and Economics*, 23–50.

[11] Oates and Schwab, 'Economic Competition among Jurisdictions: Efficiency Enhancing or Distortion Inducing?', (1988) 35 *J. of Public Economics*, 333–354; Revesz, 'Rehabilitating Interstate Competition: Rethinking the 'Race to the Bottom' Rationale for Federal Environmental Regulation', (1992) 67 *New York University Law Review*, 1210–1255.

[12] E.g. Winter, 'State Law, Shareholder Protection, and the Theory of the Corporation', (1977) 6 *Journal of Legal Studies*, 271 *et seq.*

[13] Frey and Eichenberger, 'FOCJ: Competitive Governments for Europe', (1996) 16 *International Review of Law and Economics*, 315–327; Frey and Eichenberger, 'To Harmonize or to Compete? That's not the Question', (1996) 60 *Journal of Public Economics*, 335–349; Casella and Frey, 'Federalism and Clubs. Towards an Economic Theory of Overlapping Political Jurisdiction', (1992) 36 *European Economic Review*, 639–646.

[14] Van den Bergh, 'The Subsidiarity Principle in European Community Law: Some Insights from Law and Economics', (1994) 1 *Maastricht J. of Eur. and Comp. L.*, 337–366; Van den Bergh, 'Subsidiarity as an Economic Demarcation Principle and the Emergence of European Private Law', (1998) 5 *Maastricht J. of Eur. and Comp. L.*, 129–152.

problems. Frey[15] is an exception. He acknowledges the problem, but does not consider it as market failure but rather as an unavoidable consequence of consumers having more choice (normal feature of competition). In his viewpoint, legal information costs do not differ from information costs on other markets, where consumers are confronted with plenty of choice. The solution is not to limit the choices available. If necessary, the government or private firms can offer guidance to the consumer – according to Frey.

Will similar informational problems occur on both types of markets? Are the incentives of private parties not different from public rule-makers? I will first take a closer look at the incentives of private parties behind informational shortcomings on normal markets. Second I will analyse the incentives of states to provide information on their rules to citizens and non-citizens.

On markets for 'normal' goods and services, the seller has in most cases more information than the buyer (asymmetric information) because he has produced the good, or gathered information on it as a byproduct of owning it before. Why do sellers not spontaneously reveal their information to buyers, in the absence of legal pressure? Uninformed buyers make an estimation of the value of the item. If by giving more information to the buyer, this valuation would decrease, the seller has an incentive not to give that information, as it would reduce the price of the item. So the fundamental source of informational problems is the profit maximizing behaviour of sellers.

What about the market for legal rules? Here the 'seller' is a public authority, and not an egotistic, profit-maximizing individual. Public authorities are there – in theory – to pursue the 'general' interest. In practice, public authorities consist of individuals, and their motives may be different. The public choice literature has produced overwhelming evidence of suboptimal incentives in bureaucracies and public enterprizes. Civil servants have no natural incentive to deliver an optimal quality and quantity of goods and services, unless they are forced to by the management, i.e. the politicians. But politicians in turn have an incentive to intervene only if they benefit from it in terms of votes. Until recently, reducing legal information costs was no point of discussion in electoral campaigns. The high legal information costs for citizens is the result. Recently, this issue is appearing on the political agenda in some countries. Slowly, progress is being made with respect to the simplification of legal rules and the improved availability of legal rules for citizens.

For non-citizens, i.e. persons who have no voting rights because they live in other countries, the situation is different. Politicians cannot earn votes by offering services to persons who cannot vote for them. Therefore, politicians have no direct electoral incentive to invest in reducing legal information costs for citizens of other states. Campaigning politicians will not promise to invest in translating

---

[15] Frey, 'A Europe of Variety, not Harmonization', in: Josselin and Marciano, *The Economics of Harmonizing Law in Europe* (Cheltenham, Edward Elgar, 2001).

the legal rules in English so that people from other countries have better access to them.

Do politicians have a budgetary interest, in that the use of the legal system by outsiders generates an income to the state? They have not, for three reasons. First, there is no intellectual property on legal rules, and as a consequence, one cannot make users pay (establishing intellectual property rights on legal rules is undesirable for the same reason that awarding patents on scientific theories is undesirable). Second, legal users may desire to use the court system of that state, because of its superior knowledge of that legal system (e.g. if you use German contract law, you may prefer German courts). States, however, do not make a profit on courts. On the contrary, they usually subsidize courts. Therefore, outsiders using a legal system are a cost to that legal system. Third, contrary to hotels and restaurants, states have no strong interest in attracting voters-by-feet. Though immigrants pay taxes, they also consume public funding. Though an increase of the population may create positive network externalities (more people living together may result in economics of scale), it also has negative effects by crowding scarce space. Under what condition the existing citizens of a state benefit from attracting immigrants (i.e. voters-by-feet) is a complex issue, but the fact that many countries put barriers on immigration indicates that the opportunity to attract immigrants does not create sufficient incentives to make the legal system more accessible to outsiders (unlike private firms, who usually try to increase demand for their products). In rare cases, users indirectly pay for the use of the legal system, by paying taxes. For instance, Delaware corporations pay corporate taxes to Delaware. In these cases only, states have an incentive to make their legal system accessible to outsiders.

In summary, there is such a thing as a 'market failure' with respect to providing information. Regulation of the market is necessary. As explained in section 3, this regulation should consist in a general obligation for law-makers to provide full (and clear) information on their products (legal rules). While the duty to reveal information is a duty that exists in all markets (one example is the general duty for sellers to reveal latent defects), the duty to provide *full information* (on all details) is going further than most regulatory informational requirements, where only the most important elements have to be revealed (for instance, a seller of tables is not obliged to describe the chemical components and dimensions of every screw that is used). The reason why such a far-reaching informational duty should be introduced for law rules is the nature of the product. Legal rules are techniques to change human behaviour. Legal rules can only change behaviour if the human beings for whom they are designed are able to know the legal rules.

V. MARKET FAILURE 2: STANDARDIZATION FAILURE

The fact that legal information costs are so high is mainly due to the chaotic organization of that information and the way it is published. The way of organizing legal information is not standardized among countries. Every legal system has its own structure, concepts and publication strategies. Numerous comparative lawyers have shown that with respect to the content, national rules differ very little. They are providing similar solutions to similar problems. The main differences between legal systems are differences with respect to form and technique. Yet, the fact that these differences continue to exist proves, in our opinion, that states have insufficient incentives to remove artificial differences. In short, there is a lack of international standardization with respect to classification systems, legal concepts and publication (and information technology) standards.

Given the literature on network externalities and standardization, this should not be a surprise.[16] The same problem exists in most markets. Spontaneous standardization does not take place, or takes too much time to take place, or results in the wrong standards being chosen. Two mechanisms are responsible for this special type of market failure. First, using a standard causes network externalities: every user generates a positive effect on other users (the more users, the better for all users). Externalities in general cause distortions. Second, developing standards involves costs. Since the whole industry benefits from the standard, there is a public good problem involved. Individual firms have insufficient incentives to invest in developing standards.

VI. MARKET FAILURE 3: STANDARD RULES AS NON-PROVIDED PUBLIC GOOD

As explained above, modern legal systems are extremely elaborate. They consist of hundreds of thousands of detailed legal rules. Obliging all states to carefully describe their existing rules in detail would require enormous investments. These investments for a great deal would be wasteful: since most legal rules are similar in most countries, the descriptions would largely be overlapping. The cheapest method to achieve a full description of all legal systems consists in departing from standard codes. They describe rules that apply in most countries. International standard codes not only reduce citizens' legal information costs, they also drastically reduce legal production costs. Just as suppletive rules in contract law make life easier for contracting parties, because their contracts have to include only the rules that differ from the suppletive rules, international

---

[16] Page and Lopatka, 'Network externalities', in: B. Bouckaert and G. De Geest, *Encyclopaedia of Law and Economics* (Cheltenham, Edward Elgar, 2000), 964. See also Van den Bergh (n. 14), 129–152; Van den Bergh, 'Regulatory Competition or Harmonisation of Laws? Guidelines for the European Regulator', in: Josselin and Marciano, *The Economics of Harmonizing Law in Europe* (Cheltenham, Edward Elgar, 2001) (pleading for standardizing legal concepts in order to reduce legal information costs and improve regulatory competition).

standard codes make life easier for legislators, since they only have to draft and promulgate the rules that deviate from the international standard rules. These reduced legal production costs involve enormous initial savings and facilitate regulatory competition and innovation even more.

Since all countries benefit from international standard codes, another market failure occurs. International standard codes have public good characteristics. Individual states have insufficient incentives to do the job for the rest of the world. That is why an important role has to be played by a major international organization, like the European Union.

VII. CAN THE MARKET FOR LEGAL SERVICES BE EXPECTED TO REMEDY THESE MARKET FAILURES?

Market forces create problems but also solve problems. In the Green Book[17] the Commission wonders to what extent one may expect markets to improve the current situation. Markets can refer to the market for legal systems and to the market for legal services. We have already discussed the former. Can law firms, consultancy firms, and professional organizations remove the trade barriers caused by legal information problems? While these firms and organizations can reduce legal information problems (an exporter does not himself have to study all legal systems where his products are distributed, but can buy legal advice from specialized professionals), they cannot fully remove the useless costs caused by an inefficient information system. First, what these firms produce is information. Markets for information typically work imperfectly, especially if copying information by others cannot be prevented. Nobody can stop parties from using standard contracts, without the consent of the original contract drafters. The difficulties of excluding non-payers results in the underprovision of these products. It is just another public good problem.

A second source of market failure is – again – understandardization. The costs of collecting and summarizing legal information largely depends on the way primary sources (legislation and case law) are structured and published. We have already explained why optimal standardization is unlikely to take place on markets. This also holds for the market for legal services. Without this standardization, lawyers are working in an inefficient environment.

VIII. THE ROLE OF EUROPE: EUROPEAN STANDARD CODES AS AN ALTERNATIVE TO EUROPEAN DIRECTIVES

The European Union could play a major role in setting up international standard codes, standardizing legal concepts and creating informational duties for states,

---

[17] Communication from the Commission to the Council and the European Parliament on European Contract Law, 11.07.2001, COM(2001) 398 final, sub 4.1.

at least for European Member States. The European Union is a collective actor that is well placed to solve collective action problems within Europe. As I explained in the previous sections, international standardization and public good problems between states require a supranational authority to be solved.

The European Union could finance the drafting of extremely detailed 'European standard codes'. They would apply in all EU countries, unless a Member State clearly and explicitly substitutes a different rule for the default setting. If (minimum) harmonization is considered as desirable (to solve race-to-the-bottom problems), some rules can be considered as unchangeable for EU Member States. Technically speaking, the 'authority-to-change' field for EU countries are the EU institutions only.

This solution solves the problem of Member States translating 'directives' too slowly into their legal system (if they do not do it in time the standard rule applies as long as no other rule is published). It also creates more legal certainty for citizens.

Standard Codes are a much better technique for solving legal information problems than directives. Directives are the worst of both worlds. They limit regulatory competition but do not substantially improve legal information costs problems. Dutch suppliers, for instance, have a general idea of what Italian product liability law is like (fundamentally more or less similar to Dutch product liability law), but if they want to know the exact detailed rules, their information costs remain as substantial as before. Directives can create a (minimum) harmonization. As far as the main concern is to improve legal information problems, directives are not the best technique.

24.   Toward a Multi-Layered Contract Law for Europe

*Jan Smits**

I. INTRODUCTION

There is no question that the European Commission's *Communication on European Contract Law*[1] is to be seen as the starting point of a new era in the discussion on a uniform law of contract for Europe. Until now, this discussion has been characterised by its academic character: whether a uniform or harmonised private law for Europe should be possible and what its contents should be, has been debated in the scholarly literature of the last decade. These questions, however, did not become important issues for European politics or even for legal practice. Thus, the calls from the European Parliament in 1989 and 1994[2] that work on a European Civil Code should begin, were not answered by the Commission or the Council for a long time. This has changed with the Tampere European Council of 1999, in which 'an overall study on the need to approximate Member State's legislation in civil matters' was summoned.[3] Now, the 2001 Communication invites all interested parties to give their opinion on the future of contract law in Europe. This kick-off for a political debate is most important.

In this paper, I will discuss one of the options for the future development of European contract law as sketched in the Communication. The most interesting options that are sketched in the Communication, can be distinguished in the option of a step-by-step harmonisation of consumer contract law (as practised in the past), the option of creating a binding Code of Contracts and finally the option of having an optional set of rules to which Member States or even contracting parties can adhere if they wish to do so. In my view, this last option is the most interesting one, in view not only of the present state of contract law in Europe, but also in view of its desired development.

This paper will first discuss the present state of contract law in Europe. In section 2, several diverging tendencies within this contract law are stressed. Then, in section 3, it is pointed out that the now often-defended 'generalising' approach

---

*   J.M. Smits is Professor of European Private Law at Maastricht University.

[1]   Communication from the Commission to the Council and the European Parliament on European Contract Law, COM(2001) 398 final.
[2]   (EC) OJ [1989] C 158/400 and (EC) OJ [1994] C 205/518.
[3]   See the Presidency Conclusions at http://www.europa.eu.int/council/off/conclu/oct99en.pdf.

S. Grundmann and J. Stuyck (eds.), An Academic Green Paper on European Contract Law, 387–398
© 2002 *Kluwer Law International. Printed in Great Britain.*

toward European contract law (this is the approach that seeks to formulate 'principles' of private law with a view to having national legal systems replaced by these – option 2) is not in line with this approach. Section 4 seeks to find out whether the approach of an 'Optional Code' is to be accommodated within present-day contract law and, if so, in what way.

II. GENERAL VIEW ON THE DEVELOPMENT OF EUROPEAN CONTRACT LAW: DIVERGENCE INSTEAD OF GENERALISATION

1. General

Any discussion on the future of contract law in Europe should start with an assessment of the present state of affairs in the national legal systems and at the European level. Present-day contract law is, after all, the basis on which any harmonisation of unification should take place. My evaluation of present-day contract law in Europe is entirely different from those who try to draft general principles of contract law with a view to have these replace national legal systems. In my view, contract law is more characterised by diverging tendencies than by a tendency of generalisation. Leaving aside historical aspects of the development toward a general law of contract since the sixteenth century,[4] the twentieth century has been witness of increasing divergence in contract law. At least four diverging tendencies can be identified in most, if not all, of Europe's legal systems.

2. First Diverging Tendency: the Influence of Directives on National Contract Law

In the first place, there is a tendency of divergence on a very practical level. The most successful way of Europeanising national contract law up to now has been through the use of European directives. Since 1985, a whole range of directives has been issued. These concern in particular protection of consumers in the field of doorstep sale,[5] consumer credit,[6] package travel,[7] unfair contract terms,[8]

---

[4] See J.M. Smits, 'The Future of European Contract Law: on Diversity and the Temptation of Elegance', (discussion paper presented at the conference 'Towards a European Ius Commune in Legal Education and Research', Maastricht, October 2001).

[5] Council Directive 85/577 of 20 December 1985 to protect the consumer in respect of contracts negotiated away from business premises, (EC) OJ [1985] L 372/31.

[6] Council Directive 87/102 of 22 December 1986 for the approximation of the laws, regulations and administrative provisions of the Member States concerning consumer credit, (EC) OJ [1987] L 42/48.

[7] Council Directive 90/314 of 13 June 1990 on package travel, package holidays and package tours, (EC) OJ [1990] L 158/59.

[8] Council Directive 93/13 of 5 April 1993 on unfair terms in consumer contracts, (EC) OJ [1993] L 95/29.

distance contracts[9] and sale of goods[10] as well as regulation of self-employed commercial agents,[11] timeshare,[12] electronic commerce[13] and combating late payment in commercial transactions.[14] An ever-greater part of contract law is thus governed by European legislation, be it of an often non-consistent[15] and sometimes disturbing[16] nature. This harmonisation leads away from any generalising approach because contract law at the national level is ever less governed by general principles and subdivided into separate parts, each having their own rules.[17]

This gradually leads to something that is systematically entirely different from national contract law as we have known it over the last few centuries. It used to be so that for example German, French, Dutch and English contract law were supposed to be governed by general principles: common rules governing the formation of contracts, governing the remedies of the contracting parties, governing the way of interpretation, etc., *regardless* of the type of contract involved. The Europeanisation of these national legal systems through directives leads to the contrary: not to a *uniform*, but to a *diverse* contract law, in which, for example, important remedies in case of breach of consumer contracts for the sale of movable goods[18] are governed by different rules than these same remedies in case of other contracts (commercial contracts or consumer contracts *not* for the sale of movables). Likewise, the rules governing unfair terms in consumer

---

9   Council Directive 97/7 of 20 May 1997 on the protection of consumers in respect of distance contracts, (EC) OJ [1997] L 144/19.

10   Council Directive 1999/44 of 25 May 1999 on certain aspects of the sale of consumer goods and associated guarantees, (EC) OJ [1999] L 171/12.

11   Council Directive 86/653 of 18 December 1986 on the co-ordination of the laws of the Member States relating to self-employed commercial agents, (EC) OJ [1986] L 382/17.

12   Council Directive 94/47 of 26 October 1994 on the protection of purchasers in respect of certain aspects of contracts relating to the purchase of the right to use immovable properties on a timeshare basis, (EC) OJ [1994] L 280/83.

13   Council Directive 2000/31 of 8 June 2000 on certain legal aspects of information society service, in particular electronic commerce, in the Internal market, (EC) OJ [2000] L 178/1.

14   Council Directive 2000/35 of 29 June 2000 on combating late payment in commercial transactions, (EC) OJ [2000] L 200/35. All the above directives have been reproduced in Dutch in J.H.M. van Erp and J.M. Smits (eds.), *Bronnen Europees privaatrecht* (Den Haag, Boom, 2001).

15   Also recognized in the Communication: COM(2001) 398 final, 15 *et seq.*

16   See in particular G. Teubner, 'Legal Irritants: Good Faith in British Law or How Unifying Law Ends Up in New Divergences', (1998) 61 *MLR* 11 (on the disturbing effect of the Unfair Terms Directive on English law).

17   Cf. J.M. Smits, 'A Principled Approach to European Contract Law?', (2000) 7 *Maastricht J. of Eur. and Comp. L.* 221.

18   Council Directive 1999/44 of 25 May 1999 on certain aspects of the sale of consumer goods and associated guarantees, (EC) OJ [1999] L 171/12.

contracts[19] are different from the ones governing unfair terms in other types of contracts, as there will in the near future be specific rules on the payment of debts for commercial transactions,[20] not covering consumer transactions. One could also point at the formation of distance contracts[21] or at the time of formation of contracts by electronic means,[22] both regulated in a different way than other contracts. This tendency toward divergence is reinforced by the fact that it is the European Court of Justice that has the final word on the interpretation of these directives.

I find it highly surprising that this fragmentation of contract law through directives is not taken into account by the drafters of the PECL or by those who defend any other generalising view on contract law. The PECL try to cover *all* contracts in a generalised way, reminiscent of the national private law systems as they have existed for several centuries. Even most of the directives were issued before the publication of the PECL have not been taken into account by the drafters. The directive on sale of consumer goods, as it has to be implemented by 1 January 2002, providing a detailed set of rules specifically for consumer sale of movables (including a hierarchy of actions), of course gives a much more accurate picture of what a European contract law looks like than the PECL (that still adopt the principle of free choice of action in art. 8:101).[23] The other way around, it seems that in drafting directives, the system and terminology of the PECL are not taken into account either.

3. Second Diverging Tendency: Consumer Contract Law and Business Contract Law – the Double Structure of the Law of Contract

A second tendency of divergence in contract law exists of the recognition that over time two types of contract law have come to exist in the various national legal systems. These are on the one hand a consumer contract law and on the other a specific law of contract for professional parties. Apart from the influence of European directives on contract law (mostly in the field of consumer protection), in the national legal systems a separate consumer contract law has come

---

[19]   Council Directive 93/13 of 5 April 1993 on unfair terms in consumer contracts, (EC) OJ [1993] L 95/29.

[20]   Council Directive 2000/35 of 29 June 2000 on combating late payment in commercial transactions, (EC) OJ [2000] L 200/35.

[21]   Council Directive 97/7 of 20 May 1997 on the protection of consumers in respect of distance contracts, (EC) OJ [1997] L 144/19. According to art. 6 of this directive, a consumer can still withdraw from the contract within 7 working days after delivery of the good.

[22]   Council Directive 2000/31 of 8 June 2000 on certain legal aspects of information society service, in particular electronic commerce, in the Internal market, (EC) OJ [2000] L 178/1.

[23]   Although the action for price reduction and the concept of fundamental non-performance have been laid down in both the PECL (art. 9:401 and art. 8:103 in connection with art. 9:301) and the directive.

to exist as well. This was put into place by specific statutes (in particular in the field of general conditions – like the German AGBG, the French art. L 132–1 ff. of the *Code de la Consommation* and the English Unfair Contract Terms Act – and consumer sale), but also by the national courts that tend to protect individual consumers to a much greater extent than they protect professional parties in interpreting contract terms, applying good faith, etc.

The emergence of a specific consumer contract law as distinguished from a business contract law does not come as a surprise. In 1952, Kessler pointed to the ambiguous character of contract law:[24] on the one hand it guarantees that parties are able to contract in freedom by attributing binding force to contracts validly entered into. On the other hand, it also regulates this freedom by not allowing *every* contract to be enforceable. This *double structure* of autonomy and intervention could also be phrased as one of economic rationality (efficiency) on the one hand and social rationality (distributive justice) on the other.[25]

Thus, part of contract law is governed by the morality of trade.[26] If parties contract in order to make profit, this has considerable influence on their contractual relationship. In trade, one usually does not contract in order to obtain a specific good, but is contract a means to a goal, the making of profit. If the debtor does not perform, it is only a case of bad luck: the loss should be foreseen and is usually covered by insurance.[27] If parties search for this economic rationality by making a commercial contract, the law should adjust to their wish. Thus, interpretation of contract terms should take place as literally as possible and the role of good faith should be restricted. Nineteenth century contract law was developed for this type of contracts.

This morality of trade is to be distinguished from the morality of the welfare state. There, making profit is not the goal of contracting, but it is to arrange for 'living, working, life and health'.[28] If the professional party does not act in conformity with the contract, the well-being of the individual may be threatened. Here, the law *has* to be paternalistic to serve its function. This new type of contract law is still in its infancy and should be further developed. For both moralities distinguished here, deserve to have their own contract law. What does

---

[24] F. Kessler, 'Freiheit und Zwang in nordamerikanischen Vertragsrecht', *Festschrift für Martin Wolff* (Tübingen, Mohr, 1952), 67.

[25] Cf. the writings of T. Wilhelmsson, for example 'Good Faith and the Duty of Disclosure in Commercial Contracting – The Nordic Experience', in: R. Brownsword, N. J. Hird and G. Howells (eds.), *Good Faith in Contract* (Dartmouth, Ashgate, 1999), 165; and Chr. Joerges, *The Europeanization of Private Law as a Rationalization Process and as a Contest of Disciplines* (EUI Working Paper Law No. 94/5), 15.

[26] J. Wightman, *Contract: A Critical Commentary* (London, Pluto Press, 1996), 96 *et seq.* distinguishes in this respect between 'personal' and 'commercial' contracts.

[27] Cf. Wightman (n. 26), 97.

[28] 'Wonen, werken, leven en gezondheid': see J.B.M. Vranken, *Mededelings-, informatie- en onderzoeks-plichten in het verbintenissenrecht* (Zwolle, W.E.J. Tjeenk Willink, 1989), nr. 27.

a contract with which one wants to make profit have in common with one to ensure enjoying the comfort of having a house to live in or having a medical insurance? What has marriage in common with buying shares in a company?

In any generalising approach toward contract law (such as the one envisaged by the Commission on European Contract Law), this double structure of contract law would not come to the surface. The PECL are intended to have value for any type of contract, regardless who the parties are.[29] This type of generalisation conceals the conflict between the two types of contract law. This may be done deliberately in order to give the principles universal value, or, in the words of Epstein about the people that contract law gives rules for:[30]

'These people are colorless, odorless, and timeless, of no known nationality, age, race or sex. These people are self-conscious abstractions known to be false as representations of people in the world, and useful precisely because they are so detached from any grubby set of particulars [...]. There is a cold, practical logic behind this remorseless search for abstractions. [...] This massive oversimplification of the social universe treats all persons as though they are as fungible as the letters of the alphabet, and thus ignores or rejects every effort to force the common law to take into account the difference between an individual worker of limited means and a huge industrial corporation.'

But even if done deliberately, the effect of it in the European context is doubtful. I do understand why, within one national legal system, courts are able to work with these abstractions: because they know about the national mentality underlying these. They know in their national context when the morality of the market becomes more important than the morality of the welfare state. This is the case because contract law's double structure of efficiency and distributive justice has led to a specific national fragile equilibrium that is in accordance with the socio-economic constellation of the country involved. This common socio-economic constellation is missing in Europe, which probably makes principles too abstract to build a European private law with.[31]

4. Third Diverging Tendency: the Diversity of Sources of European Private Law

Another tendency that leads rather to divergence than to unity in contract law, has to do with the sources of which European private law is made up. These sources are of a very diverse character. Apart from European directives (and

---

[29] This is different with the Unidroit Principles of International Commercial Contracts of 1994, although their content is virtually identical to the PECL.

[30] R. Epstein, *Simple Rules for a Complex World* (Cambridge, Mass., Harvard University Press, 1995), 73 *et seq.*

[31] Here, I agree with Teubner, (1998) 61 *MLR* 11, who suggests that the dividing lines in the law of Europe should not be the national frontiers, but the production regimes.

possibly regulations in the years to come), European contract law is made up of national rules on contract law (from both the national legislators and courts), international conventions, case law of the ECJ and incidentally even of the ECHR, and many other, more informal sources like commercial customary law, standardised general conditions, arbitral awards and standardised rules of professional organisations like the International Chamber of Commerce. This variety of sources is not represented adequately by any generalising approach and in particular not by laying down the present state of the law in static principles – even if these are 'designed to provide maximum flexibility and thus to accommodate future developments', as the drafters of the PECL state.[32] Looking at principles as able to replace Europe's national legal systems is adhering to the view that principles are the best way to describe the law. This may be true for some European systems, but definitely not for all. It is in any event not true for English law.[33]

5. Fourth Diverging Tendency: Multiculturalism

Finally, I hint at a fourth tendency of divergence. It is that today's Europe is not only diverse as to the different legal systems that are part of it, but that also *within* the Member States, the concepts of fairness and law many times differ. I am referring to the fact that as a result of immigration of large groups of foreigners over the last decades, there are now within the European Union many different ethno-cultural groups with their own views of what is fair. This not only applies to family law, but also to the law of contract: there *is* an Islamic view of when contracts should be binding and why this is so (just as there is a common law and a civil law view). Fairness nowadays is a pluralistic concept, or as Michael Walzer puts it:[34] 'There is no single set of primary or basic goods conceivable across all moral and material worlds – or, any such set would have to be conceived in terms so abstract that they would be of little use in thinking about particular distributions'.

The making of *general* principles, destined to govern all these different sets, is not in line with this cultural diversity. This has for a practical consequence that a future European Contract Law has to take these differences into account. The imposing of principles cannot contribute to this goal since principles are inherently unable to represent diversity, unless they are indeed – as Walzer puts it – 'abstract.'

---

[32] O. Lando and H. Beale (eds.), *Principles of European Contract Law, Parts I and II, Combined and Revised* (The Hague, Kluwer Law International, 2000), xxvii.

[33] For an elaborated version of this argument, see J.M. Smits, *The Good Samaritan in European Private Law* (Deventer, Kluwer, 2000).

[34] M. Walzer, *Spheres of Justice: a Defense of Pluralism and Equality* (New York, Basic Books, 1983), 8.

III. CONSEQUENCES OF DIVERGENCE FOR THE DEBATE ON EUROPEAN CONTRACT LAW

What does the above imply for the debate on the future of European contract law? In this section, I will focus on what a European contract law should definitely *not* be.[35] In the following section, I will investigate whether the option of an Optional Code will do justice to the present state of affairs in European contract law.

All the tendencies sketched in the above lead away from a generalised approach toward contract law. Drafting principles[36] is an example of this generalised approach; the work done within the study group on a European civil code[37] is another example. In my view, in the light of the present divergence in contract law, principles are too abstract to build a European private law with. The drafting of European principles inherently forces us to leave out as many differences between the national legal systems as is reasonably possible with the consequence that they do not give us much information anymore on what the European position actually is. They conceal the present divergence.

This analysis, for example, of the Principles of European Contract Law can be supported by philosophical insights. Presenting law through principles is what Clifford Geertz has called a 'skeletonization of fact': moral dilemmas are reduced to abstractions. Legrand rightly quotes Friedman where he says that to reduce the law in this way is very much like the work of the old system builders that 'took fields of living law, scalded off their flesh, drained off their blood, and reduced them to bones'.[38] Many details (that actually amount to national *practical wisdom*) are thus left out in an exercise that is primarily concerned with looking for *consensus*: making common principles is inherently a quest for the common denominator. This approach seems to have become the prevailing one of some leading comparatists. The well-known textbook of Zweigert and Kötz indeed departs from this '*praesumptio similitudinis*': in their functional approach, the comparatist can only be satisfied if his research leads to the conclusion that the systems he has compared reach the same or similar practical results.[39] From a pure scholarly point of view, there is nothing wrong with this because it may indeed help us to better understand the law. But if these principles or 'similar results' are subsequently used in a *political* way and prescribed to national

---

[35] The following is partly based on Smits (n. 33).

[36] Unidroit Principles of International Commercial Contracts (Rome, Unidroit, 1994); Lando and Beale (n. 32); G. Gandolfi (ed.), *Code Européen des contrats* (Milano, Giuffre, 2001).

[37] On which Chr. Von Bar, 'Le Groupe d'Études sur un Code Civil Européen', *Revue Internationale de Droit Comparé (RIDC)* [2001], 127.

[38] Friedman, as cited in P. Legrand, 'Against a European Civil Code', (1997) 60 *MLR*, 44, 59.

[39] K. Zweigert and H. Kötz, *Introduction to Comparative Law* (3rd edn., Oxford, Clarendon Press, 1998), 40.

communities (where they replace national legal systems), the warning of Paul Feyerabend becomes of paramount importance:[40] 'A society that is based on a set of well-defined and restrictive rules, so that being human becomes synonymous with obeying these rules, forces the dissenter into a no-man's-land of no rules at all and thus robs him of his reason and his humanity [...]. Remove the principles, admit the possibility of many different forms of life'.

The principles approach is thus directed toward the finding of an intermediate position. It may very well not be the *best possible rule* that prevails, but the rule on which consensus can be reached, indeed leaving out the 'flesh and blood' of national legal systems.[41]

Here, it is important to note that the present indeterminacy of national contract law at the level of rules (the too general character of contract law) does not prevent the national courts from doing justice on the basis of the value judgments (the 'national morality') that underpin each national private law system. These judgments should – in the end – be decisive for the outcomes that the courts reach. And in national legal systems, they probably *are* decisive, because of the simple fact that the courts are aware of their own national culture (if you like, morality, *Volksgeist* or *mentalité*) in which the rules are embedded. That these judgments often do not come to the surface on the level of the black letter law, does in this respect not pose a true danger for the parties' interests (although it *is* a danger from a viewpoint of a transparent and consistent national private law). This is different however if the private law rules are cut loose from their national cultural embedment and presented as European principles that are presented as being able to replace national systems. Such a venture can only be undertaken if the distilling of common denominators goes hand in hand with the development of a uniform European mentality.[42]

To sum up, replacing national legal systems with European principles will not lead to unification, but will most probably have the opposite effect. National experience in adjudicating cases will be destroyed, leaving national legal practice with no other alternative but to apply abstract norms in a European legal culture that it probably does not know and that possibly not exists. This can only have adverse effects on legal certainty and legal unity in Europe. Thus, there will only be unification at the abstract level (providing us with a 'thin description'), not in practice itself. This implies that the option of creating a binding Code that would replace existing national law,[43] has to be rejected at all times (and

---

[40] P. Feyerabend, *Against Method* (3rd edn., London, Verso, 1993), 162 *et seq.*

[41] R. Hyland, 'Comparative Law', in: D. Patterson (ed.), *A Companion to Philosophy of Law and Legal Theory* (Cambridge, Mass., Blackwell, 1996), 190, calls this 'reductionism'.

[42] Cf. P. Legrand, 'Against a European Civil Code', (1997) 60 *MLR*, 44, 60: 'What point, then, is a unitary text of reference in the absence of a unitary rationality and morality to underwrite and effectuate it?' And see Smits (n. 33), making reference to a 'programme'.

[43] COM(2001) 398 final, 17.

regardless the way in which it will be implemented: through a directive, regulation or treaty).

IV. THE IMPORTANCE OF AN OPTIONAL CODE: TOWARD A MULTI-LAYERED CONTRACT LAW

Now that the combination of imposition and general principles has been characterised as a fatal one in the European context, the question is which of the options envisaged by the European Commission is most in accordance with the state of present day contract law in Europe. The goal is to create more uniformity than there is right now, but still to take into account the diverging tendencies. In itself, the envisaged Option I of the Communication (no EC action at all)[44] could satisfy this goal, be it that there should then be more information available about the various European legal systems, as well as the possibility for the contracting parties to choose freely from these systems. Under those two conditions, the market could indeed lead to more uniformity than there is right now, while retaining national legal culture[45] and thus allowing divergence to remain intact. This option is not incompatible with the envisaged Option II to promote the development of contract law principles as a source of soft law only. If principles are only used as a checklist, a source of inspiration, a set of rules that parties can adopt or as a language for communication,[46] diversity is not hampered either.

It is, however, to be foreseen that, from a political perspective, the European Commission will go further than only Option I or II. I predict that in particular Option IV (to adopt new comprehensive legislation at EC level) will play a big role in the future discussion. Since in my view such a new set of rules should never entirely replace national legal systems, the answer to the question whether an optional Code belongs to the possibilities is important. Can such a code be accommodated within present-day contract law and, if so, in what way?

In the Communication, several scenarios regarding an optional Code are sketched.[47] The parameters are the following. First, the degree of bindingness may differ from a purely optional model by way of a recommendation or a regulation that has to be explicitly chosen by the parties to a model that applies unless it is excluded by the parties. Second, the contents of the Optional Code may differ from a set of provisions on contract law in general (I would think of

---

[44] COM(2001) 398 final, 13.

[45] For an elaboration of this argument, but focusing on the *courts* to choose freely, see J.M. Smits, 'A European Private Law as a Mixed Legal System', (1998) 5 *Maastricht J. of Eur. and Comp. L.* 328.

[46] Cf. M. Hesselink, *The Principles of European Contract Law: Some Choices Made By The Lando Commission* (Deventer, Kluwer, 2001), 25.

[47] COM(2001) 398 final, 16 *et seq.*

a set like the PECL) to a set of provisions on specific contracts or containing other specific rules. Third, an Optional Code could be optional because it can be chosen by the Member States or by the contracting parties (variable factor of who is opting in). I could imagine that a fourth variable factor (not mentioned in the Communication) would be brought in: the set could contain rules only on international contracts, but also on purely domestic ones (variable factor of which contracts are covered). This is represented in scheme 1.

Scheme 1

	Who opts in	*To what type of set*	*Covering which contracts*
1	Member States	Set of general principles	All contracts
2	Member States	Set of general principles	International contracts only
3	Member States	Sets of specific contract rules	All contracts
4	Member States	Sets of specific contract rules	International contracts only
5	Contracting Parties	Set of general principles	All contracts
6	Contracting Parties	Set of general principles	All contracts
7	Contracting Parties	Sets of specific contract rules	All contracts
8	Contracting Parties	Sets of specific contract rules	International contracts only

Generally speaking, the big advantage of an optional Code is that it can take into account the present divergence in contract law, while still allowing further unification to take place as far as the market parties wish it. Much depends, however, upon the exact combination of the variable factors. If an optional Code would exist only of general principles after the model of the PECL, the success of an optional Code would be minimal, both in the case of Member States as in the case of contracting parties opting in to such a Code. If Member States would opt in, the national wisdom as to solving concrete cases would to a large extent disappear. These principles can, after all, only be of a general nature. In the context of an optional Code, I do not see any point in the Member States deciding for the contracting parties what the law should be. If, on the other hand, it were left to the contracting parties to opt in to rather general principles after the model of the PECL, I do not think this is going to happen much in practice. The effectiveness of such a new set of rules would be minimal if compared to national legal systems that are chosen in present day practice. More probably, parties would continue to make a choice for a specific national legal system (like English law), on which there is experience as to how it works in practice.

In case there would be a choice for a more specific set of contract law rules (or rather several of such sets), this may be different. One of these sets could consist of rules on consumer contracts (of course incorporating the European directives in the field), another set could consist of rules on commercial contracts while a third set could envisage codifying a specific 'non-Western' contract view.

Thus, several sets of rules would consist next to each other in line with the divergence sketched in section 3 of this paper. These sets should preferably be chosen by the contracting parties as governing their contract, alongside with more specific provisions that govern their contract more specifically. If it were left to the Member States to opt in, the dividing lines in European contract law would still run parallel to the national frontiers, while they should instead be in accordance with the different types of contract in Europe. As to the contracts covered, it would be best not to distinguish between purely domestic and transfrontier contracts if one's goal is to create as much uniformity as possible in view of the diverging tendencies sketched. In scheme 1, option 7 would then be preferred.

This view stresses the importance of divergence, but also makes use of it to codify the separate parts of contract law along the previously sketched lines of divergence. This will result in a multi-layered law of contract for Europe,[48] not only at the level of the contents of the rules, but also as to the way contract law and the optional Code are structured. Several layers will exist next to each other with possibly one overriding layer of mandatory law (that in my view will mostly be of national origin: harmonisation of mandatory law is already highly difficult because of its relationship with public law aspects of national legal systems). This multi-layered structure reflects the pluralism in the private law of Europe much better than any approach that seeks to find general principles of contract law.

---

[48] For a similar plea for legal systems as 'multi-level frameworks', see M. Bussani, "Integrative' Comparative Law Enterprises and the inner Stratification of Legal Systems', (2000) *ERPL*, 85.

25. An Optional European Civil Code (OECC): Initiating a Learning Process

*Christian Kirchner**

I. THE PROBLEM

Drafting an optional European Civil Code (OECC)[1] is an intellectually challenging endeavour. But the success or failure of an OECC depends on the economic incentives for potential contract parties to make use of this option. Academic efforts in this field as such are not enough.

The transaction cost argument as such is not convincing. Admittedly, the transaction cost savings would be substantial: instead of applying up to 30 different civil codes or case law systems of contract law, a supplier offering goods or services in various Member States of the European Union could work with just *one* contract. Nevertheless he would be confronted with different legal norms on the implementation and enforcement of his contracts.[2] But even on the level of substantive law, new difficulties could arise having their origin in conflict of laws rules, which could lead to the substitution of clauses of the 'European' contract by those which are in line with the mandatory national law of the buyer. In effect, the 'European' contract would be split up into various national contracts. The transaction cost reduction potential would be confined to the contract; but in the moment the contract has to be enforced the transaction cost reduction would to a large degree vanish or could even be exceeded by the costs due to legal uncertainty. Thus the actual amount of transaction cost savings

---

* Professor Dr. iur., Dr. rer. pol., LL.M. (Harvard), Humboldt University, Berlin, School of Law, School of Business and Economics.

[1] The concept of European norms as options for the contracting parties has been discussed in: A. Schwartze, 'Diskussionsbeitrag', in: H.-L. Weyers (ed.), *Europaeisches Vertragsrecht* (Baden-Baden, 1997), 143–144; A. Schwartze, *Europaeische Sachmaengelgewaehrleistung beim Warenkauf* (Tuebingen, 2000), 619–623; the concept of an optional European Civil Code is one of the choices brought forward by the Commission: Communication from the Commission to the Council and the European Parliament on European Contract Law, COM(2001) 398 final, No. 66; 17. See also O. Lando and H. Beale (eds.), *Commission on European Contract Law, Principles of European Contract Law – Parts I and II, Combined and Revised* (The Hague, 2000).

[2] A. Schwartze (in his monography of 2000 – n. 1) discusses the impact of implementation and enforcement rules on rules of substantial law: 445–452.

---

would be minimal or even negative. There is hardly any incentive to make use of the OECC in the field of mass transactions.

II. SOLUTION 1: OECC AND HARMONISATION OF CIVIL LAW ORDERS

In order to overcome the problem of remaining transaction cost impediments one might try to harmonise existing civil law orders in Europe, and especially all those mandatory rules in the field of consumer protection law. Thus, the introduction of the OECC would be accompanied by approximization of national laws. But even if one were successful in harmonising the existing civil law orders in Europe in this respect, the economic problem of a supplier who wants to establish a unitary distribution system with identical contracts all over Europe would persist. Harmonisation does not mean unification; small legal differences stemming from differences within national implementations of European directives might cause important economic differences. Our supplier would still be confronted with many different solutions in the sphere of substantive civil law. On the other hand, the various national groups of buyers in different European countries would enjoy that level of consumer protection which results from a mix of the national consumer protection law of his home country and European consumer protection law harmonisation endeavours. On the other hand the consumer cannot enjoy the fruits from real transaction cost savings. The price to be paid for 'national contracts' is hidden, because nobody knows the comparable price which would have to be paid if a unitary system of contracts could be applied all over Europe.

III. SOLUTION 2: A BINDING EUROPEAN CIVIL CODE

In order to overcome these problems one could either introduce a binding European Civil Code (ECC option)[3] or a set of unified mandatory clauses which are automatically part of any contract concluded between a supplier (European or not) and a European buyer. The problems of the ECC option are well known.[4] The problems of a system of unified mandatory European civil law orders are similar; it is economically unwise to force all European consumers into the same straitjacket of one European consumer law. Their preferences, their risk propensities, their income and so on, are too different to allow one European system of mandatory European consumer law.[5]

---

[3] Discussed in the Communication from the Commission (n. 1) in nos. 61–65, 16.

[4] C. Kirchner, 'A "European Civil Code": Potential, Conceptual amd Methodological Implications', (1998) 31, *U.C. Davis Law Review*, 671–692.

[5] C. Kirchner(2001), 'Justifying Limits to Party Autonomy in the Internal Market – Mainly Consumer Protection', in: S. Grundmann, W. Kerber and S. Weatherhill (eds.), *Party Autonomy and the Role of Information in the Internal Market* (Berlin, New York, de Gruyter, 2001), s. 165–172.

IV. Solution 3: Options in the Field of Implementing and Enforcing Contracts

In order to provide incentives for applying an OECC it seems necessary to open the possibility to opt out from such parts of the national contract law system which cause the problem of not attaining the goal of real transaction cost savings: i.e. grant private autonomy to the fullest possible degree to those contract parties which are willing to apply the OECC. This seems to be a very radical proposal because it means a fundamental change in the Rome Convention[6] which in Article 5 section 2 grants the consumer the right to opt for that legal regime which appears most favourable for him. Whereas in Article 3 of the Rome Convention it is stated that a contract shall be governed by the law chosen by the parties (freedom of choice), Article 5 section 2 states that notwithstanding the provisions of Article 3, a choice of law made by the parties shall not have the result of depriving the consumer of the protection afforded to him by the mandatory rules of the law of the country in which he has his habitual residence. This holds true (1) if in the home country of the consumer the conclusion of the contract was preceded by a specific invitation addressed to him or by advertising and if the consumer had taken in that country all the steps necessary on his part for the conclusion of the contract, or (2) if the other party or his agent received the consumer's order in that country, or (3) if the contract is for the sale of goods and the consumer travelled from his home country to another country and there gave his order, provided that the consumer's journey was arranged by the seller for the purpose of inducing the consumer to buy.

The consumer – well protected by Article 5 section 2 of the Rome Convention – enjoys a quite favourable position. Why should he be willing to give up this position? Why should the law-maker allow him to renounce this favourable position? Economically, the answer is very simple: there is a hidden price the consumer has to pay for this favourable position. Let us assume a world without Article 5 section 2 of the Rome Convention (or a similar device which is made up to maximise the protection of consumers). But let us link this waiver of this type of consumer protection to a positive option for the OECC. Let us assume the following rule: if the contracting parties are opting for the OECC the consumer may waive their protection under Article 5 section 2 of the Rome Convention.

If such a rule has been created, the incentive to apply the OECC is being changed radically. If the European supplier is able to base his contracts on the OECC (and on nothing else) he can now save enormously on transaction costs. Let us imagine a big supplier of furniture who is sending to the buyer the parts of furniture which the buyer has to assemble on his own; he has been selling a

---

[6]   1980 Rome Convention on the law applicable to contractual obligations (consilidated version), (EC) OJ [1998] C 027/34–46.

certain table for 40 €. If the supplier is able to sell this table under *one* contract valid all over Europe he could reduce the price to 39 €. He now introduces a dual price system, 40 € for the table sold under the national contract system – with the given level of consumer protection – and 39 € for the table sold under an OECC contract. Why should a consumer be willing to buy the table under an OECC contract if he does not know the risk inherent of that contract compared to the old familiar contract law? There are two factors which are important for that decision: the risk propensity of an individual buyer and the terms offered by the seller. Under a contract governed by private autonomy the seller is free to offer favourable terms to the buyer. He can, for example, offer a money-back guarantee if the buyer should have problems in assembling the parts of the table. He may invent other devices as well. The advantage under the OECC regime is that the seller is now able to devise a unitary system for all sales in Europe. And this option would be open to sellers from other regions of the world who sell to European consumers as well. Thus a market for contract clauses is being established which – together with the price differential vis-à-vis old national contracts – should provide an incentive for a group of consumers to opt for OECC contracts.

V. INITIATING THE LEARNING PROCESS

In the moment this new market is established there is hardly any information on the expected cost of waiving the consumer protection granted to consumers by national law. But when there is not too small a group of buyers (who may not be the highly risk aware buyers), who opt for the unitary contract, it is possible to compare the results of both markets. A *learning process* can be started. In this learning process the seller might experiment with new clauses favourable for consumers and nevertheless extract the transaction cost reduction rent. What clauses will be decisive for consumers which they would not like to give up? The number one clause will be the jurisdiction clause. In mass contract cases consumers never will give up their right to sue the seller at the local court. Thus the seller who offers this jurisdiction clause must be aware that the unitary contract might be interpreted differently in different European countries. The whole transaction cost saving potential can thus only be realised if the OECC forms part of the European law under the jurisdiction of the European Court of Justice so that the Court may give preliminary judgments under Article 234 EC. Such a system carries the advantage that national courts are more and more confronted with the OECC and that on the other side a body of European case law is being built. The contract parties are now able to compare both types of contract. This type of market test is combined with the transaction cost savings potential of the OECC so that a win-win solution should result.

This type of learning process should result in considerable cost savings on the level of European law-making, because endeavours to harmonise consumer protection law would no longer be necessary. These resources could better be transferred to the drafting of the OECC. Such a learning process would give enough incentives to establish the OECC after two or three decades as the 'law in action' in the European Union, so that it would automatically without any top-down approach complement or partially substitute the national contract laws. But in essence these national contract laws could survive. No political act of substituting those national contract laws by the OECC would be necessary. And there would be no necessity to come to a European Civil Code with binding force, because a combination between party autonomy and private autonomy would lead to a working system of European contract law without further interventions of the legislator.

VI. POTENTIAL OBJECTIONS: DILUTING CONSUMER RIGHTS UNDER THE ROME CONVENTION

The solution proposed makes it necessary to change Article 5 section 2 of the Rome Convention. Adherents of consumer protection might oppose such a step, because they could argue that consumer rights are being diluted. They give up their option granted for consumer contracts under the Rome Convention. Under Article 5 section 2 of the Rome Convention a consumer enjoys the choice of law option *ex post*, after having concluded the contract. Under the proposed new rule he would have to exercise the choice when he is concluding the contract. But he is being remunerated by the price differential which is being made possible by real transaction cost reductions. It can be predicted that consumers who are quite risk aware would rather opt for old national and more expensive contracts; they have to pay a kind of insurance premium. But under the new regime not everyone is forced against his free will to pay this premium. With the ongoing learning process more and more consumers would become aware of the price to be paid for the choice being granted to them in the old Article 5 section 2 of the Rome Convention. And they would then be in a position to make their own judgements in the light of the experience made with the two competing regimes. The driving force in that competitive process are the transaction cost reduction potentials. They will lead in an evolutionary process to a European civil law.

26. Codifying European Private Law: Top Down *and* Bottom Up

*Walter van Gerven**

I. CODIFICATION IN THE PRESENT AND IN THE PAST

1. The European Commission's Four Options

On 11 July 2001 the Commission of the European Communities issued a Communication to the Council and the European Parliament on *European contract law*.[1] It intends to broaden the debate on the approach which is to be applied for the approximation of contract law at EC level. So far, the EC legislation has followed a selective, or piecemeal, approach adopting directives on specific contracts or specific marketing techniques where a particular need for harmonization was identified.[2] That approach is not so much the result of a deliberate strategy as it is the legal consequence of the limited number of competences which the European Treaties, mainly the EC Treaty, has attributed to the Community and its institutions. In consequence, the European legislature is enabled only to lay down rules where that is needed, to put it broadly, for the establishment and/or the functioning of the common, that is, the internal market (cf. Articles 94 and 95 EC). That is mainly, in the area of contract law, insofar as needed to remove obstacles to the free movement of goods, persons,

---

* Professor em. K.U. Leuven and U. Maastricht, Visiting professor at King's College, U. Ghent and K.U. Brussels. Member of the Belgian, Dutch and European Academies of Sciences, formerly Advocate General at the European Court of Justice (ECJ). This article is the text of the Jean Monnet lecture delivered at Groningen University on 13 September 2001 and, in a modified version, of a lecture at the ERA in Trier on 28 September 2001. I am grateful to all those with whom I could exchange views at those two occasions which helped me greatly in coming to the conclusions reflected herein.

[1] COM(2001) 398 final. For an explanation of the background and the aim of the Communication, see D. Staudenmayer (head of the working group within the Commission which was responsible for the drafting of the Communication) 'Die Mitteilung der Kommission zum Europäischen Vertragsrecht', *EuZW*, 2001, 485–489.

[2] In Annex I to the Communication the Commission enumerates and describes the various instruments, mainly directives, of existing EC legislation in the area of contract law primarily. In Annex II it enumerates the international instruments relating to substantive contract law issues. Annex III contains a list in which the documents referred to in the preceding Annexes are grouped under different headings.

S. Grundmann and J. Stuyck (eds.), An Academic Green Paper on European Contract Law, 405–432
© 2002 *Kluwer Law International. Printed in Great Britain.*

services and capital, to ensure that competition in the internal market is not distorted, and to strengthen consumer protection (Article 3(1), litt. c, g and t, EC). Beyond those objectives (and others enumerated in Article 3 EC) the Community and its institutions do not have legislative, executive or judicial competences (Article 7(1) EC, last sentence). More specifically, there is no jurisdiction within the Community that is broad enough to enact a Civil Code with the same scope of application as, for example, the Dutch, German or French Code. This limitation of Community jurisdiction constitutes a crucial point which cannot be disregarded in the discussion about codification at EC level.

The Commission's Communication hardly mentions that issue (at para. 41) but does not ignore it entirely. It is reflected indeed in the necessity of finding information 'as to whether problems result from divergences in contract law between Member States and if so, what [divergences]'. More particularly, the Commission wants to receive concrete information from all 'stakeholders, including businesses, legal practitioners, academics and consumer groups' as to whether 'the proper functioning of the internal market may be hindered by problems in relation to the conclusion, interpretation and application of cross-border contracts'. It also 'seeks views on whether the existing approach of sectoral harmonization of contract law [which is the result of the Community's limited jurisdiction] could lead to possible inconsistencies at EC level, or to problems of non-uniform implementation of EC law and application of national transposition measures'.[3]

The information sought thus focuses on the identification, in the area of contract law, of *concrete* problems, as is required by the European Court of Justice (hereafter ECJ)'s case law (see *infra*, at II 2), in view of eliminating obstacles to the proper functioning of the internal market which are due to divergences in national legislation, and to inconsistencies in existing EC legislation and the implementation thereof. The possible solutions which the Commission wants to define with the assistance of 'stakeholders', are formulated in broader terms however (that is particularly so for the second and the fourth option). They are: (i) 'to leave the solution of any identified problems to the market'; (ii) 'to propose the development of non-binding common contract law principles, useful for contracting parties … national courts and arbitrators … and national legislators'; (iii) 'to review and improve existing EC legislation … to make it more coherent or to adopt it to cover situations not foreseen at the time of adoption'; (iv) 'to adopt a new instrument at EC level';[4] whereby the Commission means 'an overall text comprising provisions on general questions of contract law a well as specific contracts', such overall text to be either

---

[3] Quotations in this paragraph come from the Communication's Executive Summary, at p. 2 of COM(2001) 398 final (not published in the OJ).

[4] The quotations in this paragraph are also drawn from the Communication's Executive Summary.

purely optional, i.e. at the discretion of the contracting parties, or suppletive, applicable unless the contracting parties have discarded it, or mandatory, in which case the text would replace national laws.[5] Let me point out immediately that these options are of a different character: the first, doing nothing, is hardly an option (but see *infra*, at II 3 *in fine*); the second, proposing non-binding common principles, refers to intiatives already realized (see *infra*, at III 2); the third, improving the quality of existing legislation, is a matter of necessity and should obtain priority (*infra*, at III 1); and the fourth, enacting comprehensive legislation, if it is to be binding, needs a firm legal basis in Community law (which cannot be found now in Article 95 EC, as exposed *infra*, at II 2). As pointed out later (at III 1 and 2) I suggest that the third and the second option be combined and put into effect before the fourth option.

2. Modernizing Private Law in a Democratic Fashion: the Dutch Code, an Example to be Followed

In 1992 the main part of the new Dutch *Burgerlijk Wetboek* (BW) entered into effect, thus offering the Netherlands the most recent code in a long row of precedents on the European continent. The BW's most significant characteristics are its comprehensive character covering civil, commercial law, consumer law and labour law, and the large amount of discretion which it grants to the courts: 'on the one hand the courts are free to further develop the law where its provisions are silent; on the other they are explicitly authorized to derogate from specific provisions of the law or of a contract if necessary to avoid an unjust result in the specific circumstances of the case'.[6] The work started with the appointment in 1947 of Professor E.M. Meijers as government commissioner. The new Code is the result of manifold drafts prepared by legal experts on the basis of a well-prepared memorandum and replies from Parliament to specific questions as to the foundations of the new Code (52 questions to be precise), followed later by extensive parliamentary discussions, first concerning draft bills (*vaststellingswetten*) relating to the introductory part and the eight substantive law parts of the Code, and then concerning the final draft bill of enactment (*invoeringswet*), all this under the stewardship of successive government commis-sioners.[7] On 1 January 1992 the central part of the Code[8] came into effect, i.e. 45 years after the official start of the work.

---

5   Paragraphs 65 ff. of the Communication.

6   Thus, Arthur Hartkamp, 'Statutory Lawmaking: the new Civil Code of the Netherlands' in: *De Lege, Towards Universal Law* (Uppsala, 1995), 151–178, 152.

7   See A.S. Hartkamp, *Compendium, Vermogensrecht volgens het nieuwe Burgerlijk Wetboek*, 5th edn. (Kluwer, 1999), 2–3 *et seq*.

8   The central part contains the general part of patrimonial law, the law of property, the general part of the law of obligations and the law of some special contracts, such as sale and agency: Arthur Hartkamp (n. 6), 156.

Obviously, the enactment of such a comprehensive code takes more time than enacting less extensive legislation for limited areas of private law (and moreover parts which, like contract law, concern less controversial matters than, e.g., family law); but, on the other hand, enacting a European code will raise 'sensitivities' which are more difficult to cope with than those arising in a purely national context. That is certainly the case if codification it is to be the product, as it should, of extensive discussions in parliamentary groups and consultations with various groups of 'stakeholders'.[9] Differences in legal mentality will not facilitate that task especially so because in some Member States (that is in the common law countries,[10] and in the Nordic countries)[11] codification is a technique which does not belong to the constitutional traditions.

3. Building a Nation-State by Enlightened Leaders: the French and German Codes, Examples not to be Followed in that Regard

The French and the German Civil Codes are products of Enlightenment at a time when democracy, as we understand it now, was not yet in place.[12] The codification phenomenon is characteristic for continental thinking in the centre and the south of Europe for more than two centuries now. Let me just recall the two most famous examples. On 1 January 1900 the German *Bürgerliches Gesetzbuch* (BGB) entered into force, that is almost one century before the Dutch BW and almost one century after the *Code Napoleon* – which in its final version was adopted by law of 21 March 1804 as the *Code civil des Français*.[13] Both Codes are of a completely different vintage. Whereas the French *Code civil* deals with particular issues in a clear and concrete manner, and is (at least in some respects, not for example with regard to gender) 'instinct with the ideal of equality

---

9   T. Koopmans, 'Towards a European Civil Code?', *ERPL*, [1997], 541–556, 541.

10   For a polite reaction against codification in a common law context, see Lord Goff, 'Coming Together the Future' in: *The Coming together of the Common Law and the Civil Law*, The Clifford Chance Millenium Lectures (ed. B.S. Markesinis), Oxford, Hart Publishing, 239–249, 241.

11   On the situation in the Nordic countries, see L. Sevón, 'Statutory Lawmaking: A Nordic Perspective' in: *De Lege* (n. 6), 179–191.

12   K. Zweigert and H. Kötz write: Codification, i.e. 'the idea that the diverse and unmanageable traditional law could be replaced by comprehensive legislation, consciously planned in a rational and transparant order' is a product of the Enlightenment: *An Introduction to Comparative Law*, 3rd edn. transl. T. Weir, 1998, 135–136, where the varying impact of rationalism inherent in the Enlightenment on German, French *and* English law is further explained. See also R.C. Van Caenegem, *Geschiedkundige Inleiding tot het Privaatrecht* (Story-Scientia, 1995), 121–155, where the role played by Jeremy Bentham, the most skillful defender of codification and his impact on the common law of England is summarized at 146–150. See further the writings of P.A.J. van den Berg (n. 16).

13   Zweigert and Kötz (n. 12), 83.

and freedom among citizens', the German BGB, for being 'the child of the deep, exact, and abstract learning of the German Pandectist School',[14] adopts throughout an abstract conceptual language and, instead of endorsing progressive tendencies in society, 'seeks to maintain a situation favourable to the establishment'.[15] In other words, whilst the French code contains (a few) revolutionary ideas and is written to be understood also by citizens, the German code was a conservative code written by and for professors. Where the two codes do resemble each other is that they had the same political goal which was to put an end to legal differentiation and thus to contribute to the shaping of a centralized Nation-State.[16] Obviously the Dutch BW had a completely different function: it was no longer intended to achieve unity or to strengthen the concept of Nation-State but constituted an undertaking carried out by lawyers in view of modernizing private law by turning judicial and doctrinal innovations into codified law.

If the German example is specifically mentioned here, it is not for style or content of the BGB but because of a controversy which took place long before its enactment. I refer to the 'famous confrontation' in 1814 between von Savigny, the unquestioned head of the Historical School of Law, and Thibaut, a professor at Heidelberg, on the desirability of a unified German civil code (to replace, among other sources of law, the Prussian *Allgemeines Landrecht* of 1794). Thibaut had proposed 'in the wave of patriotism which swept Germany after the Wars of liberation ... to replace the intolerable diversity of the German territorial laws by a general German civil code, on the pattern of the Code civil, and thus to lay the basis for the political unification of Germany'.[17] Apart from political circumstances (Napoleon's defeat in Waterloo in 1815) which were not propitious to his idea, Thibaut was fiercely opposed by von Savigny who in the name of his concept of the law, seen as a product of history, rejected the idea 'that legislation, being inorganic and unscientific, was not the right way to create a common German law and would do violence to the traditions it opposed'.[18] He maintained that the time was not ripe for the production of a unified civil code. Strangely enough, von Savigny and his followers did not revert to studying the Germanic sources of the law but turned exclusively to ancient Roman law as it appears in the *Corpus Iuris Civilis* of Justinianus, which they regarded as

---

[14]   Zweigert and Kötz, *o.c.* (n. 12), 144.

[15]   *Ibid.*, 143.

[16]   For an exhaustive analysis, see P.A.J. van den Berg, *Codificatie en staatsvorming* (Wolters Noordhoff, 1996) and, especially on the role of Jeremy Bentham, 'Staatsvorming zonder codificatie, Een vergelijking tussen het codificatiestreven op het continent en in Engeland, met bijzondere aandacht voor Jeremy Bentham en Henry Peter Brougham' in: *Recht en geschiedenis, Bijdragen tot de rechtsgeschiedenis van de negentiende en twintigste eeuw* studiedag Utrecht 1997 (red. C.J.H Jansen en M. van de Vrugt), (Nijmegen, 1999), 11–30, 11.

[17]   Zweigert and Kötz (n. 12), 139.

[18]   *Ibid.*

a 'store of legal institutions of eternal validity'.[19] So it was 'that the Historical School of Law produced the Pandectist School whose only aim was the dogmatic and systematic study of Roman material'.[20]

4. Savigny v. Thibaut, a Controversy that Bears no Repetition

The opposition between von Savigny and Thibaut, regarded as an opposition between law, seen as a product of *history*, and law, seen as a product of *reason*, is somehow reflected in the opposition nowadays between those who believe that cultural differences between Member States and legal mentalities are such that no codification at European level is possible,[21] at least not for the time being, and those who believe that codification has to come about without further delay, at least in those areas of the law, like contract, tort and property, where patrimonial considerations prevail. Those are the areas where common rules are most likely to emerge for reasons of facilitating trade relations and, nowadays, economic integration. There is however another opposition which this controversy brings to the fore, as is shown by the following description of the von Savigny/Thibaut confrontation in R.C. Van Caenegem's *Goodhart Lectures* 1984–1985:[22]

'... It is when Savigny addresses the question of where the "law of the folk" is to be found and who is to determine what its content is, however, that the modern reader is in for a great surprise, for it turns out that the learned jurists, the professors of law, are best placed to ascertain this folk-law, a task that cannot be left to ordinary people because of the "complexities of modern life". Thus the professors who in Germany were all steeped in Roman law...were proclaimed as the natural oracles of what the people felt. In the background, of course, was the struggle for control of the law. In this case the struggle was between the professors and the legislators (the enlightened princes or the deputies of the people). Savigny was particularly frightened of democratic legislatures as in the French republic. He was a deeply conservative man, believing in noble leaders knowing the law best and speaking for the people: evidently professors of aristocratic descent, as Savigny himself ...'.

---

[19] *Ibid.*, 140. It should be recalled that the *Corpus Juris* was not a real code but a collection of existing texts, some old and some recent, some legislative texts and some writings of jurists arranged according to subject matter: R.C.Van Caenegem, *Judges, Legislators and Professors. Chapters in European Legal History* (Cambridge, Cambridge University Press, 1987), 41. In other words a collection which would be called nowadays a Source- or a Casebook rather than a Code.

[20] *Ibid.*.

[21] Cf. the extreme position of someone like P. Legrand, 'Against a European Civil Code' in: (1997) *MLR*, 44.

[22] (n. 19), 51–52.

Savigny's outdated opinion concerning the role of professors, as inspired by his contempt for 'democratic' legislatures, finds of course no parallel in contemporary society. It is nevertheless worthwhile to mention it in a context of European law-making as it raises the issue of democratic legitimacy in a context of codification – an issue which is also present in the discussion of the so-called democratic deficit characterizing the European Community's legislative process as it now stands.[23] However that is, there is no reason whatsoever to re-open the Thibaut/von Savigny controversy but to combine both approaches, the top-down and the bottom-up approach, as we will see hereafter (at 13–14).

5. Themes and Propositions: Codification Defined

The foregoing brings me to present four *themes* for further consideration. Those are: (i) European codification, possible and desirable?; (ii) preserve and improve the legislative *'acquis communautaire'*; (iii) democratic legitimacy of European codification; and (iv) flanking measures to prepare and accompany codification. The general *propositions* which I would like to put forward herinafter are: 1) that there is a need for European codification, i.e. comprehensive legislation as defined hereafter, in areas of 'patrimonial' private law (mentioned *infra*, at 6); 2) that the *first stage* of European codification consists in improving and broadening existing Community directives and case law in specific areas by turning those directives and their implementing national legislation resp. such case law into Community regulations (*infra*, at 10); 3) that the most appropriate, and presently the only legal, way to carry out the *second stage* of European codification – which consists in general (i.e. not 'internal market related') law-making – is, by way of an agreement between Member States, either to amend the existing Treaties or, alternatively, to conclude a Treaty *ad hoc*; and 4) that it is imperative to prepare, accompany and follow up European codification, certainly in the second stage, by flanking measures intended to create the proper environment for European codification to succeed.

Before proceeding any further I should point out that, as a working *definition*, I understand hereinafter under (full) codification (i.e. the first and second stage taken together): legislation which is part, or drafted to be part, of a larger whole and which does not focus on the protection of specific interests, such as consumer, workers or competitors interests, but tries to take a global view of all interests involved. Codification is therefore 'comprehensive' in two regards: first, in that it is conceived and structured as a whole which implies that it normally includes, or is intended to include, more than one chapter of *in casu* private law; and secondly, in that it takes a global view which does not mean that rules focusing

---

[23] The 'democratic deficit' existing in the Community has many facets: see P. Craig and G. de Búrca, *EU Law* 2nd edn. (Oxford, Oxford University Press, 1998), 155–161.

on the protection of specific interests cannot, and preferably should, be incorporated in the larger whole (as the Dutch BW demonstrates). In consequence, to unify the general part of contract law and certain specific types of contract only, is not codification in the proper sense of the word whilst unifying large parts of 'patrimonial' law, as referred to hereafter, may deserve that denomination.

II. EUROPEAN CODIFICATION, POSSIBLE AND DESIRABLE?

1. There is no 'Epistemological' Impossibility to Reach Convergence

Let me first point out that I am not one of those who believe that codification at the European level is impossible because of cultural differences, or differences in legal mentalities or internal moralities, existing between the legal systems involved (those of the European Union). That is certainly not the case where codification is limited – as is envisaged by all those engaged in the debate presently – to the core 'patrimonial' parts of private law, such as the (at least general) law of contract, the law of tort (or at least the most important torts), the law of unjust enrichment and what I would call the law of fiduciary relations (rather than the law of property)[24] – by which I refer to techniques of *fiducia cum amico* relating to the administration of someone else's assets as well as to techniques of *fiducia cum creditore* relating to collateral for the repayment of money lent.[25] Indeed, the proposition that 'epistemological' difficulties constitute insurmountable obstacles to promote convergence between the legal systems of the common law and those of the civil law, is continuously contradicted by experience to the contrary of practitioners and down-to-earth academics working in European or international surroundings. That does not mean that those difficulties should not be taken seriously, especially because they are part of an

---

[24] It would be counterproductive, I think, to try to bridge the deep conceptual cleavage between civil and common law in the area of property. See G. Samuel, 'English Private Law in the context of the Codes' in: *The Harmonisation of European Private Law* (ed. M. Van Hoecke and I. Ost), (Oxford, Hart Publishing, 2000), 47–61, 52–58. In contrast, it should be possible, I think, to achieve commonality in regulating fiduciary relations, first, because civil and common law countries share the common a concept of *fiducia* (*fiducie, Treuhand,* trust) and, secondly, because contemporary legal practice has devised a large variety of banking and investment instruments which fulfill similar needs in the area of both categories of *fiducia,* i.e. *cum amico* and *cum creditore.* For an attempt to formulate common rules, see D.J. Hayton, S.C.J.J. Kortmann and H.L.E. Verhagen, *Principles of European Trust Law* (Kluwer Law International, 1999).

[25] As the 'Study Group on a European Code', initiated by professor C. von Bar, intends to do by and large. See C. von Bar, 'A new Jus Commune Europaeum and the Importance of the Common Law' in: *The Coming together of the Common Law and the Civil Law, Clifford Chance Millennium Lectures* (ed. B.S. Markesinis), (Oxford, Hart Publishing, 2000), 67.

ongoing discussion among European and American experts in legal theory which demonstrates in itself the universality of the law. What must be retained from that discussion is that codification, starting with the use of the instrument itself, should not ignore differences in legal mentalities; however, at the same time, it helps proponents of codification to realize that 'solutions found in different jurisdictions must be cut loose from their conceptual context, stripped of their national doctrinal overtones, and seen [...] in the light of their function, as an attempt to satisfy a particular need'.[26] What we need therefore is an intellectually revolutionary process which is part of an ongoing and all-encompassing process of integration 'among the peoples of the Europe' (Article 1, para. 2, TEU).[27]

2. Nationalistic Reflexes to be Overcome and Legal Basis Constraints not to be Ignored

To prepare uniform legislation in a truly European perpective is not self-evident. Even for comparative lawyers, trained to look beyond their national borders, it remains difficult not to be guided too much by one's own legal system and to avoid that 'the debate on the need for a European Civil code [...] be spoiled by veiled preoccupations with cultural hegemony'.[28] Any attempt, or even appearance, to transplant such feelings of cultural or legal hegemony unto the European level or, even worse, simply to create the impression of European codification to be part of some Fortress Europe, must be avoided by all means. Moreover, merely to raise expectations of civil codification to be an exponent of 'nation-state' – building at the European level, is already inconsistent with legal reality since, due to the aforementioned principle of attribution of competences, there

---

[26] Thus H. Kötz in 'Comparative Legal Research and its function in the development of harmonized law. The European Perspective' in: *De Lege* (n. 6), 21–36, 35. Kötz's description is cast in somewhat provocative terms as a reply to L.M. Friedman and G. Teubner's equally provocative criticism according to which, in the words of H. Kötz, 'a European common law would amount to the resurrection of the conceptual world of the nineteenth century'.

[27] This view corresponds with the paradigm of the EU as a 'multi-level system of governance' highlighting the erosion of Nation-States (without accepting however their transformation into a new European superstate). See amongst other writings, C. Joerges: 'The Impact of European Integration on Private Law: Reductionist Perceptions, True Conflicts and a New Constitutional Perspective' in: *Private Governance, Democratic Constitutionalism and Supranationalism* (eds. O. Gerstenberg and C. Joerges), (European Commission, 1998). For further references, see J. Wouters, 'Institutional and constitutional challenges for the European Union: some reflections in the light of the Treaty of Nice', (2001) *ELR*, 342–356, 355, n. 75.

[28] Thus U. Mattei, 'A transaction costs approach to the European Code' in (1997) *ERPL*, 537–540, 539 who proposes, as the title indicates, to examine the desirability of European codification from a transaction-costs perspective.

is no legislature at the European level which is empowered to enact comprehensive legislation covering all areas of private patrimonial law. I will return to that subject below (at IV 1). It may suffice here to refer to the ECJ's *Tobacco* judgment of 5 October 2000 where the Court held that 'a mere finding of disparities between national rules and of the abstract risk of obstacles to the exercise of fundamental (economic) freedoms or of distortions of competition liable to result therefrom, [is not] sufficient to justify the choice of Article [95] as a legal basis ...'.[29] Although that judgment relates only to Article 95 EC (which allows measures to be adopted by qualified majority in the Council in accordance with the co-decision procedure of Article 251 EC, and thus in cooperation with the European Parliament; see *infra*, at IV 1), it clearly underlines the general principle of specific and therefore *limited* competences which the Community institutions have for the purpose of approximation of national laws. That principle has for consequence that, e.g., in the field of contract law, none of the Community institutions has the authority to bring some unity into the various sets of rules which regulate, in a varying degree, the different 'categories' of contract: international contracts,[30] EU interstate contracts, commercial contracts between economic operators with equal rather than unequal bargaining power, consumer contracts and 'purely private' contracts.[31]

3. Transaction Costs and Legal-Cultural Constraints of Comprehensive v. Fragmented Legislation

Apart from the question of epistemological and legal feasibility of European codification, there is the issue of desirability which can best be resolved, as suggested in legal literature, by a transaction costs approach, that is by comparing the input of resources to be applied to bring about unity and the output in terms of results.[32] Where, as under the third option of the Commission's

---

[29] Case C-376/98, *Germany v. Parliament and Council* [2000] ECR I–8419, para. 84. See also paras. 106–107 of the judgment where it is added that the distortions of competition must be significant, and Advocate General Fennelly's Opinion, paras. 82–98 where it is underlined, at para. 93, that the *concrete* harmonization measure proposed by the Community must be compatible with the objective of the internal market or, in the terms of Article 95, must 'have as [its] object the establishment and functioning of the internal market'.

[30] For an impressive list of international instruments relating to substantive contract law issues, see Annex II to the Commission's Communication of 11 July 2001, referred to *supra* in n. 2.

[31] Thus the distinction made by L. Sevón in 'Statutory Lawmaking. A Nordic Perspective' in: *De Lege* (n. 6), 179–191, 186–189 who rightly observes that, to make general rules for these various categories, there will be a need to resort to standards with an open texture, such as reasonable time, due diligence or, one may add, good faith, which because of their open texture can be adapted to the concrete circumstances of a specific relationship.

[32] See the article of U. Mattei (n. 28).

Communication,[33] limited legislation is envisaged to improve the quality of existing consumer law directives, it is not unlikely that the transaction costs criterion would favour more harmonization, or even unification, taking into account the (relatively) limited resources needed therefore and the obvious advantages of eliminating inconsistencies and promoting coherence. But where it is envisaged to undertake the 'daunting task' (as professor Markesinis calls it), inherent in extensive codification of large parts of private law, to conceive and elaborate rules as part of a well structured code interconnecting different parts, sections and books, and not loosing sight of constitutional, institutional and public law aspects surrounding private laws and reconciling different styles of codification,[34] the cost of academic, political, administrative and judicial efforts to prepare, to adopt, implement and apply legislation may be such, that they do not necessarily outweigh the advantage of unification.

At the end of the day the desirability issue turns around the question of how much fragmentation a legal system is able to support or, in other words, how coherent a legal system must be. That is a question not only of efficiency (i.e. of limiting transaction costs due to superfluous disparities) but also of fairness and justice (i.e. of treating similar situations equally and different situations unequally). It is here that cultural differences and differences in legal mentality may come to the fore between common law and Nordic countries, on the one hand, which are used to more fragmentation of laws, and the other European countries, on the other hand, where a more comprehensive approach is favoured (although also there unification is far from being achieved, even at the European level, because of mundialization on the one hand and compartmentalization on the other).[35] I am afraid that there is no rule of thumb to reconcile, or choose between, these two attitudes save for the general principle that efforts must be made to avoid differences for which there is no objective 'particular justification'.[36]

All things considered (and leaving apart for now the issue of legal basis) the decision as to how much fragmentation a legal system can tolerate, is very much influenced by one's legal background. As an academic trained in a system of codified law, and therefore 'naturally' imbued with the ideals of rationalization,

---

[33] Communication (n. 1), paras. 57–60.

[34] B.S. Markesinis, 'Why a code is not the best way to advance the cause of European legal unity', (1997) *ERPL*, 519–524, 520–522.

[35] On the subject of fragmentation, see G. Samuel, 'English Private law in the context of the Codes' in: *The Harmonisation of European Private Law* (ed. M. Van Hoecke and F. Ost), (Oxford, Hart Publishing, 2000), 47–61.

[36] Thus the ECJ in its *Brasserie* judgment of 5 March 1996 [1996] ECR I–1029, para. 42 with respect to homogeneity between extracontractual liability rules for Community institutions as laid down on the basis of Article 288, para. 2 EC, and extracontractual liability rules for Member States as adopted by the ECJ in *Francovich* and many subsequent judgments.

unification and legal certainty, my gut reaction would be in favour of codification. However, knowing that, as mentioned above, unification remains a relative notion and, moreover, for having practised law in an international context in different occupations, I have some doubts as to how much disparities (which legal practice is unable to set aside at a reasonable cost) actually, and substantially, hinder interstate commerce. That is particularly doubtful in an area such as contract law where – subject to exceptions to protect consumers or workers – parties may, anyway, modulate their relationship in accordance with their wishes and elect the legal system which they want to apply.[37] And indeed, it may well be that 'in the past ... there has been a tendency to overrate the benefits of legislative unification and to underrate its cost'.[38] As it may also be that the assumption that disparities of rules hinder interstate commerce is often documented in a fairly abstract way (also sometimes in preambles to directives) whilst the ability to cope with differences (an ability which the principle of free movement of services has considerably strenghtened, albeit only within the internal market) is underestimated.[39] Economic research should help us to calculate more accurately the cost of divergences as compared with the cost of coping with differences.

III. PRESERVING AND BROADENING THE LEGISLATIVE 'ACQUIS COMMUNAUTAIRE'

1. Improving and Consolidating Existing Legislation in the Area of Contract Law and Consolidating and Implementing Case Law in the Area of Competition Law by means of Directly Applicable Regulations

If it is correct to assume (*supra*, at II 3) that the criterion of transaction costs supports the desirability of improving the quality of existing Community directives in the areas of *consumer, labour, public procurement, e-commerce* contracts,

---

[37] A matter for which Community jurisdiction and legislation now exist: see Articles 61(c) and 65 EC, and for which uniform rules were established by the Rome Convention on the law applicable to contractual obligations. See further O. Remien, 'European Private International Law, the European Community and its emerging Area of Freedom, Security and Justice', (2001) *CMLRev*, 53–86; also J. Basedow, 'The Communitarization of the Conflict of Laws under the Treaty of Amsterdam', (2000) *CMLRev*, 687–708.

[38] H. Kötz (n. 26), 36 who also quotes in that regard the famous comparatist, professor Kahn-Freund, according to whom the selection of areas where codification may be desirable must 'be dictated by practical requirements and nothing else'. See also Lord Goff in his conclusion on 'Coming together – the Future' to the *Clifford Chance Millennium Lectures* mentioned (n. 10), 241–249, who writes, commenting on the work of the 'Study Group' (n. 25), that: 'Uniformity as an end in itself is an ideal which is not shared by all', 241.

[39] W. van Gerven, 'A common law for Europe: the Future meeting the Past?' in (2001) *ERPL*, 485–503, 492.

etc., then the question arises how to proceed; more particularly whether it would be appropriate or not to also include in that undertaking the national legislation implementing the Community directives. In other words, whether the third option in the Commission's Communication must be understood in a minimal way, i.e. as an invitation to streamline existing directive law,[40] or in a more extensive way, i.e. as an incentive to take a further step by replacing the current directives by regulations. The latter would have for result, in the areas now covered by directives, not only to achieve more coherence between *Community* rules laid down in directives but also to unify the *national* rules now implementing those directives. From a viewpoint of legal basis that should not in itself raise problems in the important sector of consumer protection since Article 95 EC to which Article 153 EC refers allows for regulations as well as directives. However, after the *Tobacco* judgment a difficulty may generally arise with the legal basis in that area, where Article 95 (or 94) is invariably used as a legal basis for directives, unless Article 153 EC is acknowledged to be a autonomous legal basis (as I submit it does).[41] Apart from the issue of legal basis and because of the degree of convergence already existing between the implementing national rules of existing directives, to aim at unification rather than harmonization of national laws in the area of consumer law, might be easier (and from a viewpoint of transaction costs be less expensive) than directly codifying national rules which have not yet been the object of harmonization. And also psychological obstacles on the part of the Member States may be overcome more easily in areas where harmonization has already taken place than where that did not occur. Moreover, to undertake codification in those areas first, i.e. before taking on codification in areas where no prior harmonization did occur, would help to understand the kind of problems and difficulties of European codification generally and may serve as a learning experiment for more far-reaching codification efforts.

Consolidation of existing directives and implementing national rules in the areas of *contract law* just mentioned would be a first pillar in the construction of European private law in specific areas. However, thanks to case law of the Community courts,[42] there is another specific area where unification of national laws can and should be achieved. That is with regard to contractual and delictual

---

[40] From the contributions made to the colloquium held at ERA on 27/28 September 2001, it would appear that the existing directives can be put fairly well into a general framework.

[41] In Article 153, para. 1, EC the protection of the safety and the economic interests of consumers is designated as an objective without reference to any limitation regarding transborder aspects whilst the reference in para. 3 to Article 95 concerns 'procedural' aspects. But see W-H. Roth, *Europäischer Verbraucherschutz und BGB*, JZ 10/2001, 475, 477–479.

[42] See in general W. van Gerven, 'The ECJ Case-law as a means of Unification of Private Law?' in: *Towards a European Civil Code* (ed. A. Hartkamp *et al.*), second revised and expanded edition (Kluwer Law International, 1998), 91–104.

remedies to be made available to private individuals who have sustained damage as a result of breaches of Community *competition* rules (Articles 81 and 82 EC) committed by other individuals. Regarding such breaches, the ECJ has stated in a recent judgment of 20 September 2001,[43] that 'the full effectiveness of Article 81 of the Treaty and, in particular, the practical effect of the prohibition laid down in Article 81(1) would be put at risk if it were not open to any individual to claim damages for loss caused to him by a contract or by conduct liable to restrict or distort competition'.[44] That judgment implies that individuals who could already claim damages in tort, as a matter of Community law, against Member States and national public authorities for breaches of Community law (the so-called 'Francovich' liability),[45] may now also claim compensation, in contract or in tort, as a matter of Community law as well, from other individuals who have caused them damage as a result of breaches of Articles 81 and 82 EC. The conditions for such (contractual or delictual) liability to arise will have to be fleshed out further by the ECJ in later case law. It would be preferable however, that the Community legislature itself were to take the initiative to lay down such uniform Community rules in a regulation taken on the basis of Article 83 EC. Such regulation should then provide in uniform rules not only for the remedy of compensation but also for the remedy of nullity – which is explicitly foreseen in Article 81(2), as implemented by case law of the ECJ – as well as for the remedies of restitution, restitutionary (and eventually exemplary) damages, interim relief and, possibly, collective claims to protect diffuse interests. In the not unlikely event that the Commission's 'Modernization' proposals to replace the existing Regulation 17,[46] will be adopted and that private enforcement of Community competition rules will therefore be attributed fully to the national cartel authorities *and* to the national courts (including the competence to grant exemption under Article 81(3)), there will be an urgent need for such a 'remedies regulation' in order to facilitate the task of national courts and to make enforcement of competition rules by those courts more efficient than it is now.[47] Such a regulation would be the second pillar on which European private law can be

---

[43] Case C-453/99, *Courage and Crehan*, [2001] ECR I-6297.

[44] Para. 26 of the judgment. In my Opinion as Advocate General in the *Banks* case (Case C-128/92, *Banks v. British Coal Corporation* [1994] ECR I-1209 para. 36) I had encouraged the Court to do so, advice which it has now followed.

[45] See further W. van Gerven, J. Lever and P. Larouche, *Cases, Materials and Text on National, Supranational and International Tort Law*, second expanded edition (Oxford, Hart Publishing, 2000), 889–930, where 'Francovich' liability is seen in context with the liability of Community institutions under Article 288, para. 2, EC.

[46] First Regulation implementing Articles [81] and [82] of EC treaty, (EC) JO [1962], 13.

[47] See further my article on 'Substantive Remedies for the private Enforcement of EC Antitrust Rules before national Courts' to be published in *European Competition Law Annual 2001* (ed. C.D. Ehlermann and I. Atanasiu). See also the contribution of F. Jacobs on procedural aspects, to be published in the same *Annual*.

built, this time in the field of contractual *and* delictual liability,[48] for breaches of statutory duty by private or public persons. Such a specific Community tort would then come in addition to the liability regulated in the directive on liability for defective products[49] which concerns another type of ('strict') liability in contract or in tort.

2. Law-Making 'By Exception' (i.e. Only, or First, in Specific 'Internal Market-Related' Areas) can be Supplemented by Existing Non-Binding General Principles

If the above proposals were to be effected, and a first part of private law therefore constructed through regulations in 'internal market-related' areas of contract and tort law, such as consumer and competition law, the question arises whether such 'codification by exception' (by anology with 'management by exception') is acceptable. And indeed, the normal way to proceed is first to lay down general rules and only then special rules for specific situations. However, in the present state of Community law, the procedure would be different because of the existence of Community directives, and implementing national legislation, in specific areas for which there is a legal basis that can also be used, as suggested above, to turn the existing rules into directly applicable Community regulations. Since the existing rules are limited in scope, and part of a well established '*acquis communautaire*', the issue of democratic legitimacy raised hereafter in connection with new and more general legislation (*infra*, at II 3) should not arise here either.[50] That is not so much because in those specific areas 'differences in ethics

---

48 The *Courage and Crehan* judgment mentioned in the text relates to a matter of contractual law but is coached in general terms to include both contract and tort claims for breaches of Article 81 EC. The question submitted to the ECJ by the English Court of Appeal was whether a contracting party to a tied house agreement (in a brewery contract) which is prohibited by Article 81 EC, may rely upon that article to seek relief from the courts from the other contracting party, more specifically whether he is entitled to recover damages alleged to result from his adherence to a price maintenance clause in the agreement. In its judgment the ECJ had therefore to deal with the protection of a weaker contracting party and with issues of unjust enrichment and of '*nemo auditur*' or '*in pari causa*' (prohibiting a contracting party to profit from his own unlawful conduct: paras. 30 and 31).

49 Council Directive 85/374/EEC of 25 July 1985 concerning liabilities for defective products, (EC) OJ [1988] L 3.7/54, as amended by EP and Council Directive 1999/34/EC of 10 May 1999.

50 For consumer law there is Article 153 EC in conjunction with Article 95 EC which provides in any kind of measure to be taken in co-decision between the Council and the EP and allows qualified majority in the Council. For competition law, there is Article 83 EC which allows regulations or directives to be taken by qualified majority in the Council but provides only in consultation of the EP.

and legal values (would not be) considerable',[51] for indeed they are, to a certain extent at least, since also in those areas which concern the interests of weaker parties, or diffuse interests, in other words which intend to protect social, consumer and environmental 'citizen' rights,[52] there is no unanimity as to the degree of protection in all Member States. However, because of the existing *'acquis communautaire'* in Community and national statutory and case law, there is a sufficiently solid ground to take a further step in those areas.

As a matter of fact, to start with codification in those fields may have the beneficial effect that, when general codification is prepared – and there is no reason to wait for that even in the absence of a sufficient legal basis[53] – it can be effected in a more 'value-oriented' or 'policy-minded' perspective because of already agreed exceptions to the propositions of more general legislation to come.[54]

From a more practical viewpoint, the objection to 'codification by exception' can also be overcome by giving full support, in line with the second option of the Commission's Communication,[55] to initiatives aimed at drafting non-binding general principles. In the area of general contract law two sets of principles have already been elaborated: the *Principles for international commercial contracts* prepared by UNIDROIT ('Institut pour l'Unification du droit privé') and the *Principles of European Contract Law* prepared by the Commission on European Contract law (the 'Lando group').[56] Both initiatives show that, and how much, uniformity can be achieved; moreover, they already offer guidance to all those looking for uniform law in whatever capacity,[57] especially because 'they resemble

---

[51] Thus O. Lando, 'Why codify the European Law of contract?' in (1997) *ERPL*, 525–535, 530.

[52] On these rights, see N. Reich, *Bürgerrechte in der Europäischen Union* (Nomos Verlagsgesellschaft, 1999).

[53] That is the position I expressed in the study preliminary to the work of the 'Study group on a European Civil Code' (cf. n. 25; see concluding remarks in paras. 87–88). That preliminary report has been submitted to the European Parliament (Directorate General of Science, project nr. IV/98/44).

[54] For instance when issues arise concerning the scope of the *'pacta sunt servanda'* principle, the exception of 'public policy' or 'mandatory rules', theories relating to abuse of circumstance by a contracting party, to name only a few.

[55] Referred to in n. 1, paras. 52–56.

[56] On these two initiatives, see A. Hartkamp, 'Principles of Contract Law' in: *Towards a European Civil Code* (ed. A. Hartkamp *et al.*), second and expanded edition (Kluwer Law International, 1998), 105–120; and 'Perspectives for the Development of a European Civil Law' in: *Making European Law, Essays on the 'Common Core' project* (eds. M. Bussani and U. Mattei), (Università degli Studi di Trento, 2000), 39–60 where a complete overview is given of the various initiatives and projects of binding law, case law, soft law and scientific/ educational projects which are underway (see also *infra* in the text).

[57] See the Introduction, at pp. xxiii–xxiv, of the *Principles of European Contract Law*, Part I and II, edited by Ole Lando and Hugh Beale (Kluwer Law International, 2000). The Unidroit principles are commented on by M.J. Bonell in 'The need and possibilities of a codified European contract law' in (1997) *ERPL*, 505–517.

each other, not merely in the editorial form ... but also in substance'.[58] Actually, also the work undertaken by the 'Study Group on a European Civil Code'[59] will probably come up with similar results in the area of contract law, and will in the other areas of private law which it intends to cover (tort, unjust enrichment and collateral to secure debts) adopt the same methodology (including the non-binding character of the rules for the time being). The same methodology was also followed by the group drafting *Principles of European Trust Law*.[60] All of those principles may help, as explicitly intended by the authors of the 'Lando' *Principles of Contract Law*, to provide an infrastructure for the as yet dispersed Community law rules governing contracts;[61] an objective which should compensate for the 'piecemeal' approach which existing Community legislation is forced to apply.[62]

In the absence, so far, of a valid legal basis in Community law for general legislation, it will not be possible to turn those *Principles*, or others, into binding law. Accordingly, it must suffice to endorse them informally, in one way or another,[63] e.g. as 'guidelines' to be taken into account, where possible, in drafting or redrafting future or existing Community law, possibly also of implementing national legislation.[64] The European Commission could also choose to designate the principles as applicable law in contracts concluded by or on behalf of the Community[65] (see Article 288, para. 1).[66]

---

[58] A. Hartkamp in the first publication referred to in n. 56, at 119.

[59] n. 25. The name of the group is unfortunate, as pointed out by Lord Goff at 241 of his contribution referred to above in n. 10. And see the response of professor von Bar, at 78 of his contribution referred in n. 25.

[60] Referred to in n. 24.

[61] Referred to in n. 43, at xxii.

[62] See also the Commission's Communication (n. 1), where the advantages of such an approach are enumerated at paras. 52–56.

[63] For instance as part of an 'assessment of draft legislation programme'. See in that connection *Improving the Quality of legislation in Europe*, T.M.C. Asser Instituut (ed. A.E. Kellermann *et al.*), (Kluwer Law International, 1998).

[64] At the ERA conference in Trier, mentioned in the note accompanying the title of this contribution, many reporters explored ways to achieve consistency between existing legislation and underlying general principles. See also the overview contained in Annex III of the Commission's Communication concerning the 'structure of the acquis'. O. Lando in his article mentioned in n. 51 also refers to a list of 70 Principles, Rules and Institutions that was prepared by K.P. Berger, as a common core already applied by legal systems and the business community, in: *Formalisierte oder 'schleichende' Kodifizierung des transnationales Wirtschaftsrechts* (1996).

[65] As I suggested in my contribution mentioned above in n. 42, 99.

[66] See also Article 238 EC pursuant to which the ECJ can be given jurisdiction in repect of such contracts by virtue of an arbitration clause.

IV. THE ISSUE OF DEMOCRATIC LEGITIMACY

1. The Principle of (Procedural) Democracy and the (Now Lacking) Legal Basis for European Codification

The principle of democracy is one of the foundations of the European Union (Article 5(1) TEU).[67] Even before the entry into force of the Treaty on European Union the ECJ used it, where it had to choose between two possible legal bases, to give preference to the legal basis with the highest involvement of the European Parliament.[68] The procedure laid down in Article 95 EC complies with that procedural aspect of the principle of democracy, as it refers, for the adoption of measures of harmonization (through directives) or of unification (through regulations), to the co-decision procedure of Article 251 EC. Under that procedure, the Council is forced 'to treat the Parliament with the requisite respect'.[69] However, as already mentioned, in the *Tobacco* judgment[70] the Court has interpreted Article 95 EC in a way that it does not allow for codification of core provisions of private law if they do not have 'as their [concrete] object the establishment and functioning of the internal market' (Article 95(1) EC).[71]

Even assuming that Article 95 EC were to offer a sufficient legal basis, it might be inappropriate to use it as a legal basis for general private law codification, *ie.* beyond the scope of 'internal market related' matters (dealt with *supra*, at III 1). That is because Article 95 allows for measures to be taken by a qualified majority in the Council, in addition to an absolute majority in the Parliament.[72] Since 'qualified majority' implies presently that, where a majority of Council members (i.e. Member States) *and* 62 (out of 87) votes are in favour of a proposal from the Commission, that would be sufficient for a measure to be adopted (Article 205 EC). That means that it is possible to impose codification of core provisions of private law on all of the (supposedly) 'non codification minded' Member States.[73] I wonder whether it would be desirable to apply that procedure in an area so 'close to the citizen' as codification of private law (Article 1, para. 2

---

[67] On the issue of democratic legitimacy within the Community, see P. Craig and G. De Bùrca (n. 23).

[68] Case C-300/89, *Commission v. Council* [1991] ECR I–2867, para. 20.

[69] Thus P.J.G. Kapteyn and P. VerLoren van Themaat, *Introduction to the Law of the European Communities*, 3rd edn., edited and further revised by L.W. Gormley (Kluwer Law International, 1998), 430–439, 437, where the procedure is thoroughly analysed.

[70] *Supra*, n. 29.

[71] In the same sense S. Leible, 'Die Mitteilung der Kommission zum Europäischen Vertragsrecht – Startschuss für in Europäisches Vertragsgesetzbuch?', in *EWS* 10/2001, 471–481, 479; also N. Reich, *Some critical comments*, pro manuscripto.

[72] S. Leible (n. 71).

[73] Of a total of 87 votes, the UK, Ireland, Denmark, Finland and Sweden have 23 votes and could thus be 'out-voted' (if the Nice Treaty is adopted votes will be weighted differently).

TEU) and regarding an issue which the Member States concerned, at least some of them, may deem to be of 'constitutional' importance (affecting, as it does, the institutional balance between the legislature and the judiciary).[74] That would be different, of course, if the Member States were to decide, at the occasion of a next Intergovernmental Conference (IGC) and therefore unanimously, to amend the EC Treaty in order to bring codification of core provisions of private law within the scope of Community law.[75] Since such an amendment must be ratified by all Member States in accordance with their constitutional requirements, and therefore with the approval of the national parliaments, the requirement of democratic legitimacy would then be fully preserved.

For completeness' sake it should be pointed out that, apart from Article 95 EC, there is also Article 94 EC which could procure a legal basis for codification. It provides in approximation of national laws which 'directly affect the establishment or functioning of the common market' and may therefore offer a broader basis than Article 95 which is limited to (Community) measures which 'have as their object the establishment and functioning of the internal market'. However, Article 94 is less flexible than Article 95 in that it only allows the enactment of directives (and therefore only harmonization but no unification). Furthermore, it does not require co-decision from the European Parliament which must only be consulted (thus providing in less democratic legitimacy at the European level) but requires unanimity in the Council instead (thus providing in more 'indirect' legitimacy at the national level in sofar as national parliaments may have an impact on the vote of their Member State's government representative in the Council). The same procedural rules apply to measures taken on the basis of Article 308 EC (except that also regulations may be enacted under it).[76] Furthermore, Article 308 does not permit the Community institutions to exceed the limits of competences imposed by the Treaty,[77] and it may certainly not be used for changes which have a constitutional dimension.[78]

---

[74] On the doctrine of binding precedent and statutory interpretation in English law, see I. Mcleod, *Legal Method*, 3rd edn. (Macmillan Law Masters, 1999), 131 ff., resp. 227 ff.

[75] As has been decided in the Amsterdam Treaty with regard to 'judicial cooperation in civil matters having cross-border implications ... and insofar as necessary for the proper functioning of the internal market': see Article 65 (ex 73m) EC and n. 37.

[76] See further my contribution on 'Coherence of Community and national laws. Is there a legal basis for a European Civil Code?' in (1997) *ERPL*, 465–469, 467–468.

[77] See also para. 79 of the *Tobacco* judgment (n. 29).

[78] See the ECJ's Opinion 2/94 of 28 March 1996 [1996] ECR I–1789, para. 35 (a dimension which codification may eventually have for the non-codification Member States, as indicated in the text above).

2. Involving the European and the National Parliaments as an Expression of the Principle of (Participative) Democracy

Besides a 'procedural' facet, the principle of democracy has also a 'participative' (or 'deliberative') facet according to which all layers of government likely to be concerned by proposed codification, should be allowed to participate as much as possible (even in the absence of an explicit legal competence) in deliberations preceding or accompanying the decision making process. That applies particularly to elected parliaments, whenever decisions are envisaged which imply the making of value judgments and/or the taking of policy decisions, especially when they are of a nature to touch upon national sensitivities – as the codification of basic principles of private law at the European level is likely to do. That the principle of participative democracy plays a role in the European Union was confirmed by Declarations 13 and 14 which the Member States agreed to attach to the Maastricht Treaty. Declaration 13 tends to strenghten the role of national parliaments in the European Union whilst Declaration 14 invites the European and the national parliaments to meet 'as necessary' as a Conference of Parliaments. According to the first declaration, the involvement of national parliaments must be encouraged by stepping up 'the exchange of information between national parliaments and the European Parliament' and ensuring '*inter alia*, that national parliaments receive Commission proposals for legislation in good time for information of possible examination' whilst according to the second declaration a conference of (European and national) parliaments should be convened as necessary in order to consult them 'on the main features of the European Union'. Even more so, at the recent IGC in Nice, the role of national parliaments was retained as one of the four themes which are of particular importance for the future of the Union and will therefore be submitted to the next IGC to be held in 2004.[79]

If the involvement of national parliaments is a political objective to be pursued in matters for which the EU is competent, that must be so *a fortiori* for matters for which Community competences do not exist[80] – as is the case for codification of core provisions of private law as long as that issue is not brought within the scope of EC jurisdiction by amending the EC Treaty (*supra*, at III 2). In the

---

[79] Declaration 23 adopted by the Conference. See further K. Lenaerts and M. Desomer, 'Het verdrag van Nice en het "post-Nice"-debat over de toekomst van de Europese Unie', *Rechtskundig Weekblad*, 2001–2002, 73–90, 89–90. Also in the same issue the remarks of J. Meeusen and J. Wouters, 107–111, 109–110.

[80] In areas where no Community jurisdiction international principles may apply, more particularly the principle of international comity to which case law of the Community courts refers in competition cases: see recently the judgment of 25 March 1999 of the CFI in T-102/96, *Gencor v. Commission*, [1999] ECR T-II-753. For a comment see Y. van Gerven and L. Hoet, 'Gencor: Some Notes on Transnational Competition Law Issues' in (2001) *Legal Issues of Economic Integration*, 195–210.

absence of such an amendment, the only way to enact core codification is by means of an international agreement in which the Code provisions are incorporated, or to which they are attached. Such an agreement should be prepared in accordance with an 'ad hoc' procedure – modelled, for example, after the procedure followed for the Dutch Civil Code in order to ensure legitimacy and acceptability[81] – in which both the European and the national parliaments would play a role. Under that procedure codification could be prepared by experts designated by the Member States who, at an early stage, would take the advice from parliamentary commissions in the European Parliament and the national parliaments on the basis, for example, of a questionnaire approved by the European Parliament concerning important value judgments to be made or policy decisions to be taken. Once answers would have been received from those parliamentary commissions, draft bills could be prepared, on any one subject, by committees of experts, and then made public to invite comments from all segments of society. After such broad consultation and ensuing amendments, the draft bills would be submitted to final deliberation in a 'Convention' (which may take the advice of any group or person it wants to hear) and finally adopted, in view of submission to approval by the Member States, by the Council and the European Parliament. As was the case of the special body set up for the drafting of the European Charter of Fundamental Rights, the 'Convention' would be composed of representatives from the Community institutions and the national parliaments.[82] Obviously, the agreement should provide in a preliminary ruling procedure before a Community court to maintain uniformity of interpretation.[83] After it has been approved by all Member States, the agreement would come into force, e.g. when half of them have ratified it, on those Member States' territory.[84]

---

[81] Cf. *supra*, at 2. See also W. Snijders, 'The organisation of the drafting of a European Civil Code: a walk in imaginary gardens' in (1997) *ERPL*, 483–487 who stresses the fact, not to be forgotten, that 'legislation, after all, is essentially a political activity', 484.

[82] On the ('self titled') Convention, see J. Shaw, 'The Treaty of Nice: Legal and Constitutional Implications', (2001) *European Public Law*, 195–215, 212–213. The Convention comprised 15 representatives of the national governments, 16 representatives of the EP, 1 representative of the Commission and 30 members of the national parliaments (and observers from the ECJ and from the Council of Europe). Obviously the composition, and the numbers of the delegations, should be adapted to the special needs of the codification project and to ensure more specifically a larger representation from the Commission taking into account that that institution would play a crucial role in the consolidation of 'internal market related' legislation. For a favourable appraisal of the Convention instrument, see G. de Burca, 'The Drafting of the European Charter of Fundamental Rights', (2001) *ELR*, 126–138.

[83] Because of the overload of the existing Community courts, that may have to be a new court, or an extension of the present ones, which may require, depending on the scope of the envisaged codification, the allocation of important additional resources and therefore a political decision giving high priority to the codification project.

[84] Compare the provisions of Article 34, para. 2(d), *jo.* Article 35 TEU.

Some may argue that the use of an international agreement as an instrument for codification, may tend to 'bury' the project for many years or decades. However, as suggested above (*supra*, at III 1 and 2), the codification of core provisions of private law would in my view be facilitated by the fact that it would occur *after* the consolidation (by means of regulations) of existing legislation in the 'internal market related' sectors of private law (which, as already mentioned, should not preclude general codification from being prepared forthwith, in tandem with the more specific internal market related legislation). Moreover, if, in the course of preparation of general codification, it would appear that there is a broad political consensus to provide in a solid legal basis for general codification by an amendment of the EC Treaty, the prior work will not have been in vain, as it can then be used within the framework of the novel legal basis. And indeed, that has happened in the area of conflict of laws where, following the entry into force of the new Articles 61 (c) and 65 EC, Treaty provisions contained in external Conventions were transformed into regulations.[85]

V. FLANKING MEASURES NOT TO BE NEGLECTED

1. European Codification may not Start from Scratch

Assume for the sake of argument that codification of core provisions has been carried out in large parts of private law and brought to an end, where is a teacher, a judge, a legislator supposed to look when (s)he must explain, apply or elaborate European codified rules? In other words new rules will need to be seen in context, and can and may not be conceived, as one author puts, as principles, how well drafted they are, which are 'scraped off' from internal moralities, underlying value judgments and policy decisions which accompanied them in the national context from which they are drawn.[86] Or, to quote an historian, professor Zimmermann: 'The idea that a codification should be able to cut off the continuity of historical development, has proved to be a rather simplistic illusion. Even in a codified legal system the re-appearance of ideas and solutions from the treasure-house of the ius commune is by no means a rare – although it is usually an unacknowledged – phenomenon'.[87] That is already true in a purely national context as appears from the following statement of W. Snijders, the Vice-president of the Netherlands' Supreme Court who was actively engaged in the (last stages) of the drafting of the new Dutch civil code: 'An effective unification depends not only on general principles [a reference to

---

[85] See O. Remien (n. 37), 57.
[86] J.M. Smits, *The good Samaritan in European Private Law* (Kluwer, 2000), passim.
[87] R. Zimmermann, 'Roman Law and European Legal Unity' in: Hartkamp *et al.* (eds.), *Towards a European Civil Code*, 2nd edn., 1998, 21–39, 33–4.

the Principles of Contract Law of the Lando group], but can often be obtained only through detailed rules, making clear what is meant ... (E)ven a clear text cannot solve all implementation problems, linked as they are to the danger of disparity of interpretation ...'.[88] Moreover:

> '[I]t requires the re-education of judges, lawyers and other practitioners, of a kind that must not be underestimated. In the Netherlands in the years before 1992 this was a major operation, even though it was facilitated by the fact that new *textbooks* and other *literature* were available on a large scale, that practice, in the first place the *courts*, had already anticipated the new rules to a large extent and that the *law faculties* had already adapted their teaching to the code before it entered into force' (italics added).[89]

What is true for national codification (admittedly, a very comprehensive one encompassing all subjects of private law and taking more than fourty years to prepare it[90]) will be true *a fortiori* for European codification (albeit less extensive) where no comparable support can be found in national legal traditions, mentalities and sources, and where no comparable assistance is to be expected from courts, practitioners and academics.[91] Quite to the contrary, a new kind of lawyer will have to be educated, and throughout the EU considerably revised academic curricula will have to be agreed and applied in view of creating the legal environment – before, during and after codification – which should allow European codification to function in sustained continuity with the past and to take solid roots in the legal systems of the Member States. In Professor Coing's words,[92] here lies an immense role which academic learning (and teaching) has fulfilled in the past and will have to fulfill again for many years, or rather decades, to come:

> '[that role existed] in the formation of our common legal heritage, in the Middle Ages as well as in the Age of Enlightenment. It was academic training based on European ideas that created a class of lawyers animated by the same ideas, and it was the European lawyer who preceded the European law. This is the point, I think, at which our academic responsibility begins ... The curricula of our law schools must not be restricted to the study of national law, and not even to national law combined with a certain seasoning of comparative law. What is necessary ... is a curriculum where the basic courses present the national law in the context of those legal ideas which are present

---

[88]   W. Snijders (n. 81), 485.

[89]   *Ibid.*.

[90]   *Ibid.*, 484.

[91]   Drawing on his vast experience W. Snijders suggests setting up a permanent central institute which would coordinate and prepare the work of working groups and drafting committees: *ibid.*, 485. See further *infra*, at VI 1 of the present text.

[92]   Quoted by H. Kötz (n. 26), 28–29.

in the legislation of different nations, that is, against the background of the principles and institutions which the European nations have in common'.[93]

Work that is already underway (see *infra*) should therefore be continued on an even larger scale with 'the aim of finding a European common core of legal principles and rules' and starting with the modest task of

> 'mark(ing) out areas of agreement and disagreement, to construct a European legal *lingua franca* that has concepts large enough to embrace legal institutions which are functionally comparable, to develop a truly common law literature and the beginnings of a European law school curriculum, and thus to lay the basis for a free and unrestricted flow of ideas that is perhaps more central to the idea of a common law than that of identity on points of substance'.[94]

And above all, to educate lawyers who are ready and capable of leaving behind the 'provincialism and narrowness' of past legal education with its 'emphasis on formal dogma, on legal technique, on subtle doctrinal distinctions'.[95] Lawyers also, whose future it is to study and practice law in the political, economic and cultural context of a growing European integration, and to look for similarities and commonalities in goals, principles and solutions in the national and supranational legal orders which make up the legal heritage which they have in common.

2. The 'Bottom-Up' Approach of Codification to Accompany and Support the 'Top-Down' Approach

As mentioned, many projects are already underway to unearth, understand and rebuild a European common legal heritage.[96] They have in common that they intend, in varying degrees and with differences in methodology, to produce truly European doctrinal writings and materials for use by teachers and students, by judges and other practitioners, by legislators and administrators. Textbooks

---

[93] Quotation from Coing, 'European Common Law: Historical Foundations' in: Cappelletti (ed.), *New Perspectives for a Common Law of Europe* (1978), 31–44, 44, quoted in full (without the omissions in the excerpt above) by H. Kötz (n. 26), 28–29.

[94] Cited in n. 26, 36. That this is not an easy matter appears from the literature on Community law which now flourishes abundantly in any one Member State, but unfortunately very often in a closed national, or single language, circuit without reference to literature published in other Member States or other languages.

[95] H. Kötz (n. 26), 29.

[96] Together they form a new field of legal studies: European Private Law. For an overview of the various projects, see A. Hartkamp, *Perspectives for the Development of a European Civil Law* (n. 54), where in addition to the already mentioned drafting of 'Principles' projects, the ongoing scientific and educational projects are briefly described at 55–60.

written from a European perspective are published[97] as well as legal periodicals,[98] and research groups are set up, such as the Trento Group on *The Common Core of European Private law* (General Eds. M. Bussani and U. Mattei) and the Vienna/Tilburg group (Eds. J. Spier *et al.*) which engage in extensive comparative research around hypothetical cases discussed under various legal systems. It is in the same vein that I started in 1994, in cooperation with a group of distinguished judges and professors and with the financial assistance of the University of Maastricht (and during the first years of operation also from the European Commission),[99] with the preparation of a series of *Casebooks for the common law of Europe*. The first book on *Tort Law* was published, first in 1998 in an abbreviated edition, and then in 2000 in a complete and largely expanded edition,[100] whilst the books on *Contract Law*[101] and *Unjust Enrichment*[102] are ready for publication in 2002 and 2003 respectively. The books intend to 'uncover' similarities and differences between legal systems whereby the number of legal systems dealt with varies depending on the subjects and on the (large) amount of materials to be treated; but they all include the legal systems representative for the three major law families. The methodology applied is to compare judicial decisions often rendered in similar 'daily life' situations, as well as other sources (statutes and legal writings). The books wish to demonstrate how, notwithstanding existing differences in legal reasoning, very similar solutions are

---

[97] Thus H. Kötz, *Europäisches Vertragsrecht* (Tübingen, J.C.B. Mohr, I, 1996), translated by T. Weir and published as *European Contract Law* (Clarendon Press, 1997); and C. von Bar, *Gemeineuropäisches Deliktsrecht*, I and II (München, Verlag C.H. Beck, 1998–2000), translated by the authors and published as *The Common European Law of Torts*.

[98] *ERPL* (from 1993); *ZeuP* (from 1993); *Europa e Diritto Privato* (from 1998).

[99] The initiative drew its inspiration from the teachings, in the 1960s, of Professor Max Rheinstein at the University of Chicago whose assistant I had the privilege of being in 1959–60 and his successor in 1968. During his courses American postgraduate students were required to solve, and discuss in the classroom, concrete hypothetical cases under the US, French and German law of contracts and torts. It has convinced me since that the case method is the best way to learn one's own legal system and that of others. The initiative of the casebooks took concrete form after the conference held in Maastricht in 1991 on *The Common Law of Europe and the Future of Legal Education* (ed. B. De Witte and Caroline Forder), (Kluwer, 1992), where Professor Kötz delivered one of the keynote speeches along the same lines as referred to in the text above.

[100] W. van Gerven, J. Lever and P. Larouche, *Cases, Materials and Text on National, Supranational and International Tort Law* (Hart Publishing, 2000), xcix + 969 pp and more materials on the Internet site *http://www.rechten.unimaas.nl/casebook*. The first shorter edition, limited to the subject of scope of protection of tort law (now incorporated in the second edition) was published in 1998 by the aforementioned authors in cooperation with G. Viney and C. von Bar.

[101] Main eds.: H. Beale, A. Hartkamp, H. Kötz and D. Tallon. Hart Publishing, 2001, xciv + 993 pp.

[102] Main eds.: E. Schrage and J. Beatson.

often found, and how Community and ECHR law tend to stimulate convergence, especially in tort and contract law. All of the materials are reproduced in excerpt and preceded or followed by introductory, accompanying and concluding comparative notes and overviews, in which the excerpted documents are situated in the perspective of the legal system concerned, as compared with others.[103]

Obviously, the work done so far is only a start and will have to be followed up by research which, with the help of legal theory, economics and other social sciences, delves even deeper into the phenomenon of convergence and divergence with a view of sorting out differences which are artificial, i.e. maintained for no objective reason, and those which are not. It cannot be stressed sufficiently however, that without flanking measures as described above, European codification would be an enterprise that is carried out in the abstract, *ie.* with no past and probably no future.

VI. BY WAY OF CONCLUSION: LEGISLATE EFFICIENTLY AND NOT IN HASTE

1. Setting Up an Independent European Law Commission and European Curriculum Commission

Codification is not a 'mission impossible' if it is well prepared. It is not an easy task though, and should not be carried out in haste and without providing efficient flanking measures, as emphasized above. And indeed, as the American example shows, codification of private law at the European scale cannot be attained by 'mandatory top-down measures' only and, in order to be successful, i.e. in order not to be perceived as a *Fremdkörper* in the Member States, must be supported by 'voluntary bottom-up measures' deeply rooted in the traditions of both civil and common law countries.[104] Moreover, some institutional measures must be taken to carry out the whole, and lengthy, codification process *and*

---

[103] For a presentation of the project, see (1996) *European Review of Private Law*, 67–70 where the names of the members of the steering committee and of the research coordinator (A. Alvarez) are mentioned at 70 (also on the back cover of the books). See also P. Larouche, '*Ius Commune* Casebooks for a common law of Europe: Presentation, Progress, Rationale', (2000) *ERPL*, 101–109. The management of the project is presently in the hands of a joint Leuven/Maastricht committee set up in cooperation with the *Ius Commune* research school in which the Universities of Maastricht, Utrecht and Leuven participate.

[104] Compare M.A. Eisenberg, 'The Unification of Law' in: *Making European Law* (n. 56), 15–26, 26 who explains, 19–23, that an American 'national' law transcending that of the Federation and of the States came about in the US in much the same way as a common European law is to emerge: that is under the influence of economics, common history, legal education and scholarship, judicial practice and, last but not least, because of aspirations among lawyers to be part of a common legal culture.

its flanking measures. To quote, once more, W. Snijders, one of the craftsmen of the Dutch Code:

> '[The] more or less political activities (of codification) need careful coordination and political insight ... This can only be done by a permanent institute, where legal scholarship ... and managerial qualities are united ... There are ... important arguments for such an institute. They are related to a series of intertwined difficulties ... In the first place, there is the element of time ... [which] will be a matter of decades ... Secondly the work must be done in segments ... Thirdly, those employed on the code will have to deal with the general problem of the role that pressure groups and lobbyists usually play a role in the legislative process, certainly when it comes to more specific subjects ... We meet here in fact three problems: the need for continuity, the need for coordination and the need for continuous well-sifted information.'[105]

What Snijders has in mind is the setting up of a permanent institute 'where the work of different working groups or drafting committees can be prepared and attended to and where a permanent secretary and his assistants can do what is necessary for continuity ...'. Moreover, because general principles, of the Lando Commission type, will gradually lose their attractiveness as they will need detailed rules, there will be a constant need to accompany problems of implementation and interpretation in the Member States, or at least 'to serve as a kind of rallying point where assistance can be given when this is requested'.[106] And indeed, as was already referred to in an earlier quotation, there will be an urgent need to re-educate judges, lawyers and other practitioners, to revise law school curricula and to provide textbooks and other literature at a large scale.[107] To provide also for this need, the existence of a permanent secretariat will be required.

This well-taken advice from someone who has lived with, and during the last stages has directed, a major codification process, as carried out in the context of a modern and democratic society, brings me to my last point. That is to insist on the need to set up an independent law commission where legislative work can be organized and coordinated, and from where follow-up assistance can be supplied, *and* to set up an equally independent law curriculum commission from where not only the revision of university curricula would be guided but also the setting up of permanent education curricula for judges, advocates and other practitioners would be organized, in close cooperation with law schools, continued education centres and existing 'bottom-up' research projects in the Member States. All this in order to anticipate, accompany and follow-up codification by preparing, as of now, present and future generations of lawyers for

---

[105] (n. 81), 484–485.

[106] *Ibid.*, 485.

[107] *Ibid.*.

a new area of law practice, that is 'against the background of the principles and institutions which the European nations have in common'.[108] Such commissions must consist of members appointed by the Member States in Council, preferably financed directly by the Member States and must be independent from, but working closely together with, the EU Commission and the national administrations.[109]

2. *Festina lente*

All this, codification in two stages, as exposed above, and flanking measures, will take much time and, in order to succeed, must be done with moderation and without obstinacy. *Festina lente* should be the maxim. Just as Rome was not built in a day, it will take time and patience for a common law of Europe to emerge. Time is of the essence, but to put that factor in perspective, one must recall, to quote Lord Bingham of Cornhill, the Senior Law Lord in the House of Lords (as he now is) that:

> 'We are right to continue to worry away at the unnecessary divergences which continue to divide us. But the things which unite us, are greater than the things which divide us. The dawning of the new millennium should, no doubt, act as a spur to further endeavour; but it is also an opportunity to reflect on the extraordinary progress already made during what, historically speaking, is like an evening gone'.[110]

---

[108] Coing in the excerpt quoted earlier in the text accompanying n. 93.

[109] Thus also Snijders (n. 81), 486 who warns against the tendency of bureaucracy.

[110] 'A New Common law for Europe', 35, of *The coming together of the Common law and the Civil law* (n. 25.).

Private Law in European Context

KLUWER LAW INTERNATIONAL – THE HAGUE / LONDON / NEW YORK